Vocational Education for Persons with Handicaps

Edited by
Robert Gaylord-Ross
San Francisco State University

Mayfield Publishing Company
Mountain View, California

To Cory

Library of Congress Cataloging-in-Publication Data:

Vocational education for persons with handicaps.

Includes bibliographies and index.
1. Handicapped—Vocational guidance—United States.
2. Handicapped—Employment—United States. 3. Vocational
rehabilitation—United States. I. Gaylord-Ross, Robert.
HV1568.5.V615 1988   362.4'0484   87–15368
ISBN 0-87484-757-5
Manufactured in the United States of America

10 9 8 7 6 5 4 3 2 1

Mayfield Publishing Company
1240 Villa Street
Mountain View, California 94041

Sponsoring editor, Franklin C. Graham; production, Miller-Scheier Associates;
manuscript editor, Carol Dondrea; text designer, Richard Kharibian; cover
designer, Michael Rogondino; cover painting, Eva Brown, Creative Growth Art
Center. The text was set in Palatino by Editorial Associates, Los Altos, California,
and printed on 50# Finch Opaque Book by R.R. Donnelley & Sons, Inc.

Preface

Freud has said that the key to a successful life is *lieben und arbeiten:* love and work. For many persons with handicaps, however, attaining a job or a career is merely a dream—one that is not likely to be realized. In fact, about 70 percent of disabled adults are currently unemployed. Why has unemployment been the mode for disabled persons? In spite of the publicity and lip service given to the concept of employing persons with handicaps, we as a nation have failed to realize this goal. Yet, many professionals and employers have been working hard to vocationally train and place persons with disabilities. Over the past five years has emerged the notion of supported work to provide the necessary employment services to ensure that disabled persons find and maintain work. An increase in work experience programs during the secondary years has enabled handicapped youth and their families to be better prepared for the world of work. Also, career education efforts in the primary and middle school years are orienting disabled children to the types of occupations they may strive for and attain in later years. Thus, despite difficulties in employing persons with disabilities, there has been much promising activity in vocational preparation.

Vocational Education for Persons with Handicaps describes the multifaceted process of career preparation. The field is diverse, encompassing information and methods from teaching, business, counseling, administration, psychology, and economics. The contributors provide state-of-the-art information about the practice of vocational special education. This volume will serve as a text for the student in training as well as a resource for the practitioner in the field. Emphasis is on describing effective vocational programs; in addition, current research and policy is often cited. Each chapter offers case studies that illustrate and clarify the authors' main points. A number of topics, such as legislation, are covered in more than one chapter. The unique perspective that each author brings to these important topics will help the reader understand the many sides of each topic.

This work is organized into four sections. Part I, Policies and Professional Roles, presents an historical overview of vocational education policy and program development. During the past thirty years a definitive career education movement has emerged that emphasizes life-span preparation for employment. Career education focuses on instructional and counseling activities that begin in the primary school and continue through the adult years. Recent attention has been given to the transition phase, when handicapped youths leave their school programs and enter the adult world. Career education also stresses the interrelationship between work and community living. The family plays an important role in assisting work activities and in ensuring a quality of life in the employment, residential, and community living domains. Finally, effective vocational education, especially during the transition phase, requires that different professions and institutions work together in a cooperative fashion. Teachers, rehabilitation counselors, and employers, to name just a few, must be aware of each other's roles and collaborate directly. Often, formal interagency agreements must be written to clarify just what services will be provided by each institution. Thus, the role of the contemporary vocational educator involves delivering instructional programs and coordinating services among different agencies.

Part II, Vocational Assessment and Preparation, deals with designing and implementing effective instructional programs. First, it is necessary to assess the individual's current level of abilities and interests. While standardized vocational assessment instruments may be of value, a curriculum-referenced approach to assessment appears to provide program planners with more useful information. There are many instructional approaches to teaching vocational tasks, but the behavior analytic view has accumulated the largest demonstrated data base. Besides teaching the acquisition of new skills, instructional programs should promote the generalization and maintenance of these skills. In addition, it is important to enable the individual to function independently in the workplace. Self-instructional procedures are showing increasing promise in attaining this objective.

While career/vocational education spans the primary through adult years, the greatest efforts have been during the secondary years. Relatively different secondary program models have evolved for the student with mild versus severe handicaps. The importance of community vocational training has taken on increasing importance, though, for both populations. Occupational training and counseling services for disabled youths have also played important roles in their transition to adult employment.

Adult Employment Programs and Issues, Part III, addresses the many factors affecting the successful employment of disabled adults. Interested and willing employers are needed to hire and retain workers. Often, a number of economic factors may influence an employer's hiring decision. In many cases, for example, a disabled individual may need considerable on-the-job instruction in learning and maintaining job skills. The supported employment model provides intensive longitudinal services for individuals with serious vocational handicaps. An important aspect of on-the-job support is to analyze the social ecology of the workplace. Then, coworkers can be utilized to supervise and socialize with the handicapped employee.

Although the vocational education of persons with handicaps has been approached as a generic undertaking, it is useful to understand the characteristics of different types of disabilities. Part IV, Type of Disability and Vocational Education, presents specialized information that is keyed to programming for mild, severely, physical, and sensory handicapped individuals. A large proportion of vocational special education efforts has been conducted with students having mild handicaps. Yet, individuals with physical handicaps can present great challenges to successful employment because of simple barriers, such as transportation to the workplace. Individuals with visual and hearing impairments may also require special adaptations at the work site to accommodate their sensory limitations. Finally, persons with severe handicaps usually need intensive vocational training programs to make a successful transition to nonsheltered work.

It will be necessary to prepare personnel to implement vocational programs if the burgeoning career education and supported employment movements are to train and place handicapped persons successfully in nonsheltered work. Personnel will be needed from a variety of disciplines: education, rehabilitation counseling, administration, and business. Text materials are needed to reflect this interdisciplinary effort. This work incorporates information from a wide range of topics. Although previous texts have done a fine job of giving a particular focus to career education or adult employment, the broader array of vocational education topics presented here should be particularly appealing to students and practitioners. Although the book does not provide practicum exercises, instructors should be able to derive field assignments from the descriptions of instructional methods, program models, case examples, and references; or from their own experiences. We hope the clarity and comprehensiveness of the material will enable personnel in training and practitioners in the field to develop innovative vocational education programs.

Robert Gaylord-Ross

ACKNOWLEDGMENTS

An edited volume represents the efforts of many persons, most importantly the chapter author contributors. I would also like to acknowledge the many persons who stimulated and encouraged me in my own career in vocational special education. These individuals include: Tom Bellamy, Kathryn Davy, Joyce Forte, Chris Hagie, Bill Halloran, Norris Haring, Devi Jameson, Melanie Lee, George Noceti, Valerie Pitts-Conway, Joanne Prieuer, Ian Pumpian, Blair Roger, Bill Rosenberg, Keith Storey, Bill Wilson, and Gail Zittel. I must also give special acknowledgment to my supportive coworker, Shep Siegel. Of course, the greatest inspiration in this field derives from observing the vocational development of individuals with handicaps. In this light I must acknowledge Adam, David, Fred, and Mark.

Contents

Foreword
Gary M. Clark (University of Kansas)   ix

Part I   Policies and Professional Roles   1

1 Legislative and Policy Aspects of Vocational Special
Education
L. Allen Phelps and James R. Frasier (University of Illinois)   3

2 Career Education for Students with Handicaps
Warren J. White (Kansas State University) and Ernest Biller
(Ohio State University)   30

3 Professional Roles and Practices in the Provision of
Vocational Education for Students with Disabilities
Jan Nisbet (University of New Hampshire)   65

4 Community Living and Work
David W. Close and Thomas J. Keating (University of Oregon)   87

Part II   Vocational Assessment and Preparation   109

5 Vocational Assessment in School and Rehabilitation
Programs
Larry Irvin (Oregon Research Institute)   111

6 Instructional Programming in Vocational Education
David M. Mank and Robert H. Horner (University of Oregon)   142

7 Secondary Vocational Training
Robert Gaylord-Ross, Shepherd Siegel, Hyun Sook Park, and
William Wilson (San Francisco State University)   174

Part III Adult Employment Programs and Issues 203

8 Adult Employment Programs
Paul Wehman and John Kregel (Virginia Commonwealth
University) 205

9 Ecology of the Workplace
Janis Chadsey-Rusch and Frank R. Rusch (University of
Illinois) 234

10 Economic Issues in Employing Persons with Disabilities
Justin O'Brien (Indiana State University) and
David Stern (University of California, Berkeley) 257

11 The Business Perspective on Employing Persons with
Disabilities
Gopal Pati (Indiana University Northwest) 296

Part IV Type of Disability and Vocational Education 329

12 Vocational Education of Persons with Mild Handicaps
Susan Brody Hasazi and R. Brian Cobb (University of Vermont) 331

13 Vocational Education of Persons with Severe Handicaps
Ian Pumpian, Elizabeth West, and Holly Shepard
(San Diego State University) 355

14 Vocational Education of Persons with Physical Handicaps
Jo-Ann Sowers, Chris Jenkins, and Laurie Powers
(Oregon Research Institute) 387

15 Vocational Education of Persons with Sensory Handicaps
Sharon Zell Sacks (San Francisco State University) and
Michael Bullis (Teaching Research Division, Oregon State
System of Higher Education) 417

Index 445

Foreword

Fortunately, writing forewords is not restricted to the old or the wise. Otherwise, I would not have been asked to write this one. My qualification is my background, which draws on my observations and experiences of the past twenty-four years. Being a part of recent history allows me to view this book in the context of that history.

The historical context for vocational education for persons with handicaps is the evolution of an idea over the past forty years. The idea, of course, is that schools and community agencies can make a difference in the adult outcomes of the lives of persons with handicapping conditions. The book you are about to read is an important contribution to the evolution of this idea. In my opinion, the book comes at a significant time.

Earlier versions of the idea of effecting positive adult outcomes for persons with handicaps emerged in various forms: occupational core curriculum, persisting life functions curriculum, cooperative work-study, career education, special needs vocational education, and life career competencies education. Each one built on the previous conception and moved the field ahead to a new level. In time, each lost its momentum. It is not surprising that no one wants to appear outdated these days and talk about work-study programming, career education, or even special needs vocational education. But we must, and now is the time to do it.

Today, we are riding a crest of enthusiasm and optimism regarding the opportunities available for the successful transition of persons identified as mentally or physically handicapped from school to adult life. The transition concept is the newest version of the idea noted earlier. This aura of hope and readiness stems not only from the developments of the decades just past, but from current events. Some of these events include the following:

- Federal initiatives stimulating programs and services in employment training of special education students in their transition to the adult world

- State legislative actions (in at least four states at this writing) mandating some level of transition services

- The demonstration of the effectiveness of the philosophy and technology associated with transition models such as competitive and supported employment training with students of moderate to severe levels of mental retardation

- The beginnings of a consensus on what the scope of the transition concept is

- A growing body of literature in employment training providing a rich source of information on models, perspectives on problems and issues, and recommended practices

Unfortunately, in the enthusiasm for new initiatives, we tend to reject or move away from valid forms. We must recognize both the contributions of our recent history to the transition movement as well as how integral earlier concepts are to the current concepts. No one knows for sure what the state of the art in transition programming will be in the 1990s and beyond. The career education movement had about as much support as could have been asked for from the President, Congress, business and industry, the U.S. Chamber of Commerce, and labor unions. Still, it had only about a ten-year life as a visible movement with potential to make major educational reforms. We must incorporate the best of our earlier visions into the transition concept or we may lose our momentum even sooner than that.

Some of what we have learned from recent history in career and vocational programming for special populations suggests that the future holds these specific challenges for the successful transition of persons with handicaps from school to adult living:

- Disability groups such as those with learning disabilities and behavior disorders, the hearing impaired, and the visually impaired need to be included in the mainstream of vocational education as much as the mainstream of regular education. The authors in this book discuss this.

- High school courses of study and curricula for students with handicaps must include training in transition skills. Reform in this direction is directly contradictory to the reforms of the excellence in education movement. The book addresses this.

- Interagency cooperation is the keystone to effectively planning and implementing transition. What can be learned from interdisciplinary and interagency efforts in career and special needs vocational education in the past? The book speaks to this issue also.

What I see, then, in this book is a timely response to the need for a rational move from ideas of the past to the present. Such a move will have to address ideology and practical policies and procedures that work. Career and vocational education advocates were a practical lot. The ideological commitment of today's transition advocates is awesome. If the creative energy and leadership skills of current spokespersons for transition programming and the perspectives of contributors to the fields of career and vocational education can be tapped to bring us back to our roots, the future of handicapped persons in transition will be brighter. Happily, this book does that, and does it well.

Gary M. Clark
University of Kansas

THE CONTRIBUTORS

Ernest Biller is an assistant professor of Rehabilitation Services in the College of Education at Ohio State University. His professional experience includes teaching and counseling disabled youths. He has also published several intellectually based curriculum materials.

Dr. Biller's interest in working with disabled persons evolved from a summer spent with his brother-in-law David, then 16 years old. David, who is developmentally disabled, was home from an institution in Oklahoma, where he had been sent because psychometric testing indicated his inability to do any kind of work. Dr. Biller, who was then preparing to be employed in a vocational trade, set out to teach David certain basic skills for work and everyday living and discovered that David was able to learn almost anything he was taught.

Michael Bullis is an associate research professor at the Teaching Research Division of the Oregon State System of Higher Education. His interest in career/vocational education for persons with special needs developed from an earlier position in a rehabilitation facility, where he worked extensively providing work training to adolescents with handicaps. He was surprised at how little vocational training was incorporated in their high school experience. Later this surprise caused him to seriously question why vocational education was not an option open to these students. It seemed eminently logical that preparation for work would help these persons to succeed in work and community.

Dr. Bullis's experience with individuals and staff at the University of Arkansas Research and Training Center on Deafness and Hearing Impairment further influenced his commitment to vocational training, providing academic and personal insight into the field that he could not otherwise have obtained. The most powerful feature of this position was his exposure to service personnel in the field of deafness. It is Dr. Bullis's impression that teachers and counselors of students with deafness are among the most committed in education.

Daniel Close is a research professor at the Rehabilitation, Research, and Training Center of the University of Oregon. He has published a number of articles and is co-author of the book *On My Own*, (Baltimore: Paul H. Brookes Publishing Company). His interest in special education arose from his experience as an undergraduate student in psychology working with mentally retarded persons. In graduate school he worked as a behavioral specialist in a workshop professionally affiliated with Dr. Marc Gold, a national leader in the emerging field of vocational special education. Under Dr. Gold's direction, he learned how to develop community-based programs that focus on human values and quality instructional methods.

Since graduate school, Dr. Close has pursued applied research and program development. His work emphasizes development of an array of supported living situations for persons with disabilities. His chapter in this book reflects some of his ideas on the creation of support networks to facilitate the quality of life for persons in integrated community settings.

Brian Cobb is an assistant professor in the College of Education at the University of Vermont. He considers himself a vocational education teacher/trainer. His public school experience includes teaching beginning and advanced cabinet-making to high school students and to adults. His trade experience combines several years of rough and finish carpentry, including designing and building several homes on his own.

In 1983, Dr. Cobb completed his graduate work in the area of vocational special needs education. Looking back on his teaching and trade experience, he realized that many of his and his co-workers' assumptions about disability and work were unfounded and unfair. As a result, he has maintained a professional interest in improving employment and employment-training opportunities for disabled students by focusing on the ways secondary special and vocational educators can improve the delivery of their instruction.

James Frasier is currently a doctorate student in vocational education at the University of Illinois at Urbana-Champaign. He has been a vocational special needs teacher, has directed adult and continuing education services, and has published a number of articles in vocational education journals. He recently received the 1986 Award for Outstanding Service from the Special Needs Division of the American Vocational Association.

Robert Gaylord-Ross is a professor and coordinator of the Vocational Special Education Program at San Francisco State University. He has written a number of articles dealing with social skill training, behavior treatment, and vocational education. He has also co-authored a book,

Strategies for Educating Students with Severe Handicaps (with J. Holvoet; 1985, Little, Brown). Gaylord-Ross was a Fulbright Senior Research Fellow.

Dr. Gaylord-Ross' original interest in the field relates to his personal experiences with his cousin, Mark, who is mentally retarded. Although Mark had many splinter skills that enabled him to follow news events and the like, he was resigned to working in a sheltered workshop as an adult. As Gaylord-Ross saw through his own professional experiences, how disabled persons could learn with behavior analytic techniques, he knew persons like Mark were capable of becoming gainfully employed in nonsheltered settings.

Susan Hazasi is a professor in the College of Education at the University of Vermont. Her interest in vocational education and employment opportunities for individuals with handicaps began when she was a high school-level special educator working with students having mild and moderate handicapping conditions. Her students taught her that they, like most adolescents, valued work, particularly its social and financial benefits. Since then, she has been concerned about the limited opportunities for young people with handicaps to participate in vocational education, training, and employment.

For the last five years, Dr. Hazasi and her colleagues in Vermont have been conducting a series of follow-up studies on former high school students having handicaps who exited high school between 1978 and 1986. These studies have revealed several vocational education and employment experiences, which occurred during high school, that seem to increase the likelihood of future employment following school. Recently, Dr. Hasazi and her colleagues have been assisting school districts in developing curriculum and program options that include the promising practices identified in their follow-up research.

Robert Horner is an associate professor and director of the Specialized Training Program at the University of Oregon. He has published a number of books and articles on the subject of vocational training and stimulus generalization and is currently editor of the *Journal of the Association of Persons With Severe Handicaps*.

Dr. Horner's interest in vocational education stems from a belief that education should change the way people live. His experiences as a special education teacher, a "parent" in a group home for "emotionally disturbed" children, and as the manager of a small work program employing people with severe disabilities have shaped his philosophy, convincing him that education should do more than teach skills. Education should result in clear changes in where a person lives and works; changes in the opportunities for social interaction; and changes in the level of personal independence.

Larry Irvin is a research associate at the Oregon Research Institute and a research professor at the University of Oregon. He has been involved for a number of years in developing assessment instruments designed to be useful with people who have disabilities. His professional training and experience in applied measurement and developmental disabilities have provided many opportunities for this involvement. Dr. Irvin has been influenced in all of these efforts by what he calls the "Gospel according to St. Marc"—Marc Gold's clear insistence on a "train, don't test" philosophy for our field. Thus, Dr. Irvin describes here a curriculum-based approach to vocational assessment. In this approach, assessment is guided clearly by instructional considerations, not vice versa. The content and instructional technology for teaching vocational or career education are always of primary importance. The nature of assessment is guided by teaching decisions that need to be made regularly: identifying the needs for, and outcomes of, instruction.

Chris Jenkins is a research assistant at the Oregon Research Institute. He has just completed his doctoral studies at the University of Oregon and has accepted an instructor position in a junior college in Canada, where he will train personnel in educating students with severe multiple handicaps.

Dr. Jenkins' past experience as a teacher of severely, multiply disabled students made him realize that there were no expectations of meaningful employment for this population. While working in the Oregon Transition to Employment program, he has been able to demonstrate that individuals with severe multiple and physical disabilities are able to succeed in nonsheltered employment.

Thomas Keating is currently pursuing a doctorate degree in special education and rehabilitation at the University of Oregon. His interest in supported living systems that meet the lifelong needs of persons with disabilities and their families is rooted in his experience growing up in a family of ten children, one of whom, James, has a cognitive impairment. Mr. Keating's parents were normalization proponents ahead of their time, believing that James would be a full-fledged participant in the family and community. Mr. Keating inherited from his parents a specific concern for James' welfare and a more general interest in learning and teaching. On the other hand, he experienced the frustration of ignorance of his brother's condition and anger at the way society segregates and devalues persons with disabilities.

Mr. Keating's experience indicates that families are essential partners in the process of developing effective human services and assuring valued roles in society for all citizens.

John Kregel is Research Director of the Rehabilitation Research and Training Center at Virginia Commonwealth University. He also directs a Master's degree program to train supported employment specialists and co-directs a demonstration program to place individuals with severe mental retardation into competitive employment. These positions provide a unique opportunity to participate in the unprecedented revolution occurring in this country in employment options for adults with severe disabilities. The movement to convert our existing segregated workshops and activity centers into integrated, supported employment opportunities is a vital component in the overall process of moving individuals with disabilities more into the mainstream of society.

Formerly, Dr. Kregel was a teacher of adolescents with severe handicaps and the foster parent of an institutionalized young man. He has shared the frustration of many parents who often must wait years once their children leave public school programs until space becomes available in inadequate sheltered employment programs. He views supported employment as an opportunity to change and improve this situation.

David Mank is a research professor in the Specialized Training Program at the University of Oregon. He has published many articles on the subjects of applied behavior analysis, vocational training, and self-instruction. Dr. Mank considers himself to be a student of behavior. Many years ago that interest combined with a concern for persons with disabilities, especially the state of employment realities for persons with the label "disabled." Although Dr. Mank does not believe that meaningful employment is the only thing in life, an acceptable quality of life clearly is in jeopardy without the benefit of a decent job.

Jan Nisbet is Director of the Institute for Developmental Disabilities at the University of New Hampshire, Durham. She has published several articles in the *Journal of the Association for Persons with Severe Handicaps*.

Prior to her work at the University of New Hampshire, Dr. Nisbet taught in the Area of Rehabilitation Services at Syracuse University. She has received professional training in the fields of physical therapy and special education. Most of her research and program development interests are in the areas of community/vocational education, placement of adults with severe disabilities into integrated work environments, community integration, and co-worker support systems. She has served as director of several model demonstration and/or personnel preparation projects that focus on youths and adults with severe disabilities.

Justin O'Brien was Assistant Professor in the Department of Special Education at Indiana State University. His concern for the vocational education of handicapped persons grew out of his own experience as a soldier in Vietnam. After the military, he became a special education teacher and worked in a residential program for emotionally disturbed youths. He subsequently entered the joint doctoral program in special education at San Francisco State University and the University of California, Berkeley. In 1984 he completed his doctoral research on the excess costs of employing handicapped individuals in the Targeted Jobs Tax Credit program; he testified in Congress on this issue. Professor O'Brien died in 1987.

Hyun-Sook Park is a doctorate student in the joint doctoral program between San Francisco State University and the University of California, Berkeley. She is also the project coordinator of the Social Support Project, a federal research program that is investigating social skill training and support networks among disabled youths.

Ms. Park's interest in vocational education for persons with severe disabilities developed when she did her practicum as part of the requirements for her master's degree. One of the students she worked with was Ed, a 19-year-old, who was capable of performing very complex tasks, although he was classified as severely handicapped. Ms. Park was told that Ed would go back to the institution he just came from after graduation from school. He was living in a group home at the time. After further inquiry Ms. Park was surprised and disappointed to discover that Ed would be given no opportunity to prove himself in a job situation before being returned to the institution. She realized the need for a program that could help disabled students remain integrated in the community after graduation from public school. It had to be a vocational program; if Ed were given vocational training from an early age, he could have obtained a job in a nonsheltered setting and remained in the community.

Gopal Pati is a professor in the Department of Management at Indiana University Northwest. He has participated in many projects concerning the employment of handicapped persons. Dr. Pati is widely published, including an article in the *Harvard Business Review* and a chapter in *Managing and Employing the Handicapped: The Untapped Potential* with J.I. Adkins, G. Morrison (Brace-Park Press, Lake Forest, Ill). His goal is to sensitize people to the qualities of individuals with disabilities so that they will be considered a reliable, dependable source of labor. Individuals with disabilities need jobs, and employers need dependable persons to do quality work. Furthermore, Dr. Pati believes marketable education and training are keys to the success of persons with special needs. Now that opportunities for work are just opening up for individuals with disabilities, special education professionals should be encouraged that the products of their commitment, their students, are proudly being utilized by many thoughtful employers.

L. Allen Phelps is Associate Dean and Professor in the Department of Vocational and Technical Education, College of Education, at the University of Illinois at Urbana-Champaign. He is the author of forty professional articles, nine chapters, six monographs, and two professional texts; he was also Editor of the *Journal of Vocational Educational Research.* Dr. Phelps's interest in the vocational education field has been developed and maintained from his interactions with students with handicaps from his early days of teaching. He has pursued a range of topics related to improving employment opportunities for youths with special needs.

Laurie Powers is a research assistant at the Oregon Research Institute. Her interest in the provision of vocational training to individuals with physical and cognitive disabilities originated from her recognition of the lack of access to such opportunities for this group. She has since discovered that vocational training for persons with multiple disabilities can be viable, cost-effective, and very reinforcing for everyone involved. Application of the general principles of systematic behavioral training, in association with the use of alternative motor strategies and minor adaptations, provides the necessary prerequisites for vocational success for most multiply disabled workers. Personal experience with her own physical disability has heightened Ms. Power's sensitivity to the needs and aspirations of disabled persons with whom she works; she believes that success is achievable when creativity and commitment are present.

Ian Pumpian is an associate professor in the Department of Special Education at San Diego State University. He coordinates the teacher training program in the area of severe disabilities. In addition to his preservice training responsibilities, he is actively involved in research, demonstration, and inservice with a number of schools and adult service agencies throughout the greater San Diego area. He participates on various committees and provides presentations and technical assistance across the country. Formerly, he was a teacher in the Madison Metropolitan School District.

Dr. Pumpian's involvement in special education and employment activities is based on two basic beliefs: (a) that the more diverse a community is, the more exciting and interesting it can become; and (b) that the strength and integrity of a community can be measured by the degree to which it acknowledges, respects, and constructively utilizes this diversity. He takes great pride in being a part of efforts that enable people with severe disabilities to live, work, and play as accepted, productive, and involved members of the community. Such accomplishments should not only make a great impact on those individuals and their families, but on the community as a whole.

Janis Chadsey-Rusch is an assistant professor and **Frank Rusch** is a professor in the Department of Special Education at the University of Illinois. Frank is Director, and Janis a Research Associate, at the Transition Institute at that university.

Their interest in the ecology of the workplace has emerged from an understanding of human behavior, achieved through earlier work experiences in Oregon and Washington. In the past they learned about communicative intent, language development, and how to observe, record, and analyze behavior. Their most recent work has been decidedly cooperative, drawing on their basic understanding of human uniqueness as they study social integration.

Because employment structures people's lives so profoundly, their research focuses on the workplace. In this context, they contend that successful adjustment may depend more on the match between people and their environments than on the personal characteristics of the individual. They believe that physical, social, and organizational dimensions contribute to successful matches between individuals and jobs and that a better understanding of the ecology of the workplace will enable more individuals to obtain and retain jobs. Employed persons with handicaps can be assets to their employment communities, as well as deriving important benefits from their involvement in valued work.

Sharon Sacks is an instructor at San Francisco State University. She is also Project Coordinator of the Visually Impaired, Social Skills Training Project. Her experiences as a teacher of visually impaired persons and her personal experiences as a low vision individual are the foundation for her deep interest in the functional and vocational needs of visually handicapped students.

Throughout her teaching career, Dr. Sacks recognized that her role as a special educator went beyond the classroom environment. Although many of her students functioned well academically, they exhibited many "splinter skills" and demonstrated lags in social development, self-help skills, and independent thinking skills. In order to prepare these students for adult life, it was necessary to develop and implement curricular strategies that would enhance their vocational potential throughout the school years. Dr. Sacks's personal vocational experiences helped to reinforce her strong belief that functional learning endeavors are the foundation for successful independent living. Although her education was purely academic, her family encouraged independence and self-sufficiency. She was given the opportunity to pursue a variety of paid and unpaid jobs (many secured on her own). She quickly learned the value of doing a job well and experienced the positive impact of receiving a salary. These experiences gave her a sense of control and helped her make choices regarding her future goals.

Holly Shepard is Systems Coordinator for the State-Wide Systems Change Project at the Mississippi University Affiliated Program of the University of Southern Mississippi. In this capacity her responsibilities include data collection and comprehensive model development for districts in Mississippi that serve students with severe handicaps; providing technical assistance to state and local agencies and districts; and developing a service provider's guide of agencies in Mississippi that offer services for individuals with severe handicaps. Through previous professional experience as Transition Coordinator of Youth Employment and Independent Living Skills, a federally funded project in San Diego, she has developed and implemented chronologically age-appropriate, integrated programs for students with severe handicaps at the elementary, junior high, and secondary levels, with transitioning into supported adult work programs. She was an active executive board member in the California state chapter of The Association for Persons with Severe Handicaps and is a member of numerous national, state, and local organizations and task forces.

Shep Siegel is a doctorate student in special education in the joint doctoral program between San Francisco State University and the University of California, Berkeley. He is currently the project coordinator of the career ladder program, a model demonstration transition program for mildly handicapped youth.

His first teaching assignment was with adjudicated youth in Santa Cruz County, who were on probation but living with their parents or in a group home situation. One student, in particular, made it clear that he no longer (and perhaps never had) wished to be a student in a classroom. In fact, he communicated this through overt and troubling behaviors that were beyond Siegel's abilities to teach at that time. Partly out of frustration, and partly in respectful response to his position, Mr. Siegel found the student a part-time job in a bicycle repair shop down the block from the school. Their relationship, and the student's overall behavior and attitude toward his own future, took a miraculous turn for the better. He was a model employee and seemed to understand (indeed, it was only in the context of paid employment that he *could* understand) that his and Mr. Siegel's purposes were not in conflict.

Jo-Ann Sowers is a research scientist at the Oregon Research Institute. After receiving her master's degree in Applied Behavior Analysis, she worked with Frank Rusch at the University of Washington on the development of a model to train and place persons with severe and moderate mental retardation into competitive employment. She was excited to demonstrate the applicability of the behavioral technologies to the unique problems encountered when placing and training persons with disabilities into nonsheltered work settings.

In subsequent years, Sowers had the opportunity to develop vocational preparation programs for school-aged students with severe disabilities. During this time, many of the teachers with whom she worked asked for assistance in providing vocational training to students with physical and multiple disabilities. Sowers realized that there had been little attention given to this issue, and she became increasingly interested in what she considered a new challenge to those of us who believe that everyone, regardless of the nature or extent of their disability, should have the opportunity to work in integrated, community-based settings.

David Stern is Associate Professor in the Graduate School of Education at the University of California, Berkeley. He earned a doctorate in Economics and Urban Studies from M.I.T. and previously taught in the Department of Economics at Yale. His research on the economics of education includes studies of vocational education and the relation between schooling and labor markets. He has also been interested in school-based enterprises as a tool for vocational education. His interest in special education stems in part from serving as chairman of Justin O'Brien's dissertation committee.

Paul Wehman is Director of the Rehabilitation Research and Training Center on Employment of Persons with Mental Retardation. He is also a professor of Special Education and Rehabilitative Medicine. He has published numerous articles and books dealing with supported employment and transition. His greatest professional interest and excitement over the past decade is watching people go to work competitively for the first time. Observing the changes in self-perception and dignity, Wehman feels, is a real joy and reinforcer to professionals working in the field. Dr. Wehman believes there is an enormous national momentum in the civil rights of persons with severe handicaps, and he feels privileged to be part of it.

Elizabeth West is Program Manager of a San Diego–based adult service agency that provides community integration and supported employment options to a wide range of individuals with severe disabilities. She also serves as a transition coordinator to a grant-funded program entitled "Project Work." Both programs allow for her participation in demonstration, inservice, and research-based activities with school and adult agencies. She is a member of various committees and local, state, and national organizations.

Her philosophy regarding supported life for individuals with severe disabilities evolved from her master's degree coursework at San Diego State University, from her teaching experience, and from her interactions with family/consumers whom she has come to know over the years. Her beliefs are based on respect and normalized opportunities for all consumers, regardless of the severity of their disability. She contends that the active participation in society of individuals with handicaps is a definite asset.

Warren White is an associate professor in Special Education at Kansas State University. He has published several articles on career education. He is head of the research division of the Division of Career Development, Council for Exceptional Children.

Dr. White's interest in vocational and career planning for handicapped individuals began when he was an undergraduate with a psychology/special education major. A requirement of this major included spending a minimum of 180 hours of "observation and participation" time divided between a preschool for developmentally delayed children and a sheltered workshop for adults with developmental disabilities. Although he enjoyed the hours he spent in the preschool, the sheltered workshop made a lasting impression. He was so impressed with the staff of that little workshop in rural Kansas that he has been searching for better methods and models ever since.

William Wilson is a professor and chairperson of the Department of Special Education, San Francisco State University. He was previously employed by the Bureau of Education for the Handicapped and the National Association for State Directors of Special Education.

His interest in vocational and career planning originated in his experience as a teacher of children with severe disabilities and as an administrator with involvement in public policy and implementation of federal mandates. One of the primary concerns of families of children with severe disabilities is what will happen to their children once they are no longer eligible for public school service. In Dr. Wilson's experience the answer usually included a segregated recreational program, a sheltered workshop, or an institution. Very few children were eligible for rehabilitation services' discriminatory criteria, based on employability. The problem was exacerbated for the mildly disabled population because of placement in programs consisting of "watered down" academics or placement in a traditional vocational education track that provided few skills transferable to the world of work.

Dr. Wilson feels that we must remain vigilant throughout this decade to ensure that federal policies are carried out at the program level. He will continue to be involved and feel gratified that the transition and supported employment initiatives have forced policy makers in special education, regular education, vocational education, and rehabilitation services to develop strategies that will assist young people with disabilities to lead productive adult lives.

Part I   Policies and Professional Roles

The vocational education of students with handicaps is a multilevel process. On one level, a teacher may have an instructional interaction with a student, or a student may manipulate a tool. On another level, a special education teacher may be planning instructional and counseling activities for a student soon to be leaving school. On still another level, an adult employment agency administrator and a school administrator may be forging interagency agreements to provide follow-along services for handicapped youth in transition from school to work. Clearly, vocational special education is a multilevel and complex process. To become educated in this field one must absorb a variety of information from many disciplines.

In this part the reader is introduced to the many aspects of vocational special education. Phelps and Frasier describe the history of vocational special education and discuss the parallel yet interrelated disciplines of special education, rehabilitation, and vocational education. The growth of these fields coincided with particular historical events, such as the Russian success with the *Sputnik* Satellite in the 1950s, which caused a policy shift in the United States on education that led to an emphasis on educating specific sectors of the population. Policy priorities led to federal legislation, which, in turn, funded new service programs.

Phelps and Frasier, as well as Nisbet, point to the importance of getting professionals from different agencies to cooperate in providing designated services. The recent focus on transition has brought to light the problem of the school years, ending with possibly no continuing educational and vocational services for those who need them. The plea for interagency cooperation has been made to facilitate such continued programming, avoid duplication of service, encourage long-term program planning, and prevent competition among similar program offerings.

White and Biller describe a life-span, career education model that identifies learning activities at different stags of development. The strength of this career education approach is in its curricular planning and cumulative activities, which move the student from the primary to middle school, through secondary, and finally to adult years. Although career education and the career development curriculum have been primarily validated with mildly and moderately handicapped students, the approach has far-reaching implications for persons with all types of disabilities. The pioneering career development work of both Brolin and Clark (cited in several chapters) has led to the recent advances in curriculum-referenced assessment, work experience, and occupational training.

Contemporary vocational special education programs must articulate the relationships among the employment, residential, and social/leisure sectors of a person's life. Nisbet has advanced a functional curricular model which addresses these sectors and that has been validated with persons with the most severe handicaps.

Although this text focuses on preparation for employment, Close and Keating address the relationship between work and living in the community. Experience has shown that without strong family support for employment, the handicapped individual often fails in the work setting. In this regard, Close and Keating cite Halpern's model of transition, which focuses on the interrelationships among work, residential, and social networks. Although work can bring a great deal of satisfaction and elevated self-esteem, a person can still be generally unhappy because of social isolation or a lack of leisure activities.

1 Legislative and Policy Aspects of Vocational Special Education

L. Allen Phelps and James R. Frasier
University of Illinois at Urbana-Champaign

INTRODUCTION AND OVERVIEW

As a result of several legislative and policy initiatives, educational and employment opportunities currently abound for handicapped and other special needs of youth and adults. Important provisions for equality of educational opportunity were established in the early 1960s at the beginning of the civil rights movement. During the 1970s, these provisions were extended to minorities, women, and handicapped individuals via federal legislation, amendments, and significant court decisions. Initially, the legislation focused on eliminating discriminatory practices and providing access to programs that previously had been closed to handicapped youth. Over the past twenty years, these policies have been expanded and refined to include affirmative action in employment, essential related services, and provisions ensuring the quality and appropriateness of education and training experiences.

This chapter provides an overview of legislative efforts and subsequent policies related to vocational education for persons with special needs. An understanding of the historical, present, and emerging policy frameworks for vocational special education is essential for practitioners, administrators, counselors, and others involved in programming for handicapped youth and adults. Knowledge of legislation dealing with special education, vocational education, rehabilitation, and job training can provide one with valuable insights into intended program policies, federal program purposes, anticipated client outcomes, and the degree to which civil rights assurances that have been accorded to handicapped individuals served with public funds have been met. Knowledge of the legal and policy framework can also provide guidance for evaluating and improving the mandated policies and programs, as well as the direction in which programs are moving. Equally important, a broad base of knowledge helps one to understand the multiple roles played by the different education, rehabilitation, and employment agencies that serve handicapped youth through interagency programming. And finally, insight into legislation and policy helps one understand the specific responsibilities of state agencies, universities, and local agencies in providing comprehensive programming and services to the handicapped population.

While laws, regulations, and policies help provide a basis for programming and services, they should not be mistaken for a complete philosophical framework. By design, federal and state legislation leaves open many issues and decisions about programming that are best handled at the community and program level. For example, the content of the vocational or related academic curriculum and the focus of the vocational assessment services are best determined with local input from parents, employers, and educators. Also, since local taxpayers bear most of the educational costs in our nation, many of the fundamental decisions regarding educational practices and policies are left for local determination.

Readers should also be aware of the diverse and complex influences that various economic, social, political, and professional factors have on the development and implementation of legislation and policy. These influences change continuously as economic, social, and political situations change within the United States and around the world. Policy is also heavily influenced by research, evaluation, and policy developments within the profession. As medical research has produced new knowledge concerning the treatment of diseases, laws and regulations have been instituted to ensure that new drugs and treatment programs are appropriately dispensed. The rapidly expanding knowledge base regarding effective training strategies for moderately and severely handicapped individuals has influenced the development of federal policies and programs created to provide competitive and supported employment for these individuals rather than sheltered employment and day-care services.

The major sections of this chapter provide a historical review of vocational education and employment-related policies in the United States; examine each of the major federal-state-local programs designed to assist in the vocational preparation of handicapped youth; and review current policy developments and likely future directions.

Throughout, we use the term *vocational special education* to refer broadly to those programs and services designed to assist in the employment of all *handicapped* youth, including those mildly, moderately, and severely handicapped. As will be noted in the discussion of federal vocational education legislation, considerable attention is given in that legislation to serving *persons with special needs*—a term that encompasses handicapped as well as disadvantaged, limited-English proficient, and other individuals requiring special assistance to complete an educational program. For the most part, our focus will be on legislation and policy serving handicapped youth, and where appropriate, the connections to and parallels for other special population groups will be noted.

HISTORICAL PERSPECTIVE

Societies have always been concerned, in some way, with the preparation and training of youth to carry on the work that is indigenous to the society. In early civilizations much of this preparation was handled informally by families. Sons and daughters simply learned the crafts and trades of their parents, and these became their lifetime careers. In European cultures of the eighteenth and nineteenth centuries, individuals were trained primarily through apprenticeships.

Early
Developments
In the latter part of the 1800s, public concern over the formal preparation of skilled workers for agriculture and industry, as well as for the broader preparation of girls for homemaking, grew in the United States. The Morrill Act of 1856 and the Land Grant College Act of 1862 established land grant colleges in each state whose primary mission was to provide advanced instruction in agricultural and mechanical arts. During the early part of the nineteenth century, the public common school movement was begun by Horace Mann in Massachusetts, a first step in implementing the states' constitutional responsibility to provide for the education of its citizens. The common schools and emerging high schools of the mid-1800s provided a standard curriculum oriented toward preparation for college. There were no alternatives for those youth interested in entering employment at the completion of their schooling, a situation for which the schools were later criticized. Finally, during the late 1800s, the manual training movement began, led by Calvin Woodward and John Runkle. The manual training curriculum was introduced in many secondary schools to provide students with psychomotor development experiences in the practical arts (for example, gardening, construction, drawing, cooking and sewing, farming). This curriculum also helped prepare youth for technical and advanced studies at the college level.

The Smith–Hughes Act of 1917 was enacted following the work of the Commission on National Aid to Vocational Education. The commission, appointed by President Wilson in 1914, examined the growing industrialization of the cities and the increased mechanization of agriculture. In the cities, manufacturing entrepreneurs were interested in having youth trained to enter various trade and industrial occupations following their formal schooling. In rural communities, families were increasingly interested in having their sons and daughters learn more about the new developments in agriculture and farming. Labor unions embraced vocational education as a safeguard against control by employers. Social reform advocates hailed the alternative curriculum as serving the needs of the poor and the newly arrived immigrants (Greenwood, 1982). As noted in the commission's report:

> The social and educational need for vocational training is equally urgent. Widespread vocational training will democratize the education of the country . . . by recognizing different tastes and abilities and by giving an equal opportunity to all to prepare for their life work. (Commission on National Aid to Vocational Education, 1914, p. 12)

Following the commission's recommendation that the federal government enter into a partnership with the states to begin providing specific vocational training programs at the high school level, the Smith-Hughes Act specifically focused resources on preparing youth for work rather than college. Mandating a federal-state-local public education partnership, the legislation required states to match federal vocational education funds. Funds were allocated to states on the basis of population, and state boards of education were required to submit state plans for their programs. The Act also established a federal board for vocational education, which was directly responsible to the Congress.

At the same time, the federal government was studying ways it could serve the needs of disabled World War I veterans. The Smith–Sears Act of 1918 and the Vocational Rehabilitation Act of 1920 initiated rehabilitation programs and provided funding to assist disabled war veterans and disabled civilians in returning to the workforce.

From 1917 to 1963, federal interest in vocational education grew steadily. Both federal and state funding increased as did the number of new programs within the scope of vocational education. In 1936 the George–Deen Act encouraged states to provide training for personal service and public service occupations and distributive (marketing) occupations. The 1956 amendments to the Health Act provided funds for practical nurse training. The George–Barden Acts in 1946, 1956, and 1959 provided support for vocational guidance, state-level administration for the growing program, and funds for construction of vocational facilities (David and Hendrickson, 1981).

During the late 1950s, the USSR's successful space program revitalized the nation's interest in technical, scientific, and higher education. Major concerns were voiced everywhere regarding the space race and its implications for national defense. Personnel shortages in the fields of aerospace engineering, electronics, mathematics, and foreign languages were cited as weaknesses in the educational system. The National Education Act of 1958 emphasized the importance of occupational preparation by providing funds for the training of skilled technicians, support for students interested in higher education, and $15 million for the construction of area vocational education programs (Nystrom and Bayne, 1979).

During the early 1960s, when the nation was in the throes of growing unemployment, underemployment of skilled workers, and a crucial civil rights movement, the landmark Vocational Education Act of 1963 was passed. This legislation represented a major philosophical redirection for the federal vocational education program away from preparation in specific occupational fields, such as agriculture and home economics, and towards a focus on the diverse needs of the youth and adults to be served by vocational education. The need to provide adults with more retraining opportunities, to open programs to the disadvantaged, and to include more vocational guidance and career planning services for youth was significant. The Act also emphasized greater program flexibility to better serve a dynamic and rapidly changing labor market. As noted by Nystrom and Bayne (1979, p. 39), the basic purpose of the Act was to provide:

> vocational training or retraining which is of high quality, which is realistic in the light of actual or anticipated opportunities for gainful employment, and which is suited to their needs, interests, and ability to benefit from such training. (Public Law 88-210, Section 1)

Among special populations, the Act provided that funds could be used by states for persons with academic, social, or other handicaps that prevent them from succeeding in regular vocational education programs. The Act also provided for curriculum development, research, demonstration and experimental programs, more extensive teacher training, and program evaluation—all done within the framework of a state plan. In addition, a national advisory council was created under the auspices of the commissioner of education.

In 1968 the Congress made several major amendments–essentially refinements and supplements to the 1963 act. These 1968 amendments provided for special programs and also funding for consumer and homemaking education, cooperative education, and leadership and professional development. Requirements were also enacted for state-level advisory councils that would help evaluate programs. Concerning special needs populations, the Congress had found that few if any states had implemented programs and services for the disadvantaged and handicapped populations. Therefore, states were directed to spend a minimum of 10 percent of their federal funds annually on programs for the handicapped and 15 percent on programs for the academically, economically, and socially disadvantaged.

In summary, the federal-state vocational education program has become well established in both rural and urban communities. Program focus, which originally included agriculture, home economics, and industrial trades, has been expanded to reflect the growing diversity in the nation's economy. As jobs have become increasingly complex, new legislation has provided for vocational guidance services, vocational education programs that directly involve employers in the training process, and technical education, as well as greater flexibility in planning programs to meet state and local employment needs. Beginning in the early 1960s, vocational education legislation was further expanded to provide vocational and technical education to special populations, including adults enrolling in postsecondary vocational programs, individuals identified as handicapped or disadvantaged, women, and the limited-English speaking.

Vocational Rehabilitation

The declared purpose of the first Vocational Rehabilitation Act (1920) was "to provide for the vocational rehabilitation of persons disabled in industry or otherwise and their return to civil employment." The Act specified that rehabilitation services were to be provided by the states and that state requests for federal appropriations were to: (1) list the rehabilitative services that would be undertaken; (2) identify courses of study; and (3) describe efforts that would be undertaken to place disabled persons in gainful employment. The act also prohibited states from using appropriated funds for the purchase or rental of buildings, land, or equipment.

Although the Vocational Rehabilitation Act of 1920 was sustained through funding by subsequent amendments (1924, 1930, 1932), federal legislative initiatives for the disabled were not undertaken again until the Vocational Rehabilitation Act Amendments of 1943. Addressing the needs of physically disabled individuals, these amendments stipulated that vocational rehabilitation services were to include: corrective surgery and/or therapeutic treatment necessary for correcting a handicap for employment, and associated hospitalization costs; transportation expenditures related to training; prosthetic devices essential to obtaining or retaining employment; and guidance and placement services.

In a departure from the act of 1920, the Vocational Rehabilitation Amendments of 1954 provided that federal funds could be used for the purchase or rental of existing buildings and equipment. This meant that federally mandated services could be expanded through the acquisition of (1) equipment and supplies for use by handicapped individuals in any type of small business; (2) rehabilitation facilities for the physically handicapped; and (3) employment workshops for adults with severe handicaps (such as mentally retarded individuals) who could not be readily absorbed into the competitive labor market.

The 1954 amendments also undertook to promote employment opportunities for handicapped persons. First, the secretary of health, education, and welfare and the secretary of labor were directed to jointly develop policies and procedures for facilitating the placement of handicapped individuals who had received rehabilitation services. Second, the U.S. Employment Service Act of 1933 was amended to provide that at least one individual in each state and federal employment office be designated as responsible for the development of employment opportunities, job counseling, and placement of handicapped individuals.

Further refinement of vocational rehabilitation services to include reader services for blind persons was made by 1965 amendments. Seeking to identify how structural barriers impeded employment of handicapped persons, these 1965 amendments created the National Commission on Architectural Barriers to Rehabilitation of the Handicapped. Many of this commission's recommendations were ultimately manifested in the Architectural Barriers Act (1968).

Employment and Job Training

During the early 1960s public concern arose over the severe economic deprivation being felt in certain areas of the nation, most notably in Appalachia and the South. Due to their inability to attract or retain business and industry, these areas experienced high levels of poverty and unemployment. It was generally believed that economic development was not occurring in many of these areas because the workforce was unskilled or skilled in inappropriate areas–and that this factor, in essence, created worker shortages. With the Area Redevelopment Act of 1961 and the Manpower Development and Training Act of 1962 (MDTA), the Congress and Department of Labor sought to provide job training and employment for unemployed, underemployed, and economically disadvantaged adults.

The 1963 amendments to the MDTA provided support for courses and on-the-job training for individuals who would be unable to qualify for employment without such training. Support services provided by the 1963 amendments included testing to determine training needs, occupational training (such as public school vocational education courses, on-the-job training), counseling, and job placement for those who completed the training. Many of the MDTA programs were conducted in the evenings in the vocational education facilities of local schools or the emerging area vocational centers. Various classroom training programs were administered by the state agencies responsible for vocational education. Training allowances to defray transportation and subsistence expenses were made available to persons who had not graduated from high school provided that: (1) the individuals had not attended school for a period of less than one year, and (2) all guidance and counseling efforts had determined that further attendance was no longer practical.

Transition-to-work services were further expanded by the MDTA amendments of 1966. Individuals who did not require occupational training but who did need basic education, communication, and employment skills to render them employable were designated as eligible for MDTA services. Physical examinations, medical treatments, and prostheses were also defined as appropriate MDTA client-related expenditures–a development that reflected a growing interest in disabled youth and adults who were poor and economically disadvantaged.

The Economic Development Act of 1964 was an additional effort undertaken specifically to strengthen employment and training opportunities for poor and disadvantaged youth. Many of the youth served in these programs were also mildly handicapped, but, for the most part, had not yet been served in fledgling special education programs at the high school level. The Job Corps, work training, and work-study were among the significant programs authorized by the Economic Development Act.

The Job Corps established urban and rural residential training centers for disadvantaged youth between the ages of 16 and 21. The centers provided enrollees with personal maintenance (such as clothing, medical services, and living allowances), education, vocational training, and work experiences. Enrollees who completed the Job Corps program were given a readjustment allowance of $50 for each month of satisfactory participation. Later amendments expanded the program to include youths who were 14 and 15 years of age, established nonresidential centers, and added job placement services for completers. Although highly successful in placing program graduates over the years, the Job Corps continues to draw extensive criticism for its high costs–approximately $15,000 per annual training slot (Committee on Government Operations, July 22, 1985).

The Economic Opportunity Act also provided work experience and training opportunities in public agencies and nonprofit organizations to encourage disadvantaged youth 16-22 years of age to resume or maintain school attendance. Participants in these programs were provided with vocational interest testing, counseling, and job placement services, as needed. In 1966, the program was reconstituted as the Neighborhood Youth Corps and services were expanded to include basic literacy instruction and occupational training courses. In these important initial programs, youth were given extensive training, support services, and transitional public service jobs with the expectation that they would eventually obtain employment in the private sector.

To help college students from low-income families who needed part-time employment to continue their studies, the Economic Opportunity Act set up work-study programs. Jobs were to be related to the student's program of study and were not to exceed fifteen hours per week while classes were in session.

Congress moved to consolidate programs developed under the MDTA and the Economic Opportunity Act by passing the Comprehensive Employment and Training Act (CETA) of 1973. In reality, much of the language from each of the earlier acts was simply transferred verbatim or with only minor refinements. Support services for participants in Job Corps programs, transitional public service employment, and work and training programs remained intact.

CETA was authorized to alleviate both the cyclical and structural problems of unemployment and underemployment of the disadvantaged. The structural problems of disadvantaged youth were addressed more extensively in 1977 with the passage of the Youth Employment and Demonstration Projects Act, which supplemented the earlier efforts under CETA. The new amendments called for transitional public service employment under a program entitled Youth Community Conservation and Improvement Projects. A residential program modeled in part on the Job Corps was initiated under the Young Adult Conservation Corps title. The Employment and Training Programs provided general work and training programs for non-school-age youth (over 16), as well as part-time employment programs for high school students from low-income families under the Youth Incentive Entitlement Projects program. The CETA amendments of 1978 also established a summer youth program to provide unemployed youth from low-income families with work, basic education, and sufficient on-the-job training to sustain a participant's summer employment.

Special Education

Special education programs in the nation's public schools began to develop in the 1930s and 1940s as a result of the growing knowledge base in child development and developmental and clinical psychology. However, for the most part, severely handicapped children continued to be institutionalized and those less severely handicapped were still kept at home by their parents. Early treatment and educational programs focused heavily on specific disabilities, such as mental retardation, emotional disturbance, and physical handicaps. Through collaborative efforts with vocational rehabilitation funding programs, high schools in major cities began to develop work-study programs for handicapped youth that provided part-time work experiences (initially in-school jobs and then community-based jobs) for youth with mild handicaps.

Following several major court decisions affirming the rights of handicapped children and youth to equal educational opportunity, many states moved to enact mandatory special education laws. Essentially, these laws stipulated that handicapped children receive equal and appropriate treatment by local educational agencies. In some states, such as Michigan, the legislation provided for educational programs and support services for handicapped individuals from birth through 26 years of age. During the late 1960s and early 1970s the federal government became increasingly interested in the educational needs of handicapped youth. In 1965 a small bureau was established within the U.S. Office of Education, and shortly thereafter the Congress began funding projects for demonstration programs, research, and teacher training. In November 1975 the Congress enacted the Education for All Handicapped Children Act, which signaled the beginning of the contemporary era in legislation and policy affecting the education and vocational preparation of handicapped individuals.

THE CONTEMPORARY LEGISLATIVE AND POLICY FRAMEWORK

Most of the landmark legislation and policies formulated for special education, vocational education, vocational rehabilitation, and employment and job training during the mid-1970s remain in effect. Indeed, the Education for All Handicapped Children Act and Sections 503 and 504 of the Rehabilitation Act were enacted as permanent civil rights legislation and do not have an expiration date as do traditional pieces of authorizing legislation. In this section we review the major contemporary pieces of legislation that guide the implementation of vocational programming for persons with special needs, and discuss their interaction.

Vocational Education

The contemporary legislative arena for vocational education is described by two major pieces of legislation: Title II of the Education Amendments of 1976 and the Carl D. Perkins Vocational Education Act of 1984. Since the Perkins Act has repealed the earlier vocational education legislation, it will be our primary focus.

Title II of the Education Amendments of 1976 was the second major revision of federal legislation reflecting new social and civil rights concerns for vocational education. The two major themes of the 1976 amendments were: (1) Strengthen the capacity for planning and evaluating vocational education programs, and (2) effectively serve special populations. In addition to sustaining many of the earlier state grant programs, new initiatives were created by the Amendments that focused on eliminating sex-role stereotyping in vocational programs, increasing to 20 percent the amount of federal funds set aside by each state for the disadvantaged, developing local plans for vocational education, and establishing local advisory councils composed of representatives of business, industry, and labor. At the national level, new programs were launched that focused on bilingual vocational training and provided vocational education to Native Americans.

Based on the 1976 amendments, the National Institute of Education conducted a study of vocational education. This report, released in September 1981 (David and Hendrickson, 1981), was instrumental in Congress's revision of the law. Among the major findings from the NIE study of the federal role in vocational education were the following:

- Federal grants, the instrument for assisting states, were too limited in scale to help states with the task of realizing *all* the diverse objectives of federal policy.

- Policies for distributing funds within states allowed funds to be allocated for purposes that might or might not have been congruent with the purposes of federal policy.

- Although states made greater efforts to serve students with special needs, the manner in which excess costs and matching requirements were interpreted sometimes inhibited localities from spending federal funds for these populations, thus creating a disincentive to mainstreaming these students in regular classes.

These and other findings are reflected in the Carl D. Perkins Vocational Education Act of 1984 (P.L. 98-524).

P.L. 98-524 narrows the federal role in vocational education to two areas: program improvement and serving special populations. As in prior legislation, funds are allocated to states on the basis of population and unemployment levels and upon submission of an approved state plan for distribution and use of the funds. Under the new law, 57 percent of the funds received by states must be allocated for vocational programs and support services that serve an array of special groups, including the handicapped, disadvantaged, limited-English proficient, adults in need of retraining, single parents and displaced homemakers, incarcerated individuals, and students enrolled in programs leading to nontraditional careers based on their sex. Of these funds, 10 percent are earmarked for handicapped students and 22 percent for disadvantaged individuals.

Annually, each local educational agency (local school or postsecondary institution) receives a funding allocation based on the number of disadvantaged and handicapped individuals served in the previous year and the number of economically disadvantaged individuals residing within their district. These funds are to be equally matched from state and local funds, and must be used only to support the costs of special supplemental services or modified special programs for the handicapped or disadvantaged students.

Section 204 of the Act also requires local schools (but not postsecondary institutions such as community colleges or technical institutes) to provide each handicapped and disadvantaged student with several specific services, including:

- Assessment of interests, abilities, and special needs
- Special services, including adaptation of curriculum, instruction, equipment, and facilities
- Guidance, counseling, and career development activities
- Counseling services designed to facilitate the transition from school to postschool employment and career opportunities.

In previous legislation the nature of the specific services and evaluations to be provided were not specified. Further, the act requires coordination of the programs and services for handicapped youth with the IEP and least restrictive environment provisions of the P.L. 94-142. The requirement that parents and handicapped and disadvantaged youth must be informed of the options available in vocational education programs prior to the ninth grade is also an important, new addition to the act.

Vocational Rehabilitation

The federal role in vocational rehabilitation was significantly modified with the passage of the Rehabilitation Act of 1973 (P.L. 93-112). The term *vocational* was removed from the title to reflect the broadened scope of rehabilitation, with a particular emphasis on the provision of services leading to gainful sheltered or homebound employment. The primary goal continued to be employment, which participants would enter after receiving the services, provided by the Act, but the policy no longer precluded services for other, interim outcomes. Generally, the Act extended funding for previously identified services that would enable handicapped individuals to overcome barriers to employment. Table 1.1 summarizes the services typically provided to eligible clients.

Provisions for the continued use of an individualized written rehabilitation program (IWRP) were also included in the Act to ensure that services would be based on an appropriate assessment and intervention plan. Similar to the IEPs required in P.L. 94-142, the IWRPs required the following: (1) a statement of long-range rehabilitation goals and related objectives; (2) a statement of specific rehabilitation services to be provided; (3) projected dates for initiation and duration of services; (4) objective evaluation criteria; and (5) where appropriate, a detailed explanation of the availability of a client assistance project.

P.L. 93-112 also addressed for the first time the problems of employment faced by handicapped individuals. Section 503 of the Act stipulates that any businesses or agencies contracted by the government to provide goods and services at a level in excess of $2,500 must have affirmative action guidelines relating to the employment of handicapped persons. Further, those contractors whose contracts exceed $50,000 annually or have at least fifty employees must develop affirmative action programs. Affirmative action programs identify appropriate recruitment and hiring procedures, specify how the business

TABLE 1.1. Services for rendering handicapped individuals employable as listed in the Rehabilitation Act of 1973

Evaluation of rehabilitation potential

Counseling, guidance, referral, placement, and follow-up assistance

Vocational and other training programs

Personal and vocational adjustment costs (such as books)

Corrective surgery or therapeutic treatment

Hospital costs in connection with surgery or treatment

Prosthetic and orthopedic devices

Medically prescribed eyeglasses and visual medical treatment

Treatment costs associated with end-renal disease

Diagnosis and treatment for mental and emotional disorders

Subsistence living allowance during rehabilitation

Interpreter costs for deaf individuals

Reader costs for blind persons

Training of individuals for new careers (such as in health, welfare)

Orientation and mobility services for blind individuals

Occupational licenses, tools and equipment costs

Initial stocks and supplies for small business ventures

Transportation costs associated with rehabilitation services

Costs for telecommunications, sensory and other aids and devices

Other goods and services necessary to render a client employable

or agency will make "reasonable accommodation" to the job and work environments, and describe the training opportunities that will be provided to handicapped workers. The President's Committee on Employment of the Handicapped has estimated that approximately half the private businesses in the United States are subject to the requirements of Section 503.

Section 504 of this landmark legislation seeks to eliminate discrimination on the basis of handicap in any program or activity that receives federal financial assistance. The Rehabilitation Act (1973) mandates that individuals who are otherwise qualified shall not be "excluded from participation in, be denied the benefits of, or be subjected to discrimination under any program or activity receiving federal financial assistance." While regulations implementing this section were not issued until 1977, the impact of the provision on schools, social service agencies, institutions of higher education, and community organizations has been quite profound. Among the major provisions of the federal rules are the following:

- Opportunities, benefits, aids, and services must be provided for handicapped individuals that are equal to those provided for nonhandicapped individuals.

- Aids, benefits, and services must be provided in the same setting as that experienced by the nonhandicapped, except in cases where their effectiveness is jeopardized by doing so

- Barrier-free environments must be provided to ensure full access to facilities and programs.

- Equal recruitment, training, promotion, and compensation opportunities must be provided to the handicapped.

The Rehabilitation Act Amendments of 1974 (P.L. 93-516) reaffirmed the broadening of rehabilitation services. Title IV of the 1974 amendments provided community service employment and projects for training the severely disabled in the "real work" settings of business and industry.

Finally, the passage of the Rehabilitation, Comprehensive Services, and Developmental Disabilities Amendments of 1978 (P.L. 95-602) broadly expanded services for the full range of handicapped youth and adults. These amendments established major new program thrusts through pilot employment projects; comprehensive services for independent living; and special service programs for deaf individuals, blind individuals, and handicapped Native Americans. The law also established the National Institute for Handicapped Research and the National Council on the Handicapped, and strengthened the provisions afforded handicapped persons under the affirmative action programs. In many instances, this law has been interpreted as an entitlement piece of legislation that allows handicapped persons to receive services under the banner of a right rather than a privilege (Kiernan and Payne, 1982).

Employment and Training Legislation

In 1982, Congress enacted the Job Training Partnership Act (JTPA) to re-place the CETA programs. Seeking to shift training and employment programs away from public and nonprofit organization employes, the JTPA emphasized private sector involvement in all aspects of planning and implementing job training programs for the unemployed, underemployed, and economically disadvantaged. More specifically, the Act continued the Job Corps program, refined and expanded supportive

TABLE 1.2.   JTPA support services for youth

Job search and counseling assistance

Outreach to encourage use of employment and training services

Work experience and vocational exploration

Remedial education and institutional skill-training courses

On-the-job training

Client participation in private sector training programs

On-site, industry-specific training programs

Assistance to enable individuals to retain employment

Programs to develop work habits needed to obtain and retain work

Skill upgrading and retraining

Education-to-work transition activities

Literacy and bilingual training

Attainment of certificates of high school equivalency

Job development and employment-generating activities

Advanced training programs using on-the-job and institutional facilities

Needs-based payments necessary for client participation in program

Customized training with employer commitment to hire upon completion

Preapprenticeship programs

Follow-up services with participants placed in unsubsidized employment

Coordinated programs with other federal employment-related activities

Use of advanced learning technology for education and skills training

services for eligible participants (see Table 1.2), provided for exemplary programs, and extended summer programs for disadvantaged youth.

The JTPA required that states establish service delivery areas (SDA) (that is, local units of government with a population base of 200,00 or greater), and that each SDA establish a private industry council (PIC).

The PIC, which has major responsibility for planning and overseeing the programs, is to be composed mainly of individuals representing the private sector. Representatives of education, rehabilitation, and community-based organizations are also represented on the PIC to help ensure appropriate program coordination.

Most states have adopted the "family-of-one rule," which allows handicapped individuals to be considered as a family of one when income is used as the criterion for determining client eligibility. In these states the income of parents is not a factor in considering the program eligibility of handicapped individuals. Additionally, handicapped persons are targeted as a special population for JTPA services. In the last several years, special educators have become increasingly knowledgeable about JTPA programs and policies and have been successful in convincing PICs to fund special programs for handicapped youth. Tindall (1985) noted that participation by handicapped youth and adults in job-training programs has begun to increase under the JTPA.

To encourage employers to hire handicapped and disadvantaged individuals, Congress included provisions with the Tax Reduction and Simplification Act of 1977 entitled "New Jobs Credit." Commonly referred to as the "targeted jobs tax credit" (TJTC), this incentive provided a tax credit of up to 50 percent on the first $4,200 of wages earned by economically disadvantaged individuals 16-25 years of age. Employers who provided employment to individuals referred by a vocational rehabilitation agency received an additional 10 percent credit.

The Revenue Act of 1978 repealed the 10 percent credit to employers for hiring vocational rehabilitation referrals, but increased to $6,000 the wage limit of the TJTC employees used for calculating employer tax credits. This Act also expanded the TJTC to include any individual–regardless of income–between 16 and 18 who was enrolled in a qualified cooperative education program. In 1981, the Economic Recovery Tax Act narrowed the TJTC eligibility standards for cooperative education students to only those who were economically disadvantaged.

The current legislation, the Tax Equity and Fiscal Responsibility Act (1982), expanded the ranks of those eligible for TJTC certification to include summer employees between the ages of 16 and 18 who were also economically disadvantaged. Of particular significance to employers, TJTC enabled them to receive an 85 percent tax credit on the first $3,000 the youths (hired for the period between May 1 and September 15) earned in summer wages.

Special Education

Both the Education for All Handicapped Children Act of 1975 (P.L. 94-142) and the Education for the Handicapped Act Amendments of 1983 (P.L. 98-199) are focal points of current federal policy. Both will be described and discussed, with particular regard for their implications for handicapped youth and the transition of such youth from school to work.

With the passage of P.L. 94-142, Congress mandated a national special education law charging state and local education agencies with providing a free and appropriate education for handicapped youth between the ages of 3 and 21. Hearings regarding the new law revealed that there were more than eight million school-age handicapped youth who were not receiving an adequate education, and one million who were excluded from school entirely (Nystrom and Bayne, 1979). Additionally, many mildly handicapped youth who were in school were being served solely in self-contained, separate special education programs.

The Act provides several assurances and protective measures for handicapped children and their parents. These provisions form the basis for guaranteeing a free and appropriate education:

- Comprehensive due process procedures
- Development of an individualized educational program (IEP) for each student
- Assurance that each student will be placed in the "least restrictive environment," meaning that, to the maximum extent possible, handicapped learners are to be educated with their nonhandicapped peers. Students will be placed in special schools or separate classes only when the severity of their handicap is such that supplementary aids and services provided in regular classes are not effective.
- Policies and procedures that ensure the confidentiality of student records
- Testing and evaluation procedures and materials used to determine the appropriate educational placement for handicapped youth that will not be racially or culturally discriminatory

The IEP provision has major implications for coordinating programs and services for handicapped youth. The rules and regulations of both P.L. 94-142 and the current Carl Perkins Vocational Education Act urge vocational educators, special educators, counselors, administrators, parents, and other appropriate personnel to be involved in developing the instructional plan and needed support services for handicapped students. The IEP is to be a written statement that translates evaluation information on the student into a practical plan for instruction and delivery of services. In addition to assessing the student's current level of educational performance, the IEP must also include a statement of annual goals and short-term instructional objectives, the special education and related services to be provided, dates for initiation and duration of services, and criteria and schedules for annual evaluation of the student's progress. While the act does not require the inclusion of "vocational" goals or objectives, it is difficult to imagine an IEP as being "appropriate" without the inclusion of some career or vocationally oriented goals, especially for older handicapped youth.

The least restrictive environment (LRE) provision has major implications for the roles of regular education and vocational education teachers, as well as for the curricula that are provided to handicapped youth. First, vocational teachers and regular educators are expected to modify their teaching procedures and materials to the extent appropriate to accommodate handicapped learners within regular classrooms. Because mechanisms for accomplishing these goals are not specified in the legislation or regulations, vocational, regular, and special educators should work cooperatively and closely in individualizing instruction and providing related educational and counseling services to students with special needs. Administrative mechanisms and support for achieving this flexibility are also essential. Second, the LRE provision clearly suggests that, for older handicapped youth, the least restrictive and most responsive environment should include vocationally related goals and objectives. In response to this provision, major efforts have been undertaken to develop community-based training programs for moderately and severely handicapped youth who have not historically been served in high school vocational education programs (Vogelsberg, 1986; Rusch, 1986). Personnel from sheltered workshops, residential schools, and adult service centers have taken the lead in developing these programs and services.

Another important link to vocational education programming is the full educational opportunity provision of P.L. 94-142. Specifically, the federal rules and regulations state that "state and local educational agencies shall take steps to insure that handicapped children have available to them the variety of programs and services available to non-handicapped children, including . . . industrial arts, home economics, and vocational education" (Federal Register, August 23, 1977). This provision extends the obligation for cooperative programming and serving special students to those vocational programs that may not be receiving federal funds.

Finally, P.L. 94-142 focuses on personnel development. The law requires that each state formulate a comprehensive system of personnel development that provides both in-service and preservice training to special educators, parents, and other educators to help them implement the provisions of the law.

The Education of the Handicapped Act Amendments of 1983 (P.L. 98-199) extended and revised a number of special federal programs focusing on research, personnel preparation, and demonstration programs for children with learning disabilities and young handicapped individuals. A new program was also initiated that provides grants for developing model programs for secondary special education and transitional services. Targeted at reducing the continuing high levels of unemployment and fragmented delivery of services found in many communities, this $6 million program annually provides grants to local and state education agencies, institutions of higher education, public and private nonprofit organizations, and job-training service providers. More specifically, the program supports demonstration projects that "strengthen and coordinate education, training, and related services for handicapped youth to assist in the transitional process to postsecondary education, vocational training, competitive employment, continuing education, or adult services." In fiscal years 1984 and 1985, approximately 120 demonstration projects were awarded in competitions focusing on postsecondary programs, youth employment programs, and cooperative planning models for state and local agencies (Decoteau, Leach, and Harmon, 1986).

In summary, the legislative framework of the 1980s for responding to the education and employment problems faced by handicapped youth and adults has become increasingly complex. Prior to the early 1960s, these problems and related issues were given only limited recognition in federal policy. Since then, the various pieces of legislation focusing on special education, rehabilitation, job training, vocational education, and employment have been refined and now offer a clear framework for monitoring and strengthening state and local employment and educational efforts. The major task facing professionals and policymakers remains one of fully informing local officials and employers about the various legislative and policy initiatives, and then assisting them with programming efforts designed to facilitate effective implementation.

RECENT POLICY DEVELOPMENTS AND FUTURE DIRECTIONS

Within the contemporary policy and legislative framework, states and local communities have developed several exciting and innovative approaches to vocational program development for handicapped youth and adults. Although vastly different in design, most of these state policy initiatives and new programs directly address the problem of increasing educational and employment opportunities in order to create a smooth transition from school to work. At the state level, new efforts have been launched to create statewide transition plans, revise or expand cooperative interagency agreements, strengthen professional and personal development, and provide technical assistance to local schools and communities in expanding and improving programs. Locally, the most promising new initiatives have focused on expanding IEPs to include transition planning, developing postsecondary options and appropriate cooperative agreements, and increasing program involvement by business and industry. These and other policy developments will be discussed in this concluding section.

Cooperative Agreements The use of cooperative or interagency agreements has been a popular policy mechanism for several decades in both federal and state legislation for stimulating program and/or fiscal cooperation. Most often they are developed between or among agencies with clearly interactive missions or functions. For instance, the 1968 vocational education amendments encouraged state boards of vocational education to develop cooperative agreements with state vocational rehabilitation and state special education agencies to describe how vocational programs for handicapped individuals would be coordinated with the programs and services provided by their respective agencies. Such agreements were often appended to the state plans and considered an essential part of state policy.

In 1978 the U.S. commissioner of education and the commissioner of the Rehabilitation Services Administration of the then Department of Health, Education, and Welfare issued a memorandum to state leaders calling for the development of state-level interagency agreements involving rehabilitation agencies and focusing on the delivery of comprehensive vocational education services to handicapped individuals (U.S.O.E., 1978). The policy memorandum was based, in part, on an earlier position statement from the Office of Education acknowledging the importance of cooperative planning in providing comprehensive vocational education to handicapped persons (Federal Register, September 25, 1978). The memorandum was followed by a national conference for state directors from the three agencies; it was held in 1979 in Washington, D.C., to provide guidance to states in developing or revising such agreements. The conference was aimed at assisting states in:

> development of new interagency agreements among state departments of special education, state boards of vocational education, and state rehabilitation agencies . . . during fiscal year 1979. (U.S.O.E., 1978)

The memorandum specified or urged that: (1) minimum services be included in the agreements, (2) collaborative implementation of IEPs and IWRPs begin at the earliest possible age, (3) cooperative funding be considered, and (4) pertinent information between agencies be shared (Tindall, 1982).

More recently, the U.S. Office of Special Education and Rehabilitative Services (formerly the Bureau of Education for the Handicapped and the Rehabilitative Services Administration) undertook a major policy initiative to strengthen the transition from school to work of handicapped youth (Will, 1984). The policy statement broadens the earlier focus of cooperation to include the private sector:

> Cooperative relationships between special education, vocational rehabilitation, and vocational education can do much to facilitate vocational planning and ensure smooth changes in service responsibility. . . . Efforts to improve employment opportunities will involve cooperative initiatives with other agencies. Of particular concern to OSERS is development of a broader range of incentives for employers who offer jobs to individuals who may require special

equipment, building modifications, longer training periods, or other investments. (pp. 4-5)

Many of the cooperative agreements now being developed at the state level involve a growing number of agencies. Agreements and cooperative activities seem to be most prominent among vocational education, rehabilitation, JTPA agencies, and special education. In most instances, the cooperative agreements are among two or three agencies. It is not uncommon to find state agencies having agreements with multiple agencies rather than single, large multiagency agreements. Cooperative agreements concerning the vocational preparation of handicapped individuals might also involve agencies responsible for developmental disabilities, the Job Corps, corrections, mental health, and a host of other appropriate human service providers.

North Dakota has undertaken innovative and unique cooperative planning activities under a recent grant from the Secondary and Transition Program sponsored by the U.S. Office of Special Education and Rehabilitative Services. Following an interagency conference to identify the problems and issues affecting the transition of secondary age handicapped youth to postschool adjustment, a transition-related services agreement was developed and adopted by the state education and rehabilitation agencies. The sponsoring agencies include: North Dakota Department of Public Instruction, Special Education; State Board for Vocational Education, Vocational Special Needs; Department of Human Services, Developmental Disabilities Services; and the Department of Human Services, Division of Vocational Rehabilitation. A full-time transition services staff member has been employed by the project to travel throughout the state assisting local schools and community agencies in developing and implementing similar local agreements (Decoteau, Leach, and Harmon, 1986).

Professional Development

Over the past decade state and local agencies and universities have significantly increased their efforts at professional development in the field of vocational special education. Realizing that the quality of programs and services depends heavily on the skills and knowledge of professionals, paraprofessionals, and parents, various special training programs have been launched to provide training and assistance to practitioners. Due to the large number of teachers, counselors, and administrators who entered the field prior to the landmark legislation of the late 1970s, most resources for professional development since then have been spent on in-service programs. However, in the past five years universities and colleges have begun increasingly to address the implications of vocational special education in their undergraduate teacher education and other professional education programs (rehabilitation, social work, and so on).

Significant funds have been available from discretionary grant programs of the U.S. OSERS as well as through state vocational education and rehabilitation agencies for personnel training and technical assistance programs. Two such programs are described below.

The Leadership Development Program in Vocational Special Education at the University of Illinois assists teams of vocational and special educators from ten to fifteen communities each year in developing and implementing local program improvement plans. Participant teams attend two intensive summer workshops to broaden their knowledge and expertise in vocational special education as well as in specific areas of programming, such as vocational assessment. By the conclusion of these summer workshops, each team has carefully assessed their own program and community and developed an action plan, which they implement during the following school year to strengthen and expand their programs and services for handicapped and disadvantaged students. Faculty members from various departments, graduate assistants, and consultants provide technical assistance and workshops for the participants throughout the school year as well. Participants receive tuition and fee waivers for graduate course credit from the university, and each participating agency receives approximately $2,000 to assist in the implementation of the action plan (Schutz, 1986).

With funding from the California Office of Vocational Education, the Institute on Human Services at Sonoma State University has established the Vocational Education Resource System (VERS). VERS assists vocational education personnel in their efforts to integrate students with special needs into regular vocational education programs and services. The system provides both comprehensive technical assistance and information referral for teachers, counselors, and administrators. VERS has trained a group of resource facilitators who meet with local administrators, teachers, and special needs staff to conduct self-assessments of the local program and develop improvement plans. Over the past two years, program improvements have focused heavily on identifying appropriate instructional materials, strengthening vocational assessment efforts, providing appropriate career counseling, and delivering in-service training to staff. Schools can request various kinds of materials and assistance through VERS to move forward with planned program improvements. VERS also disseminates a comprehensive newsletter throughout the state (California Institute on Human Services, Winter 1986).

Special Projects

Several states have established special projects or programs designed to be implemented on an optional basis by local agencies and schools. These projects and programs tend to be found in states where: (1) state government has historically taken a major interest in education, (2) extensive local program planning to obtain federal or state funds is not required by state statute, and (3) strong interdepartmental or interagency cooperation exists at the state level. Ballantyne (1985) recently reviewed several of these state-local programs involving special education and rehabilitation service providers.

An example of a state-initiated special program is Project Workability (Zittel, 1985). This project is a statewide job training and job placement program representing an interagency effort of educators, employment specialists, and rehabilitation counselors in California. Begun in 1981, three state agencies–education, rehabilitation, and employment development–combined financial resources and offered grants to local schools to pay for the "excess costs" incurred by the local schools in providing job development, student stipends, job placement, and job follow-up services to place disabled youth between 16 and 21 years of age in private sector jobs or continuing education.

Local Project Workability programs differ in design depending on the urban-rural-suburban nature of the community, the personalities of the local project leaders, the types of students being served, employment opportunities, and the needs of the local school board. However, common performance criteria are applied to all programs, which currently include 112 projects serving approximately 500 schools and 5,000 students. Special educators, vocational educators, or regular education teachers must assist students in either obtaining employment or ensuring that they pursue continued education beyond high school. After local projects are under way, many obtain continuing funding from the local JTPA Private Industry Council. The cooperative spirit developed by aligning vocational and special educators with rehabilitation counselors, employment specialists, and local employers has been very beneficial to all who are involved. In 1985-1986, fifty new projects were initiated through an additional $3.5 million in state funds, $1.25 million in federal special education funds, and $500,000 from the Department of Employment Development. Federal rehabilitation funds are also being used to start Workability Projects in the regional occupational programs and centers.

Transition-Focused Programs

In 1984 the U.S. OSERS adopted a new initiative focused on the transition from school to adult working life. Based on the realization that the number of handicapped adolescents nearing graduation or completion of high school has rapidly increased each year as a result of the implementation of P.L. 94-142, many local schools and rehabilitation agencies have focused heavily on the question of what happens to individuals after high school. Two of the projects recently funded by the OSERS as part of this initiative are examined here to illustrate some of the alternative approaches that can be taken within the policy arena.

Project INTERFACE seeks to design, implement, and evaluate a model postsecondary demonstration project focusing on minority disabled youths (D'Alonzo, Owen, and Hartwell, 1985). Funded at Arizona State

University in 1983, Project INTERFACE links disabled youth who exit secondary school and who are not yet ready for competitive employment to community-based training programs and services. This linkage occurs through the development of a job bank and information clearinghouse. Disabled students between the ages of 18 and 22 are served using four major program components: identification, intervention, employment, and evaluation. The intervention component includes vocational evaluation, employment training, and job placement. Individualized transition education plans are developed and used for each client. Employment assistance is provided through individual counseling, working closely with employers, and providing crisis intervention as needed.

Project Transition into Employment (TIE), located at Virginia Commonwealth University (VCU), assists states in developing inter-agency teams that facilitate school-to-work transition for persons with severe disabilities (Rehabilitation Research and Training Center, 1986). Teams of professionals from vocational rehabilitation, special education, vocational education, and developmental disabilities are trained to serve as statewide trainers for local transition teams. During a week-long intensive course at VCU, participating TIE teams develop expertise in: training local transition teams to write and implement effective transition plans, training teachers and adult service providers to implement school employment training programs and supported work programs, and providing technical assistance to others in establishing transitional services. The programming process used in Project TIE includes: establishing an individual transition team; preparing an individual transition plan involving key professionals, parents, and the student; identifying goals and procedures for community-based vocational training; identifying a job as the student begins his or her last year of school; and providing supported employment services as needed following graduation.

Future Directions

As can be seen from this brief review of selected projects and policy initia-tives, considerable differences exist in the ways in which states and local communities are implementing efforts in vocational special education. Many of the initiatives are clearly based on comprehensive efforts to interface with the various federal programs described earlier. These diverse yet comprehensive initiatives are a strong endorsement for state and local leadership, as well as for policy flexibility. Clearly, the nation has developed over the past two decades a comprehensive policy framework for dealing with the education and employment difficulties faced by handicapped youth. As each year passes, this policy framework appears to be more clearly understood and appropriately implemented by state and local leaders.

Although major amendments and refinements have been added in the past three years (for example, the Carl D. Perkins Vocational Education

Act, the Secondary and Transition Services Program in the Education of the Handicapped Act Amendments of 1983), the overall framework appears to be operating with increased effectiveness. What appears to be lacking and clearly needed, however, is a comprehensive policy evaluation study that examines the collective effects, costs, and benefits of these initiatives on the employment of persons with special needs, including mildly, moderately, and severely handicapped youth and adults. However, since both the federal and state governments have begun to invest more heavily in programs and services for these populations, it is likely that such careful evaluation of the policies and programs will be required at all levels in the coming years.

A number of other future directions also appear likely. As the disabled youth population grows older (along with the rest of the baby boomers), greater attention will need to be directed toward the employment and retaining problems of disabled adults. The changing nature of employment (including job sharing, flex-time, deskilling in certain industries) and the impact of technology on the workplace will likely create significant problems for handicapped persons that will need to be addressed by employer-based training, community colleges, or other post-secondary training agencies. Finally, the current emphasis in secondary schools on academic excellence poses a severe threat to vocational education and other specialized curricula that are often viewed as nonessential elements of a general or liberal education. The extent to which the secondary school curriculum of the future can provide high-quality, comprehensive educational experiences for *all* of the nation's youth will most surely have an impact on the employability of youth with handicaps in the year 2000 and beyond.

REFERENCES

Area Redevelopment Act of 1961, U.S.C. 42 2513 (Supplement V 1959-63).

Ballantyne, D. (1985). *Cooperative Programs for Transition from School to Work.* Washington, D.C.: National Institute for Handicapped Research.

California Institute on Human Service. (Winter 1985-86). *Working Together.*

Carl D. Perkins Vocational Education Act of 1984 (P.L. 98-524).

Commission on National Aid to Vocational Education. (1914). *Report of the Commission on National Aid to Vocational Education* (together with hearings held on the subject). U.S. House of Representatives, 63rd Congress, Second session, Doc. No. 1004. Volume 1, p. 12. Washington, D.C.: U.S. Government Printing Office.

Committee on Government Operations. (July 22, 1985). *Jobs Corps Program: Its Benefits Outweigh the Costs.* 14th report. Washington, D.C.: U.S. Government Printing Office.

Comprehensive Employment and Training Act of 1973, U.S.C. 29 874, 918, 919 (1976).

Comprehensive Employment and Training Act Amendments of 1978, U.S.C. 29 893, 899, 906, 942, 991 (Supplement V 1981).

D'Alonzo, B., S.D. Owen, and L.K. Hartwell (1985). Transition models: An overview of the current state of the art. *Techniques 1* (6), 429-436.

David, H. and G. Hendrickson. (1981). *The Vocational Education Study: The Final Report.* Washington, D.C.: National Institute of Education.

Decoteau, J.P., L.G. Leach, and A.S. Harmon. (1986). *Handbook for Project Directors.* Champaign: Transition Institute at Illinois, University of Illinois.

Economic Opportunity Act of 1964, U.S.C. 42 2711, 2731, 2751, (1964).

Economic Opportunity Act Amendments of 1966, U.S.C. 42 2732 (Supplement II 1965-66).

Economic Opportunity Act Amendments of 1967 U.S.C. 42 2713, 2723, 2738 (Supplement III 1965-68).

Economic Recovery Tax Act of 1981, U.S.C. 26 51 (1982).

Education for All Handicapped Children Act of 1975, 20 U.S.C. 1410(i), 1412(2) (A), 1414(a) (i) (C), (1982).

Education for the Handicapped Act Amendments of 1983 (P.L. 98-199).

Federal Register, September 25, 1978). Comprehensive vocational education for handicapped persons..43(186).

Federal Register. (August 23, 1977). Implementation of part B of the education of the handicapped act. 42(163), p. 42488, 1212.305.

Greenwood, K.B. (1982). An historical look at politics in vocational education. In American Vocational Association, *Politics of Vocational Education.* Arlington, Va.: American Vocational Association.

Job Training Partnership Act of 1982, 29 U.S.C. 1512(a) (b), 1604, 1605, 1632 (1982).

Kiernan, W.E., and Pyne, M.E. (1982). Hard to train: A history of vocational training for special needs youth. In K.P. Lynch, W.E. Kiernan, and J.A. Stark (eds.), *Prevocational and Vocational Education for Special Needs Youth.* Baltimore: Paul H. Brookes.

Manpower Development and Training Act of 1962, U.S.C. 42 2571 (1970).

Manpower Development and Training Act Amendments of 1963, U.S.C. 2583, 2584 (1964).

Manpower Development and Training Act Amendments of 1966, 42 U.S.C. 2581, 2583 (Supplement II 1965-66).

Nystrom, D.C. and G.K. Bayne. (1979) *Occupation and Career Education Legislation* 2nd ed. Indianapolis, In.: Bobbs-Merrill Educational Publishing.

Rehabilitation Act of 1973, 29 U.S.C. 723(a), 721(a) (9), 793, 794, 795(a), 795(g) (1982).

Rehabilitation Act Amendments of 1978, U.S.C. 29 795 (1982).

Rehabilitation Act Amendments of 1984 (P.L. 98-211).

Rehabilitation, Comprehensive Services, and Developmental Disabilities Amendments of 1978, U.S.C. 29 796 (1982).

Rehabilitation Research and Training Center. Virginia Commonwealth University. (1986). *Project TIE–Transition into Employment, i(i).*

Revenue Act of 1978, 26 U.S.C. 51 (1982).

Rusch, F.R. (ed.). (1986). *Competitive Employment Issues and Strategies.* Baltimore: Paul H. Brookes.

Schutz, R. (1986). *Leadership Development Program in Vocational Special Needs Education: Final Report.* Champaign: Office of Career Development for Special Populations, University of Illinois.

Smith-Hughes Act of 1917, U.S. Statutes at Large, Volume 39. (1917).

Tax Equity and Fiscal Responsibility Act of 1982, 26 U.S.C. 51 (1982).

Tax Reduction and Simplification Act of 1977, 26 U.S.C. 44B (1982).

Tindall, L.W. et al. (1982). *Handbook on Developing Effective Linking Strategies.* Madison: University of Wisconsin, Vocational Studies Center.

Tindall, L.W. (September 1985). The Job Training Partnership Act and transition from school to work for handicapped youth. Paper presented at the Forum on School-to-Work Transition for Handicapped Youth, University of Illinois.

U.S. Office of Education. (1978). Memorandum on cooperative agreements. In L.A. Phelps (ed.), *A Compendium of Interagency Agreements: Vocational Education, Special Education, and Vocational Rehabilitation.* Champaign: Leadership Training Institute/Vocational and Special Education, University of Illinois.

Vocational Education Act of 1963, 26 U.S.C. 5 (1964).

Vocational Education Act Amendments of 1968, 26 U.S.C. 1262(c), 1263(b) (F), (1970).

Vocational Education Act Amendments of 1976, 20 U.S.C. 2310(a) (b) (1982).

Vocational Rehabilitation Act of 1920 (P.L. 236).

Vocational Rehabilitation Act Amendments of 1924 (P.L. 209).

Vocational Rehabilitation Act Amendments of 1930 (P.L. 317).

Vocational Rehabilitation Act Amendments of 1932 (P.L. 4743).

Vocational Rehabilitation Act Amendments of 1943 29 U.S.C. 40 (1946).

Vocational Rehabilitation Act Amendments of 1954 29 U.S.C. 41(a) (7) (A), 41(f), 38 (1958).

Vocational Rehabilitation Act Amendments of 1965, 29 U.S.C. 41, 41 (D) (1964 Supplement II).

Vogelsberg, R.T. (1986). Competitive employment in Vermont. In F.R. Rusch (ed.), *Competitive Employment Issues and Strategies.* Baltimore: Paul H. Brookes.

Will, M. (March/April 1984). Bridges from school to working life. *Programs for the Handicapped* 2.

Youth Employment and Demonstration Programs Act of 1977, 29 U.S.C. 801 (Supplement V 1981).

Zittel, G. (Winter 1985-86). Handicapped youth prove their "work-ability." *Working Together.*

2 Career Education for Students with Handicaps

Warren J. White
Kansas State University

Ernest Biller
Ohio State University

"Career education" began as a response to a growing dissatisfaction with American schools. In the late 1960s and early 1970s many educators and educational organizations became disenchanted with the structures and outcomes of contemporary educational institutions and policies. During this period, educational critics were concerned about the authoritative and oppressive nature of schooling, an overemphasis on abstract knowledge, and the absence of alternatives for students with different goals, backgrounds, and ability levels. A document adopted by the U.S. Office of Education succinctly summarized the opinions of many professionals at that time:

1. Too many persons leaving our educational system are deficient in the basic academic skills required for adaptability in today's rapidly changing society.

2. Too many students fail to see meaningful relationships between what they are being asked to learn in school and what they will do when they leave the educational system. This is true of both those who remain to graduate and those who drop out of the educational system.

3. American education, as currently structured, best meets the educational needs of that minority of persons who will someday become college graduates. It fails to place equal emphasis on meeting the educational needs of the vast majority of students who will never be college graduates.

4. American education has not kept pace with the rapidity of change in the postindustrial occupational society. As a result, when worker qualifications are compared with job requirements, we find overeducated and undereducated workers are present in large numbers. Both the boredom of the overeducated worker and the frustration of the undereducated worker have contributed to the growing worker alienation in the total occupational society.

5. Too many persons leave our educational systems at both the secondary and collegiate levels unequipped with the vocational skills, the self-understanding and career decision-making skills, or the work attitudes that are essential for making a successful transition from school to work.

6. The growing need for and presence of women in the workforce has not been reflected adequately in either the educational or career options typically pictured for girls enrolled in our educational system.

7. The growing needs for continuing and recurrent education of adults are not being met adequately by our current systems of public education.

8. Insufficient attention has been given to learning opportunities [that] exist outside the structure of formal education and are increasingly needed by both youth and adults in our society.

9. The general public, including parents and the business-industry-labor community, has not been given an adequate role in the formulation of educational policy.

10. American education, as currently structured, does not adequately meet the needs of minority or economically disadvantaged persons in our society.

11. Post high school education has given insufficient emphasis to educational programs at the sub-baccalaureate degree level. (Hoyt, 1975, pp. 1-2)

Various educational movements began as a result of these criticisms. Open schools, schools without failure, and incidental education, among others, were all designed to address the ills of what was perceived as an educational system that was failing to meet the needs of many children. Career education was also proposed as a solution to these problems.

Sidney P. Marland, Jr., is credited by many educators with beginning the current career education movement in the United States. In a 1971 address to the National Association of Secondary School Principals, Dr. Marland applied the label "career education" to his proposed solution to the pervasive lack of curriculum relevance for a great majority of youth. Since that time, career education has grown at a remarkable rate. For example, in 1973 a Center for Career Education was established within the Bureau of Occupational and Adult Education. During 1974 an Associate Commissioner for Career Education was appointed and the newly passed Education Amendments of 1975 (PL 93-380) authorized the establishment of a U.S. Office of Career Education, funded up to $15 million for career education each fiscal year until 1978, and authorized the appointment of a National Advisory Council on Career Education. Part C of Title III (Career Education and Career Development) of the Education Amendments of 1976 (PL 94-482) authorized $10 million in federal assistance to states for planning and developing career education programs. Additional legislative support for career education is evidenced by the passage of the Career Education Incentive Act (PL 95-207) in 1977. This law authorized $325 million for career education for the years 1979 to 1983. At present, career education is eligible for funding in the block grant program of the Omnibus Reconciliation Act of 1981.

Career education has also been proposed by many special educators as a viable response to a growing concern that special education programs are not meeting the needs of handicapped children and youth. This concern has resulted, in part, from a recent body of literature reporting on the postschool occupational adjustment of handicapped persons. For example, it has been predicted on the basis of students records that, in spite of special education, about 2 million handicapped persons left school between 1973 and 1977 without the skills necessary for productive work (Schworles, 1976) and that only 4 million of the 11 million handicapped adults capable of competitive employment are actually working, and many of these are underemployed (Viscardi, 1976).

THE CONCEPT OF CAREER EDUCATION

Although first formally introduced more than a decade ago, career education still has no single, universally accepted definition. Early proponents of career education felt that an "official" definition at that time might adversely affect the career education movement and restrict its growth. It was hoped that a meaningful definition would result from the debate of divergent groups evaluating the concept from different viewpoints. Instead of resulting in one accepted definition as planned, however, the process of debate has resulted in a number of definitions, each supported by various groups of professionals (Clark, 1979).

Career education received its initial conceptual and financial thrust from vocational education (Bailey, 1985; Hoyt, 1976). This influence may be seen in the U.S. Office of Education policy statements regarding career education. Kenneth Hoyt, then the Associate Commissioner for Career Education in the U.S. Office of Education, first advanced a definition in 1972:

Career education represents the total effort of public education and the community to help all individuals become familiar with the values of a work-oriented society, to integrate those values into their personal value structure, and to implement those values in their lives in ways that make work possible, meaningful, and satisfying to each individual. (Budke, Bettis, and Beasley, 1972, p. 3)

According to Hoyt (General Learning Corporation, 1972), work values in this definition encompass a wide variety of motivations, including but not limited to, the "Protestant work ethic." This definition was severely criticized by some authors (e.g., Goldhammer, 1972; Gordon, 1973) for its almost exclusive emphasis on work.

A second definition was presented in 1975 in a U.S. Office of Education policy paper:

Career education is the totality of experiences through which one learns about and prepares to engage in work as part of one's way of living. (Hoyt, 1975, p. 4)

This new definition softened the strong emphasis on work found in the earlier definition but still remained heavily oriented toward preparation for work as the primary component of career education.

Some professionals rejected Hoyt's almost exclusive emphasis on the work aspects of career education (e.g., Gysbers and Moore, 1974; Hansen, 1977). They argue that career education encompasses more than simply work orientation and training. It also includes other life roles: social, leisure, and interpersonal. Goldhammer, for example, identified several "life careers" in which individuals engage: (1) producer of goods and renderer of services; (2) member of a family group; (3) participant in social and political life; (4) participant in avocational pursuits; (5) participant in the regulatory functions involved in aesthetic, moral, and religious concerns (1972, p. 129). Clark (1976) summarized his position by stating that one's career goes beyond one's occupation to include all the roles and experiences one may encounter in life. Gordon suggested that "career" be defined as "the course by which one develops and lives a responsible and satisfying life" (1973, p. 59). By this definition, career education should encompass such possible roles as learner, producer, consumer, citizen, family member, and social-political being. Kokaska and Brolin do not discount the importance of the work component of career education, but believe personal, social, and daily living skills are of equal importance. Their definition, stated here, is the definition upon which this chapter is based:

Career education is the process of systematically coordinating all school, family, and community components together to facilitate each individual's potential for economic, social, and personal fulfillment and participation in productive work activities that benefit the individual or others. (Kokaska and Brolin, 1985, p. 43)

Evaluation of this definition reveals that it is both broad and comprehensive. In it, not only must the school be involved in the career education activities of an individual, but so must the family and community. In addition, this definition recognizes that *occupations* are only one part of the total career development needs of an individual: Social and personal fulfillment are also integral components. This emphasis helps to distinguish career education from vocational education, which is primarily concerned with specific vocational training.

To further clarify the concept of career education, it is often useful to specify the competencies students achieve in career education programs. Although many authors have published detailed lists of career education competencies, the list that is probably most often quoted is the one developed by Brolin (1976). He divides career education competencies into three broad categories or curriculum areas. Each curriculum area contains from six to nine competencies:

Daily Living Skills
    Family finances
    Home furnishings
    Personal needs
    Children and family living
    Food
    Clothing
    Civic activities
    Recreation and leisure time
    Mobility

Personal-Social Skills
    Self awareness and appraisal
    Self-confidence and self-concept
    Socially responsible behavior
    Appropriate interpersonal relationships
    Independent functioning
    Problem solving
    Communication with others

Occupational Guidance and Preparation
    Occupational awareness and exploration
    Job selection
    Appropriate work habits
    Necessary skills
    Entry-level skills
    Vocational adjustment

As can be seen from this list, career education is as concerned with the "process of living" as with the "process of making a living" (Clark, 1974).

On the basis of this or a similar list, some professionals have decided that instruction and training in these competencies is the responsibility of the secondary schools. Nothing could be further from the truth. Instruction in these competencies *must* begin early for all students. This is particularly true for handicapped students, whose rate of learning and ability to generalize is often much less than normal students. For example, while young elementary students obviously will not be involved in specific job skill training, they should be developing an *awareness* of the world of work. Later, they can *explore* the world of work, searching for an occupational area in which they are interested. Then, in the secondary school, they can begin the process of skill training. The key point is that too much valuable time is lost if career education is not included in the curriculum until junior or senior high school (Kokaska and Brolin, 1985).

A RATIONALE FOR CAREER EDUCATION

The swift acceptance of career education by governmental and educational agencies can be largely attributed to the timing of its introduction. As previously mentioned, career education was introduced at a time when many groups (e.g., parents, teachers, employers, and students) were voicing dissatisfaction with educational practices and outcomes. Though these criticisms alone constitute a severe indictment of American education, statistics are often quoted, as well, to strengthen the rationale for career education. Some of the most quoted statistics include the following:

- In the 1980s, it is predicted that 80 percent of all job openings will require less than a college education. (Russo, 1972)

- The average person must go back to school or receive some kind of training or retraining seven to nine times in her or his lifetime. (Russo, 1972)

- General education enrolls 25 percent of those who graduate from high school, but (1) it produces about 70 percent of all high school dropouts; (2) it produces about 88 percent of all Manpower Development Act trainees; (3) it produces at least 78 percent of the inmates of correctional institutions. (Pucil, 1968)

- Two and one-half million students left the formal education system of the United States in 1970-1971 without adequate preparation for careers. Of these, 850,000 were dropouts from elementary and secondary schools, 750,000 were general high school graduates who did not enter any postsecondary training and had no marketable skills, and 850,000 were dropouts from college or other postsecondary programs. (Marland, 1971)

Similar statistics are often used to strengthen the rationale for career education for the handicapped. Barone (1973) estimated that only 21 percent of the handicapped students leaving school systems in the mid-1970s would be fully employed or in college, while 40 percent would be underemployed and at the poverty level and 26 percent would be unemployed. Levitan and Taggert (1976) report that only 40 percent of all disabled adults are employed, compared with 74 percent of the nonhandicapped population. Among the employed disabled, 85 percent have incomes of less than $7,000, and 52 percent of these make less than $2,000 per year (Biklen and Bogden, 1978). Although the need for vocational programming for the handicapped is widely recognized, only 2 percent of those enrolled in secondary vocational programs in fiscal 1978 were identified as handicapped (Razeghi, 1979). To further illustrate the importance of career education, a more specific discussion of various categories of handicapped individuals follows.

Mildly Mentally Retarded Persons

Early studies on the occupational and community adjustment of the mildly mentally retarded persons tended to suggest that these individuals were making a satisfactory transition from school to adult life. However, more recent research has revealed that a majority has had problems after leaving school. For example many surveys have found that the majority of mildly retarded persons have the ability to secure—and have secured—employment, but that the nature and satisfactoriness of that employment varies considerably. Herber and Dever (1970) found retarded persons to be at the bottom of the scales of occupational and social adjustment. They found retarded persons to be employed primarily at unskilled and semiskilled, low-paying jobs. Many were not performing at a level the investigation considered minimally adequate, although it could be said such retarded persons were "nominally assimilated" into the community. Thus, although employed, many of the retarded have been found to be working in marginal positions for inadequate wages.

Many of the studies have indicated that inadequate interpersonal relations account for most vocational failures among the mildly retarded persons. Poor working habits and inadequate social skills are frequently cited reasons for job failure. Job success tends to be related to dependability, the ability to accept criticism, and attempts at doing a good job (Stephens and Peck, 1968; Windle, Stewart, and Brown, 1961).

Severely Disabled Persons

Historically, habilitation efforts with severely retarded persons have, at best, consisted of prolonged prevocational training, day-care activities, and intermittent remunerative employment at piece-rate wages. While sheltered workshops offer the only service option emphasizing vocational development for many handicapped persons, severely retarded adults are often totally excluded from such sheltered workshop programs (Lynch and Graber, 1977).

Several recent trends are beginning to change this situation, however. First, the concept of normalization described by Nirje (1969) and Wolfensberger (1972), and Perske's (1972) defense of the dignity of risk, have focused professional attention on the issues of values and objectives in treatment programs. Habilitation efforts are increasing because of an emphasis on access to normalized experiences and opportunities for individual choices. Second, research and demonstration efforts in the last few years have provided many examples of vocational competence through structural training of the severely retarded. Loos and Tizard (1955) apparently started this trend by demonstrating that not only could severely retarded adults learn vocational tasks, they could produce them as rapidly as other workshop employees. Since then, a number of research studies have demonstrated that severely retarded persons can master complex tasks in a vocational setting (Bellamy, Peterson, and Close, 1975). In a national survey of exemplary vocational practices, Cook, Dahl, and Gale (1977) found severely retarded adults employed in sheltered and competitive settings in the following occupations: duplicating-machine operator, sorter, order clerk, sandwich-board carrier, houseworker, dining-room attendant, cafeteria counter attendant, salad counter attendant, fountain server, kitchen helper, orderly, cleaner, groundskeeper, farm worker, baker's helper, cook's helper, collator, printer, stapler, eyelet-machine operator, racket stringer, woodworking shop helper, upholstery sewer, painter's helper, and screen printer.

Hearing-Impaired Persons

Little definitive information about the general occupational patterns of deaf and hard-of-hearing individuals is found in the research literature. Of the studies found, many report contradictory results because of variance in the definitions of "unemployed," "labor force participation," and "employed." Most authors do agree that many employed deaf workers are actually underemployed. Schein and Delk (1974) report that 43 percent of deaf adults with thirteen or more years of schooling are employed in clerical, transit and nontransit operation, manual labor, and service and household labor positions.

One of the areas in which authors most frequently disagree is in the unemployment rate of deaf adults. Berger, Holdt, and Le Forge (1972) report an unemployment rate of 21 percent (this sample was limited to Oregon), Bigman and Lunde (1959) state that 6.3 percent are unemployed, the Texas School for the Deaf (1972) reports a 21 percent rate, and Schein and Delk (1974) state that only 3 percent of the deaf males and 10 percent of the deaf females in their sample are unemployed. Again, variance in the definitions of "unemployed" may make these statistics appear to be more divergent than they really are.

Another area of disagreement in the literature is the level of income of deaf workers. Schein (1968) and Schein and Delk (1974) report the average income to be approximately 84 percent that of the general population, while Crammette's (1968) results suggest a level comparable to, and for some categories of workers higher than, the general population.

Learning Disabled Persons

The field of learning disabilities is relatively young, and only in the last several years have youth identified by schools as learning disabled begun to graduate from high school and enter the labor force. Therefore, few studies reporting occupational characteristics of learning disabled persons can be found. Menkes, Rowe, and Menkes (1967) report a twenty-year follow-up study of adults retrospectively diagnosed has having shown symptoms of hyperactivity and minimal brain dysfunction as children. The study indicates an apparent persistence of neurological symptoms over time, the severity of which affected later adjustment. Positive correlations were found between adult and childhood I.Q. scores, independent living, and socioeconomic status; that is, those scoring highest were most able to support themselves. It should be noted that the children in this study did not receive specialized education for their symptoms.

Several studies have focused on the relationship of reading-related skills to adult outcomes. Preston and Yarrington (1967) demonstrated that reading disorders could be successfully remediated, and remediation could have lasting effects into adulthood. They did not find reading disabilities to detrimentally affect later vocational and social adjustment. Rogan and Hartman (1976) conducted an extensive study into the adult adjustment of children classified as learning disabled who had experienced reading difficulty in childhood. Of the sample of 91 adults, 60 percent were employed, 16 percent were in college, and 55 percent independent of parental supervision.

In another recent study, White et al. (1980) surveyed randomly selected learning disabled and non-learning disabled young adults who had been out of school from two to six years. The employment status of both groups at the time of the study were similar in most respects. Similar proportions of the groups were working (LD = 76%; non-LD = 66%), at about the same number of hours per week. However, after the jobs reported by both groups were transformed to a socioeconomic index, the learning disabled individuals displayed a significantly lower than average job status than the non-learning disabled group. Unemployment statistics for the groups were also similar.

One of the most striking differences among the vocational characteristics of the two groups was the extent to which they were happy with their current employment/unemployment situation. The learning disabled sample reported they were neither happy nor unhappy, while the non-learning disabled sample seemed to be fairly content with their employment situation. The degree of happiness reported by each group was apparently unrelated to earned income, since the distributions of income for each group were very similar. Approximately 75 percent of both groups earned $7,500 or less, and nearly 60 percent of both groups earned $5,000 or less.

Summary of Occupational Characteristics

In summary, research relating to occupational characteristics and accomplishments of handicapped persons foresees a less-than-optimal outlook for successful adult adjustment. Despite the efforts of professionals, not only are significantly fewer disabled adults employed than nondisabled adults, but the handicapped persons also frequently face significant obstacles in gaining access to high-status, high-paying occupations. As indicated by this discussion, these obstacles are not limited to one or several groups of disabled individuals, but apply to all groups. The research reported underscores the importance of career education for handicapped persons.

CAREER EDUCATION AND CAREER DEVELOPMENT: IS THERE A DIFFERENCE?

As previously mentioned, the concept of emphasizing "preparation for work" (career education) as a primary goal for public education was advanced in the early 1970s to counter public dissatisfaction with the performance and direction of America's schools during the preceding decade. This singular focus for schooling was not accepted, however, by all sectors of the American academic community and, even in the middle 1980s, it is a source of controversy among school reformers. In point, the U.S. Department of Education (U.S.D.E.) has recently released a booklet on what it calls school programs that work, entitled: *What Works: Research About Teaching and Learning* (1986) in which, under the section title "Preparation for Work," it is stated that the "best vocational education will be solid preparation in reading, writing, mathematics, and reasoning" (p. 62). Does this mean that public schools should now disassociate themselves from the concept of career-related programming and focus only on teaching those "basic academic skills" through twelve years of schooling.

The answer to this question lies, perhaps, in explaining the misunderstandings that have evolved between what has been referred to as career education and what has been denoted as career development. For example, since the early 1900s American education has been providing career assistance to students through two very distinct programs over and above normal academic offerings. Historically, these two school programs have been identified as career guidance counseling and vocational education. Not all students in the public school system, however, have taken or had access to these two "nonmandatory" programs–in fact, they were not intended for all students. But, with the 1970s promotion of the concept of "preparation for work" as a primary goal of public education, these two program areas were repackaged and infused as a K-12 curriculum that all students would participate in. Thus, it is not difficult to understand why the term *career/vocational* is so often used when discussing this topic. Nevertheless, it is an unfortunate development because, as education research reports (such as the U.S.D.E. publication mentioned) continue to reject the 1970s career education focus, many who supported and/or tolerated these career-related programs may now find it necessary to dissociate themselves not only from the more recent concept of "career education" but also from these original and historical programs as well.

The term *career development* was born in the field of career guidance psychology during the early 1950s, created by career behavior theorists who advocated that "matching a student's interests, aptitudes, and values to jobs with similar ecologies" was the best way of obtaining a career. The more current view regarding career behavior, as popularized by Donald Super (1977, 1984), states that one's career acquisition path occurs through stages over the life span (rather than as a "one-time matching decision), while career, used in the broader developmental sense, means the sequence of roles (of which occupation is only one) played over the life span. Many of the "career education" programs that emerged in the 1970s and early 1980s cited the "developmental" concept. However, when these respective curricula are closely examined, it becomes apparent that they are much too narrow in their occupational role focus and begin an occupational emphasis much too early in the curriculum sequence to be "true" developmental models of career formation. This outcome occurs primarily because of the lack of understanding about and between the historical underpinnings of career behavior theory and the educational reform movement called career education. In summary,

Career education refers to educational programs and curricula at many developmental levels, and provided by several types of delivery systems, which provide experiences designed to help individuals become oriented to, select, prepare for, enter, become established, and advance in an individually satisfying and productive career.

Career development is a term used to describe the accumulation of individual behaviors related to work, both before and after entry into an occupation. It is a developmental, continuously iterative process which progresses from infancy throughout adulthood like an expanding spiral. In curricular terms, career development refers to the behavioral outcomes of career education, primarily those related to self-development; career planning and decision-making; and the development of work attitudes, values, concepts, and skills. (Bailey & Stadt, 1973, p. 346-347).

In distinguishing between the two definitions, the difference between means and ends becomes apparent. With regard to means, career education refers to topics, activities, materials, instructional methods, programs, and services. With respect to ends, career development refers to the various types of concepts and skills students will develop.

CAREER DEVELOPMENT

While career education has its roots in the educational reform movement of the 1970s (Hoyt, 1985), career development has its roots in America's early concern for the occupational placement of the large number of immigrants who arrived during the Industrial Revolution. More specifically, the roots of career development theory and practice, as an individual occupational guidance concern, are attributed to Frank Parsons, through the classic work, *Choosing a Vocation* (1909). According to Brown and Brooks,

> Parsons believed that, if a person would choose a vocation rather than merely hunt for a job, worker satisfaction and success would increase, and employer cost and inefficiency would decrease. (1984, p. 2)

Gysbers (1984) notes that over the two years following publication of Parsons' work, career concerns, as Parsons viewed them, led to a broader, more comprehensive view of individuals and their occupational development over the life span. Gysbers further notes that occupational choice was beginning to be viewed as a developmental process, with the term *vocational development* becoming popular as a way of describing the expanding view of occupational choice. He summarizes this transitional period of career choice development:

> By the 1960s, knowledge about occupational choice as a developmental process had increased dramatically. At the same time, the terms career and career development became popular. Today, many people prefer them to the terms vocation and vocational development. This expanded view of career and career development was more useful than the earlier view of career development as occupational choice because it broke the barrier that previously restricted the vision of career development to only a cross-sectional view of an individual's life. As Super and Bohn (1970, p. 15) pointed out, "it is well . . . to keep clear the distinction between occupation

(what one does) and career (the course pursued over a period of time)." It was also more useful because it made it possible for career development to become the basis for organizing and interpreting the impact that the role of work has on individuals over their lifetimes . . . . (Gysbers, 1984, p. 17)

The current National Vocational Guidance Association (NVGA) definition for career development reflects this life-span perspective: Career development is the "total constellation of psychological, sociological, educational, physical, economic, and chance factors that combine to shape the career of any given individual over the life span" (Sears, 1982, p. 139).

In sum, career development comprises two components. The first component, career, refers to all the major positions a person occupies in a lifetime; the second, development, refers to growth that helps the individual move to a more complex level via stages (Bradley, 1984). Super (1984) has conceptualized these life stages, beginning in adolescence, into five areas: (1) growth, (2) exploration, (3) establishment, (4) maintenance; and (5) decline. Table 2.1, which is adapted from Super, describes these life stages and their corresponding developmental tasks.

TABLE 2.1.   Super's Life Career Stages and Developmental Tasks

| | Age | | | |
Life Stage	Adolescence (14-25)	Early Adulthood (25-45)	Middle Adulthood (45-65)	Late Adulthood (over 65)
Growth	Developing a realistic self-concept	Learning to relate to others	Accepting one's limitations	Developing non-occupational roles
Exploration	Learning more about more opportunities	Finding opportunity to do desired work	Identifying new problems work on	Finding a good retirement spot
Establishment	Getting started in a chosen field	Settling down in a permanent position	Developing new skills	Doing things one has always wanted to do
Maintenance	Verifying current occupation	Making occupational position secure	Holding own against competition	Keeping up what is still enjoyed
Decline	Giving Less time to hobbies	Reducing sports participation	Focusing on essential activities	Reducing working hours

Source: Adapted from D.E. Super, *"Career and Life Development,"* in D. Brown, L. Brooks, and Associates (eds.), *Career Choice and Development* (San Francisco: Jossey-Bass, 1984).

Listed in Table 2.2 are the specific substage tasks of the exploration stage.

TABLE 2.2   Exploration Stage

Ages 15-24		
Exploring the world of work		
A. Tentative substage Age 15-17	B. Transition substage Age 18-21	C. Trial substage Age 22-24
1. Needs, interests, capacities, values, and opportunities become basis for tentative occupational decisions.	1. Reality increasingly becomes a basis for vocational thought and action	1. First trial job is entered after the individual has made an initial career commitment.

Source: Adopted from D.E. Super, *"Career and Life Development,"* in D. Brown, L. Brooks, and Associates (eds.), *Career Choice and Development* (San Francisco: Jossey-Bass, 1984).

Career Awareness and the Growth Stage

According to Jordaan and Heyde (1979), the primary task of the first stage is to develop a picture of the kind of person one is, as well as an understanding of the nature an meaning of work. In the early school grades (K-6) this can be done by ensuring that students develop independent school work habits (autonomy), allowing them to participate in a wide range of activities to learn their strengths and weaknesses (exploration), allowing them to conduct and be responsible for classroom duties, and rewarding them for those efforts that can lead to the development of positive levels of self-esteem. Failure to successfully accomplish these early tasks results in a lack of readiness (career maturity) to cope with the middle school or early adolescence tasks of the exploration stage.

Career Exploration Stage

Exploration refers to
   activities, mental and physical, undertaken with more or less con-
   scious purpose or hope of eliciting information about oneself or one's
   environment, or at verifying or arriving at a basis for a conclusion or
   hypothesis which will aid in choosing, preparing for, entertaining,
   adjusting to or progressing in an occupation. (Jordaan, 1963, p. 59)

As noted in Table 2.2 under the tentative substage column, it is necessary, as a prerequisite in making meaningful career decisions, to be aware of one's needs or values, interests, and abilities, as well as the requirements of anticipated careers.

Longitudinal research begun in the 1950s on factors related to the career choice of high school youth culminated in results indicating that while the majority of boys in the ninth and twelfth grades expected to accept responsibility for their career choices, their use of appropriate resources, their knowledge of the world of work, and their plans for achieving their goals were seriously deficient (Jordaan, 1977). Similar research findings on the lack of readiness of adolescents to cope with career choice within the exploration stage have been reported by Gribbons and Lohnes (1968, 1969), Crites (1973), and Westbrook (1976). As summarized by Super, adolescents during the exploration stage "should know the options available when entering high school; they should look ahead to a variety of choices in curricula offering different types of training institutions and occupations" (1977, p. 297). For many handicapped persons, these curricular choices are prerequisites for entrance into future academic and technical programs, as well as prerequisites to occupations themselves.

Career Options Limited

Many career options are not available for handicapped students because of the belief commonly held by the public that they lack adequate academic or physical abilities for such careers (Deshler, 1978) and because of the corresponding decision on their part to choose less demanding courses or curricula because of past learning failures. However, if handicapped adolescents have developed an average or above-average level of career decision-making maturity, they may make wiser choices, and thus accrue the motivational benefits derived from making competent career-related selections. This increase in motivation may, along with appropriate academic help, assist handicapped adolescents in completing the more demanding courses and curricula. The availability of increasing numbers of postsecondary opportunities for handicapped students is evidence that, when encouraged to do so, these students can successfully attempt a wider range of courses and curricula.

Career Readiness of the Mildly Handicapped Adolescent

Although limited in scope, research studies conducted with respect to the career maturity of mildly handicapped youth have indicated that they are less career mature than their nonhandicapped peers (Bingham, 1978, 1980; Fafard and Haubrich, 1981; Kendall, 1980). Why mildly handicapped adolescents are less career mature has yet to be empirically demonstrated; however, Deshler (1978) describes personality-related characteristics that could contribute to the problem. Deshler notes that there is a high probability that in adolescence mildly handicapped students will experience the indirect effects of a handicap: poor self-perception, lowered self-concept, reduced motivation. And given that many mildly handicapped adolescents:

are likely to have experienced many years of viewing themselves and being viewed by others as ineffective, marginal, and unsuccessful, it is not surprising that some of those feelings are being incorporated into their perceptions of themselves as potential workers. (Bingham, 1980, p. 68)

Career Preparation and Placement

If a student has been guided through the previous two life career stages and has accomplished most of those tasks, the student will probably have some idea of what career he or she would like to pursue, and, in fact, may have even specified one or more career options. Thus, the student may be ready to begin implementing or preparing to enter this particular career. For the student leaving middle school, this preparation may mean entering the first sequence of college prep algebra or the first course in the construction cluster within the vocational education curriculum. For some special education students, this preparation phase may not occur until just before their final year of high school. For students who complete their particular vocational cluster, obtaining employment is the next step. For others, the next step may involve going on to vocational school, junior college, or four-year college. Of course, this normal developmental sequence will vary for the type and degree of handicap a student possesses. For more severely disabled persons, this process works best if combined with "supported work training models" (Wehman, Kregel, and Barcus, 1985) and community-based vocational training.

IMPLEMENTATION OF CAREER EDUCATION

A number of career education models have been developed and field tested that correspond to carrying out the tasks given in Table 2.1 for each of the career development stages. Those discussed here are Brolin's (1978) *Life Centered Career Education* model for mildly mentally retarded persons, Biller's (1975) *Life Stage Model for the Career Development of Individuals with Specific Learning Disabilities,* Clark's (1979) model for handicapped students in the elementary classroom, and Wehman, Kregel, and Barcus's (1985) model for transitional life skill development for the severely handicapped persons.

Brolin's Life Centered Career Education (LCCE) Model

Brolin (1978) took the 1970s perspective on the role of career education that career education is an "educational reform movement." Brolin stated that his LCCE curriculum "is more than just a part of the educational program–it is the program" (p. 9). And because the LCCE curriculum covers much more than just "occupational" readiness and preparation, the claim may be justified.

The LCCE curriculum consists of twenty-two student competencies, which are organized into three primary categories: daily living skills, occupational guidance and preparation, and personal and social skills. Academic skill development is the basis for developing in each of these three categories.

The daily living skills component includes competencies in such areas as managing family finances, maintaining a home, caring for personal needs, raising children, engaging in civic activities, and utilizing recreation and leisure time. Brolin believes that all students, including most educated retarded students, have the potential to become independent citizens, and these daily living skills activities support that effort.

In the second category, occupational guidance and preparation, Brolin asserts that many people do not attain their true potential in the labor market and are relegated to unskilled and skilled labor. To assist in overcoming this lack of attainment into more skilled jobs, the LCCE curriculum includes skill development in such areas as knowing and exploring occupational possibilities, selecting and planning occupational choices, exhibiting appropriate work habits, obtaining vocational skills, and seeking and maintaining work.

The final category, personal and social skills, is aimed at developing independence, self-confidence, and socially acceptable behaviors, and at maintaining personal friendships. LCCE competencies to promote these skills include achieving self-awareness, acquiring self-confidence, achieving socially responsible behavior, and communicating with others.

An Exploration Career Life Stage (ECLS) Curriculum for the Learning Disabled

Responding to the lack of secondary educational materials for assisting the student with specific learning disabilities, Biller (1985) has developed a model for implementing a career development program for the secondary or postsecondary level. The model is based on Super's developmental model and is combined with the known characteristics of adolescents with specific learning disabilities. The primary focus of the ECLS is on promoting student development in the three areas referred to by Jordaan and Heyde (1979) as crystallization, specification, and implementation of a career option or choice. As noted earlier, in order for these three adolescent life stage tasks to occur, a student must have successfully completed the prerequisite tasks of developing autonomy, developing positive self-esteem, and developing a belief in the importance for work. Therefore, Biller has used a major portion of the ECLS to address this type of readiness, referred to in the curriculum as career maturity. Career maturity has five dimensions: (1) planfulness, (2) exploration, (3) information, (4) decision making, and (5) reality orientation. For the dimension of planfulness, there is considered to be at least three determinants: (1) autonomy or internal locus of control, (2) time perspective, and (3) self-esteem–all areas that Biller noted are weaknesses in students with learning disabilities.

Theoretical assumptions and research results presented by Biller show that many learning disabled adolescents are not ready (career mature) to cope with the career decision-making tasks required in the adolescent life stage. Super also noted "that to people to whom work does not seem important, the attitudes and information that constitute career maturity must seem irrelevant" (1983, p. 558). Ruling out socioeconomic status and sex as correlates of one's career maturity, Super also maintained that for some people work and careers do not appear as a personal reality. Thus, it seems that readiness for career decision making encompasses more than the dimensions included in Biller's construct of career maturity; that is, adolescents must also be motivated to want a career. Spreen's (1983) data on the job-related aspirations of learning disabled young adults suggest that this motivation is lacking.

Clark's School-Based Career Education Model

Given the importance of the developmental perspective of career information, Clark (1979) developed a sequential model for educators working with special education students that begins at the kindergarten level and extends through adulthood. As with the Brolin model, Clark (1974) assumes that career education for handicapped persons should encompass the broader perspective of all life roles, not just awareness, exploration, and preparation for work. In his model of the structure of career education within the public school, Clark (1979) maintains a focus on work careers but also gives equal value to other competencies essential to life-role careers, including: (1) attitudes, values, and habits; (2) human relationships; (3) occupational information; and (4) acquisition of job and daily living skills.

The objectives of the elementary school (K-6) should emphasize occupational roles, occupational vocabulary, awareness of occupational alternatives, and general familiarity with some of the realities of the world of work. In grades 7 to 9, objectives would shift to focus on occupational exploration, initial matching of job requirements to personal interests and abilities, and more specific coverage of the realities of the working world. With specific reference to handicapped children, Clark (1979) believed that the goals of career awareness leading to career identify, and self-awareness leading to self-identity, are vital to career development.

Supported Work Transition Model (SWTM) for the Severely Handicapped

The earlier descriptions of career development stages and tasks tend to be less generalized when applied to youth and young adults who are severely restricted by their cognitive ability. The approach of Wehman, Kregel, and Barcus (1985) to serving the life skill needs of moderately and severely handicapped persons is based on the normalization concept, which includes competitive employment as a primary goal. Wehman, et al. presented the supported work model in the context of a vocational transitional model; that is, competitive employment should be made available to handicapped individuals who need more help than even the mildly handicapped in getting a job, learning and adjusting to a job, and holding a job (Revelli, Wehman, and Arnold, 1984; Wehman, 1981; Wehman and Kregel, 1984).

It is apparent from previously reported placement experiences that many young adults with mild, moderate, and severe mental handicaps, autism, behavior disorders, or multiple handicaps, do not fare well in competitive employment. Generally, there are difficulties in learning and performing the job, parental concerns, transportation problems, and also fears of losing social security payments. Currently there are programs and efforts taking place that demonstrate how "supported work," through the use of an ongoing job coordinator, can assist this mostly unemployed population gain access to the labor force (Brickey and Campbell, 1981; Rusch and Mithaug, 1980). According to Wehman and Barcus (1985), three major assumptions underlie the use of a "supported work model": (1) A community labor environment has been studies for those jobs experiencing higher than average turnover that incorporate tasks within the range of the handicapped population of concern; (2) a prevocational program has already begun to develop skills related to the types of jobs identified in the first assumption; and (3) student adaptive behaviors, parent/caregiver, and mobility concerns have been reviewed and such data are available to staff working within the supported work model. According to Wehman and Barcus, if these assumptions are not met, placement, retention, and costs of the program will be negatively affected.

A strong focus of the SWTM model is helping individuals maintain their jobs. To some this might appear too expensive; however, there is evidence that significant cost savings occur with this approach compared with the cost of rehabilitating this population by making social security transfer payments (Hill and Wehman, 1983; Wehman and Hill, 1985).

Career Assessment Approaches

Psychological testing, work samples, community or situational assessments, and on-the-job tryouts are the basic assessment formats used in evaluating abilities, interests, and levels of occupational functioning. Career assessment activities have primarily relied on a sample of student behavior in order to make predictions about an individual's work potential. Those using career assessment instruments have primarily been concerned with identifying static student characteristics rather than gaining a better understanding of the dynamic exchange between student behavior and environmental conditions. However, if used appropriately, and if the data is considered in proper perspective, traditional career assessment methods should yield useful information for planning a school's career development program. This career information will be even more valuable if it is strengthened by alternative assessment data that includes information on student performance over time and under varying environmental conditions. Following is an overview of the major components of a traditional career assessment.

Psychological Tests. Psychological tests are usually included as part of a comprehensive career assessment. The tests typically involve paper and pencil assessments of cognitive, attitudinal, and affective traits that are reported to be important in job performance. Frequently used psychological tests include the *Wechsler Adult Intelligence Scale*, the *Strong-Campbell Interest Inventory*, the *Iowa Test of Basic Skills*, the *General Aptitude Test Battery* (GATB) and the *Differential Aptitude Test Battery* (DAT).

An implicit assumption in psychological testing is that knowledge of an individual's personal characteristics will enable accurate prediction of behavior in a variety of situations. According to Neff (1968), this assumption is the "psychologist's fallacy," which occurs when professionals fail to appreciate the critical importance of the interaction between individuals and environment. Further, the face validity of psychological tests is weak because the tests do not simulate, in any way, community employment conditions. Also, many students have exhibited low motivation and apathetic responding in the testing situation due to previous failure experiences with written evaluations. Many students have a difficult time associating their performance on these assessments with improved prospects of being employed. However, although there are significant limitations to reliance on psychological test data in career program development, data from these tests can be valuable if used in proper perspective. Teachers do need to recognize the situational specificity and abstract nature of such tests, though.

Work Sample Evaluation. Work samples have been defined by Neff as a "mockup, a close simulation of an industrial (actual) operation, not different in its essentials from the kind of work a potential employee would be required to perform on an ordinary job" (1968, p. 178). Their most unique feature, when compared to other assessment methods, is that they are intended to approximate real-life situations. A number of work samples have been developed and used in the vocational assessment of handicapped persons [e.g., Vocational Information and Evaluation Work Samples (VIEWS); Wide-Range Employment Sample Test (WREST); Talent Assessment Programs (TAP); Valpar Component Work Sample Series (VCWSS); and the McCarron-Dial Work Evaluation System]. The reader is referred to Botterbusch, *A Comparison of Commercial Vocational Evaluation Systems* (1980), in which these and other such systems are compared along such dimensions as work evaluation process, administration, scoring and norms, client observation, and other technical considerations.

The work sample evaluation assesses a student's performance on a well-defined activity involving tasks, materials, and tools that are highly similar to those in a job or group of jobs located in the community. The Vocational Evaluation Project Final Report (1975) recommended the work sample be (1) an actual job moved into an evaluation unit, (2) a trait sample designed to assess a single factor such as finger dexterity, (3) a simulation of an actual job operation, and (4) a cluster of trait samples that measures a group of traits for specific skills. The work sample evaluation should approximate the range of vocational behaviors that are important for success on a particular job or group of jobs.

Work sample assessments represent an attempt by teachers and counseling personnel to apply the testing approach to actual job performance. In contrast to psychological testing, which is abstract in nature, work sample evaluation requires that students actually manipulate real work materials. The work sample is usually a discrete task from a specific work area (e.g., small parts assembly, clerical work, food service work). The format for assessment on these tasks is standardized, and student performance is measured in comparison to norm groups that have been evaluated previously. Often individual work samples are incorporated into more general test batteries. The Institute for the Crippled and Disabled (ICD) developed the first work ample battery in 1937. This system was the Test Orientation and Work Sample System (TOWER). Since the origination of the TOWER, over ten major work sample systems, have been developed.

This method of assessment does provide data for student's career program development beyond that which is available from pencil and paper assessments. However, since these assessments are usually conducted in artificial work environments, they can measure only limited aspects of the total work repertoire required for success in community employment.

Situational Assessment. Situational assessment refers to the practice of conducting a twenty- to thirty-day evaluation of a student's performance in a structured vocational setting. In these assessment situations, the student is given an actual job to perform, and information is collected on work skills and other work-related behaviors. Work skills include the time required to learn new tasks, speed of performance, and accuracy. Examples of work-related behaviors are direction following, frustration tolerance, safety, motivation, punctuality, dependability, perseverance, and social-interpersonal skills.

According to Brolin (1976), situational assessment is primarily subjective and anecdotal. At the completion of the situational assessment period, a staffing is usually held, and the student's vocational education program is modified according to his or her individual needs. Although situational assessments do not follow any standard format, the reality of the job situation results in the collection of information that may closely approximate a student's performance in an actual employment situation. If student data can be collected across a variety of different situations, educators are able to acquire extensive information regarding the relevance of their vocational preparation programs. The value of this data can be increased by efforts to quantify aspects of a student's work personality and by repeated measurement techniques. Potential limitations of situational assessment methods relate to logistical problems in collecting data across a large range of occupations. In response to these limitations, on-the-job tryouts have often been used to increase the reality factor of assessment and to expand a student's exposure to different jobs.

On-the-Job Tryouts. Of all the traditional methods for conducting vocational evaluation information, the on-the-job tryout provides the most realistic setting in which to assess vocationally relevant behaviors. This method of evaluation gives the teacher an opportunity to determine students' ability to work in different settings. Further, this method allows students to be exposed to a variety of occupations.

In an on-the-job tryout, students are evaluated by the actual supervisory staff and by school personnel. These school personnel may include classroom teachers, vocational educators, and vocational counselors. The characteristics of on-the-job assessment typically involve the following: (1) students are not paid; (2) placement is for the students' benefit and not the employers; (3) placement is for experience, not employment; (4) the student becomes an addition to the work force; (5) close supervision is given; and (6) the students' performance is critically evaluated by both the employer and education personnel.

Information that is typically collected in an on-the-job assessment includes work skill performance, social-interpersonal skills, vocational interests, and work habits (e.g., punctuality, compliance, dependability). From the students' exposure to a series of community employment experiences, school personnel are provided with assessment data from which they can further develop the relevance and quality of their career and vocational education program. For specific students, this information will be extremely useful in planning the vocational component of their individualized education plan (IEP).

Nontraditional Career Assessment Techniques. Since career evaluation needs to be more sensitive to the interaction of student behavior and environmental conditions, alternatives to traditionally used methods are needed. Such alternatives should be dynamic as opposed to static. Furthermore, these assessment techniques need to include repeated measurements across an extended period of time. As a first step in developing more appropriate career assessment techniques, a detailed analysis of employment situations in the community should be conducted. This assessment can be used to identify the criteria for successful vocational performance across a variety of occupational areas.

Vocational preparation programs in the public schools must be responsive to an ever-changing job market. The content of these programs should reflect those occupations that are presently in demand and those that are projected to become available on the local, regional, and national levels. For handicapped students, vocational mobility beyond the local community may be limited. Consequently, vocational programs for handicapped students need to be closely aligned with those specific occupations that are realistically available in the students' home community. Local job availability must be continually assessed by school personnel. Assessment activities include monitoring listings of employment situations where former students have succeeded, help wanted ads in local newspapers, and job service listings; consulting with rehabilitation counselors; conducting telephone and written surveys; having discussions with friends and service clubs; maintaining personal contacts with employers; and reviewing other vocational training programs. Career assessment should also include the opportunity for students to participate, where possible, in industrial tours and visits to community job sites, and to be exposed to the many activities and courses offered in the secondary school environment. Classroom experiences would include learning about the opportunities and requirements of a broad range of occupations. Community business representatives and parents should be invited into the classroom to provide information about their particular careers.

For the employment options that have been identified for a student or groups of students, a detailed aptitude assessment of the specific skills that are required in the occupation is generally conducted. This assessment should result in the identification of specific skills for the actual performance of the job(s) and of specific work-related behaviors that have been determined to be prerequisite for minimal employment adjustment.

As part of the total assessment, concern for the handicapped individual's functional level in the nonwork life roles of consumer, leisure user, community member, and resident should be included. Examples of competency skills found in these life roles include: (1) managing family finances; (2) selecting, managing, and maintaining a residence; (3) caring for personal needs; and (4) raising children, enriching family living, buying and utilizing recreation and leisure, and getting around in the community. An example of a functional and ecological based assessment approach in "caring for personal needs" of a severely handicapped individual would be to conduct an on-site visit to a number of eating establishments frequented by the target population. In a representative sample of those establishments, observe the type of equipment used in their respective washroom facilities. Note in checklist form the operational nature of such items as soap dispensers, faucet types, and equipment for drying hands. Using these data, construct a series of tasks approximating the most common operations found across environments. Then assess students in classroom settings on how well they are able to perform these "most used" procedures. Similar procedures should be used for consumer and leisure skills.

After environmental assessment, the next best assessment is to use Halpern, et al's *Social and Prevocational Information Battery* (1975) to assess these non-work-related life skills. According to these authors, the SPIB contains nine tests designed to assess knowledge of certain skills and competencies regarded as important for the community adjustment of mildly mentally retarded students at the junior and senior high levels.

The areas measured by SPIB reflect five long-range educational goals that are considered important for the successful postschool adaptation of mildly retarded adolescents and young adults. These goals, when reached, should result in grater success in the areas of: (1) employability skills, (2) economic self-sufficiency skills, (3) family living skills, (4) personal habit skills, and (5) communication skills.

To approximate environmental criteria in the form of a paper and pencil test, Halpern et al. initially identified eight long-range goals with fifty-four more specific environmental domains by collaborating with over twenty-five Oregon teachers engaged in school district work-study programs for mildly mentally retarded students. Nine of the domains were finally chosen for inclusion in the assessment battery.

Let us now present a case study of vocational assessment information. The different types of vocational information we just discussed is presented.

CASE STUDY: William Smith

Disability: Reading Disability with Associated Emotional Problems

Background of Case

William was referred to the high school guidance counselor for career assistance as he was nearing the end of his public school career but failing a number of his classes. On the basis of testing for occupational aptitudes, William was considered for the first time as a person who is fairly capable, but whose reading failure and generally low verbal and language abilities might be related to emotional problems connected with his past home life.

Test History: Academic

Testing done at grade six using the *Stanford Achievement Test* reveals grade equivalents between 2.9 and 4.8 on the various subtests, with reading related scores being the lowest. The *IOWA Silent Reading Tests* given at grade nine resulted in percentiles of 33, 22, 28 and 62 for vocabulary, reading comprehension, directed reading, and rate, respectively. The *WAIS* was given in William's junior year, and scores were in the average range although subtests related to spatial relations and quantitative reasoning were in the superior range. On the *Kuder Personal Preference Survey* given at grade eleven, William ranked highest to lowest on being: agreeable, theoretical, practical, dominant, and sociable.

Test History: Vocational

William's scores on the *Differential Aptitude Battery Testing* (DAT) reflect his overall low poor reading skills, being at third percentile in both reasoning and language usage. Highest scores on the DAT were in abstract reasoning, space relations, and clerical speed and accuracy; each of these three aptitudes were in the 80th and above percentile range. Obviously, poor reading skill prevents the verbal and language measures from being assessed reliably. On the *Kuder General Interest Survey*, William, at grade nine, had percentiles of 47, 40, 31, 86, 84, 21, 55, 70, and 60, in mechanical, computational, scientific, persuasive, artistic, literary, musical, social, and clerical, respectively.

Personal Background

William is a white male who comes from a lower middle-class family. His parents are divorced and the father has been treated at various times in the state hospital for emotional problems. The mother has remarried. There are two brothers, ages 22 and 11. Overall, the family situation is now stable but certainly could account for part of William's early school difficulties.

Educational History

At grade nine William was referred for remedial reading. At referral, William was reading at approximately grade two level. After one year, he has increased his reading skills to almost grade six.. At grade eleven, William's reading level has improved to about a ninth grade level. Grades at that time were still Cs and Ds and Fs in some of the reading-related classes. Despite his academic weaknesses, William is a popular student, which perhaps accounts for why he did not come to the attention of school staff as needing academic assistance until late in junior high school.

Vocational Recommendations

William's aptitude for observing relationships between objects in terms of their size, shape, position, and so on would be important to the assessment of machinery or electronic malfunctions by mechanics or scientists; logical thinking is the key factor. Similarly, the ability to visualize or imagine the shape and surfaces of a finished object before it is built merely by looking at drawings would be useful to a broad array of mechanical/electronic technical fields. Finally, William's higher score in aptitudes for record-keeping, addressing, pricing, order-taking, filing, and keeping track of tools or supplies would be useful in occupations associated with low language oriented tasks. William's high Kuder interests in *persuasive* and *artistic* might suggest an occupation in becoming a technical illustrator for industrial product sales.

The occupational groups that are most compatible with William's higher vocational aptitudes are *technical occupations* and *crafts and trades*. Each of these two groups load heavily on spatial relations and mechanical reasoning. William's scores are average in mechanical reasoning and high in spatial reasoning. To enter technical fields, William will need, however, to complete high school and at least two years of vocational-technical school. The second area, crafts and trades, would also require high school and completion of an apprenticeship. William's aptitude in clerical detail might also support an occupation of technical illustrator.

To collaborate the findings of the DAT, the counselor may also want to have a more in-depth vocational evaluation that would include William's overall behavior performance in an actual work setting. From this environmental assessment, important data about on-the-job behavior, as well as vocational aptitude, can be gathered. If the school/agency has access to a work evaluation unit, the environmental assessment may be completed after the "in-house" work evaluation. Based on the data gathered from this evaluation, an individualized vocational plan can be constructed for William's remaining year of high school. Based on this assessment, it is hoped that William would see the benefit of staying in school and graduating.

As part of William's vocational plan, he should also be given a functional academic assessment to determine the specific academic areas in which he will need to become proficient when beginning a postsecondary technical training program. Contact should be made with the area vocational-technical school to determine what skill levels William will need for making a smooth transition. These deficit areas should take precedent over all other curriculum except those required for graduation. By guiding William into a low demand reading occupation, his immediate disability, reading, can be lessened.

Counseling for William's possible emotional problems should also be considered. The on-the-job assessment should reveal if these emotional overlay problems will manifest themselves as work-related behavior problems.

Separate Programming Versus Infusion

There are two major approaches to the delivery of career education programming. The first, separate programming, separates career education content from other school content. For example, separate programming might consist of a short unit specifically designed to teach certain money skills or a semester-long course on personal finances. In this approach, the goals and objectives of the career education content are the primary focus.

Infusion, the second major approach, integrates career education concepts into other subject matter content. With infusion, the primary learning objectives remain with the subject matter content but career education content is incorporated. To use an example from Clark, "When an instructional objective in a science class focuses on the concept of toxicity, instructional activities can include learning about poisons found in the home. This presents a science concept in the context of a daily living skill (1980, p. 68).

There are advantages and disadvantages to both approaches. With separate programming, evaluation of student mastery of the material is easier because the focus is on the career education concepts. Also separate programming tends to communicate to pupils the importance of career development (Clark, 1980). However, developing separate units of instruction for career education will place these units in competition with all the other curricular demands increasingly faced by schools. Separate programming may also make generalization of content from one setting to another more difficult for handicapped students, who often find it difficult to generalize unless explicitly taught to do so. Infusion has the advantages of making abstract academic content more concrete and making it easier to incorporate generalization activities into the lessons. However, with infusion it is much more difficult to evaluate student mastery of career education content because the primary focus of the lesson is on other content (Clark, 1980).

The choice of which approach to use will somewhat depend on the severity of the handicaps and the grade level of the students in question. A viable alternative to the exclusive use of either approach is to combine the two. In this way a teacher may be able to capitalize on the advantages and neutralize the disadvantages of the separate approaches.

Let us close this chapter by presenting a case example of a career education program.

The Pleasant Valley Oregon Career Education Program

1974–1978

A Case Example of How One School District
Integrated Career Education Without Excluding Their
Mildly Handicapped Population

CASE STUDY: A Totally Mainstreamed K-12 Career Education Program in Oregon

Background of Program

In the years 1972-75 a few states were taking Sydney Marland's 1971 remarks seriously about career education being an educational reform movement. One of these states, Oregon, was one of the first to adopt a statewide mandate requiring a competency based education including the requirement that there be two full units of career education completed by the student.

Pleasant Valley School District (1200 students in grades K-12) quickly moved into a leadership role by being one of the first districts to adopt and develop a set of high school (9-12) competencies that included a full range of career education competencies. A career education grant was written and a new career education director, with a special education background, was hired to implement the total Career Education Program. Following is a description of the program beginning at the elementary level. It should be noted that all of the district's mildly handicapped students were fully mainstreamed. The severely handicapped students were always bused to a larger nearby school system for services. The only major special education change that was made in 1977, when P.L. 94-142 IEP's had to be in place, was at the high school level, where a full-time resource room teacher was hired. However, even after this addition the mildly handicapped and the physically disabled students still maintained full integration in the district's academic and career education programs.

Pleasant Valley Career Education in Grades 1-6

Part of the state grant that Pleasant Valley School District received was used to provide teacher in-service time to develop career education modules. The modules were centered around five themes representing the career awareness concept. The five themes were: (1) awareness of one's ability and those of others, (2) assumption of responsibility for one's actions, (3) realization that decisions can be made and problems can be solved, (4) awareness that one is both a consumer and a producer, and (5) awareness that there are a number of different workers.

The Pleasant Valley elementary school teachers integrated these themes into their daily teaching curriculums. There were some teachers who felt that teaching or emphasizing these career education themes in the regular education content were taking away from the goals of "basis education" but most teachers endorsed and used the curriculum activities.

Pleasant Valley Career Education in the Middle School

Consisting of only two grades (7 and 8), the middle school prior to the new career education program had all girls attending home economics and typing classes and all the boys attending woods and mechanical drawing class. These classes were a year long and you could take Woods I for a year and mechanical drawing for a year. It was the same for home economics and typing.

The major reform at the middle school was to implant a computer career guidance system in the counseling office and to shorten all of the industrial arts and typing courses to one semester. Both boys and girls were strongly urged, but were not forced to participate in all of the courses, i.e., home economics and typing for the boys and industrial arts for the girls. Most of the boys and girls were quite willing to do this once it became an openly endorsed practice by the school administration and counselors. All of the school's mildly handicapped students participated in this cross-pollination of career centered curriculum.

Career Education at Grade Nine

Because of the many programs offered at Pleasant Valley High, it was decided that all of the ninth grade courses that offered vocational skills would be reformulated into six-week mini-units. All incoming freshmen were previously given aptitude and interest tests at the end of eighth grade and were randomly assigned to one of the six six-week mini-courses. Each six weeks, all of the students would rotate. One of the six-week units was a career guidance unit in which the students used the results of their aptitude and interest tests to formulate a four-year high school course plan. These plans were developed with assistance from the school guidance counselors who taught the six-week guidance unit. The students' parents had to review and sign off on these "tentative" long range high school plans. The high school special education teacher assisted the mildly handicapped students in formulating their plans in conjunction with their IEP's.

Career Education Program at Grade Ten

Previous to the new career education plan at Pleasant Valley, the tenth grade consisted of year-long courses, including the classes for art and music. In keeping with a career exploration theme, all of the occupational and fine arts classes were shortened to one semester. This allowed the students who had completed the six-week mini-units to have a broader variety of courses to explore in more depth. If the tenth grade classes would have remained as year-long courses, the offerings would have been greatly restricted and the objective of career exploration defeated.

Grade Eleven Career Education

This was the first year of a 2-year in-depth instruction in a trade or business area. The Pleasant Valley career goal stated: "all students at Pleasant Valley High School would leave with one marketable skill" e.g., typing, bookkeeping, building construction, etc., regardless if they were going to college. However, on the basis of interests, there were many students who did not like what was offered in the traditional Pleasant Valley programs. To circumvent this problem a new program called Diversified Occupations (DO) was implemented. Using the staff time of the Career Education Coordinator, all students needing to complete their final unit of career education, but not interested in the traditional offerings, signed up for DO. Individualized occupational programs (IOP) were developed for each student. In the IOP was a set of reading materials and a series of community explorations in diesel mechanics, air traffic controller, veterinary assistant, child care, auto mechanics, and hotel-motel management. Interestingly, DO students included dyslexic, emotionally disturbed, and academic honor students. The DO class met twice a week. In those class meetings, students shared experiences, developed their job seeking and keeping skills, and studied about their occupational areas of interest.

Grade Twelve Career Education

In most all of the occupational related programs, the senior year included a combination of in-class and community work experience in their respective occupational fields. Students who had been in the DO program during their junior year often signed up for another year or held part-time jobs if they had met their high school credit requirements.

The dropout rate prior to the career education program was running just over twenty percent but after the new career education program was instituted, that figure dropped to about twelve percent. A large percentage of the dropouts were the school's disadvantaged population. Most all of the mildly handicapped students were accommodated in whatever program they wanted, and only a few of the behavior-disordered students experienced dropout problems.

The key to the success of the Pleasant Valley program was the willingness of most of the instructors to accommodate the changes brought about by the new career education philosophy, but also their willingness to accept all types of students in their classes, including the handicapped. However, the positive attitude about handicapped students was present long before the career education changes were begun. The key to this positive attitude was perhaps to be found in the close knit ties of the community. If you were born and raised in Pleasant Valley, you were accepted regardless of your mental or physical differences. This was true, both in the Pleasant Valley academic and vocational programs, but also in their sports programs; all students who wanted to, could participate. In follow-up studies in the immediate years following the first graduates of the new career education programs, unemployment rates were no greater or no worse than the regional average. Any real advantages to be accrued to the Pleasant Valley career education program will have to be borne out over a longer time period.

REFERENCES

An Employment Analysis of Deaf Workers in Texas. (1972). Austin, Tex.: Texas School for the Deaf and Texas Education Agency.

Bailey, L.J. (1985). *Career Education for Teachers and Counselors: A Practical Approach.* Cranston, R.I.: Carroll Press.

Bailey, L.J., and R.W. Stradt. (1973). *Career Education: New Approaches to Human Development.* Bloomington, Ill.: McKnight.

Barone, C.S. (1973). Paper presented to a forum of national organizations sponsored by the Vocational Education and Work Adjustment Association, the National Rehabilitation Association, and the President's Committee for the Employment of the Handicapped.

Bellamy, T., L. Peterson, and D. Close. (1975). Habilitation of the severely and profoundly retarded: Illustrations of competency. *Education and Training of the Mentally Retarded 10*, 174-186.

Berger, D.G., T.J. Holdt, and R.A. Le Forge. (eds.). (1972). *Effective Vocational Guidance of the Adult Deaf.* Eugene, Ore.: Oregon State Board of Control, Special Schools Division.

Bigman, S.K., and A.S. Lunde. (1959). *Occupational Conditions Among the Deaf.* Washington, D.C.: Gallaudet College.

Biklen, D., and R. Bogden. (October 28, 1978). *Handicappism in America Win.*

Biller, E.F. (1985). *Understanding and Guiding the Career Development of Adolescents and Young Adults with Learning Disabilities.* Springfield, Ill.: Charles C. Thomas.

Bingham, G. (1978). Career attitudes among boys with and without specific learning disabilities. *Exceptional Children 44*, 341-342.

Bingham, G. (1980) Career maturity of learning disabled adolescents. *Psychology in the Schools 17*, 135-139.

Botterbusch, K.F. (1980). *A Comparison of Commercial Vocational Evaluation Systems.* Menomonie: University of Wisconsin, Materials Development Center.

Bradley, L.J. (1984). Lifespan career assessment for counselors and educators. *Counseling and Human Development 16(5).*

Brickley, M., and K. Campbell. (1981). Fast food employment for moderately and mildly retarded adults. The McDonald's Project. *Mental Retardation 19*, 113-

Brolin, D.E. (1978). *Life Centered Career Education: A Competency Based Approach.* Reston, Va.: Council for Exceptional Children.

Brolin, D.E. (1976). *Vocational Preparation of Retarded Citizens.* Columbus, Ohio: Charles E. Merrill.

Brown, D., and L. Brooks. (1984). Introduction to career development: Origins, evolution, and current approaches. In D. Brown, L. Brooks and Associates (eds.), *Career Choice and Development.* San Francisco: Jossey-Bass. Pp. 1-7.

Budke, W.E., G.E. Bettis, and G.F. Beasley. (1972). *Career Education Practice.* Columbus, Ohio: ERIC Clearinghouse on Vocational and Technical Education.

Clark, G.M. (1979). *Career Education for the Handicapped Child in the Elementary Classroom.* Denver: Love Publishing.

Clark, G.M. (1974). Career education for the mildly handicapped. *Focus on Exceptional Children 5(19)*, 1-10.

Clark, G.M. (1976). Career exploration: An integral part of the career education program. In G. Blackburn (ed.), *Colloquim Services on Career Education for Handicapped Adolescents.* West Lafayette, In.: Purdue University.

Clark, G.M. (1980). Methods of implementing career education into the schools. In G.M. Clark and W.J. White (eds.), *Career Education for the Handicapped: Current Perspectives for Teachers.* Boothwyn, Pa.: Educational Resource Center.

Cook, P., P. Dahl, and M. Gale. (1977). *Vocational Training and Placement of the Severely Handicapped: Vocational Opportunities.* Palo Alto, Calif.: The American Institute for Research in the Behavioral Sciences.

Crammette, A.B. (1968). *Deaf Persons in Professional Employment.* Springfield, Ill.: Charles C. Thomas.

Crites, J.O. (1973). *The Career Maturity Inventory.* Monterey, Calif.: McGraw-

Deshler, D.D. (1978). Psychoeducational aspects of learning disabled adolescents. In *Teaching the Learning Disabled Adolescent.* Dallas: Houghton Mifflin.

Fafard, M., and P.A. Haubrich. (1981). Vocational and social adjustment of learning disabled young adults: A follow-up study. *Learning Disability Quarterly 4,* 122-130.

General Learning Corporation. (1972). *Career Education Resource Guide.* Morristown, N.J.: General Learning Corporation.

Goldhammer, K. (1972). A careers curriculum. In L. Goldhammer and R.E. Taylor (eds.). *Career Education: Perspective and Promise.* Columbus, Ohio: Charles E. Merrill.

Gordon, E.W. (1973). Broadening the concept of career education. In L. McClure and C. Buen (eds.), *Essays on Career Education.* Portland, Ore.: Northwest Regional Educational Laboratory.

Gribbons, W.D., and P.R. Lohnes. (1969). *Career Development from Age 13 to Age 25.* Washington, D.C.: U.S. Department of Health, Education, and Welfare.

Gribbons, W.D., and P.R. Lohnes. (1968). *Emerging Careers.* New York: Teachers College Press, Columbia University.

Gysbers, N.C. (1984). Major trends in career development theory and practice. *Vocational Guidance Quarterly 3 33,* 15-25.

Gysbers, N.C., and E.J. Moore. (1974). *Career Guidance, Counseling and Placement Elements and Placement Elements of an Illustrative Program Guide.* Career Guidance Counseling and Placement Project, University of Missouri-Columbia.

Halpern, A., P. Raffeld, L.K. Irvin, and R. Link. (1975). *Social and Prevocational Information Battery.* Eugene, Ore.: University of Oregon, Rehabilitation Research and Training Center.

Hansen, L.S. (1977). *An Examination of the Definitions and Concepts of Career Education.* Washington, D.C.: U.S. Government Printing Office.

Herber, R.F., and R.B. Dever. (1970) Research on education and rehabilitation of the mentally retarded. In H. Carl Haywood (ed.). *Social-Cultural Aspects of Mental Retardation.* New York: Appleton-Century Crofts.

Hill, M., and P. Wehman. (1983). Cost benefit analysis of placing moderately and severely handicapped individuals into competitive employment. *Journal of Association for Severely Handicapped 8,* 30-38.

Hoyt, K. (1985). Career guidance, educational reform, and career education. *Vocational Guidance Quarterly, 34,* 6-10.

Hoyt, K. (1975). *An Introduction to Career Education: A Policy Paper of the U.S. Office of Education.* Washington, D.C.: U.S. Government Printing Office.

Hoyt, K. (1976). *Relationships Between Career Education and Vocational Education.* Washington, D.C.: U.S. Government Printing Office.

Jordaan, J.P. (1977). Career development: Theory, research, and practice. In G.D. Miller (ed.), Developmental theory and its applications in guidance programs. (Special issue.) *Pupil Personnel Services Journal 6*(i).

Jordaan, J.P. (1963). Exploratory behavior: The formation of self and occupational concepts. In D.E. Super, R. Starishevshy, N. Matlin, and J.P. Jordaan (eds.), *Career Development: Self-concept Theory.* New York: College Entrance Examination Board. Pp. 42-78.

Jordaan, J.P., and M.B. Heyde. (1979). *Vocational Maturity During the High School Years.* New York: Teachers College Press.

Kendall, W.S. (1980). *Affective and Career Education for the Learning Disabled Adolescent.* Prairie View, Tex.: Prairie View A&M University. (ERIC Document Reproduction Service No. ED 181 772).

Kokaska, C.J., and D.E. Brolin. (1985). *Career Education for Handicapped Individuals.* 2d. ed. Columbus, Ohio: Charles E. Merrill.

Levitan, S.A., and R. Taggert. (1976). *Jobs for the Disabled.* Washington, D.C.: George Washington University Center for Manpower Policy Studies.

Loos, F., and J. Tizzard. (1955). The employment of adult imbeciles in a hospital workshop. *American Journal of Mental Deficiency 59,* 395-403.

Lynch, K., and P. Graber. (1977). *Survey of Michigan Rehabilitation Facilities: Implications for the Developmentally Disabled.* Research Monograph, ISMRRD. Ann Arbor: University of Michigan.

Marland, S.P. (1971). *Career Education Now..* Speech presented at the convention of the National Association of Secondary School Principals, Houston, Texas.

Menkes, M., J. Rowe, and J. Menkes. (1967). A 25 year follow-up study on the hyperkinetic child with MBD. *Pediatrics 39,* 394-399.

Neff, W.S. (1968). *Work and Human Behavior.* New York: Atherton Press.

Nirje, B. (1969). The normalization principle and its human management implications. In R. Kugel and W. Wolfensberger (eds.), *Changing Patterns of Residential Services for the Mentally Retarded.* President's Committee on Mental Retardation, Washington, D.C.

Parsons, F. (1909). *Choosing a Vocation.* Boston: Houghton Mifflin.

Perske, R. (1972). The dignity of risk and the mentally retarded. *Mental Retardation 10(i),* 24-26.

Preston, R., and D. Yarrington. (1967). Status of 50 retarded readers eight years after reading clinic diagnosis. *Journal of Reading ii,* 122-129.

Pucil, D.J. (1968). Variables related to MDTA trainee success in Minnesota. Unpublished manuscript, University of Minnesota.

Razeghi, J. (1979). *Education of the Handicapped 5* (22), 9.

Revelli, G., P. Wehman, and S. Arnold. (1984). Supported work model of employment for mentally retarded persons: Implications for rehabilitative services. *Journal of Rehabilitation 50,* 33-39.

Rogan, L.L., and L.D. Hartman. (1976). *A Follow-up Study of Learning Disabled Children as Adults.* Final Report, Project No. 443Ch 60010 USDE, Department of Health, Education, and Welfare.

Rusch, F.R., and D.E. Mithaug. (1980). *Vocational Training for Mentally Retarded Adults.* Champaign, Ill.: Research Press.

Russo, M. (1972). Speech presented to Governor's Conference on Career Education, Manhappan, Kansas.

Schein, J.D. (1968). *The Deaf Community.* Washington, D.C.: Gallaudet College Press.

Schein, J.D., and M.T. Delk. (1974). *The Deaf Population of the United States.* Silver Spring, Md.: National Association of the Deaf.

Schworles, T.R. (1976). Increasing the opportunities through vocational education. In J.E. Wall (ed.), *Vocational Education for Special Groups*. Washington, D.C.: American Vocational Association.

Sears, S. (1982). A definition of career guidance terms: A National Vocational Guidance Association perspective. *Vocational Guidance Quarterly 31*, 137-143.

Spreen, O. (1983). *Learning Disabled Children Growing Up: A Follow-Up into Adulthood* (Grant MA-6972, & Grant 81/2). Toronto: University of Victoria.

Stephens, W.B., and J.R. Peck. (1968). *Success of Young Adult Male Retardates*. Washington, D.C.: The Council for Exceptional Children.

Super, D.E. (1983). Assessment in career guidance: Toward truly developmental counseling. *The Personnel and Guidance Journal 61*, 555-561.

Super, D.E. (1984). Career and life development. In D. Brown, L. Brooks and Associates (eds.), *Career Choice and Development* San Francisco: Jossey-Bass. P/. 192-234.

Super, D.E. (1977). Vocational maturity in mid-career. *Vocational Guidance Quarterly 25*, 294-302.

Super, D.E. (1957). *The Psychology of Careers.* New York: Harper & Brothers.

Super, D.E., and M.J. Bohn. (1970). *Occupational Psychology.* Belmont, Calif.: Wadsworth.

Texas School for the Deaf and Texas Education Agency. (1972). *An Employment Analysis of Deaf Workers in Texas.* Austin: Tex.

U.S. Department of Education (1986). *What Works: Research about Teaching and Learning.* Consumer Information Center, Pueblo, Colorado.

Viscardi, H. (1976). Speech presented at the annual meeting of the President's Committee on Employment of the Handicapped, Washington, D.C.

Vocational Evaluation Project Final Report. (1975). Menomonie, Wis.: Materials Development Center.

Wehman, P. (1981). *Competitive Employment: New Horizons for the Severely Disabled.* Baltimore, Md.: Paul Brooks.

Wehman, P., and J.M. Barcus. (1985). Unemployment among handicapped youth: What is the role of the public schools? *Career Development for Exceptional Individuals 8*, 90-101.

Wehman, P., and J. Hill. (1985). *Competitive Employment for Persons with Mental Retardation from Research to Practice.* Richmond, Va.: Virginia Commonwealth University, Rehabilitation Research Training Center.

Wehman, P., and J. Kregel. (1984). A supported work approach to competitive employment for persons with moderate and severe handicaps. Manuscript submitted for publication.

Wehman, P., J. Kregel, and J.M. Barcus. (1985). From school to work: A vocational transition model for handicapped students. *Exceptional Children 52*, 25-37.

Westbrook, B.W. (1976). Criterion-related and construct validity of the career maturity inventory competency test with ninth grade pupils. *Journal of Vocational Behavior 9*, 377-383.

White, W.J., J.B. Schumaker, M.M. Warner, G. R. Alley, and D.D. Deshler. (1980). The current status of young adults identified as learning disabled during their school career. Research Report No. 21. Institute for Research in Learning Disabilities, University of Kansas.

Windle, C.D., E. Stewart, and S.J. Brown. (1961). Reasons for community failure of released patients. *Education and Training of the Mentally Retarded 66*, 213-217.

Wolfensberger, W. (ed.). (1972). *The Principle of Normalization in Human Services.* Toronto, Canada: National Institute on Mental Retardation.

3

Professional Roles and Practices in the Provision of Vocational Education for Students with Disabilities

Jan Nisbet
University of New Hampshire

NEW TRENDS DICTATE NEW ROLES, SKILLS, AND DIRECTIONS FOR PROFESSIONAL EDUCATION

In 1985, federal and state programs spent more than $14 billion on services to people with mental retardation. Additional dollars were allotted to persons with different and varying labels. This amount of money included supplemental social security income (SSI), which goes specifically to unemployed workers. Recent government studies report that between 50 and 80 percent of all working-age adults with disabilities are unemployed and underemployed (President's Committee on Mental Retardation, 1983; Will, 1984). In order to combat this disturbing trend, Madeline Will, Assistant Secretary of the Department of Special Education and Rehabilitation Services, has allotted $5 million to experimental job projects that include vocational education for school-age students and those transitioning into adult environments. In addition to these monies, Congress has allotted $6.3 million to develop special job training and transition services, including vocational education, professional development, and interagency collaboration. These monies combined with systematic improvements in vocational curricula and supported work opportunities will improve the employment status of many persons who have been labeled as disabled and who have previously been excluded from vocational education.

65

Exclusion from vocational education and community opportunities is reminiscent of times when students were labeled ineducable and excluded from public schools. Now, expectations for all persons with disabilities have changed, and there is an increasing emphasis on community integration and employment in business and industry. Unfortunately, legislation forbidding the exclusion of students and adults with disabilities from vocational services, and mandates for providing education and services in integrated environments do not functionally exist. Traditional vocational and day treatment services continue to provide most students graduating from high school with "day," "prevocational," or "work" programs. These programs function from a notion that persons must acquire certain skills before they will be able to work. This situation results in such labels as "unemployable," "incapable of consequential work," and "not ready" for community employment. Brown et al. (1986) suggest that these labels limit opportunities and are the result of: (1) the societal assumption that students and adults with more severe disabilities are not capable of performing meaningful work in the real world; (2) laws and regulations for providing services that have evolved that minimize the possibilities of functioning anywhere but in sheltered and segregated environments; and (3) the belief by many professionals that sheltered environments are the most appropriate daytime environments. In order to change these assumptions and traditional orientations to delivering vocational education and postschool services, new models for professional preparation and vocational service delivery, including elements of interagency collaboration, must be developed. These models should be based on the following important themes.

Vocational Education Curricula Should Reflect Integrated Community Environments

When students with disabilities became involved in the public educational system under the mandate of P.L. 94-142, many special and vocational educators adopted curricula designed for typical students. This situation resulted in students (throughout their public education careers) being exposed to math, reading, science and social studies—subjects that were not directed to future skill acquisition for community work, living and involvement. In addition, students with disabilities were integrated into typical vocational education classes or attended the same vocational-technical education centers as their nondisabled peers. These attempts at integration were extremely important, but unfortunately resulted in students either not learning meaningful skills or learning hotel/motel management, automotive, clerical, horticulture, and food service skills in classrooms where the same expectation for generalization to community environments was held for them as for nondisabled students. As a result, students with disabilities had few if any opportunities to learn and demonstrate skills learned in community environments. In the infrequent situations where students became employed in one of the occupations taught in vocational schools, poor job retention and failure frequently resulted (Greenspan and Schoultz, 1981). Rather than identifying the failure as a training and curricular problem, vocational educators frequently blamed students for the failure.

Some students, especially those labeled severely disabled, often did not have opportunities to be integrated into vocational education classes. Instead, because of perceived incompetence, a vocational component was not included in their individual education plan (IEP). They often received in their classrooms training such as sorting nuts and bolts and stuffing envelopes. These skills were directed at the performance expectations of day habilitation centers or sheltered workshops.

All traditional vocational educational models have one flaw in common: they lack community reference and thus do not provide the longitudinal community instruction that is critical for the development of job-related skills such as transportation, communication with nondisabled coworkers and employers, time and money management, and coordination with home and family. These elements missing in traditional vocational education programs have led educators to implement community-based curricula directed at skill acquisition in integrated businesses and industries. It is no longer acceptable to provide vocational instruction only in a school or a vocational-technical center. Ecological and community-based orientations are replacing school-only models. Vocational skills must be taught systematically and verified in the actual work environments in which they are acquired (Brody-Hasazi, Salembier, and Finck, 1983). This requires vocational educators to reevaluate the nature of the assessment instruments and procedures being used to determine students' vocational curriculum and employability.

Vocational Assessment Should Emphasize Ecological Approaches

Vocational evaluation has been used to identify individual strengths and weaknesses and the potential work performance of persons with disabilities. Many school systems, in attempts to facilitate the transition to adult life for students with disabilities, conduct vocational evaluations as part of the vocational education process. However, in doing so, many, students fail or do poorly and are thus referred to sheltered workshops or non–work site situations. According to the President's Committee on Employment of the Handicapped:

> The majority of tests and evaluation procedures that are used to select qualified students for occupational training opportunities are designed to constitute a nearly insurmountable barrier to handicapped applicants. . . . Tests and evaluation procedures have been tailored to the needs of the nonhandicapped. Such tests and procedures do not measure the capacity for success that can be achieved through special education and rehabilitation. (1980, p. 14)

Murphy and Ursprung (1984) reported that evaluations that take place in self-contained rooms or in sheltered facilities often result in recommendations for programs and services that are also segregated in nature. This clearly raises concerns whether evaluation results are based on agency or individual needs. Additionally, the tools used for vocational evaluation such as paper and pencil tasks, artificial work samples, and evaluation instruments such as the Singer, Valpar, and McCarron-Dial have well-documented problems with reliability, validity, and generalizability when used with students who are severely disabled (Schalock and Karan, 1983). Interpretation of the scores of these assessment tools frequently results in low expectation of work performance for students with more severe disabilities.

Because integrated work opportunities for students with disabilities are being increasingly emphasized, evaluation procedures should reflect this orientation. Vocational educators should move away from self-contained evaluation centers and measure students' performance in relation to actual skills required in business and industry. Evaluation can be conducted only in combination with systematic instruction in community-based work environments. Therefore, vocational evaluators must also be vocational teachers and act as community liaisons.

Vocational Educational Programs Should Reflect The Community

Vocational educators must move from the confines of special education classrooms and vocational centers to explore the vast potential of the community. O'Brien (1986) defines "community" as being an alternative to an "institution, a direction of service delivery, as sponsored by local rather than state authorities. All of these descriptions are appropriate in the discussion of vocational education, but more importantly,

> Community is based on peoples, common desires for decent housing, good work, opportunities to learn, mutual support in difficult times, friendship, intimacy, and celebration. Services that transform these ordinary desires into commodities that can only be properly supplied to handicapped people by professionals encourage passivity and create a scarcity of "appropriate" professional resources (Illich, 1978; McKnight, 1977). Programs that recognize ability in many community members—including people with mental retardation and their families—and distribute information, authority, and tools widely build community competence. (O'Brien, 1986, pp. 3–4)

Community members such as parents and guardians, businesspersons, neighbors, bus drivers, coworkers, friends, and adult service personnel can provide valuable information and support for meaningful vocational education programs. Valuable information held by community members includes job preference and interests (provided by families), skills required for job routines, appropriate bus-riding skills and schedules, ongoing job performance and payment mechanisms for students with different levels of productivity. In addition, these individuals can provide natural support and supervision in vocational training to a student with a disability. Parents and guardians can help students get to work on time and manage their money. Employers can assess a student's performance within the job site and give directions and feedback. Bus drivers can give information on the appropriate stop and on key landmarks. Coworkers can help with teaching job and break-time skills, and adult service personnel can provide critical information on SSI, payment mechanisms for minimum and subminimum wages, financial supports, and job coaches. Vocational educators must involve these persons in the training programs. By doing so, they are expanding the intensity and comprehensiveness of the program and maximizing students' chances for success.

In sum, vocational educators must recognize the need for changes in vocational curricula, become evaluators and instructors within community contexts, and learn to use their communities as active resource and supports for vocational preparation of students with disabilities. The skills and values that vocational educators must learn in order to develop longitudinal vocational curricula that results in students with disabilities working in community environments are the focus of the following sections.

PROFESSIONAL TRAINING PROGRAMS FOR VOCATIONAL EDUCATORS

Preparation to become a vocational educator includes understanding educational practices, vocational curricula, community resources, business and industry, and the need for community. Knowledge of systematic training techniques is critical to the success of students with various disabilities. However, a vocational educator must also be able to rely on the natural supports available in the community and in businesses. For example, a supervisor or a coworker may also train and supervise the student. A parent may help reinforce new skills at home. A friend or neighbor can be supportive after work. Such support essentially means the "professional" is no longer operating in a solitary role. Facilitating this transfer of responsibility is also a skill and must be emphasized within professional training programs. In sum, the vocational educator must not only be a job developer, trainer, supporter, and community organizer, he or she must also know how to work with coworkers and employers and others in the community in order to gain their help in the vocational educational process.

Douglas Biklen writes:

The fields that fashion themselves in the business of disability treatment (e.g., special education, psychology, and rehabilitation) operate on a model of individual assessment, diagnosis, and placement. That is, in order to determine the best strategy for educating, rehabilitating, or otherwise serving persons with disabilities, the professions must first consider individual needs and the finding of research on what constitutes best approaches for meeting such needs. If the truth be known, however, no matter how reasonable and appealing this approach, in reality it is little more than a mythology. True, on a day-to-day basis professionals do make placement decisions. But what are the range of options available to them? Are the best practices typically among their choices? Usually not. Certainly there are professionals who find themselves in situations where they indeed have choices. In many states or regions, however, largely as a function of economic policy, options are limited and individualization is severely constrained. Consumers of service find themselves squarely in the midst of a single-option, love-it-or-leave-it bind. . . . The data seem to suggest that a child's geographic location and the degree to which the jurisdiction funds segregated services outweigh professional judgement. To continue to believe that professional, clinical judgement does anything more than fashion itself to the imperative of finding (and therefore service) pattern is akin to believing that individual bank tellers can set their own interest rates. ("The Myth of Clinical Judgement," 1986, pp.8–15).

This statement regarding the roles of professionals in developing services for persons with disabilities should lead vocational educators to closely evaluate their own practices. Vocational educators must actively set policies toward developing integrated work options and, at the same time, must advocate within-system change. Biklen's statement appropriately challenges the notion of professional judgment; however, he does not acknowledge the ability of a single person or a task force of persons to actually change curricula, educational practices, and service delivery systems. In many school districts across the country, individual teachers or small groups of professionals and parents have, in fact, successfully pushed for community-vocational education. These demonstrated successes in developing vocational training and placement opportunities have resulted in school systems making systemic changes toward integration and community-vocational instruction (Taylor, 1983). These changes have involved first recognizing the underlying values of integration, chronological age appropriateness, natural proportion, and meaningful work, and then modifying practices to fully realize those values. These efforts point to the specific changes necessary in professional preparation programs for vocational educators. First, vocational educators must be educated to understand the key underlying values, and second, they must have technical skills to facilitate acknowledgement of those values.

Many authors have provided lists of skills needed by vocational education professionals. Batsche (1980) listed several topics to be included in personnel training for programs for learners with special needs. These include: (1) techniques for identifying and assessing student needs; (2) strategies for individualizing instructional procedures and for acquiring up-to-date knowledge of available resources and support services; (3) attitude development of staff and students; (4) techniques designed to maximize student behavior in the classroom and on the job; (5) procedures for articulating and coordinating in-school and out-of-school resources; (6) procedures for modifying curriculum, equipment, and teaching materials; and (7) services to enhance job placement, school-to-work transition, and job maintenance.

Brolin, in a description of George Washington University's Masters Program in the Vocational/Special Education Teacher Program, reports that graduate students are trained in the following areas: assessment; individual educational planning; prevocational educational; prevocational enabling skill development; supportive vocational education; functional life skills and academics; interdisciplinary planning, development and cooperation; curriculum development; materials development and instructional methodology; behavior control and classroom management techniques; work/study and community placement procedures; and legislative implications and practice (1982, p. 306). However, values directed at integration and meaningful work are not included. In a similar vein, Brolin, citing a Council on Exceptional Children (CEC) Policy Manual, lists placement options that vocational educators should consider for students:

1. Placement in regular vocational classroom with:
   a. Consultative assistance for teachers
   b. Provision to direct services to students by itinerant specialists
   c. Resource room help for students
2. Placement in separate vocational classroom with:
   a. Students (being) part-time in regular class
   b. Self-contained class in regular education facility
   c. Self-contained class in special education facility
3. Placement in a sheltered environment:
   a. Residential
   b. Hospital
   c. Other institution
   d. Sheltered Workshop
   e. Work Activities Center
4. Placement in work/study or cooperative education program
5. Homebound instruction (1982, pp. 298–299)

These placement options are discussed by students as part of many professional training programs. It is important to encourage students to strive for the least restrictive placement, or, as vocational educators, they may accept the status quo of single-option, segregated offerings. The following section describes those underlying values and technical skills that vocational educators need in order to assist students with disabilities achieve meaningful work in integrated work environments.

THE EVOLVING ROLE OF THE VOCATIONAL EDUCATION PROFESSIONAL

In the past, vocational educators primarily served students labeled mildly mentally retarded and learning disabled. Students with severe disabilities were labeled "unemployable" or "marginally employable" and were the responsibility of special educators who, in their professional certification programs, were rarely exposed to vocational curricula. This situation frequently resulted in haphazard efforts to help these students develop the vocational skills needed for sheltered workshop functioning.

Today, these practices are changing. Vocational educators are now serving more students with severe disabilities, and special educators are being exposed to vocational curricula in university preparation and in-service training programs. As a result, more students with disabilities are receiving necessary and appropriate vocational services and are graduating into integrated employment rather than into sheltered segregated work. What changes in professional preparation programs have already occurred and what changes are still needed to facilitate the inclusion of all students with disabilities into community-vocational employment? The following areas should be included in professional preparation programs.

Development of Positive Values Toward Students with Disabilities

Positive values toward students with disabilities is the most important feature and knowledge base of a vocational educator. When integration for all students is considered valuable, vocational curricula are more likely to be designed to facilitate movement and placement into environments that contain nondisabled persons. If integration is not considered valuable, decisions are often made to place students in sheltered workshop and day treatment centers. Few of those in such environments are fortunate enough to receive training and placement opportunities in typical businesses and industry. Similar discrepancies exist if a vocational educator does not place a high value on the concepts of natural proportion, chronological age appropriateness, meaningful work, and individualization.

Natural proportion describes community environments that contain a typical distribution of the population (Brown et al., 1983). Because only 1 percent of the population would be labeled severely disabled, then the natural proportion would be maintained if only 1 out of a group of 100 persons was considered severely disabled. Because of the need to maintain reasonable student–instructor ratios, this is a difficult concept for a vocational educator who provides community instruction. For example, for students who are 13 and 14 years old and engaged in their first community work experience, a reasonable student–supervisor ratio that ensures that all students receive the appropriate level of instructional intensity may be 3:1. Although the natural proportion is violated in this case, attempts should be made to maintain such reasonable ratios so that when these students graduate from high school they will have received sufficient amounts of instruction to work in environments that most closely approximate the population norm.

Chronological age appropriateness is a concept that guides educators and service providers to develop training and placement opportunities commensurate with students' chronological age. This translates into 14-year-old students delivering papers on a paper route rather than stacking rings. Similarly, a 6-year-old child should be responsible for cleaning up his or her room and picking up the toys but not assembling a complex circuit board.

Meaningful work refers to the concept that identified tasks within a job or a job itself should be one "that if a nondisabled person doesn't perform it, someone else will have to." A vocational educator can translate this concept into practice only by identifying the skills required by a business. For example, dusting church pews is not a job that is assigned to maintenance staff since the work is usually done naturally by the parishoners. If a student with a disability is assigned this task, then it would be considered nonmeaningful work. Conversely, meaningful work would be bussing tables at a sandwich shop because this is a task required in order to keep the tables clean and the customers happy.

Individualization is another critical value. Viewing, assessing, developing curricula and instructional strategies, and finding appropriate jobs and careers for students with disabilities requires a thorough knowledge of the student, including family, preferences, interests, skills, and future goals. It should translate into IEPs and placement decisions that reflect the individual rather than the preferences of the vocational educator or the public educational and vocational system. Lack of individualization can result in vocational educational curricula that include hotel/motel management and clerical skill development for all students. Students who are poorly matched in job sites may indicate disinterest, dislike, lack of attentiveness, and even behavioral difficulties. Unfortunately, these behaviors may be viewed as indicators of lack of employability rather than as job or curricular dissatisfaction due to lack of consideration of individual needs.

Knowledge of Community Resources

Knowledge of community resources including vocational services, businesses, and other services is critical for a successful vocational educator. This knowledge must go beyond weekly analyses of the employment advertisements in the newspaper. Direct contact with employers and with Office of Vocational Rehabilitation and Department of Labor and Social Security personnel is necessary for a comprehensive understanding of an area's employment situation. Vocational educators serving students with disabilities must become an integral part of the service community and bridge the gap between schools and the community at large. For example, a close working relationship with the area business council can lead to information on available jobs, upcoming industry, and potential employer concerns. With this information the vocational educator can plan meaningful curricula, placement strategies, and support service development.

Knowledge of Assessment and Evaluation Procedures

Vocational assessment and evaluation procedures have been used to identify the strengths and weaknesses and potential work performance of students with disabilities. The correct use of systematic, curriculum and community-based, criterion referenced, and individualized vocational evaluation can result in the most appropriate vocational training and placement environment. Vocational educators must rely on community-relevant and community-referenced measures of performance. Job inventories (Belmore and Brown, 1978) have served as useful tools for valuating the skills of students and adults with disabilities and then directing appropriate intervention at performance deficits. In the inventory process, a job is analyzed according to the way in which it is performed by a nondisabled worker. Then, evaluation proceeds as follows: (1) A worker with a disability is observed performing the target job in a specific work environment; (2) discrepancies in performance are noted; (3) strategies for increasing skills are developed; and (4) adaptations are developed for skills that the disabled worker is unlikely to acquire. This process allows ongoing evaluation of the worker in the environment in which the job is required. Below is a selected sample of skills assessed using a discrepancy analysis format.

Knowledge of Appropriate Intervention Methodology

After a vocational educator has identified strengths, preferences, and skill deficits, remediation must be planned. How does one systematically address skill deficits and capitalize on strengths? What cueing, correction, and reinforcement procedures are most effective? Intervention procedures result from a thorough knowledge of the individual and a clear understanding of the variety of instructional techniques that are

Skills Required	Performance	Teaching Strategies	Adaptations
1. Determines when table needs to be cleared	(–) Student attempted to clear the table when customer was at the salad bar.	1. Teach student a scanning strategy. Point to examples of other persons who leave their table only temporarily.	1. Based on student's performance and learning characteristics, no adaptations are necessary.
2. Clears table at acceptable rate	2. (+)	2. Student has mastered the skill.	2. No adaptations are required.
3. Brings tray of dirty dishes to kitchen	3. (–) Student has difficulty carrying tray while avoiding customers; has problems with balance.	3. Will not teach this skill. Balance problems persist; there is too great a risk of broken dishes.	3. Will propose the use of a basin for dirty dishes to prevent dishes from falling on the floor; will teach the use of a basin.

available for teaching new skills. When a student is unable to produce at the desired rate, what can a vocational educator do? The following interventions should be considered: repositioning materials to improve efficiency; analyzing the correctness of the method used to complete the job; establishing a reinforcement system to increase rate; or developing an adaptation to improve productivity. Any of these interventions may be appropriate depending on the reason for the performance discrepancy. A motoric difficulty may be helped by the development of an adaptation or the repositioning of materials, whereas a motivation problem may warrant the development of a reward system. These intervention decisions are key to the success in the workplace of students with disabilities. Any difficulty experienced by a student should first be viewed in light of the intervention strategies used.

Knowledge of Placement Techniques

The ability to find a training experience or a job for a student with disabilities requires knowledge of how to conduct ecological inventories and job analyses of work environments, how to contact employers by phone or in person, how to present the purpose and components of the vocational training, and how to involve the employers as much as possible in the vocational education process.

The environment selected for vocational training, and possibly long-term placement, should be one that matches both the student's and family's interests and needs. Placements should not be selected solely on availability of jobs because this often results in a mismatch between the student and the job. Failure on a job that results from a mismatch may be interpreted as a student problem rather than as a service problem. This inappropriate interpretation may, in turn, lead to a decision that the student is "not ready" for work and may result in a segregated placement.

The importance of the placement process must be underscored and emphasized in all undergraduate, graduate, and in-service training programs.

Decisions regarding the type of job, the nature of the work, the number of hours of work, the amount of pay, the nature and intensity of supervision, interaction and social skills, the type and intensity of training, and family concerns, all require careful analysis and, ultimately, an informed decision. Systematic methods of analyzing decisions that frequently must be made in training and employment should be part of the repertoire of the vocational educator.

Ability to Work with Employers and Coworkers

Ultimately, employers and coworkers become the central figures in the employment of adults with disabilities. Therefore, their participation in the development and implementation of community-vocational education programs is essential. How can professionals secure the participation of employers and coworkers? How can professionals best communicate the goals of their programs to employers and coworkers? How can employers and coworkers be involved in the training and placement process? All these questions must be addressed by vocational educators and professional preparation programs.

Educational professionals have been taught to use terminology that is inconsistent with that of business and industry. For example, terms such as *systematic instruction, task analysis, multiply disabled, augmentative communication,* and *fading* may not be understood by employers and coworkers. Instead, terms such as *training, job analysis, persons with more than one handicap, a way to assist persons to communicate,* and *reducing the amount of supervision* should be used. Language in itself can present a major barrier to developing relationships. Thus, vocational educators should become familiar with the terminology used in the world of work before they attempt to develop relationships.

Vocational educators must also understand the essential needs of employers (Nisbet and Callahan, 1986). Some of these essential needs include: quality; safety; performance of work that meets a "real need"; and satisfactory relations with customers and coworkers (p. 10). Successful negotiations with employers that include discussion of these needs can result in employers understanding: that work skills and productivity can be developed through training and appropriate support; that they can provide essential evaluation, training, and support to a student and adult with a disability; and that jobs can be individually tailored to an individual and adaptation developed. When employers are approached by vocational educators as participants in the process rather than receivers of commodities, then vocational opportunities for persons with disabilities are enhanced.

Ability to Communicate with Persons with Disabilities, Their Families, and Other Agency Personnel

Everyone has a different communication mode and style. Understanding that differences exist and that it is necessary to receive and impart information to people is important for the vocational educator. The vocational educator must be able to solicit interest, concerns, and preferences from families, persons with disabilities, and other agencies. Because interagency coordination is a critical component of a successful vocational educational training program, effective communication strategies and coordination strategies with personnel who may have different interests and philosophies must be part of the vocational educator's repertoire. How does one deal with a vocational supervisor who resists integration? What is the best strategy for communicating with a parent who does not want her daughter riding a public bus? How can information be solicited from a student with a disability regarding a preferred job? All of these situations require carefully analyzed responses and strategies. Without them, a vocational educator may face barriers that ultimately interfere with vocational success.

Consider the following example. Recently a vocational educator had to confront the real situation in which her supervisor maintained that some students with severe disabilities are best served in self-contained classrooms. The vocational educator collected all the information available on successful community-based programs, compiled a brief report of these findings, and proposed an alternative trial program that would be evaluated after six months. This systematic approach, which went beyond philosophical beliefs, was enough to convince the supervisor to at least try this "new idea."

The above critical values and skills provide a foundation for developing longitudinal and meaningful vocational opportunities for students with disabilities. This foundation in combination with a coordinated service delivery system will maximize the success of students.

Knowledge of System Change and Advocacy Strategies

Many professionals believe that the system changes as a result of policy decisions made by upper level bureaucrats. This belief can lead to a feeling of impotence on the part of the vocational educator. Small changes in the service system often influence the ways in which persons view the larger system. For example, if a vocational educator develops a successful placement and training opportunity for a student who has been labeled "unemployable" by traditional assessment measures, then others can see that those assessment and evaluation systems lack reliability. This, in turn, could result in the Office of Vocational Rehabilitation developing a policy to fund on-site and extended evaluations. Clearly, in such a case, the vocational educator will have influenced the service delivery system and engaged in change strategies. This realization can assist the vocational educator in communicating successes and problems to persons who are in a position to influence policy and funding patterns.

INTERAGENCY COLLABORATION: A PRACTICE FOR PROMOTING INTEGRATED VOCATIONAL EDUCATION AND EMPLOYMENT OPPORTUNITIES

How can agencies work together to create the most integrated and beneficial opportunities for young adults with disabilities? What agency is ultimately responsible for vocational education, placement, and follow-up? If agencies have overlapping goals, how can they create interagency agreements? The agencies involved in the community in vocational preparation and follow-up of students with disabilities typically include special education agencies, vocational rehabilitation agencies, the Office of Developmental Disabilities and Mental Retardation, public health services, community colleges and adult vocational-technical schools, and private nonprofit agencies such as the Association for Retarded Citizens and United Cerebral Palsy. Although the names of individual agencies may vary among states, their goals are basically similar. These agencies were created to promote an increased quality of life and movement toward independence for youth and adults with disabilities. Questions regarding responsibility of service delivery must be addressed effectively. If they are not, then students graduating from high school may "fall through the cracks" and be denied opportunities for meaningful lives. In order to understand how agencies can work together, their missions, according to federal regulations, will first be presented. By defining "missions," it will be clear where overlapping goals and potential conflicts exist.

Vocational Education

Vocational education includes federal, state, and local programs at less than a baccalaureate level that are designed to prepare individuals for occupations and work. The Vocational Education Act of 1963 mandated that opportunities be provided for persons with disabilities. In 1968, amendments to this act designated that 10 percent of federal funds allocated under Part B be spent on persons with disabilities. In 1976, new amendments required that each state match the 10 percent of federal funds and thereby substantially increase the amount of monies available to persons labeled as disabled. These monies can be used only for students who require special education and related services, and who are not expected to succeed in a typical vocational education program without assistance or modifications. In 1978, some $5.5 billion in taxes were spent to support vocational education (Weisgerber, Dahl, and Appleby, 1981). In 1979, unfortunately, the President's Committee on Employment of the Handicapped reported that (1) only 2 percent of all vocational education students were disabled; and (2) only 3 percent of the community college students were disabled (Brolin, 1982). When these figures are compared with those of the Department of Special Education and Rehabilitation Services, which indicate that 80 percent of students with disabilities are unemployed after graduation from high school, the discrepancies between need and services (practice) are stunning. These discrepancies may reflect the lack of appropriate vocational options available. Many vocational education programs include only persons who can benefit from traditional curricula—and not those who require ongoing and systematic community vocational instruction.

According to P.L. 94–482, the Vocational Education Act Amendments, vocational education requires conformity to the requirements of P.L. 94–142 in order that

> those with special education handicaps will have ready access to vocational training which is of high quality, which is realistic in light of actual or anticipated opportunities for gainful employment, and which is suited to their needs, interests, and ability to benefit from such training.

This requirement should expand the vocational options to students with disabilities perceived as too severe to benefit from traditional vocational curricula.

Special Education

P.L. 94–142, the Education of All Handicapped Children Act, mandates free and appropriate education for all handicapped children between the ages of 3 and 21. The law requires zero exclusion of students with disabilities, parental participation, nondiscriminatory evaluations, individualized educational programs (IEPs), placement in the least restrictive environment, and the right to due process. Because vocational instruction is a critical component of an appropriate education, it ought to be included in the IEP and should reflect parental and family concerns, individual learning and performance characteristics, and the "criterion of ultimate functioning" (Brown, Nietupski, and Hamre-Nietupski, 1976). This means that vocational instruction should reflect future requirements for working in integrated community environments and thus prepare a student for adult life and the world of work.

Vocational Rehabilitation

The Office of Vocational Rehabilitation, a federal and state program, is mandated by the Rehabilitation Act of 1973 to provide vocational services to persons with disabilities. These services typically include:

(a) Evaluation of rehabilitation potential, including diagnostic and related services;

(b) Counseling, guidance, referral, and placement services for handicapped individuals, including follow-up, follow-along, and other post-employment services necessary to assist such individuals to maintain their employment, and services designed to help persons with disabilities secure needed supports from other agencies for services which are not available under the Rehabilitation Act itself;

(c) Vocational and other training services, which include personal and vocational adjustment and other training material and services to the families of individuals with disabilities;

(d) Physical and mental restoration services, including but not limited to:

- Corrective surgery or therapeutic treatment
- Necessary hospitalizations for reducing or preventing disability
- Prosthetic or orthotic devices;
- Eyeglasses and visual services;
- Special services (including transportation and dialysis, artificial kidneys and supplies necessary for the treatment of individuals suffering from end-stage renal disease); and
- Diagnosis and treatment for mental and emotional disorders by a physical or licensed psychologist;

(e) Maintenance, not exceeding the estimated cost of subsistence during rehabilitation;

(f) Interpreter services for deaf individuals, and reader services for those persons determined to be blind;

(g) Recruitment and training services;

(h) Rehabilitation teaching services and orientation and mobility services for persons who are blind;

(i) Occupational license, tools, equipment, and initial stocks and supplies;

(j) Transportation in connection with the rendering of any vocational rehabilitation service; and

(k) Telecommunication, sensory, and other technological aids and devices. (29 U.S.C. 723)

Section 504 of the Rehabilitation Act mandates that all children and adults with disabilities be served regardless of family income, severity of disability, type of handicap, geographical location, or any other limiting criteria. However, vocational rehabilitation requires that an individual show potential for competitive employment. This potentially excludes a large number of persons labeled severely disabled who are in need of long-term services, since the nature of the service delivery is short-term transitional, or time-limited. Ironically, in 1973 the Rehabilitation Act was amended to state that persons with the most severe disabilities be given priority for services. This automatically creates a conflict between the nature of the service delivery model, which is time-limited, and the targeted priority group.

Although there are no age limits for vocational rehabilitation services, referrals are frequently not accepted until an individual is a minimum of 14 and frequently 18 years of age. Additionally, independent living services are available to persons "who cannot potentially benefit" from employment services but require some other form of financial or program support. Laski (1979) reported that it is often determined that persons with developmental disabilities and severe physical disabilities will not benefit, and thus they are frequently excluded from vocational rehabilitation services. When this happens, they may be referred to sheltered work, day activity, or day treatment services. Clearly, a contradiction in service delivery exists. Those who are the most severely handicapped have been targeted for vocational rehabilitation services and yet are frequently considered too disabled to benefit. This contradiction has been and should continue to be resolved by trained personnel able to meet the challenge presented by persons labeled severely disabled.

Interagency Agreements

Professionals too often attend only to interventions directed at individuals and forget that knowledge of systems and change strategies are equally important. In the fields of vocation education and rehabilitation, one change strategy frequently proposed is the development of interagency agreements. Much attention is currently being devoted to interagency agreements because of the need to coordinate services for persons with disabilities. Schalock (1984) contends that awarding services based on categorical diagnoses and single-agency service delivery is not a viable option. Elder, Conley, and Noble believe that services to children and adults are disorganized and inefficient. They presented a real-life situation in which one person could receive Social Security Childhood Disability Beneficiary payments supplemented by SSI benefits, Medicare benefits supplemented by Medicaid, food stamps, help from social service agencies, and possible vocational rehabilitation services. This person could therefore be involved with five separate agencies. Based on this wide array of services, they conclude that "each program not only has an independent effect but also displays interactive effects with other programs" (1986, p. 65). Consequently, they suggest that efficient policies that reflect the combined and interacting effects of all programs that may affect employment must be developed to promote employment of adults with mental retardation. Responses to this and other findings and suggestions have resulted in written joint policy statements among the Offices of Special Education and Rehabilitation Services, Vocational Education, and Community Health Services. The implication for persons receiving vocational education services is that special education and rehabilitation will be included in some form of interagency agreement.

Approximately thirty-five states have some form of interagency agreements (Wehman, Kregel, Barcus, and Schalock, 1986). However, many agency administrators are suspicious of each other's intentions and potential financial gains and losses. Schalock (1984) argues that agencies must proceed into interagency agreements with a clear understanding of their positive results and, at the same time, they must reconceptualize the service delivery system. Interagency agreements should reflect a commitment to integration, least restrictive environment, and consumer and family rights (Biklen, 1973, 1976; Schalock, 1983, Wilcox and Bellamy, 1983; Wolfensburger, 1972).

Noble, Conley, and Elder (1986) propose that the integration and coordination of programs be improved so that the system of services operates in a unified and consistent way. One method for accomplishing this would be to require unified and comprehensive plans for each client that would include the input of special education, vocational education, vocational rehabilitation, adult social services, health care, income support, and other services (1986, p. 89).

In many states, according to Noble, Conley, and Elder, joint planning among state and local agencies currently exists, and a plan is not valid until approved by the representatives of the different agencies. These authors propose that this type of effort become mandatory in order to ensure consistency among plans and to ensure that all agencies share in the responsibility of service delivery rather than being responsible for one isolated service delivery system (1986, p. 89). These agreements should include at least the following benefits: increased staff productivity, improved utilization of resource capacity, lower staffing requirements, reduced unit costs from joint activities, financial advantages, staffing benefits, organizational growth and survival, improved resource allocation, improved distribution of health personnel, increased availability of services, and broader and more comprehensive scope of services (Schalock, 1984, p. 54).

Ultimately, interagency agreements must have positive results for the persons for whom they were created. Persons with disabilities are victims of our disorganized service delivery system. Professionals must take care not to create interagency agreements without first carefully evaluating the fundamental premises upon which those services were created. It would not make sense to create an interagency agreement between two agencies that supported segregated services and exclusionary practices. In such a case the interagency agreement would not serve the consumer, but would rather serve the system.

Although some of the advantages of interagency collaboration have been listed, there have been few recognized models in the area of vocational education and employment. The following model is one example of how agencies can collaborate in order to maximize effective service delivery to persons with disabilities.

CASE STUDY:

Joseph is 20 years old. He lives at home with his two parents and younger sister. No alternative living arrangements are being considered because of the strong support he receives from his family, neighbors, and other friends. He is in his final year of school and is currently involved in a community-vocational program funded jointly by special education and vocational education. He is receiving training in a community business five half days per week in preparation for future employment. He works at a printing company where he collates and packages printed materials. He dislikes doing physical work but prefers to do a number of tasks throughout the day. The nature of this job and its location on a bus line seem a good match to Joseph's preferences. The site is supervised by the transition teacher (a jointly funded position between vocational education and special education) and an Office of Vocational Rehabilitation job coach. The job coach program is funded through OVR and is available to students for up to two years, if necessary. This cooperative agreement is meeting the vocational training needs of the student.

When Joseph graduates from high school, he will no longer be eligible for special education and vocational education funding. OVR has an agreement with the Office of Mental Retardation and Developmental Disabilities (OMR-DD) to provide the initial intensive employment services and then turn over long-term follow-up activities to OMR-DD. This model, supported by Wehman and Kregel (1985) and currently being implemented in supported work efforts in many states, has been effective and efficient in providing initial intensive training and followalong services. The cooperative agreement will ensure that Joseph's postschool vocational needs are being met. The vocational service agency is attempting to involve coworkers with Joseph. This will not only help with the fading of external supervision but will help to fully integrate him into the workplace. He will continue to live at home with his parents and take the bus to and from work. Because his parents are flexible, Joseph's six-hour workday (rather than eight) does not present a problem. He has reported satisfaction with his job and living situation.

SUMMARY

Educators are part of the rapidly changing field of vocational training and placement for students with disabilities. In order for educators to become the "innovators" rather than responders to the concerns of parents and others, vocational education curricula must include knowledge of critical values and techniques for evaluation, training, placement, and community agency communications and coordination. Curricula changes in personnel preparation programs will result in an increasing number of professionals who look beyond traditional in-school and in-class instruction to providing meaningful work opportunities for all students and adults in integrated community businesses and industries.

REFERENCES

Ashbaugh, J.W. (1981). Accountability of community providers for services to the mentally retarded and other developmentally disabled persons. In T.C. Muzzio, J.J. Koshel, and V. Bradley (eds.), *Alternative Community Living Arrangements and Nonvocational Social Services for Developmentally Disabled People.* Washington, D.C.: Urban Institute.

Batsche, C. (1980). Personnel preparation for serving special vocational needs populations. In G.D. Meers (ed.), *Handbook of Special Vocational Needs Education.* Rockville: Aspen Publications. Pp. 245–266.

Belmore, K., and L. Brown. (1978). Job skills inventory strategy for use in a public school vocational training program for severely handicapped potential workers. In N. Haring and D. Bricker (eds.), *Teaching the Severely Handicapped.* Vol. 3. Seattle: American Association for the Education of the Severely/Profoundly Handicapped.

Biklen, D. (1976). Advocacy comes of age. *Exceptional Children 42,* 308–313.

Biklen, D. (1973). Human report: I. In B. Blatt (ed.), *Souls in Extremis: An Anthology on Victims and Victimizers.* Boston: Allyn and Bacon.

Biklen, D. (1968). The myth of clinical judgement. In preparation.

Brody-Hasazi, S., G. Salembier, and K. Finck. (1983). Directions for the 80's: Vocational preparation for secondary mildly handicapped students. *Teaching Exceptional Children 15,* 206–210.

Brolin, D.E. (1982). *Vocational Preparation of Persons with Handicaps.* 2d ed. Columbus, Ohio: Charles E. Merrill.

Brown, L., J. Nietupski, and S. Hamre-Nietupski. (1976). The criterion of ultimate functioning and public school services for severely handicapped children. In M.A. Thomas (ed.), *Hey, Don't Forget about Me!* Reston: Va.: Council for Exceptional Children. Pp. 2–15.

Brown, L., J. Nisbet, A. Ford, M. Sweet, B. Shiraga, J. York, and R. Loomis. (1983). The critical need for nonschool instruction in educational programs for severely handicapped students. *Journal of the Association for Persons with Severe Disabilities 8*(3), 71–78.

Brown, L., B. Shiraga, A. Ford, P. VanDeventer, J. Nisbet, R. Loomis, and M. Sweet. (1986). Teaching severely handicapped students to perform meaningful work in nonsheltered vocational environments. In R. Morris and B. Blatt (eds.), *Perspectives in Special Education: State of the Art.* Glenview, Ill.: Scott-Foresman. In press.

Elder, J.K., R.W. Conley, and J.H. Noble. (1986). The service system. In W.E. Kiernan and J.A. Stark (eds.), *Pathways to Employment for Adults with Developmental Disabilities.* Baltimore: Paul H. Brookes. Pp. 53–67.

Falvey, M., P. Ferrara-Parrish, F. Johnson, I. Pumpian, J. Schroeder, and L. Brown. (1979). Curricular strategies for generating comprehensive longitudinal and chronological age appropriate functional individual vocational plans for severely handicapped adolescents and young adults. In L. Gruenewald (ED.), *Strategies for Teaching Chronological Age Appropriate Functional Skills to Adolescent and Young Adult Severely Handicapped Students.* Vol. IX, Part 1. Madison: Wi.: Madison Metropolitan School District. Pp. 102–309.

Ford, A., and P. Mirenda. (1984). Community instruction: A natural cues and corrections decisions model. *Journal of the Association for Persons with Severe Handicaps 9*(2), 79–88.

Greenspan, S., and B. Schoultz. (1981). Why mentally retarded adults lose their jobs: Social competence as a factor in work adjustment. *Applied Research in Mental Retardation 2*, 23–28.

Hasazi-Brody, S., G. Salembier, and K. Finck. (1983). Directions for the 80's: Vocational preparation for secondary mildly handicapped students. *Teaching Exceptional Children 15*, 206–210.

Illich, I. (1978). *Toward a History of Need.* New York: Bantam Pres.

Laski, F. (September/December, 1979). Vocational rehabilitation services for severely handicapped persons: Rights or reality. *Amicus*, 237–245.

McKnight, J. (1977). Professionalized service and disabling help. In I. Illich (ed.), *Disabling Professions* London: M. Boyes. Pp. 69–91.

Murphy, S., and A. Ursprung. (1984). The politics of vocational evaluation: A qualitative study. *Rehabilitation Literature 44*(44 (1–2), 2–13.

Nisbet, J.A., and M.J. Callahan. (1986). Elements of vocational services which assist persons with severe disabilities to achieve success in integrated workplaces. In preparation.

Noble, J.H., R.W. Conley, and J.K. Elder. (1986). Where do we go from here? In W.E. Kiernan and J.A. Stark (eds.), *Pathways to Employment for Adults with Developmental Disabilities.* Baltimore: Paul H. Brookes. Pp. 85–103.

O'Brien, J. (1986). Discovering community: Learning from innovations in services to people with mental retardation. Atlanta: Responsive Systems Associates.

President's Committee on Employment of the Handicapped. (1980). Washington, D.C.: U.S. Government Printing Office.

President's Committee on Mental Retardation. (1983). The mentally retarded worker: An economic discovery. Report to the President. Washington, D.C.: U.S. Department of Health and Human Services.

Rand Corporation Study. (1983)

Schalock, R.L. (1983). *Service for the Developmentally Disabled Adult: Development, Implementation and Evaluation.* Baltimore: University Park Press.

Schalock, R.L. (1984). *Services for Developmentally Disabled Adults.* Baltimore: University Park Press.

Schalock, R.L., and O.C. Karan. (1983). An ecological approach to assessing vocational and community living skills. In O.C. Karan and W.I. Gardner (eds.), *Habilitation Practices with the Developmentally Disabled Who Present Behavioral and Emotional Disorders.* Madison, Wi.: Rehabilitation Research and Training Center in Mental Retardation.

Sweet, M., B. Shiraga, A. Ford, J. Nisbet, S. Graff, and R. Loomis. (1982). Vocational training: Are ecological strategies applicable for severely multihandicapped students. In L. Brown, J. Nisbet, A. Ford, M. Sweet, B. Shiraga, and L. Gruenewald (eds.), *Educational Programs for Severely Handicapped Students.* Vol. XII Madison, Wi.: Madison Metropolitan School District. Pp. 99–131.

Taylor, S.J. (1983). From segregation to integration: Strategies for integrating severely handicapped students in normal school and community settings. *Journal of the Association for Persons with Severe Disabilities* 7(3), 42–50.

Wehman, P., and J. Kregel. (1985). A supported work approach to competitive employment of individuals with moderate and severe handicaps. *Journal of the Association for Persons with Severe Disabilities* 9(5).

Wehman, P., J. Kregel, J.M. Barcus, and R.L. Schalock. (1986). Vocational transition for students with developmental disabilities. In W.E. Kiernan and J.A. Stark (eds.), *Pathways to Employment for Adults with Developmental Disabilities.* Baltimore: Paul H. Brookes. Pp. 113–129.

Weisgerber, R.A., P.R. Dahl, and J.A. Appleby (1981). *Training the Handicapped for Productive Employment.* Rockville, Md.: Aspen Systems Corp.

Wilcox, B., and G.T. Bellamy. (1983). *Design of High School Programs for Severely Handicapped Students.* Baltimore: Paul H. Brookes.

Will, M. (1984). OSERS programming for transition of youth with disabilities: Bridges from school to work life. Position paper. Washington, D.C.: Office of Special Education and Rehabilitation Services.

Wilms, W. (1984). Vocational education and job success: The employer's view. *Phi Delta Kappan* 65(5), 347–350.

Wolfensburger, W. (1972). *The Principle of Normalization in Human Services.* Toronto, Canada: National Institute on Mental Retardation.

4 Community Living and Work

Daniel W. Close
Thomas J. Keating
University of Oregon

INTRODUCTION

The current emphasis on transition from school to adult life has generated much interest within the field of special education and rehabilitation. In part, this interest is a natural outgrowth of the emphasis on mainstreaming and integration of students with disabilities in the schools. As the children served under P.L. 94-142 have matured, awareness by parents and professionals of the lack of coordinated planning and service delivery for adults with disabilities has increased. In response to this concern, the Federal Office of Special Education and Rehabilitative Services (OSERS) produced a series of documents that describe a model of transition from school to adult life (Will, 1984a, 1984b).

Will's model (Figure 4.1) proposes a schema that describes the transition from school to work. The process is defined as an array of service bridges that link the high school years with the world of employment. Will defines these service bridges as: (1) generic services available to all citizens in a community, such as community college programs; (2) time-limited services provided for a fixed term, contingent on the existence of a disability for program entitlement, such as the State Vocational Rehabilitation Program; and (3) ongoing support services provided for an extensive time period, such as the new "supported employment" initiative.

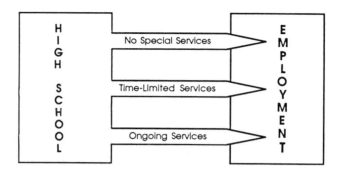

Figure 4.1 Will Model

The Will model provides a structure for planning and evaluating the government role in the employment of persons with disabilities. This recognition of an active role for government at federal, state, and local levels is valuable. Generic services, such as adult basic education, and time-limited resources, such as state vocational rehabilitation services, will continue to train many persons with disabilities for meaningful employment. Long-term services to support employment of persons with disabilities is a truly innovative idea, however, and has breathed new life into secondary school special education and adult service programs.

Halpern (1985) has proposed a model of transition from school to adult life (Figure 4.2) that incorporates the Will services bridges with other valued outcomes. The Will (1984) thesis focused attention on services needed for the successful transition from school to work. Halpern attempts to incorporate other equally valued dimensions of adult life, proposing a three-component model that includes: (1) employment and finances, (2) residential environments, and (3) social and interpersonal networks. This expanded concept is consistent both with current literature on adult adjustment (Heal, Sigelman, and Switzky, 1981; Lakin, Bruininks, and Sigford, 1981) and with current findings on the adjustment of adults with disabilities in less restrictive residential environments (Halpern, Close, and Nelson, 1986).

In an effort to expand Will's notion of ongoing support services and Halpern's thesis of multiple dimensions of adult adjustment, it is necessary to identify additional avenues of support that may be provided to persons with disabilities. One important dimension stems from the work of Halpern, Nave, Close, and Nelson (1986), which suggests family support as a crucial component of successful adult adjustment for persons in semi-independent living programs. Given the current emphasis on incorporating parents and other family members into the educational process, it is useful to look beyond the resources of the social service system toward family support in the transition from school to adult life.

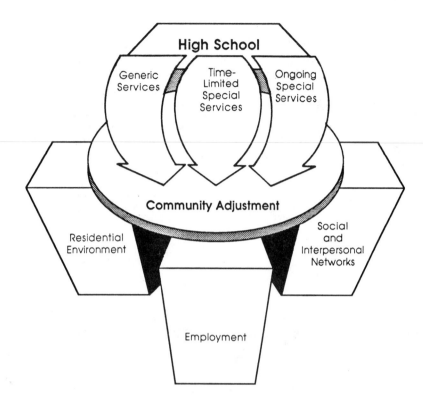

High School

Generic Services

Time-Limited Special Services

Ongoing Special Services

Community Adjustment

Residential Environment

Social and Interpersonal Networks

Employment

Figure 4.2 Halpern Model

There are several reasons to incorporate family support systems into the transition process. Families are a powerful and enduring source of support for their children with disabilities (Baller, Charles, and Miller, 1967). Early efforts to secure jobs for graduates of special education programs often called for family members to locate and obtain employment (Deno, 1965). Likewise, Edgerton (1967) reported that family members were instrumental in assisting with the employment, money management, and overall community adjustment of adults with mild retardation who had been released from institutions. Recent work by Schalock, Harper, and Genung (1981) and Halpern, et al. (1986) documents the critical role families play in the successful employment of young adults with disabilities.

Thus, a synthesis of the Will (1984a, 1984b) and Halpern (1985) concepts produces yet another model of adult adjustment. This model (Figure 4.3), referred to as "supported living" (Close and Halpern, in press), draws a distinction between the formal services provided by government-funded agencies, and the informal assistance provided by families and friends. Graphically, the model incorporates elements from the perspectives of both Will (1984) and Halpern (1985). The model acknowledges the cooperative nature of service delivery between government and private sources. This cooperation does not imply that families need to take the lead role in providing adult services for their children with disabilities. Rather, families act as advocates to ensure access to high-quality services, and they play a supportive role in the ongoing delivery of services. This "supported living" model incorporates the best ideals of government assistance and family support for successful adult adjustment of persons with disabilities.

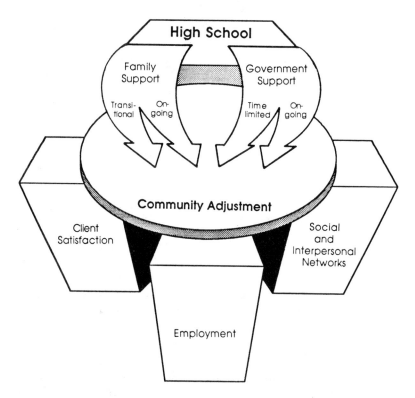

Figure 4.3 Supported Living Model

STATEMENT OF PURPOSE

While the "supported living" concept has intuitive and political appeal, much work is needed to clearly define the roles of government and family in the transition from school to adult life. Our purpose here is to articulate such a model with regard to family support and quality of life for adults with disabilities. To this end, empirical evidence from an intensive study on the adult adjustment of persons with mental retardation will be provided. These individuals were clients of semi-independent living programs (SILPs) in California, Washington, Oregon, and Colorado (Halpern, et al., 1986). In addition, we will present anecdotal information from an OSERS-funded postsecondary program that teaches vocational, residential, and social skills in a community college setting to persons with disabilities. These data will be discussed in terms of the model of "supported living." Specifically, a discussion of the function of government in training and encouraging parents to fulfill their supportive roles will be provided. Finally, we will describe current efforts to incorporate parents in the planning and implementation of programs for transition from school to adult life.

RESEARCH FINDINGS

The research literature on the transition from school to adult life has produced a number of reports detailing the accomplishments and problems of persons with disabilities. When one analyzes this literature, it is clear that a variety of research designs have been utilized to study this area. A common design measures the life adjustment of individuals following graduation from high school. Recent studies by Hasazi, Gordon, and Roe (1985), Wehman, Kregel, and Barcus (1985), and others provide quantitative data on number of persons employed, manner of exit from programs, and type of work experience program employed during the high school years. Other studies have followed more qualitative approaches to describe the life situations of persons following high school (Kernan and Koegel, 1984; Nelson, 1984). These participant observation approaches provide a wealth of information on relatively few people, while the quantitative studies provide less detail on a greater number of people.

Here we will provide a balance between information collected from both large-scale quantitative studies and small-scale qualitative sources. The present treatment of the subject is not intended to be comprehensive or exhaustive. Rather, it is our desire to report on a series of studies conducted at the Rehabilitation Research and Training Center in Mental Retardation at the University of Oregon. The research program in community/adult adjustment at the Research and Training Center at the University of Oregon is presently in its twentieth year of operation. This experience will be utilized in presenting both quantitative and qualitative information on the role of social support and employment in the lives of adults with disabilities.

The purpose of the first study (Halpern, Close, and Nelson, 1986) was to identify the descriptive factors associated with semi-independent living programs (SILP) for persons with mental retardation. The design used several sources of information to identify both person-specific attributes and service-setting characteristics affecting semi-independent living for this group. Carefully formatted interviews and questionnaires were utilized to collect information from three sources; persons with mental retardation, SILP service providers, and SILP program administrators.

Halpern's study (Halpern, Nave et al., 1986) produced a wealth of descriptive statistics in the areas of employment, residential environment, social support, and client satisfaction. Information in the employment area uncovered both positive and distressing facts for persons with disabilities. For example, 25 percent of the sample worked in nonsubsidized competitive settings. These individuals in competitive jobs earned far more money than those who were employed in a sheltered setting or who were unemployed. Specifically, a person with a competitive job typically had a monthly income of $360 after payment for housing. Clients in sheltered workshops averaged $292, and unemployed persons $247 a month.

Persons in competitive settings also sharply differed from other individuals in amount of time spent with nondisabled persons. Individuals in competitive employment situations spend 250 percent more time with nondisabled persons that individuals in sheltered workshops. Further, unemployed individuals spent 50 percent more time with nondisabled persons than did clients in sheltered workshops.

Additional analysis of the jobs in the competitive sector indicates, however, that most of those workers were employed in low-skill, low-pay jobs. Also, nearly half of the people in competitive jobs had worked in them for less than a year. Nelson (1984) comments on this dilemma by stating, "The ability of adults with mental retardation to make a successful transition . . . in the labor market is thwarted by their placement in a sector of the occupational structure marked by instability and low wages" (p. 10).

Another disturbing finding from Halpern, Nave et al. (1986) is that almost one-third of the individuals studied were unemployed. Of those individuals, approximately two-fifths were either in training for work or were exploring job opportunities. Of those still seeking work, inadequate job placement services and lack of available employment (either sheltered or competitive) were primary obstacles. Unfortunately, over 50 percent of the unemployed had given up searching for work or were not motivated to choose work over reliance on income maintenance programs such as Supplementary Security Income (SSI) or welfare.

The Halpern study (Halpern, Nave et al., 1986) also provided information on social support and client satisfaction. Support is defined as the friendship, family involvement, intimate relationships, and sexuality experienced by people with retardation. Client satisfaction is defined as the personal feelings and impressions of semi-independence by persons with retardation. Ninety-five percent of the sample had some direct contact with family members. Not surprisingly, mothers were the most frequent source of contact with the SILP participants. Nearly half of the clients perceived their families as having a positive influence on their lives, while the influence was viewed as negative in only one-fifth of the cases. Further, over three-fourths of the service providers reported that families provided valuable assistance to their clients. The primary sources of assistance provided by family members were advice, social and leisure opportunities, money, and assistance with job placement.

More detailed information on the relationship among employment, social support, and self-satisfaction is provided by Halpern, Nave, et al. (1986). Individual items from the Halpern, Nave et al. (1986) study were organized into the four variables: employment, residential environment, social support, and self-satisfaction. The items that contributed to each variable were then subjected to psychometric analyses. Measures of internal consistency, reliability, and stability over time were more than adequate for all items and resultant variables.

The outcome variables of particular interest here are employment, social support, and self-satisfaction. Statistical analyses indicate little correlation between employment status and the other variables. For example, indices of social support and satisfaction remain constant across all three categories of employment. Further inspection revealed that the only variable to correlate significantly with satisfaction was social support. Persons receiving a high level of social support expressed greater satisfaction, while persons with lower levels of social support expressed lower satisfaction. When the social support variable was further analyzed, the family support component in particular showed a significant relationship with self-satisfaction.

The two studies provide much descriptive and correlational information regarding the adult status of persons with disabilities. The implications of these data are critical for current efforts to promote the transition from school to adult life. Clearly, efforts to promote competitive employment must be emphasized because of the benefits of increased wages and opportunities for social integration. Likewise, equally concerted efforts must be directed to developing a full range of government and private social supports to enhance the quality of life and self-satisfaction of persons with disabilities.

Anecdotal Support

The following three case studies were drawn from a sample of adults who have participated in supported living services offered through the University of Oregon. They represent a range of employment situations and different levels of family support. These accounts are intended to illustrate the relationship between social support and quality of life.

CASE STUDY 1

Jane is 40 years old and was raised in a small farming community in the Northwest. She attended public schools for only one year as a young girl and, not surprisingly, failed to learn to read or perform simple academic tasks. Her mother died when Jane was 20 and she lived with her father until she was about 21. At that time, he became unable to care for her and Jane was sent to live in a large, state-operated institution for persons with developmental disabilities. Jane had little further contact with her father after being placed in the institution. Nor did she have any contact with an older sister, who had married and left home. Jane speaks harshly of her experience at the institution, referring to it as a "prison" where she was lonely and had few friends. At a time when most people her age are making a change to greater independence and opportunity, Jane was headed in the opposite direction.

After several years there, Jane benefited from an early effort at deinstitutionalization. She was placed in a nursing home, where she developed a close relationship with another resident and his brother. When the nursing home closed down, all three were scheduled to return to the institution. At that point, the case management system arranged for foster care where Jane and her two friends could live together, in close proximity to the stepmother of the two men. After a short time in the foster home, the stepmother arranged for the three of them to rent their own house.

Jane and her housemates receive a variety of formal and informal supports. The brothers' stepmother provides ongoing support and assistance with such things as budgeting and bill paying and, occasionally, with advice on interpersonal matters. Jane has a small income from Social Security Disability. She receives neither support nor training from the developmental disabilities system.

Jane has been unemployed for the past twenty years. She worked briefly in a number of sheltered employment settings but, each time, she quickly became bored by the "lousy work they give you." In addition, she says she "make(s) more money on Social Security" than she thinks she can reasonably obtain in the secondary labor market.

Though Jane does not have a paying job, she works full-time as a volunteer and does an impressive amount of work to help other persons with disabilities. She has been a member of her State Developmental Disabilities Council, and she has served on the advisory board for a major research center in mental retardation. Jane has even served as a state president of a support group for persons with disability called "People First." As president she learned to make speeches, organize and run meetings, and plan for a large convention. She actively recruited members and participated in a variety of ticket sales and other fund-raising activities. She also provides informal support on a regular basis to other individuals in her community who are trying to make it on their own.

Commenting on her life, Jane says, "I feel just great! I have so much to do. I don't have time to work." Her relationship with her boyfriend is also a source of pride and satisfaction. Jane has dedicated her life, "to helping all the handicapped people do what they want to do." Jane is succeeding because of enormous personal drive and a supportive social network that was lacking in her natural family. She has found an occupational niche that is meaningful and important but, unfortunately at present, not remunerative.

CASE STUDY 2

Gil is 24 years old, and was born and raised in western Oregon. His parents separated when he was 12, and he spent his high school years living alternately with each of them. His mother has since moved from the area, but his father remains nearby, an important source of stability and support for Gil. During high school has was "mainstreamed" into a resource room program for students with mild handicaps. When he was 20, Gil graduated with a diploma of completion.

After graduation, Gil, with his father's encouragement, enrolled in a vocational training program at a local community college. This training prepared him for work as a kitchen aide in a restaurant or food service. Gil successfully completed the community college program and obtained a full-time job washing dishes in a local restaurant.

While he was attending the community college, his father consulted with the local office of developmental disabilities to determine what residential opportunities were available. As a result, Gil moved into an adult foster home where he shared a room with another man. This home was designed to teach the skills needed for independent living, but it was only moderately successful in doing so. In the meantime, Gil and his roommate had become good friends. After living in the foster home for a little over a year, they took an opportunity offered through a new semi-independent living program (SILP) and rented an apartment together. While Gil seemed able to live in an unsupervised setting, he had several problems that required training and support. One of the most significant of these was his lack of money management skills. He had no knowledge of budgeting or bill paying, and he had a string of unpaid bills from various health care and leisure companies.

Once in the SILP, Gil enrolled in an adult education program to learn money management and social survival skills. A quick learner, he rapidly picked up the skills needed to live in an apartment with minimal assistance. Gil's SILP coordinator assisted him in organizing and paying his bills, helping him apply the skills he had learned, and reinforcing the rule of "not buying anything from strangers." A substantial portion of Gil's financial difficulties stemmed from his susceptibility to sales pitches by strangers calling either at the door or on the phone.

Gil sees his father regularly. Gil's father is very supportive and his role is generally a positive one, although Gil at one point discovered that if he failed to plan his budget correctly, or if he overspent his father would bail him out. Gil's father was inadvertently encouraging Gil's dependence. When the SILP coordinator became aware of the situation, she discussed it with Gil's father. He was quite responsive to the suggestion that Gil be allowed to experience the consequences of poor spending habits (e.g., having his cable television cut off) as a step toward improving them.

Gil has worked forty hours per week at the same local restaurant for the past three years. He manages his own affairs, with three–four hours of assistance a month by the SILP coordinator. He worked the 11:00 P.M. to 7:00 A.M. shift at the restaurant, and he has an active social life. Physical exercise is his main form of recreation.

Gil reports that his life is "just super!" He is justifiably proud of his work record, his success at the community college, and the fact that he lives "on his own." He even extols the virtue of working at night, saying, "I can do so many things I want during the day, and I like the people I work with." Gil clearly has achieved a degree of success and personal satisfaction in his work, residence, and social life. His father remains an important source of friendship and support, and one would be challenged to overestimate the importance of his role in facilitating the various transitions in Gil's life.

CASE STUDY 3

Mark is a 28-year-old man who is moderately mentally handicapped. He attended special high school classes in New York City. Graduating at the age of 18, he entered an occupational training center (OTC), an intermediate placement for persons who graduate from high school but are either unprepared or must wait to enter other vocational programs, such as work activity centers, or sheltered workshops. Though the OTC was ostensibly a "pre-vocational" skills program, he emerged at the automatic release age of 21 no better prepared for a vocation than when he entered. Further, a variety of acting-out behaviors that had created problems in his middle and high school years had increased in both intensity and frequency.

Mark proceeded to work at several sheltered workshops in the New York City area, traveling independently every day as much as an hour and a half each way. At this point Mark could handle the complexities of the subway and bus systems, had basic reading and writing skills, participated in social and recreational activities, and could do all these things on a regular basis. He was, however, severely limited in all areas by a variety of behaviors that included yelling, banging, spitting, hitting, throwing things, and talking loudly to himself in public places. It was these behaviors that overshadowed his good basic skills and vocational potential. By the age of 25 he had been fired from a succession of sheltered workshops.

At the time Mark moved from his parents' home in New York to live in the Northwest with two older brothers, one of whom worked in special education and had some teaching and behavior management skills. The family felt that Mark could benefit from a more structured and supportive environment, and Mark had long expressed an interest in living with his brothers. Several months after arriving in the Northwest, and while still in a period of adjustment to the increased structure of his new environment, Mark was placed in a work activity center (WAC) at a local community college. After two or three days at the WAC, his aggressive and destructive behaviors intensified. This quickly escalated beyond the tolerance and programming abilities of the WAC staff, and Mark's dismissal was imminent. At this time, Mark's brother suggested a behavior management program to the staff. The program, a token economy, was implemented, and it proved effective both in reducing inappropriate behavior and increasing appropriate ways of dealing with anger. The program required a concerted effort and cooperation between the home and work settings. Mark's brother and the WAC staff communicated regularly in order to make necessary modifications in the program and to keep behavioral contingencies consistent in both places.

Mark remained at the WAC for two and a half years. He then was evaluated and accepted into a sheltered workshop. Permanent acceptance, however, was dependent on the results of a thirty-day evaluation period during which his vocational potential and social behavior were to be assessed. Mark did very well on the vocational measures, but his acting-out behaviors emerged again in the less structured workshop. Once again, despite his vocational abilities, the workshop staff was unable to allow an extensive transition and adaptation period. The staff did not have sufficient resources to deal with the problem. The evaluation recommended that he be sent back to the WAC. Mark had expressed a strong preference for the sheltered workshop, where he knew he could at least earn some money. Still, he continued to engage in disruptive behavior. His brother was interviewed once again and he and the staff designed a simple behavior management plan. The workshop staff agreed to implement the program and postponed firing Mark dependent on the results. Mark's behavior improved rapidly. He has now been working at the workshop for over one year, and is doing so well both vocationally and socially that one case manager commented at a recent evaluation, "Mark, I'm sure glad we kept you around." There continues to be cooperation between the home and workplace, though the focus is usually on less critical issues.

Mark says he is satisfied with his work and the social atmosphere of the workshop. Despite his contentment, however, Mark often asks questions about various other jobs. He expresses an interest in doing everything from pumping gas to performing surgery but doesn't comprehend the skill differences represented by such a continuum. While it is possible that his behavior would improve of its own in an integrated setting, it is perhaps more likely that any competitive job placement he obtains will have to take into account the need for periodic attention to his social behavior. His brother remains supportive, and continues to advocate to obtain appropriate residential and vocational services for Mark. Informed family support is an important complement to the efforts of service providers.

FAMILY SUPPORT

Both the empirical and anecdotal data indicate that social support—more specifically family support—is a key variable affecting clients' satisfaction with their lives. There is a little difference among unemployed individuals, sheltered workshop employees, and competitively employed persons on measures of satisfaction. There are, however, significant differences in satisfaction between persons with high levels of family support and those with less.

The conclusion to be drawn from these findings should in no way impede efforts to secure meaningful employment opportunities that include competitive wages in integrated settings. We must, however, also consider those variables that are associated with clear differences in personal satisfaction in the lives of individuals with disabilities. If persons working in competitive employment have less contact with friends and feel more isolated than persons working in a sheltered workshop (Halpern, Nave et al., 1986), it does not mean that working in a sheltered workshop is better. It does, however, suggest that we must attend to all meaningful variables in an attempt to improve the quality of life attainable by any individual.

The fact that family support is correlated with satisfaction, irrespective of employment status, suggests that families play an important role in meeting the social needs of persons with disabilities, as they do in the lives of many of us. This may be especially true for individuals in integrated settings who have difficulty establishing social relationships with their coworkers. The availability of support from one's family and the kinds of services that are the object of their advocacy depend on family awareness and professional attitudes. It is worth asking whether families are realizing their full potential both as social support agents and as aware advocates who will ensure that valued vocational and residential options are made available throughout their relatives' lives.

Rationale for Family Support

Recognition of the need for community-based, family supported services has developed as greater numbers of families have rejected the option of institutionalization for persons with disabilities. Initial supports were focused on the medical and educational needs of the child, with little formal help aimed at other family members. Early descriptive studies of the effect on other family members of a disabled member concluded that intervention was warranted (Rosen, 1955). The rationale for providing services to other members of the family was based initially on the concept of deviant development. That is, the presence of someone with a disability was likely to result in abnormal relationships and development for the rest of the family (Farber and Ryckman, 1965). In practice, though, interest was primarily in the mother–child relationship (Lamb, 1983).

More recently, a family systems approach to service provision (Jaffe-Ruiz, 1983; Zigler, 1984), and the demonstrated use by families of effective teaching and behavior management techniques (Patterson and Broadsky, 1966; Becker, 1971; Schreibman, O'Neill, and Koegel, 1983), have broadened the scope of services deemed essential to effective family support. The view of the family as an interactive system where all members are challenged by the presence of a relative with a disability is increasingly accepted (Gentry and Olson, 1986), and has resulted in concern for fathers, brothers and sisters, and grandparents, as well as mothers (Ogle and Powell, 1985; Meyer et al., 1985; Lamb, 1983).

The kinds of services available have also been expanded to include: information and counseling services to assist families in adjustment; instruction in effective teaching approaches families can adopt; and more formal avenues for support and advocacy. Integral to this shift has been a focus not on deviant development but on provision of needed skills and information. Family development will certainly be different, but need not be considered deviant or abnormal, if necessary services are provided.

While there has been much progress in the development of family support, however, there remain some problems of communication and conflict between families and professionals (Schulz, 1985). Some parents still experience the "run around" phenomenon, receiving inconsistent information that is delivered with varying degrees of insensitivity by human services professionals (Warren, 1985). Parents often still feel they are on an unequal footing with professionals in consideration not only of their needs and problems, but in the value attached to their choices, skills, and observations (Schulz, 1985). Finally, despite the recent interest in family members other than the mother and child, groups such as fathers and siblings remain largely unserved (Seligman, 1983), as do older persons with disabilities and their families.

Common to many of these difficulties is a tendency to view families as a homogeneous group, when this is clearly not the case (Perske and Perske, 1981). It would be difficult to obtain unanimity among families on any given issue. There is support as well as opposition, for instance, to various community-based services (Boggs, 1985). There are families who wish to be thoroughly involved with school and community programming and some who do not. There is also variability among members of any one family. According to Bradley and Agosta (1985), factors that affect how families interact with their disabled relatives include: the seriousness of the disability, presence of difficult behavior, the family's emotional status, other family characteristics such as size, and level of community services available.

In addition to the incorrect view of families as a homogeneous group, there is confusion about the relationship between government and family in service planning and implementation. Agosta, Jennings, and Bradley emphasize that government policies should be directed to "support not supplant" (1985, p. 107) the family in service delivery. They note that society has not reached consensus over the public's role in private family affairs. Parents receive services to improve the quality of life for their children, yet a balance is necessary between service and interference. Despite the controversy, pressures will persist for additional training and education for families during the transition from school to adult life. There is reason to believe that the relationship between parents and professionals will continue to improve, however, and that better support services will result (Darling, 1985).

The family is the object of much recent interest due to increased awareness of family issues by professionals, increased activism by family members, and various political legislative factors (Agosta, Jennings, and Bradley, 1985). First, families accustomed to the increased level of involvement mandated by P.L. 94-142 for their school children are faced with a paucity of services as their children reach adulthood. Parent groups are increasingly involved in an attempt to make valued services available during and after the high school years (Wilcox and Slovic, 1986), The current emphasis on transition services is one response to this deficit. The political momentum of the proposed Community and Family Living Amendments (S. 873) is another factor. If passed, the legislation would mandate a shift in spending of federal Medicaid funds from large institutions to small community-based programs. It would also require a thorough assessment of the needs of families with disabled persons at all stages of life (Weinberg, 1985).

Another reason for the turn to family support is the necessity born of fiscal austerity. Overburdened human resource systems find that families can actively participate in program planning and service delivery, and that cooperation and training yield greater dividends than mere tolerance. Many families remain intimately involved with their members over the long term (Bank and Kahn, 1982; Gentry and Olson, 1986). While the economy or the service delivery apparatus cycle ebbs and flows, family support remains relatively constant. Families necessarily deal with family business regardless of the amount of outside help. Given the likelihood, however, of accelerated development of services in this area and a legislative request for information to guide that process (Chaffee, 1986), let us consider the role to be played by families in supported living for persons with disabilities.

What Role Do Families Fulfill

Clients of SILPs who participated in the Halpern study (Halpern, Nave et al., 1986) indicated by more than 2 to 1 that their family relationships were positive, an impression also supported by anecdotal data. Of those interviewed, 42 percent considered help received from family to be adequate, 16 percent received too little, and 16 percent received too much. Even in the absence of substantial family intervention and training programs, then, the overall impact of family support for these persons is positive. Still, there is much room for improvement. What should be the role of family support as part of a comprehensive planning effort?

In the case studies, a variety of family members make an essential contribution to the quality of each person's life. Jane receives assistance, with money matters and personal affairs from her companions stepmother. Given her limited income, budgeting and bill paying help are crucial in allowing her to pursue her volunteer activities and maintain a satisfactory home life. We can't tell from the story what may happen when the stepmother can no longer provide assistance. Will Jane eventually be able to manage her own affairs or will she remain dependent on outside help, family or otherwise? Could the service system provide guidance in such a situation? We may also wonder about Jane's natural family; and whether appropriate services might have resulted in maintenance of family ties.

Gil maintains regular contact with his father and, thanks to his employment and his participation in a semi-independent living program, does not rely on his family to meet his basic needs. The regular social contact is important to him, however, and his relationship with his father is a good illustration of a relationship that facilitates Gil's development without limiting him or creating undue dependence. This is seen in his early movement into an independent living situation, and in his father's responsiveness to the programming suggestions of the SILP coordinator. When the coordinator explained that budgetary bailouts were hindering Gil's progress in money management, his father was willing to arrange a more constructive form of assistance. The family support received by Jane and Gil is not intensive in nature, but it clearly facilitates their efforts at independent living, and reduces the extent to which they rely on the traditional service delivery system.

Mark's case is somewhat different in that the family support is more intensive and facilitates his efforts at independence in spite of the limitations of the adult service system, which has difficulty dealing with his deficits. Without the intervention and continuing advocacy of his brother in the vocational setting, Mark's employment prospects would be poor, indeed, even in a sheltered workshop. Mark is in a sense overly dependent on his family, but it is because the assistance he requires is not available in other ways.

Mark is also atypical in using an often wasted part of the family support network, brothers and sisters. As pointed out by Powell and Ogle (1985), siblings play an important and unique role in many of our lives. Siblings contribute to each other's social and cognitive development as children, and they continue as a source of love and support throughout life. According to Bank and Kahn (1982), this relationship may be taking on even greater significance in contemporary society for several reasons: increased mobility of families, resulting in greater reliance on intra-family relationships; smaller family size with more closely spaced children and more intense contact between them; and increased longevity, making longitudinal support even more important.

Whether persons with disabilities and their families can realize the full benefits of their unique positions depends on the support services available throughout life. Using all family resources and addressing their needs is certainly desirable, for family members can be teachers, advocates, and friends. This will not happen, however, without an increase in the scope and level of coordinated efforts by families and professionals.

Need for Parent/ Professional Partnership in Adult Services

If families are to fulfil their potential, a continued rethinking of the relationship between the human services system and the family will be necessary. Families must be regarded as important allies in providing high-quality services for persons with disabilities. As such, the level of support and training must be increased beginning with the primary diagnosis of a disability and continuing throughout the life span (Zigler, 1984). This intervention should be aimed at all members of the family, including parents, brothers, sisters, and extended family where appropriate.

Family support across the life span can build a constructive relationship between the family and service providers. In addition, such support provides a long-range perspective that prepares the family for important transitions in a disabled relative's life. This preparation should enable family members to actively seek the best possible services and stimulate the creation of new ones where necessary. During this period of change, many families are overwhelmed by the complexity of service delivery systems (Rubin and Quinn-Curran, 1983). The family is often willing but unable to participate because they don't know how.

One goal of support should be to assist families in being positive, skilled, and informed in their roles of teacher, counselor, and advocate for their disabled relatives. The service system should show families how to help meet day-to-day needs, how to participate in program decisions, and how to procure and maintain client-centered services.

A second goal should be to provide the educational and counseling resources families need in their ongoing adjustment to the unique needs of a disabled family member. The family should be as much a client of the service system as the person with a disability. This approach should begin early and continue in all later programming efforts.

Without education and encouragement, parents cannot know how to increase opportunities and assist their sons and daughters on the way to independence. Neither parents nor professionals have resources or time to do everything that is needed. The two groups must work together, complementing each other's efforts and striving toward the same goals (Turnbull, 1985).

A clear shift in public policy appears to be on the horizon. The policy initiative on transition by the Office of Special Education and Rehabilitation Services (OSERS) has resulted in the funding of over 125 new projects focusing on the interface between secondary special education and adjustment to work and community after graduation. These projects are primarily intended to develop policies and procedures that help students with disabilities to graduate from school into valued adult roles. The Department of Special Education and Rehabilitation at the University of Oregon has received two projects that highlight the role of families in facilitating the transition from school to adult life. One project has resulted in the development of a series of parent support groups referred to as the Parents Graduation Alliance (Wilcox and Slovic, 1985). The other project has resulted in the organization of the Adult Skills Development Program (ASDP), a postsecondary educational program that taught vocational and independent living skills to students with disabilities and their families (Close, Auty, and Keating, 1985). In the following section, we describe one of these projects, showing how families can plan and implement programs that support the transition of persons with disabilities from school to work and adult life.

Parents Graduation Alliance

In January 198 the Parents Graduation Alliance (PGA) was formed to provide support to families of students who are disabled and who face the transition from school to work and adult life (Wilcox, Slovic, and Hennessy, 1985). The PGA is based on three beliefs:

1. Following graduation from high school, young adults with disabilities should actively participate in integrated community activities.

2. The transition years before and after graduation from school require decisions that may have long-term consequences.

3. Families of students with disabilities have interests that transcend those of school and adult service professionals.

The PGA has several goals related to ensuring that there is a smooth transition from school to work and adult life. These include: family education, improvement of secondary and postsecondary special education curricula, expanding work and residential options in community settings, coordinating service delivery between school and adult service agencies, participating in boards of directors of state and local community agencies, and political involvement in state and local legislative efforts for person with disabilities.

Family Education The PGA is centrally organized with a paid professional staff at the University of Oregon. Local teams of parents and professionals operate throughout Oregon. During an impressive first year, the PGA developed nine parent teams whose membership totaled over 400 parents. Team leaders receive specialized training on a variety of issues, including: citizen advocacy, program ideology, the family role in the IEP, transition planning, and indicators of the quality of vocational and residential services. Team leaders return to their local communities following training, and provide instruction to local team members, who are parents of students or recent graduates of secondary school special education programs.

PGA staff and local team leaders produce "fact sheets" listing different issues of concern to alliance members. The "fact sheets" provide detailed explanations of the problems that students and families encounter during the transition process. They also offer information on characteristics of good quality vocational and residential programs, and ideas for local community action. The "fact sheets" provide the basis for communication between PGA staff and members of local teams.

Program Improvement Local teams of parents and professionals participate with school and adult service agencies to improve course content and methods of instruction. Team leaders and project staff provide training and technical assistance to individuals and local PGA groups to handle issues ranging from choosing instructional methods, designing the IEP, changing the high school curriculum, and planning the transition from school to adult life. The advocacy program often focuses on implementing methods and materials that have been effective in other school districts. Examples of this advocacy include suggestions for creating social and interpersonal networks among students after school and on weekends. In addition, the development of standards for school programs in the work and independent living area is continuing.

A key to improving program activities is developing formal strategies for making the transition from school to adult life. In this regard, PGA teams advocate establishing transition planning groups including the PGA and local school district and adult service agency personnel. The goal of this activity is to develop formal mechanisms for transition planning. Such mechanisms include formal guidelines that specify school and agency roles, time lines for implementation of plans, and procedures to evaluate the results of activities.

Another important element of program improvement is advocacy for improved work and residential options for high school graduates. Project parents and staff work closely with adult service agencies to encourage the development of approaches that emphasize the goals of productivity, integration, and independence. In addition, PGA advocated that available data on wages and other valued outcomes from existing programs be made public. In this way, parents and advocates can select appropriate programs and monitor the effectiveness of services (Wilcox and Slovic, 1985). The result of these program improvement efforts is the development of family- and consumer-oriented curricula to enhance the transition from school to adult life.

Political Involvement A natural outgrowth of these family education and program improvement activities is involvement in the political arena. The newsletters produced by PGA lament poor levels of funding for school programs and adult service options for persons with disabilities. For example, a recent newsletter said, "Each year nearly 100 Oregon high school students with severe handicaps turn 21 and leave school only to join over 200 individuals already on wait lists for work and residential placements" (Wilcox and Slovic, 1985, p. 1).

PGA members pursue a range of political activities including: (1) seeking membership on local school boards and boards of directors of adult service agencies; (2) testifying before legislative hearings to advocate increased community services; (3) seeking membership on state level boards and advisory committees responsible for planning, monitoring, and evaluating the provision of services to persons with disabilities; and (4) participating in coalition efforts with other state and local organizations to promote a broad political agenda.

Until recently, families of young adults with disabilities did not have an advocacy group organized specifically for their needs. The focus of PGA is to provide such a structure during the last years of school and the first few years following graduation. Local teams of parents and professionals supported by a centralized staff are able to address critical local and statewide issues. No doubt such a structure will encourage the development of similar support groups for families of adults who have graduated already. Through this process, parents can assume their legitimate role as informed and organized advocates for their children.

SUMMARY

In this chapter, we have presented research findings to substantiate the value of family support for persons with disabilities and their families. A significant relationship between family support and self-satisfaction of adults in semi-independent living programs is supported by both correlational data and anecdotal accounts. We have also discussed the nature of that support and the need for a cooperative working partnership between government and families in developing services that will enhance supported living options for persons with disabilities. Particular emphasis must be placed on the period of transition from school to adult life. The Parents Graduation Alliance is presented as a model parent advocacy program that illustrates a cooperative approach to program planning and service delivery in addressing this need.

REFERENCES

Agosta, J.M., D. Jennings, and V. Bradley. (1985). In J. Agosta and V. Bradley (eds.), *Family Care for Persons with Developmental Disabilities: A Growing Commitment*. Cambridge, Mass.: Human Services Research Institute.

Baller, W.R., D.C. Charles, and E.L. Miller. (1967). Mid-life attainment of the mentally retarded: A longitudinal study. *Genetic Psychology Monographs 75*, 235-329.

Bank, S., and M.D. Kahn. (1982) *The Sibling Bond*. New York: Basic Books.

Becker, W.C. (1971). *Parents Are Teachers: A Child Management Program*. Champaign, Ill. Research Press.

Boggs, E.M. (1985). Who is putting whose head in the sand? In H.R. Turnbull and A.P. Turnbull (eds.), *Parents Speak Out: Then and Now.* Columbus, Ohio, Charles E. Merrill. p. 39-54.

Bradley, V.J., and J.M. Agosta. (November 1985). Keeping your child at home: The case for family support. *Exceptional Parent 15* (7), 10-22.

Chaffee, J.H. (February 1986). Senator asks your help. In *Together: News for the Rehabilitation Community.* (Available from Information Center for Individuals with Disabilities, 20 Park Plaza, Room 330, Boston, MA 02116.)

Close, D.W., and A.S. Halper. Transition to supported living. In M. Janicki, M. Krauss, and M. Selzer (eds.), *Here to Stay: Operating Community Residences.* In press.

Close, D.W., W.P. Auty, and T.J. Keating. The adult skills development: Community college classes as a resource for adults with developmental disabilities. Paper presented at Oregon Conference, Eugene, Oregon.

Darling, R.B. (1985). Parent-professional interaction: The roots of misunderstanding. In M. Seligman (ed.). *The family with a Handicapped Child: Understanding and Treatment.* Orlando, Fla. Grune & Stratton. p. 95-121.

Deno, E. (1965). *Retarded Youth: Their School Rehabilitation Needs.* Minneapolis: Minneapolis Public Schools.

Edgerton, R.B. (1967). *The Cloak of Competence: Stigma in the Lives of the Mentally Retarded.* Berkeley: University of California Press.

Farber, B., and D.B. Ryckman. (1965). Effects of severely mentally retarded children on family relationships. *Family Relations 2,* 1-17.

Featherstone, H.F. (1981). *A Difference in the Family: Living with Disabled Child.* New York: Penguin.

Gentry, D., and J. Olson, (eds.). (1986). *The Parent Family Support Network Series: Best Practices and Available Resources in Parent/Family Services.* Vol. 1. (Available from Warrent Center, College of Education, University of Idaho, Moscow, ID 83842.)

Halpern, A.S. (1985). Transition: A look at the foundation. *Exceptional Children 51,* 479-486.

Halpern, A.S., D.W. Close, and D.J. Nelson. (1986). *On My Own: The Impact of Semi-independent Living Programs for Adults with Mental Retardation.* Baltimore: Paul H. Brookes.

Halpern, A.S., G. Nave, D. Close, and D. Nelson. (1986). An empirical analysis of the dimensions of community adjustment for adults with mental retardation. Paper presented at the Annual Conference of the American Association on Mental Deficiency, Denver, Colorado. Published as: An empirical analysis of the dimensions of community adjustment for adults with mental retardation in semi-independent living programs *Australia and New Zealand Journal of Developmental Disabilities, 12* (3), 147-157.

Hasazi, S., L. Gordon, and C. Roe. (1985). Factors associated with the employment status of handicapped youth exiting from high school from 1979 to 1983. *Exceptional Children 51* (6), 455-469.

Heal, L.W., C.K. Sigelman, and H.N. Switzky. (1978). Community residential alternatives for the mentally retarded. In N.R. Ellis (ed.), *International Review of Research in Mental Retardation.* Vol. 9. New York: Academic Press.

Jaffe-Ruiz, M. (1983). A family systems look at the developmentally disabled. In M. Screiber (ed.), *Proceedings of First Annual Seminar on Siblings of Mentally Retarded and Developmentally Disabled Persons.* Siblings Conference, c/o AHRC, 12 Floor, 200 Park Avenue South, New York, NY 10003. Pp. 79-93.

Kernan, K.T., and D. Koegel. (1984) Employment experiences of community-based mildly retarded adults. In R.B. Edgerton (ed.), *Lives in Process: Mildly Retarded Adults in a Large City.* Washington, DC: American Association on Mental Deficiency.

Lakin, C.D., R.H. Bruininks, and B.B. Sigford. (1981). Deinstitutionalization and community-based residential adjustment: A summary of research and issues. In R.H. Bruininks, C.E. Meyers, B.B. Sigford, and K.C. Lakin (eds.), *Deinstitutionalization and Community Adjustment of Mentally Retarded People.* Washington, DC: American Association on Mental Deficiency.

Lamb, M.E. (1983). Fathers of exceptional children. In M. Seligman (ed.), *The Family with a Handicapped Child: Understanding and Treatment* Orlando, Fla.: Grune & Stratton. Pp. 125-146.

Meyer, D.J., P.F. Vadasy, R.R. Fewell, and G.C. Schell. (1985) *A Handbook for the Fathers Program: How to Organize and Program for Fathers and Their Handicapped Children.* Seattle: University of Washington Press.

Nelson, R. (1984). Retarded adults in the competitive employment sector: A descriptive analysis of deviance and occupations. Doctoral dissertation, University of Oregon.

Patterson, G.R., and G. Broadsky. (1966). A behavior modification program for a child with multiple problem behaviors. *Journal of Child Psychology and Psychiatry, 7,* 277-295.

Perske, R., and M. Perske. (1981). *Hope for the Families: New Directions for Parents of Persons with Retardation or Other Disabilities.* Nashville, Tenn.: Parthenon.

Powell, T.H., and P.A. Ogle. (1985) *Brothers and Sisters: A Special Part of Exceptional Families.* Baltimore: Paul H. Brookes.

Rosen, L. (1955). Selected aspects in the development of the mother's understanding of her mentally retarded child. *American Journal for Mental Deficiency 59,* 522-529.

Rubin, S., and N. Quinn-Curran. (1983). Lost, then found: Parents' journey through the community service maze. In M. Seligman (ed.), *The Family with a Handicapped Child: Understanding and Treatment* Orlando, Fla.: Grune & Stratton. Pp. 63-94.

Schlock, R., R. Harper, and T. Genung. (1981). Community integration of mentally retarded adults: Community placement and program success. *American Journal of Mental Deficiency 85* (5), 478-488.

Schreibman, L., R.E. O'Neill, and R.L. Koegel. (1983). Behavioral training for siblings of autistic children. *Journal of Applied Behavior Analysis 16*(2), 129-138.

Schulz, J.B. (1985). The parent-professional conflict. In H.R. Turnbull and A.P. Turnbull (eds.), *Parents Speak Out: Then and Now.* Columbus, Ohio: Charles E. Merrill. Pp. 3-9.

Seligman, M. (1983). Siblings of handicapped children. In M. Seligman (ed.), *The Family with a Handicapped Child: Understanding and Treatment*. Orlando, Fla.: Grune & Stratton. Pp. 147-174.

Turnbull, A.P. (1985). From professional to parent–a startling experience. In H.R. Turnbull and A.P. Turnbull (eds), *Parents Speak Out: Then and Now*. Columbus, Ohio: Charles E. Merrill. Pp. 127-135.

Warren, F. (1985). A society that is going to kill your children. In H.R. Turnbull and A.P. Turnbull (eds.), *Parents Speak Out: Then and Now*. Columbus, Ohio: Charles E. Merrill. Pp 201-219.

Wehman, P., J. Kregel, and J.M. Barcus. (1985). From school to work: A vocational transition model for handicapped students. *Exceptional Children* 52(1), 25-37.

Weinberg, N.M. (October 1985). Creating community. Presentation at Washington State Residential Services Conference, Ellensburg, Washington.

Wilcox, B., and R. Slovic. (1985). *From School to What?* Eugene, Ore. Specialized Training Program, University of Oregon.

Wilcox, B., R. Slovic, and R. Hennessy. (1985). *The Parents' Graduation Alliance: Transition Support for Students Who Are Severely Handicapped*. Eugene, Ore. Specialized Training Program, University of Oregon.

Will, M. (1984a). Bridges from school to working life. *Programs for the Handicapped 2*, 8-9.

Will, M. (1984b). *OSERS Programming for the Transition of Youth with Disabilities: Bridges from School to Working Life*. Washington, D.C.: Office of Special Education and Rehabilitation Services.

Zigler, E. (1984). Handicapped children and their families. In E. Schopler and G.E. Mesibov (eds.), *The Effects of Autism on the Family*. New York: Plenum. Pp. 21-39.

Part II   Vocational Assessment and Preparation

As the often stated phrase goes, "When all else fails, teach!" Notwithstanding our complex policy and interagency flowcharts, vocational development ultimately boils down to the successful teaching of a number of valuable skills and attitudes. The power of our instructional procedures are obviously paramount to effective teaching. Before instruction occurs, though, it is necessary to adequately assess the abilities and preferences of the handicapped individual. Irvin outlines the different approaches to vocational assessment. Recently, the value of standardized, summative assessment in program planning has been questioned. Irvin favors a curriculum-referenced approach that stresses the repeated measurement of pupil performance with real work materials and in actual vocational settings. He feels that the functional purpose of the assessment increases the likelihood that assessment information will be utilized in the planning and instructional process.

Although there are many ways to learn vocational skills, the behavioral approach has been the most visible and has received the most empirical validation. Mank and Horner describe the basic principles of behavior analytic instruction and apply them to vocational activities. After successfully acquiring a new skill, it is important that students generalize the skill to other vocational settings and maintain over a long period of time. Mank and Horner present their general case model for promoting generalization. Self-management is a new method used for maintaining performance in work and other settings. The authors describe how persons with handicaps can be taught to monitor, cue, and reinforce their own performance.

Although instruction in career and vocational education takes place at all age levels, most occurs during the secondary school years. Educators have felt that students nearing graduation must be given training for a specific occupation. Since there have been two generally different approaches to secondary vocational training, Gaylord-Ross, Siegel, Park, and Wilson describe the characteristics of programs for students with mild handicaps and students with severe handicaps. The former program balances occupational training for a specific vocation with work experience and career counseling. The program for severely handicapped students depends heavily on a series of community work experiences to prepare the individual for entry-level employment positions. For all types of handicapped students, there has been an increasing focus on the transition from school to the adult world. An individual transition plan should be incorporated within a student's IEP to reflect planning for the exit from school and entrance into the adult world. Effective secondary programs will enable the graduate to be employed and function as independently as possible in the local community.

5 Vocational Assessment in School and Rehabilitation Programs

Larry K. Irvin
Oregon Research Institute

Vocational assessment is a comprehensive, multidisciplinary process that educators and rehabilitation professionals can use for a variety of purposes. It can be used, for example, to identify vocationally relevant characteristics of students. It can also be used to document relevant educational, training, and placement needs of individual students. Finally, it is appropriate as a strategy for identifying the necessary and available resources to address those needs.

In this chapter, an effective approach is detailed for conceptualizing and implementing the vocational assessment process. The primary emphasis is on vocational assessment within school programs for students with special needs. In addition, the application of vocational assessment in the vocational rehabilitation process is described briefly. A proposal is made for reconciling the processes of vocational assessment in both school and rehabilitation settings, in order to maximize their coordination, and therefore their impact, across settings.

GUIDING PRINCIPLES

First and foremost, vocational assessment must focus on both individuals *and* settings. Assessing individuals outside the context of real (or

111

potential) work environments leads to incomplete and limited information. As Sitlington and Wimmer (1978) have maintained, vocational assessment should provide, at the minimum, relevant information on:

1. *Individual competence in prevocational areas,* such as work habits and attitudes

2. *Training needs of individuals in specific vocational areas*—that is, skills for specific job roles instead of training on generic "tool use" or "equipment operation"

3. *Characteristics of training strategies that are effective* for an individual in school and other settings

4. *Placement options* during and at the end of training

Most commonly, these types of information are derived by combining a variety of measures from the medical, educational, personal-social, and occupational domains. Various types of assessments are used, including medical protocols, paper and pencil achievement and aptitude tests, manual dexterity performance tests, commercially or locally developed work performance samples, observations and/or ratings of behavior in simulated or real work environments, and analyses of job requirements.

A second guiding principle is that vocational assessment is most useful when it is carried out *within* the context of ongoing educational or rehabilitation program-planning and implementation activities. Well-informed decision making requires valid assessment across the range of academic, social, and vocational domains. Thus, vocational assessment must be integrally related to an individual's educational and training programs. It should be a continuous, ongoing process that occurs *as part of* a training program, and that derives directly from the components of that program. When vocational assessment occurs in this manner, it can be described as "program-related" or "curriculum-referenced" (Cobb, 1983). These terms, used interchangeably in this chapter, describe the basic concept underlying the material presented here.

POSITION OF THE DIVISION ON CAREER DEVELOPMENT

The Division on Career Development (DCD) of the Council on Exceptional Children has adopted an official position on "career/vocational assessment in the public school setting (Sitlington, et al., 1985). That position clearly establishes a contemporary framework for accomplishing effective vocational assessment, and is summarized here.

The DCD statement stresses the importance of using the specific purpose or purposes for a vocational assessment to guide the selection of content, methods, process, and personnel to be used in any assessment activities. The importance of this point cannot be overemphasized. Useful assessment simply cannot be accomplished outside of the context of the clear purpose of assessment. Without clarity of purpose, decisions about appropriateness of instruments cannot be made, specific assessment strategies cannot be devised, and valid interpretations of results are impossible. A strong rationale for emphasizing this aspect of the DCD position is that test validity information should provide evidence for the *validity of the uses of a measure*. For example, commercially produced work sample instruments (or any other measurement devices) are useful only if the information they provide can be applied to make some type of educational decision about students and if documentation exists that these instruments are valid for those purposes.

The DCD statement also asserts that the specific content of a career assessment process should be determined by the components of the career education model being implemented. Ideally, the career education program addresses *all* the roles or "careers" commonly assumed by adults in our society—worker, family member, citizen, and participant in leisure and recreational pursuits (Sitlington et al., 1985). In any case, though, the assessment activities should derive from the content of the program and be the continuous foundation for individualized educational placement and program planning throughout the school years. The actual goals and objectives that guide instructional services should also serve as indicators of assessment needs. Use of aptitude, interest, work sample, or other instruments is not justifiable unless their contents match the content of the instructional program to some degree.

Though DCD does not endorse any particular model for implementing career assessment, its position does stress that any assessment approach must be decision-based: Assessment needs should be determined by the types of educational decisions that are to be made. No assessment should be undertaken that is not firmly linked to educational decisions such as: (1) how to develop, implement, and/or modify curriculum and instructional technology based on student strengths and needs related to ultimate roles or "careers"; or (2) how to match students' abilities to learn and profit from specific instructional strategies with the assets and requirements of both training and placement environments.

Finally, DCD does not promote any specific methods for accomplishing career assessment. It does, however, endorse the use of both the following concepts in selecting and applying assessment methods and instruments. First, assessment strategies must be determined by the nature of information and decision needs. Decisions about whether to use tests, ratings, or observations must be based on the types of decisions that need to be made. Although more informal assessments may serve well for monitoring progress during instruction, more formal, standardized measures may be required for selecting students for programs. Second, assessment instruments should be selected based on their appropriateness for the learning and performance characteristics of an individual to be assessed. Factors such as students' reading, motor, and attentional skills must be considered in instrument selection. If these skills are lacking, then assessments of other skills that depend on this first set (e.g., knowledge of consequences of appropriate/inappropriate social behavior) do not provide valid results because student performance is being limited by factors extraneous to the focus of the assessment. Third, the assessment program must use instruments and methods that incorporate tasks that are very similar to those in the training program. Programwide assessment with manual dexterity measures, for example, is not useful unless the instructional program is prepared to address such skill areas. Without a match between program and instrument content, the usefulness of the assessment outcomes is limited. Fourth, as much of the assessment as possible should be conducted *within* the environments where ultimate performance is desired. Otherwise, generalization of student competencies is not likely to occur. And finally, student behavior must be assessed through multiple and representative samples over time (Sitlington et al., 1985). If this is not done, valuable instructional time can be lost because single assessments may be the result of a "bad day" (or other nonrelevant factor) for a student.

The vocational assessment strategy advocated here has been developed to meet these kinds of criteria in various school settings over the past five years. In the next section, we review briefly the different vocational assessment approaches that have been implemented in school settings.

VOCATIONAL ASSESSMENT IN SCHOOL PROGRAMS

School-based Models of Vocational Assessment

A fair amount of diversity exists in the implementation of vocational assessment within school settings. All currently used approaches, however, derive, at least in part, from the vocational evaluation process that that occurs within vocational rehabilitation settings: a sequence of gathering and reviewing background information, interviewing the client, and assessing both the client and work/job characteristics with a variety of psychological tests, work samples, and tryouts in simulated and real work settings, along with individual counseling throughout the process. As Peterson (1985) notes, though, educators agree that the rehabilitation model for vocational evaluation must be adapted somewhat if it is to be useful in school settings (Cobb, 1983; Sitlington, 1979; Stodden, 1981). In particular, the model must be modified to enable users to derive their assessments directly from the range of educational activities that occur in school programs: academic, prevocational, and social.

A case can even be made that the whole rehabilitation approach to vocational assessment must be reconceptualized if it is to be optimally functional (program-related) even in rehabilitation settings. A proposal for such a change is detailed later in this chapter, in the discussion on the current process of vocational assessment in rehabilitation settings.

Vocational Evaluation Center Model In some school settings, vocational assessment is accomplished primarily through vocational evaluation centers. In this approach, students are referred to an evaluation center that typically functions outside of the ongoing educational program. A standard battery of assessments is administered to all referred students (e.g., aptitude tests—verbal, spatial, motor; work sample tests—sorting, folding, tool use; and interest inventories). Effective and useful application of this model in school rather than rehabilitation settings requires (1) a greater emphasis on the use of evaluation results to direct specific skill-training instructional activities (Peterson, 1981), (2) use of classroom tryouts and work samples based directly on the contents of vocational training programs (rather than on the contents of standardized work samples), and (3) use of vocational evaluation as part of a comprehensive support service for students receiving special education (Peterson, 1985).

Curriculum-based Model In recent years, a number of educators have suggested that for vocational assessment to be useful it must be gathered primarily in the classroom, school, and community settings in which career education occurs (Cobb, 1983; Phelps and McCarty, 1984). Team input and decision making are the cornerstones of this approach; all staff—special and vocational educators, as well as regular educators, para-professionals, and specialized service staff (e.g., speech and language specialists, physical therapists)—participate in assessment, *in the settings where they provide educational services*.. Only in this way can vocational assessment be most instructionally relevant and most cost-effective.

Those who do the training are those who do the assessments and decision making. In fact, training and assessment occur simultaneously and continuously within this approach. The major emphasis is on an instructional approach in which competencies, interests, and values are addressed within a comprehensive scope and sequence of curriculum throughout the school years; assessment follows the directions provided by curriculum and the IEP process (Peterson, 1985; Phelps and McCarty, 1984). A persuasive argument is offered by Cobb (1983) that *a curriculum-based model for vocational assessment is the only approach that has proven functional*—that is, highly useful and prescriptive for application by special and vocational educators.

Comprehensive Model Some program developers have designed models of vocational assessment that blend the features of both center- and curriculum-based approaches (Peterson and Hill, 1982; Roberts et al., 1983). These models use the curriculum-based assessment just described briefly as the primary strategy for educational decision making about vocational development. When curriculum-based measures fail to provide enough information for placement and/or training, or when additional, perhaps specialized, information is required, referral to an evaluation center is suggested (Peterson, 1985; Peterson and Hill, 1982; Roberts et al., 1983). For example, trained staff in an evaluation center might use applied assessments to determine appropriate instructional strategies for individual students—reinforcement preferences and schedules—or necessary levels of assistance—verbal, demonstration, physical guidance. In this comprehensive approach, *vocational assessment information collected in center-type settings must be communicated actively to instructional personnel* to facilitate its use in the IEP planning and instructional implementation processes (Peterson, 1985). Interdisciplinary team meetings with liaison vocational assessment staff are essential if center-based results are to be utilized effectively (Patten, 1981; Peterson, 1985).

Conceptual Model. In an in-depth discussion of the career/vocational assessment of individuals who have special needs, Stodden and Ianacone (1981) noted that assessment methodology and technology, rather than conceptualization of purposes and structure of assessment, have historically been emphasized in vocational evaluation activities. Current school-based vocational assessment programs appear to have selected assessment strategies and instruments somewhat randomly from rehabilitation models, without directing due consideration toward students' career development processes and toward the requirements of specific educational, training, or placement settings. As the DCD position on vocational assessment emphasized, the purposes for assessment activities provide the only legitimate foundation on which to determine their validity, utility, and efficiency. Thus, those purposes must provide the conceptual basis for any assessment activity or instrumentation.

Stodden and Ianacone (1981) have delineated a three-stage conceptual model that addresses purposes, sequence of implementation, and contexts of valid, effective, and efficient vocational assessment. Their model is summarized here. It is entirely consistent with a basic curriculum-referenced approach to vocational assessment, and provides a conceptualization of its purposes and structure.

The first stage of this model is labeled "Readiness" and involves preassessment activities addressing student awareness, exploration, and decision making. In practical terms, this Readiness component involves providing opportunities for elementary (grades K–3) and middle school (grades 4–9) students to explore, become aware of, and learn about the values, roles, and nature of work in our society. Essentially, educators must plan and implement instructional units to accomplish this. For example, awareness activities provide information about the changes people go through in life, the many kinds of work that people do, and the preparation required for various types of work roles. Values activities can consist of units on the value of yourself and others as unique persons, roles of learning, work and leisure as part of living, and concepts of quality and responsibility.

As a result of these activities, students and educators will have a clearer understanding of values, roles and interests, and students will know more about employability issues, personal-social behaviors, and general academic preparation. Peterson (1985) notes that these components should be initiated no later than the middle school years as curriculum-referenced guides to ongoing IEP development and implementation.

Though the activities in this first stage are more exploration- and instruction-oriented than assessment-oriented, they are necessary to provide the foundations for subsequent meaningful interpretation of more traditional assessment information on interests, aptitudes, knowledge, and performance. The general idea underlying the Readiness component is that vocational assessment of students' interests, knowledge, and skills provides useful information *only after* students are exposed to the world of work. Assessment must have a context, and Readiness activities provide that context.

The second stage of the Stodden and Ianacone conceptual model is labeled "Assessment," and involves an in-depth assessment of students' performance of work roles and specific work-related and work skills. Within the secondary school program (grades 9–12), students are introduced to tasks and equipment that are optimally representative of both the outcomes of readiness activities and, most importantly, locally available employment opportunities. For example, if the local job market for students and graduates consists largely of fast food service, janitorial, and recycling work, the school program must familiarize students with the requisites for those types of jobs. The content of instruction on tasks and equipment must come from those settings: dishwashing, mops, brooms, bundling, and so on. Students are provided with multiple opportunities over time to experience the information, skill, value, and role demands of real work contexts in classroom, school, and community settings throughout the secondary school years.

Typical administrative and program structures should include traditional classroom learning in regular, vocational, and special education program settings, work experience placements in and outside of the school, and crew work. These opportunities are simultaneously both instructional and assessment activities. Assessment should be continuous, curriculum-referenced, and derived from multiple sources in multiple settings—for example, observations, ratings, psychometric tests, performance samples, and job analyses in classroom, school, and community work settings.

The third component of the model is labeled "Application," and involves formatting and interpreting assessment information for use in the secondary school program. Assessment information is organized and communicated to meet the needs of multiple audiences (evaluation team, instructional staff, parents, support services staff, employers, and administrative personnel). Interdisciplinary staffings are conducted to plan and implement assessment-based programming. And, ongoing assessment is conducted within instructional programming. It is clear that the second-stage activities (Assessment) and the third-stage activities (Application) in this approach must occur continuously and interactively to be useful for instructional staff.

Extended Example

Within a local education agency (LEA), implementation of a comprehensive vocational assessment effort that conforms to Stodden and Ianacone's conceptual model would include the following program elements.

Readiness To address the Readiness component, the LEA will develop and implement structured educational activities at the elementary and middle school levels in at least four general areas: awareness, exploration, understanding, and decision making (including information gathering). The emphasis for students will be on learning about the interactions in their environment among all of the important aspects of the world of work, such as roles and functions, values, interests, actual work activities, decision making, job seeking, personal-social behavior, and limitations.

A list of specific goals and objectives will provide the structure and guide the progression of Readiness educational activities. Goals, objectives, activities, and materials should address such content areas as: values, attitudes, and habits; human relationships; occupational information; and acquisition of job and daily living skills. Regular and special education classroom programs will be used as the primary educational settings, with Readiness activities occurring across all typical academic content areas: language, mathematics, science, social studies, and so on. Examples of goals and related objectives are as follows:

Values

K–3:   awareness of self and responsibility for own actions

4–6:   understanding concepts of quality, opportunity, planning one's time

7–9:   individual inquiry and problem solving

Human Relationships

K–3:   awareness of behavior standards, cooperative social behavior

4–6:   self-control and development of personal relationships

7–9:   socially responsible behavior

Occupational

K–3:   awareness of different types of occupational roles, respect for others and work that they do

4–6:   knowledge of occupational clusters, development of work attitudes/ethics

7–9:   knowledge of economic concepts, development of work environment behavior

Job and Daily Living Skills

K-3:   skill in using money and caring for equipment

4–6:   skill in home and school safety, skill in responsibility for younger children

7–9:   skill in banking and purchasing, skill in specific job requirements

These are only examples and are not comprehensive. Clark (1979) and Lamkin (1980), as well as Brolin (1982), offer very detailed specifications of the appropriate scope and sequence for Readiness activities.

Different settings and instructional activities are appropriate as learning environments for students of different ages, and for different objectives (e.g., knowledge vs. performance-based objectives). For example, in the Values and Human Relationships areas, young children (grades K–3) will be involved in the school and home in stories, role playing games, recordings, and films—activities where the emphasis is on personal and interpersonal values and relationships. Children in grades 4-6 will be involved in individual and cooperative in- and out-of-class project activities, where an emphasis is placed on quality of product, interpersonal cooperation, and planning. Middle school students (grades 7–9) will examine their own and peers' social behavior in guided discussions and practice positive behavior in simulated and actual situations (e.g., refusal of tobacco or alcohol offers, acceptance of invitations to join activities, abiding by rules, handling peer distractions).

In the Occupational area, young children (grades K–3) will be involved in drawing pictures of (or role-playing) work situations, as well as reading about and listening to parents' or others' descriptions of work. Children in grades 4–6 will simulate various aspects of work in a community (e.g., interdependence of roles), conduct community surveys of occupations, sponsor school demonstrations of work-related programs, and visit workers on the job. In addition, they will begin to "work for pay" in the home (e.g., chores) and community (e.g., paper routes, babysitting). Middle school students will continue actually working, observe systematic differences in job roles (cafeteria worker vs. janitorial worker vs. school bus driver vs. secretary vs. teacher, and so on), and begin to apply economic practices (e.g., accounting for proceeds from newspaper sales).

In general, Readiness activities can be home, school, and/or community-based, depending on the Readiness objective involved. In any case, broad exposure of students to the values, roles, and nature of work in our society, in order for subsequent assessment results to be placed into a known context of students' experiences, is the goal for Readiness activities.

Assessment To develop and implement the Assessment component, secondary-level staff (special and/or vocational educators) will complete a market analysis of the local employment area and design an instructional program that prepares students for job roles within that area. Toward that end, staff will survey local employers regarding work role needs within the community and necessary entry-level task and equipment skills and behaviors for specific work roles. In addition, staff will get information enabling them to develop jobs and redesign job activities as needed, as well as information regarding any work site, station, and task accommodations necessary to enable students with various disabling conditions to work effectively. Finally, staff will undertake job placement activities as appropriate.

The Assessment component will be designed to occur within the context of the ongoing instructional program. Classroom and community-based educational experiences will be designed to prepare students for actual work in the community. A major purpose of this approach to assessment is to allow students to explore and experience specific work role requirements, and to begin to make choices then can pursue further. In the course of that preparation, multiple ongoing opportunities for relevant assessment will occur regularly. For example, a student who is interested in food service work (waiting tables, dishwashing, cashiering) may discover that either or both verbal skills and a willingness to stand or sit upright for long periods of time —job-specific skills—are required. Thus, assessments will be aimed not only at actual job performance skills, but at ongoing and changing interests and motivation as well. On the basis of such assessment, further exploration activities by a student may well be indicated—for example, if a student doesn't like to stand for long periods while working.

For each instructional component, the LEA staff (regular, special, and vocational educators) will:

1. Design relevant assessment content that samples the range of content in the instructional curriculum

2. Identify and obtain relevant assessment information, or design and use new data-gathering systems such as ratings, observational systems, and direct tests for that purpose

3. Validate data collection systems—that is, document that they provide the desired information

Application In the Application component, the LEA staff will evaluate the outcomes of Readiness and Assessment activities by interpreting assessment information and formatting it properly for use by all appropriate users. As a student becomes aware, explores, and understands general work opportunities and requirements, as well as specific work role demands, she or he acquires an increasing foundation of skill, interests, attitudes, and behaviors. The relevant information must be compiled in formats that the student and appropriate others can use to plan subsequent programming and placement opportunities. Each participant in the decision-making process has "specialized needs" (Stodden and Ianacone, 1981, p. 607) as to how assessment information relates to their involvement in the planning and implementation processes. Each participant must receive appropriately formatted data in order to participate fully and effectively in those processes.

Petzy (1983) has described a straightforward and comprehensive approach to analyzing and using vocational assessment data. In this approach, there are five major ways in which data are used. First, educators use assessments to *describe student competencies, behaviors, and preferences in relation to specific learning situations*. Data can be drawn from formal and informal observations, student input, tests, and ratings. Strengths and weaknesses are described, as are likes and dislikes, with reference to specific learning situations, such as units in home economics, health or vocational education courses, or work experience. Over a school year or more, reasonable overall judgments about strengths and weaknesses can be made across broad program components such as industrial arts or career education programs.

Second, educators use assessments to *describe capabilities, interests and attitudes that underlie performance across tasks in a learning situation*. The emphasis is on factors such as verbal ability, manual dexterity, and interpersonal skills. Again, formal and informal observations, ratings, and tests may be used as data sources. Over time, these data should clarify students' variations in performance, interests, and attitudes. Then, instructional and other services can be selected carefully to optimize performance and remediate problems.

The final three approaches to using vocational assessment data involve interpreting and applying them by comparing them to data from a variety of relevant situations outside the instructional program. Students' competencies, interests, and attitudes are compared to other learning situations, to course or program requirements in vocational and/or comprehensive high school programs, and to requirements in nonschool programs such as sheltered or competitive work.

By *comparing vocational assessment data across a variety of learning situations*, information relative to specific prevocational and vocational factors can be combined to document prevailing patterns for individual students. For example, information on level and type of interpersonal interactions, on- and off-task behaviors, competence with tools or other equipment, distractability, and punctuality can be collected from many program components. Teachers and counselors can use such data in an ongoing manner to help students make appropriate vocational development and adjustment progress.

By *comparing data to school-level standards*, special and vocational educators, along with counselors, can help students make program choices based on the extent of the match between entry criteria for various school programs and the students' own development. For example, some school courses require certain levels of reading ability, motor skill, or competence at social interaction. By comparing a student's skills to such criteria, informed decisions can be made (by students, parents, and program staff) about appropriate placements. To do this, staff must first develop valid entry and success indicators for all potential school-based learning opportunities, and use such information in conjunction with outcomes of the first three types of vocational assessment.

Finally, by *comparing assessment data with requirements in nonschool programs* (especially sheltered or competitive employment options), educators can help students develop requisite skills for entry into postschool opportunities. Staff must be careful, though, not to use criteria from outside the school program to eliminate student options within the school program. That is, students should still be provided with opportunities to try to learn desirable and necessary skills, no matter how low their perceived competence or how severely their disabling condition appears to impair their functioning.

In summary, the special and vocational educators in the LEA will use assessment data to: (1) conduct conferences with staff, students, and others in order to determine ongoing programming and placement needs and options; (2) format assessment information to suit the needs of various participants, including parents and employers; and, very importantly, (3) assist with implementation based on the outcomes of assessment within school programs. The multiple participants will include (in various ways at various times): multidisciplinary evaluation team members, administrative placement decision-makers, vocational educators, special educators, academic educators, employers, parents, counselors, school psychology staff, and other service providers, as appropriate (e.g., vocational rehabilitation personnel, speech and language specialists).

In order to implement the types of vocational assessment and application activities required within the Stodden and Ianacone conceptual model, educators will need to accomplish several specific steps. These are detailed in the following section.

Process of Vocational Assessment

Determining Relevant Student Characteristics Prior to implementation of any type of assessment activities in school and other settings, educators need to determine the extent to which student characteristics are relevant assessment considerations. In particular, the implications of various handicapping conditions for valid assessment must be determined. The major criticisms of traditional vocational assessment technology, as applied to individuals with handicapping conditions, have focused on the lack of established validity of most of the instruments commonly employed with these individuals (See Brolin, 1982; Browning and Irvin, 1981; Cobb, 1983; Irvin and Halpern, 1979; Phelps and McCarty, 1984; Schalock and Karan, 1979; Sitlington and Wimmer, 1978; Stodden, Casale, and Schwartz, 1977).

Unless appropriate instruments are used with students (and this appropriateness is established), assessment results simply will not be valid—inappropriate normative comparisons, assessment format demands that are inconsistent with student response capabilities (e.g., reading, motor, and/or memory requirements unrelated to assessment purposes), or lack of relationship between student performance with assessment materials and performance in real life settings will result. Instruments that require reading, motor, and/or memory skills in order to assess other competencies (social, communication, prevocational) cannot provide valid measures of those competencies of interest. Rather, such instruments only provide measures of students' reading, motor, and/or memory deficits.

Determining Vocationally Relevant Instructional Options After establishing student characteristics that are relevant for decisions about vocational assessment instruments and strategies, it is essential to determine the array of possible instructional opportunities and other vocationally relevant options available to students in the program. Selecting assessment instruments outside the context of the settings where these program components and options are available is to guarantee that most, if not all, vocational assessment will never be used for program-related decisions.

As described in other chapters in this book, it is important to view career education in the widest possible manner. Just about any component in the school program can be considered vocationally relevant, depending on the prior experience and achievement of a given student. However, someone must identify, organize, and coordinate the vocational education activities that occur across various program components, in order to place students appropriately and monitor their progress effectively.

Specific prevocational/vocational educational opportunities are usually easy to identify—for example, industrial arts, career education courses/experiences, and work experience opportunities. In addition, objectives such as completion of tasks and general direction following are examples of the many possible basic educational objectives that are clearly vocationally relevant, and that can be addressed in just about any program component within a school. Regardless of specific objectives that are eventually developed, though, the in- and out-of-school settings where they can be addressed must be identified before appropriate curriculum-referenced assessment can occur.

Determining the Skill Demands of Instructional Options Once the realistic array of vocationally-relevant instructional options is identified for students with special needs, educators should assess characteristics of in- and out-of-school settings in order to identify student instructional needs prior to and/or during placement within those settings. Examples of useful types of such information are: reading and/or writing requirements on tasks within the setting, provision of an aide or tutor for students who need it, motor performance requirements of tasks within the setting, competence of regular educator at effective consequation and structured instruction for special needs students.

Structured rating, observation, and interview formats can be developed to use in collecting such information. Rusch and Mithaug (1980) have detailed this process thoroughly as it applies to adults. Their procedures and formats can be adapted easily for students in school programs. They present and discuss formats for documenting various aspects of work (and instructional) settings: available supervision, social environment, physical conditions, nature and sequence of task performance, training resources available, requirements of workers (or students), and expectations and concerns of staff.

Similarly, Petzy (1983) provides a thorough description of a rationale, strategy, and applied examples from multiple school-based vocational assessment and instructional programs in Massachusetts. These are summarized here for their clear practical value and because they represent a solidly curriculum-referenced approach. The logic of this approach is that if learning activities can be identified for secondary-level students, the objectives of which are consistent with entry skills in vocational education and/or work placements, then those learning activities can and should be structured also as assessment opportunities.

Within this approach, teachers and other educational staff identify sequences of short-term units of instruction that are a sample of their program components and that are related to broader vocationally relevant programs. Thus, within a home economics course, a unit on baking cupcakes can offer multiple assessment opportunities, depending upon level of entry skills required within the course: reading recipes, measuring ingredients, motor performance, following instructions, and so on. A variety of these samples of short-term units can be identified for assessing the skill demands within various instructional opportunities.

Assessment and training are interdependent and continuous. When this approach is applied across multiple content domains and instructional experiences, a match can be made ultimately between requirements on the one hand and student skill levels, interests, attitudes, and responsiveness to differential approaches to instruction on the other.

Applying a curriculum-referenced strategy in this manner enables clear recommendations for program placement, specific learning and performance objectives, and useful instructional technology to be identified. Specifically, these recommendations can address vocational education programs, job or work experience placement, support services, teaching techniques and vocational curriculum modifications, vocational information and exploration experiences, work adjustment training, academic course selection, and functional living skills training (Peterson, 1985).

Implementing Ongoing Training and Assessment Once in-school and/or out-of-school placements and their associated skill demands have been identified, students can be placed, based on availability and on reasonable matches between student skills/needs and requirements/ resources in those placements. Then, ongoing training and related assessment are implemented simultaneously and continuously. All educational and training experiences offer continual opportunities for program-related and curriculum-referenced assessment.

In any school-based assessment program, decisions about instruction and/or placement should always be the foundation of any assessment activities. Essentially, no assessment should occur without an identifiable rationale.

The most common rationales are: needs assessment, program planning, program monitoring, and outcome evaluation. These four stages involve eight interrelated components. In Figure 5-1, the sequence of assessment-related steps within these four stages is illustrated.

ACTIVITY   **STAGE IN PROGRAM RELATED ASSESSMENT MODEL**

Needs Assessment	Program Planning	Implementation and Monitoring	Outcome Evaluation

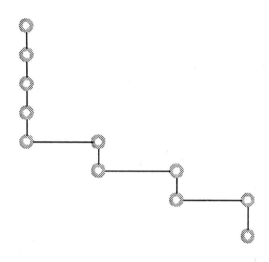

(1) Select appropriate content domains

(2) Select appropriate instruments for populations and content domains

(3) Measure current knowledge, performance, learning skills

(4) Determine needs for instructional and other services

(5) Determine priorities for instructional and other services

(6) Develop goals and objectives to guide instruction and other services

(7) Implement and monitor instructional and other programs

(8) Evaluate outcomes of instruction and other services

Figure 5.1 Program-Related Assessment

Users of this approach will realize an important benefit. A clear linkage exists between assessment-related activities in the four major stages. The final step in any stage is also the initial step in the next stage. For example, the final step in the needs assessment process—determining priorities for instruction and other services—is also the starting point for program planning. Similarly, the development of goals and objectives links the program planning and implementation processes, and the monitoring of programs serves as a natural link between the implementation and evaluation stages. Finally, the results of evaluation of program outcomes can and should be "recycled" to serve as the basis for ongoing needs assessment.

In a program-related or curriculum-referenced assessment approach, assessment activities addressing each of these types of necessary decisions are viewed as sequential and interdependent. Needs assessment information is gathered to identify necessary instructional and other service emphases for individuals and groups of students. Decisions about eligibility for, and placement in, curricula and/or settings are a common result of needs assessment. Several factors usually influence these decisions, including the values and preferences of educators, students, and parents, as well as availability of program options and resources. In fact, eligibility is essentially determined by the relationship between individual needs and environmental opportunities. The results of needs assessment activities, ideally, should also be useful for accomplishing program planning and, ultimately, for guiding the development of the IEP (goals, objectives, instructional strategies, and evaluation methods and criteria).

Once a program is underway in any content domain, assessment activities are implemented to track or monitor student progress as instruction takes place. These activities are typically perceived as the curriculum-referenced assessments in a program. However, the needs assessment and program-planning activities that precede monitoring should also be based directly on and referenced directly to curricular and instructional programs. In any case, monitoring is required in order to determine to what extent the planned program of services actually has occurred. By using information from program monitoring, professionals and others can modify either or both plans and programs when desired effects are not being achieved.

Finally, as major segments of an instructional program are completed, assessment is used to determine the overall impact of the instructional program. This outcome evaluation process results in new information to use for needs assessment in order to continue the program-related cycle.

Assessment activities associated with each of these types of decisions should be ongoing throughout the school program. At any given time, the assessment needs of any individual student or group of students are likely to be multiple and varied. For any student, there may be a need to collect initial needs assessment information, in one or more content domains, at the beginning of a school term or year. In other content domains, however, there may be a need only for ongoing monitoring of short-term achievement/learning. This is often the case when students change educational levels (e.g., move from middle or junior high to senior high school settings). At that time, new assessment information is often needed in prevocational/vocational areas not previously addressed within non-senior high programs (e.g, work experience, tool use, job interview skills), but is not required in other areas that represent continuations of previous curricular emphases and instructional efforts (such as social studies or language arts). Other occasions arise when new assessment information is needed for some students but not for others in the course of a school term or year, as students are placed differentially into various prevocational opportunities in in- and out-of-school settings. For example, information is required for some students and not for others at different times during the school year regarding necessary levels of instructional support after placement in work experience opportunities.

In a curriculum-referenced approach to vocational assessment, not all needs assessment occurs at the beginning of the year, just as not all program monitoring occurs during the middle of the year and not all outcome evaluation occurs at the end of the year. Rather, assessment is individualized for students, and various types of assessment are implemented differentially in different program areas as placement and instructional needs dictate throughout the school year. The sequence of needs assessment, program planning, program monitoring, and outcome evaluation occurs continually as instruction is implemented. Decisions about ongoing student needs, and about necessary curriculum and instructional adaptations, can be made at any time in this approach.

Generally, assessment must focus on at least four features that should occur within most, if not all, curriculum areas: *knowledge* of critical concepts, *performance* of essential behaviors, *competence at learning* new concepts and behaviors, and *environmental features or instructional technology* that can serve as resources for students who need to acquire, maintain, and generalize necessary concepts and behavioral skills. The assessment emphasis should always be an applied one. That is, it should address ultimate performance criteria, whether explicit or implicit, that are usually associated with any instructional activity. For example, units on job interview skills are implemented by educators who at least assume that what is taught and learned will have some impact on eventual student job interview behaviors. Those job interview behaviors, and their knowledge requisites, should be the focus of criterion assessment as well.

The role of assessment during instruction is to document student achievement of those implicit or explicit criteria from as many perspectives as are instructionally relevant and integral to ultimate performance. Only in this way can instructional resources be identified as precisely as possible and related instructional resources be mobilized effectively. Students' ongoing performance of desired skills within criterion contexts (the settings where they are ultimately desired) is the highest level of achievement that must be documented. No less important, however, is documentation of four other types of student behavior:

1. Acquisition of performance skills

2. Maintenance of performance in simulated settings (often classroom or other instructional environments)

3. Knowledge of the nature, consequences, or other aspects of performance

4. Nature and quality of learning skills related to acquiring and performing the criterion behavior skills

The major steps in the assessment-training process have been detailed here. Next, a brief discussion is presented regarding the features of exemplary vocational assessment.

Exemplary Vocational Assessment Instrumentation

A number of sources exist that serve as annotated compendia of vocational assessment instruments and strategies (e.g., Botterbusch, 1980; Brolin, 1982; Halpern et al., 1982; Phelps and McCarty, 1984; Roberts et al., 1983; Sitlington and Wimmer, 1978). These sources describe general sequence and/or specific types of instruments available for assessment in vocationally relevant medical, educational, and personal-social domains. The assessment of interests, work habits/attitudes, general and specific aptitudes, and learning styles is addressed in these sources, and all of the major techniques of traditional vocational assessment are described: paper and pencil tests, manual dexterity tests, commercially available and locally developed work samples, behavior analysis, situational assessment, and job/task analysis. The formats and contents of the instruments are detailed, necessary considerations in their use are outlined, the nature of the information they provide is discussed, and the advantages/disadvantages of applying them to special needs students are identified.

These descriptions and reviews will not be reiterated here. Readers are referred directly to those sources for that information. Here we describe the features of exemplary instrumentation, and discuss how to utilize such instrumentation and strategies, along with more informal approaches, *within* a curriculum-referenced vocational assessment program.

A variety of assessment strategies and related instruments can be used. Several exemplary ones are described here in order to identify key characteristics that users should attend to when selecting instruments. As Cobb (1983) has noted, teacher-made tests, observations, interviews, standardized tests, and rating scales are all potentially useful strategies as long as their formats (response requirements) do not place students with handicaps at a disadvantage and as long as their contents can be referenced to some aspect of the curriculum.

Several standardized instruments clearly meet these criteria. For knowledge assessment, the Social and Prevocational Information Battery—Revised (SPIB-R) (Halpern, Irvin, and Munkres, 1986) and the Tests for Everyday Living (TEL) (Halpern, Irvin, and Landman, 1979) offer examples of measures that cover multiply relevant content domains and that have established and adequate psychometric characteristics. These tests cover such daily living and prevocational content domains as purchasing, banking, budgeting, job search skills, and home management, in an orally administered, true-false (SPIB-R) or multiple-choice (TEL) format.

For direct testing of applied performance in criterion and instructional settings, the Mid-Nebraska Competitive Employment Screening Test and Remediation Manual (Schalock, 1976; Schalock and Harper, 1977), the Vocational Behavior Checklist (Walls, Werner, and Bacon, 1977; Walls, Zane, and Werner, 1978), and the Florida International Diagnostic-Prescriptive Vocational Competency Profile (1980) all offer vocationally relevant and criterion-referenced behavioral test items that are amenable to further task analysis across multiple content domains. Each item in these instruments is a statement of a behavioral performance that is observable, measurable, and teachable. A criterion for performance is stipulated for every item (users can substitute their own criteria) and data collection formats are provided. The greatest utility of these performance measures is that users can tailor content to their own needs; that is, users can choose the assessment contents that can be referenced to their own curricula.

For observational assessment of performance, Glascoe and Levy (1985) have described a multidimensional approach. They have developed an observational coding system that can be applied in any setting to measure the frequencies and intensities of a variety of work-related skills via cross-referenced "interactive/noninteractive" and "on-task/off-task" measures. Interactive refers to working with others, and noninteractive measures assess independent functioning. The categories within these dimensions were derived from participant observation in a number of placement settings.

Finally, the Trainee Performance Sample (TPS) (Irvin, et al., 1982) is an example of a standardized measure of learning progress. The TPS was designed to assess the resources necessary to accomplish successful vocational training with severely mentally retarded individuals on benchwork-type tasks. Every item in the TPS includes an opportunity for the student to profit from instruction. Indeed, this is the focus of the assessment: to measure what types of training will be required to enable students to acquire vocationally relevant skills. For example, one item in the TPS requires examinees simply to bend a copper wire into a U shape. The examiner shows the examinee how to do the item *before* asking that the examinee do it. If the examinee does the item incorrectly, the examiner physically guides a correct performance, and then asks again for the examinee to bend the wire. By analyzing how examinees perform on a number of similar items, the user of the TPS can determine how well the examinee can imitate demonstrations and repeat guided practice.

All of these examples were selected because their *validated uses are consistent with a curriculum-referenced, applied behavioral analysis approach to assessment and instruction.* The critical components of that approach have been detailed comprehensively by Schalock and Karan (1979) and comprise the technology of instruction described elsewhere in this volume. Underlying that technology is the premise that work and work adjustment are "complex sets of specific behaviors that must be broken into sequential component parts for both assessment and training" (Schalock and Karan, 1979, p.39). Behavior is evaluated in relation to what is required by instructional and work placements. Further and continuous instructional programming and related assessment proceed on a "step-by-step basis toward prespecified behavioral objectives derived from actual job requisites" (p.39).

This approach to vocational assessment allows those who employ it to accomplish both the cataloging of current competencies at any point within the educational process *and*, by introducing training into the evaluation, to assess the effects of various instructional experiences on student learning and/or performance.

| Criteria for Selection of Vocational Assessment Instruments | Using only the instrumentation briefly described above (or only very similar measures, for that matter) is not essential. Those were offered as examples of currently available, standardized instruments that meet or exceed the criteria for selection discussed here. Schalock and Karan (1979) have proposed a set of five explicit criteria upon which such selection should be based. According to these criteria, the utility of vocational assessment instruments is maximized when they enable: |

1. *Criterion sampling*—analysis of actual task and environmental requirements into behavioral units (or chains)

2. *Ecobehavioral analysis*—specification of student and setting characteristics to facilitate eventual generalization of learner competencies to the settings where they are intended to be used

3. *Competency assessment*—a focus on functional skills—that is, skills required in settings where students live and work

4. *Operant and respondent behavior assessment*—continuous measurement of the relationships between behavior and environmental/training events

5. *Tailored assessment*—measures that fit the specific characteristics of settings, target skills, and individuals.

By using these criteria as standards in selecting vocational assessment strategies and instruments, educators can ensure that their vocational assessment programs provide information that is directly relevant for educational decision making. Assessment results will be referenced directly to program components (content *and* process of instruction), and will be functional for guiding student-oriented decision making within instructional and work experience or placement settings.

CASE STUDY: Application of Program-Related Assessment Model

Robert is a 15-year-old who has been classified as having mild mental retardation (I.Q. between 55 and 70, with documented deficits in adaptive behavior at home and in school and community settings). He is entering a senior high school program after being served in special education programs throughout elementary and middle school years. For Robert, applying a curriculum-referenced and program-related assessment approach would involve the following components.

First, some needs assessment activities must occur in order to match Robert's instructional needs to the resources available in various school program components. Thus, the coordinator of career education services for students with special needs must identify the content domains where needs assessment information is required. Previous school records provide basic academic achievement data—language, reading, and computational skills—and document that Robert participated in career education exploration activities over a two-year period. He is aware of different general job types and requirements, gets along moderately well with peers and supervisors (except in his reaction to criticism, which involves arguing and sulking), can use money, and wants to "get a job."

Program-related needs assessment for Robert, at entry into high school, consists of observing his competencies at basic entry-level skills required by the various school program components—applied ("survival") reading for courses such as health and home economics, physical dexterity, safety and tool handling for industrial arts; basic computational skills for consumer math; and knowledge of social skills in work environments. Some of these assessments are paper and pencil [e.g., knowledge tests such as the Social and Prevocational Information Battery (Halpern, et al., 1986)}; some are from previous records (e.g., basic academic or achievement records); some are direct observations of performance on an array of samples of entry-level skill criteria for prevocational/vocational program components, such as following verbal instructions and using measurements in meal preparation, from criterion-referenced measures such as the Mid-Nebraska instrument (Schalock, 1976). Finally, some are ratings or reports from parents or teachers (e.g., informal measures of independent community mobility performance). Results of these assessments are used to make decisions regarding which program units Robert can function in without additional support, which will require a special education aide or peer tutor to assist Robert and/or the instructional staff, and which he is not ready for yet.

Robert is then placed into a combination of regular (e.g., physical education and home living), special (on-the-job social skills instruction), and vocational (food service crew) education program components, based on assessment results, his own and his parents' wishes, and program coordinator perceptions of Robert's needs and available program resources.

Annual goals and shorter-term objectives that derive from the needs assessment are the foundation of Robert's individual education plan (IEP). These IEP goals and objectives guide the content of instruction throughout the year. In the home living area, for example, Robert's lowest performance on needs assessment activities was in the areas of: (1) knowledge and performance of how to acquire help for problems with home utilities and accidents, and (2) overall meal preparation skills. Thus, the annual goal and short-term objectives for the first of these areas in home living are as follows: **Annual Goal 1:** Robert will demonstrate knowledge and performance of acquiring assistance with utility and emergency needs.

> **Short-term objective 1a:** Robert will name the providers of utility and emergency services for his family home and for the school.

> **Short-term objective 1b:** Robert will locate the telephone numbers of such providers in the local telephone directory.

> **Short-term objective 1c:** Robert will call providers of services for assistance with utility or emergency problems.

Robert's IEP document also includes statements of evaluation criteria associated with each short-term objective (e.g., "four consecutive times" or "with 80 percent accuracy" or "without error").

Very importantly, needs assessment is ongoing within each unit as instruction is implemented. That is, instructional staff use formal and informal behavioral observations, ratings, and paper and pencil tests to monitor performance and identify ongoing needs for further instruction.

Finally, in this program-related assessment approach, the program staff accomplish outcome evaluation, or an overall assessment of the effects of units of instruction. In Robert's case, outcome evaluation consists of several elements, such as (1) analysis of how many or what proportion of short-term objectives were met within each longer range (annual) goal area, (2) year-end posttesting on overall knowledge measures such as the Social and Prevocational Information Battery (Halpern, et al., 1986), a measure that is independent of instruction and, perhaps, (3) "social validity" measures—ratings from Robert, his parents, and his teachers of the value, effectiveness, and satisfactoriness of educational experiences. These outcome evaluations are used to document both the impact of the instructional program components on Robert's achievement and the ongoing needs that Robert has for additional instruction.

In this way, the program-related assessment cycle is complete. All elements of the cycle are linked to subsequent steps. Outcome evaluation results are recycled as ongoing needs assessment information, just as initial assessment provides information for program planning and implementation, and program implementation provides a structure for program monitoring.

Advantages of Curriculum- Referenced Vocational Assessment

A number of advantages accrue when the approach described here is implemented. First, and most importantly, vocational assessment of this kind is relevant to educational decision making *by definition*. When the content and formats of assessment are derived directly from the scope, sequence, and process of instruction, the results of assessment have immediate implications for educational decisions such as what to teach, how to teach, and where to teach.

Second, any of the necessary types of educational decisions can be informed by such assessment. The utility of the sequence of needs assessment, program planning, program monitoring, and outcome evaluation is enhanced by a uniform, curriculum-referenced foundation for all assessment.

A third advantage is that there is a focus on competencies. What students cannot do is not relevant. What students can do, and what resources are required to enable students to achieve various competencies are the emphases within this approach.

Fourth, vocational assessment reflects a comprehensive, developmental approach to vocational education. All levels of curriculum (elementary through postsecondary) can be addressed. Appropriate instructional/training content, process, and opportunities can be easily identified, regardless of student age or grade.

Fifth, the curriculum-referenced approach is applicable to all special needs students, regardless of handicapping condition. It is especially important, however, to students with severe and multiple handicaps because no assumptions about "functioning level" are necessary. Assessment of effective instructional/learning processes is as important as assessment of already acquired skills.

A sixth advantage is that assessment has implications for ultimate placement in local work and training opportunities, again regardless of age or grade of student. Each element of the curriculum is related ultimately to local opportunity, and any assessment addresses some aspect of development toward that goal.

Another advantage is that a curriculum-referenced approach is the strategy of choice to best conform to the assessment-related requirements of P.L. 94-142 (which requires nondiscriminatory, valid, multiple, and educationally-relevant evaluation) and Section 504 of P.L. 93-112, the Rehabilitation Act of 1973 (nondiscriminiation in evaluation). See Galagan (1985) and Stodden and Ianacone (1981) for thorough discussions of this point.

A final advantage of the curriculum-referenced approach to vocational assessment is that it can result in information applicable in postschool rehabilitation settings. For young adults to accomplish successfully and efficiently the transitions from school to the world(s) of adult work and community living, immediate postschool rehabilitation services must overlap with school services *before and at the time students leave school.* Curriculum-referenced assessment results can provide a useful developmental context as well as an ongoing and continuous foundation for directing the necessary collaboration between educational and rehabilitation service providers.

Personnel in the Vocational Assessment Process

The Division on Career Development (DCD) of the Council on Exceptional Children has taken a strong and clear position regarding who should be responsible for actually doing vocational assessment activities (Sitlington et al., 1985). DCD maintains that the professionals who are responsible for students' vocationally oriented education should be equally responsible for vocational assessment during any particular phase of students' development. At the elementary level, those who do career/vocational assessment should be certified in special education and have backgrounds in career development and informal assessment. At the secondary and postsecondary levels, they should be certified as vocational special needs/secondary special educators or rehabilitation professionals, and have training that meets at least the minimal standards for certification in vocational evaluation.

DCD has summarized the competencies that are essential for meeting these criteria (Sitlington et al., 1985, p.5):

1. Analysis of entry-level competencies needed by students in the career development program

2. Implementation of job analysis procedures

3. Identification and selection of assessment procedures appropriate for students of different ages and functioning levels

4. Selection and administration of appropriate assessment instruments

5. Construction of instruments for situational assessment and behavior observations related to all career roles

6. Integration and interpretation of assessment data

7. Application of assessment data to instructional programs

DCD and others (Peterson, 1985; Roberts et al., 1983) have also recognized and detailed the roles that other professionals must assume if vocational assessment is to be most effective. Administrators of regular, special, and vocational education programs must provide the necessary coordination, staff training, and other administrative support services. Vocational evaluation specialists, school psychologists, and counselors must provide necessary adjunct and specialized services such as focused individual and family counseling, specialized testing when needed, career awareness opportunities via information and counseling services, and staff consultation and development services. DCD has acknowledged the need to integrate professional standards across the education, rehabilitation, and psychology professions involved in the vocational assessment process in public school settings.

VOCATIONAL ASSESSMENT IN VOCATIONAL REHABILITATION

Students with special needs often require continuing vocational training, placement, and support services after completing high school. Many qualify for, and are served by, their state vocational rehabilitation agency during the last year or two of high school The process of vocational rehabilitation services is summarized here, with an emphasis on the vocational assessment activities that are integral to that process.

Ideally, in order to optimize the usefulness of school outcome for subsequent rehabilitation efforts, and to maximize the positive impacts of both, provision of vocationally relevant services is coordinated by school and rehabilitation professionals.

Case Recording and Assessment in Vocational Rehabilitation

The vocational rehabilitation case recording process offers a succinct structure for describing the sequence of rehabilitation services. Conveniently, it is useful also for structuring a program-related assessment strategy for application within the context of rehabilitation services. Case recording is the method by which the agency defines, tracks, and evaluates the relationship between clients and the agency. Recording is accomplished by means of a numerical status designation (00,02,08, and so on) and a narrative entry in the client's file. There are fourteen statuses, each of which characterizes a current stage of the rehabilitation effort. Figure 5-2 is an annotated diagram of the nature and sequence of rehabilitation case recording and services.

As a client progresses from Applicant (02) through Eligibility (10) to Closed (26, 28, 30), the numerical designation serves as a flag regarding current level of rehabilitation service provision and as an indication of ongoing evaluation needs to inform future decisions about service provision. Input to the decision-making process may come from any or all of several sources: the client and/or a guardian; other agencies or case records; formal assessment procedures conducted by rehabilitation agency staff or through private contract; or the counselor's own knowledge of the nature of client needs and the available service options.

The current practice of vocational assessment and other evaluation activities in the vocational rehabilitation process may be divided roughly into three parts. First, the vocational rehabilitation counselor must determine client eligibility. Second, a series of activities is focused on developing a plan for, and providing, actual services. Finally, a decision must be made about termination or "closure" of services.

The needs of the rehabilitation counselor for formal assessment data are mostly met by subcontracting evaluation responsibilities to appropriate medical, psychological, or vocational evaluators. In practice, formal assessment data are used primarily in the eligibility determination stage, though such data could certainly be useful at any stage. Some formal assessment data is mandated for eligibility

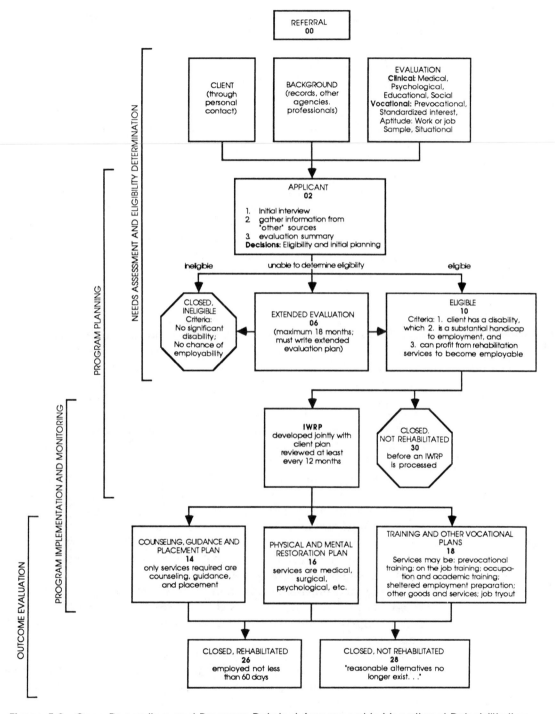

Figure 5.2 Case Recording and Program-Related Assessment in Vocational Rehabilitation

purposes—for example, certain score or cut-off points on specific measures such as an intelligence quotient score from a standardized individual test to certify clients as mentally retarded. Otherwise, the counselor typically gathers informal assessment information through direct contact with the client and others in interviews, and from existing documents.

The counselor acts primarily as interpreter of records from evaluators and as coordinator of the great variety of other informal and formal assessment information used in the development of eligibility determinations, subsequent program planning, and eventual closure of services. As a result, while counselors seldom carry on formal assessment activities personally, their roles and responsibilities require several abilities that are directly related to formal assessment and evaluation skills: ability to interpret the results of formal assessments; knowledge of existing instruments and strategies in order to be able to request specific information from assessments and evaluations; and ability to use assessment and evaluation results for programming purposes to establish objective criteria for planning, monitoring, and evaluation services.

Program-Related Assessment in Vocational Rehabilitation

The primary involvement of vocational rehabilitation counselors in assessment activities, then, is as interpreters and decision makers regarding applicant status and client service needs. As a result, assessment facilitates and justifies their decisions, which are made at regular and predictable intervals within the vocational rehabilitation process. In that respect, assessment in vocational rehabilitation is somewhat comparable to the curriculum-referenced approach described earlier as essential for school programs. That is, it is implemented to facilitate program-related decisions. A program-related assessment strategy is a decision-based approach.

Essentially, four types of decisions must be made within the vocational rehabilitation process: eligibility, development of an individual written rehabilitation plan (IWRP), training and placement, and closure of services. These decisions, and their related evaluation activities, can be conceptualized and structured into the program-related (or curriculum-referenced) model that was defined and detailed earlier: needs assessment, program planning, program implementation and monitoring, and outcome evaluation. In this highly functional model, all assessment is related to some aspect of decision making about services to clients, and each stage of the process is integrally related to the previous and next stages.

As the headings on the left side of Figure 5-2 demonstrate, eligibility determination and the initial steps in the program-planning process can constitute a through needs assessment. In fact, the Extended Evaluation (06) status offers a formal opportunity for rehabilitation counselors to make data-based decisions. Before determining client status, counselors can actually try out various training and other services to assess directly the benefit to the client. This opportunity is especially important for more severely disabled clients who might be perceived intuitively as "not able to benefit from rehabilitation services" when, in fact, they may well be able to benefit if appropriate services are provided.

The other three stages of the program-related assessment model can be applied within a rehabilitation services context in much the same manner. Program-planning comprises the same activities as needs assessment, with the addition of the individual written rehabilitation plan (IWRP) process, which leads to a clear, written specification of goals, objectives, and evaluation criteria for services.

Implementation and monitoring are guided by the contents of the IWRP process and are accomplished via placement, training, counseling, and/or restorative services. Monitoring focuses on both features of training or placement sites (e.g., employer concerns, social-prevocation expectations—interpersonal skills and punctuality, on-site needs for support), and on client performance (job roles defined as behavior—knowledge, performance, learning skills).

Outcome evaluation can be based directly on goals, objectives, and training plans developed in the IWRP, and also can be, in part, a compilation of program monitoring results. Outcome evaluation can and should be both:

1. Client-centered—that is, provide data for answering questions such as: What goals have been met/unmet? What needs were not planned for? What assistance is still required?

2. Agency-oriented—that is, provide data for answering questions such as: How does client data help the agency evaluate its own planning efforts? What information contributes to evaluating the implementation of services?

Finally, the results of outcome evaluation can and should be used to facilitate ongoing needs assessment.

The point of this brief description has been to demonstrate that current practice of assessment in vocational rehabilitation can be conceptualized in a program-related fashion (or in a "curriculum-referenced" fashion by viewing the "curriculum" as a program of placement, training, counseling, and restorative services). When this is accomplished, assessment is always functional for its consumers—clients, counselors, educators, trainers. It serves clear, specific, and applied purposes, and is not simply "data in a file somewhere." To the extent that both educators in vocational preparation programs for students with special needs and rehabilitation professionals in any local area apply a basic curriculum-referenced or program-related assessment strategy, they ensure that students/clients are optimally served by the outcomes of assessment.

REFERENCES

Botterbusch, K. (1980). *A Comparison of Commercial Vocation Evaluation Systems.* Menomonie, Wis.: Materials Development Center, Stout Vocational Rehabilitation Institute, University of Wisconsin-Stout.

Brolin, D. (1982). *Vocational Preparation of Persons with Handicaps.* 2d ed. Columbus, Ohio: Charles E. Merrill.

Browning, P., and L.K. Irvin. (1981). The vocational evaluation, training and placement of mentally retarded persons: A research review. *Rehabilitation Counseling Bulletin 24,* 374–408.

Clark, G.M. (1979). *Career Education for the Handicapped in the Elementary Classroom.* Denver: Love Publishing.

Cobb, B. (1983). Curriculum-based vocational assessment. *Teaching Exceptional Children 15,* 216–219.

Florida International Diagnostic-Prescriptive Vocational Competency Profile. (1980). Chicago: Stoelting Company.

Galagan, J. (1985). Psychoeducational testing: Turn out the lights, the party's over. *Exceptional Children 52*(9), 288–299.

Glascoe, F., and S. Levy. (1985). A multi-dimensional, observational approach to vocational assessment and placement. *Career Development for Exceptional Individuals 8*(2), 73–79.

Halpern, A.S., L.K. Irvin, and J.T. Landman. (1979). *Tests for Everyday Living.* Monterey, Calif.: CTB/McGraw-Hill, Publishers Test Service.

Halpern, A.S., L.K. Irvin, J. Lehmann, and T. Heiry. (1982). *Contemporary Assessment of Adaptive Behavior of Mentally Retarded Adolescents and Adults.* Baltimore: University Park Press.

Halpern, A., L.K., Irvin, and A. Munkres. (1986). *The Social and Prevocational Information Battery—Revised.* Monterey, Calif.: CTB/McGraw-Hill.

Irvin, L.K., R. Gersten, V. Taylor, T. Heiry, D. Close, and G.T. Bellamy. (1982). *Trainee Performance Sample.* New Berlin, Wis.: Ideal Developmental Labs.

Irvin, L.K., and A. Halpern. (1979). The process model of diagnostic assessment. In G.T. Bellamy, G. O'Connor, and O. Karan (eds.), *Vocational Rehabilitation of Severely Handicapped Persons: Contemporary Service Strategies.* Baltimore: University Park Press. Pp. 55–70.

Lamkin, J. (1980). *Getting Started: Career Education Activities for Exceptional Students (K–9).* Reston, Va: Council for Exceptional Children.

Patten, M. (1981). Components of the prevocational/vocational evaluation. *Career Development for Exceptional Individuals 4,* 81–87.

Peterson, M. (1981). Developing a model of vocational assessment for use in public schools in Texas. *Vocational Evaluation and Work Adjustment Bulletin 14*(3), 100–107.

Peterson, M. (1985). Models of vocational assessment. *Career Development for Exceptional Individuals 8*(2), 110–118.

Peterson, M., and P. Hill. (1982). *Vocational Assessment of Students with Special Needs: An Implementation Manual.* Commerce: East Texas State University Occupational Curriculum Laboratory.

Petzy, V. (1983) Vocational assessment for special needs students in the middle/junior high school. *Career Development for Exceptional Individuals 6*(1), 15–24.

Phelps, L.A., and T. McCarty. (1984). Student assessment practices. *Career Development for Exceptional Individuals 7*, 30–38.

Roberts, S., D. Doty, S. Santleben, and T. Tang. (1983). A model for vocational assessment of handicapped students. *Career Development for Exceptional Individuals 6*(2), 100–110.

Rusch, F., and D. Mithaug. (1980). *Vocational Training for Mentally Retarded Adults.* Champaign, Ill.: Research Press.

Schalock, R. (1976). *Competitive Employment Screening Test and Remediation Manual.* Hastings, Neb.: Mid-Nebraska MR Services.

Schalock, R., and R. Harper. (1977). Three track approach to programming MR. In P. Mittler (ed.), *Research to Practice in Mental Retardation.* Baltimore: University Park Press. Pp. 369–394.

Schalock, R., and O. Karan. (1979). Relevant assessment. In G. T. Bellamy, G. O'Connor, and O. Karan (eds.), *Vocational Rehabilitation of Severely Handicapped Persons.* Baltimore: University Park Press. Pp. 33–54.

Sitlington, P. (1979). Vocational assessment and training of the handicapped. *Focus on Exceptional Children 4.*

Sitlington, P., D. Brolin, G. Clark, and J. Vacanti. (1985). Career/vocational assessment in the public school setting: The position of the Division on Career Development. *Career Development for Exceptional Individuals 8*(1), 3–6.

Sitlington, P., and D. Wimmer. (1978). Vocational assessment techniques for the handicapped adolescent. *Career Development for Exceptional Individuals 1*(2), 74–87.

Stodden, R. (1981). Planning vocational assessment within education settings: An interdisciplinary focus with handicapped students. *Vocational Assessment: Policy Paper Series Document 6*, Urbana-Champaign: University of Illinois, Leadership Training Institute.

Stodden, R., J. Casale, and S. Schwartz. (1977). Work evaluation and the mentally retarded. *Mental Retardation 15*, 25–27.

Stodden, R., and R. Ianacone. (1981). Career/Vocational assessment of the special needs individual: A conceptual model. *Exceptional Children 47*(8), 600–608.

Walls, R.T., T. Werner, and A. Bacon. (1977). Behavior checklist. In R. Coe and P. Hawkins (eds.), *Behavior Assessment.* New York: Brunner/Mazel. Pp. 77–146.

Walls, R.T., T. Zane, and T. Werner. (1978). *The Vocational Behavior Checklist.* Morgantown: West Virginia University, Rehabilitation Research and Training Center.

6 Instructional Programming in Vocational Education

David M. Mank and Robert H. Horner
University of Oregon

INTRODUCTION

Vocational education for students with severe handicaps is successful when students are gainfully employed soon after leaving school. The strategies needed to produce this result involve a wide variety of processes including individual planning, development of work sites, and the use of instructional strategies that yield a range of job-related skills. Vocational education includes preparing a student for a wide range of locally available jobs, and actually assisting the student to obtain a paying job toward the end of his or her education. The success or failure of vocational education has lifestyle implications that extend far into adulthood. Students well prepared to face working life are more likely to move into the mainstream of their communities. Students poorly prepared for a lifetime of working may well find the realities of adulthood to be unforgiving. In meeting the needs of working life, the role of careful vocational instruction cannot be overlooked (Wilcox and Bellamy, 1982).

THE OBJECTIVE OF VOCATIONAL EDUCATION

Successful employment requires ongoing performance of the job tasks and other behaviors needed by competent employees. Too often young adults

142

fail in employment as a result of instruction that did not build a core set of skills needed in real jobs (Hill, Hill, Wehman, and Banks, 1985; Sowers, Thompson, and Connis, 1979). What is needed is instruction that builds competent work behaviors.

A careful look at the requirements of any job can provide important information about the skills needed for successful employment. In most jobs it is necessary to do several things well. First, an employee must be able to meet the demands of every task associated with the job. Second, an employee must be able to move from task to task at the appropriate times. Third, an employee must be able to deal with the social contingencies in the job setting. Fourth, an employee must be able to handle exceptions and day-to-day variations that inevitably arise in any job. Finally, an employee must be able to perform the job competently over time without constant supervision. An analysis of job requirements makes clear much of what is needed for successful instruction in vocational education.

Vocational education should build behavior that generalizes across untrained situations and maintains over time without continuous supervision. In developing such work behavior, instruction must address generalization and maintenance issues as well as the initial acquisition of job skills (Mank and Horner, 1987).

This chapter addresses the elements of instructional programming needed to build competent work performance. It begins with a brief introduction to the principles of applied behavior analysis, which forms the cornerstones of successful instruction. This is followed by a discussion of procedures for analyzing jobs prior to actually beginning instruction. Next comes a discussion of basic training procedures for acquiring needed behaviors, and, finally, a discussion of strategies for promoting the generalization and maintenance of job behavior and techniques of self-management.

THE TECHNOLOGY OF VOCATIONAL INSTRUCTION: APPLIED BEHAVIOR ANALYSIS

Applied behavior analysis is a technology based on the assumption that the causes or determinants of behavior can be identified and isolated (Kazdin, 1980). A behavioral approach assumes that patterns of behavior can be understood by defining biological and environmental conditions. Behavior is not random. Rather, it occurs in response to stimuli present in the environment, and is maintained as a result of the consequences following the behavior.

A Behavioral Approach

A behavioral approach to vocational instruction calls for attention to detail at several initial points in developing vocational behaviors (Rusch, and Mithaug, 1980; Wehman, 1981; Bellamy, Horner, and Inman, 1979). First, it is necessary to define precisely the goal of any specific job-related instruction. While vocational education is aimed at building a set of work skills, specific instruction should focus on the development of previously defined behaviors that together contribute to successful vocational life. Second, the requirements of tasks for instruction must be identified carefully. It is only after developing a thorough understanding of the task or behavior at hand that an instructor is able to impart information to the learner. Third, an analysis of the specific responses required to perform a task is needed for successful instruction. With a careful response analysis, it is possible to build chains of behaviors that result in successful acquisition by the learner. Finally, attention must be directed toward understanding and providing the reinforcers that are likely to maintain specific behaviors.

An overview of a behavioral approach to instruction is provided in the following scenario.

CASE STUDY: Keith

Keith is a high school student with severe disabilities. As a part of his education plan Keith spends three hours a day in a work experience program. He recently has been assigned job tasks in a photocopy department. A trainer skilled in vocational instruction using a behavioral approach has been assigned to teach the job to Keith and build his competence at it.

Keith's trainer approaches the task systematically and begins a sequence of activities that will result in Keith's ability to perform this job competently to the satisfaction of the copy room supervisor. Keith's trainer first schedules time with the copy room supervisor to gather information about the job and the working conditions. The purpose of the preparation on the part of the trainer is twofold: (1) to become familiar with the specific tasks and behaviors required for successful performance of the job; and (2) to understand the pace, working conditions, quality standards, and social contingencies associated with the job. Through careful preparation and analysis of the job demands, the trainer can expect success in building Keith's performance. During this process, the trainer will become familiar with the job and perform it long enough to construct a specific task analysis of its requirements; develop instructional plans for teaching Keith; and identify the consequences and contingencies of the job. This preparation occurs before the trainer begins instructing Keith on how to do the job. Once the analysis is complete, the trainer introduces Keith to the situation and actually begins imparting information about the job to Keith.

The trainer begins systematically teaching Keith the entire job and each specific task within the job by providing information, assistance, and feedback. Once Keith begins to gain independence in using the photocopy machine, organizing orders, filing, and so on, the trainer gradually fades the assistance and feedback provided until Keith performs the task without input or assistance from the trainer. When instruction is completed, Keith performs correctly on all aspects of the job. The trainer has built competence on the range of time management, task variation, and coworker interactions needed for successful employment.

This case study provides a brief look at the process and the outcome of job specific instruction. The following sections of this chapter describe a range of issues and strategies for delivering quality instructional programming in vocational education for students with disabilities.

Response Analysis A response analysis is a critical component of effective vocational education. A response is a basic unit of behavior that can be identified, specified, and measured (Johnston and Pennypacker, 1980). The size of a response can vary. We could define a response as the successful completion of an entire job task or as one small piece of a job task. For example, picking up a single sheet of paper to photocopy could be the response of interest. Alternatively, photocopying a ten-page document could be considered the response of interest. The size of a response depends on the purpose of the analysis, the competence of the individual to be instructed, and the demands of the task (Bellamy, Horner, and Inman, 1979). Where instruction is concerned, it is necessary to define response units that are sufficiently small to allow monitoring of student acquisition.

Responses occur in the context of a set of environmental conditions and are maintained (or not maintained) as a result of the consequences of the behavior. Stimuli or events that occur following a response are referred to as *consequences*. In applied behavioral analysis, the probability of a response occurring in the future is affected by the type and nature of the consequence that follows it. There are several kinds of consequences. A consequence can be a reinforcer if it increases the probability that the response will occur again in the future. A consequence can be a punisher if it decreases the probability of the behavior occurring again. Finally, a consequence can be neutral, having no discernible effect on the future probability of a response (Kazdin, 1980; Schoenfeld and Farmer, 1970).

This discussion of response analysis points out the importance of understanding that most vocational behaviors are composed of specific responses. For each response there is an antecedent condition that should act as the signal for the occurrence of the response. After the response occurs, it is followed by some consequence.

Operant Chains Many vocational tasks require performance of a complex sequence of behaviors. This sequence of behaviors can also be referred to as an *operant chain* of specific and identifiable responses. An operant chain, however, is different from just a series of independent responses. Rather, an operant chain is a series of responses that are

Discriminative Stimulus / Response

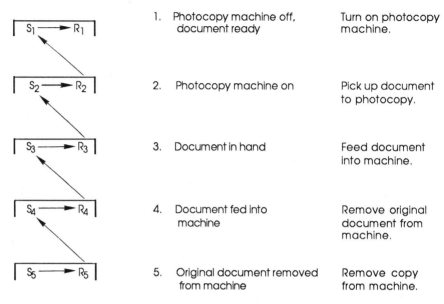

$S_1 \longrightarrow R_1$	1. Photocopy machine off, document ready	Turn on photocopy machine.
$S_2 \longrightarrow R_2$	2. Photocopy machine on	Pick up document to photocopy.
$S_3 \longrightarrow R_3$	3. Document in hand	Feed document into machine.
$S_4 \longrightarrow R_4$	4. Document fed into machine	Remove original document from machine.
$S_5 \longrightarrow R_5$	5. Original document removed from machine	Remove copy from machine.

Figure 6.1   An Operant Chain: Antecedents-Responses-Consequences

repeated in the same sequence, and in which the completion of one response leads to the performance of the next response (Bellamy, Horner, and Inman, 1979). Operant chains are evident in many activities of day-to-day life. Returning to the example of photocopying: The first antecedent or discriminative stimulus (SD) could be the machine off and not yet ready to use. This signals that the machine should be turned on. Turning on the machine by flipping the appropriate switch is the response made to the SD of the machine being off. In turn, the response results in the machine activating, which reinforces the response of flipping the switch. In addition, the machine now being turned on acts as the next discriminative stimulus for engaging in the next response (picking up a document to photocopy), and so on. The proper sequence of antecedents-responses-consequences is an operant chain (Gollub, 1977). Such an operant chain is represented in Figure 6.1. In order to complete an entire task successfully, each response must be performed in the proper way and at the proper time.

Responses occur in a continuous flow of behavior. An individual performs a response at particular times before some responses and after other responses. A response occurs at the appropriate time if the conditions are right for that response. Using the photocopying example: it is appropriate to insert a new page into the photocopy machine only if the previous page has already been copied. In other words, the response should occur based on the appropriate *antecedent* conditions. An antecedent condition or stimulus is said to control a response if the response is more likely to occur in its presence (Kazdin, 1980).

Defining tasks as operant chains in work situations is useful for instruction and when tasks are lengthy or complex in nature. It is possible to consider the task of copying a document as a single response having many parts. The sequence of the responses chosen for analysis will depend on the purpose of the analysis. On a larger scale, the copying of a single document could be viewed as one response of an entire job that includes picking up documents to be copied from other buildings, photocopying the documents, recording the number of copies made, and delivering the copies as appropriate. These larger response units may be useful in analyzing a total job but may not be sufficient to teach the specific behaviors an individual needs to use the photocopy machine correctly and efficiently. The most important purpose of defining the size of the response unit is related to planning training activities around the operants chosen.

Defining tasks as operant chains can be useful for activities other than job tasks. For example, if an employment situation calls for a student with disabilities to use the employee dining room at lunch time, an operant chain can be specified for the responses needed in that situation.

Although this description of operant chains includes a focus on the consequences of responses, the presence of reinforcers and other consequences that help build or maintain behavior should not be assumed. Rather, successful instruction in vocational direction calls for systematic management of reinforcers and contingencies (Rusch and Mithaug, 1980; Bellamy, Horner, and Inman, 1979).

Managing Contingencies   The previous section focused on the importance of developing operant chains to produce successful task performance by the student. Specific strategies for further analyzing tasks and conducting training will be discussed later in this chapter. There is, however, a set of principles related to reinforcement, providing consequences, and managing contingencies that must be discussed first. Reinforcement refers to an increase in the frequency of a response when it is followed by some given consequence. The consequence following the behavior or response in question must be contingent on the behavior. *Contingency* refers to the rule that defines when a consequence should be delivered. If a contingent event increases the frequency of a behavior, it is considered a positive reinforcer (Kazdin, 1980). Reinforcers can be presented after small units or chunks of behavior or after larger sequences of responses. For practitioners and teachers, it is important to manage the nature of the consequences and contingencies provided to the learner during and after instruction.

Recent literature has shown the effectiveness of a wide variety of reinforcers in teaching and maintaining the behavior of persons with disabilities (e.g., Gifford, et al., 1984). In general, teachers must develop the skills to effectively provide appropriate consequences during instruction. Teachers must respond differentially to the learner's behavior. During instruction an effective teacher will provide positive consequences or positive reinforcers for correct or improved performance. In response to incorrect responses or errors, effective teaching calls for correction. One of the most important strategies of instruction is related to a teacher's ability to find ways to reinforce successful performance and provide information and correction for errors or unsuccessful performance.

Managing contingencies is not merely a matter of providing reinforcement indiscriminately. Rather, successful contingency management calls for delivering consequences contingent on the behavior of the learner; reinforcement and corrections are constantly adjusted, related to type and frequency of reinforcement delivered. The focus is to build increasingly large sequences of independent behaviors. As training progresses, trainer-provided assistance and consequences should be faded to approximate the conditions of the natural environment.

Contingency management is needed in instruction, not only in building and maintaining performance. In many situations, the same principles can be applied to managing inappropriate behaviors. A thorough discussion of reinforcement theory and contingency management is beyond the scope of this chapter; for a more complete discussion of behavioral principles, the reader is referred to Kazdin (1980).

ANALYSIS OF JOBS

A job is a set of behaviors that result in a vocationally meaningful outcome. Jobs are usually composed of tasks, and tasks are further broken down into responses. One of the most important steps that must be taken before instruction is actually begun is to conduct a thorough analysis of the job and all tasks that compromise the job. It is not possible to deliver quality instruction without a thorough understanding of the job to be performed. As a result, the trainer must assess the demands of a job, just as he or she assesses the skill level of the learner. A job analysis must be detailed enough to allow the trainer to impart information to the student about each behavior required for each task of the job. In addition, the instructor's design and analysis must be comprehensive enough to ensure that all components of a job are addressed and that the student develops competence at performing the entire job in addition to competence and independence at performing each specific task.

For example, consider the situation of instruction related to custodial jobs in a local hospital. The job requires that the student keep the floors clean, empty trash containers, clean railings and walls, and wash inside windows. At the task level, the student must develop competence at each specific task. That is, the student must learn to use a broom, mop a floor, use a buffing machine, care for the equipment, locate and use trash collection equipment, use rail polishers, and so on. Each of these tasks should be the focus of specific analysis and instruction. It is not enough, however, to learn merely how to do each task. In addition, the student must also learn to do the entire job: performing each task at the right time and in the right way in order to meet both the quality standards of the job and the supervisor's standards. Therefore, a thorough analysis must be specific to each task yet build the student's ability to move from task to task appropriately and fulfill the role specified by the job. Each level of such an analysis is discussed below.

Task Design Most jobs and tasks can be performed in several ways. The instructor's task is to select a method, or design, that is best suited to the situation for the student and the job. For example, if a job calls for sweeping and mopping the floors in four hospital rooms, the design could call for the student to sweep the first floor, put aside the brooms and immediately mop the first floor. This approach, properly executed, will result in clean hospital rooms. It may not, however, be the most efficient design. An alternative design might be more appropriate. For example, the requirements of the job might be met more effectively if the student swept all four hospital rooms before doing any mopping. This latter design could reduce the time the student spends changing equipment. While the ultimate outcome, clean floors, may be the same, complexity and efficiency is likely to vary depending on the design. At issue for the trainer, then, is to select a method that will result in the desired outcome that takes into account the abilities of the student and efficiency requirements. Several guidelines can be identified when addressing design issues.

1. Increase efficiency by selecting a method that, once taught, will result in the most rapid completion of the task.

2. Use appropriate equipment whenever possible if the equipment can be expected to increase efficiency or make performance easier.

3. Select a method that can be learned by the student. In some cases, the most efficient process may be one that is extremely difficult to learn.

Task Analysis A task analysis is a process of breaking a task into its required component responses, and listing these responses in an appropriate sequence (Bellamy, Horner, and Inman, 1979). A task analysis is a complete description of each and every behavior needed to accomplish a specific

Discriminative Stimulus	Response
1. Ready to clean floor	Procure broom, dust pan, mop, and mop bucket
2. Materials ready	Go to dining room
3. In dining room	Put chairs on tables
4. Chairs on tables	Go to far corner with push broom
5. In far corner	Sweep under tables
6. Under tables swept (entire area)	Go to far corner
7. In far corner	Sweep aisles toward door
8. Aisles swept	Sweep debris into single pile
9. Debris in single pile	Pick up dust pan
10. Dust pan in hand	Sweep debris into dustpan
11. Debris in dust pan	Empty dust pan in trash receptacle
12. Dust pan emptied	Return broom and dust pan to door
13. Broom and dust pan at door	Get and fill mop bucket
14. Mop bucket filled	Take mop and bucket to far corner
15. Mop and bucket in far corner	Mop under all tables
16. Mopping under tables completed	Go to far corner
17. In far corner	Mop aisles from corner toward door
18. Aisles mopped	Empty mop bucket
19. Mop bucket emptied	Gather all implements
20. Implements gathered	Return implements to custodial closet
21. Implements in closet	Go to next task

Figure 6.2 A Sample Task Analysis: Cleaning a Floor

and discrete task (Popovich, 1981). The purpose of task analysis is to facilitate training by focusing the instructor's attention on the specific demands of a task and by providing a method for gathering data during training about the acquisition of the task by the student. A variety of systems for task analyses are described thoroughly in available literature (e.g., Wehman, 1981; Rusch and Mithaug, 1980; and Bellamy, Horner, and Inman, 1979). A sample task analysis for the task of cleaning a floor is included as Figure 6.2.

In developing a task analysis, an instructor should consider the following points:

1. The specific objective for the task should be identified and recorded.

2. The person who will be doing the training should perform the task several times before constructing a task analysis.

3. The person who will be doing the training should analyze the task and construct the task analysis.

4. The tasks should be broken down into response units small enough to instruct the student successfully.

5. The steps in the task should be sequenced in exactly the order in which they will be performed.

6. The discriminative stimulus, or the antecedent condition, for each step should be identified.

7. The criterion for successful completion of each step should be identified.

8. The sequence of steps should be used to construct a data collection format for use during training.

9. The trainer should verify that the sequence of steps does result in completion of the task.

These guidelines provide important rules for building task analyses. A task analysis is a tool for the person who will be training the student with disabilities. Construction of a task analysis before instruction begins meets two training needs. First, it increases the likelihood that the instructor has a thorough understanding of the task in question. Second, the task analysis provides the basis for a system for data collection. For a discussion of a data collection format, the reader is referred to Bellamy, Horner, and Inman (1979) and Saunders and Koplik (1975). Task analysis provides the basis for training. It is important to reiterate, however, that most jobs are composed of a number of tasks, and the student must learn the entire job as well as each task.

Job Analysis The task design and task analysis process just described has focused on specific tasks and the importance of breaking tasks into component steps for instruction. Job analysis on the other hand, can be considered to be more complicated and of greater scope, with specific tasks compromising job duties. A logic similar to that for task analysis is useful here (Buckley, Sandow, and Smock, in preparation). That is, the tasks associated with successful job completion must be identified and sequenced. A job analysis is conducted to ensure that the requirements of the employment position are met. In other words, the tasks must be performed at the proper time and in an acceptable way in order to result in completion of the entire job. A job analysis tends to focus on the decision rules concerning which tasks come next and the sequence of task performance, whereas task analysis focuses on the specifics of "what to do" for each step of component tasks. A sample job analysis composed of multiple tasks for a custodial job is presented in Figure 6.3a. Of course, each task of the job would require a task analysis. This job analysis

Job/Custodial/Time Health Corp.

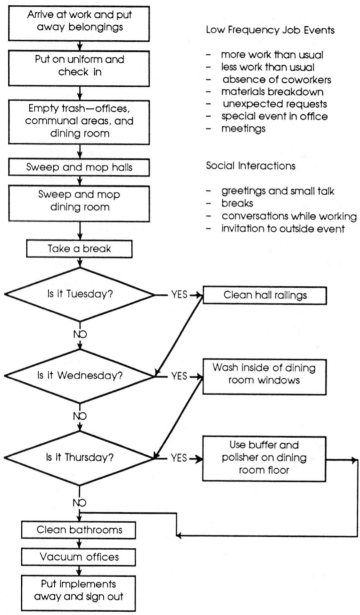

Low Frequency Job Events

- more work than usual
- less work than usual
- absence of coworkers
- materials breakdown
- unexpected requests
- special event in office
- meetings

Social Interactions

- greetings and small talk
- breaks
- conversations while working
- invitation to outside event

Figure 6.3a Job Analysis Summary

Use a new sheet for each day you work the job during analysis

Date: 11/11/86
Job: Custodial
Analyst: Hal

Employer: Time Health Corp
Data Source(s) Supervisor: Ken
Working Job: _____
Coworker: Freda

Actual Time	Task	Location	Natural Task Cue	Feedback Received	Criteria — Quality	Criteria — Time	Social Interactions — Person	Social Interactions — Frequency	Social Interactions — Type Interaction	Low Frequency Job Events — Event	Low Frequency Job Events — Frequency
12:30	Arrive & get set up	Break room	Time	None	—		Freda	Daily	Greeting		
12:35	Put on uniform			·			·				
12:38	Empty trash	Offices; communal areas & dining rm	Completion of prior task	·	Empty cans		Ken	Occasional	Small talk	More trash than usual	1 time bi-weekly
1:15	Sweep and mop halls	Halls	·	·	Clean halls	by 2:00	·	·	·		
2:00	Sweep & mop dining room	Dining room	·	·	Clean floor in dining room	by 2:30					
2:30	Break	Break room	Time	—	—	Stop by 2:45	Freda and others	Daily	·	Special event / Absence of co-workers	Monthly
2:45	Clean railings	Halls	Tuesday	Social	Rails shine	by 3:45	Ken	Daily	—	Special event	Bi-weekly
	Wash windows	Dining room	Wednesday	Social	Windows clean	by 3:45	—	—	—		
	Buff & polish	Dining room	Thursday	Social	Floor shines	by 3:45	—	—	—	Special event	Bi-weekly
3:34	Clean bathrooms	Bathrooms	Completion of prior task	Social	Bathrooms clean	by 4:10	—	—	—	Bathrooms in use	Varied
4:10	Vacuum	Offices	·	·	Clean carpet	by 4:30	Staff	Daily	Small talk	Meeting in progress	Weekly
4:30	Put things away and check out	Break room	Time	—	—	4:30	Freda & Ken	Daily	Goodbyes	Extra work	Bi-weekly

Figure 6.3b Job Analysis Worksheet

includes a job summary and a completed job analysis worksheet Figure 6.3b, that identifies conditions for each task for the job.

A few guidelines contrasting job analysis and task analysis help point out the difference. These include:

1. The focus of task analysis is the component responses required for completion of a specified and discrete task.

2. The focus of job analysis is the performance of requisite component tasks in successful performance of the responsibilities of all job duties.

3. The steps of a task analysis specify precisely "how" each component behavior is performed and the sequence of responses for task completion.

4. The components of job analysis focus on the tasks that comprise the job and the decision rules for when and how to perform the tasks.

5. Task analysis can usually be constructed for specific tasks that specify a consistent sequence of performance of the steps of a task.

6. Job analysis must be comprehensive enough to include and identify the decision rules, the if-then decisions, required for successful job performance.

These considerations concerning the analysis of job and task requirements set the stage for the instructional procedures to be employed in teaching a student with disabilities to perform a job. Basic training procedures are addressed next.

TRAINING PROCEDURES FOR VOCATIONAL INSTRUCTION

The strategies described in this section are the basis of instruction that builds competent job performance by students with disabilities. It is in the delivery of instruction that information is imparted to the student. It is in the delivery of instruction–in the process of training on vocational tasks–that the understanding of a behavioral approach and the preparation via job and task design and analysis come together in such a way that job competence can be developed. There is one and only one criterion for successful vocational training: successful acquisition and performance of vocational skills by the student.

Building operant chains of responses is the heart of successful vocational training. During training, the instructor must impart to the student the specifics of what to do and when to do it for each step of each task for the entire job. The focus of the following discussion is on the skills and procedures used by the instructor during training sessions. For more information on training procedures, the reader is referred to Bellamy, Horner, and Inman, (1979); Rusch and Mithaug, (1980); and Wehman, (1981).

Format for Training

Specific training on job and task performance is best conducted in a small group or one-to-one format. Further, training is best conducted in the same environment in which performance is expected of the student. Although training in simulated settings may be useful under certain conditions (Horner, McDonnell, and Bellamy, 1985), it is generally preferable to conduct training, as noted, in the same setting and under the same conditions that the student is expected to perform the job. If training is conducted in the performance setting, problems associated with transfer of skills and generalization can be minimized.

Training Skills

Efficient training calls for consistency in providing information, providing assistance, and managing contingencies. Such training is conducted most appropriately in a forward chain approach–that is, training that starts at the beginning of a task and continues to the completion of a task. All training should be as positive as possible. A basic characteristic of successful training is that it is a reinforcing experience. In general, in training situations presumed reinforcers should be delivered several times as often as corrections for errors or inappropriate responses. Teaching people who have difficulty learning involves delivering information with precision and clarity. Five skills are critical for a trainer: (1) delivering unambiguous assistance; (2) providing corrections; (3) delivering reinforcement; (4) providing ongoing assessment; and (5) pacing during training.

Providing Information and Assistance

Instruction involves the transfer of information from the instructor to the student. The instructor can provide information in a variety of ways at different times during instruction. All tasks contain information that any competent performer uses when doing a task correctly and consistently. During instruction, the trainer provides additional information (verbal cues, gestures, and so on) to help the student to learn the task. An instructor skilled in vocational training varies the kind of assistance provided, the method by which it is provided, and the amount provided.

Purpose of Assistance The purpose of assistance is to increase the likelihood of a reinforceable response from the learner. An instructor provides assistance about when a response should be performed (discrimination), how a response should be performed (manipulation), and the criterion for correct performance (when a response should stop). Assistance emphasizing *when to respond* involves providing information about the cue or discriminative stimulus for performing a response. Assistance emphasizing *how to respond* focuses on providing information about the movements needed for successful performance of a response. Assistance emphasizing the *criterion* for correct performance provides information about when a response or behavior should end (e.g., when is a window clean enough?).

Methods of Assistance   The demands of tasks and the abilities of the student will help determine which method of assistance is most appropriate at specific moments of instruction. There are four major methods of providing assistance. These include:

- *Verbal cues:* The instructor provides information by delivering verbal instructions about what should be done.

- *Modeling:* The instructor provides information by performing the exact movements required for a response or set of responses while the student observes.

- *Physical prompts:* The instructor points to or gestures toward a characteristic of the task or part of the task.

- *Physical guidance:* The instructor physically moves the body of the student through the movements required by a response.

Some students learn more effectively via one method or another. The instructor must decide the amount and the kind of assistance needed and the method of assistance to be used, based on the improving performance of the student. To provide more than is needed will result in unnecessary dependence of the student on the instructor rather than building independence and competence.

Amount of Assistance   Assistance provides information. The amount of information provided varies with the amount of assistance provided. Regardless of the method of assistance an instructor employs, the amount of information delivered can vary. The objective of quality vocational instruction is to provide the minimum information and assistance needed for correct performance.

Providing
Correction

It is likely that the student will make errors in task performance during instruction. When errors occur, a correction procedure should be used that allows the student to try it again while the instructor provides just enough additional assistance to ensure correct performance. Correction is provided using the same methods of assistance noted earlier. There are three purposes for correction during instruction: (1) It allows the student to perform correctly; (2) it prevents any reinforcement of the incorrect response; and (3) it allows the student more practice on a response that may be difficult.

When errors occur, the instructor backs up in the operant chain–that is, returns the stimulus conditions to those for the response on which the error occurred. Then the instructor provides enough assistance to ensure correct performance. As with all instruction, correction should be delivered with the least assistance possible that results in correct performance.

Providing Reinforcement and Contingencies

Reinforcement refers to the presentation of a positive event (e.g., praise, tokens, and so on) after the student performs a behavior or response appropriately. The instructor must define the behaviors that will be reinforced during instruction and make clear the contingencies on which reinforcement is delivered. In all cases, the reinforcer should be age-appropriate; be delivered easily (that is, reinforcers should be delivered in a way that does not distract the instructor or the student from the task); be desirable by the student; and not interrupt the work behavior. Reinforcement is most effective when delivered immediately after the desired behavior is performed. A skilled instructor continuously assesses and adjusts the type, amount, and schedule of reinforcement during vocational instruction. The following seven points provide guidelines for managing consequences during instruction.

1. *Teach skills that will produce positive consequences in the performance setting.* The most successful strategies for building work behavior in vocational instruction are based on teaching in contexts that provide positive consequences for learning and performing work tasks. That is, the most successful instruction occurs in settings where quality performance will naturally result in positive consequences, or positive feedback, for the student over time.

2. *Contingencies should be planned.* Skilled trainers will arrange consequences and provide reinforcement in a way that takes into account the abilities of the learner and the demand of the tasks. Based on this information, the trainer can plan for the management of contingencies, an ability that builds independence.

3. *Contingencies should be used to build competent performance.* Once a specific instructional objective is chosen, contingencies should be used to build competent performance by reinforcing increasingly independent performance. Systematic use of reinforcers for correct or improved performance will assist in training independent performance.

4. *Contingencies must be thinned.* As independent performance emerges on a vocational task with a student with disabilities, the instructor must plan to thin the presence of continuous or excessive reinforcers. The student can be considered independent

on tasks when performance occurs in the absence of the contingencies that were used to help build independent performance.

5. *The use of contingencies should be individualized.* The specific reinforcers employed should be chosen with attention to the likes and dislikes of the student. It cannot be assumed that all learners will respond similarly to praise, points systems, or any other single reinforcer. Rather, the reinforcers used to build or maintain performance must take into account the preferences of each student.

6. *Contingency management can be used to develop appropriate behaviors and decrease inappropriate behaviors.* Reinforcement procedures can, of course, be useful in addressing needs a student may have related to responding appropriately in social contexts or reducing inappropriate or maladaptive behavior. However, even when the intention is to reduce inappropriate behavior, the focus of contingencies should be positive.

7. *Reinforcement should be age- and situation-appropriate.* Reinforcers delivered in work settings are most appropriate to the extent that they match the nature of reinforcement typically available to others in regular work settings.

The present section of this chapter has provided a brief overview of important principles of applied behavior analysis. These principles guide the use of strategies for building and maintaining vocational abilities with students having disabilities. These principles, however, must be applied in the specific contexts in which vocational behaviors are developed.

Providing Ongoing Assessment

During instruction, the student gains information about the task. As a result, the instructor must alter the way in which instruction occurs by adjusting the information and feedback provided. The instructor must continuously select the type, method, and amount of assistance and the type, amount, and schedule of reinforcement delivered during instruction. An instructor makes these decisions based on information provided during instruction by the student. The competence the student develops and the errors that emerge give the instructor information about the assistance and feedback that will promote further independence. Thus, the instructor must continually assess the student's performance and adapt the instruction to meet current student needs.

During instruction the instructor must monitor the student's progress. The instructor gathers information in order to make good decisions about changes needed in instructional strategies. Progress is monitored in two ways: (1) by using a task analysis data collection format for recording changes in independent performance, and (2) by closely observing the details of the student's performance that are not captured by a data recording system.

Pacing During Training

Work must continue smoothly from response to response and task to task if students are to develop competent and fluent work behavior. The delivery of pacing prompts can improve work rate by helping to reduce and eliminate pauses. The pace needed for a given job should be built into training right from the beginning in order to reduce the likelihood of a student's learning that a slow pace is acceptable. For example, pacing prompts might be needed during instruction if the learner slows in moving from response to response. A pacing prompt can be provided verbally with a direction (e.g., "keep working") or a gesture from the instructor toward the task. In all cases, the purpose is to increase work rate and prevent pauses. Pacing prompts are most effective if provided just as the student correctly finishes one response and is being reinforced for independent initiation of the next response.

If pace is attended to during instruction, the student is likely to work more quickly, without pauses. This means that the student with disabilities will work at a higher production rate, earn more money, and meet the speed requirements a job may have.

Fading Assistance

Training is successful when the learner performs all target responses to the vocational criterion, and does so using information naturally available in the work setting with all other information and assistance faded.

It is during the final phase of training that the instructor can make the training environment as similar as possible to the performance environment. If the student is expected to perform the job with only occasional contact with a supervisor, then instruction is not completed until the instructor has systematically faded all cues, corrections, and consequences to those available in the performance conditions. Of course, this fading must occur as the student maintains quality performance.

Five major guidelines can be identified that enhance transfer of new skills from training settings to performance settings.

1. Identify antecedent events and consequences that differentiate instruction from performance conditions.

2. Vary antecedent conditions that are irrelevant to task and job performance.

3. Provide differential reinforcement for consistent and acceptable work place.

4. Gradually and systematically fade the type, amount, and schedule of reinforcement to those that can be expected on the job.

5. Expose the student to the competing stimuli and reinforcers that can be expected under performance conditions.

Successful training, as noted, calls for the instructor to deliver as little assistance as possible in order to increase the student's independent performance on the job. The following example shows how the instructor (1) modifies instruction to impart information about the task and (2) provides and then fades assistance and contingencies in order to promote independent performance.

CASE STUDY: Nancy

Nancy has been assigned a custodial job in a health-care facility. Instruction begins after the trainer conducts the job and task analyses to ensure that she thoroughly understands the task. Then the trainer can introduce Nancy to the job. On the first day, the trainer shows Nancy all parts of the job, models task performance for Nancy, and requests participation in order to get an idea of the type and method of assistance that will be most useful for instruction on various tasks. The initial go-through on each task provides valuable information to the trainer. For example, the trainer can discover whether the student may learn more effectively through verbal cues, physical prompts, or models. He can discover if the student will be likely to require intense instruction if the tasks seem difficult for the student. The trainer will also get information about the type, frequency, and intensity of reinforcers that may be useful during instructions. Although some instruction certainly takes place during the initial trial, this first training period is most important as the time when the trainer can gather information about the expected performance of the student and the interaction of the student and the job tasks.

During the initial training trial on the task of sweeping and mopping the dining room floor, the trainer discovers that Nancy is having difficulty with mopping the floor in a way that is thorough yet efficient. Thus, the trainer continues the instruction by carefully modeling the required movements. When Nancy attempts it again, the trainer observes errors. In response, the trainer provides more information via specific physical guidance: He shows Nancy exactly how to hold the mop and how to move the mop head in a specific arc. After providing this physical guidance for a while, the trainer begins to relax the guiding of Nancy's arms through the movements. This is done gradually, with the trainer constantly checking to see if Nancy continues to perform correctly as the physical guidance is slowly reduced. If Nancy ceases to respond correctly, the trainer will increase the assistance provided. If Nancy continues correctly as the trainer fades, then fading continues. In all cases and without regard for the method of assistance in use at the time, the trainer should provide the minimum assistance necessary that results in correct performance on the part of the student. The trainer cannot know if too much assistance has been provided. However, the trainer will know immediately if too little assistance and information is provided.

When a trainer provides too little assistance, the student performs incorrectly. As errors occur, the trainer considers the nature of the error. The purpose here is to decide if Nancy is exhibiting a manipulation error (that is, does not know how to perform the needed behavior) or a discrimination error (that is, does not know what to do or when to do it). If the error seems to be related to *how* to perform, the trainer provides additional assistance on the physical movements required for successful performance. If the error seems to be related to a discrimination, additional assistance can help clairify the criterion for successful performance or draw attention to *when* to perform the response.

Throughout the training effort, the trainer provides reinforcement. At first, the trainer might delivery praise for attempts to perform correctly as well as for correct responses. Over time, the trainer will thin the reinforcers by giving praise only for successful responses, and then for larger and larger chunks of correct responses.

As errors occur during training with Nancy, the trainer takes care to stop Nancy immediately and back up in the operant chain in order to provide enough assistance and information to produce correct performance.

From the very beginning of instruction, the trainer attends to the pace of performance. Pauses can be treated as incorrect responses requiring additional assistance. The pace for moving from step to step and from task to task should approximate the pace that will be required when training is completed.

As Nancy gains competence on the task, the trainer begins to reduce systematically the assistance and reinforcement provided. During the initial training sessions the assistance provided and reinforcement delivered is increased to promote correct responding. However, Nancy will be independent and competent on each task only when she performs the tasks correctly while receiving the assistance and reinforcers that are available in the performance environment–when a trainer is not present.

Successful performance of job skills requires good instruction based on the principles and guidelines discussed here. Many vocational settings, however, call for generalized skills. Further, for vocational success, any competent employee must be able to maintain performance over weeks and months. While the preceding techniques help build performance, additional strategies may be needed to increase the generalization and maintenance of work behavior.

STRATEGIES FOR PROMOTING GENERALIZED PERFORMANCE

Students with disabilities can learn and perform a broad range of jobs in community settings. Procedures and strategies for systematic instruction have been developed that will result in students' performing trained tasks independently. However, important questions remain as to the effectiveness of instruction in allowing students with disabilities to generalize performance in situations other than training situations (Horner and Bellamy, 1983; Wacker and Berg, 1986). In fact, the literature suggests there is often a lack of generalization beyond the situations in which training occurs (Stokes and Baer, 1977). Even so, promising strategies are emerging that will help teach persons with disabilities behaviors that are performed reliably and consistently across the range of natural situations.

General case instruction is a strategy for teaching generalized skills to students with disabilities. Recent literature supports the utility of this approach (Pancsofar and Bates, in press; Horner, Bellamy, and Colvin, 1984; Horner, Eberhard, and Sheehan, 1986; Sprague and Horner, 1984). It has been used to teach such skills as telephone use (Horner, Williams, and Steveley, 1984), street crossing (Horner, Jones, and Williams, 1985), vocational behaviors such as table bussing (Horner, Eberhard, and Sheehan, 1986), and circuit board component preparation (Horner and McDonald, 1982). This process emphasizes the role of selecting and sequencing teaching examples so students who complete training perform new behaviors across all appropriate stimulus conditions *and* do not perform these new behaviors in inappropriate stimulus conditions. The focus of general case instruction is on understanding the range of conditions under which a behavior needs to occur as well as the range of similar but inappropriate situations in which the behavior should not occur. Specific guidelines are proposed for selecting and sequencing teaching examples that will result in generalized skills. This emerging technology has clear implications for instructional programming in vocational areas.

The discussion here provides a brief overview of the process of general case programming. Readers interested in this topic are referred to Englemann and Carnine (1982); Horner and McDonald (1982); and Horner, McDonell, and Bellamy (1985) for more thorough discussions.

There are five important steps in building general case programs (Horner, McDonnell, and Bellamy, 1985): (1) defining the instructional universe; (2) selecting teaching and test examples; (3) sequencing teaching examples; (4) teaching; and (5) testing.

1. *Defining the instructional universe.* The first step in general case instruction is to define the set of stimulus conditions across which the target skill should be performed. A student being trained to mop floors may have an instructional universe that includes the floors of all rooms on the third floor of a hospital, or the floors of all classrooms at an elementary school. Each "universe" of instruction defines a set of stimulus conditions within which the student should perform "floor mopping." The instructional universe chosen defines conditions that are functional for the student yet may vary widely as to the range with which the student must work. Defining the instructional universe allows the instructor to specify the functional outcomes of the general case program and provide the detail that will be needed to select training examples.

2. *Selecting teaching and testing examples.* General case training always requires instruction with more than one example so the student may sample the range of relevant stimulus variation. The point is to

develop adaptable skills that will be performed across a range of appropriate situations. It is neither reasonable nor possible to teach a student one or two examples and expect the skills to generalize across a wide range of nontrained situations. General case instruction addresses this problem by teaching with multiple examples.

The first step in selecting the teaching examples is to analyze each response the student must learn. For each response, the stimulus conditions that should control it must be defined. Next, how that stimulus changes across different conditions within the instructional universe must be examined.

A large number of teaching examples is not necessary in order for general case instruction to be successful. Rather, a relatively small number of well-chosen examples will usually suffice to develop a generalized skill. For example, Horner, et al. (1986) taught generalized table bussing with just six types of training examples. The skill of generalized street crossing was taught to students with moderate and severe retardation using twenty examples (Horner, Jones, and Williams, 1985). Generalized crimp-cutting of biaxial circuit board components was taught with only four teaching examples (Horner and McDonald, 1982). Five criteria for selecting examples for instruction can be identified. The first three are provided by Engelmann and Carnine (1982, p. 8). The last two are provided by Horner, Sprague, and Wilcox (1982).

a. The set of positive examples should be similar only with respect to relevant stimuli. Irrelevant stimuli should be as different as possible across examples.

b. The set of positive examples should sample the range of stimulus variations across which the learner is expected to respond (that is, across the instructional universe).

c. A range of negative examples should be included (where appropriate) that are maximally similar to positive examples (e.g., when teaching table bussing skills, the set of examples used included tables that should *not* be bussed (Horner et al., 1986).

d. Select a set of positive examples that include significant exceptions.

c. Select examples that are feasible in terms of cost, time, and location.

Once the set of teaching examples has been selected, the instructor can use the same process to select a set of examples (different from the teaching examples) to test for generalization. These "test" examples will be used at the completion of instruction to determine if the student can perform the skill in new situations.

3. *Sequencing teaching examples.* The sequence in which the teaching examples are presented will affect how the skill generalizes, and the efficiency of instruction. Five suggestions for sequencing have been developed based on recent research:

a. Teach multiple components of a skill within each instructional session.

b. When the entire skill is taught, use multiple examples with individual training sessions. Specifically, do not train one example at a time in an easy-to-hard sequence.

c. Present maximally similar positive and negative examples sequentially so that the student's attention is drawn to how these examples are similar and how they are different.

d. Review examples learned during previous instructional sessions.

e. Teach the general case before teaching exceptions. That is, if there are exceptions to the rule, teach using the regular examples first.

4. *Teaching.* Once the universe for instruction has been defined and the examples for teaching and testing have ben selected, the next step is to begin instruction. Once the examples and the sequence are chosen, the instructor has only to utilize the teaching techniques described previously.

5. *Testing.* The next and final stage for general case instruction calls for testing the student with the set of selected "test" examples. This is to ensure that a generalized skill has, in fact, been learned. The student's performance during training does not ensure generalization competence in novel situations that may arise at a later time. After the student has met the specific training criterion, the instructor must probe for generalized performance with test examples. It is critical to follow success in instruction with test probes under natural performance conditions.

Those situations in which vocational instruction is conducted will vary. The point is that students must develop vocational abilities if working life is to be enhanced. The use of general case instruction can be applied to job settings in which students work in order to build performance that is as generalized as possible given the appropriate criteria.

Generalization of work behavior is an important aspect of competent work performance, but another facet of working life must also be addressed, and that is the maintenance of learned behaviors over time. The next section discusses strategies for promoting learned behavior maintenance.

STRATEGIES FOR PROMOTING MAINTENANCE

The long-term maintenance of learned behavior is a problem frequently cited and rarely managed. While it is clear that persons with disabilities can learn many jobs, all too often those acquired skills are not maintained by example to facilitate new lifestyles (Mank and Horner, 1987; Rusch, Martin, and White, in press; Sowers, Thompson, and Connis, 1979). In normal job settings, a lack of maintenance has been shown to interfere with successful long-term employment (Hill and Wehman, 1983; Sowers, Thompson, and Connis, 1979).

Maintenance is defined as "a stable pattern of responding in the presence of constant stimuli" (Horner, Bellamy, and Colvin, 1984). In considering the problem of maintenance of learned work behaviors it must be assumed that in order to be functional, appropriate work behaviors must be maintained sufficiently to show continued performance over relatively long periods of time without continuous supervision.

Williams and Horner (1984) discuss three classes of variables related to maintenance: training variables, transfer variables, and performance variables. Each of these can be expected to have an impact on the maintenance of learned behaviors.

Training Variables

Training is a process in which an individual learns how to perform certain responses and when those responses should be performed (that is, establishing stimulus control). To some extent, the stimulus control developed during training will be maintained over time as a function of the level or strength of the stimulus control established during training (Engelmann and Carnine, 1982; Haring, Liberty, and White, 1980). Stimulus control must be established and the controlling stimuli must be present in the maintenance environment if maintenance is to occur (Koegel and Rincover, 1977).

Transfer Variables

Transfer variables refer to the procedures used at the end of training to shift stimulus control from stimuli unique to the training setting (e.g., trainer prompts) to stimuli that are available in the performance setting. These procedures involve the gradual removal (fading) of both trainer prompts and the physical presence of the trainer. Positive reinforcers are also thinned to approximate the type, level, and schedule of consequences experienced in the performance setting. Finally, the frequency of opportunity for performing the behavior in question should be adjusted gradually from the initial training levels needed to establish stimulus control to the levels naturally experienced in the performance setting (Koegel and Rincover, 1977).

Performance Variables

Performance variables include those factors related to antecedent and consequent events present in the performance setting. Assuming that adequate stimulus control has been established, behavior cannot be expected to continue without ongoing consequences. Critical to promoting maintenance is determining the type, amount, schedule, and method of delivering positive consequences (Bellamy, Inman, and Yeates, 1978). In addition, more powerful reinforcers for competing or incorrect responses should be absent or minimized.

Wacker and Berg (1986) have suggested three methods for managing the consequences in performance settings: (1) introducing naturally maintaining consequences, (2) intermittent reinforcement, and (3) consequence regulation.

1. *Use naturally maintaining consequences.* Several such strategies are available for promoting maintenance: using consequences in training that are routinely available in work settings; teaching students to engage in behavior that normally receives reinforcement in a given setting; and teaching students to solicit feedback from the natural work environment. Each of these strategies focuses on natural consequences in environments.

2. *Use intermittent reinforcement schedules.* Several other strategies for maintenance focus on the use of reinforcement schedules that are less predictable. These include gradually shifting the available reinforcers from continuous to intermittent, and gradually increasing the amount of time or work that must be completed before reinforcement is available.

3. *Use consequence regulation.* A third category of maintenance strategies is related to consequence regulation. This focus involves procedures to shift from externally provided consequences to self-administered consequences (that is, teaching students to reinforce themselves). Implied in this approach are self-management techniques.

These ideas provide guidelines for strategies to promote long-term maintenance of learned behaviors. Clearly, additional efforts are needed to develop and document variables contributing to maintenance. One set of procedures mentioned in promoting maintenance has shown promise with persons with disabilities—that is, self-management techniques.

Self-Management in Vocational Settings

Self-management refers to an individual's engaging in a response or responses in order to monitor or manage his or her own behavior (Litrownik, 1982). The behaviors included as self-management techniques are many and varied. These include self-assessment, self-recording or self-monitoring, prearranged stimuli or consequences, self-determined reinforcers, self-delivered reinforcers, self-determined and self-delivered punishers, and self-instruction (Mahoney and Thoresen, 1974). Some of these techniques have been used in vocational settings with persons with disabilities.

The Promise of Self-Management Procedures The literature available suggests that self-management techniques may promote independence for students with disabilities. Common points of agreement include:

1. Self-management procedures can be used with a variety of behaviors to promote independence in work settings.

2. Recording systems can be devised that are manageable by students with disabilities. That is, systems have been used to allow persons with disabilities to monitor their own performance.

3. Self-monitoring data can be used to make decisions. Available data show that persons with disabilities can accurately monitor their own performance. While the act of self-monitoring may have an impact on behavior, it also can provide accurate information about performance for teachers or supervisors who are not continuously present.

4. Self-management procedures can reduce dependence on external supervisors. Several studies have shown that their use has resulted in increased independence and decreased reliance on external supervision (Shafer and Brooke, 1984; Zohn and Bornstein, 1980).

Self-Management Techniques A number of self-management techniques have been used in the vocational context with persons with disabilities. These include the following.

Self-monitoring refers to behaviors associated with identifying some aspect of one's own behavior, detecting the occurrences of the behavior, and recording whether or not that behavior has occurred (Kendall and Williams, 1982). It is considered a first step in many self-management interventions. Several research studies have shown the capacity of persons with disabilities to monitor their own behavior (Bornstein and Zohn, 1980; Brooke and Shafer, 1984; Goyos, Michael, and Martin, 1979). These studies suggest two main points. First, work rate increases, at least temporarily, when individuals self-monitor. Second, persons with disabilities can accurately track the occurrences of specified behaviors.

Self-delivered reinforcement refers to the ability of an individual to actually deliver reinforcers to himself or herself, based on a specified criterion for performance. Studies with self-delivered reinforcers suggest that this strategy is at least as effective as externally provided reinforcers (Wehman, 1981; Hanel and Martin, 1980; Horner and Brigham, 1979). In most cases, however, this strategy includes some use of additional reinforcers provided by supervisors. The strategy emphasizes the potential of shifting control for performance from instructors and supervisors to the individual with disabilities.

Antecedent cue regulation refers to teaching individuals to control the cues for performance. For example, small cards with pictures of job tasks have been used by students with disabilities to increase independence in going from task to task within a job (Sowers et al., 1985; Berg and Wacker, 1983). This strategy focuses on having the individual control, from day to day, the stimulus conditions in performance environments. Unlike the former self-management techniques, this approach focuses on the antecedent conditions for performance rather than on the consequences for performance.

Self-instruction is yet another technique that falls under the rubric of self-management. This approach teaches individuals to "coach" themselves through a set of specified behaviors. This strategy can include teaching individuals to ask a question of themselves about what to do next or to state the task that should be performed next. This technique also can include self-delivery of verbal reinforcement for successful completion of tasks (Rusch, Martin, and White, in press).

Self-recruited feedback is another self-management strategy. Self-recruited feedback (Mank and Horner, 1987) refers to individuals self-monitoring work performance, evaluating their work rate against a predefined criterias, and reporting their performance to a supervisor for feedback.

Self-recruited feedback is one example of a procedure that incorporates several self-management techniques, including self-monitoring, self-evaluation of performance, and self-recruitment of feedback from external agents. Mank and Horner (1987) documented a functional relationship between the use of self-recruited feedback and maintenance of jobs such as washing dishes, scrubbing pots and pans, and bussing tables. For example, one student washed dishes in a local restaurant. First, a unit of measure was established for the task. One load of dishes equaled one unit of work. With a unit of work established, it was possible to train the student to self-record the number of units of work completed. The student was given a small counter and then trained to depress the button each time a load of dishes was completed. The student stopped the stopwatch and recorded in a small notebook the number of units completed and the amount of time spent working. These constituted the self-monitoring component of the self-recruited feedback strategy.

Next, the student was taught to evaluate whether or not he had worked fast enough. For the task of washing dishes, a matrix was drawn listing minutes worked on the horizontal axis and units completed on the vertical axis. The cells in the matrix were shaded in to show acceptable work rate vs. a work rate that was too slow. At the end of the work period, the student would line up a ruler with the number of minutes worked and the number of units completed. If the corner of the ruler fell in the shaded areas, the student knew he had worked fast enough on that day and recorded a + (plus) in his notebook. If the corner of the ruler did not fall in the shaded area, the student knew he had not worked fast enough and recorded a − (minus) in his notebook. This portion of the strategy allowed the student with disabilities to evaluate his own performance against a criterion that had been set in conjunction with the restaurant supervisor.

The final component of self-recruited feedback called for the student to approach the supervisor with his notebook and indicate whether or not he had worked "fast" that day. The supervisor differentially praised the student depending on what the student indicated about his performance. This process required little time and effort from the supervisor, yet resulted in improved work rates for students who initially failed to maintain the skills they had learned during instruction.

Self-management strategies demonstrate an important, and exciting, new approach to teaching and supporting vocational skills. First, the antecedent cue regulation and self-instruction strategies provide ways to incorporate self-management into initial instruction in order to give the student methods whereby he or she can manage antecedent units. Second, the strategies that include self-monitoring are a source of information to instructors and supervisors about the performance of the individual when the instructor is not present. Third, self-management strategies offer opportunities for independence by teaching individuals with disabilities to manage some of the consequences of their own behavior, shaping independence rather than ongoing dependence on others.

SUMMARY

The extent to which we are successful in imparting to students information and methods for independence in the vocational area helps define the extent to which students with disabilities will be successful working adults. To fail in instruction is to doom students with disabilities to lives of unnecessary reliance on others. This chapter has provided an overview of current technology in instructional programming. This technology is based on principles of applied behavior analysis, analysis of the requirements of jobs, and basic teaching and behavioral principles. It is buttressed by emerging strategies for generalizing learned behaviors and for maintaining vocational competence in the long term. It is further supported by developing self-management strategies that show great potential for transferring control of ongoing performance to the individual.

The ultimate outcome of vocational education is clear. Students with disabilities must learn the behaviors needed to work successfully in adult life without undue supports.

REFERENCES

Becker, W.C., and S.E. Engelmann. (1978). Systems for basic instruction: Theory and applications. In A. Catania and T. Brigham (eds.), *Handbook of Applied Behavior Analysis: Social and Instructional Processes.* New York: Irvington Publishers.

Bellamy, G.T., R.H. Horner, and D. Inman. (1979). *Vocational Habilitation of Severely Retarded Adults: A Direct Service Technology.* Baltimore: University Park Press.

Bellamy, T., D. Inman, and J. Yeates. (1978). Evaluation of a procedure for production management with the severely retarded, *Journal of the Association for Persons with Severe Handicaps,* 17(1), 37–41.

Berg, W., and D.P. Wacker. (1983) Effects of permanent prompts on the vocational performance of severely handicapped individuals. Unpublished manuscript, University of Iowa, Iowa City.

Buckley, J., D. Sandow, and K. Smock. (in preparation). *Job Analysis for Supported Employment.* Eugene, Ore.: University of Oregon.

Englemann, S., and D. Carnine. (1982). *Theory of Instruction: Principles and Applications.* New York: Irvington Publishers.

Gifford, J.L., F.R. Rusch, J.E. Martin, and D.M. White. (1984). Autonomy and adaptability: A proposed technology for maintaining work behavior. In N. Ellis and N. Bray (eds.), *International Review of Research in Mental Retardation.* Vol. 12. New York: Academic Press. Pp. 285–314.

Gollub, L. (1977). Conditioned reinforcement: Schedule effects. In W. Honig and J. Staddon (eds.), *Handbook of Operant Behavior.* Englewood Cliffs, N.J.: Prentice-Hall.

Goyos, A.C., J.L. Michael, and G.L. Martin. (1979). Self-recording training to teach retarded adults to reinforce work behaviors of retarded clients. *Rehabilitation Psychology,* 26, 215–227.

Hanel, F., and G. Martin. (1980). Self-monitoring, self-administration of token reinforcement, and goal-setting to improve work rates with retarded clients. *International Journal of Rehabilitation Research 3,* 505–517.

Haring, N.G., K.A. Liberty, and O.N. White. (1980). Rules for data-based strategy decisions in instructional programs: Current research and instructional implications. In W. Sailor, B. Wilcox, and L. Brown (eds.), *Methods of Instruction for Severely Handicapped Students.* Baltimore: Paul H. Brookes.

Hill, M., J. Hill, P. Wehman, and D. Banks. (1985). An analysis of monetary and nonmonetary outcomes associated with competitive employment of mentally retarded persons. In P. Wehman and J.W. Hill (eds.), *Competitive Employment for Persons with Mental Retardation.* Richmond, Va.: Virginia Commonwealth University, Rehabilitation Research and Training Center. Pp. 110–133.

Hill, M., and P. Wehman. (1983). Cost benefit analysis of placing moderately and severely handicapped individuals into competitive employment. *The Journal of the Association for the Severely Handicapped 8*(1), 30–39.

Horner, R.H., and G.T. Bellamy. (1983). *The Transition to Integrated Neighborhoods Project.* U.S. Department of Education, Grant Ho. 1-963001786-A8. Eugene, Or.: University of Oregon Center on Human Development, Specialized Training Program.

Horner, R.H., G.T. Bellamy, and G.T. Colvin. (1984) Responding in the presence of nontrained stimuli: Implications of generalization error patterns. *Journal of the Association for Persons with Severe Handicaps 9*, 287–296.

Horner, R.H., and T.A. Brigham. (1979). Self management and on-task behavior in two retarded children. *Education and Training of the Mentally Retarded 14*, 18–24.

Horner, R.H., J. Eberhard, and M.R. Sheehan. (1986). Generalization of table bussing skills with moderately and severely retarded adolescents. *Behavior Modification, 10*, 457–471.

Horner, R.H., D. Jones, and J.A. Williams. (1985). Teaching generalized street crossing to individuals with moderate and severe mental retardation. *Journal of the Association for Persons with Severe Handicaps 10*, 71–78.

Horner, R.H., and R.S. McDonald. (1982). A comparison of single instance and general case instruction in teaching a generalized vocational skills. *The Journal of the Association for the Severely Handicapped 7*, 7–20.

Horner, R.H., J.J. McDonnell, and G.T. Bellamy. (1985). Teaching generalized behaviors: General case instruction in simulation and community settings. In R.H. Horner, L.H. Meyer, and H.D. Fredericks (eds.), *Education of Learners with Severe Handicaps: Exemplary Service Strategies.* Baltimore: Paul H. Brookes.

Horner, R.H., J. Sprague, and B. Wilcox. (1982). General case programming for community activities. In B. Wilcox and G.T. Bellamy (eds.), *Design of High School for Severely Handicapped Students.* Baltimore: Paul H. Brookes. Pp. 61–98.

Horner, R.H., J.A. Williams, and J.D. Steveley. (1984). *Acquisition of Generalized Telephone Use by Students with Severe Mental Retardation.* Submitted to *Applied Research in Mental Retardation.*

Johnston, J.M., and H.S. Pennypacker. (1980). *Strategies and Tactics of Human Behavioral Research.* New Jersey: Lawrence Erlbaum Associates.

Kazdin, A. (1980). *Behavior Modification in Applied Settings.* Homewood, Ill.: Dorsey Press.

Kendall, P.C., and L.L. Williams. (1982). Assessing the cognitive and behavioral components of children's self-management. In P. Karoly and F.H. Kanfer (eds.), *Self-management and Behavior Change: From Theory to Practice.* New York: Pergamon Press. Pp. 24–284.

Koegel, R.L., and A. Rincover. (1977). Research on the differences between generalization and maintenance in extra-therapy responding. *Journal of Applied Behavior Analysis 10*, 1–12.

Litrownik, A.J. (1982). Special considerations in the self-management training of the developmentally disabled. In P. Karoly and F.H. Kanfer (eds.), *Self-management and Behavior Change: From Theory to Practice.* New York: Pergamon Press. Pp. 315–352.

Mahoney, M.J., and C.E. Thoresen. (Eds.). (1974). *Self-control: Power to the Person.* Monterey, Calif.: Brooks/Cole.

Mank, D.M., and R.H. Horner. (1987). Self-recruited feedback: A cost-effective procedure for maintaining behavior. Research in Developmental Disabilities, 8(1), 91–112.

Pancsofar, E.L., and P. Bates. (in press). The impact of the acquisition of successive training exemplars on generalization by students with severe handicaps. *The Journal of the Association for the Severely Handicapped.*

Popovich, D. (1981). *Effective Educational and Behavioral Programming for Severely and Profoundly Handicapped Students.* Reston, Va.: The Council for Exceptional Children.

Rosine, L.P.C., and G.L. Martin. (1983). Self-management training to decrease undesirable behavior of mentally retarded adults. *Rehabilitation Psychology 28,* 195–205.

Rusch, F.R., J.E. Martin, and D.M. White. (in press). Competitive employment: Teaching mentally retarded employees to maintain their work behaviors. *Education and Training of the Mentally Retarded.*

Rusch, F., and D. Mithaug. (1980). *Vocational Training for Mentally Retarded Adults: A Behavior Analytic Approach.* Champaign, Ill.: Research Press.

Saunders, R., and K. Koplik. (1975). A multi-purpose data sheet for recording and graphing in the classroom. *AAESPH Review 1,* 1–8.

Schoenfeld, W.N. and J. Farmer. (1970). Reinforcement schedules and the "Behavior Stream." In W.M. Schoenfeld (ed.), *The Theory of Reinforcement Schedules.* New York: Appleton-Century-Crofts. Pp. 215–246.

Shafer, M.S., and V. Brooke. (1984). The development of punctuality in a mentally retarded worker through self-recording. Unpublished manuscript, Virginia Commonwealth University, Rehabilitation Research and Training Center, Richmond.

Sowers, J., L. Thompson, and R. Connis. (1979). The food service vocational training program. In G.T. Bellamy, G. O'Connor, and O. Karan (eds.), *Vocational Rehabilitation of Severely Handicapped Persons: Contemporary Service Strategies.* Baltimore: University Park Press.

Sowers, J., M. Verdi, P. Bourbeau, and M. Sheehan. (1985). Teaching job independence and flexibility to mentally retarded students through the use of a self-control package. *Journal of Applied Behavior Analysis 18,* 81–86.

Sprague, J.R., and R.H. Horner. (1984). The effects of single instance, multiple instance and general case training on generalized vending machine use by moderately and severely handicapped students. *Journal of Applied Behavior Analysis 17(2),* 273–278.

Stokes, T.F., and D.M. Baer. (1977). An implicit technology of generalization. *Journal of Applied Behavior Analysis 10,* 349–367.

Wacker, D.P., and W. Berg. (1986). Generalizing and maintaining work behavior. In F. Rusch (ed.), *Competitive Employment Issues and Strategies.* Baltimore: Paul H. Brookes. Pp. 129–140.

Wehman, P. (1981). *Competitive Employment: New Horizons for Severely Disabled Individuals.* Baltimore: Paul H. Brookes.

Wilcox, B., and G.T. Bellamy. (1982). *Design of High School Programs for Severely Handicapped Students.* Baltimore: Paul H. Brookes. Pp. 1–60.

Williams, J.D., and R.H. Horner. (1984). Variables related to maintenance with persons with severe handicaps. Unpublished manuscript, University of Oregon, Center on Human Development, Eugene.

Zohn, J.G., and D.H. Bornstein. (1980). Self-management of work performance with mentally retarded adults: Effect upon work productivity, work quality and on-task behavior. *Mental Retardation 18*, 19–24.

7

Secondary Vocational Training

Robert Gaylord-Ross, Shepherd Siegel,
Hyun Sook Park, and William Wilson
San Francisco State University

During recent years the career/vocational education field for persons with handicaps has grown. Its initial appearance in the 1960s was given impetus by Kenneth Hoyt, Donn Brolin, and Gary Clark. Career education originally focused on students with mild and moderate handicaps. In the past five years, however, an increasing emphasis has been given to the vocational education and employment of persons with severe handicaps. Central to this movement has been the notion of transition from school to work. Although adult employment and transition are newly emerging fields, vocational education at the secondary level has benefited from a lengthy service and research effort. In fact, when the notion of career/vocational education arises, one is likely to think of some kind of craft training or work experience at the high school level. Unfortunately, relatively few advances have been made in career education at the primary level (Clark, 1979).

In this chapter, different kinds of program models for secondary vocational training are examined. Separate analyses are made of programs for students with mild and severe handicaps—the two populations for whom most program efforts have been advanced. There should be implications from these models for students with other disabilities, such as sensory and physical impairments. Before describing the program models, though, the conceptual and policy developments in secondary vocational training are discussed.

POLICY AND VOCATIONAL EDUCATION

Vocational training in the secondary years is predicated on the assumption that it is possible for the student to obtain employment as an adult. In the past, the potential for employment was not a given for most persons with handicaps. Society conceived the adult years as a time when the handicapped person would live in a residence, possibly attend a day program, and enjoy recreational and other activities in the community. With advances in instructional technology and increasing demonstrations of the abilities of persons with handicaps, the potential for work became more evident. Once this potential for work became culturally accepted, a substantial effort for vocational preparation began. Since the secondary years were contiguous with the beginning of the adult years, it made more sense to focus training efforts here. Since work is valued in our culture, and once the potential for work by handicapped persons was accepted, a whole host of policy developments appeared to facilitate the vocational training of persons with handicaps.

FEDERAL LAWS AND PROGRAM IMPLICATIONS

Figure 7-1 illustrates the federal laws influencing vocational special education. It is important to recognize that both P.L.94-142, the Education for All Handicapped Children Act, and P.L.98-524, the Carl D. Perkins Vocational Education Act, are amendments to earlier legislation. The original legislation for these amendments was the Education of the Handicapped Act (P.L.91-230) and the Vocational Education Act (P.L.88-210) respectively. P.L.94-142 primarily amended Part B (the state grant program) of the Education of the Handicapped Act, while various sections of P.L.98-524 expanded the opportunities available to handicapped people in the Vocational Education Act.

The most recent amendments to the Education of the Handicapped Act are included in P.L.98-199. These amendments provide for grants and contracts to be awarded by the federal government for training, research, and demonstration in the areas of secondary education and transition for handicapped individuals. P.L.98-199 extends the case for secondary vocational education and authorizes appropriations; however, the legal mandates for direct service to handicapped individuals are still found in the state plan provisions of both P.L.94-192 and P.L.98-524. Both laws require the state to submit a plan that must be approved by the U.S. Department of Education before dollars are allocated to the state. The state must provide assurances that it will properly assess and develop appropriate individual education programs for those individuals who

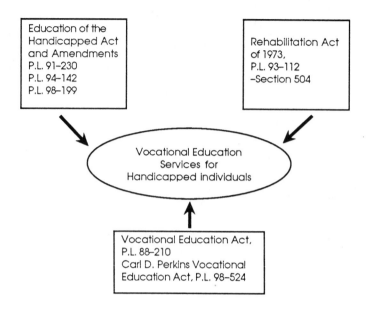

Figure 7.1   Federal Laws Influencing Vocational Education
for the Handicapped

will receive services. This is the legal basis upon which all handicapped individuals receiving vocational education services have the right to an appropriate and complete program.

Although many school districts throughout the nation have yet to fully develop programs that comply with these mandates, the service and assessment provisions of P.L.98-524, the state plan provisions of P.L.94-142, and section 504 of the Rehabilitation Act state that individuals with disabilities are entitled to participate in any vocational education program funded through the Vocational Education Act. This right is affirmed in section 2(2) of P. L. 98-524, which states that one of the purposes of the act

> is to assure that individuals who are inadequately served under vocational education programs are assured access to quality vocational educational programs, especially individuals who are disadvantaged, who are handicapped (1984).

Comparing the language of this provision with section 504 shows that the Rehabilitation Act of 1973, which was concerned with the civil rights of handicapped individuals, was a foundation upon which amendments to existing legislation were based.

Section 201 of P.L.98-524 continues the theme of service provision to handicapped persons. It requires, through subsection (c), that states receiving federal funds for vocational education programs use a portion of those funds (10 percent) to meet the special needs of handicapped individuals participating in vocational education programs. This 10 percent of the state's federal allocation must be spent specifically for supplemental or additional staff, equipment, materials, or services needed to meet the special needs of this population. Special and vocational educators refer to this as the "10 percent set aside" (as specified in section 202).

These funds have been responsible for states beginning to initiate programs for handicapped individuals within vocational education. Certainly the cost may go beyond 10 percent of the federal share. If so, the state and local jurisdictions are responsible for the funding. P.L.94-142 funds may also be used for vocational activities as stated in the student's individual education program. Figure 7-2 presents a model for a state's plan for a sequence of vocational activities.

Vocational Education Opportunities

Program planners should keep in mind that regardless of funding, all handicapped individuals may by law participate in vocational education, and according to section 504 of the Rehabilitation Act, cannot be denied the right to participate on the basis of their handicap. The underlying principles of both P.L.94-142 and section 504 indicate that handicapped individuals should be afforded the same basic educational opportunities and rights as nonhandicapped individuals in federal vocational educational programs. Thus, handicapped individuals have the right to participate in basic as well as specialized programs. Handicapped individuals cannot be excluded from the following opportunities on the basis of their handicapping condition: the Job Training Partnership Act; vocational education programs for training or retraining adults, including programs for older individuals and displaced homemakers; programs that require school facilities to stay open longer; community-based activities; child-care assistance; support services; and contracts with vocational training institutions. In addition, handicapped individuals participating in vocational education programs are entitled to participate in on-site work programs such as cooperative vocational education, work-study, and apprenticeship programs. Federal dollars allotted under the Vocational Education Act may also be spent for placement activities for handicapped individuals who have completed vocational education programs. This is an important funding allowance in that a number of activities, all of which are high cost items, are necessary in order for placement to be successful.

```
┌─────────────────────────────────────────────────────────────┐
│           STATE PLAN FOR VOCATIONAL EDUCATION                 │
│                                                               │
│      —Must assure handicapped persons equal access to:        │
│                                                               │
│                      1.    Recruitment                        │
│         STATE        2.    Enrollment                         │
│                      3.    Placement                          │
│                      4.    Services                           │
│                                                               │
│              FEDERAL APPROVAL OF STATE PLAN                    │
│                                                               │
│              STATE LEVEL IMPLEMENTATION OF PLAN               │
│  ───────────────────────────────────────────────────────     │
│                                                               │
│                    LOCAL IMPLEMENTATION                       │
│                                                               │
│              IEP DEVELOPMENT ASSESSMENT                       │
│                  Goals,                                        │
│                  Objectives                                   │
│                  Services                                     │
│                  Evaluation                                   │
│                                                               │
│         LOCAL    SPECIAL SERVICES            LEAST            │
│                  Counseling                  RESTRICTIVE      │
│                  Curriculum adaptation   ENVIRONMENT         │
│                  Adaptive equipment                          │
│                  Career Opportunities                        │
│                                                               │
│                  PLACEMENT                                    │
│                  School                                      │
│                  Off-Campus Training Site                    │
│                                                               │
│              POSTTRAINING JOB PLACEMENT                       │
└─────────────────────────────────────────────────────────────┘
```

Figure 7.2 Sequence of Activities Within P.L. 98-524 Pertaining to Handicapped Individuals

Least Restrictive Environment

Special educators often refer to a full range of services as a continuum, and vocational education services for handicapped individuals may be viewed in this way. Section 204 (of P.L.98-524) requires that all services within the continuum be provided in the least restrictive environment and be included as a component of the individual education program, when appropriate. For the secondary education student the least restrictive environment may well be a community work training setting. Placing handicapped individuals side by side with nondisabled individuals in community training sites in supported employment programs and in competitive employment illustrates the intention of the least restrictive environment language in the various laws. Vocational education programs that maintain the least restrictive alternative will willingly choose to integrate both programs as well as students. Progressive programs will not allow segregated facilities where handicapped individuals are placed only with other handicapped individuals for training or to complete sheltered contract work.

Likewise, the secondary classroom setting where training is to take place should be situated on a regular school campus. The regular vocational educational program should be accessible to handicapped individuals who can participate. This may require modifying the vocational and technical program so as to allow their participation. If supportive aides, special equipment, and special instruction are necessary in order for handicapped individuals to participate, funds from either P.L.94-142 or P.L.98-524 may be utilized for these purposes.

Most handicapped individuals may participate in the regular or modified vocational education program, but severely handicapped individuals may require special classrooms and facilities. Such programs should be integrated—that is, located on the regular school campus, with participants having access to all regular campus programs. Programs that fail to integrate limit the person's potential and are in conflict with section 504 of the Rehabilitation Act (P.L.94-142), as well as section 204 (a)(3)(A) of the Carl Perkins Act, which states that:

> vocational education programs and activities for handicapped individuals will be provided in the least restrictive environment in accordance with section 612(4) and section 614(a)(5) of such Act. (1984)

Individualized Education Programs

In addition to providing services within the least restrictive environment, section 204 of P.L.98-524 requires that whenever appropriate, vocational education services should be provided to handicapped individuals as part of the individualized educational plan, in accordance with procedures in P.L.94-142. When developing the IEP, an adequate vocational assessment is first needed. Once the assessment has been completed, a meeting should be held to formulate objectives and activities. In many cases it is appropriate and helpful to include the secondary student in the meeting. Other key individuals to be included are vocational and special education personnel, parents, a school official who is responsible for providing or supervising services, and any persons knowledgeable of the student's assessment results. Many manuals on the IEP process are available to the reader (NASDE, 1976; HEW, 1978). However, IEPs reviewed by author Wilson during federal monitoring site visits to states in 1980 and 1981 seldom included vocationally oriented objectives, results of vocational assessments, or evidence that secondary students had been included in the IEP meeting. Apparently, more in-service for educators is needed to ensure that vocational education is included in the student's program. After an appropriate vocational program is developed, parents should be kept informed of the progress the student is making. An annual meeting to update or amend any services is required. The meeting provides a formal time for evaluating the goals and objectives that have been set for the student as well as an opportunity to reassess the strengths and weakness of the individual's skills in both vocational and related areas.

Program Implemen-tation

The vast majority of vocational special education programs are still in the process of creating new and effective vocational services for handi-capped youth out of previous systems that were less than ideal for nonhandicapped students. Prior to the federal initiative (Will, 1984), vocational education services seemed designed for two distinctly different types of students. The first was the student who would fail in the regular high school college preparatory curriculum. The second was the student with a high aptitude for technical skills who could meet entrance requirements for technical vocational schools. Vocational education for handicapped students usually meant prevocational, segregated training leading to sheltered workshop-type activities. Students with less severe handicaps, but those who could not participate in regular vocational education programs, were often systematically excluded from vocational education because they could not meet entrance requirements.

Under the mandate of P.L.94-142, some school districts chose to develop a continuum of vocational services for handicapped youth on a voluntary basis, while others did so only after compliance visits from the U.S. Department of Education. Few compliance reviews during the first five years of implementation examined vocational education issues other than the one requiring that 10 percent of the vocational education funds be spent on programs for handicapped individuals. During the late 1970s, identification, assessment, IEP development, due process, and basic service provisions were the major issues.

Prerequisite to effective vocational special education services is cooperative or interagency planning among various service providers. As long as there are different agencies with overlapping responsibilities, there will be a need for planning before service is implemented. When adequate planning is completed, an adequate service system should follow.

In presenting only a basic framework for the provision of vocational special education, the federal government has made it clear that states and local systems may choose a variety of ways to implement the requirements of the various federal laws. Leaders in vocational education have begun to implement these requirements with a great deal of enthusiasm. Research continues in both the special education and vocational education field. New programs, such as those described in other parts of this chapter, are the result of educators' endorsing the applicable federal laws in spirit as well as meeting their required minimum standards. For full program implementation to occur, however, consumers, parents, and professionals will have to insist that state and local systems provide opportunities for handicapped students in vocational education.

SECONDARY VOCATIONAL TRAINING FOR STUDENTS WITH MILD HANDICAPS

Probably the greatest amount of effort in vocational education at the secondary level has been put into working with students with mild handicaps. This might be due to the fact that some students could be mainstreamed into existing occupational training and work experience courses that had been set up for regular education students. Also, new work experience programs, which followed regular education models, were sometimes developed for handicapped students.

This section describes two aspects of vocational education. One aspect deals with vocational preparation, or the skill training needed for particular employment opportunities. The second aspect deals with career counseling and affective education. Here, the role of employment is one important piece of the individual's personal growth. Thus, a comprehensive vocational education provides both essential components. Career counseling without specific job training may result in an aware but unemployable youth. Vocational skill training without career counseling may get the student a particular job, but he or she may have no insight into long-term career development and interests.

A Functional Curriculum Model

The mildly handicapped student participates in the regular academic curriculum throughout his school years. Yet, as the student moves from the primary to secondary years, there should be a relative deemphasis on pure academics and a shift to a functional, life skills curriculum (Brolin, 1982). The curriculum should prepare the student for adult community living. There should be a major emphasis on work skill training, but there should also be education in the areas of residential living, social skills, affective development, and so on.

The Adult Performance Level Survey (University of Texas, 1977) identifies five major life skills that are comprehensive and emphasize areas appropriate to the mildly handicapped person. These are:

1. Community Resources: understanding how to use transportation systems, public agencies and services, recreation and entertainment, and informational resources.

2. Occupational Knowledge: which increases awareness of job opportunities and job skills.

3. Consumer Economics: knowing how to manage a family economy and demonstrating an understanding of sound purchasing practices; budget planning; effective use of money, money substitutes, and financial services; principles of consumerism, economic factors involved in maintaining consumer goods, and a consumer's understanding of marketing techniques.

4. Mental and Physical Health: understanding the principles and practices that lead to good mental and physical health; knowing where, when, and why to seek medical help; personal habits that promote good health; applying principles of health to planning and raising a family; and dealing with potential hazards and accidents.

5. Government and Law: understanding how the structures of government and the functions of the legal system delineate rights and obligations; the structure and functioning of the federal government; the relationship between individual citizens and the selection and maintenance of government; the relationship between individual citizens and the legal and penal systems; and the relationship between individual citizens and government services.

Each of these five skills is significantly important for the successful transition and community adjustment of mildly handicapped students. Unfortunately, Occupational Knowledge is often treated as the sole component of career education. From the time students are in their teens, teachers should plan for the achievement of competency in all five areas. Academic tasks can be keyed to these life skills and can be included in the student's IEP. Progress in all life skills should be monitored and coordinated from year to year so that competency is reached by the time students graduate from high school.

A Sequence for Career Education Activities

In the following sections a sequence is described for career education activities for mildly handicapped students. Although this chapter focuses on secondary training, middle school activities are described because of their preconditional relationship with secondary school. Also, the first steps in postsecondary career education are described in the transitional phase activities.

Middle School The middle school years are transition years from primary school, where students should have been made aware of occupations, (Clark, 1979) to high school, where they begin to get some direct experiences with vocations. Career awareness activities should continue in the middle school. Successful adults from the same racial, ethnic, or handicap group should be invited to speak to the students about how they succeeded and what obstacles they had to overcome. Students should be encouraged to read materials about the type of work and experiences that different kinds of vocations entail. The school counselor can begin to discuss curriculum options available in high school and long-term career plans. The total career awareness process continues from primary school through secondary school. At the middle or secondary level, a typical career awareness activity is job fairs, where employers display booths or give lectures about employment opportunities in their occupational fields.

Middle school is a time when mildly handicapped students can begin to have direct experiences with work activities. Career exploration entails having students experiencing a job firsthand. Students may take a field trip, for instance, to a factory to see how cars are made and to observe what assembly-line workers do. Or students may experience *job shadowing* in which a single student goes to a work site and is paired with a particular worker. Throughout the day the student follows, or shadows, the worker. For example, the student may shadow a carpenter who is remodeling a house. The student would get the feel of the job, observe what specific skills are needed, and have a role-modeling experience with an adult. Career exploration activities should continue at the secondary level, but the mildly handicapped student should have at least one job shadowing experience per year in the middle school.

The middle school should also be a time when general work behaviors can be developed. Numerous surveys of employers have pointed out their need for workers with good general work habits and attitudes. While employers are willing to teach the new employee the specific job skills needed, they view the school's primary job as providing a pool of employees with fine work attitudes and habits. These general work behaviors include skills in: attendance, punctuality, following directions, stamina, accuracy, and getting along with coworkers. These general work behaviors should apply to just about any job. During middle school is a fine time to begin training on general work behaviors; during the secondary years, training continues at an even more intense level.

During the middle school, IEP goals may relate not only to learning new tasks, but also to producing already learned tasks at an acceptable rate and for a reasonable duration. Many students with handicaps are pampered at home and at school, so they do not have the stamina to work for consecutive hours or for a complete workday. Thus, duration, rate, and accuracy are important general work skills that can be targeted for instruction in the middle school.

Middle School (11–14)	Secondary School (15–18)	Transition to Adulthood (18–22)
Career awareness	Career awareness	Job placement
Career exploration	Career exploration	Job-keeping skills
Production rate, stamina, and accuracy	Career counseling	Job search skills
	Work experiences	Transition plan and services
Working in group	Job-keeping skills	Family involvement
Consumer economics	Occupational courses	Continuing education
Health education	Law and government	Community resources
Academic remediation	Health education	
	Consumer economics	
	Community resources	
	Family involvement	
	Academic remediation	

Figure 7.3 The Phases and Curriculum Components of Secondary Vocational Training for Mildly Handicapped Youth

Figure 7-3 presents a listing of the other career education activities that can be addressed in the middle school. Although they will not be elaborated upon here, it should be pointed out that health education needs to carefully address the issue of narcotics use. Many mildly handicapped youth are poor and live in crime-ridden neighborhoods. The school has increasingly taken on the responsibility of making students aware of the pitfalls of narcotics. Unfortunately, the role models of drug pushers may compete with appropriate models for the attention and affection of these youth. An effective career education program should provide information and offer a variety of viable role models for the student. This activity may begin in the middle school (or primary) years but will certainly continue into the secondary years.

Secondary Career Education

For mildly handicapped youth, secondary career education will branch into three coordinated segments: career counseling, occupational training, and work experience.

Career Counseling Career awareness and career exploration activities will heighten the awareness and knowledge of the mildly handicapped youth. In addition, however, there needs to be intensive career counseling experiences during the secondary years. The career counselor should be pooling vocational assessment information related to the interests and abilities of the student. There should be discussions about the type of occupation the student might select. The counselor also needs to make the student aware of the type of businesses present in that community region, as well as the type of vocational training courses offered at the high school. In the career selection process, the parents should become active participants. Parents may want the student to continue postsecondary training at a community college. The premature tracking of a student in a specific career might meet family resistance and be undermined.

Career counseling must also address the affective development of the student. Many mildly handicapped students drop out of high school or are terminated from jobs because of personality and behavioral problems. The career counselor or the school psychologist may counsel the student concerning emotional disturbances. The counselor may develop support groups for group counseling. Specific behavior problems at school or in the community may be targeted for behavior modification. Social skill deficits may be remediated through role-playing exercises.

Career counseling is an important component of secondary vocational training. Too often, because of decreased funding, not enough counseling services are provided. However, when they are needed, it is important to include counseling services in the student's IEP.

Occupational Training Fortunately, a good deal of money has been allocated for equipment and instructors in vocational education. Many high schools attended by mildly handicapped students have occupational training programs in: automotive mechanics, computer operation, electronics, graphics, and so on. Considerable program development in recent years has allowed handicapped students to participate in these occupational course offerings.

For example, Gary Moe and David Craft have developed an exemplary resource specialist program at Richmond High School in Richmond, California. The school has numerous occupational training courses and programs of study. Moe and Craft have mainstreamed a large number of mildly handicapped students into these courses, while resource specialists modify the occupational class curriculum as necessary. The regular education teacher in the classroom assists the student in both academic and social areas. The resource specialist not only helps the individual handicapped student, but also assists the regular education teacher with instructional activities for all the students. In this way the regular education teacher is less likely to view the handicapped student as an unwanted addition to an already heavy teaching load. The Richmond High School program serves over 150 handicapped students per year. Many of the handicapped and nonhandicapped students travel from surrounding high schools in the large urban school district to enroll in the occupational education courses. The mainstreaming of mildly handicapped students into occupational training courses at high schools, vocational technical centers, and community colleges is an option that should be actively explored.

Work Experience The mildly handicapped student in secondary vocational training engages in one or more work experiences at a real work site. Although vocational educational courses can teach specific occupational skills, they cannot simulate the work climate of a real factory or office. The best place to teach a student the various general work behaviors required for employment is in actual work settings. General work behaviors can be taught in school contexts, but it is questionable whether the handicapped student could transfer these behaviors to a job setting. In contrast, all work settings have certain environmental similarities that contrast with school settings. For example, those present are all adults; there are serious production demands; stringent academic tasks like those in school usually do not exist. Also, when students have a work experience in the same type of business in which they will be ultimately employed (e.g., a factory), the similarities between the training setting and the ultimate work setting are plentiful and a transfer or generalization of work behaviors across the two settings will likely occur.

Thus, in terms of learning and generalization, the advantages of on-the-job work experiences should be evident. A school cannot simulate an office or a factor. Also, many mildly handicapped students have come to associate school with a series of failures in academic tasks. When they get to a work setting they are often more motivated because they sense they are in the real, adult world. In addition, they often learn to successfully perform nonacademic work tasks. Thus, they feel competent as they become part of the adult world. Creative teachers, furthermore, can often take advantage of this heightened motivation in the work setting by introducing academic tasks in the nonschool setting. For example, mathematical calculations may need to be done in a laboratory. Passages of information may have to be accurately read in an office. Thus, work experiences do not necessarily mean a break from academic activities. The latter can sometimes be best taught in the motivating context of work.

Project Workability is an example of an effective work experience program. It is a statewide program that was developed by Gail Zittel in California, and presently serves 150 school districts throughout the state. A student is individually placed at a work site for three to ten months. The student goes to that site three to five days a week, working twelve to twenty hours per week. He or she works as a regular employee and is paid at least the minimum wage of $3.35 per hour. The positions vary from stock clerks, to cashiers, to food service workers, to manual laborers. A work experience is primarily a training experience, and it is possible for students to have two or three different work experiences during their high school years. In some cases, the work experience results in a permanent position with the employer where training occurred. For example, the student might have been a clerical assistant in a pharmaceutical company between February and June of his senior year.

The work experience may have been so successful that the employer decides to hire the student upon graduation as a regular employee.

Work experiences can be invaluable training grounds and introduce the person into the world of work. The student may also learn what he or she does *not* wish to do. For example, she might have done well at a work experience in a factory but decides she would really like to work in an office. She might also decide that she would like to receive more higher education and not work immediately after graduation. A whole range of things can be learned outside the classroom in real work sites.

Transition to Work and Adulthood

The period of transition to adulthood is receiving increasing attention from special educators and rehabilitation counselors. Those guaranteed educational services for school-aged, handicapped persons are not available for adults. Cessation of services and high unemployment rates have led many people to call for an emphasis on programming for the transition from school to adulthood. Such programming may take the form of career counselors working with the student to identify a particular occupation and a specific place to live upon graduation. It may entail the delineation of an individualized transition plan, which lists goals and activities to ensure a successful transition. It may involve a specific job-training program that secures permanent employment for the student after graduation.

The Community Vocational Training Program in the San Francisco Unified School District (Siegel, et al., 1986) is an example of an effective transition program for students with mild handicaps. In this program, students are identified in their senior year of high school to be trained at one of two work sites in the community. One work site is the large office building of California Automobile Association of America. Here, the student is trained in clerical skills such as filing, typing, and message delivery. At each site, a community classroom model is set up (Gaylord-Ross, Forte, and Gaylord-Ross, 1986) where an instructor works with a group of six students. The instructor teaches the students the specific job tasks involved in being, for example, a clerical assistant. The instructor also teaches general work behaviors. The students go to the work sites four days a week, in the afternoon, for three to four hours. Initially, the instructor works in close proximity with the students, carefully supervising them. As the four-month training period progresses, the student moves more independently throughout different parts of the work site. The instructor gradually turns supervision over to the coworkers. Thus, the artificial supervision of the instructor is transferred to the natural supervision of the employer.

Employers have agreed to hire students who meet their standards for employment. Thus, not every student is automatically hired. Yet, the transition program provides a direct connection between school and business that increases the chances of permanent employment for the participants. Also, some students are counseled into other, more appropriate positions.

On the fifth day of training the twelve students from the two work sites meet in the afternoon at a school for career development sessions. At this time instructors lead discussions about what the students did at the workplace during the previous week. The discussions are keyed around task performance and general work behaviors, with a particular emphasis given to social relations with coworkers. In addition, a social skills training program is used, where students rehearse a variety of social interactions that may appear at the workplace, such as socializing at break time or disagreeing with a supervisor. Thus, the discussions and role plays are keyed to job-keeping skills at the work site, with the hope that these social behaviors will generalize to future work sites.

Finally, the career development sessions work on job-seeking skills. The Azrin and Besalel (1980) job club technique is taught so that students can generate potential jobs through contacting businesses, family, and friends. Role-playing interactions for job-interviewing techniques are rehearsed. Also, students write their own resumes. The hope is that students will obtain a permanent job at their respective work sites, but if they are not able to or do not wish to, they are directed to seek employment or continuing education elsewhere. The job search skills may generalize to the future, so that students who have left the program will be able to find a job in later years.

SUMMARY

A model has been presented for the secondary vocational training of mildly handicapped students. Figure 7-3 summarizes this model by listing the curricular components of the middle school, secondary, and transition phases. This career education curriculum emphasizes life skills, career counseling, occupational training, work experience, general work behavior, and job search skills. A functional approach to curriculum generation is used as the emphasis on academic remediation is gradually reduced during the secondary years.

CASE STUDY: JJ

JJ is a youngster who has faced some difficult life events, ranging from his own premature birth to the sudden death of his father. Though hindered by vision and learning problems, as well as difficult and sometimes violent surroundings, JJ has managed to plot a course for his life that now includes full-time employment and a nurturing family life. In fact, though vocational and special education services played a role, a glimpse at some of his life events shows how decisive a supportive family and early participation in community activities can be for successful career development.

JJ was born prematurely due to a fall by his pregnant mother, Alicia. Learning problems and low test scores were attributed to this fall. JJ's parents separated when he was 5 years old. He lived in a tough neighborhood in a large city and learned quickly to fight back when bullied. He also showed an early interest in books and reading, partly because he did not want or get the type of play experiences offered in his neighborhood. In elementary school, JJ preferred to get to know the teachers rather than his peers. He received certificates for his shop projects and made the honor roll. He was bused to a distant school as part of a mandated integration plan. There, toward the end of the fifth grade, he was first referred to a special education program. Though he was behind in reading and arithmetic, the referral was actually prompted by behavioral incidents in which JJ was distracted by the antics of another boy sitting near him.

He responded well to the resource rooms at his elementary and middle schools. That is, he liked the extra attention and perceived himself as working hard, but his performance remained at least two years below grade level. Though academic learning was a frustrating problem, and would continue to be throughout JJ's school career, he was supported in the formation of a positive and purposeful attitude towards school. His mother would remind him and his brother and sister: "You better do well in school. I can only carry you for so long, and then you have to carry yourself." JJ thus learned to value his education at an early age, and also to apply common sense to decisions in his daily life. In his own words: "Look and listen, see what people say. . . by lookin' on the streets, you get to know what's right and what's wrong. . . if you go wrong, you never know where you're gonna end up at." Even though school was difficult, and the temptations of truancy were great, seeing another classmate fail a class was enough to convince JJ to stick with it.

JJ's brother, who was two years older, had verbal behaviors that earned him a negative reputation in the neighborhood, and this made JJ subject to harassment by other boys. His friend Kirk offered JJ activities that were alternatives to hanging out on the streets: building model race cars and boats, and drawing, which has since become a major interest and hobby of JJ's. JJ's mother was very supportive of his relationship with Kirk, and the two young men are still friends today.

Other activities helped JJ maintain a positive outlook on his future and develop a socially supportive network around himself, even though he was described as being shy and a loner during the middle school years. These networks included participation in basketball and drama programs at the local YMCA, art, recreation leadership for younger children, games and sports at his neighborhood community center, and membership in the Boy Scouts.

School activities during this period were less rewarding. Today, JJ's mother attributes these difficulties to the fact that JJ had a learning disability, and would not learn academics as quickly as other students. But she also feels very strongly that he was not receiving the best education possible, and that the school could have done a better job of teaching. She had always supported and actively participated in the educational choices made at the school, that is, referral to special education, repeating the fifth grade. Yet, frustration with his slow progress culminated in an initial refusal to sign his seventh-grade IEP. She demanded that his instruction in measurement and reading improve. Feeling somewhat powerless, she eventually relented and signed, figuring that what was offered was "better than nothing."

Some of the difficulty of the period centered around JJ's need to pass exams and the anxiety related to taking them. He needed to memorize his multiplication tables before he could graduate from the fifth grade. His repetition of that grade led to his first of many efforts to advance academically through extra study sessions at home. His mother supported, encouraged, and occasionally demanded the extra work from JJ. She enrolled herself in an adult school algebra class so that she could help JJ with his math assignments.

The high school stage of JJ's academic career continued to present hurdles. His awareness of the need to pass the high school proficiency exam, combined with low grades—JJ was not to receive a grade above a C until the eleventh grade—compounded his problems. Through the counseling efforts of his resource room teacher, JJ was able to persevere. On his third effort, and with differential standards applied, he passed his high school proficiency exam.

JJ had shown definite talent as an artist and woodworker, and he began his freshman year with a shop class—but he lost his eyeglasses that semester and could not see the blackboard in the woodshop. Later he had an accident where he cut his fingers on a table saw, which curtailed woodshop activities in school. It was not until his junior year in high school that JJ enrolled in an art class—and got A's and B's.

Another place where JJ's woodworking skills developed was in his backyard. Steven, a friend of his mother's, would come to make driftwood sculptures with JJ. This was an important activity for JJ, who was beginning to feel some of the boredom of adolescence. Other outlets included bicycle riding, a part-time job at a nearby car wash, and frequent visits to his father, for fishing, conversation, and hanging out.

The fine relationship with his father came to an abrupt end at the age of 14 when his father was shot and killed in a neighborhood dispute. JJ felt the loss acutely, and restricted his social circle to only close relatives. However, he also sought counseling from the peer counseling center at his high school. Through that program he eventually made new friends at his school. The counseling center also played a role in providing some security for JJ. There was a serious outbreak of violence among the students in his school that year. Wanting to avoid the fights, JJ would spend his lunch and free time drawing at the counseling center.

JJ took advantage of vocational opportunities through the school as well. He participated in the Mayor's Summer Youth Employment Program for two summers, working for the municipal transit system (doing clerical work). During one semester, he took an inside work experience class where he was on the phone asking guest speakers to come to the school and talk about their work.

JJ was recommended for the community vocational training program during his last semester of high school. He went to the work site, the central office of a major insurance firm, for a half day each school day, and received instruction from an on-site teacher. While JJ initially seemed to be socially withdrawn, and had some minor grooming problems, he overcame these and was hired as a full time employee upon his graduation from high school. JJ had always been described as restless and "fidgeting" by his teachers. When asked how he adapts to sitting all day doing filing tasks, JJ said: "Work keeps me busy. There's always more to do, and if I do finish early, I give other people help 'til I get more." He claims that he has had no problems making friends at the work site because he likes the work, and therefore feels better about himself and can enjoy meeting people. He likes working around people older than himself. He also feels that the counseling he got in high school, which enables him to speak about himself and get to know people, was the most valuable thing he learned there. He is now planning to enroll in a night class in art, and to take his first paid vacation to Hawaii!

SECONDARY VOCATIONAL TRAINING FOR STUDENTS WITH SEVERE HANDICAPS

The emphasis on functional curriculum for mildly handicapped students is even greater for students with severe handicaps. By the time the latter enter the secondary years, almost all curricular activities should be focused on preparation for community living in adulthood. The student should spend very little time in the special education classroom, practicing leisure, social, vocational, and other community skills instead on the school campus and in the surrounding community. This section describes the characteristics of a community vocational training model for students with severe handicaps. The types of training activities that are carried out during the secondary years take the student to the point of transition into adulthood.

Community-based vocational programs have emerged as a new service delivery model for severely handicapped students and are being supported by a growing data base (Bellamy and Wilcox, 1982; Forte, Storey, and Gaylord-Ross, 1985; Sailor et al., 1985; Sprague, Paeth, and Wilcox, 1984). The following sections describe the purpose, principles, planning process, implementation strategies, and evaluation procedures.

Purpose

Community vocational training attempts to:

1. Teach functional skills curriculum

2. Facilitate the generalization of learned skills to other settings and persons

3. Promote positive attitudes on the part of nondisabled persons toward the employment capabilities of disabled persons.

The use of a functional skills curriculum has been identified as one of the critical components of secondary educational programs that are necessary for the transition from school to work (Bellamy and Wilcox, 1982). Functional curriculum entails learning the specific job tasks and general work behaviors needed for real work environments. As with mildly handicapped students, classrooms cannot simulate real work settings. Since severely handicapped students have such slow rates of learning, and generalize learned skills only poorly, it is particularly important that they learn functional vocational skills in the actual work setting.

Community vocational training should help these students generalize work-related skills as much as possible to other work settings. Persons with severe handicaps do not transfer learned skills well to new environments, or to other persons, materials, or language cues (Coon, Vogelsberg, and Williams, 1981; Hill, Wehman, and Horst, 1982; Horner, McDonnell, and Bellamy, 1985). Thus, in-classroom simulation training is likely to have limited transferability to work settings [although it might play some role in generalization training (Horner, McDonnell, and Bellamy, 1985)]. By providing the student with a series of work experiences, however, the student is likely to generalize a number of learned skills to untrained contexts (Horner, McDonnell, and Bellamy, 1985).

Finally, community vocational training seems to positively affect the attitudes of nondisabled persons toward the employment potential of severely handicapped students. Bates, (1984) and Forte, Storey, and Gaylord-Ross (1985) found that nondisabled persons perceived severely disabled students to be more vocationally capable when the students were engaged in functional tasks in real work settings. Also, parents' low perception of their child's employment potential can be raised by the results of community vocational training—for example, as they observe their child in the workplace (Wershing, Gaylord-Ross, and Gaylord-Ross, 1986). By positively affecting the attitudes of nondisabled persons, including the disabled students' own parents, the employment options and quality of life experiences for handicapped persons may also be approved.

Principles

Several principles should be kept in mind in providing community vocational training to severely handicapped students. First, the student should be involved in a series of community vocational training programs during the secondary school years. Gaylord-Ross, et al. (1987) suggest that at least three or more training experiences should be provided during the secondary years. Each training experience should last three to nine months, be one to six hours per day, and two to five days per week. Each training experience should differ in terms of the nature of the work (e.g., office, restaurant, factory). One of the purposes of community vocational training is to expose a student to a variety of work experiences so that job preferences can be identified. This process will later help to place the student in an appropriate job setting. Also, training in different jobs enables students to practice previously learned skills and general work behavior in different work environments, which facilitates the generalization and maintenance of their learned skills. Additionally, the jobs performed at different work sites should reflect a range of task difficulty. Varying the difficulty of tasks allows a classroom teacher to determine the types of jobs that are best matched to a student's ability. The secondary years also offer an opportunity to push the student to the maximum of his or her capability. A work setting with difficult tasks can assess the limits of a student's work capacity.

Finally, community vocational training should be incorporated into the student's IEP. Vocational activities should form the core of educational programs for severely handicapped high school students. Incorporating community vocational training activities into the IEP facilitates the planning process and increases support from parents and administrators. Also, funding for the program can be more easily obtained once community training is documented in the IEP (Sailor et al., 1985).

Planning Process

Administrative Support   Administrative support is essential in carrying out a successful community vocational training program, since such a program involves many issues related to activities held outside the school environment (e.g., insurance and liability), and it may require many adaptations to current administrative policy. One issue relates to the supervision of off-campus activities and the supervision of the students who remain in class. It may not always be possible for all the students in a class to participate in a community vocational training program at the same time. When a classroom teacher accompanies the community vocational training group, a flexible policy is needed to permit paraprofessionals (e.g., aides) to supervise the students who are left behind. The job description of paraprofessionals may need to be revised accordingly. Also, nondisabled high school students working as peer tutors or foster parents working as volunteers should be permitted to accompany instructors with students for off-campus community vocational training (Sailor et al., 1985).

In terms of insurance and liability, all staff, including volunteers and peer tutors, should be protected under the school or district insurance policy when they accompany a vocational training group off the school grounds. Even though there are no clear guidelines regarding insurance for the students or their liability for accidents (Brady and Dennis, 1984), Wershing, et al., (1986) suggest that the status of a student as an employee of the business or a nonemployed trainee should settle most legal questions. If a student is a paid employee, his or her accident insurance and liability should be paid for by the employer. If a student is not a paid employee and the community vocational training program is part of the IEP, he or she should be covered by the school insurance policy.

Parental permission for community vocational training should also be dealt with. While some schools require classroom teachers to obtain parental permission for each community vocational training activity, other schools may simply require a yearly "blanket" off-campus permission form (Sailor et al., 1985). If the community vocational program is included in an IEP, this matter becomes very simple. A parent's signature on the IEP serves as a substitute for a parental permission form for each community training activity.

Transportation to community work sites may be a real barrier to training. Work sites may not always be within walking distance of the school. The students may need to learn how to travel to work sites. While public transportation, particularly buses, may be the least restrictive way of traveling, there are alternative solutions (Sailor et al., 1985). The classroom teacher or aides may transport small groups of students to the work site in their own vehicles. Parent volunteers may be recruited for the same purpose. A school bus also can be used to transport students directly to the work sites in the morning and to pick them up at the same or different sites at the end of the day.

The issue of payment to the students in the community vocational training must also be considered. Although wages are a significant aspect of work life, the primary focus of community vocational training is in teaching a variety of job skills and general work behaviors. This is not to say that paid work is not encouraged. Earning a paycheck is indeed a natural reinforcement, and it may provide students the opportunity to learn about the value of money and money management. However, the matter of wages should not limit the work opportunities for students with severe handicaps. When a student does begin to approximate the production of a nonhandicapped employer, he or she must be paid. Wershing, et al., (1986) have suggested the following guidelines for work and pay:

1. If a student is performing at a very low rate (e.g., less than 25 percent of the rate of nondisabled coworkers), the student can be viewed as working toward mastery of an IEP goal. While a wage may not be given, it is desirable to subsidize unpaid training through special program funds when possible.

2. If a student is performing between 25 and 90 percent of the rate of his nondisabled coworkers, some payment should be provided by the employer. In most cases, it is likely to be a subminimum wage. It is important to get clearance from the Department of Labor for subminimum payments. Subsidies from special educational funds may supplement payment from employers.

3. If a student is performing equally with his nondisabled coworkers, he should be paid at least the minimum wage level or at a similar rate as the nonhandicapped employees. To violate such a principle would be a form of peonage.

Site Procurement It is important to identify appropriate work sites in the community. Sites may be identified in the following ways:

1. Vocational special education personnel in the school district office can provide information on potential work sites. Also, career education teachers for nondisabled students may share work site information. If there is no vocational education staff, classroom teachers should develop work sites on their own. In such cases, administrators should give the teachers time during the school hours to search for potential work sites.

2. Information about possible work sites can be solicited from parents, family members, or friends by means of personal interviews or questionnaires.

3. Another source of information is the local chamber of commerce, which probably publishes employer directories and provides information on industrial councils or employer organizations.

4. Employers that a teacher has already worked with may supply referrals.

5. Local newspapers or Yellow Pages ads are another source of information on work sites.

Once the teacher obtains a list of possible employers, he or she should interview these employers in person or on the telephone. The teacher should explain the rationale for the community vocational training program and give the employers a brief description of the students. He should also obtain information regarding the job, available space, materials needed, quality and time standards, training hours, and the presence of nondisabled coworkers. The issue of insurance and liability should also be discussed during the interview. Further points in site development are:

1. Contact personnel in the highest executive position.

2. Stress that an instructor is responsible for providing supervision and teaching the students at the work site.

3. Use a prepared written outline or handout.

4. Present pictures of the students performing vocational tasks.

Site Selection   After interviews have been conducted and employers have indicated an interest in participating, sites should be finally selected according to the following criteria:

1. A work site should provide students an opportunity to learn a variety of jobs.

2. The work site should ideally be close to the school so that an excessive amount of time is not spent on travel.

3. The availability of public transportation is also important, both because it gives students the opportunity to learn how to use such transportation and because private staff vehicles may not always be available.

4. An ample amount of space must be available at the work site both for instruction and so the program will not interfere with production.

A parental permission form should be completed during this stage of site selection and should be kept in a student's file along with an emergency information card listing a contact person, medical information, and procedures to be used in case of emergencies. The site selection procedure will be completed when the teacher and the employer have signed a training contract for the students.

Implementation Strategies

Before actual training begins, a specific training program should be written out, with the information obtained through a job analysis and an ecological inventory of the work site. The job analysis includes task analyses, identification of performance standards for nonhandicapped employees, and determining if any equipment or adaptations are required for student performance besides those provided by the employer. The teacher will need to learn to perform the job task in order to teach it. Effective correction cues and reinforcers also need to be determined (Gaylord-Ross and Holvoet, 1985). The ecological inventory should include information related to the time and place for breaks, the location of the lunch area, the clothing and equipment that will be needed, the time and place for training, and coworker attitudes toward disabled workers. All this information is utilized in identifying the general work behaviors to be taught, such as appropriate dress, appropriate break-time behavior, and socialization with coworkers. A training program is not complete until the specific job tasks and the general work behaviors have been clearly identified.

Scheduling   When implementing a community vocational training program, scheduling can be hectic, since it involves coordinating transportation schedules, staff schedules, individual student's schedules for related services, and available time at work sites. A time schedule for community vocational training should include travel time, set up/clean up time, and break or lunch time, in addition to the time required to complete the job tasks. The following matters must be given special attention:

1. A student should receive at least two to three hours of training per day. This will allow adequate time for performing real work tasks (Sprague, Paeth, and Wilcox, 1984).

2. Scheduling small groups at different sites may be necessary when it is not possible to place students at one work site. This will largely depend on staff resources. Staff ratios of 1:4 or less are generally recommended for community vocational training. Heterogeneous groupings across a range of severe disabilities may also facilitate the management and instructional process (Sailor et al., 1985). Peer tutors, foster parents, and other staff should be utilized for community instruction when possible.

3. The work at each site should occur at the same time of day, if possible. This will eliminate the need to create different schedules for the students every day.

4. Scheduling at the work site is also important, since a well-coordinated schedule will allow the teacher and the students to use their time most effectively. It may be helpful to develop an individual schedule (e.g., a picture sequence chart) so that the student can follow the order of the tasks independently as much as possible. This will allow a teacher to provide individual training to those students who need more assistance.

Instruction When a complete training program and schedule have been developed, actual instruction at the work site may begin. The teacher should provide instruction on specific job tasks and general work behaviors. The transferability of general work behaviors to different employers, coworkers, and work settings should always be emphasized. While the teacher may need to prompt or assist severely disabled students to perform tasks during the initial stages of community vocational training, she should fade out intensive supervision as soon as possible. The ultimate goal of community vocational training is to teach students to work independently. Students should be encouraged to perform tasks with the least possible assistance. Self-management procedures should be introduced to help them toward this goal (Sowers et al., 1985); Sprague, Paeth, and Wilcox, 1984). As the teacher fades out her assistance, supervision should be transferred to the appropriate coworker at the site.

Evaluation Procedures

All data regarding a student's performance at the work site should be kept in a file. Periodic evaluations of the student's progress should be conducted by examining the individual performance data sheets and graphs. Questions should be raised concerning whether a student's performance is improving and whether it approximates the standard of a nonhandicapped employee. If a student is not progressing, different instructional techniques may be needed. When a student has mastered the performance of a task, a decision must be made as to whether new tasks will be taught or the student will continue to perform previously learned tasks. The classroom teacher should communicate regularly with the employer regarding each student's performance. The student's progress at the work site should be summarized and documented in the IEP.

CASE STUDY: Lisa

Lisa was 16 years old and diagnosed as severely mentally retarded. She had minimal speech but was able to express her basic needs verbally and to follow simple directions. She lived in a group home with five other mentally retarded persons. Even though she was liked by others, she demonstrated few social interaction skills with peers or adults. When frustrated, she exhibited behavioral problems such as pinching herself and others. Her work endurance was very low and she needed constant supervision.

In her first community vocational training program she was trained to collate and package notecards in a local stationery store. She went to the site for three hours a day, four days per week. The paraprofessional supervised Lisa and two other students at the store. Her work routine consisted of: punching a time card, performing the collating and packaging tasks, socializing with coworkers during breaks, and undergoing a behavior modification program for her pinching. The teacher initially would cue her verbally to perform a task and physically correct errors. Also, she was positively reinforced with edibles for correct responses. By the end of the semester, Lisa was able to perform the tasks in her work routine independently with the aid of a picture sequence chart. The teacher did not have to cue her and the cards indicated the next task to do. She learned to use a vending machine to get soda during breaks and to exchange simple greetings and conversations with coworkers. Her pinching behavior decreased to a near-zero level through the use of a differential reinforcement of other behavior program. She also learned to take a public bus from school to the work site with another student.

After successful completion of her first community vocational training program, Lisa entered another training program during the second year of high school. She worked in a laundry room at a local hospital, where she learned to use a washer and dryer, to fold gowns, sheets, and towels, and to sort them according to category. She was under less intensive supervision by her teacher. She was able to transfer to the new work setting some skills learned during the previous training such as greetings, and use of a picture sequence chart.

During her last year of high school, Lisa participated in her third community training program, in a fast-food restaurant. She learned to prepare food and to do the kitchen chores. She was under minimal supervision by a teacher's aide. By the end of the semester she was completely supervised by the restaurant manager. She was paid at below the minimum wage since her production rate was 50 percent of that of her nondisabled coworkers. A work stipend was also given to her from Vocational Education Act funds.

At the end of her last year of school careful consideration was given to Lisa's future employment plans. Her teacher talked with her parents, who were quite pleased with Lisa's vocational development. They reported that Lisa was quite motivated to go to work. The teacher noted that she seemed happy when she worked at the restaurant and had developed genuine friendships with some of her coworkers. The manager stated that he was pleased with Lisa's performance and had a position available at minimum wage for twenty five hours per week.

An individual transition plan was developed whereby an adult service agency funded by the Department of Vocational Rehabilitation would provide follow-along job training. The employment agency would also coordinate communication between the family and the employer. The transition plan also identified a day program for developmentally disabled adults that was located at the local community college. It was planned that Lisa would participate in that program when she was not working in order to advance her education and quality of life in the community living and recreational domains.

CONCLUSION

Community vocational training offers students with handicaps many benefits that cannot be offered in traditional in-class, simulated vocational training. It also opens an avenue for future employment options for the individual in transition. However, given the advantages of community vocational training programs, it is unfortunate that many classroom teachers are caught in the inertia of in-class instruction. Through the coordinated efforts of teachers, administrators, parents, and employers, the operational barriers to community-based vocational training can be overcome.

REFERENCES

Azrin, N.H., and V.A. Besalel. (1980). *Job Club Counselor's Manual: A Behavioral Approach to Vocational Counseling.* Baltimore: University Park Press.

Bates, P., S.A. Morrow, E. Pancsofar, and R. Sedlak. (1984). The effect of functional vs. non-functional activities on attitudes/expectations of non-handicapped college students: What they see is what they get. *Journal of the Association for Persons with Severe Handicaps 9,* 73–78.

Bellamy, G.T., and B. Wilcox. (1982). Secondary education for severely handicapped students: Guidelines for quality services. In K.P. Lynch, W.E. Kiernan, and J.A. Stark (eds.), *Prevocational and Vocational Education for Special Needs Youth: A Blueprint for the 1980s*. Baltimore: Paul H. Brookes. Pp. 65–80.

Brady, M.P., and H.F. Dennis. (1984) Integrating severely handicapped learners: Potential teacher liability in community based programs. *Remedial and Special Education 5*, 29–36.

Brolin, D. (1982). *Vocational Preparation of Persons with Handicaps*. Columbus: Ohio: Bell & Howell.

Bronfenbrenner, U. (1979). *The Ecology of Human Development: Experiments by Nature and Design*. Cambridge: Harvard University Press.

Clark, G.M. (1979). *Career Education for the Handicapped Child in the Elementary School*. Denver: Love Publishing.

Coon, M., T. Vogelsberg, and W. Williams. (1981). Effects of classroom public transportation instruction on generalization to natural environment. *Journal of the Association for the Severely Handicapped 6*, 46–53.

Flynn, R.J. (1982). Effectiveness of conventional and alternative vocational education with handicapped and disadvantaged youth: A research review. In K.P. Lynch, W. E. Kiernan, & J.A. Stark (eds.), *Prevocational and Vocational Education for Special Needs Youth: A Blueprint for the 1980s*. Baltimore: Paul H. Brookes.

Forte, J., K. Storey, and R. Gaylord-Ross. (1985). Social validation of community vocational training in technological work settings. In R. Gaylord-Ross, J. Forte, K. Storey, A Wershing, C. Gaylord-Ross, S. Siegel, D. Jameson, and J. Pomies (eds)., *Community Vocational Training for Handicapped Youth*. (Monograph). San Francisco: San Francisco State University, Department of Special Education.

Gaylord-Ross, C., J. Forte, and R. Gaylord-Ross. (1986). The community classroom: Technological vocational training for students with serious handicaps. *Career Development for Exceptional Children 9*, 24–33.

Gaylord-Ross, R., J. Forte, K. Storey, C. Gaylord-Ross, and D. Jameson. ((1987). Community-referenced instruction in technological work settings. *Exceptional Children*.

Gaylord-Ross, R., J. Forte, K. Storey, A. Wershing, C. Gaylord-Ross, S. Siegel, D. Jameson, and J. Pomies. (eds.). *Community Vocational Training for Handicapped Youth*. San Francisco: San Francisco State University, Department of Special Education.

Gaylord-Ross, R. and J. Holvoet. (1985). *Strategies for Educating Students with Severe Handicaps*. Boston: Little, Brown.

Grasso, J.T., and J.R. Shea. (1979). Effects of vocational education programs: Research findings and issues. In *The Planning Papers for the Vocational Education Study*. Vocational Education Study Publication No. 1. Washington, D.C.: National Institute of Education.

Harter, J., D. Stern, and T. Strano. (1984). *Enterprises for Learning*. Albany, Calif.: Rosenberg Foundation to the Youth Project, Inc.

HEW. (1987). IEP, *Developing Criteria for the Evaluation and Documentation of IEP Provisions*.

HEW. (1978). Office of Civil Rights, DHEW Vocational Education Programs. *Guidelines for Eliminating Discrimination and Denial of Services on the Basis of Race, Color, National Origin, Sex and Handicap.*

HEW, Office of the Secretary. (May 4, 1977). *Nondiscrimination on the Basis of Handicap.*

Hill, J., P. Wehman, and G. Horst. (1982). Toward generalization of appropriate leisure and social behavior in severely handicapped youth: Pinball machine use. *Journal of the Association for the Severely Handicapped 6*(4), 38–44.

Hobbs, N. (1983). *The Troubled and Troubling Child.* San Francisco: Jossey-Bass.

Horner, R.H., J.J. McDonnell, and G.T. Bellamy. (1985). Teaching generalized skills: General case instruction in simulation and community settings. In R.H. Horner, L. Meyer, and H.D. Fredericks (eds.), *Education of Learners with Severe Handicaps: Exemplary Service Strategies.* Baltimore: Paul H. Brookes. Pp 289–314.

Horner, R.H., J. Sprague, and B. Wilcox. (1982). General case programming for community activities. In G.T. Bellamy and B. Wilcox, (eds). *Design of High School Programs for Severely Handicapped Persons.* Baltimore: Paul H. Brookes. Pp. 61–98.

Jones, R. (Ed). (1983). *Reflections on Growing Up Disabled.* Reston, Va: Council for Exceptional Children.

Kelly, Jeffrey A. (1982). *Social-Skills Training: A Practical Guide for Interventions.* New York: Springer.

Kelly, W.J., C.L. Salzberg, S.M. Levy, R.B. Warrenteltz, T.W. Adams, T.R. Crouse, and G.P. Beegle. (1983). The effects of role-playing and self-monitoring on the generalization of vocational social skills by behaviorally disordered adolescents. *Behavioral Disorders 9*, 27–35.

NASDE (1976). *Functions of the Placement Committee in Special Education.* Washington, D.C.

Peycha, J.A. (October 1980.) *A National Survey of Individualized Education Programs for Handicapped Children.* Research Triangle Park, N.C.: Research Triangle Institute.

Phillips, E. (1978). *The Social Skills Bases of Psychopathology.* London: Grune and Stratton.

P.L. 88–210. Vocational education act of 1963.

P.L. 91–230. Education of the handicapped act.

P.L. 93–112. Rehabilitation act of 1973, section 504.

P.L. 93–380. Education amendments of 1974.

P.L. 94–142. Education for all handicapped children act of 1975.

P.L. 97-300. Job partnership training act.

P.L. 98-199. Amendments to EHA 1984.

P.L. 98-524. Carl D. Perkins vocational education act.

Rusch, F.R., R.P. Schultz, and M. Agran. (1982). Validating entry-level survival skills for service occupation: Implications for curriculum development. *Journal of the Association for the Severely Handicapped 8*, 32–41.

Sailor, W., A. Halvorsen, J. Anderson, L. Goetz, K. Gee, K. Doering, and P. Hunt. (1985). Community intensive instruction. In R.H. Horner, L.H. Meyer, and H.D. Fredericks (eds.), *Education of Learners with Severe Handicaps: Exemplary Service Strategies.* Baltimore, Paul H. Brookes. Pp. 251–288.

Siegel, S., K. Deuter, J. Prieuer, and R. Gaylord-Ross. (1987). The community vocational training program. Unpublished manuscript, San Francisco State University.

Sowers, J., M. Verdi, P. Bourbeau, and M. Sheehan. (1985). Teaching job independence and flexibility to mentally retarded students through the use of a self-control package. *Journal of Applied Behavior Analysis 18*(1), 81–85.

Sprague, J., M.A. Paeth, and B. Wilcox. (1984). Community work crews for severely handicapped high school students. Unpublished paper, University of Oregon.

Storey, K., J. Forte, and R. Gaylord-Ross. (1985). Measuring the community-based vocational training gains of disabled persons: A behavioral checklist approach. In R. Gaylord-Ross, J. Forte, K. Storey, A. Wershing, C. Gaylord-Ross, S. Siegel, D. Jameson, and J. Pomies (eds.), *Community Vocational Training for Handicapped Youth.* (Monograph). San Francisco: San Francisco State University, Department of Special Education.

U.S. Department of Education. Child count—1983, 1984, 1985.

U.S. Department of Education. Letters of findings—1980, 1981.

U.S. Department of Education, Office of Vocational and Adult Education. Final regulations, August 16, 1985.

University of Texas. (1977). *Adult Performance Level Survey, Users Guide.* Iowa City, Ia.: American College Testing Service.

Wehman, P. (1981). *Competitive Employment: New Horizons for Severely Disabled Individuals.* Baltimore: Paul H. Brookes.

Wehman, P. (1984). Transition for Handicapped Youth from School to Work. Conference Proceedings Document: I. *Enhancing Transitions from School to the Workplace for Handicapped Youth.* Champaign: University of Illinois.

Wehman, P., J. Kregel, and J.M. Barcus. (September 1985). From school to work: A vocational transition model for handicapped students. *Exceptional Child 52*(1).

Wershing, A., C. Gaylord-Ross, and R. Gaylord-Ross. (1986). Implementing a community vocational training model: A process for systems change. *Education and Training of the Mentally Retarded 21*, Pp. 130–137.

Will, Madeline. (1984). *OSERS Programming for the Transition of Youth with Disabilities: Bridges from School to Working Life.* Washington, D.C.: Office of Special Education and Rehabilitative Services.

Part III Adult Employment Programs and Issues

The ultimate validation of a vocational education program is whether a substantial proportion of the student participants become employed. The rates of unemployment among handicapped adults indicate that most previous vocational training programs have been lacking. Wehman and Kregel describe a new model for employment training that has reported considerable success in job placement, training, and retention. The supported work approach provides additional staff, like job coaches, to ensure that the individual procures a job, learns the job skills, adjusts to the work setting, and maintains job performance over the long run. Wehman and Kregel describe the different types of supported work models, such as the enclave, and issues in staffing related to these programs.

A successful employment experience entails more than learning a particular set of job skills. Chadsey-Rusch and Rusch describe the major variables to consider when analyzing the ecology of the workplace. They outline assessment and intervention factors involved with the physical, social, and organizational ecology of the workplace. Successful employment means not only doing the job well but also having a relatively enjoyable quality-of-life experience. Quality of life at the workplace often revolves around the types of social interactions that occur between the handicapped worker and nonhandicapped coworkers. Many strategies are being developed to facilitate coworker interaction and advocacy behavior.

In spite of our advanced instructional technology in vocationally training persons with handicaps, serious economic barriers to their employment remain. O'Brien and Stern describe these economic issues in considerable detail. Fortunately, despite barriers such as the general unemployment rate and social security insurance, progressive incentive programs like the Targeted Jobs Tax Credit encourage employers to hire handicapped workers. In addition, many companies have set aggressive and positive policies to hire handicapped employees. With an upbeat style, Pati cites the many ways that disabled persons have become a human resource in the workplace. His interviews with corporate leaders and the examples of job accommodations that he describes are a source of inspiration for those trying to place and train handicapped employees.

8 Adult Employment Programs

Paul Wehman and John Kregel
Virginia Commonwealth University

In the United States today there is a civil rights movement occurring for adults with disability who historically have been either unemployed or grossly underemployed. Millions of people with mental, physical, sensory, and health-related disabilities would like the opportunity to work but are being denied this opportunity. There are many reasons for this such as limited expectations and attitudes of professionals in the field, the unwillingness of business to make reasonable accommodations for people with disabilities, lack of sufficient funds for training and placement, and government disincentives to work.

It is our belief that these problems are being overcome and will be overcome dramatically in the near future. A recent Harris Poll indicating that two out of three persons with disabilities are not working is simply unacceptable. Furthermore, it is highly inconsistent with what astute professional, advocates, and persons with disabilities themselves know is possible based on research and innovative practices currently in place in some parts of the country.

We believe that society is not openly opposed to persons who are disabled working; furthermore, our experiences suggest that business persons can and will be highly accommodative given sufficient labor demand. However, we do believe that professionals in the field, special educators, rehabilitation counselors, adult educators, vocational, and so on themselves have low vocational expectations for the people with disabilities they serve. These expectations are shaped by antiquated or inadequate training experiences or lack of exposure to what is possible when the right program elements are in place. In a very real sense, this civil rights movement is a plea to professionals in the field to seriously evaluate their ways of delivering vocational services and creating real work opportunities.

This chapter describes services that currently exist and examines ways in which they can be improved as totally new opportunities are developed. We will base the chapter on two themes: (1) appropriate values of normalization—that is, real work for real pay, and (2) existing research which provides an underlying empirical base for the type of adult/vocational service. It is noteworthy to remember that tens of thousands of handicapped youngsters leave school each year and require one or more of the alternatives that will be discussed.

Within the chapter we describe numerous types of adult service options and conclude with a discussion of the important interrelationships among different state agencies. The combined efforts of different agencies will greatly influence vocational outcomes in respective states for persons with disabilities. What follows is a rationale for adult employment programs and a discussion of vocational service alternatives.

EMPLOYMENT FOR INDIVIDUALS WITH DISABILITIES: A RATIONALE

Employment is a major part of the lifestyle of all people, with or without handicaps. Type of employment, amount of money earned, and advancement opportunities directly affect how we look at ourselves, how society evaluates us, and the amount of freedom we have financially and socially. Meaningful work that pays a fair wage in settings where there are predominantly nonhandicapped people plays a pervasive part in the quality of life we enjoy.

Let us consider some of the points more closely. For example, how much does type of employment affect our behavior and the behavior of others toward us? Often, entry level manual labor is seen as less desirable and more physically straining than office work, assuming the amount of wages earned is equivalent. On the other hand, consider the prospect of someone who is restricted to a developmental adult day program that serves only persons with mental and physical handicaps and who has no opportunity for employment. Someone in that position might find entry level manual positions much more attractive, not only financially but also socially in terms of family and community acceptance. The opportunity to make nonhandicapped friends would be a major advantage to nonsheltered employment. Hence, type of employment can be an important feature in how we evaluate ourselves.

The amount of money that can be earned is another critical indicator of quality of life. If we work for free or volunteer our services all the time, our outlook and society's perceptions of us will be different than if we earn a wage comparable to that earned by nonhandicapped workers performing the same job. Generally, the more money we earn, the more freedom we have to purchase desired and necessary items in the community and to establish personal independence. Someone who earns $5 per week in a day program or sheltered workshop will probably have a lower perception of herself than a person who earns $190 per week as a micrographics camera operator. Unfortunately, many disabled people earn very little money and this becomes a real problem. Wolfe (1980) reports that disabled persons, on average, earn $2.25 per hour compared with over $4.50 per hour by nondisabled people. This type of significant wage discrepancy cannot help but significantly influence the quality of life of individuals with disabilities.

The opportunity to switch jobs and move to a more favorable work setting in terms of work conditions and job stability as well as dollars earned must also be assessed as we look at the importance of employment in the lifestyles of persons with handicaps. Advancement and career mobility also need to be made available to people with disabilities. Again, certain types of jobs in real work settings that yield a decent wage often lead the way ultimately to better jobs with more pay.

The astute reader will observe that the word *opportunity* has been used several times already. No one has a right to a job. Jobs are not available for everyone and a person must demonstrate a certain degree of skill and aptitude to have a job. However, all nonhandicapped people have an opportunity to work if they choose and we should provide no less for the thousands of individuals with handicaps who would like to work and who can work if given the opportunity. To emphasize this, there is an abundance of literature spanning the past twenty years that consistently shows the vocational potential of handicapped people as workers. This literature indicates progressively greater vocational competence on the part of individuals with both mild and severe disabilities. What is unfortunate, however, is that there is an enormous difference between what we know can be done and what is actually happening in practice. What follows is a discussion of several of the most pressing concerns related to the employment of handicapped individuals.

UNEMPLOYMENT: A SERIOUS PROBLEM

In the United States today, from a variety of accounts, the unemployment of disabled people is at an unconscionably high level: anywhere from 50 percent to as high as 90 percent. The United States Commission on Civil Rights (1983) reports a level of 50 percent to 75 percent. This assessment is up from a 1979 U.S. Department of Labor estimate of 59 percent disabled unemployment. As high as this seems, similar data from states such as Vermont, Missouri, Virginia, and Maryland seem to corroborate these figures.

In Maryland, for example, a sample of over 1400 developmentally disabled individuals was studied in terms of large number of variables (Smull and Sachs). Only 7 percent of the individuals were found to have regular jobs. Hill and her colleagues (Hill, et al., in press) surveyed 263 parents of adult mentally retarded persons in Virginia and found that only 13 of the 263 had a son or daughter who was competitively employed. Well over one-third indicated no employment of any type for their son or daughter.

Hasazi and her colleagues (Hasazi, Gordon, and Roe, 1985) in Vermont did a follow-up study of recently graduated special education students. Through an elaborate telephone interviewing system, they found that over half were not competitively employed. In Virginia Wehman, Kregel, and Seyfarth (1985) completed a similar postsecondary follow-up study of 300 young adults with mental retardation between 20 and 24 years old. (Wehman, Kregel, and Seyfarth, 1985). The parents of these adults were surveyed by trained interviewers. More than 40 percent, it was found, had never held a regular job at any time. Mithaug, Horiuchi, and Fanning (1985) report similar discouraging results from the state of Colorado. In short, the current employment of disabled people is quite limited when it comes to placement in regular jobs. Futhermore, it seems as if all too many professionals and parents are unaware of this high level of unemployment.

One cannot study the employment picture of disabled people without looking carefully at sheltered workshops, which number well over 5,000 nationally. In 1977, the U.S. Department of Labor reviewed a large sample of sheltered workshops (600) and reported a significant increase in their client population: from 39,254 in 1968 to 156,475 in 1977, an increase of 300 percent. This increase illuminates the pattern of many people and agencies choosing the sheltered workshop for employment services for disabled people. Since sheltered workshops have traditionally been a major source of employment for many significantly disabled people, this selection is less an option than it is a predestined track. Fortunately, the evaluation of programs designed to serve persons with disabilities is also receiving increased attention.

However, several studies of sheltered programs indicate that there are significant problems involved with depending on the workshops to meet the needs of all handicapped persons, especially those with severe handicaps. For example, in the U.S. Department of Labor study (1977) only 12 percent of regular program workshop clients were placed into competitive employment (this study did not discuss retention rate past the initial employment period); hourly wages increased only 9 percent in five years, and the average hourly wage for all mentally retarded clients was $.58 per hour. These data support the contention that retarded individuals are underemployed, underutilized, and underpaid. Furthermore, research shows that the longer one is placed in a day program with only other disabled persons, the lower the probability for success in a regular job (Wehman, et al., 1985). This finding is also supported by the Buckley and Bellamy (1985) survey.

Sheltered workshops have not been successful in moving disabled people into competitive employment and maintaining this employment. However, workshops have had to face significant disincentives. Some of these are as follows:

1. Financial support has not typically been provided for competitive job placements.

2. Financial support has not typically been provided for client training at job sites in the community.

3. Monetary support is not provided for follow-along services; that is, funds have not been provided for maintenance services designed to help difficult-to-train clients hold their jobs.

4. State and federal funding patterns have not typically encouraged workshops to allocate much more of their time and resources to competitive employment.

While there continues to be an expanding controversy between those who feel sheltered workshops and other adult day programs are not consistent with the best employment needs of most disabled persons and those who feel that these types of sheltered programs are a necessary part of the vocational alternatives available, two points related to this controversy are increasingly clear. These points, which are discussed throughout this chapter, are briefly described here:

1. Perhaps the true point of contention is not always to debate what the best *setting* is to accomplish desired vocational outcomes. Instead we need to decide on which *outcomes* we want for persons with disabilities. For example, assume that competitive employment is a highly desirable outcome. If this is the case, what are the placement, training, and follow-along conditions necessary to effect that outcome regardless of the setting? This is not to say that a community-based vocational training site will not be superior for client placement success than sheltered workshop benchwork activity or adult activity center arts and crafts program. However, perhaps that very same adult activity center can convert itself to an employment oriented placement program with specific employment outcomes accomplished for clients.

2. The second point that cannot be overlooked is that there are 5,000 sheltered workshops and over 2,000 adult day programs (Buckley and Bellany, 1985) nationally. These programs are the principal service delivery mode of vocational services for significantly disabled adults. Although they must be changed, modified, and improved, the changes will not happen overnight. Therefore, it is more constructive to identify the best ways their role in stimulating desired employment outcomes, which are characterized by decent pay and integrated employment, can be facilitated.

THE COSTS OF DISABLED UNEMPLOYMENT

As we consider the seriousness of the unemployment problem for persons with disabilities, it will be helpful to review the costs of unemployment to society, and business, as well as to individuals with all types of disabilities. It is not difficult to see how the impact of this pervasive high level of unemployment can affect thousands of people in addition to persons with disabilities themselves. The points that follow address just some of the adverse effects that occur when meaningful employment opportunities are not made available to capable handicapped persons.

Human Dignity

Without meaningful employment opportunities, human dignity and the self-worth of individuals with disabilities are not enhanced. The opportunity and ability to work in a real job that pays a fair wage is a major part of everyone's life, not just persons with disabilities. It is apparent to many after talking with persons with disabilities and friends of individuals with handicaps that sustained employment is a critical avenue to other successful aspects of life such as health, friendship, self-esteem, and a feeling of purpose. Employment is often the key to improving self-perceptions, reducing feelings of loneliness, and moving toward a richer quality of life (Matson and Rusch, 1986).

Family Concerns

The concern and doubts of families and friends of persons with disabilities must also be considered. These concerns often center around the question of: "What will happen to my son or daughter after I'm gone?" or "Will my son or daughter be able to get a job after he completes school?" These are legitimate and serious questions that sustained employment can help address. Although a job may not solve all problems, it will be a major step in the right direction. Families need our support and assistance in helping individuals with disabilities enter the labor force (Seyfarth, et al, in press; Venn, DuBose, and Merkler, 1977).

Earning Power

As noted earlier, wages for individuals with disabilities are poor. However, earning competitive unsubsidized wages provides the person an opportunity to have more independence in his or her lifestyle. Even at minimum wage levels of $3.35 per hour, the wage accumulation over time is considerable and allows workers with disabilities to have money to spend on housing, meals, and other discretionary items. Often fringe benefits are made available as well. Wages and benefits provide greater independence on the part of citizens with disabilities and improve their quality of life.

Economic Benefits to Society

Wages earned by citizens with disabilities typically flow back into the local and state economy. The impact of these wages being spent should not be minimized. When combined with the taxes that are paid, it is apparent that significant reductions in the disabled employment rate would benefit state and federal budgets and the economy in general.

There are other economic benefits of employment as well. For example, there are significant costs to taxpayers in subsidizing restrictive "prevocational" or work adjustment programs that often do not lead to the employment of persons with disabilities who have the potential to work. In addition to these program costs, the supplemental security income savings to the government for those who are able to work can be tremendous. While it is vitally important not to take away social security benefits from those in need, it is also fiscally and morally necessary to help those work who can. Thus, service agencies need to move toward joint development of training efforts with industry. These training efforts need to culminate in employment that is not government subsidized.

Impact on Business and Industry

Business and industry lose out on an excellent source of good labor when competitive employment opportunities are not made available to citizens with disabilities. For example, one industry in which many workers with mental handicaps are employed is the hotel and restaurant industry. In a recent study conducted by the National Hotel and Restaurant Association (1983), it was found that the average length of employment for over 2,000 nondisabled workers was only five months; yet data from the supported competitive employment efforts in Virginia (Wehman, Kregel, and Seyfarth, 1985) indicate that the average tenure for 150 workers with mental handicaps in similar jobs was almost nineteen months. Consider further that the well-known fast-food chain of McDonalds, Inc., had turnover rates of over 175 percent in 1981. This type of turnover is terribly expensive to business and industry and can be partially offset by a pool of well-trained workers with disabilities.

Expectations of Family and Friends

Finally, the attitudes and expectations of family and friends, professionals, and the citizens with disabilities are greatly influenced negatively when persons with handicaps continually are shut out from opportunities to earn decent wages and have meaningful jobs. People are often viewed by others in the context of whether they have a job, how much money they make, how long they have their job, what work they do, and so on. Chronic unemployment of persons with disabilities when it is frequently not necessary or warranted casts an unfair light on the capabilities of these persons.

MAJOR VOCATIONAL ALTERNATIVES FOR ADULTS WITH DISABILITY

The following section describes three traditional vocational alternatives currently available to individuals with disabilities. The section describes the basic nature of each alternative, the research findings underlying the alternatives, and the major strengths and weaknesses of each.

Adult Developmental Programs

In most cities and towns young adults with mental and physical handicaps go to special centers after they finish school. Many go to places that are variously called adult activity centers, developmental achievement centers, stimulation centers, and the like. These day programs have grown enormously in number, with approximately 2,000 in the country. Many other young adults are accepted in work activity or sheltered workshop programs. Sheltered workshops number well over 5,000. Many more young adults are at home because services are unavailable.

Within these day programs participants receive the opportunity to engage in recreation, learn activities of daily living, learn academics, and be involved in some work skill activity. Sheltered workshops, on the other hand, provide for contract benchwork under sheltered conditions, and only with other persons with mental or physical disabilities. Sheltered workshop employees typically earn an average of $1 to $4 per day. Most parents and young people with severe handicaps, as well as professionals, have come to expect this form of service. With increasing numbers of students leaving school and needing adult service, a move has been made by some to further expand segregated adult day programs. In most states, adult activity centers cost annually anywhere from $4,200 per client (Virginia) to $7,500 per client (Maryland). Sheltered workshops usually cost more in the range of $2,500–$3,000 annually per client.

The special day program that takes place in a segregated center must come to an end. This arrangement focuses too many fiscal resources into buildings, not staff. A more significant disadvantage results from the segregation of people with severe handicaps away from the community.

Furthermore, the emphasis of these programs is not on finding employment with decent pay in the community—in spite of the many successful programs demonstrated through research. Instead, the underlying assumption has been that clients are not "ready" and need much more training.

In the period of time between 1955 and 1979 there were very limited data and published research to suggest that individuals with significant mental and physical handicaps could benefit from real work opportunities yielding unsubsidized pay. There was no question that during this time establishment of a special day center where individuals could go for continued special education and developmental activities was considered the best option—in fact, often the only option. Unfortunately, this alternative is still very much in practice nationally since the thinking of many adult service administrators reflects a center-based ideology.

What needs to be considered alternatively is how to best convert these existing centers from day-care activity to supported employment activity. The emerging initiative toward supported employment—that is, supported competitive employment, enclaves, and workcrews—provides a basis for alternative day activity that is much more productive. Adult service administrators must evaluate and review the following issues as they consider converting center-based day program activity to industry-based supported employment:

1. Staff training needs necessary to develop new skills and philosophies in service staff.

2. Analysis of funding streams and determination of the best ways to utilize resources from different agencies.

3. Ability to mobilize staff opinion, parent attitudes, and the business community to accept the employability of clients with no previous work histories.

These issues are on the cutting edge of what will be required to begin the long-term conversion from day programs to industry-based supported employment.

Sheltered Workshops

Sheltered workshops have for a very long time been considered the foundation of our nation's vocational service system for adult persons with disabilities. Over the past two decades the number of sheltered workshops in the country has grown tremendously. Recent data indicate that the number of sheltered workshops has risen to over 5,000 nationally (Bellamy, et al., 1986). At the same time that the number of sheltered workshops in the country has risen substantially, these programs have come under attack from a number of different government agencies, professionals, and advocates (U.S. Department of Labor, 1977;

Whitehead, 1979). This public outcry over the limited outcomes obtained by sheltered workshop clients has left the movement in a state of confusion. Many sheltered workshops are facing increasingly greater financial constraints while at the same time struggling to find a role within newly emerging community-based employment programs for persons with disabilities.

Sheltered workshops vary considerably in terms of their size and the type of services they provide, but all workshop programs must meet the criteria of the Fair Labor Standards Act regulating the payment of subminimum wages to individuals with mental or physical impairments. The Department of Labor has authorized five different types of subminimum wage certificates to provide payment to persons with disabilities in sheltered workshop settings.

1. *Regular work program*—The regular workshop program provides a minimum wage floor of 50 percent of current minimum wage for individuals or an entire shop. This option is designed to provide long-term employment for individuals at a wage commensurate with their productivity.

2. *Training*—Training certificates (usually limited to twelve months) are designed to provide work adjustment or specific skill instruction to clients with disabilities in transitional workshops. The purpose of this option is not to maximize the amount of client earnings, but rather to "prepare" the worker for subsequent employment.

3. *Evaluation*—Evaluation certificates issued to clients for the work performed are used to determine their potential for subsequent employment. Evaluation certificates allow workers to be paid at a rate far less than that which they might earn if paid on the basis of productivity. Evaluation certificates are generally provided on a six-month basis, but may be extended for up to eighteen months for a specific individual.

4. *Work activity center*—Work activity programs are designed for clients "whose physical or mental disabilities are so severe as to make their productive capacity inconsequential." It is this type of program that has seen the greatest amount of growth over the past decade. It should be clearly understood that these programs, for clients with supposedly "inconsequential" productive capacity, are the very programs from which clients are frequently placed directly into competitive employment using the supported competitive employment model described later (Wehman, 1981; Wehman, et al., 1985).

5. *Individual rate*—Individual rate certificates allow two specific types of exceptions to the regulations just described. First, clients in regular workshop programs who do not produce at fifty percent of minimum wage may be paid at a rate of 25 percent of minimum wage with the prior approval of the state rehabilitation agency. Second, workers in work activity centers who produce at 50 percent of minimum wage or above may remain in work activity centers if no other appropriate alternative is available for them.

Operational Problems in Sheltered Workshops Major criticisms of the existing sheltered workshop system were described earlier. Clients in these programs generally earn insignificant wages; in addition, client earnings have not risen at a rate comparable to overall wages for workers in our country. Sheltered workshops by their very nature are segregated facilities, with no mission to provide clients regular contact with nondisabled individuals. These programs have come to be viewed as "dead end" facilities with little client movement into competitive employment. The U.S. Department of Labor (1977) study cited previously found that only 12 percent of regular program clients were placed into competitive employment annually. Furthermore, for clients who had remained in workshops for over two years, the placement rate dropped to 3 percent annually. In addition to these frequently cited concerns, sheltered workshops have traditionally been plagued by operational and organizational problems that have contributed to their shortcomings.

Sheltered workshops have generally been underfunded. Funding levels provided to sheltered workshops have often been inadequate to meet the actual costs of these programs. Workshops have too frequently been forced to rely on United Way contributions, fund raising activities, or other charitable contributions to support wages, staff salaries, and overhead costs. This situation has lead many workshops to focus their efforts on "keeping their doors open"—that is, keeping the workshop operating—rather than on facilitating the movement of clients into competitive employment.

Sheltered workshops have failed to incorporate the most efficient business and industrial technologies. Sheltered workshops are generally labor intensive, nonautomated industries. Many times workshops fail to incorporate state of the art practices in marketing, production, and management. This situation is frequently caused by a lack of available work. In order to provide work for the greatest number of individuals for the greatest amount of time, workshops divide jobs into small units that provide "activity" for the largest number of clients. They may fail to procure equipment or machinery that would make production more efficient, or rely too frequently on items for which they are the prime manufacturer, such as crafts or other low-profit merchandise.

Sheltered workshop staff are frequently not prepared to perform the marketing and production management activities necessary to maximize profits and client wages. In many instances workshop and work activity center staff are human service professionals who do not possess the industrial management skills required in contract procurement and production activities. These staff members are frequently hired because they possess the skills and motivation to work in settings that serve persons with disabilities. While these individuals are highly dedicated and skilled in working with individuals with disabilities, the lack of business knowledge, coupled with the low salaries they generally receive, limit the ultimate financial and employment outcomes for workshop clients.

The Future of Sheltered Workshops   The preponderance of problems associated with sheltered workshop programs has led many to advocate that these programs be phased out or eliminated entirely. This argument, however, should be viewed with caution. A more effective view may be to assist these facilities in making the transition into programs that provide an array of the supported employment options. This approach would allow these programs to transfer their resources into options that hold the promise of greater client outcomes at equivalent or reduced public costs. Start-up monies may need to be provided to assist workshops in making this transition. Parent and consumer education programs should be initiated to assist clients and caregivers in accepting the risks and challenges associated with such a change. Finally, staff development programs must be designed to prepare existing workshop staff for the new roles and job responsibilities associated with the supported employment movement.

Placement into Competitive Employment   The majority of students with special needs who exit public school special education programs will be able to enter competitive employment with the assistance of a vocational rehabilitation counselor. This traditional approach to competitive employment placement involves providing individuals with a variety of *time-limited* services—that is, services that may be intensive, but that are provided only for a specified, short period of time. Traditional placement services have their greatest applicability for individuals with mild disabilities.

Vocational rehabilitation services can be divided into four categories:

1. *Evaluation* services intended to identify client strengths and weaknesses and to identify potential job placement alternatives and the services required to secure these alternatives.

2. *Preplacement* services designed to allow individuals to maximize their employment potential.

3. *Placement* services to assist individuals in securing a job that allows them to realize their vocational potential.

4. *Postemployment* services to enable the client to maintain employment and assist in future career enhancement.

Vandergoot and Worrall (1979) describe this process as (1) preparation for a job, (2) finding a job, and (3) keeping a job.

Time-limited placement services are most frequently initiated through a comprehensive vocational evaluation. While a tremendous amount of professional and financial resources continues to be expended in the evaluation process, in recent years this activity has seriously been called into question. Critics have charged that the outcomes derived from this activity do not justify the large expenditures, and that financial resources should be channeled to other components of the placement process. Wehman and McLaughlin (1979) have identified four types of vocational evaluation data. These include:

1. Clinical assessment, which addresses formalized testing regarding medical conditions, educational skills, adaptive behavior, vocational interests and aptitudes, and other factors.

2. Work samples, which are simulated activities that attempt to assess an individual's capacity for and interest in tasks associated with various job clusters.

3. Situational assessment, in which clients are placed in employment settings to assess their general work behaviors, skills, and attitudes.

4. Job tryout, which focuses on an individual's ability to adjust to a natural job setting.

Preplacement services refer to a variety of activities that vary in length and intensity. For example, clients may receive counseling services to help them develop appropriate work attitudes and to provide them information regarding the types of jobs that might be available. Some individuals may be placed into a transitional workshop to receive work adjustment training—that is, training designed to improve general work skills and attitudes. Other individuals may be placed into more formal types of training programs, including community colleges, vocational-technical centers, or college or university programs.

Placement services lie at the heart of the time-limited services approach. Generally, placement strategies fall into two categories: client-centered or selective placement. The client-centered approach focuses on teaching the client general job-seeking skills. Rather than trying to obtain a job for the client, the rehabilitation professional tries to develop the client's own job-seeking skills to the point where the client can locate and obtain his or her own job. In the selective placement approach, the rehabilitation professional takes a much more directive role. In selective placement the counselor attempts to match the skills and needs of a particular client with the requirements and rewards of a specific job in the local community.

Postemployment services are an area that has traditionally been underemphasized in the vocational rehabilitation process (Dunn, 1979). Postemployment services refer to the follow-up activities that may be provided after an individual has successfully secured a job. These activities may include assessing client and employer satisfaction with job performance, initiating needed work adjustment, and preparing the client for future career enhancement and job mobility.

The key feature of all these services is their *time-limited* nature. After an individual has successfully adjusted to the initial job, services are terminated after a short period of time. Although this feature may exclude many individuals with severe disabilities from success within this model, for others it may be entirely adequate. Some individuals may require assistance in determining the job for which they are best suited, need additional training to prepare themselves for the job, require specific help in obtaining their first job, and need support to adjust to the performance and social demands of the job. For these individuals, the traditional approach to competitive placement continues to meet their needs.

However, this approach has several shortcomings. The typical vocational rehabilitation counselor may have an active caseload of well over 100, which makes it impossible for the counselor to be actively involved in all facets of the placement process for all individuals. Thus, the counselor is forced to purchase services from a variety of different providers for a given individual, a situation that too often results in disjointed and uncoordinated service programs. Another major shortcoming focuses on the lack of postemployment follow-up services provided in the model. Services to many individuals are terminated after the client has completed just two months of successful employment. However, research on the placement of persons with mental retardation using a more intensive placement approach (referred to as supported competitive employment) and a six-month employment criterion indicates that individuals with mild mental retardation are no more likely than persons with moderate or severe mental retardation to be successfully retained in competitive employment (Hill, et al., in press). While the time-limited approach may be appropriate for many individuals with mild handicaps, it seems clear that other mildly handicapped individuals require more intensive services in order to adjust to and maintain employment for extended periods of time.

SUPPORTED EMPLOYMENT

The preceding discussion related to adult developmental programs, sheltered workshops, and placement into competitive employment points up the reality that many persons with substantial handicaps will never gain entrance to employment in industry under the current service delivery system. Also, many significantly impaired persons will never earn money at a real job in the community without professional support. Hence, the concept of supported employment has evolved within recent years as an alternative for severely disabled persons. Supported employment offers work in nonsheltered settings through provision of necessary services such as on-site instruction. Supported employment provides opportunities for many people who are at substantial risk of gaining and maintaining employment to work for the first time. The program may involve a host of difficult arrangements within industry or outside of industry, in different occupations, and with different staffing patterns.

Paid Employment

Supported employment is paid employment. The federal government has suggested that an individual should be considered to meet the paid employment aspect of supported employment if he or she engages in paid work for at least an average of four hours each day, five days per week, or follows another schedule offering at least twenty hours of work per week. This standard does not establish a minimum wage or productivity level for supported employment.

The number of hours worked should not be viewed as the only criterion for supported employment because some people (such as adolescents with severe handicaps) may choose to work only fifteen hours a week. The stipulation of number of hours worked, however, does convey the seriousness and impact that paid employment may have on the young person with disabilities.

Community Integration

Work is integrated when it provides people with disabilities with frequent daily social interactions with people without disabilities who are not paid caregivers. The federal government has suggested that integration in supported employment programs be defined in terms of a place (1) where no more than eight people with disabilities work together and where the site is not immediately adjacent to another program serving persons with disabilities, and (2) where persons without disabilities who are not paid caregivers are present in the work setting or immediate vicinity.

For example, an individual with severe cerebral palsy who works in a local bank creating microfilm records of transactions clearly meets the integration criterion for supported employment. So may four individuals with severe emotional disorders who work together in an enclave within a manufacturing plant; a mobile janitorial crew that employs five persons with moderate mental retardation in community work sites; and a small bakery that employs persons with and without disabilities.

Ongoing Support

Supported employment exists only when ongoing support is provided. In contrast to the time-limited support, which may be provided for only a few months, ongoing support continues as long as the client is employed. An individual should be considered to be receiving ongoing support when public funds are available on an ongoing basis to the individual or to a service provider who is responsible for providing employment support, and when these funds are used for specialized assistance directly related to sustaining employment.

The nature of ongoing support—which is ongoing, as noted, through the entire span of the individual's employment—differs markedly from the time-limited nature of traditional rehabilitation services. This characteristic positively influences the concerns of parents and employers.

Severe Disability

Supported employment exists when the persons served require ongoing support; it is inappropriate for persons who would be better served in time-limited preparation programs leading to independent employment. The most significant way to describe who should receive supported employment is to assess how much an individual is at risk of gaining and maintaining employment. Youths who are highly likely to lose jobs shortly after placement because of their disability may be prime candidates for supported employment. This means that individuals labeled autistic; moderately, severely, or profoundly mentally retarded; and multiply handicapped would be the principal target groups for this approach. These individuals would not be able to hold jobs without permanent, long-term follow-along at the job site.

The following sections describe several emerging supported employment models.

THE SUPPORTED COMPETITIVE EMPLOYMENT MODEL

A supported work approach to competitive job placement requires specialized assistance in locating an appropriate job, intensive job-site training for clients who are usually not "job-ready," and permanent ongoing follow-along. A qualified staff person essentially establishes a 1:1 relationship with a client in need of individual employment services and provides placement and ongoing training right at the job site. *The person is employed immediately, with wages paid by the employer.* Follow-along is differentiated from follow-up in that with the first there is daily and weekly on-site evaluation of how the client is performing while with the second, checking occurs only periodically, at established intervals of time. Competitive employment is defined in this chapter as a real job providing the federal minimum wage in a work area with predominantly nonhandicapped workers.

In the supported competitive employment model, all workers are paid at or above minimum wage. A closely related model is termed supported employment or distributed work (Mank, Rhodes, & Bellamy, 1986); in this model workers are employed in competitive settings, but work at subminimum wages. Although the distributed work model is a very appropriate alternative for certain individuals, employment at or above minimum wage should be the first priority of all supported employment programs.

Supported competitive employment is contrasted with traditional placement into competitive employment in that the latter is time-limited. That is, once the client has been placed and trained at the job site to the satisfaction of the employer, the service is terminated. With supported employment there is a permanent commitment to follow-along services provided by professional staff. In approach that has worked well in Virginia, the Virginia Department of Rehabilitative Services funds the initial job placement and intensive job site training costs through case service funds. The permanent follow-along component is then paid for through local and state mental health/mental retardation funds. This interagency shared responsibility is now happening in at least four areas of Virginia (Hill, et al., in press).

The Need for Supported Competitive Employment Services

One question related to supported employment that vocational rehabilitation experts who have been in the field for a long time are asking is: Why do we need another service when we barely have enough case service dollars now to meet the increasing demand for services? There are several answers to this question. First, most persons with truly severe disabilities will not be able to obtain a real job without ongoing professional assistance. Substantial planning and direct assistance is required to overcome transportation difficulties, parental concerns, employer skepticism, and location of an appropriate job. A specialized and individualized approach is required to ensure job retention.

A second reason for this approach is that many persons with severe disabilities will be unable to maintain employment without professional support. The amount and nature of support will vary from person to person and, of course, be influenced by the nature of the disability. For example, the amount of intervention required by an individual with severe cerebral palsy would be expected to decline over time, reaching a point of very little follow-along. However, an individual with a history of long-term institutionalization and a dual diagnosis of mental retardation and emotional disturbance would require greater periods of long-term support (Anthony and Jensen, 1984).

The inability of many persons with severe disability to transfer to real jobs and skills learned in special centers is a third reason for using a supported employment approach. Although "readiness" is a long and timehonored concept of vocational preparation in day programs, in reality, it has not helped. Clients do not "flow" from work activity to workshop to competitive employment (Whitehead, 1979); furthermore, studies by Sowers, Thompson, and Connis (1979) and Wehman, et al., (1985) clearly show that many persons who are purported to not be ready for competitive employment do quite well with a supported competitive employment approach.

A fourth rationale for consideration of supported competitive employment turns out what is the most effective use of limited case service dollars. Setting aside one's professional biases toward one adult service or vocational rehabilitation service or another, the successes of supported competitive employment [see Rusch (1986) for a description of many of these programs or McLeod (1985)], suggest strongly that the outcomes and costs associated with day center nonvocational skill programming, vocational evaluation, or work adjustment should be contrasted with those outcomes and costs related to supported competitive employment. That is, why spend $2,000-$3,000 on "preemployment" preparation activity for a given client if roughly the same amount of money can be spent immediately on job-coaching services (Wehman and Melia, 1985) in supported competitive employment? These are the types of questions and decisions that rehabilitation administrators and counselors increasingly will need to face.

A final rationale for use of this specialized placement approach is to meet the labor demands and needs of certain businesses and industries. The hotel and restaurant industry and cleaning industry are two high-growth areas in entry-level service occupations. Similarly, micrographics and entry-level computer skills are also growth industries in which persons with severe physical disabilities might be able to enter with support. Previous experiences in Virginia (Wehman and Hill, 1982) suggest that, because of the training and follow-along components, business personnel welcome this approach.

Staffing Issues Traditionally, neither rehabilitation counselors nor special education teachers—two professional groups that might meet staffing needs in this area—have been completely trained in the skills necessary for successful supported competitive employment. As a result, university field-based training programs will need to be developed in business settings. This need is based on the following: (1) Close relationships must be established with business and industry, and (2) professionals working in supported competitive employment must understand personnel practices in business.

The success of the entire supported employment initiative, in fact, is highly dependent on (1) the willingness of business to hire disabled persons and (2) the likelihood that business will allow professional staff to work at job sites. Our experiences in Virginia as well as around the country (Rusch, 1986) seem to support the high level of business support.

It is probable that two types of job coaches are necessary: a senior person with either a bachelor's or master's degree, and a junior person. The senior person would provide job development, job placement, and initial intensive training and employer relations work. Once the client became "stabilized" at the job site with greatly reduced staff assistance, then a less skilled job coach could be employed for follow-along (Harold Russell Associates, 1985). Much more emphasis must be placed on job development and placement skills, behavioral training, and work with parents, social security representatives, and other key agencies. In short, rehabilitation, special education, business, and social work skills are essential for effectiveness in this role.

There are, of course, a number of ways to provide this service. For example, there is the intact unit approach, which many rehabilitation facilities and other special center-based programs might find attractive. With this approach, approximately $20,000 (including fringe benefits) would be allotted for the senior staff person, $10,000 for the junior person, and $5,000 for travel and supplies for a total of $35,000. This group could expect to place approximately twelve persons with severe mental disabilities annually. Data from the Virginia group show 66 to 75 percent six-month job retention at the end of such a program (Wehman, 1981).

A second approach might be to deploy a small team of senior job coaches who, upon completion of client placement and training, turn over their cases to follow-along and retention specialists who have a much larger caseload of businesses, all geographically close to each other. There undoubtedly is no shortage of ways to resolve the problem of best staff deployment.

The Best Settings from Which to Establish Supported Competitive Employment Programs

Supported competitive employment programs are labor intensive, not capital intensive. Therefore, there is no need for a large physical space in which to house persons with disabilities during the day—work with clients will take place directly in business and industry. From a cost standpoint, this factor is an attractive feature of this type of vocational option. Many supported employment programs (e.g., Rusch, 1986) are established on this basis. On the other hand, there is no reason why effective placement and training programs cannot also occur from community-based adult day programs, rehabilitation facilities, schools, and vocational technical centers. If, in fact, an aggregate of professional personnel already exist in a given setting, then it may be possible to redeploy some of these persons into supported competitive employment activities.

In Virginia local rehabilitation facilities receive rehabilitative case service funds to provide supported competitive employment for at-risk clients (Hill, et al., in press). As noted earlier, facilities may become vendored in transitional and supported employment services until clients become stabilized in their new job. This may last from four to twelve weeks. At this point, the participating staff and business decides the level of involvement necessary by the supported employment specialist. Follow-along employment support services are then funded by the local mental retardation/mental health services. These costs are typically much less expensive (Wehman and Hill, 1982). This approach has been one apparently successful way to implement the program, but it is probably too early to evaluate these efforts. Schools can also be logical settings from which supported competitive employment efforts can occur. With such a major push nationally toward transition from school to work, many schools are feeling a great deal of pressure to provide placement for students with severe handicaps before graduation.

In short, we do not know yet which settings are ideal—but in all likelihood, all of those just described may be appropriate at a given point in time with the right staff attitudes, funding base, and local economy.

Supported Competitive Employment and Different Severe Disabilities: Needs and Concerns

A supported work approach to competitive employment has definite applicability to the needs of individuals with several types of severe disabilities. While the majority of the supported competitive employment programs nationally have focused on persons with mild, moderate, or severe retardation, individuals with autism, severe physical disabilities, head injuries, and significant psychiatric impairments can also benefit. Each of these populations exhibits characteristics in travel, social skills, communication, and other adaptive behaviors that have typically reduced their likelihood for competitive employment. What is not fully understood yet is how much staff intervention is necessary with each of these disabilities. Also unknown is how much of this staff intervention would be distributed over the life of an individual's employment. Furthermore, the necessity of specific job coach competencies may vary according to type of disability.

The overriding issue, however, is not what the disability is but rather—is this person at serious risk for gaining employment and maintaining employment? If so, then a supported competitive employment arrangement may be planned and undertaken by an appropriate service provider.

MOBILE WORK CREWS AND ENCLAVES

Mobile work crews and enclaves are employment options for adults with disabilities that have existed for many years (McGee, 1975), but they have recently received renewed attention within the supported employment initiative (Mank, Rhodes, and Bellamy, 1986). Enclaves and work crews both allow individuals previously served in sheltered employment alternatives an opportunity for meaningful employment in more integrated community-based settings. In both options, individuals with severe disabilities are provided continuous ongoing support by a human services professional that enables them to succeed in more challenging employment settings. Workers are paid based on performance, and wages are commensurate with those paid to nonhandicapped workers performing the same duties. While similarities exist between the two models, each will be discussed separately to differentiate the array of alternative approaches currently used to implement enclave and work crew options.

Mobile Work Crews

Mobile work crews or work force teams are generally comprised of four to six individuals with severe disabilities who spend their day away from a center-based rehabilitation facility or adult vocational program performing service jobs in community settings. Mobile work crews may operate independently as private, not-for-profit corporations, or may be part of a large array of employment options operated by a rehabilitation or adult service agency. Whatever the organizational structure, the sponsoring agency contracts with community businesses or individuals to perform groundskeeping, janitorial, home maintenance, or similar tasks. Workers are generally paid by the sponsoring agency based on productivity. A training supervisor or manager accompanies the crew and is responsible for training work crew members, providing ongoing supervision to maintain productivity and quality control, and guaranteeing that the contracted work is completed to required standards.

The work crew is staffed by a single supervisor or manager. The supervisor is responsible for all aspects of the operation, including securing and negotiating contracts, training and supervising crew members, and maintaining program records. While the small size of the crew allows for intense supervision and the inclusion of individuals with significant learning and production problems, the reliance on a single staff member makes the operation of the crew challenging. Since the crew functions away from the service agency or rehabilitation facility, the manager is often isolated from other professionals. Also, the need to provide continuous supervision to crew members often makes it difficult for the supervisor to perform the required contract procurement and administrative activities. In larger communities, establishing a number of crews may be one way in which direct service and management functions may be shared to maximize total program effectiveness.

The flexibility of the work crew, both in terms of the type of work performed and the make-up of the crew, allows the model to accommodate the needs of individuals with a wide array of disabilities.

The majority of work performed is in the areas of buildings and grounds maintenance, housecleaning, farm work in rural areas, and motel room cleaning in areas with large tourist industries have been identified as successful alternatives (Mank, Rhodes, and Bellamy, 1986). A crew may have contracts with a number of different agencies and may perform work in a large number of settings over the course of a week. While work crews have been successful in areas with high unemployment rates, securing enough contracts to provide work during all standard work hours is frequently a problem (Mank, Rhodes, and Bellamy, 1986).

Mobile work crews are an option that may have particular applicability in small communities and rural areas. Service agencies in rural areas attempting to provide supported employment alternatives to persons with severe disabilities face a unique set of challenges. Many rural areas often have a relatively high unemployment rate. With little or no industrial base, service agencies encounter serious problems accessing an adequate amount of work. The small number of individuals to be served within a large geographical area creates severe logistical problems for the agency. In addition, it is often difficult for the areas to identify and recruit highly trained staff with the skills necessary to implement supported employment alternatives. A major part of the strength of the mobile work crew is its ability to provide stable employment for a small number of workers with severe disabilities in the types of found work in a local area.

Enclaves

Enclaves are employment options in which small groups of workers with disabilities (generally six to eight) are employed and supervised among nonhandicapped workers in a normal business or industry. Continuous long-term supervision is provided on-site by a trained human service professional or host company employee. Workers may be employed directly by the business or industry, or remain employees of the not-for-profit organization that supports them (Rhodes and Valenta, 1985). Enclave members work alongside others performing the same work, although in some situations workers with disabilities may be grouped together to facilitate training and supervision.

Enclaves provide an excellent alternative to both supported competitive employment and traditional sheltered employment. The model provides intensive on-site supervision designed to maximize worker productivity and prevent job termination. It allows access to community-based employment settings for workers with substantial handicaps who might otherwise be unsuccessful when daily training and supervision is faded during the follow-along state of supported competitive employment. At the same time, enclaves provide extended employment in an integrated community setting for individuals who traditionally have been served exclusively in segregated workshops or work activity centers. The model may also be contrasted with the mobile work crew approach. Within mobile work crews, workers generally move to different work settings on a daily basis, or may work at several different sites in the course of a single day. Enclave employees are able to work in a single setting for a prolonged period of time. Additionally, enclave employees in some instances will be paid wages and receive benefits directly from the company, whereas work crew members will remain employees of the sponsoring service agency indefinitely. In one demonstration (Rhodes and Valenta, 1985), workers who had reached 65 percent of standard productivity were hired as employees of the host company at a competitive rate and with full fringe benefits.

The critical feature of the enclave model is the extended training and supervision provided to address low worker productivity and difficulties in adapting to changing work demands. Systematic intervention is necessary to allow workers to acquire all needed skills and produce at an acceptable rate. This extra support may in some cases be provided by the host company, but in most instances is the responsibility of the sponsoring service agency. The enclave supervisor is the key to providing this support. It is a major commitment for the company to hire a group of workers with severe disabilities and allow the involvement of an outside service organization. The enclave supervisor must be highly skilled in effective instruction and supervision techniques while also being sensitive to the production demands and concerns of the host company.

Major Outcomes Associated with Mobile Work Crews and Enclaves

Major positive outcomes associated with mobile work crews and sheltered enclaves are the physical and social integration of individuals with severe disabilities into natural work settings and the opportunities this provides them to earn significant wages. Wages paid to work crew and enclave members are based on productivity, with members earning a percentage of the standard hourly wage for individuals performing similar work. Since the workers in most instances are clients of a not-for-profit service agency, fringe benefits are generally not provided. Mank, Rhodes, and Bellamy (1986) report data from two mobile work crew agencies in which individuals earned from $130 to $185 per month. Rhodes and Valenta (1985) report wages of $295 for six individuals in an enclave after eight months of employment. Public funds are required to make up the excess costs incurred in both models due to low worker productivity and the need for intense, continuous supervision (Cho, 1983). While these figures may not seem particularly high, they are quite significant when compared to earnings of clients in sheltered employment alternatives (Noble, 1985). For example, in the enclave described by Rhodes and Valenta (1985), the individuals involved had averaged less than $40 per month prior to placement in the enclave.

The outcomes associated with the work crew and enclave options must be evaluated in the context of the individuals served by these models. In most cases workers are not making minimum wage or making only a percentage of the prevailing competitive wage, and public costs for the programs are not significantly reduced from the costs of traditional workshop programs. In spite of this, the models are very justifiable on the grounds that they are providing employment in integrated settings for individuals who traditionally would have no opportunity for such work. Individuals who may have medical conditions such as seizure disorders or severe diabetes, or individuals who may exhibit significant maladaptive behaviors such as stereotypic or inappropriate behavior may at long last now have an opportunity to secure and maintain employment in a natural work setting.

CASE STUDY: Michael

Michael is a 22-year-old student currently in his last year of school at a segregated special education center that he has attended since he was 6 years old. Testing psychologists have assessed him, based on scores on standardized intelligence tests, as having moderate to severe mental retardation. Michael's medical records report no significant sensory, perceptual, or motor problems, but he has a history of epilepsy, which has been successfully controlled for three years through daily medication. His school records indicate that his speech is clear and he interacts minimally with others using short, incomplete sentences. Michael has acquired simple counting skills, basic word recognition skills, some coin discrimination, and can tell time to the hour. He has a history of aggressive behavior. His family is very supportive and encourages Michael to interact with nonhandicapped persons and to use the public bus system.

Michael has participated in a community-based vocational training program through his school for three years. Three days a week, Michael and four other students practice janitorial skills at a local business under the supervision of their special education teacher. Michael's major responsibilities include buffing, mopping, dusting, vacuuming, and emptying trash. His teacher describes Michael as a slow, steady worker who can complete up to three tasks independently with minimal supervision and reinforcement.

At the age of 21, Michael was referred to the vocational rehabilitation agency for employment services by the special education teacher at his school. The rehabilitation counselor made arrangements to provide Michael with transitional supported work services. A job coach met with Michael, his special education teacher, vocational teacher, rehabilitation counselor, and family to discuss specific vocational goals and employment options. The transition team decided that a part-time job utilizing Michael's janitorial skills would be an appropriate and desired employment outcome.

After a thorough job/client match was completed by his job coach, Michael was hired as a maintenance worker in a local department store for twenty hours a week at a starting salary of $3.35 an hour. His job included all employee benefits—medical, dental, vacation, sick leave, and an employee discount. As a maintenance worker, his major job responsibilities were to vacuum the carpet in nine departments of the store four days a week and once a week to move the clothing fixtures and vacuum underneath them. Prior to Michael's placement on the job, the job coach spent several days learning the job and developing a task analysis for use in training Michael. The job coach also established the production rates of coworkers and planned strategies for training Michael in job skills and increasing his production rate. School and transportation arrangements were made so that Michael could walk to work in the morning and ride the bus back to school in the afternoon.

A job coach accompanied Michael to work every day to provide training, and support services, and to model appropriate interactions with coworkers and customers. Training and production data were recorded daily to monitor his progress. Michael had acquired basic vacuuming skills in his vocational training program, but had difficulty generalizing these skills to a new environment and needed assistance with learning new patterns. Because Michael was easily distracted and failed to look at the clock, he was often unable to complete the job or take his break at the appropriate time. The job coach developed a work schedule based on the average time needed by Michael, the job coach, and his coworkers to complete the job. The schedule helped Michael to take his break and leave work after he had completed designated sections of work. If production rates were maintained, Michael would finish in time to take a break with his coworkers and leave in time to stop at a fast-food restaurant for lunch before catching the bus back to school.

By the end of four weeks, Michael was completing the job with 95 percent to 100 percent accuracy and maintaining the established competitive performance rates. The job coach gradually began to fade the amount of time spent training Michael directly, but remained on the job site to provide reinforcement, collect data, and provide supervision as needed. Over the next few weeks, the job coach continued to reduce intervention time with Michael, but continued to make monthly follow-up visits to the job site. After three months of employment, Michael's salary was raised to $3.60 an hour and his supervisor reported that his work was "better than required."

Michael's teacher and family describe him as more social and mature since he began working. Additionally, they report that he is interacting with his nonhandicapped peers more frequently, participating in more community activities, and independently initiating grooming skills. Michael has learned to independently cash his paycheck at a local bank each payday, and voluntarily offers to contribute a portion of this salary toward his family's household expenses. He independently purchases clothing, records, and food with the remainder of his money. His teachers report that he is envied and admired by his peers at school whom he frequently advises about the role of a working adult. His job coach, rehabilitation counselor, special education teacher, and family continue to work cooperatively with Michael to provide ongoing support services and to plan for independent living goals as he prepares to leave school.

CASE STUDY: Kathy

Kathy, a 21-year-old student with Down's syndrome, is currently finishing her final year of public school in a self-contained class for the trainably mentally retarded that is situated in an elementary school. She spends most of her school day learning preacademic and prevocational skills and has minimal interaction with her nondisabled peers or with her local community. Kathy speaks in short sentences, but her speech is difficult to understand for people who do not know her well. Kathy's records report no significant medical, academic, or psychological problems, other than obesity. Her teacher and family report that she is independent in many self-care skills, but that she often needs verbal prompting to initiate and complete routines. Her teacher describes her as "stubborn, and often flirtatious."

During her last year of school, Kathy was referred for supported employment services offered by her school system. At a transitional IEP meeting, Kathy, her special education teacher, vocational rehabilitation counselor, parents, and job coach targeted a part-time position in a fast-food restaurant near Kathy's home. Because Kathy had no previous vocational training, the job coach spent a great deal of time assessing her work skills and her related vocational skills to ensure an appropriate job match. Kathy's family was hesitant and required reassurance by the job coach that Kathy would not lose her social security benefits and would receive continued support while employed.

Kathy's job coach identified a "crew member" position at a fast-food restaurant near her home and school. The job coach spent several days task analyzing the position and developing a strategy for training Kathy before she was actually employed. The job coach also targeted city bus training for Kathy so that she could eventually ride to and from work independently. Kathy was hired to work five days a week, for a total of thirty hours. Her salary was set at $3.50 an hour without benefits because she was a part-time worker.

During the first month of Kathy's employment, her job coach accompanied her to work every day and assisted Kathy in completing nearly 90 percent of the job. Kathy's job duties included bussing tables once customers were through eating, washing and drying food trays, and emptying the trash from the kitchen and eating area. The job coach used verbal, model, and in some instances, physical prompting to train Kathy to complete her job sequence. The job coach designed a series of picture cue cards to help Kathy follow her schedule to complete her work and take a break appropriately. Kathy's special education teacher and job coach, in cooperation with her family, trained Kathy on independent grooming skills, such as makeup, hair styling, and clothing, to improve her appearance on the job.

Gradually, over the next two months, Kathy's job coach reduced the intervention time spent directly with Kathy. Now, Kathy is able to complete almost 60 percent of her job and is able to ride the bus to and from work with minimal assistance from the job coach. With the assistance of the coach, Kathy is learning to interact appropriately with her coworkers during her break, and they in turn are learning how to interact with her. In addition, the job coach is modeling appropriate social skills so Kathy is learning to respond and interact politely with the restaurant's customers. The job coach still accompanies Kathy daily at work, but now spends more time observing and collecting production data than actually assisting her in completing the job.

Kathy has received favorable evaluation from her work supervisor who was at first reluctant to hire an individual with a severe disability. Through the use of the supported work model, Kathy is quickly becoming a productive employee. Her parents, teacher, vocational rehabilitation counselor, and job coach anticipate that she will be successfully employed with minimal support services from the job coach by the time she leaves school at the end of the school year.

CONCLUSION

This chapter has described the importance of real work for real pay for people with disabilities. The chapter outlines the many different vocational alternatives available and provides a critique of each. An in-depth look at sheltered workshops, which has been a major source of employment of disabled people, was undertaken. In addition, supported employment, a new concept gaining attention, was also reviewed and evaluated. Finally, two case studies were presented describing how supported competitive employment can be implemented for youth with mental retardation.

REFERENCES

Anthony, W.A., and M.A. Jensen. (1984). Predicting the vocational capacity of the chronically mentally ill. *American Psychologist 39*(5), 537–544.

Bellamy, G.T., L.E. Rhodes, P.E. Bourbeau, and D.M. Mank. (1986). Mental retardation services in sheltered workshops and day activity programs: Consumer benefits and policy alternatives. In F. Rusch (ed.), *Competitive Employment Issues and Strategies.* Baltimore: Paul H. Brookes. pp. 257–271.

Buckley, J., and G.T. Bellamy. (1985). National Survey of day and vocational programs for adults with severe disabilities: A 1984 profile. Unpublished manuscript. The Johns Hopkins University, Baltimore, Md.

Cho, D.W. (1983). An alternate employment model for handicapped persons. *Journal of Rehabilitation Administration 8*, 55–63.

Dunn, D.J. (1979). What happens after placement? Career enhancement services in vocational rehabilitation. In D. Vandergoot and J.D. Worrall (eds.), *Placement in Rehabilitation.* Baltimore: University Park Press. Pp. 167–196.

Harold Russell Associates. (1985). *Supported and Transitional Employment Personnel Preparation Study.* Boston, Massachusetts.

Hasazi, S., L. Gordon, and C. Roe. (1985). Factors associated with the employment status of handicapped youth exiting high school from 1979 to 1983. *Exceptional Children 51*, 455–469.

Hasazi, S., H. Reskill, L. Gordon, and C. Collins. (1982). Factors associated with the employment status of handicapped youth. Paper presented at the American Educational Research Association, New York, New York.

Hill, J., D. Banks, P. Wehman, and M. Hill. (In press). Individual characteristics and environmental experiences related to competitive employment success of persons with mental retardation. *American Journal of Mental Deficiency.*

Hill, J., J. Seyfarth, P.D. Banks, P. Wehman, and F. Orelove. (In press). Parent/guardian attitudes toward the working conditions experienced by their adult children with mental retardation. *Exceptional Children.*

Hill, M., J. Hill, P. Wehman, G. Revell, J. Noble, and A. Dickerson. (In press). Supported employment: An interagency funding model for persons with severe disabilities. *Journal of Rehabilitation.*

McGee, J. (1975). *Work Station in Industry.* Omaha: University of Nebraska.

McLeod, B. (March, 1985). Real work for real pay. *Psychology Today,* Pp. 42–50.

Mank, D., L. Rhodes, and G.T. Bellamy. (1986). Four supported employment alternatives. In W. Kiernan and J. Stark, *Pathways to Employment for Developmentally Disabled Adults.* Baltimore: Paul H. Brookes.

Matson, J., and F. Rusch. (1986). Quality of life: Does competitive employment make a difference? In F. Rusch (ed.), *Competitive Employment Issues and Strategies.* Pp. 331–337.

Mithaug, D., and C. Horiuchi. (1983). *Colorado Statewide Follow-up Survey of Special Education Students.* Denver: Colorado State Department of Education.

Mithaug, D., C. Horiuchi, and P. Fanning. (1985). A report on the Colorado statewide follow-up survey of special education students. *Exceptional Children, 51* 397–404.

National Hotel and Restaurant Association. (1983). Personal communication with Dr. Philip Nelan, Washington, D.C.

Noble, J.R. (July, 1985). A comparative cost-benefit analysis of adult day programs, sheltered workshops, and competitive employment. Paper presented at VAF Leadership Seminar. Richmond, Va.: Virginia Commonwealth University.

Rhodes, L., and L. Valenta. (1985). Industry based supported employment. *Journal of the Association for the Severely Handicapped 10,* 12–20.

Rusch, F. (1986). *Competitive Employment Issues and Strategies.* Baltimore: Paul H. Brookes.

Seyfarth, J., J. Hill, J. McMillen, F. Orelove, and P. Wehman. (In press). Factors influencing parents' vocational aspirations for their mentally retarded children. *Mental Retardation.*

Smull, M., and M. Sachs. (1983). Update: NRDD reports on persons with developmental disabilities. Unpublished manuscript. University of Maryland School of Medicine, Baltimore, Md.

Somers, J., L. Thompson, and R. Connis. (1979). The food service vocational training program: A model for training and placement of the mentally retarded. In G.T. Bellamy, G. O'Conner, and O.C. Karan (eds.), *Vocational Rehabilitation of Severely Handicapped Persons.* Baltimore: University Park Press.

U.S. Commission on Civil Rights (September, 1983). *Attitudes Toward the Handicapped.* Washington, D.C.: U.S. Government Printing Office.

U.S. Department of Labor (March, 1979). *Sheltered Workshop Study. Vol. II.* Washington, D.C.

U.S. Department of Labor (1977). *Sheltered Workshop Study. Workshop Survey: Volume I.* Washington, D.C.

Vandergoot, D., and J.D. Worral. (Eds.). (1979). *Placement in Rehabilitation: A Career Development Perspective*. Baltimore: University Park Press.

Venn, J., R. Dubose, and J. Merkler. (1977). Parent and teacher expectations for the adult lives of their severely and profoundly handicapped children. *AAESPH Review* 2(4), 222–238.

Wehman, P. (1981). *Competitive Employment: New Horizons for Severely Disabled Individuals*. Baltimore: Paul H. Brookes.

Wehman, P., and J. Hill. (1982). Preparing severely and profoundly handicapped students to enter less restrictive environments. *Journal of Association for Severely Handicapped* 7(1), 33–39.

Wehman, P., M. Hill, J. Hill, V. Brooke, P. Pendleton, and C. Britt. (1985). Competitive employment for persons with mental retardation: A follow-up six years later. *Mental Retardation* 23(6), 274–281.

Wehman, P., J. Kregel, and J. Seyfarth. (In press). What is the employment outlook for young adults with mental retardation after leaving school? *Rehabilitation Counseling Bulletin*.

Wehman, P., and P. McLaughlin. (1979). Teacher's perceptions of problem behavior in severely and profoundly handicapped students. *Mental Retardation* 17, 20–21.

Wehman, P., and R. Melia. (1985). The job coach: Function in transitional and supported employment. *American Rehabilitation* 11(2), 4–7.

Whitehead, C.W. (1979). Sheltered workshops in the decade ahead: Work, wages, and welfare. In G.T. Bellamy, G. O'Connor, and O.C. Karan (eds.), *Vocational Rehabilitation of Severely Handicapped Persons*. Baltimore: University Park Press.

Wolfe, B. (September, 1980). How the disabled fare in the labor market. *Monthly Labor Report: Research Summaries*, 48–52.

9 Ecology of the Workplace

Janis Chadsey-Rusch and Frank R. Rusch
University of Illinois

Most people will hold more than one job during their lifetime. In a follow-up study conducted in the state of Vermont, 23 percent of the youth with handicaps were shown to change their employment status over a two-year period of time and 63 percent changed their status over a four-year period of time (Hasazi, Gordon, and Roe, 1985). People change their jobs for various reasons. For example, some people change jobs because they are not paid enough, they do not like their working hours, they do not like their boss, they find their work too boring, or they find that their job interferes with other aspects of their life. Similarly, people may get fired because they do not perform their job at an acceptable rate, they do not follow directions, they show up late for work too often, or they do not get along with their coworkers. In other works, employment status changes because the match between the individual and the job is not ideal.

It is the premise of this chapter that there will be less employment turnover if there is a good "match" between employees and their jobs. A central question that must be addressed with regard to this premise, however, is whether high employment turnover is desirable or undesirable. That is, is long-term job maintenance desirable or undesirable. The answer to this varies depending on your perspective. From the perspective of the employee, job turnover may be desirable in some instances and not desirable in other instances. If the worker is not making enough money to pay for essentials such as food, clothing, and shelter, then securing a new and higher paying job would seem to be very desirable. However, being fired from a job or electing to quit a job without having another job prospect could be very undesirable.

From the perspective of employers, job turnover may be desirable to some because they could continue to pay the same salary over time without having to offer pay raises. However, job turnover would be undesirable for positions that were difficult to fill and/or were crucial to production.

For persons with special needs, job maintenance is seen as desirable. Part of this is based on the fact that the unemployment rate for individuals with handicaps is quite high. The U.S. Commission for Civil Rights (1983) reported that unemployment for persons with handicaps was between 50 and 80 percent. One possible way to decrease unemployment is to ensure a better match or fit between the worker and the job. From the perspective of service providers, who assist individuals with handicaps in job placement, training, and follow-up, job fit also decreases the likelihood of job separation.

In this chapter, we discuss several of the ecological dimensions that should be considered to achieve a good match between a job and a person with special needs. These dimensions are discussed in relation to two basic groups of skills crucial to job acquisition and maintenance: work performance skills and social-interpersonal skills (Rusch, 1979). First, a rationale is given as to why the workplace should be viewed from an ecological perspective and how this can enhance the match between the worker and the job. The ecological perspective is defined and three dimensions of ecology are described. Second, each ecological dimension is discussed with respect to potential assessment factors and intervention strategies.

ECOLOGICAL PERSPECTIVE

Sharon is a 22-year-old female with mild mental retardation. She is employed at a pizzeria, where she is responsible for prepping the salad bar, washing dishes, and bussing tables. Sharon has held this job for the past nine months. During this time, she has not missed one day of work and has never been late. If you ask her how she likes her job, Sharon will tell you that she likes it a lot.

Prior to her present job, Sharon had worked at another pizzeria in the same town. Her duties were the same. But, she was fired because she always came in late. Also, if you asked her, Sharon would tell you that she did not particularly like her first job.

What are the differences between these two jobs? The job tasks were the same, the product that was sold was the same, the pay was similar, and so was the working schedule. In addition, Sharon was equally competent in both settings in performing her job duties. What was going on in these jobs that made Sharon get fired from one and not from the other, and like one and not like the other? Viewing Sharon's two jobs from an ecological perspective will help provide the answers.

ECOLOGY DEFINED

The ecological perspective has its roots in ecological psychology. Ecological psychology studies the interrelationships and the interdependencies between individuals, their behavior, and their physical and social environments (Barker, 1968; Schoggen, 1978). Behavior is viewed as a dynamic part of the interaction between the person and the environment—that is, people influence environments and environments influence people. For example, when we attend a football game we know that in this context it is appropriate to yell and clap our hands. But when we go into a library, we know by observing the people around us that we would be reprimanded (or possibly asked to leave) if we displayed the same rowdy and noisy behavior.

If ecologists were to study a restaurant setting as a potential job site for a student with special needs, they would go into that setting and observe directly ongoing streams of events. They might describe the physical layout of the restaurant, the specific job tasks, the types of customers, the pace of the work, the managerial style used by the supervisor, and interactions between coworkers. If special educators were to study the same restaurant setting as a potential job site, they might study only the specific job tasks that would need to be accomplished in order to get the job done. But there is more to finding and keeping a job than just being able to perform specific job duties. For example, research has suggested that many individuals with special needs lose their jobs because of inappropriate social behaviors (Brickey, Browning, and Campbell, 1985; Greenspan and Shoultz, 1981; Hanley-Maxwell, et al., 1986). Thus, potential job sites need to be assessed from more than just a job task perspective.

Studying employment contexts via an ecological perspective implies that successful adjustment to employment may depend more on the match between people and their environments than on the personal characteristics of individuals (Berkson and Romer, 1980; Schalock and Jensen, in press). The goal of job placement and maintenance is to maximize the fit, or the congruence (Thurman, 1977), between the worker and his or her environment. According to Thurman (1977), congruence (or fit) occurs when an individual's behavior is in harmony with the expectations of the environment. Workers with special needs may display behaviors that vary considerably from established expectations in employment settings or they may lack the particular skills necessary to function adequately. If incongruencies occur, then the behavior of the individual will have to be changed, or the context, (that is, employment setting) in which the deviant or incompetent behavior occurs will need to be altered, or both the person and the environment will need to be transformed. Generally, in special education, we have tended to focus our efforts on changing the behavior of target students and have not given very much thought to environmental variables that might need changing.

ECOLOGICAL DIMENSIONS

In order to make a match between the student with special needs and a job, several ecological dimensions of the employment context need to be considered. Although numerous ecological dimensions are probably relevant (e.g., Moos and Lemke, 1983), three are defined and discussed in this chapter: (1) physical ecology, (2) social ecology, and (3) organizational ecology. It must be stated at the outset that few of these dimensions have been defined and described in relationship to employees with handicaps in the context of employment settings. Thus, the examples described must not be thought of as definitive, but should serve to illustrate the broad range of dimensions relevant to this area. In addition, these three dimensions are not mutually exclusive; they overlap and are interrelated.

PHYSICAL ECOLOGY

Physical ecology refers primarily to the architectural and physical designs of environments that may affect behavior. For example, we have all probably had trouble working on hot summer days when there has been no air conditioning. Similarly, we may have had difficulty concentrating on our assigned work when our coworkers were making a great deal of noise. Other variables such as ventilation and design and comfort of machines, tables, and chairs can potentially influence work efficiency.

Physical arrangements can also influence interaction patterns in work settings. For example, if employees are placed in areas that are far apart from one another, there is probably less interaction occurring between these employes than if the same employees were working side by side. Similarly, comfortable chairs arranged in a circle may be more likely to encourage conversation during a break than chairs that are arranged in rows.

Physical ecological variables deserve careful consideration when a match is being made between a person and a job. Such variables are particularly important when the match involves individuals with physical handicaps (see Chapter 14). Fortunately, a growing body of literature has addressed many of the physical ecological variables that need to be assessed in job settings, especially with regard to production skills. Another body of literature has begun to specify ways to adapt and redesign jobs to enhance the match between a worker and the job if a discrepancy occurs. Unfortunately, little work has been done with regard to physical ecological factors and social behaviors.

Production
Skills

The architectural and physical designs of work environments have been the focus of study by industrial engineers, efficiency experts, and industrial managers since Frederick Taylor's work in the 1800s, which focused on production requirements irrespective of psychological and social influences. Taylor's work preceded modern-day time-in-motion studies (Vandergoot and Worrall, 1979). Frank and Lillian Gilbreth are credited with extending Taylor's work to include social factors associated with employment. In fact, the "therblig" ["Gilbreth" spelled (almost) backwards], which refers to the units of motion needed to accomplish tasks, heavily influenced early efforts in special education to develop task analyses associated with job analysis (Mithaug, 1981).

Today, job analysis is the method most often used to obtain information related to physical ecology variables. *Job analysis* is the process through which accurate and complete information about the requirements of a job can be identified so that the functional abilities and limitations of the individual with handicaps can be matched to these requirements. An emerging trend in rehabilitation engineering is to identify potential problems through job analysis and to make appropriate accommodations. Job analysis is straightforward and has been dealt with extensively in the literature (e.g., Engelkes, 1979; U.S. Department of Labor, 1979).

Assessment Variables   A job can be described as a composite of tasks requiring various skills sequenced to produce a specific result. The results of employee efforts are referred to as production. Consequently, production skills have been a primary focus of job analysis. A job analysis is conducted through direct observation and interview techniques, basic methods of gathering information that are widely accepted throughout industry. Occasionally, a job coach who is conducting a job analysis will actually perform the tasks associated with the target job to better understand the demands of the job.

When assessing job requirements, a number of factors should be considered, including:

1. How the tasks are accomplished

2. The physical movements and/or mental processes involved in the work activity

3. The degree of physical effort and/or the complexity of mental processes involved in the job

4. The time involved in performing each task

5. The frequency with which each activity is performed (U.S. Office of Personnel Management, 1984).

Comparing these job requirements with individual abilities allows potential functional incompatibilities to surface so that appropriate intervention strategies may be applied to reduce or eliminate the incompatibilities.

All jobs require the completion of a series of tasks (that is, methods, techniques, tools, or equipment employed by a worker to complete work tasks). One focus of job analysis has always been to identify precisely what an employee will be required to do when placed in a particular job. Typically, job tasks are identified according to the time and sequence in which they are to be completed throughout a work shift. For example, a janitor may be required to complete preassigned tasks within a specific time frame. Failure to do so may result in job termination.

Identification of the tasks associated with a job is made through direct interview and observation of employees performing the target tasks. Identification of job tasks is important to defining the target employee's role. Sowers, Thompson, and Connis (1979) indicated that absence of job sequence descriptions appeared to correlate highly with shorter employment periods. Typically, employers identify tasks associated with a particular job; however, they do not always identify all the tasks. Sowers, Thompson, and Connis (1979) found that incomplete lists of tasks hindered the ability of target employees adjusting to their new jobs. Furthermore, if these tasks were identified but not sequenced in the order that the employer wanted them performed, the target employee was at risk of losing his or her job. Clearly, the existence of a job sequence helps follow-up trainers in teaching target employees to perform their jobs.

The physical movements and/or mental processes involved in the work activity usually include descriptions of physical motions such as pulling, lifting, sorting, sitting, walking, and matching; the mental processes can include reading, interpreting, answering questions, and solving problems. The degrees of physical effort and/or the complexity of mental processes can be extended to include such factors as weight or type of problems to be solved. For example, an employee might be required to lift tools or equipment that weighs forty pounds or to reach and strike a keyboard. Mental involvement might include reading complex instructions associated with software programs or discarding templates with soldering imperfections at any one of several points.

The total time involved with a task and the frequency with which the task is performed can vary immensely across jobs. For example, a task may require ongoing involvement throughout the day or various tasks may be required to be performed frequently according to customer demands. In the former example, a worker may survey respondents through a telephone interview format. In the latter example, the employee may wipe tables as a function of the number of customers who eat in a restaurant.

The work environment alone poses demands on an employee. In fact, work activities may present fewer functional problems for an employee with handicaps than the environment. For example, an employee who is capable of following simple instructions provided by a supervisor may be distracted by excessive noise at the work site; an employee in a wheelchair who is capable of cataloging and shelving reference material in one library may not be able to do so in a second library where isles are too narrow or shelves are too high. When considering the work environment, attention must be paid to the location of work stations (e.g., on the third floor versus on the first floor), mobility barriers (e.g., steps, narrow passageways, steep grades), physical design of the work station (e.g., furniture dimensions, floor coverings, proximity to coworkers), climatic conditions (e.g., temperature ranges, humidity, drafts), atmospheric conditions (e.g., odors, dust, ventilation), presence and level of noise (e.g., how many coworkers work within an area and the number of potential disruptions in the work environment), and potential hazards (e.g., wiring, heaters, explosives, machinery) (U.S. Office of Personnel Management, 1984).

Intervention Strategies   The purpose of intervention strategies is to redesign jobs in situations where the match between job requirements and potential employees' abilities is not ideal. The intervention should be job-oriented and *not* focused solely on the characteristics of the employee. Focusing on employee characteristics has usually led job placement personnel to develop employee solution criteria that are used more often to discourage than encourage employment. The job-oriented analysis is more appropriate for designing intervention strategies. As discussed, job analysis is suited to identifying tasks associated with a position and the functional demands placed on employees by the tasks and the environment. Job requirements are derived through careful observation of employees performing job tasks at the actual work site. These observations will provide the service provider with firsthand information needed to plan interventions.

Careful job analysis and job modification are often critical to the employment success of the individual with handicaps. Wershing (1984) cited the need to critically analyze requirements for job performance and compare these with the capabilities of the individual with handicaps. She suggested the use of the Available Motions Inventory (Malzahn, 1979) as a method of analysis. Additionally, she cited a variety of studies that investigate the effects that particular job modifications have on the ability of target workers to perform job tasks.

A careful comparison of job analysis data and the characteristics of a potential employee help us to understand incompatibilities that exist between the known physical and/or mental demands, as well as capabilities. Typically, a list of potential remedies or accommodations are listed as potential interventions that could resolve identified problems. There are a number of possible solutions to problems, and the best choice must be made based on the individual being considered for placement. When deciding among potential interventions, the employer and potential employee should be included in the final determination.

Numerous job accommodations can be made to enhance matches between employees and their jobs. For example, if an employee is totally deaf and is being considered for a job that requires some telephone use, the phone could be adapted to include a light that flashes when the phone is ringing, or a secretary could be assigned to take incoming calls. If an employee cannot grasp a pen hard enough to hold it, a hand orthosis might be designed to allow writing with a pen. If an employee cannot reach shelves because they are too high, the employee could be reassigned to shelving reference materials at a lower level or additional bookcases with shelves at an appropriate height could be obtained. Thus, jobs can be redesigned in situations where the match between the job requirements and the employee's abilities is not ideal.

Social Skills

As indicated, little information is available regarding the influence that physical ecological variables have on social behaviors and social interaction patterns in employment settings. Thus, what is presented here are some possible considerations with respect to assessment variables and intervention strategies.

Assessment Variables Research in other areas (e.g., Littleson, Proshansky, and Rivlin, 1972) has reported the effects of physical ecological variables on social behavior. Ittelson, Proshansky, and Rivlin (1972) studied psychiatric wards in New York by categorizing the nature and location of social behavior in relation to different physical arrangements. For example, after recording how bedroom space was used depending on the number of people assigned to a room, they found that activities were more varied when one to three people were assigned to a room than when more than three people were assigned to a room. Thus, contrary to what most people might believe, more social interactions took place when fewer people were assigned to rooms.

Few investigations have specifically assessed the effects of physical ecological variables on the social behaviors of special needs workers in employment settings. However, Salzberg, Agran, and Linugaris/Krafter (1985) surveyed employers from five different jobs to obtain their opinions regarding social behaviors that may differ across jobs. While these researchers confirmed that social factors were critical for success in all jobs studied, there were differences between jobs. For example, social behaviors were more important for kitchen helpers and food service workers than for janitors, dishwashers, and maids. These differences were attributed to the fact that some jobs (such as kitchen helpers and food service workers) occurred in more of a physical-social context, where workers frequently interacted with coworkers and customers.

In a preliminary analysis regarding the effects of physical ecological variables on the social behaviors of employees with mental retardation and their coworkers, Chadsey-Rusch (1986) observed more frequent social interactions occurring in smaller employment settings (such as a fast-food pizza restaurant) than in larger employment settings (for example, a university food service setting). In addition, most of these interactions took place when workers were involved in production tasks. That is, conversations appeared to revolved around work-related matters rather than social-related matters (e.g., how something looked when it was put together versus what somebody watched on television the night before). Thus, it may be that when employees work in physically smaller environments, they interact more due to the very fact that they are in closer proximity to one another.

Intervention Strategies   Assessing the effects of physical ecological variables on social behaviors has several implications for intervention strategies that may enhance the match between employees with handicaps and their jobs. For example, if a service provider is looking for a job placement for a student who has good social skills and likes to interact with others, a physically small working environment with high interaction rates between coworkers may be an important factor to consider. However, placing the same individual into a setting that is physically arranged so it discourages interactions (e.g., a large space or one that is very noisy due to heavy machinery) may not be desirable.

The service provider cannot do much to change the physical ecology of an employment setting. That is, little can probably be done to rearrange space unless the service provider happens to work initially with the architect and contractor while they are designing and building a work site. However, there may be times when the service provider can rearrange workers' positions in relation to one another by moving a table or equipment or changing a job task. Thus, the best intervention strategy may be to assess physical ecological variables prior to making a job placement so that these variables "match" the desires and characteristics of the special needs worker.

Summary

Job analysis is an important procedure for identifying variables associated with physical ecology and for identifying the intervention strategies that will result in an improved match between an employee's performance of production skills and his or her social-interpersonal skills. Regarding production skills, several dimensions of a job analysis were presented. These included job tasks and the work environment. The intervention strategies presented included strategies designed to identify potential remedial approaches to functional problems.

There is a likelihood that physical ecological variables can have an effect on social interaction patterns in employment settings as well, but little research has been done in this area. However, the arrangement and size of physical space may cause an increase or decrease in the frequency of interactions displayed. Many effects, though, are unknown. For example, little is known about the effects of heating, lighting, noise level, number of people, and staffing patterns on social interaction behaviors. Clearly more research is needed to identify which are the important physical ecological variables to assess before effective intervention strategies can be designed for special needs workers.

SOCIAL ECOLOGY

For the purposes of this chapter, *social ecology* refers to the interactions and interrelationships that exist between and among individuals and/or groups within the employment context. As stated previously, social ecological variables are important for enhancing matches between workers and their jobs because many handicapped workers have lost their jobs because of inappropriate social behaviors (e.g., Brickey, Browning and Campbell, 1985; Greenspan and Shoultz, 1981; Hanley-Maxwell, Rusch, and Rappaport, 1986). In addition, social interactions occur with great frequency in some job sites (Chadsey-Rusch, 1986a).

Production
Skills

Little information is available regarding how social ecological variables might affect production skills. In terms of assessment, only a few variables are discussed. Intervention strategies are discussed more completely within the social skills section.

Assessment Variables The relationship between social ecological variables and production skills has not been well studied. For example, even though some workers have been fired from their jobs for inappropriate social behaviors, little is known about whether or not these individuals also had poor production skills. In the Hanley-Maxwell, Rusch, and Rappaport (1986) study, however, nineteen of fifty-one job terminations were due to both social and nonsocial reasons, which suggests that poor production and social skills may be interrelated. What we do not know, however, is whether poor production skills leads to poor social skills or whether poor social skills leads to poor production skills. Similarly, if an individual is judged to have good social skills, we do not know if that necessarily makes that person a more competent employee. However, there is certainly a possibility that the better one gets along with his or her coworkers and supervisor, the happier, and perhaps more productive, a worker will be (House, 1981).

Intervention Strategies To date, little research has been done on the effects on production skills of manipulating social ecological variables. For example, if handicapped workers are taught to carry on conversations with their coworkers at break time, what effect might this intervention strategy have on speed of production? Little is known about the effects of such strategies. Generally, when social ecological variables are manipulated in employment settings, data is collected on social skill measures and not usually on production measures. It is unlikely that different social skill intervention strategies would be used to change social or production skills; the primary problem is that the effects of these strategies are not usually assessed on work performance. Thus, potential social ecological intervention strategies that might have an effect on production behaviors are discussed more fully in the following section.

Social Skills When making a match between a worker with special needs and a job, it is important to consider the effect that social ecological variables can have on social skills. This is important not only because of the relationship between these skills and job tenure, but also because of the increasing attention being placed on social-support networks and their relationship to quality of life issues. Social-support networks are defined by the interaction between individuals and groups that improve adaptive competence in dealing with short-term crises, long-term stresses, and life transitions. These networks include "emotional, informational, and material support that is provided by friends, relatives, neighbors, service providers, and others with whom (the target employee) has an ongoing relationship, and to whom one can turn in times of need or crisis" (O'Connor, 1983, p. 187).

Recently, Karan and Berger (in press) cited several studies that highlight the importance of developing social-support networks in everyday situations, such as in the employment setting. In fact, studies conducted with nonhandicapped persons have shown that certain types of social support can reduce various types of occupational stress and improve certain health indicators (House, 1981). Similarly, O'Connor (1983) concluded that social support can lead to reduced stress, enhanced well-being, and better outcomes for physical health problems. Finally, Romer and Heller (1983), in a review of studies examining the role that peers play in the successful adjustment into community settings of adults with mental retardation, concluded that individuals with more peer contact were more likely to remain in the community, transfer to less restrictive settings, demonstrate independence in self-care skills, earn more money, and transfer out of sheltered workshops into less restrictive employment settings.

If mismatches occur between employees with handicaps and their jobs, and the mismatches are due primarily to social ecological variables, it should be clear from the literature just cited that there will be different ways of viewing assessment and intervention strategies. That is, one might assess and design intervention strategies for the individual with handicaps or one might assess and design intervention strategies that affect social-support networks or the employment context. As discussed previously, when ecological incongruencies occur, matches can be enhanced by changing the individual, by changing the context, or by changing both the individual and the context. Special education has not always assumed an ecological perspective, and thus, when mismatches occur, assessment and intervention strategies have focused primarily on changing the individual with the handicap (Hanley-Maxwell, Rusch, and Rappaport, 1986). In the area of social skills assessment and training in employment settings, this has also been the trend.

Assessment Variables There have been only a few studies that have identified the types of social behaviors that will enhance matches between employees and their jobs in competitive employment settings. Again, it has been the premise of these studies that it would be the social skills of the worker with special needs that would need assessing rather than the social interaction patterns of others within the employment context.

In an investigation done by Rusch, Schutz, and Agran (1982), questionnaires were sent to 120 potential employers in Illinois from food service, janitorial/maid service, and light industrial occupations regarding their expectations for entry into employment. The results of the survey indicated that 90 percent of the employers agreed on sixteen social behaviors they felt were important. Two social behaviors in particular (reciting full name on request by verbal means and following one instruction provided at a time) were mentioned by every employer as being critical in competitive employment settings.

In another study, Salzberg, Agran, and Linugaris-Krafter (1985) also surveyed employers from five different jobs to obtain their opinions regarding social behaviors important for entry-level work. The results of this study indicated that social behaviors related to worker productivity (e.g., asking supervisors for assistance, following directions, responding to criticism, getting information before a job, offering to help coworkers) were rated higher in importance than general personal-social behaviors (e.g., listening without interrupting, acknowledging, and expressing appreciation to coworkers). Interestingly, there was little relationship between the frequency of occurrence of a behavior and its rated importance.

In addition to looking at the social behaviors that employers have identified as being important for matching up with jobs, we can also look at the reasons that employers have fired handicapped workers when obvious mismatches have occurred. For example, Greenspan and Shoultz (1981) conducted a study to determine the primary reason for job termination from competitive employment of thirty individuals in Nebraska with mild to moderate mental retardation. They found that seventeen of the thirty subjects lost their jobs for social reasons. In a more detailed analysis, Greenspan and Shoultz further sorted the social reasons for job loss into three categories: (1) character or moral reasons (e.g., stealing, assaulting others, sporadic work attendance), (2) temperament or affective reasons (e.g., yelling, banging head, hallucinations), and (3) social awareness reasons, or not understanding people and work settings (e.g., walking into a meeting and talking about a television program, being very inquisitive about other people's business). The study results revealed that three persons lost their jobs for reasons of character, five lost their jobs for reasons of temperament, and nine individuals lost their jobs for social awareness reasons.

Brickey, Browning, and Campbell (1985) also looked at the social reasons for the job loss of fifty-three adults with varying levels of mental retardation who had been placed in Projects with Industry or competitive employment. Social behaviors that contributed to job terminations were: relations with peers and supervisors, inappropriate behaviors, absenteeism and tardiness, poor motivation and attitude, hypochondria, gross insubordination and abusive behavior, and refusal to accept instructions. [For a more detailed review of studies that have investigated the social reasons for job loss, see Chadsey-Rusch (1986a)].

Clearly, these studies suggest that a number of social skills have been identified as being important to successful matches between workers with special needs and their jobs. In addition, several studies have also pinpointed the types of social behaviors that, if displayed, are likely to cause job terminations. It seems logical that if a target employee were assessed and found to be lacking in a particular social skill required for a job, then the individual would be taught this required skill. But what if an employee was assessed and found to have all the necessary social skills needed for the job, but still ended up being fired for social reasons? A possible answer to this question requires that we assess other social ecological variables, such as the social context in the employment setting.

For the purposes of this discussion, *social context variables* in employment settings will refer to the personal characteristics of its members (that is, the employer and coworkers) that may influence the "climate" of the setting, which, in turn, may influence the level and type of social support that a worker with special needs is likely to encounter on the job. Personal characteristics were described by Moos and Lemke (1983) as suprapersonal factors. They include such things as educational history, functional abilities, activity level, friendship patterns, physical appearance, and interests (e.g., job and leisure), as well as attitudes of the employer and coworkers. Few personal characteristic variables have been assessed with respect to matching workers with jobs. The area that has received the most attention is employer attitudes. For example, in a recent survey Shafer and Banks (1986) reported that 71 percent of the employers they surveyed had favorable or noncommittal attitudes toward hiring employees with handicaps. This figure represents responses from employers who had prior experience working with employees with handicaps and employers with no prior experience. It is possible that the employers with more favorable attitudes toward working with employees with handicaps are more likely to provide social support on the job, which may, in turn, influence the "goodness" of the job match.

Remember Sharon who was discussed earlier? As you recall, she was fired from one job (job A) for always coming in late but had never been late for her new job (job B). Both of her jobs were similar with respect to hours, pay, and task responsibilities. But obviously, differences were occurring in the settings that caused Sharon to like job B and dislike job A. One big difference between the jobs was the attitude and interactional style of the employers. In job A, the employer did not have a very favorable attitude about hiring Sharon in the first place, but in job B, the employer was more than willing to work with handicapped workers, had worked with them in the past, and had liked the advantage of being able to use the targeted-job-tax credit. In addition, the employer in job B often worked side by side with her employees and frequently told stories and jokes. It was also evident that this employer provided social support for Sharon on the job because she had been observed defending Sharon after a coworker had yelled at her.

One more interesting note about Sharon. At the same time that Sharon was working at job B, she was kicked out of her group home for breaking curfew. Some nights, Sharon stayed out all night. But even though Sharon stayed out all night, she was never late for job B. It may be that Sharon uses the same tactic (violating time) to get out of situations that she does not like. That is, she did not like job A, so she frequently came to work late, and she did not like her group home, so she never came home on time.

Although we know that employer attitudes may affect the job match, we don't know very much about coworker attitudes. In the only study to date, Hill and Wehman (1980) reported that coworkers have a predominantly positive perception of the handicapped worker. Coworkers seemed to value the work attitudes and positive personality characteristics of the handicapped workers more than how well they did their jobs. Like employer attitudes, coworker attitudes may affect the match between workers and their jobs.

Intervention Strategies Quite a bit of research has been conducted with respect to changing the social behaviors of workers with special needs (Chadsey-Rusch, 1986b). The majority of studies that have investigated strategies to increase social competence have used social skills training packages. These packages have typically consisted of some combination of the following components: (1) a rationale as to why the social behavior is desirable; (2) an opportunity to observe examples of the behavior (that is, modeling); (3) an opportunity to practice the behavior, usually in role-play situations; and (4) feedback regarding performance. By and large, most studies have employed these packages in analogue settings (e.g., laboratory room), but several studies have also trained and taken measures of the behavior in the natural environment (that is, on the job). While these packages have proven useful for increasing the acquisition of social skills, generalization effects to the natural environment have not been as pronounced.

Few studies have investigated strategies for changing the social context (employers and coworkers) in employment settings. In a general review on changing attitudes toward handicapped persons, Donaldson (1980) reported several intervention strategies that could be considered. One factor that emerged in successful interventions was ensuring that the person had at least equal status with nondisabled persons. By equal status, Donaldson meant that handicapped and nonhandicapped individuals should be approximately the same age and should have comparable social, educational, or vocational status. An example of nonequal status would be when a target employee worker always needed help or assistance from coworkers or employers.

Another intervention strategy that was found effective in the Donaldson (1980) review was exposing the nonhandicapped to presentations of, or experiences with, persons who represented nonstereotypic images of handicapped people. For example, media presentations might be used to convey information about what it is like to be handicapped, who the handicapped are as individuals, and how they expect nonhandicapped persons to relate to them. This type of strategy helps to reduce the discomfort, uneasiness, or uncertainty that nonhandicapped individuals may have in their interactions with persons with handicaps.

Shafer (1986) has suggested a different type of intervention tactic. He has proposed that coworkers should be taught to assume three new roles in employment settings: an advocate role, an observer role, and an intervention-agent role. By being an advocate, coworkers can help to protect the rights of target employees, can help employees from getting "stuck" with the least prestigious tasks, and can minimize practical jokes. By being an observer, coworkers can assist service providers in providing information on how the target employee is doing on the job. If coworkers assume the role of a trainer, they may be asked to assist the service provider or employer in teaching specific skills.

Summary

From the information presented, it is clear that social ecological variables can have an effect on matches between workers and their jobs. If workers display inappropriate social skills, for example, there is a strong likelihood they will be fired. Employers surveyed have identified several social skills that are crucial to employment success, such as following directions and being able to accept criticism. Thus, if certain social variables are found to be important for a job, and a worker is found to be lacking in these skills (or displays behavioral excesses), then intervention strategies will have to be designed to overcome this discrepancy. (Another strategy would be to find a different job for the worker, one that did not require the social skills the worker was lacking.)

Other social ecological variables that are important are those associated with the social context of the employment setting. That is, the personal characteristics of employers and coworkers can have an effect on job matches, particularly with regard to the issue of providing social support to handicapped workers. If a mismatch is due to social context variables, then intervention strategies will have to be designed to change the employer and/or coworker in the employment setting—or at least these variables will need to be considered when placing handicapped workers on jobs.

Although we know something about the effects of social ecological variables on social skills, we know very little about how these variables might affect production skills. Even within the social skills framework, we have little information regarding the personal characteristics of most employers and coworkers in job settings and how this might affect the social support received by handicapped workers on the job. It is clear that social ecological variables warrant further research.

ORGANIZATIONAL ECOLOGY

In this discussion, *organizational ecology* refers to those policy and program factors in an employment setting that may influence individual and group behavior. For example, the type of management or supervisory style that is used by the employer can potentially influence production skills and the social interaction patterns present in the workplace. If an employer's style is to provide constant supervision through coercion, for example, workers may be less satisfied with their jobs, and this may, in turn, cause production rates to fail. On the other hand, if employers are supportive and allow a certain degree of employee autonomy, it is likely that production rates and job satisfaction will be high.

Production and Social Skills

Little work has been done with regard to the influence of organizational ecological variables on job acquisition and maintenance by workers with special needs. Since so little work does exist in this area, assessment variables and intervention strategies are discussed with respect to both production and social skills together.

Assessment Variables   Moos (1983) has discussed a number of variables that relate to the organizational ecology dimension. For example, the size of the organization and the number of organizational levels of departments within a specific business or industry could enhance or impede a match between workers and their jobs. Some workers, for instance, may feel more comfortable working in organizations that are smaller in size and have fewer departments or bureaucratic levels.

Another variable that deserves consideration is the type of management structure present within an organization. For example, it might be important to note whether management was more centralized or more decentralized. Similarly, it might also be important to determine the span of control that exists within the organization—that is, the number of workers that each manager is responsible for supervising.

Management style, as discussed previously, is also an important feature to assess. Some supervisors prefer to interact with their employees frequently by giving many directions and continual feedback. This may be a desirable management style for some workers, but other workers may prefer a less intrusive supervisor.

Another variable that is somewhat related to management style is the degree with which a job allows employee autonomy. That is, it is important to assess the extent to which workers are encouraged to be self-sufficient and independent. Also an important feature of autonomy is the amount of freedom that workers have to make decisions and solve problems.

Two other dimensions of organizational ecology that may influence work performance and/or social behaviors are the (1) staffing ratios and work patterns in a job and (2) the salary levels, benefits, and opportunities that exist for advancement. While the importance of salary levels, benefits, and opportunities for advancement are self-explanatory, staffing ratios and work patterns may need to be more carefully defined. *Staffing ratios* refers to the number of workers assigned to complete tasks on the job that may influence levels of stress or pressure perceived by the workers. For example, if a small number of workers are always assigned to complete large tasks, they may experience high levels of stress because there are not enough workers assigned to complete the job within the time frame requested by managements. And *work patterns*, in this case, refers to the flexibility of a setting in allowing employees to work different time schedules, such as working flextime and job sharing.

Probably the key word in regard to organizational ecological variables is *flexibility*; that is, the degree to which the employment setting has clearly articulated policy and program goals that match the goals of the employees, and the degree to which the policy is flexible enough to allow input from the employees to modify goals and the working environment.

Intervention Strategies Regarding intervention strategies, alternative work patterns has probably received the most attention with respect to organization ecological variables. McMahon and Bartley (1981) suggested that for several reasons (e.g., transportation difficulties, health and stamina, skill demands) many individuals with handicaps may be unable to work traditional work hours. To accommodate this problem, two alternative work patterns have emerged: flextime and permanent part-time employment. Flextime allows employees more control over the hours they must work. Although a set number of core hours must usually be maintained to complete the work assignments, beginning and ending times are flexible. Studies examining the use of flextime have noted improved morale and productivity, and reduced absenteeism, tardiness, and turnover. Additionally, flexible scheduling allows workers to better meet unique transportation needs (e.g., bus scheduling), health needs (e.g., catheterization times, medical appointments, counseling sessions), educational needs (e.g., speech, occupational and physical therapies, community skills training), and leisure needs. Finally, flextime allows the worker time to develop social-interpersonal networks outside the work environment.

Permanent part-time employment is employment carried out in less than eight hours per day or forty hours per week. Seventy-five percent of the work force with handicaps in the United States works part-time. Numerous variations are possible. Job sharing is a version of part-time employment that is particularly attractive when dealing with job options for employees with handicaps. Job sharing requires that a full-time position be restructured into two or more part-time jobs. These part-time jobs may be worked as consecutive shifts or as concurrent shifts in which two employees, for example, collaborate on meeting the responsibilities of the job while working shorter hours. Another variation of job sharing includes sharing the responsibilities of the job as well as sharing the salary and benefits.

Each of these alternatives has some advantages. Flextime and permanent part-time employment may facilitate better job performance through a combination of shorter work hours and allocation of tasks based on ability and extent of disability. The third variation, job sharing, may open job opportunities that have previously been unavailable due to one person's inability to perform tasks associated with the job. Job sharing allows service providers to mix and match individuals to accomplish job tasks that highlight the competencies of each of the individuals rather than their incompetencies. Job sharing often reduces the need for job restructuring or modification. The following case study provides an example of how flextime and job sharing have been used.

CASE STUDY: Jane and John

Jane and John are completing their education at a local high school. Both students are physically disabled and require motorized wheelchairs. Jane and John are also mildly mentally retarded. Over the past three years both have been working in alternative businesses as part of their high school's work experience program. During this period, Jane and John have worked in traditional food service settings, laundry and maid service settings, and various small assembly businesses throughout their local community.

Jane and John have been good workers across a number of jobs. In fact, based upon attendance, social ability, and work performance, they appeared to show little variation in overall performance across each of the work settings. However, the work experience coordinator collected specific data on work performance at different times during each day. This coordinator found that Jane worked much better (that is, faster and more accurately) during the morning hours, whereas John performed better later in the day; both students appeared to slow down and make more errors after they had worked for three or four hours. This information coupled with the work experience coordinator's knowledge of available jobs allowed the coordinator to identify a job suited for both Jane and John.

Jane and John job share. They work at a local print shop for a total of thirty to forty hours a week (fifteen to twenty hours each). The positions that they now hold previously constituted a full-time position that was, for the past thirty months, held by one person working full-time. The work experience coordinator contacted the employer and discussed the possibility of two individuals holding the job, and this was agreed upon. The employer indicated that Jane and John could work flexible hours but that they had to check with the supervisor at the end of each day to discuss the print shop's workload for the following day.

Allowing Jane and John to work shorter periods of time and to arrange the hours that they work each day provides benefits to the employer as well as to Jane and John. The employer can structure her time to meet her clients' jobs because she has one employee who is willing to work early mornings as well as late mornings; she also has an employee who is willing to work late afternoons/early evenings as well as early afternoons. Jane and John are happy because they can arrange their leisure, transportation, shopping, and other daily chores around their shorter work hours. They also like their work.

Summary   Although an authoritative research literature does not exist to better define the influence of organizational ecology on work behavior, some characteristics of organizational ecology have been identified as important to assess. These characteristics include the size of the organization and organizational levels; management structure and style; degree of autonomy on the job; staffing ratios and work patterns; and salary levels, benefits, and opportunities for advancement. While few of these variables have been researched with respect to intervention strategies, modification of work patterns has the potential to enhance matches between workers and their jobs.

GENERAL SUMMARY

Two premises guided our discussion throughout this chapter. First, there will be less employment turnover if there is a good match between employees and their jobs; and second, matches can be enhanced by viewing the workplace from an ecological perspective. The ecological perspective implies that the behavior of individuals in physical and social contexts is interrelated and interdependent. If we choose to accept this perspective, then we need to take a broader look at assessment and intervention strategies. That is, rather than assessing and designing interventions only for the individual, we must also begin to assess and design interventions that affect the employment context (e.g., job tasks, supervisors, coworkers), or both the individual and the employment context.

In this chapter, three dimensions to the ecological perspective were discussed: (1) physical ecology, (2) social ecology, and (3) organization ecology. *Physical ecology* refers primarily to the architectural and physical design of the work setting. *Social ecology* refers to interactions and interrelationships that exist between and among individuals and/or groups, and *organizational ecology* refers to policy and program factors that may influence individual or group behavior. Assessment variables and possible intervention strategies were introduced for each of the three ecological dimensions.

Although a research literature is beginning to emerge concerning these ecological dimensions and their impact on maximizing matches between employees and their jobs, much work remains to be done in this area. There should be little doubt, however, that people like Sharon, Jane, and John are assets to their employment communities and, because of their involvement in valued work, they derive important benefits also.

REFERENCES

Barker, R.G. (1968). *Ecological Psychology.* Stanford, Calif.: Stanford University Press.

Berkson, G., and D. Romer. (1980). Social ecology of supervised communal facilities for mentally disabled adults: An introduction. *American Journal of Mental Deficiency 85*(3), 219–228.

Brickey, M., L. Browning, and K. Campbell. (1985). A five-year follow-up of sheltered workshop employees placed in competitive jobs. *Mental Retardation 23,* 67–83.

Chadsey-Rusch, J. (1986a). Identifying and teaching valued social behaviors in competitive employment settings. In F.R. Rusch (ed.), *Competitive Employment Issues and Strategies.* Baltimore: Paul H. Brookes.

Chadsey-Rusch, J. (April, 1986b). The relationship between social behaviors and supportd employment. Paper presented at the RRTC Third Annual Symposium on Supported Employment, Virginia Beach, Va.

Donaldson, J. (1980). Changing attitudes toward handicapped persons: A review and analysis of research. *Exceptional Children 46,* 504–513.

Engelkes, J. (1979). Job analysis in vocational rehabilitation. In D. Vandergoot and J.D. Worrall (eds.), *Placement in Rehabilitation* Baltimore: University Park Press. Pp. 127–141.

Greenspan, S., and B. Shoultz. (1981). Why mentally retarded adults lose their jobs: Social incompetence as a factor in work adjustment. *Applied Research in Mental Retardation 2,* 23–38.

Hanley-Maxwell, C., F.R. Rusch, J. Chadsey-Rusch, and A. Renzaglia. (1986). Factors contributing to job terminations. *Journal of the Association for Persons with Severe Handicaps 11*(1), 45–52.

Hanley-Maxwell, C., F.R. Rusch, and J. Rappaport. (1986). *A Multilevel Perspective on Job Terminations for Adults with Handicaps.* Champaign: Secondary Transition Intervention Effectiveness Institute, University of Illinois.

Hasazi, S.B., L.R. Gordon, and C.A. Roe. (1985). Factor associated with the employment status of handicapped youth exiting high school from 1979 to 1983. *Exceptional Children 51,* 455–469.

Hill, M., and P. Wehman. (1980). Employer and nonhandicapped coworker perceptions of moderately and severely retarded workers. In P. Wehman and

M. Hill (eds.), *Vocational Training and Placement of Severely Disabled Persons* Richmond: Virginia Commonwealth University. Pp. 73–83.

House, J.S. (1981). *Work Stress and Social Support.* Reading, Mass.: Addison-Wesley.

Ittelson, W.H., H.M. Proshansky, and L.G. Rivlin. (1972). Bedroom size and social interaction of the psychiatric ward. In J.F. Wohlwill and D.H. Carson (eds.), *Environment and the Social Sciences: Perspectives and Applications.* Washington, D.C.: American Psychological Association.

Karan, O.C., and C. Berger. (In press). Developing support networks for individuals who fail to achieve competitive employment. In F.R. Rusch (ed), *Competitive Employment Issues and Strategies.* Baltimore: Paul H. Brookes.

Malzahn, D.E. (1979). *Intra-individual Ability Evaluation Using the AMI: Problem Solving with Rehabilitation Engineering.* Wichita: Cerebral Palsy Research Foundation of Kansas, Inc., Rehabilitation Engineering Center Tech Brief.

McMahon, B.T., and P.A. Bartley. (1981). Alternative work patterns and rehabilitation. *Rehabilitation Literature* 42(1-2), 14–17.

Mithaug, D.E. (1981). *Prevocational Training for Retarded Students.* Springfield, Ill.: Charles C. Thomas.

Moos, R.H. (1983). Conceptualizations of human environments. *American Psychologist 28,* 652–665.

Moos, R.H., and S. Lemke. (1983). Assessing and improving social-ecological settings. In E. Seidman (ed.), *Handbook of Social Intervention.* London: Sage Publications. Pp. 143–162.

O'Connor, G. (1983). Presidential address 1983: Social support of mentally retarded persons. *Mental Retardation 21,* 187–196.

Romer, D., and T. Heller. (1983). Social adaptation of mentally retarded adults in community settings: A social-ecological approach. *Applied Research in Mental Retardation 4,* 303–314.

Rusch, F.R. (1979). Toward the validation of social/vocational survival skills. *Mental Retardation 17,* 143–145.

Rusch, F.R., R.P. Schutz, and M. Agran. (1982). Validating entry-level survival skills for service occupations: Implications for curriculum development. *Journal of the Association for Persons with Severe Handicaps 7,* 32–41.

Salzberg, C.L., M. Agran, and B. Linugaris/Krafter. (1985). *Behaviors That Contribute to Entry-level Employment: A Profile of Five Jobs.* Logan: Department of Special Education, Utah State University.

Schalock, R.L., and C.M. Jensen. (In press). Assessing the goodness-of-fit between persons and their environments. *Journal of the Association for Persons with Severe Handicaps.*

Schoggen, P. (1978). Ecological psychology and mental retardation. In G.P. Sackett (ed.), *Observing Behavior, Vol. I: Theory and Applications in Mental Retardation.* Baltimore: University Park Press. Pp. 33–62.

Shafer, M.S. (1986). Utilizing coworkers as change agents. In F.R. Rusch (ed.), *Competitive Employment Issues and Strategies.* Baltimore: Paul H. Brookes.

Shafer, M.S., and D. Banks. (April, 1986). Supported competitive employment: Research related to employers' perspectives on hiring workers with mental retardation. Paper presented at the RRTC Third Annual Symposium on Supported Employment, Virginia Beach, Va.

Sowers, J., L.E. Thompson, and R.T. Connis. (1979). The food service vocational training program. In G.T. Bellamy, G. O'Conner, and O.C. Karan (eds.). *Vocational Rehabilitation of Severely Handicapped Persons.* Baltimore: University Park Press.

Thurman S.K. (1977). Congruence of behavioral ecologies: A model for special education. *Journal of Special Education 11*, 329–333.

U.S. Commission on Civil Rights. (1983). *Accommodating the Spectrum of Disabilities.* Washington, D.C.: U.S. Commission on Civil Rights.

U.S. Department of Labor. (March, 1979). *Sheltered Workshop Study:* Volume II. Washington, D.C.: U.S. Department of Labor.

U.S. Office of Personnel Management. (1984). *Handbook of Job Analysis for Reasonable Accommodation.* Washington, D.C.: Selection Placement Programs.

Vandergoot, D., and J.D. Worrall. (eds.) (1979). *Placement in Rehabilitation: A Career Development Perspective.* Baltimore: University Park Press.

Wershing, A. (1984). *Engineering Technology as Applied to the Vocational Domain for Persons with Severely Handicapped Students: A Review of Current Literature.* Charlotte: Department of Special Education, University of Virginia.

10 Economic Issues in Employing Persons with Disabilities

Justin O'Brien
Indiana State University

David Stern
University of California, Berkeley

INTRODUCTION

This chapter presents a perspective perhaps not yet typical for special education teachers, but one that will surely become increasingly useful in understanding the roles they may find themselves in—as job coaches, employment associates, and transitional employment specialists. The socioeconomic dilemma of work disability, as well as the difficulties economists encounter in studying this problem, are described. Pertinent economic issues include: the financial benefits and costs related to work disability; various work incentives and disincentives; the relationship between educational programs and the skill needs of employers; public and private sector programs intended to benefit handicapped individuals; and innovative programs such as school-based enterprises and the supported employment initiative.

For most handicapped people throughout history, access to a normal social role has been acquired with great difficulty, if at all. Indeed, the needs of disabled people have seldom been among society's priorities. For most of history, to be handicapped was to be stigmatized, isolated, and expendable. The late nineteenth century witnessed the scientific formalization of the persecution of physically and mentally handicapped individuals. Social Darwinists maintained that such disabilities were the underlying source of nearly all social problems. Handicapped persons were often referred to as "animals," "subhumans," and "waste-products." Some authorities advocated institutionalization for even minor disabling conditions. Through the early 1900s, disabled individuals continued to be segregated and relegated to second-class citizenship (Burgdorf and Burgdorf, 1977; U.S. Commission on Civil Rights, 1983).

Nevertheless, in recent years, handicapped persons have seemingly gained parity with other minority groups in the public consciousness with regard to civil rights, their unique educational needs, and the difficulties they encounter in securing and maintaining stable employment. Among the more prominent events providing evidence for a greater recognition of their needs are the passage of such legislation as the Rehabilitation Act of 1973; special provisions included in the vocational education legislation, most notably in the Carl Perkins Act; Department of Labor programs such as the Targeted Jobs Tax Credit Program and the Jobs Training Partnership Act; the Education for All Handicapped Children Act of 1975; and the 1980 and 1984 amendments to the Social Security Act, the purposes of which were to reduce the work disincentives created by the Social Security insurance and supplemental security income programs.

Despite enabling legislation and government-sponsored programs, handicapped Americans continue to represent a sizable group beset by major life problems, not the least of which is potential labor market discrimination. A 1980 report by the Carnegie Council on Children, *The Unexpected Minority: Handicapped Children in America*, presented testimony to this unhappy fact (Carnegie Council on Children, 1980). According to the report, handicapped children of all types are the targets of unconscious social and political oppression that is often more damaging to their lives than their disabilities. This oppression includes outright prejudice against handicapped people of all ages, job discrimination, and, most fundamentally, well-meaning but destructive misconceptions that exaggerate the true limitations of many handicaps.

As in the case of other dispossessed groups, public awareness and statutory intentions have not been translated into socioeconomic equity. Furthermore, discussion of the employment difficulties of handicapped individuals tends to be eclipsed in the national debate on employment policy and programs. The facts, however, suggest an issue of greater significance than one would infer from the employment literature.

Approximately 37 million people—16.3 percent of the entire U.S. population—is covered by federal disability rights now in effect. Fifteen percent of the total working-age population (16 through 64) is work-disabled due to a physical or mental condition. Thus, disabled persons comprise the largest single class afforded civil rights protection (Disability Rights Education and Defense Fund, 1982). According to the 1983 report of the White House Working Group on Disability Policy, an amount equal to 8 percent of the gross national product of the United States is spent each year on disability programs, with most of that amount going to programs that support continued dependence on public funds (White House Working Group on Disability Policy, 1984). In fiscal 1985, federal spending for mentally retarded and developmentally disabled individuals alone totaled $7.8 billion. (Conley and Noble, 1985). National data compiled by the Berkeley-based Disability Rights Education and Defense Fund indicate that a "disabled" family's income is nearly three times as likely to fall below the federally defined poverty level as the average family's; "disabled" families are only half as likely to reach the level of economic well-being attained by the American population as a whole, and as a class they are the poorest single group in our country (Disability Rights Education Defense Fund, 1982).

Two factors contribute to the impoverishment of handicapped Americans: extraordinarily high rates of unemployment or nonemployment, and low wages. The U.S. Commission on Civil Rights, 1983, recently reported unemployment rates of between 50 and 80 percent among handicapped persons. In terms of wages, those of disabled men equal only 79 percent of those of nondisabled men; wages of disabled women are only 74 percent of the wages earned by nondisabled women. For many years, advocacy groups such as the President's Committee on Employment of the Handicapped and the various governor's committees have produced and distributed consciousness-raising advocacy material designed to persuade private-sector employers to hire handicapped workers. However, there is little evidence that such nonpecuniary (non-monetary) strategies have had any significant impact on the unemployment rates of handicapped individuals (Levitan and Taggart, 1976).

Major pieces of legislation such as the Rehabilitation Act and the Education of the Handicapped Act have been in effect now for many years. Despite their accomplishments, however, some 250,000 to 300,000 handicapped students continue to leave the nation's public schools each year and enter an adult society still very much unprepared to deal with most of them. To address this need, the Office of Special Education and Rehabilitative Services (OSERS) has taken the lead in promoting intervention strategies such as transitional employment programs and supported employment to assist handicapped students in successful entry into the labor market. The competitive employment and long-term labor force attachment of disabled youth leaving school has been declared a national priority (Guard, 1985).

Problems in Studying the Economics of Work Disability

Numerous difficulties characterize the employment of disabled persons and tend to hinder the effectiveness of even the most well thought-out educational strategies and programs. The first and most significant barrier is the lack of a full employment policy on the part of the national government. It has been suggested that the adoption of a total employment policy would require structural changes both in the national economy and in society as a whole. As economist Robert H. Haveman (W.F. Upjohn Institute for Employment Research, 1978) has observed:

> Social policy toward handicapped, disabled, and disadvantaged workers varies widely among countries. Those adopting full employment policies—the Eastern European countries, for example—expect all individuals, including the handicapped and disabled, to contribute to the social product, and these countries make provisions for such contribution via public enterprises, state-supported cooperatives, or home work. The social welfare states of Western Europe—for example, Sweden and the Netherlands—generally take the "right to work" concept as a fundamental principle and seek to provide employment for anyone who wishes to work. In the United States, many handicapped and disadvantaged persons are guaranteed some income support, but *not* employment. (1978, p. 242)

Within the context of an economy not based on full employment, the effects of work disability on employment is studied by economists using models representing supply and demand in the labor market (Johnson, 1985). The labor supply model represents the work activity of a disabled individual as the outcome of: (1) economic incentives and disincentives (e.g., wages vs. nonwage income such as SSI); (2) personal preferences (e.g., the preference for the time off vs. material goods acquired through wage income), and (3) a set of personal (e.g., nature and severity of handicap, work readiness) and environmental (e.g., geography, architectural, and transportation barriers) characteristics that influence the choice an individual makes between work and other alternatives.

The labor demand model analyzes the influence of variables such as labor market discrimination, and the effects of employment programs on hiring and training decisions. We will examine the variables that these models incorporate, but mainly from the perspective of an educator rather than an economist. While it is the critical role of the economist to construct such models to explain or predict employment outcomes, it is useful for educators to understand these labor market forces. The economist develops models to perfect macroeconomic (major economic aggregates) truths. To the extent that we comprehend the forces at work in the labor market that affect the employability of our handicapped constituency, we will achieve greater insight into the instructional and programmatic needs of special education students. Before reviewing specific issues in greater detail, let us consider the difficulties economists often encounter in conducting analyses of this type.

Conley and Noble (1985) have described the many empirical and conceptual problems associated with conducting studies in the area of work disability. These include:

1. Problems of missing data. Obviously, handicapping conditions have many effects. At best, only a few are measured, such as the resultant loss of earnings, the increase in earnings after rehabilitation, and the costs of treatment and rehabilitation. So too, it is extremely difficult to measure the effects of an individual's disability on the morale, productivity, and thus the earnings of other family members. Similar effects on the work efforts of siblings or their future college achievements are rarely examined. Even with respect to obvious variables such as the earnings of handicapped individuals themselves, only rarely is there sufficient data to estimate, without making very judgmental assumptions, the increase in earnings that will result after rehabilitation.

2. Variables without a monetary or market value. Many of the effects of handicaps do not have an easily determined value. This is obviously true for psychic costs such as mental depression or lowered self-esteem, for losses in the ability to carry on normal activities, and even for such activities as homemaking.

3. Problems of different weighting of costs and benefits. Although economists are primarily concerned with easily measured variables such as earnings and treatment costs, others, such as parents, may attach less importance to these variables and place greater emphasis on psychic costs and family stability.

4. Problems of distribution. The costs of programs are usually borne by taxpayers and the benefits are received by handicapped persons. It is difficult to compare costs borne by one group with benefits received by another. Although such information may be useful for funding decisions, it will require a judgment concerning the proper distribution of income and social responsibility.

5. Problems in defining the appropriate decision units. Although economists stress the importance of conducting benefit-cost analyses based on marginal changes in a program (that is, changes in a part of the program that are realistically subject to a funding decision), it is usually next to impossible to determine the benefits that result from changing only a small part of the program. Who can say which persons in a vocational rehabilitation program would not have been served if the program had not expanded?

6. Problems of discounting. Obviously, much of the benefit and some of the cost in rehabilitation programs will not occur until future years and must be discounted to present value. Although this is one of the most significant computations affecting the results of benefit-cost analysis, there is little consensus about what

constitutes the appropriate discount rate. Using two rates, as is sometimes done, merely doubles the number of calculations. Two sets of calculations may produce a confusing and inconclusive range of estimates of benefits, with unclear implications for policy makers.

ISSUES

These conceptual and empirical difficulties have precluded a definitive resolution of several recurrent policy issues. One such issue is how to provide for individuals' basic material needs without destroying their financial incentive to work. Another is whether training programs should emphasize specific or general job skills. A third recurrent question is whether programs to promote employment should rely mainly on training, direct job creation of jobs in the public sector, or on wage subsidies for private jobs. A fourth issue is where best to combine employment and training: in workplaces, in schools, or in some combination of the two. A fifth issue is that of supported employment in its various forms to provide training and employment opportunities for more severely disabled individuals. Finally, the question may be raised whether employing disabled persons will cost or save the taxpayers money.

FINANCIAL BENEFITS AND COST FOR SOCIETY AS A WHOLE

Placing disabled workers into competitive employment can save taxpayers money, as Hill and Wehman (1983) have shown. They found that the cost of helping a disabled person to get and hold a regular job is often (though not always) less than the sum of taxes paid from the disabled employee earnings, plus the cost of alternative programs and income support no longer required by the disabled individual who becomes employed.

However, Hill and Wehman note that "most, if not all, of the jobs held by disabled persons would be held by nonhandicapped individuals in their absence" (1983, p. 35). If the nonhandicapped individuals who are displaced by disabled workers do not succeed in finding jobs, the saving to taxpayers is substantially less than that shown by Hill and Wehman, because the nonhandicapped individuals who become unemployed now pay fewer taxes, and also may incur costs to the public for unemployment insurance payments as well as other income support and social services. (This is also true, of course, if the workers who become unemployed are themselves disabled.) To the extent that a program for placing a certain number of individuals into competitive employment causes other individuals to become unemployed, it becomes less financially advantageous from the taxpayers' point of view, and makes it less palatable politically to certain segments of society.

Some displacement is inevitable as long as the total number of people seeking paid jobs exceeds the number of jobs available in the economy as a whole. Abraham (1983) has estimated that the total number of job-seekers exceeds the total number of jobs available in the U.S. economy whenever the overall unemployment rate is higher than 3 or 4 percent. When the unemployment rate goes down to 3 or 4 percent, then 3 or 4 percent of the labor force is between jobs, but there is an equal number of jobs that are vacant. Three or 4 percent is therefore called the "frictional" rate of unemployment: When unemployment is at that rate, the total number of jobs is adequate, but the processes of recruitment by employers and job search by unemployed workers take time, and therefore not everyone is employed at every moment. In actual fact, economic policy in the U.S. has not been able to keep unemployment down to 3 or 4 percent. Inflation tends to accelerate when the unemployment rate is pushed down that far—though this is a matter of controversy among economic theorists.

As long as the national unemployment rate is above the 3 to 4 percent range, programs to promote employment of disabled persons will compete against programs for other groups, such as low-income youth, former convicts, and welfare recipients. And all such programs compete against ordinary workers and job-seekers.

If inflation could be kept at bay, so that unemployment could be maintained at the frictional rate, promoting employment of disabled persons would no longer be at the expense of other groups. With no surplus job-seekers in the labor market, the full earnings of individuals who obtain paid jobs as a result of a training program could be counted as an economic benefit to society. Under these circumstances preparing disabled persons for competitive employment would be substantially more attractive for taxpayers and society as a whole.

WORK INCENTIVES VERSUS TRANSFER PAYMENTS

The federal government conducts a wide variety of programs intended for the redistribution of income among economic classes in our society; these can be classified into three main types: (1) transfer payments in cash (e.g., SSI) or in kind (e.g. food stamps); (2) education and training programs designed to increase the labor productivity and thus the earning power of a target group [e.g., Job Corps, Jobs Training Partnership Act (JTPA), compensatory education, and vocational education]; and (3) directly increasing employment opportunities through wage subsidies (e.g., Targeted Jobs Tax Credits) or job creation.

However, different kinds of redistribution may conflict with each other. Investments in increased labor productivity, such as vocational education, may score highly in terms of developing skills that are thought to contribute to the recipient's self-respect, but they are not as cost-effective as transfer payments in raising recipients' incomes.

Education programs may not succeed in raising the earning power of the recipient by as much as the marginal cost (cost per individual recipient) of the program, whereas a direct transfer of public funds (as in the case of SSI payments) to individual recipients would do so. In an economy that has never been able to attain full employment (except in time of war), investments in training programs for those who are most likely to remain unemployed, even in the best of times, are simply not as "allocatively efficient" as pure income transfer programs (Weisbrod, 1977).

Almost fifty years ago, the first income transfer program, Social Security, was established by the federal government. Until 1974, however, federal assistance to groups such as disabled persons was channeled through grants to states for public assistance transfer payments. Beginning in that year, similar support was provided through direct grants from the federal government to individual recipients under the supplemental security income (SSI) program (Singer, 1976). By 1985, the SSI program had grown to include nearly 4 million recipients, about half of whom were of working age. (Gorski, 1985). In FY 1985, 34.8 percent of the total federal outlays for programs for the mentally retarded and the developmentally disabled—over $2.7 billion—was spent on Medicare, noninstitutional Medicaid, and direct SSI payments (Conley and Noble, 1985).

Soon after its enactment, however, it became apparent that this well-intended program contained a major disincentive for many disabled individuals anxious to go to work. If a disabled person receiving cash benefits engaged in "substantial gainful activity" (SGA) amounting to $300 per month, cash benefits and medical benefits available under medicaid were terminated. In discussing income transfers as work disincentives, Levitan and Taggart (1976) in their classic work *Jobs for the Disabled* suggested that the expansion of this income support may have been the cause rather than the effect of reduced employment, if disabled people reacted to more attractive benefits by shunning work.

While the work disincentives built into the program were apparent to many SSI recipients and their advocates, no organized attempt to modify the program occurred until 1977. In that year, the Carter administration convened the White House Conference on Handicapped Individuals. Disability advocates and organizations such as the National Association for Retarded Citizens, the California Westside Center for Independent Living, and the Berkeley Center for Independent

Living met to advocate effective work incentives in the SSI program (Gorski, 1985).

In 1980, as the result of the efforts of the disabled community and its supporters, Congress enacted section 1619, on a three-year demonstration basis, as part of the Social Security Disability Amendments (P.L. 96–265). It contains provisions that allow severely disabled SSI recipients to continue to receive some cash benefits and Medicaid services though engaging in substantial gainful employment beyond the $300 limit. Section 1619 has two parts:

1619(a) Essentially, under this first part, disabled SSI recipients may continue to receive SSI payments even though their earnings have exceeded the $300 limit and have passed a nine-month trial work period. SSI payments are reduced at a rate of $1 for each $2 earned after the first $85 per month. When earnings reach $735, the individual loses the last dollar of the basic (federal portion) SSI payment—currently $325. Because some states supplement the federal money, some disabled persons may continue to receive a cash benefit beyond the $735.

1619(b) This second part encourages higher earnings by continuing Medicaid coverage, even though the disabled individual's earnings and other income exceed the provisions of Section 1619(a). Because different states have different Medicaid eligibility rules, this section may not function the same way uniformly throughout the nation. For example, Idaho, Indiana, and Minnesota as well as seventeen other states are not necessarily affected by 1619(b) because they do not use SSI criteria to automatically establish eligibility for Medicaid. Income ceilings vary from state to state, but generally, Medicaid benefits may continue for working disabled individuals even though earnings become high enough to end SSI payments. Indeed, in some states, handicapped workers may earn as high as $20,000 per year under certain circumstances and still retain Medicaid eligibility. (National Clearing House on Postsecondary Education for Handicapped Individuals, 1985).

Aside from these major provisions, a fifteen-month reentitlement period was created. During this period, an individual's Social Security or regular SSI checks can be affected by substantial gainful activity. However, should the work effort fail, the individual has the security of knowing that he or she can return to regular benefits status without filing a new application or disability determination.

When section 1619 expired on December 31, 1983, the administration continued the effects of the provision until Congress extended it, once again on a temporary basis, through June 1987. Although the Social Security Administration has been able to provide some data on the numbers of people benefiting under these provisions, the information has been inconclusive as to the effectiveness of these new provisions as work incentives. Only about 5,000 disabled persons nationwide have taken advantage of this program to date. Two reasons have been cited: (1) lack of publicity—many counselors and other service providers, as well as disabled people themselves, have been unaware of the program and how they might benefit from it; and (2) the provision has not been permanent and many disabled people have not participated for fear of losing needed benefits if the program were discontinued. Indeed, this fear has prevented many severely handicapped individuals from leaving the disability rolls.

For example, consider the case of Guy, a young man living in Wisconsin. He is in his late 20s and is both mildly mentally retarded and physically disabled. He has worked as a clerk in his local United Cerebral Palsy program for three years. He is punctual, dependable, and works well. He could be earning at least minimum wage in competitive employment, but he cannot afford to lose his group home status nor the medical services provided by Medicaid. Thus, he works for only $50 every two weeks. It is the maximum he can earn before his benefits begin to decrease. Under the new regulations, his income may increase dramatically without a loss of eligibility for benefits (Griss, 1985).

In those reported cases in which disabled people have taken advantage of section 1619, they have benefited. For example, Peter Pointon of Arlington, Virginia, who is mentally handicapped, earns $7,000 per year and has retained Medicaid coverage. Douglas Martin, a resident of Los Angeles, is a post-polio quadriplegic. He earns $16,000 and retains both Medicaid and a small SSI monthly payment because disability-related work expense deductions are sizable enough to bring his earnings below the point at which he would lose all SSI payments. In Minneapolis, Minnesota, Clint Schultz, afflicted with a spinal cord injury, earns $9,500 per year and has retained his Medicaid (Gorski, 1985).

What role will educators and other helping professionals play in the effort to further eliminate work disincentives for disabled persons? In 1985, OSERS began a comprehensive review of this issue. Specific provisions of the proposed "Employment Opportunities for Disabled Americans Act" are related to OSERS responsibilities. Title II of the act would amend the Rehabilitation Act and establish a direct grant program in the Rehabilitation Services Administration. Authorizations of $5 million in FY 1985 increasing to $8 million by FY 1992 are planned for three separate purposes: (1) to establish a program of one-year planning grants to assist employers in planning the initiation or expansion of a comprehensive retention and reemployment program for disabled workers; (2) to establish a program of grants of not more than three years' duration to implement or substantially expand comprehensive retention or reemployment programs; and (3) to establish a program of one-time, one-year grants to assist employers in evaluating the effectiveness of any retention and reemployment program for disabled workers (Will, 1985).

These proposals obviously hold great potential for increasing the employability of handicapped individuals. They also present educators with increased opportunities to assist employers in developing the full potential of handicapped employees.

As special educators and helping professionals, we may exercise great influence with regard to the labor market "supply-side" issue of work disincentive. In our evolving roles as "employment associates" and "transition program specialists," we will be in positions to continue to provide our handicapped constituents with the encouragement and motivation to achieve a less stigmatized social role through productive employment. So too, as knowledgable advocates, we can guide our handicapped students' awareness of their opportunities under the new and permanent work incentive provisions of legislation such as H.R. 2030.

The financial benefits disabled individuals may derive from paid employment are enhanced by the increase in dignity and self-value they will most assuredly gain. Lex Frieden, Executive Director of the National Council on the Handicapped, has stated the case well:

> Employment is an essential key to successful adult integration into community life. Various forms of work are frequently associated with greater independence, productivity, self-esteem, and social and financial status. In our society, success and quality of life are often measured in terms of paid employment. While paid employment may not be a reasonable expectation for all disabled people, work remains an important component of each individual's right and obligation to live as independently and responsibly as possible in the community. (Frieden, 1985)

SPECIFIC VERSUS GENERAL WORK SKILLS

A crucial role for special educators will continue to be to provide handicapped students leaving school with appropriate job skills to facilitate successful, long-term labor force attachment. Following their best instincts down a well-traveled path, many special educators have come to view vocational education, with its emphasis on occupationally specific skill training, as an effective strategy for preparing handicapped students for employment. Opinions expressed by Marc Hull epitomize much of the literature on the subject.

> Possessing marketable vocational skills is one of the most impressive credentials that anyone can present to a prospective employer. For the handicapped, possessing marketable skills is proof of their ability to perform specific skills job functions and goes a long way in eliminating or reducing the anxieties that employers express about hiring the handicapped. (1977, p. 3)

However, the empirical evidence that high school vocational education helps its graduates get jobs is, at best, ambiguous. Reviews of local and national outcome studies of vocational education graduates conducted over the past several years have been consistently nonsupportive of vocational education as an effective strategy for improving the employment stability or earnings of its graduates or even of providing appropriate or readily salable specific job skills (Flynn, 1982; Stern, 1985).

What factors contribute to the ineffectiveness of conventional specific-skill vocational education, and what implications does this issue have for planning truly effective employment preparation of handicapped youth? Let us first review the basic concepts.

In his definitive work *Human Capital: A Theoretical and Empirical Analysis, with Special Reference to Education*, Gary S. Becker (1964) introduced the concepts of occupationally "general" and "specific" training. General training, for such tasks as typing or operating a cash register, equips the trainee with skills that may be useful for increasing productivity in many different firms. Since employers have little incentive to invest on skills that may be transferred to other firms, there is a tendency for the wages of newly hired employees who receive general training on the job to be depressed to the level of their net marginal product during the period of training. Essentially, the employee who receives general training on the job pays for it through reduced wages.

In contrast, specific training, such as that required to operate a particular firm's computer system, increases a person's productivity only if the person is employed in that particular firm. A completely "specific" skill is unique to a single job category in a single firm, whereas a completely "general" skill is requisite for every job in every firm. Becker showed that, unlike general training, specific training will be financed in part by employers.

In their description of "The Origins of the Internal Labor Market," Peter B. Doeringer and Michael J. Piore (1971) relate these concepts to the internal organization of firms' work forces, and the structure and customs that have evolved related to job training. The specificity of a job is defined in part by the particular physical characteristics of the jobs performed. The most common denominator of job specificity in any given workplace is the productive environment specific to the work tasks performed. Awareness of the routine operating characteristics of machines, as well as the functional relations between coworkers, are skills highly specific to a particular work setting.

Closely associated with job specificity is specificity of technology, which is the entire set of individual tasks that make up a work process. It utilizes skills of varying degrees of specificity. Most manufacturing jobs require both speed and accuracy, which often are the most critical factors in labor costs. Both depend a great deal on the skillful use of particular pieces of equipment, materials, products being manufactured, the length of the production run, and the environment in which the product is being produced. Many factors of a job, such as idiosyncratic sounds, smells, and so on of the work environment, require firsthand experience to appreciate. Ultimately, the unique skills required to maintain production under all these circumstances become the possession of the particular labor force in a given production process. Individual members of the internal labor force acquire their respective shares of the total repertoire of skills required to continue production through on-the-job specific-skill training. These facts enhance the importance of the internal labor market as a stable and self-perpetuating entity and, in turn, create rigidity in the rules concerning on-the-job training.

Typically, on-the-job specific-skill training is informal. It occurs as part of the production process, partly through trial and error. Participants in the training process therefore assume dual roles: as supervisors or subordinates, and as instructors or students. The process of on-the-job training blurs the distinction between jobs, creating a "rolling readjustment"—a gradual and progressive exchange of skills—between experienced workers and trainees.

In most cases, there is simply no alternative to on-the-job training. It often cannot be duplicated in the classroom. One advantage of on-the-job training is that it tends to be more economical than formal instruction because it is confined only to those skills required for that particular job. Another advantage is that it allows for individualized instruction. Costs of on-the-job training are further reduced by the output resulting from the training process.

Extensive surveys conducted by the Department of Labor on how workers learned the actual cognitive job skills they used revealed that only 40 percent of the work force indicated they were using any skill they had learned in formal training programs, and the majority of this 40 percent reported that some of the skills they were using had been learned in informal, casual, on-the-job-training. The remaining 60 percent of the workers had acquired *all* of their job skills in the latter manner. Only 12 percent of the workers indicated that formal training and specialized education programs were the "most helpful" in acquiring their current job skills, and that some of this type of training had been carried on at their places of work and was directly dependent on their already having been selected for the job in question (U.S. Department of Labor, 1964). The findings of these surveys were confirmed during a series of round-table discussions conducted at Brandeis University, in which over 200 private sector employers participated (Weisberg, 1983).

The intimate connection between specific skills and on-the-job training implies it is difficult to impart such skills through school-based vocational education. However, that is not to suggest that this activity should be ignored. To the extent that vocational education can respond to the diverse learning styles of students and increase their interest in remaining in school by providing a more interesting and stimulating school environment, it will serve a major purpose. However, the specific skills learned in the class may not be the most influential factors in affecting an employer's decision. Lester Thurow (1978) suggests, in his theory of the "labor queue," that it is certain background characteristics such as basic literacy and "industrial discipline" that employers seek in potential employees. Why? According to his job competition model of the labor market, wages are based on the characteristics of the job, and are in most cases fixed—such as in the case of the minimum wage. Individuals compete against one another for job opportunities based on their expected training costs after being hired since, as we have seen, the majority of job-related cognitive and motor skills are acquired through on-the-job training.

With other variables held constant, variations in hiring and training costs translate into variations in profit for employers. Thus, employers attempt to rank prospective employees in a "labor queue" on their estimation of the prospective employee's hiring and training costs. Lacking information on exact training costs for individuals, employers often rank potential employees according to their background characteristics, which are useful as indirect indicators of the costs required to produce standard work performance. These bases of selection may include educational attainment, innate abilities (as measured by test scores), age, sex, personal habits, and, we would suggest, a handicapping condition. If employers are aware, for example, that a prospective employee is mildly mentally retarded or has a learning disability, they may then suspect these problems would extend or complicate training and thus prove costly.

The issues of: (1) the empirically discerned ineffectiveness of traditional secondary-level vocational education, and; (2) the general, rather than specific, skill needs of employers for entry-level positions have found resonance in a recent report of the Panel on Secondary School Education of the National Academy of Sciences, "High Schools and the Changing Workplace: The Employer's View." The panel's basic findings were that the major asset required by employers is the ability to learn and adapt to changes in the workplace. It found that:

> Technical education, vocational training, and curricula providing specific job skills can enhance a student's employability, but cannot substitute for education in the core competencies. (National Academy of Sciences Committee on Science, 1984, p. xi.)

The core competencies judged by the panel to be required for successful employment include: command of the English language; reasoning and problem solving; reading; writing; computation; knowledge of science and technology; oral communications; interpersonal relationships; social and economic studies; and personal work habits and attitudes. To the extent that a secondary special education program prepares handicapped students in these general competency areas, it prepares them for employment.

Efforts must continue to integrate handicapped students into traditional school-based vocational education. However, community-based work experience programs are becoming the focal point of many local and state transitional employment programs under development. This component can provide an apprenticeship element not possible in a traditional vocational program, thus facilitating the acquisition of both general and job-specific skills (Harold Russell Associates, 1983).

TRAINING VERSUS JOB CREATION VERSUS WAGE SUBSIDIES

Eliminating work disincentives, motivating disabled students to work, informing them of their rights under enabling legislation, and providing appropriate vocationally related educational programming will not necessarily solve the unemployment problems of many disabled youth. As Lester Thurow has noted, the success or failure of efforts such as vocational education depend a great deal on the effectiveness of labor market demand-side strategies such as government jobs programs (Thurow, 1978).

Public Sector Employment During the early 1960s, concern with the labor market difficulties of groups such as the economically disadvantaged and handicapped persons inspired efforts to increase opportunities for their employment. The majority of government efforts through 1982 were concentrated on public sector employment programs, such as the Comprehensive Employment and Training Act. The goal of public sector programs has been to raise workers' skills so that their productivity at least equals the cost of employing them. These programs, which were essentially publicly funded 100 percent wage subsidies, created jobs outside the private sector, thus providing employment in a setting in which the cost of employing workers temporarily exceeded the benefits. The expectation was that over the long run, the benefits of such programs would outweigh the costs, because the workers involved gained valuable job experience that could then be transferred to the private sector (National Commission on Manpower Policy, 1978).

By 1980, public sector employment programs had consumed over $40 billion. Despite this massive effort, however, there remained a serious unemployment problem, particularly among certain subgroups (U.S.

Department of Labor, Employment, and Training Administration, 1980). Although recent retrospective evaluations of the CETA program tend to demonstrate that it held sufficient promise to be retained as a training program (Cook, Adams, and Rawlings, 1985), disillusionment with expensive, and in the public's perception, ineffective, social programs such as public sector employment has led to greater reliance on the private sector for job training.

In the 1980s public sector employment has been reduced in favor of the private sector. It is thought that one of the potential advantages of placing structurally employed persons in the private sector is that, upon successful completion of formal and/or informal training, they may be able to move directly into an unsubsidized job in the private sector, most likely with the same employer who has provided the training. By contrast, it has been found that initial employment in a public sector job is not as likely to prepare an individual for unsubsidized work in the private sector, where most of the growth of job opportunities is concentrated (Fisk, 1980).

The Job Training Partnership Act

In October 1982, the Jobs Training Partnership Act (JTPA) was signed into law by President Ronald Reagan. It represented a "landmark" in employment and training legislation because it made fundamental changes in the federal government's approach to assisting the unemployed. Among the major departures from previous practices are (U.S. Department of Labor, 1983):

- a focus on training as the primary purpose of the program, with a strict limitation of 30 percent of expenditures for activities not directly related to training. These include support services such as child care, transformation, and medical services, all of which may be supported at a 100 percent rate

- a leading role given to the private sector in the planning, operation, and administration of local training programs through Private Industry Councils

- an expansion of the state role in training and employment programs including management and oversight functions formerly carried out by the federal government

- establishment of a new training program for dislocated workers

The JTPA contains set-aside provisions, services, activities, and policies that have the potential of assisting handicapped youth to access its benefits. A variety of JTPA programs that serve handicapped youth have been developed. The Vocational Studies Center at the University of Wisconsin-Madison (Tindall, Gugerty, and Dougherty, 1985) has conducted a national search of programs considered by local Private Industry Councils as "successful" in serving handicapped students.

Although varying in design, they illustrate the different ways in which JTPA programs have been developed. They include:

1. Targeted in-school JTPA programs—designed specifically to serve the handicapped youth population through special vocational education employment programs

2. Mainstream in-school JTPA programs—designed to include youth with handicaps into the JTPA-eligible youth population served by integrating them into mainstream vocational education programs

3. School and business partnership programs—activities focus on: business personnel serving as program advisory committee members; business providing assistance to a program's pre-employment training component; employers providing on-the-job training and work experience sites for a program

4. School and city partnership programs—activities include: a city administration office being responsible for providing pre-employment skill training to a program; a city agency providing job development services to a program

5. School and community-based organization (CBO) partnership programs—activities focused on: a CBO providing the use of their facilities (e.g., a shop or food service) for training purposes; a CBO serving as a recruitment, referral, and intake agency for a program; a CBO providing a program's preemployment component and conducting the try-out employment component.

6. School and other local agency partnership programs—activities include: a local Job Service Office assuming responsibility for obtaining on-the-job training sites for a program; a local Vocational Rehabilitation Agency assuming responsibility for the assessment component of a program.

These JTPA-sponsored programs are integral to the OSERS school-to-work transition model. So-called time-limited services include opportunities presented by the Jobs Training Partnership Act. There is recent evidence, however, that the JTPA is failing in its objective of helping more disadvantaged youth. Participation and job placement rates are low among youths aged 16 through 21. High performance standards and low stipends have produced the familiar phenomenon of "creaming," in which more job-ready, employable youths are receiving services while the needs of more severely disadvantaged young persons are going unmet (Walker, Feldstein, and Solow, 1985). We may assume that handicapped persons are well represented in the latter group. Thus, the labor queue winds it way through the JTPA.

Factors Associated with Employment in the Private Sector

There are numerous problems associated with the employment of handicapped persons in the private sector, and these thwart the effectiveness of employment and training programs. Among the barriers most often cited are: less than accepting attitudes on the part of union officials, employee health insurance as well as employer's accident insurance coverage, architectural and transportation barriers; stereotyping as to the capacity of individuals with certain handicaps to perform successfully at selected occupational tasks, and the need for excessive accommodations and modifications of the work environment (Phelps, 1977; Phillips, 1977).

In the private sector, these issues imply excess costs to employers intent on minimizing costs in order to maximize profits. Since 1980, the federal government has sought to make the private sector predominant in U.S. employment policy. Advocates for disabled persons were faced in 1980 with the realization that over the previous twenty years, despite greatly expanded research on handicapped persons, data on their employment in the private sector had been virtually ignored (Berkeley Planning Associates, 1981).

Although employment discrimination against handicapped persons is an intuitively reasonable proposition, a review of the literature through the mid-1980s reveals a great deal of ambiguity. The causes of employment discrimination are subject to dispute. For some, the very existence of discrimination against most disabled job-seekers is questioned.

Advocates for disabled persons often cite the conclusions of Levitan and Taggard:

> Employer surveys evidence a general reluctance to hire the disabled when nondisabled workers are available. Many employers believe there are higher costs, such as increased worker's compensation expenses or inflated medical and life insurance premiums . . . involuntarily absenteeism and turnover . . . lack of flexibility in job assignments and the difficulty of promoting. Whether based upon reasonable best guesses by employers or on an unreasoned bias against the mentally and physically handicapped, the attitudes are facts of life that will be difficult to change. (1976, p. 8)

A 1975 report by the Urban Institute, commonly known in the field of vocational rehabilitation as the "Comprehensive Needs Study," summarized some thirty different research efforts conducted during the past few decades focusing on labor market conditions for disabled persons. It concluded:

> Virtually all the studies on employer attitudes have found that large proportions of employers disfavor hiring disabled people. There are strong indications that these attitudes are in large part based on non-rational negative feelings—prejudice—rather than on realistic fears

of low productivity, high absenteeism and high insurance rates. (Urban Institute, 1975, p. 324)

A later view of these studies by Berkeley Planning Associates (1981) reached different conclusions. It found that while a few studies reported negative employer attitudes, the preponderance of the studies concluded that employer attitudes are not negative toward the handicapped, and that the large majority of employers did not perceive the disabled to be less productive, have higher rates of absenteeism, or require more costly insurance. However, a careful caveat is proffered by BPA:

> Although formal research studies do tend to find that employers generally do not have a strong prejudice against the disabled, many of those working in the State Vocational Rehabilitation and Job Service offices will argue that objections to hiring the disabled are indeed present in the private sector . . . . while most employers will tell you they have no problem hiring the disabled, when faced with an actual applicant for a specific job, many will produce a wide range of reasons why this particular individual is not well-suited for this particular job. (p. 64)

This recent review of research by BPA found that most employers' perceptions indicated a limited assessment of the ultimate potential of disabled workers. In terms of the types of entry-level jobs disabled workers hold, employer perceptions do not appear to be negative. However, employers generally have low expectations regarding disabled persons as career employees (that is, employees who will progress through an increasingly responsible and demanding, and thus higher paying, series of positions). Perhaps as a result, work-disabled individuals are disproportionately represented in marginal, secondary labor market jobs such as manual labor and some kinds of clerical work, and underrepresented in professional/technical, managerial/ administrative, and craftsman categories.

Suspicions of extended training needs and lower productivity depresses the value of hiring disabled workers. Both law and custom have, in the past, prevented firms from lowering wages to the levels perceived to be cost-effective. Thus, the disabled represent a substantial portion of the unemployed who are unable to find steady work in a tight labor market.

The Targeted Jobs Tax Credit

Concern with structural unemployment of groups such as the disabled led the Carter administration in 1978 to enact the Targeted Jobs Tax Credit program (TJTC). The TJTC, in essence a wage subsidy, is the broadest-coverage tax credit for specific groups ever enacted in the United States. As originally enacted, the TJTC was available for wages paid before the end of 1981. The program was extended by the Economic Recovery Tax Act of 1981 (ERTA), the Tax Equity and Fiscal Responsibility Act of 1982

(TEFRA), and the Deficit Reduction Act of 1984 (the 1984 Act). Through the end of 1985 it could be claimed by private sector employers for qualified wages paid for services performed during 1986 and 1987 to individuals who began working prior to the end of 1985.

The TJTC has been available on an elective basis for the hiring of individuals from one or more of nine targeted groups: (1) vocational rehabilitation referrals; (2) economically disadvantaged youths aged 18 through 24; (3) economically disadvantaged Vietnam-era veterans; (4) SSI recipients; (5) general assistance recipients; (6) economically disadvantaged cooperative education students aged 16 through 19; (7) economically disadvantaged former convicts; (8) AFDC recipients and WIN registrants; and (9) economically disadvantaged summer youth employees aged 16 or 17.

This program provides a tax credit equal to 50 percent of the first $6,000 of qualified first-year wages subject to federal unemployment tax (FUTA) and 25 percent of the first $6,000 of qualified second-year wages. Thus, the maximum value of the credit before taxes is $3,000 for the first year and $1,500 for the second.

The actual net value of the credit to an employer is a function of the firm's tax rate. An employer with an effective corporate tax rate of 16 percent would receive a net credit of $2,250 for the first year and $1,260 for the second. By contrast, a firm with an effective tax rate of 36 percent would receive a net tax credit of $1,920 for the first year and $960 for the second. The reason for this is that a firm must reduce its tax deduction for wages and salaries paid during the year it was earned, the value of the credit being taxable is income. Thus, the credit becomes an increasingly attractive incentive for smaller firms with lower tax rates, but is less so for more highly taxed businesses. During FY 1984, 1,337,637 target group members were vouchered for the program by state employment service offices. Of that total, 95,443 were vocational rehabilitation referrals, and another 3,755 were SSI recipients (U.S. Senate, 1985).

The theoretical basis of the TJTC is the labor queue. Group affiliation can have an informational impact in the labor market that results in discrimination. Employers often view potential employees as average members of the groups to which they belong (Spence, 1972). Thus, being handicapped in a legal or educational sense may imply higher training costs to an employer, and thus a lower rank in the queue. Groups such as the handicapped have been included in the TJTC because, historically, they have endured labor market discrimination. Employers' uncertainty about, and the systematic underevaluation of, the productive potential of certain groups are both factors in such discrimination. In the specific case of the handicapped, these factors are compounded by expectations of excess costs for job modifications and so on. In a labor market where, in most cases, wages are fixed, such groups as the handicapped, stigmatized by these employer assumptions, cannot "bid down" the cost of employing them.

The economic theory of the TJTC is that these individuals whose suspected or actual employment and training costs are excessive are at a disadvantage in the labor market and require a program such as the TJTC to reduce these costs to employers. The underlying purpose is to induce firms to substitute subsidized targeted workers for unsubsidized, nontargeted workers, as well as to substitute labor (workers) for capital (equipment).

In 1985, two separate bills were submitted to extend the TJTC through the end of 1990. H.R. 983, originally sponsored by Representatives Rangel, Wheat, and Campbell, was intended to extend the program and increase the wage base from the original $6,000 to $10,000. Similarly, Senators Heinz, Domenici, and others sponsored S.1250, a bill that would have liberalized the eligibility requirements for membership in the "vocational rehabilitation referral" and "SSI recipient" target groups. Committee hearings on these two bills included testimony from administration spokespersons generally critical of the program. Among the problems identified was that of "ineffectual credits" occurring when eligible workers for whom the credit is claimed would have been hired by an employer just as another person would have been hired without the credit. Another difficulty was that no net increase in employment would necessarily occur because the credit might simply have resulted in a reallocation of employment between targeted workers who qualified for the credit and nontargeted but nevertheless low-paid individuals who were displaced by the credit (Rollyson, 1985). Although the TJTC failed to be reauthorized in 1985 (along with thirteen other tax credits), efforts continued into 1986 to extend it retroactively. The House-passed and White House–supported "Tax Reform Act of 1985" would extend the program for two years, through the end of 1987, although at a reduced rate of 40 percent of the first-year wages (U.S. House of Representatives, 1985).

Support for the TJTC draws generally from two sources: those private sector firms and organizations who stand to benefit by hiring target group members; and the targeted employees themselves. The desirability of lowered taxes to for-profit private sector firms hiring targeted workers is not easily misunderstood. However, as Senator Heinz (R-Pa.) observed, the principal beneficiaries of the program are the targeted workers themselves:

> TJTC offers a way out of poverty and joblessness for people who, for a lack of money, skills and experience, cannot compete effectively in the job market. TJTC provides the incentive to hire these individuals, thus giving these disadvantaged and, often, discriminated against people a chance to help themselves. TJTC increases employment,

decreases federal spending under entitlement programs, and results in more taxpaying citizens . . .

The five year extension of the Targeted Jobs Tax Credit program is very important to this country as a means of spurring employment and training for those people who have traditionally found it difficult to get jobs. It is a way out of poverty and joblessness for those people who, for a lack of money, skills, and experience cannot compete effectively on the job market. Rather than suffer the ignominies of joblessness and lifelong underemployment, TJTC provides the incentives to hire these individuals, thus giving these low-income people a chance to help themselves and avoid the trap of welfare dependence (Heinz, 1985, p. 6,7).

Perhaps no more poignant a statement in support of the program has been advanced than by Charles Stradford, of Downers Grove, Illinois, who testified on behalf of his son, a TJTC participant:

My son is twenty-one years old. At the time of his birth we were advised to place him in an institution because the medical authorities felt that he would never be anything more than a burden to us and our other two children. As a family unit, we refused to take the advice of the doctors.

When Ronald was five years old, he wanted to go to school because his sister and brother were in school. At that time, some of the psychological testers and school officials felt that he was not ready.

Two years later, Ronald wanted to become a Cub Scout like his brother. With the help of some of the other parents with mentally handicapped sons, we organized a Cub Scout unit for the mentally handicapped.

As Ronald has grown older, his physiological needs have changed. In order help him meet those needs, my wife and I have become active participants in encounter groups and advocacy groups of the handicapped. As I mentioned earlier, Ronald has attended school since age five. Our initial intent was for him to develop motor skills and to learn basic survival skills. Later we found that he had an aptitude for academics and we pushed for his educational development.

At age twenty-one, there is no more school for Ronald. He has proven through the Targeted Jobs Tax Credit program, however, that he has the will and ability to be a contributor in today's work force.

The point I'm trying to make Gentlemen, is that for my son, SELF ESTEEM AND SELF WORTH are important. I can also make that statement for the majority of the mentally handicapped individuals whom I've known and with whom I've worked over the past fifteen years. The attainment of these feelings comes through participating in and contributing to society. I sincerely believe that my son's positive feelings about himself are a direct result of his employment with Pizza Hut under the Targeted Jobs Tax Credit Program. I also believe that without such programs in place, the vast majority of mentally handicapped individuals would not be able to experience those feelings of self worth and self esteem.

One could contend that work may have been available for my son without the Targeted Jobs Tax Credit program and I would not disagree. I would counter, however, by saying that it is highly unlikely that there would be mentally handicapped individuals in the work force in great numbers without the TJTC program. First of all, without some tangible benefit, there is little incentive for a company to take a chance on an unknown entity. Secondly, there is little incentive for a company to compel its management and workers to adjust to the physical and mental idiosyncrasies of this unskilled labor force. Finally, without some type of program in place, there is absolutely no incentive for companies to actively seek these individuals for the purpose of hiring them only to incur the wrath of partisan groups or factions who may feel the need to pressure the companies for jobs.

In closing, I would like to say that in the opinion of this taxpayer, our tax dollars are better spent by putting them back into our employment base and providing jobs for the handicapped than by providing medicare funding for institutions and welfare programs. (Stradford, 1986, pp. 26–28)

But what of the issue of excess costs? Research conducted by O'Brien (1984) attempted to identify, categorize, and measure the disability-related excess costs of individuals employed under the TJTC (O'Brien, 1984). At the time this inquiry was planned, no studies had been conducted on the TJTC at the level of the firm and the individual. Fifteen case studies were conducted on handicapped individuals randomly selected from the TJTC files of the California Employment Development Department. These confidential files were opened for the purposes of this investigation as the result of the endorsement of the study by the California State Department of Education. These individuals, all voluntary participants, reside and work in the eight San Francisco Bay Area counties. The analytical categories (adapted from Ratner, 1978) developed for the study include:

I. Disability-related Transaction Costs

Transaction costs are those that occur when a worker's status within a firm changes. These changes may include the movement of a worker between the external labor market and the labor force of a firm, as well as between departments within the internal labor market. This construct includes only those costs that are exclusively the result of a worker's disability, and that are in excess of the average cost incurred by a firm in the employment of a typical worker. They may include:

A. Administrative costs in personnel, payroll, and other ancillary departments including:

- materials
- administrative costs for recruiting, processing, orientation, formal off-the-job training, preparation of TJTC forms, and so on
- costs of separation for disability-related terminations
- replacement costs

B. Excessive financial payments to third parties associated with accession, including:

- medical examinations
- insurance surcharges
- consultant's fees
- accountant's fees (for tax credit preparation)

II. Disability-related Productivity Costs

These costs occur within the production process itself, and are in excess of the costs incurred by a firm for the average worker. They may include:

A. Production-related ancillary costs, which may include:

- physical accommodations, work site and work procedures modifications
- off-the-job training
- preparation costs of coworkers/trainers/supervisors (to work with a disabled employee)
- costs of: material, additional premium wages for additional or overtime instruction

B. Production-process costs, which may be subdivided into two basic elements:

1. Atomistic processes

These processes refer to the productive domain of the individual worker as opposed to the effects of the worker's presence on the productivity of other workers in the same production department or in other departments within the firm. They may include:

(a) Disability-related replacement lag

When a new worker is hired to replace a worker who has left the work force, there may be a lag between the time the old worker leaves and the new worker begins work. During this time a firm may elect to maintain its customary production rate by utilizing its remaining work force more intensively. During this period, costs in the form of overtime or premium wages paid to other employees may be incurred by a firm. In the event that a replacement lag results from the disability of a worker, the costs incurred in the form of overtime or premium wages are considered to be excess costs.

(b) Disability-related supervision and instruction

Each new worker, regardless of whether he or she is disabled, requires some degree of supervision and instruction during a training or probationary period. When supervisors or others are diverted from their customary assignments, the firm incurs costs equal to the foregone value of the output of the diverted worker. To the extent that a disabled worker requires additional time, beyond the average expected for a typical new worker, excess foregone output, and thus excess costs, may occur.

(c) Disability-related production deficits

When an experienced worker leaves, a firm is forced to replace the individual with a new, less experienced worker. As a result of this replacement, the mean (average) job experience of the production unit declines. The mean skill level in a production unit is positively related to the mean length of job experience of the workers in that unit. Thus, when an inexperienced worker replaces an experienced one, the mean skill level of the firm's work force declines. Since the total value of the flow of labor services may decline as a result of the decrease in mean skill level, output may be reduced.

In the event the new inexperienced worker is disabled, a situation arises in which the firm may incur excessive costs if the handicapped individual's disability extends the required period of training beyond that usual and customary for a particular job.

2. Group processes and interdependencies, which may include:

(a) Group cohesion and intensity of effort

Labor adjustment costs may also be generated as a result of the effects of labor turnover on the morale or group cohesion of a firm's labor force. Groups typically have interdependent and interlocking social bonds based upon friendship, solidarity, and mutual need in the workplace. If the introduction of a disabled worker produces a tear in the social fabric of the work force of a production unit, the resulting decline in group cohesion could further affect productivity. Such effects could conceivably result from a new worker's disability.

(b) Functional integration

The predictability and work performance of a worker—that is, his or her habits, idiosyncrasies, speed, and so on—may, and probably do, affect to some degree the performance of his or her coworkers. It is further hypothesized that the introduction of a new, inexperienced worker reduces the level of functional integration of a production unit by decreasing the average length of time workers in the department have interacted with one another during the production process. We may extend this concept to include the disruption of the functional integration of a production unit caused by the disability of a newly hired employee. As with production deficits caused by a disruption in group cohesion, production costs may be incurred by a firm due to a disability-related functional *dis*-integration.

(c) Spillover effects

Within a firm, components of finished products move through a progression of work stations. When the output of any production entity, be it an individual work station, production unit, or an entire department, is disrupted, a firm may incur excess costs. A spillover may affect clients or customers of a firm, resulting in lost sales or contracts. It is conceivable that the disability of a new hire may produce such effects.

As might be expected, the costs incurred by the employers of these fifteen individuals varied enormously. Transaction costs occurred mainly as the result of paperwork generated by the TJTC itself (that is, secretarial and accountant's time). However, disability-related productivity costs appeared in a variety of forms. Ancillary costs included damages to work sites and materials, excessive sick leave, overtime wages for helpful coworkers, extra supervision, as well as extra instructional costs. Actual disability-related production deficits were significant in many cases. Group cohesion, functional integration, and spillover phenomena resulting from the disabilities of some of these individuals were also observed. For example, the slow work rate of a newly hired physically disabled man in the receiving unit of a microprocessor manufacturing firm slowed the rate at which raw materials were delivered to the firm's production line. In another, a disabled man's emotional problems negatively affected coworkers and their functional integration. In this latter case, the productivity of the construction firm to which they belonged was disrupted.

Many of these employers enjoyed net benefits (a case in which the net value of the TJTC exceeds the excess costs incurred by the employer) as a result of participation in the program. However, the aggregate net excess cost (total excess cost minus total net value of TJTC) to this set of employers equaled $16,382, after appropriate discounting. Thus, in the aggregate, the total excess costs these employers incurred exceeded the value of the TJTC by a significant margin.

While this study was conducted with an eye toward policy relevance and formulation, its major emphasis was on the refinement of existing analytical categories for the purpose of measuring costs. This consideration, along with the modest size of the study, militates against overamibitous generalizations with regard to the Targeted Jobs Tax Credit or the employment of handicapped individuals on a nationwide basis. The findings, however, provide clear evidence in support of continuation of the TJTC. The continuing incurrence of excess costs logically suggests a continuing program of reimbursement.

The Targeted Jobs Tax Credit has been a seriously underutilized program, the maximum benefits of which have not been fully taken advantage of on a nationwide basis by advocates for the handicapped. The program, given its continuation, has the potential to be an effective placement and jobs training device that could be incorporated into the school-to-work transition model being advocated by OSERS. Many employers of handicapped individuals do, unhappily, incur excess costs for reasons independent of the employee's willingness to work. Special education employment specialists ideally should have the skills to identify and measure such costs, and to assist employers in improving the disabled worker's repertoire of skills necessary to attain and continue successful employment. Trainer advocates and employment associates will be needed to work alongside more difficult to place workers until they learn to function at an acceptable performance rate in an entry-level job. They will serve as role models for handicapped trainees, monitor and measure productivity progress on the job, obtain written feedback from employers and coworkers, and utilize behavioral data for use in on-the-job training. TJTC-supported intervention and follow-up procedures to assist the handicapped student/worker in the acquisition of production and interpersonal survival skills is a desirable program option and one worthy of future research and development.

WORK AS A CONTEXT FOR LEARNING: PROVIDING ACCESS

As explained above, many important work skills are learned on the job. Much of this learning takes place in the beginning, when a newly hired worker has to become accustomed to the new demands of the workplace. Moreover, for a person who is new to paid employment, the first job is especially important in teaching certain generic work skills, customs, and behavioral norms. Providing initial access to paid employment as a context for learning has therefore been an important component of training programs for unemployed youth (Taggart, 1981), and is becoming an increasingly important component of programs for disabled persons (Gaylord-Ross, et al., 1985).

However, employers are not able to accommodate all new workers who want on-the-job training. Even when subsidies have been available through Targeted Jobs Tax Credits, only a small fraction of the eligible population has found jobs. This is just another consequence of the fact that the economy has not been operating at full employment.

Fortunately, a regular paid job is not the only context in which a person can acquire work skills through experience. Agencies and programs that provide education and training can also provide work experience that complements direct instruction. In so doing, these programs can impart specific and general work skills, while at the same time reinforcing necessary academic skills (Hahn and Lerman, 1985).

An example of this approach is a school-based work experience program for handicapped youth begun in 1976 in the Newark, California, school district, near San Francisco. The program, called JEWEL (Job Entry Work Experience Laboratory), was an outgrowth of a federally funded experimental program for handicapped high school dropouts. In its first year, JEWEL located twenty-two mentally and physically handicapped dropout students under the age of 21 and provided them with education, job training, and wages. Of the twenty two students, fifteen were able to move directly from JEWEL into full-time employment.

Dolores Lindsay, JEWEL's director, created work for the students by finding ways to meet community needs. JEWEL's first project involved building mobile bookcases that were purchased by the school district. Students determined their wages by deducting the cost of materials from the sale price of the bookcases. The profit was shared. Lindsay remembers that "students didn't really earn a great deal on their first project, but they did gain pride." From this modest beginning came a retail store, a furniture unit, a construction company, a janitorial service, and an employment agency. JEWEL remodeled a Mexican restaurant, then moved and remodeled a bakery.

Although JEWEL was started as a program to serve handicapped students, it grew to include other out-of-school youth. At the end of its first year, JEWEL's gross sales totalled $30,000. In the second year of operation, gross sales increased to $74,000. Because of the program's growth and its success in placing youth in full-time jobs, JEWEL was able to serve over one hundred dropouts per year. Eventually, JEWEL became a nonprofit corporation, in order to separate its financial operations from those of the school district.

The JEWEL program gave participating Newark youth the opportunity to experience social and academic success and to do productive work. Many of these students had experienced failure in the regular school program. As one student explained, "It's a whole lot better than going to Newark High School. I was only at the third grade reading level and Newark High teachers expected me to read these big old thick books, I was sick of regular school."

At JEWEL students learn reading and mathematics by reading design plans or balancing the project's books. Lindsay gives an example of how the work context can encourage students to take academic skills more seriously:

> The shop teacher asked one of the boys to cut a board 8-3/4". The boy turned to me and said, "I don't know what 8-3/4" are." We showed him, and he managed to get the board cut correctly. We asked him if he would like to learn how to use a ruler. This boy and three others met with us the following morning and we started with a ruler, then math, then English reading. They worked solidly (without even a cigarette break) for two hours every morning.

Since education is its primary purpose, a school-based work experience program can provide more learning opportunity than the jobs ordinarily available to young (or disabled people). A JEWEL student attested: "I was tired of having to wash cars for bad pay. Here I can learn enough basics in electronics to get an entry-level job in industry."

THE SUPPORTED EMPLOYMENT ALTERNATIVE

For a significant portion of the work-disabled population, traditional vocational training, public sector employment programs, private sector strategies such as the JTPA and the TJTC, and school-based enterprises are not sufficient to improve their chances of securing an entry-level or long-term labor force attachment. An increasing number of more severely handicapped children are "aging out" of special education and are seeking not only adult services, but meaningful work. In the last decade, largely as the result of the trend toward deinstitutionalization, day activity programs have become the primary community service approach for individuals whose disabilities are so severe as to preclude their eligibility for traditional vocational rehabilitation services. During the 1970s, these day programs expanded by an estimated 600 percent. By 1979, approximately 105,000 individuals were being served in such programs across the nation.

Day activity programs usually consist of groups of approximately fifty severely disabled individuals in a segregated facility, where they receive instruction in daily living skills, social activities, and prevocational skills. In those states allowing paid work activities, the average annual earnings of participants is about $160 per year. States use a variety of federal, state, and local funding sources to support these programs. Current estimates place the cost per person per year at between $3,600 and $4,000.

While originally intended to develop readiness for subsequent vocational rehabilitation and employment, these expectations have generally not been realized. For example, in 1979 the California Department of Finance reported that only 2.7 percent of the state's day program participants moved on to higher level vocational programs. In 1980, the state of New Jersey reported 3.5 percent. Day activity programs are generally thought to be habilitatively superior to institutions. However, the continued segregation of participants from their nonhandicapped peers, the paucity of earnings, as well as the lack of movement of participants to less costly and less dependent services have all served to bring these programs under increasing criticism. Sheltered workshops and work activity centers have experienced similar increases in numbers nationally, and have endured the same criticisms.

For more severely disabled adults, supported employment programs have come to be viewed as desirable alternatives to segregated, sheltered settings. During 1984, OSERS began a new program initiative to assist and encourage states to establish and expand such programs. Supported employment programs are ongoing intensive services designed to help individuals with severe disabilities gain and maintain employment in regular work settings. They are intended to provide support to whatever length and degree necessary to ensure a successful transition to employment and community independence. They may be distinguished from traditional vocational rehabilitation and day activity services by four general characteristics:

1. The service recipients are those who were previously served in day activity programs because they appeared to lack the potential for competitive employment.

2. Supported employment involves a continuing provision for training, supervision, and support services.

3. Supported employment is designed to produce the same benefits for participants that other people receive from work.

4. Supported employment is flexible; it incorporates a variety of techniques to assist individuals to obtain work and to perform work. (Office of Special Education and Rehabilitation Services, 1985)

A large variety of supported employment strategies and programmatic structures have evolved, each with potential advantages and short-comings. The key to the success of supported work appears to be its adaptability in form to local employment opportunities and individual needs. Mank, Rhodes, and Bellamy (1985) have described four supported work employment models developed by the University of Oregon's Specialized Training Program (STP) (Mank, Rhodes, and Bellamy, 1985). These are discussed in the following sections.

The Supported Jobs Model

The supported jobs model adopts the direct approach of placing individual adults in regular community jobs, with support provided at the work site as needed for the person to be productive. In this model, a not-for-profit community agency is funded by service fees from the local developmental disabilities agency on the same basis as a day activity program. However, all individuals served work in regular community jobs, typically in restaurants, offices, hotels, and similar situations. Positions usually involve three to six standard hours of work per day. Program staff are responsible for job development, on-the-job training, and ongoing support at the work site.

This employment strategy opens up employment in integrated settings to many individuals previously denied such opportunities due to low productivity. In some cases an employer may take advantage of U.S. Department of Labor Regulations, Part 524, which allows special sub-minimum wages for handicapped workers in competitive employment. By ensuring that wages paid are based on productivity, the employer is not penalized for hiring a worker who does not perform at full productivity.

Data generated from the first supported jobs model demonstration site operated by STP have been described as "encouraging." During the first seven months of its operation, five individuals were placed in jobs. Average wages were approximately $210 per worker per month, with each person putting in a four- to six-hour workday. Prior to this employment experience, two of these people had been unemployed and the other three had been in work activity centers earning less than $50 per month. Start-up and operations cost data are unknown at this time.

The Enclave Model

An enclave is a small group of work-disabled individuals who are trained and supervised among nonhandicapped workers in an industry or business. This approach provides a useful alternative to competitive employment and traditional sheltered employment. It combines the benefits of an integrated setting with the continuous, ongoing support required by more severely disabled individuals. Typically, within the enclave, payment for work performed is commensurate with pay to other, nonhandicapped workers performing the same type and amount of work. The severely disabled worker, though, usually accrues salary at a subminimum rate due to slower production rates. Disabled workers are integrated into the production process, although often within close proximity to one another for purposes of training and supervision. The enclave has two distinct advantages over the supported jobs model that makes it possible to accommodate persons with more severe handicaps. First, larger corporations tend to have work available that is relatively stable over time; and secondly, the enclave model offers the possibility of continuous supervision, essential for more severely handicapped individuals, particularly those with behavioral problems. There are limiting factors, however. One is the ability of the supervisor to manage the behavior of up to eight individuals. Another factor is the limited tolerance of the host industry for certain behavior problems of workers.

Enclave developers have a number of incentives to offer a host firm. These include: guaranteed productivity on a fixed-cost basis; effective training and supervision techniques; detailed production information; affirmative action assistance; tax credits; possible reduction in employee turnover; and improved public relations. An example of this type of supported employment program is the enclave operated by Physio-Controls, Inc., in Bellevue, Washington. Eight moderately and severely retarded adults work in a large manufacturing plant. The cost of a special trainer/supervisor is set by the state agency responsible for day activity services. Typical of work enclaves in for-profit firms, care is taken to ensure that public funds are utilized only for the excess costs of employing workers with disabilities, not to subsidize the firm itself. The average annual public cost for this enclave, in terms of tax dollars utilized to support the program, is $2,800; however, the enterprise experiences average annual earnings of $4,000.

The Mobile Crew Model

A third program model is the mobile work crew. Although it is present in urban and suburban settings, it is particularly well suited for rural areas. The mobile crew model is a combination of service and business in which service providers establish commercial enterprises and provide work opportunities as well as services. Often, a work crew will operate from a van rather than a building and perform jobs such as groundskeeping and janitorial work in community settings. This model is designed to support employment in smaller communities where there are modest service needs or where a large industrial base is unlikely. Normally, extra cost are incurred in commercial operations because workers produce at less than full productivity and require greater supervision than workers without disabilities. Public funds cover such costs. As with the other supported work models, the major outcomes of mobile work crews are wages and community integration.

The Specialized Training Program operates a custom landscape service mobile crew serving ten individuals with a variety of disabilities who would otherwise take part in a day activity program. Ongoing support is provided by the Washington State Day Service Agency. The average annual cost in public funds to support the program is $2,172. The project thus far has enjoyed average annual earnings of $3,720.

The Benchwork Model

The fourth supported model is designed to provide employment in electronics assembly work in a service agency that also functions as a business enterprise. Electronics firms and related industries provide contract work. Operated as a small, single-purpose, not-for-profit corporation, companies using the benchwork model provide employment and related services to approximately fifteen individuals with severe and profound developmental disabilities. These programs are located in separate, segregated facilities at a regular work site. Work is performed in the program's own work space, thus reducing the opportunities for social integration during the workday. While many of the antihabilitative aspects of sheltered employment are present in this model, procedures may be implemented to overcome the barriers to integration that are inherent in a separate work facility. First, integration into the community may be accomplished by maintaining small, independent programs serving smaller numbers of individuals and locating work sites close to stores, restaurants, and other community resources. Secondly, possibilities for integration during the workday are available as commercially successful programs hire workers without disabilities as regular production employees. This "reverse mainstreaming" is thought to be a helpful procedure for both handicapped and nonhandicapped alike—providing social integration opportunities for both, hopefully for mutual benefit.

The long-term costs of operating a benchwork model program are approximately the same as those of operating a day of work activity center serving similarly severely disabled individuals. The planning and start-up costs of a company using this model are a minimum of $15,000 to $25,000 for equipment and staff. Due no doubt to the severe nature of the disabilities of the workers, the annual earnings of these programs tend to be less than those of other programs. For example, the Eugene Precision Manufacturing Services of Eugene, Oregon, is an electronics assembly contract program employing sixteen severely and profoundly retarded adults. The annual public cost of the program is $3,950, with annual earnings of $1,560. Olympus Electronics, of Burien, Washington, also an electronics assembly contract shop, employs eighteen moderately and severely retarded workers, and operates at an annual public cost of $2,321, with annual earnings of $820. Dynatron, Inc., of Bend, Oregon, employs twenty moderately to profoundly retarded adults at an annual public cost of $3,245, with annual earnings of $1,006.

The federal role in the advocacy and development of supported employment programs is substantial, and efforts to establish supported employment programs are increasing. A major reason for this is that a significant portion of the public benefits of changing from day activity programs to supported employment is experienced at the federal level. The wages earned by program participants translate into substantial savings in transfer payments (e.g., SSI and Medicaid). For example, in the aforementioned STP programs, this amount has been estimated to be $516 per program participant per year (Mank, Rhodes, and Bellamy, 1985).

In comparing the benefits to participants in supported employment versus traditional programs, four measures are being taken into consideration:

1. The annual earnings of the participants and the supported employment programs

2. Other benefits, such as changes in adaptive behavior, functioning level, and the use of community resources

3. Improvements in community integration

4. Changes in family and community attitudes

In measuring the benefits of such programs in terms of public cost, the major issues involve:

1. The cost per person per year of traditional vs. supported employment programs

2. Transfer payments reductions

3. The total cost of a state's day and supported employment program

4. The cost of other public services consumed by participants

To the extent that increased earnings of disabled individuals translate into increased revenues, public funds are saved as a result of a diminishing need for sheltered facilities, and savings are realized in the form of decreased government transfers (eg., SSI, Medicare, Medicaid), supported employment programs will continue to enjoy growing support and diminishing skepticism.

However, monetary gain represents only one dimension of the supported employment experience. Whether or not this nascent movement continues to enjoy professional enthusiasm and political support will probably depend as much on social and emotional issues as on pecuniary ones. Improvements in adaptive behavior and functioning outside the immediate work environment will undoubtedly result from increased contact with nondisabled citizens. An enhanced sense of self-esteem will surely follow, as will the improved attitudes of family members, and ultimately it is hoped, the community.

SUMMARY

This chapter has described a number of economic issues related to work disability. It may be that as educators we possess limited power with which to successfully confront many of the forces that produce such extremely high unemployment rates among disabled people. However, with knowledge need not come despair. Understanding the dynamics of employment, unemployment, and the relationship between education and the labor market prepares us to deal much more realistically with those issues that are within our control. The work incentives provided under the most recent Social Security amendments may be used by knowledgeable professionals to inspire and assist handicapped adolescents to seek employment, rather than remain on public support; knowledge of research relevant to the skill needs of employers can assist us in making more informed decisions regarding students' training needs; understanding the employment programs available to handicapped students as they leave school allows us to facilitate their access to the benefits of these programs; and finally, being aware of innovative programs such as school-based enterprises and supported employment alternatives now being demonstrated equips us with an array of options for program development and student placement.

REFERENCES

Abraham, K.G. (1983). Structural/frictional vs. deficient demand unemployment: Some new evidence. *American Economic Review, 73*(4), 708–724.

Becker, G.S. (1964). *Human Capital: A Theoretical and Empirical Analysis, with Special Reference to Education.* New York: Columbia Press. Pp. 7–29.

Berkeley Planning Associates. (1981). *Final Report: Analysis of Policies of Private Sector Employers Toward the Disabled.* (Contract HEW-100-79-0180). Washington, D.C.: Department of Health and Human Services. Pp. 1–4, 64.

Burgdorf, R.L., Jr., and M.P. Burgdorf. (1977). The wicked witch is almost dead: Buck V. Bell and the sterilization of handicapped persons. *Temple Law Quarterly, 50*(2), 997–1000.

Carnegie Council on Children (1980). *The Unexpected Minority: Handicapped Children in America.* New York: Harcourt Brace Jovanovich. Pp. 3–4.

Conley, R.W., and J.H. Noble, Jr. (1985). Severely handicapped Americans: Victims of misguided policies. Paper presented at a meeting on the economics of disability. Sponsored by the U.S. Department of Education, Assistant Secretary for Special Education and Rehabilitative Services, National Institute of Handicapped Research. Washington, D.C.: Pp. 7–9, 12.

Cook, R.F., C.F. Adams, Jr., and V.L. Rawlins. (1985). *Public Service Employment: The Experience of a Decade.* Kalamazoo, Mich.: W.E. Upjohn Institute for Employment Research. Pp. 125–131.

Disability Rights Education and Defense Fund. (1982). *Socio-economic Profile of Disabled People in the United States.* Berkeley, Calif. Pp. 3, 6.

Doeringer, P.B., and M.J. Piore. (1971). *Internal Labor Markets and Manpower Analysis.* Lexington, Mass.: Health Lexington Books. Pp. 13–64.

Fisk, J. (1980). *The Economic Rationale for the Targeted Jobs Tax Credit.* (Report No. 80-196 E). Washington, D.C.: Congressional Research Service, The Library of Congress. P. CRS-40.

Flynn, R.J. (1982). National studies of the effectiveness of conventional vocational education: A research review. In K.P. Lynch, W.E. Kiernan, and J.A. Stark. (eds.), *Prevocational and Vocational Education for Special Needs Youth: A Blueprint for the 1980's.* Baltimore: Paul H. Brookes. Pp. 15–62.

Frieden, L. (1985). Executive Director, National Council On The Handicapped. Testimony presented on H.R. 2030. The Employment Opportunities for Disabled Americans Act. Subcommittee on Select Education, Committee on Education and Labor. U.S. House of Representatives.

Gaylord-Ross, R. et al. (1985). *Community Vocational Training for Handicapped Youth.* San Francisco, Calif.: San Francisco State University. Pp 1–4.

Gorski, R. (1985). 1619: Its a working number! *DISABLED USA.* Washington, D.C.: The President's Committee on Employment of the Handicapped. Pp. 1–5.

Griss, B. (1985). Testimony presented on behalf of The Consortium for Citizens with Developmental Disabilities, The Task Force on Employment, Medicaid and Social Security, on H.R.2030. The Employment Opportunities for Disabled Americans Act. Subcommittee on Select Education, Committee on Education and Labor, U.S. House of Representatives. (In press).

Guard, P. (1985). Deputy Director, Special Education Programs, Office of Special Education Programs. Keynote address: A National Conference on Secondary, Transitional, and Postsecondary Education for Exceptional Youth. Boston, Massachusetts.

Hahn, A., and R. Lerman. (1985). *What Works in Youth Employment Policy?* Washington, D.C.: National Planning Association. Pp. 37–51.

Harold Russell Associates, Inc. (1983). *Models of Exemplary/Practices in Coordinating Special Education and Vocational Rehabilitation Services.* (Contract No. 300-83-0158). Washington, D.C.: National Institute of Handicapped Research, Office of Special Education and Rehabilitative Services, U.S. Department of Education. P. 2.

Haveman, R.H. (1978). The Dutch social employment program. In J.L. Palmer (ed.), *Creating Jobs: Public Employment Programs and Wage Subsidies.* Washington, D.C.: The Brookings Institution. P. 242.

Heinz, H.J. (1985). U.S. Senator (R-PA.). Testimony in hearing before the Subcommittee on Select Revenue Measures, Committee on Ways and Means, House of Representatives, Ninety-Ninth Congress, First Session, Serial 99-12. Washington, D.C.: U.S. Government Printing Office. Pp. 6–7.

Hill, M., and P. Wehman. (1983). Cost benefit analysis of placing moderately and severely handicapped individuals into competitive employment. *TASH Journal*, 8(1), 30–38.

Hull, M. (1977). *Vocational Education for the Handicapped: A Review.* (Information Series No. 119). Columbus: The Ohio State University, ERIC Clearinghouse on Career Education. P. 3.

Johnson, W.G. (1985). Economics of work disability. *Disability and Chronic Disease Quarterly*, 5(3), 1.

Levitan, S., and R. Taggart. (1976). *Jobs for the Disabled.* Washington, D.C.: George Washington University, Center for Manpower Policy Studies. Pp. 5–10, 105–107.

Mank, D.M. L.E. Rhodes, and G.T. Bellamy. (1985). Four supported employment alternatives. In W. Kiernan and J. Stark (eds.), *Pathways to Employment for Developmentally Disabled Adults.* Baltimore: Paul H. Brookes. Chap. 10.

National Academy of Sciences Committee on Science, Engineering, and Public Policy. (1984). Report of the Panel on Secondary School Education for the Changing Workplace. *High Schools and the Changing Workplace: The Employers' View.* Washington, D.C.: National Academy Press. Pp. 17–29.

National Clearinghouse on Postsecondary Education for Handicapped Individuals. (1985). Work incentives for severely disabled persons. *Information from HEALTH*, 4(3), 1–2.

National Commission for Manpower Policy. (1978). *An Enlarged Role for the Private Sector in Federal Employment and Training Programs.* (Fourth Annual Report to the President and the Congress). Washington, D.C.: U.S. Government Printing Office. P. 15.

O'Brien J. (1984). An analysis of the excess costs in the employment and training of handicapped individuals in the Targeted Jobs Tax Credit Program: Implications for Educational Policy for the Handicapped. Ph.D. dissertation, University of California at Berkeley/San Francisco State University. In Hearing before the Subcommittee on Ways and Means, House of Representatives (1985). Ninety-Ninth Congress, First Session, Serial 99-12, pp. 140–146. Washington, D.C.: U.S. Government Printing Office. See also Hearing before the Subcommittee on Savings, Pensions, and Investment Policy of the Committee on Finance, United States Senate (1986). Ninety-Ninth Congress, First Session, S. Grg. 99–544, pp. 144–157. Washington, D.C.: U.S. Government Printing Office.

Office of Special Education and Rehabilitative Services. (1985). Supported employment of adults with severe disabilities: An OSERS program initiative. Washington, D.C. Pp. 2–3.

Phelps, L.A. (1977). Washington report expanding commitments to vocational education and training of handicapped individuals. *Education and Training of the Mentally Retarded*, 12(2), 186–192.

Phillips, L. (1977). *Barriers and Bridges: An Overview of Vocational Services Available for Handicapped Californians.* Sacramento: California Advisory Council on Vocational Education. P. ix.

Ratner, B. (1978). Costs labor adjustment and demand for labor: A case study in the micro-foundations of macroeconomics. Ph.D. dissertation, Yale University. Pp. 1–50.

Rollyson, M.M. (1985). Tax legislative counsel, U.S. Department of the Treasury, Testimony in Hearing before the Subcommittee on Select Revenue Measures, Committee on Ways and Means, House of Representatives, Ninety-Ninth congress. First Session, Serial 99-12, pp. 15–23. Washington, D.C.: U.S. Government Printing Office.

Singer, N.M. (1976). *Public Microeconomics: An Introduction to Governmental Finance.* 2d ed., Boston: Little, Brown & Company. Pp. 159–161.

Spence, A.M. (1972). Market signaling: The information impact of job markets and selected phenomena. Ph.D. dissertation, Harvard University. P. 42.

Stanford, C. (1986). Testimony before the Subcommittee on Savings, Pensions, & Investment Policy, Committee on Finance, United States Senate, Ninety-Ninth Congress, First Session, S. Grg. 99-544. Washington, D.C.: U.S. Government Printing Office. Pp. 26–28.

Stern, D. (1985). *Reconstituting Vocational Education.* Berkeley: University of California at Berkeley, School of Education. P. 5.

Stradford, C. (1986). Testimony before the Subcommittee on Savings, Pensions, and Investment Policy, Committee on Finance, United States Senate, Ninety-Ninth Congress, First Session, November 22, 1985, S.Grg. 99-544. Washington: U.S. Government Printing Office. Pp. 26–28.

Taggart, R. (1981). *A Fisherman's Guide, An Assessment of Training and Remediation Strategies.* Kalamazoo, Mich.: The W.E. Upjohn Institute for Employment Research. Pp. ix–x, 141.

Thurow, L.C. (1978). Vocational education as a strategy for eliminating poverty. Discussion paper developed for a *Plan for the Study of Vocational Education.* Washington, D.C.: National Institute of Education. Pp. 1–5, 12–13.

Tindall, L.W., J. Gugerty, and B. Dougherty. (1985). *Partnerships in Business and Education: Helping Handicapped Students Become a Part of the Job Training Partnership Act.* Produced under grant number G008302551, Office of Special Education and Rehabilitative Services, U.S. Department of Education. Madison: Vocational Studies Center, School of Education, University of Wisconsin-Madison. P. 17.

U.S. Commission on Civil Rights. (1983). *Accommodating the Spectrum of Disabilities.* Washington, D.C.: Clearinghouse Publication. Pp. 17–45, 29.

U.S. Department of Labor. (1964). *Formal Occupational Training of Adult Workers.* Manpower Automation Research Monograph #2. Washington, D.C.: U.S. Government Printing Office. Pp. 3, 18, 20, 43.

U.S. Department of Labor. (1983). *Seventy-First Annual Report FY 1983.* Washington, D.C.: U.S. Government Printing Office. P. 1.

U.S. Department of Labor, Employment and Training Administration. (1980). *A Review of Youth Employment Problems, Programs, and Policies.* Vl. 3, The Vice-President's Task Force on Youth Employment. Washington, D.C.: U.S. Government Printing Office. P. 1.

U.S. House of Representatives. (1985). Tax Reform Act of 1985. Report of the Committee on Ways and Means. House of Representatives, on H.R. 3838, together with dissenting and additional dissenting views. Washington, D.C.: U.S. Government Printing Office. P. 229.

U.S. Senate. (1985). Description of the Targeted Jobs Tax Credit and S. 1250. Prepared by the Staff of the Joint Committee on Taxation. Washington, D.C.: U.S. Government Printing Office. Pp. 1–12.

Urban Institute. (1975). *Report of the Comprehensive Needs Study.* Report to the Rehabilitative Services Administration. Washington, D.C.: U.S. Department of Health Education and Welfare. P. 324.

W.E. Upjohn Institute for Employment Research. (1977). *Work in America: Report of a Special Task Force to the Secretary of Health, Education, and Welfare.* Cambridge: The MIT Press. P. 158.

Walker, G., H. Feldstein, and K. Solow. (1985). *An Independent Sector Assessment of the Job Training Partnership Act, Phase II: Initial Implementation.* Grant No. 00-4-0794-50-325-02. Report prepared under grants from the Fork Foundation, the Charles Stewart Mott Foundation, the Rockefeller Foundation, and the National Commission for Employment Policy, New York. Pp. ii–viii.

Weisberg, A. (1983). What research has to say about vocational education and the high schools. *Phi Delta Kappa, 65*(5), 355–359.

Weisbrod, B.A. (1977). Collective action and the distribution of income: A conceptual approach. In R.H. Haveman, and J. Margolis (eds.), *Public Expenditure and Policy Analysis.* 2d ed. Chicago: Rand McNally. P. 126.

White House Working Group on Disability Policy. Cited in Madeline Will. (1984). *OSERS Programming for the Transition of Youth with Disabilities: Bridges from School to Working Life.* Washington, D.C.: Office of Special Education and Rehabilitative Services. P. 1.

Will, M. (1985). Assistant Secretary for Special Education and Rehabilitative Services, U.S. Department of Education. Statement on H.R., The Employment Opportunities for Disabled Americans Act. Before the Subcommittee on Select Education, Committee on Education and Labor, U.S. House of Representatives.

11 Business Perspective on Employing Persons with Disabilities*

Gopal C. Pati
Indiana University Northwest

You are a special education student in college. One of these days, you will finish your schooling and training as a "special educator" and assist students with special needs to acquire education and skills so that they can coexist and function with dignity side by side with those who may not have such needs. While a majority of our students may not require much assistance at all, some may. Even among those who naturally achieve, there will be days when, as students, they will ask you questions about their future:

- Will they hire me?
- How am I going to support myself?
- Am I going to be discriminated against?
- Am I going to be accepted?
- Am I going to be promoted on the job?
- What are my chances of success?
- What are my employment rights?
- Do I really have a chance?

*The author is grateful to Paul Scher of Sears, Roebuck and Company, Paul Ashton of the President's Committee on Employment of the Handicapped, Robert Salitore of Bank of Indiana, and Jay Rochlin of AT&T for taking valuable time and contributing their views to this chapter to enrich our learning experience. This type of unselfish contribution speaks very well of them as well as of their companies.

These and other concerns, of course, are very natural. You do not have to be a person with disabilities *or* have special needs to raise such issues. Most of us ask such questions *or* think them at one time or another to get some assurance. For students with special needs, such questions are pivotal to motivation—to learn, to adjust, to function, to integrate, to work, to grow and just to live!

In a society where we adore "looks," admire masculinity, seek economic and personal power, and equate material possession with status and stature as signs of success, it is not at all surprising that persons with disabilities, who are America's largest minority group, have apprehensions as students and adults. Although attitudes are changing, we still have a long way to go to convince people of the following:

- That disability does not mean inability
- That persons with disabilities need empathy not sympathy
- That persons with disabilities are precious human resources
- That both persons with *or* without disabilities have special needs
- That lack of training and education are more handicapping than the disability itself
- That properly placed, there is little difference between the person with disabilities and the person without disabilities
- That performance counts, not disability *or* personality

Special education students and teachers can play a very important role in instilling drive and positive attitudes in students with disabilities. They can do this by learning what is going on in the major institutions in our society, and through this knowledge develop the skills that will allow them to do the following:

1. Develop creative strategies to train and assimilate persons with disabilities into the mainstream of society.

2. Appreciate the needs and expectations of employers in the world of work so that students with disabilities can be better prepared to be a meaningful part of the employer's total scheme of things.

3. Facilitate the understanding of human resource planning systems within which selective placement, training, and continued employment of persons with disabilities are possible.

4. Communicate to the students, educators, and the families of students with special needs on trends in partnerships among the business world, the educational institutions, and the vocational rehabilitation communities, in order to pinpoint motivation for community linkage in hiring and managing such employees in the work systems.

5. Create a believable and workable body of knowledge that can be expanded so that special education professionals can be further motivated to continue their work of preparing and marketing a valuable product called *human resources with disabilities*, a product whose abilities can be utilized to improve productivity and profitability in the business world.

This chapter will assist you, we hope, to become a believer in the notion that indeed our society is changing , that your products are appreciated, that many businesses now welcome with enthusiasm as an important source of human resource supply, students with special needs. Furthermore, recent trends in the acceptance of workers with disabilities in the workplace, and the philosophies that go with these trends, illustrate the special education holds not only in educational and rehabilitation settings, but in the world of work as well.

THE CASE OF JAN (JOB ACCOMMODATION NETWORK)

Members of the Employer Committee of the President's Committee on the Employment of the Handicapped have created a unique national clearinghouse that offers a cost-free service to an employer wishing to make accommodation for an individual with disabilities, an existing employee, or a person anticipating return to work from injury and illness *or* just waiting to perform his or her present job more easily. JAN (Job Accommodation Network) is an informational network developed by employers for employers. The service is based at the University of Virginia in Morgantown and has been in operation since July 1984. It brings together practical information from many sources about steps employers have been taking to accommodate the functional limitation an individual may possess *or* environmental limitations one may encounter. An employer may like to place a qualified worker with a disability, but may not know how. Now, with the network in place, all the employer has to do is to call a toll-free number (1-800-526-7234). A human factor engineer answers the call and gets information on functional limitations, environmental factors, requirements of the job, and other relevant operations information. A computer does the rest. It prints out ideas for accommodations from its national data base, which listed over 4,000 experiences as of 1985. Furthermore, in the printout, the name, address, and telephone number of the company representative are included so the caller can receive further information and clarification. Again, this service is cost-free. The only requirement is that the employer commit to share accommodation information with other employers through JAN. The result? More job opportunities for people with special needs.

Some of the employers whose executives played an important role in creating JAN are AT&T, Atlantic Richfield, Continental Group, E.I. DuPont, Edison Electric Institute, Honeywell, ITT, Hughes Aircraft, National Restaurant Association, Sears, U.S. Steel, Westinghouse, and the President's Committee in Employment of the Handicapped. JAN has helped over 300 employers, large and small, to cost-effectively utilize individuals with special needs. Some specific examples follow:

- A woman who was told in her school days that she could not work after college because she had epilepsy and was in a wheelchair, now works successfully at Atlantic Richfield, with her company helping her with accommodations that cost less than $50—they bought an "amplified telephone and window blinds that she can lower when she needs to lie down."

- At Westinghouse, an engineering assistant who is paralyzed in one leg was given a desk job that requires little walking but has flexible work hours and a parking place. He is doing just fine.

- At DuPont, a blind computer programmer was given a speech computer to echo her words so that she can work more efficiently.

- At Continental, an office phone's volume was significantly increased for a hearing impaired person.

- One major insurance company (see Watkins, 1984) has provided at least fifty types of accommodations, such as providing a drafting table, page turner, and pressure sensitive tape for a sales agent who is paralyzed from a broken neck ($300 cost); changing a work desk layout for a visually impaired data entry operator (no cost); and renting a headset phone that enables an employee with cerebral palsy to write while talking ($6.01 per month).

These and other examples illustrate that accommodations are not always incredibly expensive; they do require creative thinking and teamwork, however.

The case of JAN is interesting and important for a number of reasons:

1. Many businesses and their executives want to utilize people with special needs. They are cooperating with each other and learning from each other. This is a creative business perspective in action.

2. It is possible to minimize stereotypes about people with special needs. JAN emphasizes functional limitations rather than handicaps. For example, Jay Rochlin of AT&T, one of the founders of JAN, said, "We do not accommodate cerebral palsy, but rather an inability to grasp" (Watkins, 1984).

3. There is a human side to business. With tools such as computers and other information technology, it is possible to serve both humanity and business interests by getting good and dependable people who want to work.

4. Both employers and employees gain from such partnerships. Businesses get valuable people with skills; and employees gain economic independence. In today's cost-conscious business environment, large and small businesses alike can utilize JAN without expensive modifications for accommodations or complicated solutions. This resource can significantly reduce disability costs through sharing of information.

THE BUSINESS CONNECTION: WHY EMPLOYERS UTILIZE PERSONS WITH DISABILITIES

Why do employers utilize individuals with special needs? This is a complex question. There are probably as many motivations as people. In this section we present a summary of the major external and internal developments in the business world that are causing organizations to view persons with disabilities as a viable option in recruitment. Any way one looks at the question, businesses have been evolving from a "charity" perspective to a "good business" perspective. Therefore, a summary statement would sound something like this: *It is good business to utilize people with special needs* (Pati and Adkins, 1980). In this section, we also present statements of some thoughtful executives who have demonstrated their commitment to help persons with disabilities, while at the same time serving their respective organizations.

First, during the last decade the business world has been extremely cost-conscious. Foreign competition, the cost of energy, labor shortages in certain skills, a decline in work ethics, antidiscrimination laws and regulations , the mounting costs of disability and worker's compensation, and so on (Pati, 1985) have all contributed to the realization that business must produce quality products, which means maintaining a well-motivated work force committed to productivity. Utilizing qualified people with disabilities is part of good human resource management. There are plenty of experiences to suggest that such persons make good employees and, therefore, that they can be an important resource in achieving productivity goals. For example, the Kentucky Department of Education emphasizes the use of an industrial relations manager in that state and points out that employers can be assisted by such managers from the state vocational rehabilitation agency at no cost to find competent, dependable employees. A special brochure intended for business, labor, and industry says, "The Major Factor Determining Job Success Is Capability *not* Disability." It also points out the following advantages of utilizing job-qualified individuals who happen to have disabilities:

Advantage #1—*SAVE MONEY*

Services* are provided at *no cost* to you and no fees to applicants. You will experience less turnover and absenteeism and a high rate of productivity.

Advantage #2—*TAX INCENTIVES*

Tax breaks are available for hiring individuals with disabilities, for removal of architectural barriers, and for providing accommodations.

Advantage #3—*EMPLOYER CONTROL*

You do the hiring and firing. Professional vocational rehabilitation counselors are available for consultation as requested.

Advantage #4—*CONTROLLED REFERRALS*

Only qualified applicants will be referred for consideration. Only the number of applicants you specify will be referred.

Advantage #5—*APPLICANT INFORMATION*

Professional vocational rehabilitation counselors will provide you with *essential information* on each applicant. All participants have gone through an extensive assessment of their capabilities, aptitudes, skills, and interests.

Advantage #6—*UTILIZE EXPERIENCE*

Vocational rehabilitation has over 60 years experience in meeting employer needs with job qualified workers with disabilities.

Second, employers are realizing that they must control disability costs.** Utilizing and hiring persons with disabilities is a partial solution to that problem.

---

*Services include referral of qualified persons with disabilities to an employer, vocational evaluation, providing relevant information, facilitating government support, counseling employer and supervisor, orientation for persons with disabilities for better work adjustment, and input to make accommodations, etc.

**When an employer fails to hire back an employee after he or she has been rehabilitated *or* fails to recommend an injured worker for rehabilitation, that employer is paying the worker to stay home and depend on disability payments. Such payments increase an employer's liability in terms of paying additional premiums to support nonworking workers. Through rehabilitation and gainful employment an employer can drastically cut down such costs. See the statement of Paul Scher on pages 302–304.

For example, Lee Iacocca in his autobiography said:

> When I came to Chrysler, I saw that Blue Cross/Blue Shield had already become our largest supplier. They were actually billing us more than our suppliers of steel and rubber! Chrysler, Ford and G.M. are now paying $3 billion a year for hospital, surgical, medical and dental insurance plus all pharmaceutical bills. At Chrysler, that comes to $600 million or about $600 per car. (1984)

Paul L. Scher is the manager of the Equal Opportunity /Handicapped Program at the National Personnel Department of Sears, Roebuck and Company in Chicago. He is a writer, consultant, and one of the leaders in industrial rehabilitation in the United States. In this capacity he advises Sears concerning: (1) the designing of their affirmative action program for handicapped civilians and disabled veterans; (2) the administration of services to return chronically ill or permanently disabled employees to a job; (3) the development of products for the disabled customer; and (4) participation in public service activities to develop awareness among neighbors in the business community about the skills of individuals with special needs. Scher has a functional limitation that, to him, is nothing more than what he calls "a nuisance." He is blind. He has written the following message for this chapter.

> Americans paid $387 billion in 1984 for health care services. Private insurance accounts for $102.2 billion of this figure. As we move toward the 21st century, enlightened employers will continue to take steps which will lessen the number of hospital days their employees consume. Positive efforts will increase to bring recovering employees back to a job before long-term disability provisions are invoked. Injured workers will be reassigned in preference to paying total disability as an ongoing expense. About 5% of company payroll goes to maintain those benefits which business cannot afford in a world of increasing competition.
>
> Because of this, the sight of a person with disabilities at a work station will become familiar. Their competency will be taken for granted. They will be held to the same standards as their peers and, therefore, more easily be considered for a promotion when deserved. This will happen if such employees are appropriately prepared for work.
>
> Forty-four percent of working age males with a disability are presently unemployed. Seventy percent of working age females with a disability remain outside the work force. These figures will be noticeably reduced when school counselors, vocational education faculty, principals, the State Employment Service, the Department of Rehabilitation, and organizations of parents with students with

special needs unite together so as to create the experiences which will make Vocational IEP's realistic. Plans for work should begin no later than Grade 6.

Our evolving economy has created many part-time jobs. Many of them can be performed by students with physical, mental, and learning disabilities. Part-time work experience is as important for the vocational maturity of students with special needs as it is for able-bodied individuals.

At Sears, too many applicants with disabilities are referred to me because they have no idea of what they can do. I wind up spending an hour discussing how to apply for a job, what to expect from a supervisor, what components go into a pay check, the use of a timecard, and how to explain to personnel and a potential supervisor the ways by which you overcome the handicap of your disability. While it is easy to understand why many youngsters have no part-time work experience, there is no excuse for the school system failing to teach this aspect of practical occupational information. If the student cannot describe his or her skill in an understandable manner, then personnel will only have difficulty trying to place the individual as well as determining what reasonable accommodations might be necessary. At last, there seems to be a growing variety of model cooperative education programs for the persons with disabilities. They are barely in time.

Fortunately, employers and employees are becoming as concerned about the environment where work is performed as they are in respect to the quality and quantity of output. For example, employees assigned to information manipulating jobs, where the computer is used as the basic tool, develop eye strain, back aches, stiff necks, and fatigue unless their work station is ergonomically designed. They consist of adjustable chairs, tables, VDT rack, and a reading lamp. In this atmosphere, accommodating workers with disabilities is not much different from accommodating everyone else. So the qualified person with disabilities will find it easier to obtain jobs.

How can the community create the necessary experiences for people with special needs to achieve vocational maturity? The school, Department of Rehabilitation, Job Service, and Welfare Department must network in such a way that exceptional children gain access to the knowledge and experiences needed to attain independence and a gainful employment. Within the network, turf must be inconsequential. The PTA, organization of parents of special need students and the business community can participate in civically motivated efforts to assure such graduates, in spite of their limitations, be prepared for work.

Parents of youngsters with disabilities can help by talking to their employers about participating in work-study programs. Job developers can encourage employers to cooperate and they can also feed back to the schools information about skills which must be taught if "Sam, or Sally," is to be ready for that summer job. Finally, agencies can cooperate in the administration of a job bank so that firms can deal with one or two counselors instead of representatives from many agencies. This happenstance will make more time available for employers to develop training jobs which can be filled by a succession of students with special needs. If these steps are taken, then equal opportunity will be closer to reality for America's largest minority.

Sears Tower
Chicago
January 29, 1986

Third, in an enlightened corporate culture, rehabilitation and placement of individuals with special needs are rapidly becoming important parts of the personnel/human resource department, which has itself just been regaining its rightful place in organizational decision making.

Paul Ashton, a licensed psychologist and an active member of the President's Committee on Employment of the Handicapped, is a veteran researcher and innovator in the concept of disability management and possesses a wealth of experience in the area of returning injured workers to work in business settings. Ashton has issued the following statement depicting the profit cycle as an opportunity for persons with disabilities. He also believes that effective partnerships between industry and rehabilitation may be developed.

THE PROFIT CYCLE OF INDUSTRY AND REHABILITATION

Nothing New Under the Sun:

In the early 1970's, government and private industry alike placed much emphasis upon rehabilitating workers with disabilities. Laws were enacted, and regulations were imposed. Affirmative Action programs for such individuals flourished.

In industry, these efforts answered industry's question of government. One big problem was to find the starting point. Among some of the brain storming and feverish trials were the following:

1. The establishment of return to work programs for the injured/ill employee; these programs were assigned to the charge of personnel departments in the companies insurance/benefits departments, and medical departments.

2. Rehabilitation professionals were hired in major industries as part of the return to work program.
3. Liaisons were established between industry, local rehabilitation agencies, and state offices of vocational rehabilitation.

Taking a close look at the three itemized statements, there really is nothing new, just a realignment of the forces.

A Cycle of the 80's:

In the 1980's we still have remnants of a semblance of "new" activities. However, the expression, "the more things change, the more they remain the same," is certainly true for the outcome.

Insurance companies, the legal systems (legislation, regulations, policies, and the like), are each fighting for something new, or the top of the pile. Insurance costs have escalated to new (and almost unbelievable) heights. Corporate benefits programs appear to be designed to determine who shall and shall not return to work, or who shall be hired. The problem is, it is not feasible to hire (or return to work) *an individual who cannot produce.* Most state vocational rehabilitation programs will not, or cannot, accept a client who is not vocationally feasible.

Too often the rehabilitation scenerio looks more like the saga of the film *"Clockwork Orange."* Initially, the individual had severe problems of anti-social behavior. The social systems including the church, the law, the scientists, and the news media arrived on the scene to evaluate/remedy the individual's problem behavior. The film concluded with all of the social systems blaming and destructively striking out accusatively at each other, as the client lay watching and fading away.

Documenting Success and Evaluating Failure:

What has happened? Where are the success stories? And where are the failures? Who now cares? Are positive actions initiated by the legal forces, or do we get good results because it is good business to hire disabled individuals? During the past one and a half decades, we've learned a lot about high achievers whom we were previously aware of as being disabled. We've had a great awakening of a powerful workforce within the community of disabled individuals.

Of course, not all have been highly successful. Far too many have been re-cycled through the rehabilitation centers. Far too many have been dropped from the roles of the successful when a social problem became a greater problem than the lack of vocational capability. This is where the task of research and analysis becomes more important than placement. First, find out what the problems were (if a disabled person should lose a job), work for remedies, and then proceed to the next steps.

Somewhere money must be generated. One of the primary ingredients necessary for making money is people. An understatement. People are primary movers. No industry can exist without them. Tools, material products, equipment, technology, and services, follow.

Profit makers share with the non-profit makers. But first there must be the profit makers. Our result is another cycle. Industry needs anyone who can perform a task of producing at a profitable rate.

Our recent years of experimenting and bringing the formerly "hidden profit makers" (disabled individuals) out of prisons of powerlessness should now be a wealth of research and resource material. Current research will answer the questions the business and insurance industries formerly (and still may be) asked. Research materials currently available on the market are quite sufficient for presenting the facts of how much rehabilitation pays.

Experience has proven that returning the disabled employee back to work does pay. However, that same "experience" by now should have taught us the difference between "return to a job" and placement in a carefully selected, suitable occupation. The rehabilitation process cannot be forcing an individual into a job which may never have been acceptable even before the injury or illness. This too often happens due to insurance coverage stipulations without due consideration of the complete individual.

The rehabilitation professional has to be capable of comprehending all (social, mental and physical) aspects, needs, weaknesses, and capabilities of the worker facing a potential job placement. The requirements of the rehabilitation professional cannot end there, industry demands convincing professionalism and high assurance of successful placement. Successful placement includes starting an individual at a beginning level with great potential for growth and promotion.

The Industry/Rehabilitation Connection:

The resolution of industry's quest, the frustration of applicants with disabilities, and the success of "closed cases" for the professionals led to something very positive. Communications are open. We all hear each other. We stop trying to make the other say what we want to hear. The connection is made. Industry develops a trust in the rehab professional. The professional has exercised the best of his/her career development skills and knowledge. The disabled individuals service is offered as an opportunity to the job resource. Each entity understands its role. The connection is assured success and profit. The handicapped worker profits, the employer profits, and the system profits. Rehabilitation pays.

The President's Committee on Employment of the Handicapped is another "connection" which interfaces the employer and handicapped individuals on a national, supportive scale. This organization, based in Washington, D.C., is represented by a cross section of employers, dedicated to work with every type of problem which prevents maximum functioning on the part of individuals with handicaps.

The Value of Credibility in Placement:

Industry searches for profit-makers: people, products, technologies, and services. Research of past rehabilitation successes are good sales tools. The professional has a responsibility to review track records which give evidence of both successes and failures and share the data with employers. Face the issue, sometimes applicants have been oversold, and sometimes undersold. The former usually results in the employee being unable to do the new job; the latter is often the cause for the employee becoming disenchanted, bored, and developing a loss of esteem. The employer is dependent upon the professional's skills in making proper placements, with credibility.

Rehabilitation case studies show that the successful applicant is the one who endures, has support, and uses initiative to update his /her skills. As the employer learns about the capabilities and limitations of any individual with a disability, adjustments come almost automatically (in most cases) on the part of all involved. Whether the placement is a return to a former employer, or filling a new position with a new employer, the goal must be top production and profitability, or it is not realistic. When the employer can realize definite profit, then and only then, will future placements be easy.

So , without a team-work connection, the questions regarding who has to do what about placing the disabled individual, or what industry has to do, or specific details about the role of the rehab professional, become moot. It may even sound like a dream, but even the insurance industry (which keeps the profit and loss scores without the advantage of empathic concern for the individual employee) will have no basis for exclusion when X Employee (the disabled individual) results in the same insurance experience rating as Y Employee (the "able-bodied" employee).

A Joint Venture:

The wise industry still looks for capable employees who will enhance the bottom line profits. The disabilities become inconsequential when the proper team member (the rehab professional) does a good job in introducing the capable worker for the appropriate task. Together, this growing team, (the industry, the professional, and the capable worker), earn the profits, share the profits, and in turn, appropriately redistribute the same to the non-profit enterprises in order to make more profits.

> Minneapolis
> January 28, 1986

There is another perspective. Although some may downplay it, the passage of the Vocational Rehabilitation Act of 1973 is an added force for utilizing disabled persons. Sections 503 and 504 require government contractors and subcontractors to take affirmative action in hiring and utilizing people with disabilities and to stop discriminating against them. About half of America's businesses—some 3 million—are covered by this including schools, colleges, hospitals, nursing homes, social service agencies, governments, and other establishments. Although the requirements are quite extensive, the following are emphasized:*

- Do not discriminate against a "qualified" person with a disability.
- Provide "reassurable accommodation" to accommodate special needs.
- Remove architectural barriers and promote accessibility to programs and facilities.
- Make your employment process job-related.
- Establish an "outreach"—efforts to find qualified people with special needs within and outside the organization.
- Train supervisors and managers in the concept of disability.
- Conduct "internal reviews" of the workplace to identify needless barriers and do something about them.

These laws and regulations have come to stay. Even though some employers still give only lip service to the legal requirements, rehabilitation as well as employment concerns of the disabled have bipartisan support throughout the country and they are here to stay irrespective of who occupies the White House. Some recalcitrant employers may be insensitive to the legal requirements by thinking that the laws were passed to legislate morality. But progressive employers realize that in the eyes of the law, *prejudice against persons with disabilities is not the issue—discrimination is.* Laws change behavior, not attitudes. Some employers who reluctantly hired a disabled person because of legal requirements have been pleasantly surprised by the person's accomplishments. Consequently, they have changed their attitudes and now include persons with special needs as a viable source of

---

*For detailed requirements of the 502 legislation and compliance, see Pati and Adkins (1981, pp. 35–73) and Zimmer (1981).

labor supply. Workers with disabilities also have a very positive impact on able-bodied coworkers.*

Robert Salitore, Vice President of Human Resources at the Bank of Indiana, who also teaches at Indiana University Northwest in the field of organizational development and change, believes, as does his organization, in the value of people with special needs in workplaces. Mr. Salitore has issued the following statement for this chapter:

> The hidden dividend of fuller utilization of disabled persons is in the *development* of those who work side-by-side with disabled employees. We have always felt that *quality of worklife* issues are linked inextricably with quality of life issues. As such, accommodations made for employees with disabilities never really hit home until realized one-to-one.
>
> We find that those employees who work closely with employees with disabilities get an excellent perspective on the real world. They also appreciate how "fragile" life is and, most important of all, able-bodied employees learn valuable lessons in how to integrate alternative lifestyles into their own through these interactions.
>
> The potential for fuller usage of employees with disabilities is clear, based upon the payout to the company and society in general. We find the immediate payout to coworkers to be a refreshing added dimension.

THE SELECTIVE PLACEMENT PROCESS

In the preceding section, we talked about employer motivation in utilizing persons with disabilities. What we need to learn now is the process used to accommodate this type of human resource. Many employees with little or no experience in this effort are skeptical about what kinds of employees the disabled make. Having never seen a deaf, blind, or wheelchair-bound person perform, employers naturally ask: "How can disabled workers be as productive and dependable as nondisabled workers?"

The answer to that "how" is *selective placement*. Selective placement is simply the matching of an individual's abilities with the person's accomplishments. Consequently, they have changed their

---

* See Pati and Adkins (1981, pp 35–73), Zimmer (1981), and Pati (1978). Comments on the positive impact by workers with special needs is based on the author's personal experiences and the reports of those involved in job placement. Usually, companies do not like their names mentioned. But experiences in companies such as Sears, AT&T, TVA, Miles Laboratories, 3M, Continental Bank, DuPont, McDonald Douglas, and so on show that coworkers admire a selectively placed individual with a positive attitude.

attitudes and now include persons with special needs as a viable source of person's accomplishments. Consequently, they have changed their attitudes and now include persons with special needs as a viable source of requirements of the job. Every personnel officer practices it to some degree. For individuals with special needs, selective placement requires a more precise analysis of the demands of the position and the abilities of the applicants. The rehabilitation community can be of enormous help in evaluating people. [For a detailed discussion of rehabilitation agencies who help employers, see Pati and Adkins (1981), chapter 3.] The employers must perform a job analysis, a method of studying a job in detail, keeping in mind the physical and environmental aspects of the job as well as the components of the job content. Job analysis, which is described in a later section, is extremely critical.

Once the job analysis is done, the employer has a workable set of standards for all applicants—with a much better chance of placing applicants in the appropriate job. Thus, when done well, job analysis and selective placement eliminate the disabled distinction; we have one population of employees. *When an individual is placed in a job for which he or she is fitted, the worker is no longer job-handicapped.*

In fact, when this extra care is given to the person–job matching process, work becomes a source of satisfaction for the employees. A worker satisfied with the job yields dividends for the employer in terms of: greater production, fewer accidents, less tardiness, and less absenteeism. Again, this relationship between well-placed employees and productivity holds for persons with disabilities as well as those without.

Consider the model of human resource management presented in Figure 11-1. All employees (people with or without special needs) are supported internally by certain personnel activities. The only two for which persons with disabilities receive any special consideration involve selective placement and accommodations. Selective placement is essential for everyone. Here, however, persons with disabilities have an advantage: They have been evaluated (and likely counseled and trained) by professionals in rehabilitation agencies. Accommodations, as we shall see later, are nowhere near as awesome as most people believe: extensive redesigning of jobs is not necessary and extensive modifications of work environments are not needed.

The human resource model in Figure 11-1 assumes that human beings are a good resource. Such resource formulation does not just happen. It has to be planned, developed and nurtured, and properly utilized. Activities associated with this idea are considered important investments in human capital. And the fifteen specific personnel functions that have been identified are designed to provide a climate of work where properly selected individuals can be motivated to work, survive, compete, grow, and contribute to the achievement of organizational objectives. These activities improve morale and contribute to the reduction of turnover.

All Employees—Including the Handicapped

Internal Support: Specific Activities

- Meaningful and selective placement
- Orientation nitty gritty
- Supportive supervision
- Training and development
- Opportunity for growth and mobility
- Recognition of employee uniqueness
- Fair performance appraisal
- Achievement of personal goals
- Consistency and fairness of rules
- Strong leadership to inspire and give direction
- Sense of belongingness
- Freedom to speak and participate
- Organizational receptiveness to ideas
- Organizational openness to clarify things
- Accommodations

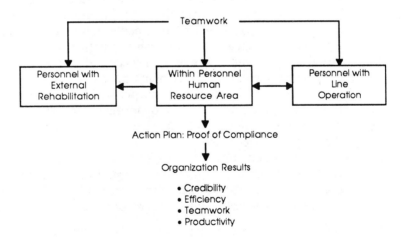

Figure 11.1 Human Resource Management Model: Internal Support

Source: Pati and Adkins, 1981.

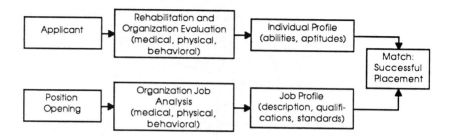

Figure 11.2 Overview of Selective Placement Process

Furthermore, the model indicates that for internal support activities to function effectively, there must be teamwork: with rehabilitation people, with line management, and within the total management system. In terms of people with disabilities, the product of this teamwork is the climate where they can work with dignity without discrimination, which is the proof of compliance with the law on nondiscrimination. In terms of the organization, the results are greater efficiency and productivity.

Since disabled applicants are evaluated by the rehabilitation service and the personnel apparatus of the organization, a detailed applicant profile is achieved; that is, the person's medical needs, physical skills, work behaviors, work attitudes are well known. For the applicant to be selectively placed, the characteristics of the person must be matched with a job profile (requirements of the job) containing the same elements: physical requirements, job skills, behavioral skills (see Figure 11-2). Such a profile can come only from a specific and detailed job analysis of what an employee at a specific job must do, what tools must be used, what movements made, what decisions made, and what the desired product should be (the job's purpose). That is, all criteria—medical, physical, behavioral—must be quantifiable and job-specific. Once the job profile is completed, a match with the potential employee (either disabled or not) can be made.

For the remainder of this section, we will discuss the five major components of a program for successfully employing persons with disabilities: (1) recruitment and outreach, (2) job analysis, (3) medical examinations, (4) placement with accommodations, and (5) follow-up.

Recruitment and Outreach

Before we can selectively place anyone, we have to acquire a pool of qualified applicants—but traditional methods of recruitment will not be adequate. Fortunately, any company wishing to employ persons with disabilities has a potential willing partner: a local vocational rehabilitation agency. The best approach is to develop a working relationship with one agency or with a small select group of agencies.

Once the agencies have been located, a company can invite the agency counselors to visit the company operation and thereby acquire a firsthand understanding of how the company works, what technology is used, the variety of positions available, and so on. Counselors will need to talk with the line managers and personnel staff as well, in order to develop as comprehensive and detailed a picture of the employer's needs as possible. Continued energetic teamwork, and a little creativity, will be necessary to select those agency clients that will make up the applicant pool (Pati, 1978).

Although a close relationship with one or more agencies is best, other options are possible. A company needs to consider all possible sources, external and internal, then develop close relationships with those who are competent and with whom the company is comfortable.

External Sources. An organization's personnel apparatus can establish and maintain contact with as many of the following sources as possible (U.S. Civil Service Commission, 1977):

- The state employment service
- Organizations providing services for the disabled and for disabled veterans
- State vocational rehabilitation agencies
- Private rehabilitation facilities
- Training schools for handicapped persons
- College and university placement services
- United Way agencies
- Unions
- Sheltered workshops
- Local or regional Veteran's Administration offices.
- Churches
- Public school systems with work-study programs
- Private Industry Council
- Project with Industry (PWI) programs

[For a review of the extremely useful PWI concept, see Watkins (1984).]

Internal Sources. The organization itself may be a good source of workers with disabilities—especially since most organizations want to promote and train from within. Any company is likely to have such individuals, but the organization may not know about them because they are reluctant to identify themselves. An honest and well-publicized commitment to utilize workers with special needs—with better placement and better work atmosphere resulting—will locate them inside the organization.

In addition, there are an increasing number of employees with special needs that the company *does* know about. Employees become injured on the job, are disabled on off-the-job accidents, or develop medical conditions. The cost of this phenomenon occurs in three areas:

1. Formerly productive people become incapacitated.
2. Valuable, trained employees are lost.
3. Compensation payments escalate enormously.

The best way to avoid those human and productivity losses is to arrange to keep these employees (who usually *want* to keep working) on the job. A good way for a large company to begin is to appoint a full-time coordinator for selective placement. The Tennessee Valley Authority (TVA) responded to the "disabled-employee" problem in this way. TVA's program attacked on three fronts:

1. It modified personnel and medical procedures to better accommodate persons with disabilities and to create closer working relationships with other departments.
2. It assessed and removed architectural barriers at several sites.
3. It implemented training programs for managers. The participants were taught about the Vocational Rehabilitation Act; types of disabilities; needs that require accommodations; the company commitment to such activities; and the value of utilizing persons with disabilities.

At the TVA, when an employee applies for disability retirement, every employing division is required to search for a job that the rehabilitated worker might perform. Only when medical information clearly indicates the impaired worker can no longer work or be retrained without injury to his health is the worker retired with disability. TVA's return-to-work process requires several related services (Pati and Hinton, 1980):

1. Interviewing and counseling to determine the individual's needs and problems
2. Evaluating the individual's vocational assets and liabilities
3. Developing a plan of action that will lead to job placement
4. Identifying appropriate job openings
5. Placing the individual in a job
6. Following up on the individual's progress and adaptation

Such a process drastically cuts worker's compensation and minimizes "free-loaders" or "chronic fakes" who find disability benefits an attractive alternative to work.

TVA's success was the result of two critical factors: (1) top management made an honest commitment to rehabilitation, and (2) the personnel, medical, and rehabilitation people developed an effective system and worked closely together. The TVA experience can be duplicated if those two criteria are met.

Job Analysis

As mentioned earlier, a good job analysis should strive to be detailed and comprehensive. As a guideline, it might answer the following questions [adopted from Human Resources Center, "Job Analysis Worksheets"; for another good source of information on conducting job analysis, see U.S. Department of Labor, (1972)]:

- What are the physical demands of the job? (How much walking, standing, bending, lifting, heaving, seeing, and so on are required?)

- What are the mental factors involved? (Reading, writing, color discrimination, judgment, and so on)

- What are the stress factors? (Repetition, high pressure, hazards, fatigue, boredom)

- How does the job break down into sequenced steps? What are the physical and time requirements of each step?

- What tools and machines are involved?

- What factors influence the work environment? (Noise, ventilation, lighting, temperature, duct, congestion, and so on)

In a world where products, technologies, methods, knowledge, and human values are constantly changing, jobs will be changing as well. When jobs change, the descriptions *should* change—and with them the qualifications of the people who perform the jobs. A job, for instance, that required high physical strength ten years ago might make far fewer physical demands today because of technological changes,

People with or without special needs alike are frequently screened out or misplaced because of outdated, vague, or inaccurate job descriptions. Such job misplacement has a high cost to employers in terms of turnover, absenteeism, accidents, bad employee attitudes, low motivation, and low productivity.

Once a job is defined, the qualifications needed in an employee can be established—this is known as the job specifications or the employee specifications. To repeat, the specifications must be precise and job-related. And, obviously, they must be revised periodically as the job analysis is reviewed.

To summarize, accurate job descriptions from rigorous job analyses can produce many benefits:

1. They help employers get the right people for their jobs.

2. They assist in identifying only job-related qualifications.

3. They facilitate career planning by identifying relationships between groups of jobs.

4. They aid in defining appropriate training and development activities.

5. They help make wage and salary structures more equitable and performance evaluations more relevant.

6. They provide a documentation of an organization's good faith attempts to be fair.

7. They help make job accommodations and job revision easier.

8. They eliminate unnecessary medical standards.

As is evident from the last item, medical considerations are part of job analysis. Just what physical abilities should an applicant have? What role should the medical department have in determining them?

Medical Examinations

No matter how gifted, knowledgeable, or experienced physicians may be, they can only make their own diagnoses of workers health conditions. And even then, diagnoses are difficult to translate into job behaviors. Physicians, no matter how capable, are not likely to be experts on job placement.

No member of an organization's medical staff, no company doctor, should make an employment decision. A doctor should be part of a team that identifies the condition of the job applicant, or the injured worker, or the employee seeking disability retirement. The doctor provides only some of the technical input: a judgment of the physical abilities and limitations of the applicant/employee.

Unfortunately, in the past, and even today in some organizations, employers inadvertently rely on the company physician to make employment-related decisions for them. We feel this must change. Although employers may have apprehensions and concerns about certain illnesses or disabilities, they must discipline themselves, and their staffs, to answering four specific questions:

1. Will the employee's condition affect his or her job performance?

2. Will the condition affect coworkers?

3. Will the condition pose hazards to any employee?

4. Will the condition create additional liability for the employer?

That last item deserves a little comment. Contrary to the prevailing myth, insurance rates do *not* go up when persons with disabilities are hired. Insurance rates are based on the nature of the hazards involved in the work and on the employer's accident record, not the employee's physical condition. Indeed, since this type of employee has good accident rates, they have good insurance rates (American Mutual Insurance Alliance [undated]).

It is the manager's job to take the medical data, the job description, and other information from colleagues, to answer those questions, and then to make the placement decision. If the answers to these questions are all no, then there is no reason to hinder or restrict placement.

Placement with Accommodations

In one sense, all life, and all business, is an accommodation. Employers make accommodations when they buy new equipment, rearrange furniture, allow flexible scheduling, or alter the work environment in any way. Reasonable accommodations for employees with disabilities need not cause any special concern. Accommodations are easier and cheaper than most employers fear.

Accommodations should be determined on an individual basis—*flexibility* and *reasonableness* are the keys. In considering an accommodation, the following needs to be asked (U.S. Office of Personnel Management, 1980, p.2):

- Is the accommodation necessary for performance of duties?
- What effect will it have on the company's operations and the employee's performance?
- To what extent does it compensate for the person's limitations, if any?
- Will it give the worker a chance to function on a more equal basis with coworkers?
- Will it benefit others (those with and without limitations)?
- Are there alternatives that would accomplish the same purpose?

Accommodation Areas. There are many creative ways to accommodate qualified employees with disabilities. Here is a review of the ten basic areas of accommodation (U.S. Office of Personnel Management, 1980, pp 4–11):

1. *Modifying written examinations*—reading for blind persons, writing for persons with some dexterity problems, and so on
2. *Modifying work sites*—widening access areas, adding braille labels, installing holding devices on desks or workbenches, and so on

3. *Making facilities accessible*—providing ramps, handrails, elevators, and so on

4. *Adjusting work schedules*—flexibility for medical treatment, avoiding rush hours, work at home, and so on

5. *Restructuring jobs*—reassigning nonessential duties, altering job procedures, and so on

6. *Providing assistive devices*—phone amplifiers for the deaf, braillewriters for the blind, and so on

7. *Providing readers and interpreters*—assigning another to help on a limited-time-per-day basis.

8. *Adopting flexible leave policies*—training on assistive devices, traveling through inclement weather, and so on

9. *Reassigning and retraining employees*—being alert to similarities in job families, and the employee's individual capabilities

10. *Eliminating transportation barriers*—forming carpools, providing close parking spaces, and so on

As with all aspects of selective placement, accommodations require teamwork among personnel officers, rehabilitation counselors, selective placement specialists, operations managers, and *the persons with special needs and their fellow workers*. Consulting with the individual workers involved can keep the accommodation specific and the cost down. Involving coworkers helps make the transition easier (and also is a source of good ideas).

Again, most accommodations involve inexpensive, one-time outlays—or no expense at all. Benefits include getting a competent, motivated employee or retraining a skilled, experienced one (and avoiding disability compensation). [For examples of accommodations and how different employees are coping, see Pati and Adkins (1981, chapters 4 and 5).]

Follow Up

Now that all the jobs are analyzed and the people have been screened and placed, there are various housekeeping chores to attend to that ensure that the whole recruitment/placement process continues to function as it should. Employers need to be able to evaluate application forms, records of employee disposition, and interviewing techniques.

Forms for employment should state clearly the company's policies regarding affirmative action and disability. These need not be elaborate or lengthy. Simply, do not ask for disability/physical-related information that is not job-related.

Keeping good records on the fate of applicants—especially applicants with special needs—is very useful for compliance purposes. It is also just one aspect of internal review that any organization would want to follow: documenting promotions, demotions, and transfers. As to employees with special needs, there should be no barriers to equal opportunity and no requirements that are not job-related.

In terms of liabilities and assets in employing persons with special needs, it should be clear that a properly placed employee with disabilities is an asset, neither a handicap nor a liability. And an improperly placed individual, irrespective of able-bodiedness or disabledness, constitutes nothing but a liability. The truth of the matter is that selective placement works for everyone.

BUSINESS AND REHABILITATION—COMMUNITY LINKAGE

Employers need qualified people; qualified people with special needs require jobs. Rehabilitation agencies must be dedicated to helping disabled persons adapt to their disabilities, train for employment (that is, become qualified), and find suitable positions. All three groups— employees, people with special needs, and rehabilitative agencies— want the same thing: competent people placed properly. Businesses are realizing how the unique services of rehabilitation agencies can be used and how they can work closely with such agencies (both public and private) to reach this commonly desired goal. A bridge of understanding is gradually developing. While there are many examples of partnerships such as Industry Labor Council; OJT's (On the Job Training); Jobs Training and Partnership Act; and programs involving NTID (National Institute for the Deaf) at the Rochester Institute of Technology, from which companies such as AT&T, U.S. Steel, IBM, Hewlett Packard, and others hire graduates with hearing impairments. We will focus on Projects with Industry (PWI's), an innovative concept that has been gaining tremendous popularity in our country today as a workable example of partnership in action (see Bowe and Rochlin, 1984).

Projects with Industry (PWIs)   PWIs are programs cooperatively administered by private industry and rehabilitation agencies. The program began in 1970 with funding from HEW's Rehabilitation Services Administration. Today, there are over a hundred programs operating successfully in all parts of the country; however, they are still relatively unknown and their benefits are not fully appreciated.

Assumptions. The desirability of a partnership between industry and rehabilitation services agencies is based on four major assumptions: [adopted from Jewish Vocational Services (1978, p. 1)]:

1. Actual work settings provide the most reliable arena for evaluating potential employees and preparing them for competitive employment.

2. Both the employer and the worker with a disability need help in the hiring and training process.

3. Employers are the best resources for identifying jobs for such workers, defining the qualifications for those jobs, and designing training programs for employees to meet those qualifications.

4. It is in the industry's best interests to institute proper employment practices for people with special needs.

Functions. Although there are a wide variety of PWI programs, they all involve (1) industry and rehabilitation personnel working closely to achieve common goals, and (2) the ultimate aim of competitive employment for individuals with special needs.

Projects with Industry, thus, perform three important and related functions (Jewish Vocational Services, 1978, p. 2):

1. They create an active and effective partnership of business, industry, and service agencies in the rehabilitation process.

2. They make rehabilitation services more responsive to the needs of employers.

3. They facilitate the tapping of the great potential of workers with disabilities.

Models. Most PWIs follow one of four basic program models: *job placement, work adjustment, skills training,* and *linkage.* The first three involve areas of direct service; the last is a referral system. They all are relevant for placement. [The following discussion is adopted from Jewish Vocational Services (1978, pp. 2–9, 17–19, 24–25, 30).]

A majority of all PWIs fall into the *job placement* category. This model attempts to place job-ready and nearly job-ready workers into positions with business or industry. Its distinguishing feature is that the participant completing the program is ready for immediate placement— to become an actual employee of the company and no longer an agency client.

The job placement model requires close cooperation between employers and agency professionals. PWI staff must be thoroughly familiar with the employer's procedures, policies, and supervisory personnel. They must understand the qualities and skills demanded by positions under consideration within the various companies in order to be able to match those positions with the workers with disabilities in their charge. And, just as important, company personnel staff have to provide accurate, up-to-date, precise job descriptions for the placement process to work.

Work adjustment programs teach clients with disabilities appropriate work attitudes and behaviors in an actual industrial or business setting. In contrast to the placement model, participants in these programs are only partially job-ready; that is, they are ready to handle part-time schedules at entry-level jobs. Beginning with such a schedule—at a real, needed job, at the going rate of pay—rehabilitation personnel can work with the employee to get him or her up to full readiness. Thus, work adjustment programs offer work experience to clients in entry-level positions that do not require much training, and at the same time, provide constant support services from the rehabilitation agency.

The work experience is valuable to the clients because it provides them an opportunity to practice promptness and reliability, to associate with coworkers, and to get accustomed to work procedures. The client may or may not be hired by the participant for a permanent job; the training position is left open for new trainees. Although the employer may not get permanent employees from the program, he is assured of a steady supply of workers in positions of high turnover. In addition, employer participation satisfies affirmative action requirements.

In contrast to the previous two models, *skills training* programs equip people with disabilities with skills that will allow them to enter specific occupations that are financially rewarding and that require technical abilities. This model is for the trainee who has mastered basic work skills and has developed appropriate work attitudes and behaviors. Instruction is, consequently, in technical fields for positions already identified and open. Instruction is in the classroom, not on the job. Instructors and advisors are recruited from the private sector so that information on occupational skills, skill requirements, and manpower needs is current.

The benefits to the client are obvious: a good job with a future. The benefits for the employer, despite the demands this model places on him, are similar and just as valuable: a chance to hire highly trained individuals to meet specifically defined needs (and, incidentally, to meet affirmative action requirements).

The fourth model, *the linkage model*, attempts to place workers with disabilities within one industry through a nationwide referral system that matches potential employees with open positions. The PWI supplies the communications network needed for this system to function.

The linkage model tends to be industry-centered rather than client-centered. Indeed, the linkage PWI we will look at in detail shortly is private and industry-administered, as opposed to agency-administered and publicly funded, which most PWIs are. Many rehabilitation facilities are applying the PWI concept without federal agency sponsorship or funding. The trend is toward more private industry involvement and more private industry control.

In the following section we will examine two significant PWI programs: one representing the job placement model, and one representing the linkage model. First, the job placement model.

Jewish Vocational Services (JVS) The Chicago JVS Project with Industry is a small part of this large and venerable agency. With help from administrative and support staff, most of the key operations are handled by the vocational rehabilitation counselors. The counselors are responsible for client evaluation, job development, training, placement, follow-up, and PWI-company relations (see Jewish Vocational Services, 1980).

The Process. Once accepted into the program, a participant (potential disabled employee) works with a counselor to establish a reasonable vocational objective. The counselor will then develop an employment opportunity for the client. Counselors are assigned to specific companies and visit those companies regularly. Once a client is placed, the counselor and an agency job coach visit the line supervisor every week to check the new employee's progress. In addition, the agency provides a crisis intervention service twenty-four hours a day, seven days a week. It is this close contact with the employer that is the key to the success of the program.

The Employers. JVS in Chicago has a continuing relationship with over 5,000 local employers, who place orders in the agency's sheltered workshop. Of these, over fifty annually commit themselves to a PWI agreement, and some of the companies have hired over ninety-five workers with disabilities since the beginning of their PWI experience.

Companies and placement positions are selected with great care. Although there are no restrictions as to the size of a company or product produced—PWI employees work for banks and insurance companies and help make gum, paper cups, and steel—each work site has to meet the following criteria:

- The position must involve real training with full-time regular employment available to a successful trainee/employee.

- PWI supportive staff must have access to company production staff, line supervisors, and clients on a regular basis at the job.

- Each client must begin at the same wage rate as permanent employees doing the same job and receive any earned raises according to permanent employee standards.

- Participating companies are asked to support the program by reviewing hiring standards, providing a representation to the PWI Advisory Council, enlisting union support (when there is a collective bargaining agreement).

However, employers are *not* required to make any firm commitments of job openings. Rather, they are encouraged to consider referrals on an individual, case-by-case basis. The PWI program is interested in placing employees with disabilities without any rigid quota system.

Midwest Association of Business, Rehabilitation, and Industry (MABRI) MABRI was created in 1980 as an independent, not-for-profit corporation to carry on the services of the JVS-PWI. In addition to training and placing handicapped persons, MABRI operates "troubled employee programs" for existing company employees. These programs deal with managing stress, personal problems, alcoholism, drug abuse, and disability. MABRI also runs seminars designed to assist management, supervisors, and workers in understanding the meaning of disability and the capabilities of people with special needs (MABRI, undated).

Costs and Benefits PWIs are good social investments: New employees earn money and pay taxes instead of squandering their potentials and receiving welfare payments. The JVS/MABRI program has been estimated to return $11.20 (earnings, taxes paid, welfare saved) for every $1.00 spent to provide the placement service.

Obviously, society gets a good return on its dollar. But what are the costs and benefits to the company to invest in this kind of labor? For MABRI, the annual membership fee is $1,000; this covers the full range of services. There are also costs in terms of personnel time and involvement. The benefits are:

1. Companies get good employees who want to work.
2. Companies receive valuable support and follow-up services from the agency (including help with affirmative action).
3. Companies have the opportunity to help the community and project a good public image.
4. Companies can take control of their own personnel needs and not wait for the government to get involved.

The MABRI program is a good example of a job placement Project with Industry. Next we review a PWI that follows the *linkage* model.

Electronic Industries Foundation (EIF)

The EIF is a nonprofit organization that was founded in 1975 to perform a variety of research and public education functions for the Electronics Industries Association, which represents approximately 300 electronic industry companies nationwide. The EIF-PWI is administered by the association, but it is funded by the federal government.

The Process EIF-PWI is a referral service. It attempts to match the manpower needs of a national industry with the employment needs of individuals with disabilities. EIF subdivided into five geographic areas

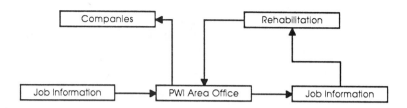

Figure 11.3 EIF-PWI Process

with high concentrations of electronics companies: Los Angeles, San Francisco Bay, Minnesota, Massachusetts, and Chicago. Employment specialists in these area offices maintain close contact with electronic companies in their area, looking to see if a client on file is qualified for a job opening.

Participating companies submit job information to the PWI area office, where information is reviewed and sent on to rehabilitation agencies. From the other direction, rehabilitation agencies identify qualified applicants and send their resume to the PWI office for evaluation. The PWI office matches applicant and job, makes a referral to the company, and notifies applicant and agency. At this point, the regular company personnel process takes over, although the PWI office can help arrange interviews. The process is shown schematically in Figure 11.3.

Training and Other Services EIF has staff specialists who work with industry to sensitize employers to the qualities of workers with disabilities. Other staff alert rehabilitation people to the precise work requirements of the industry. But the most productive activity involves training, because in the electronics industry more jobs are available than there are qualified workers to fill them.

The EIF approach is to make training specific to local job openings. To do this, EIF-PWI employs industry advisors and technicians to: (1) help assess the needs of the persons with disabilities and the participating companies, (2) review existing training programs, (3) develop new curricula as needed, (4) develop training selection criteria, (5) help select sites and implement programs, and (6) be involved in the decision making throughout the processes (see Pati, 1982).

Benefits In addition to finding good jobs for hundreds of individuals with special needs, the EIF-PWI provides useful services for the rehabilitation community and the electronics industry as well.

For the rehabilitation people, EIF

• Is a central source of current job openings

- Increases job opportunities for individuals with disabilities
- Expands contacts with employers
- Provides job market forecasts to aid in planning

For the industry, EIF

- Is a central source of qualified workers with special needs
- Is an effective outreach mechanism
- Provides information on the needs of such employees
- Facilitates communication with rehabilitation resources

Career Mobility. Equal opportunity in employment goes through three phases: entry, survival, and mobility. Some employers may initially hire a person with disabilities, but, to enjoy a satisfying career, the person must have some reasonable prospect for mobility. It is not good business to allow human beings to needlessly decay in one spot if they have abilities and training. In some businesses mobility is important. In the following statements, Jay Rochlin, a human resource executive at AT&T, addresses this issue. Currently, Rochlin is on a leave of absence and serving on the President's Committee on Employment of the Handicapped.

Washington, D.C.
February 18, 1986

THE NEXT FRONTIER: UPWARD MOBILITY

For years the rehabilitation system in this country has focused on obtaining employment in entry level jobs for people with disabilities. More recently, a concern for retaining employees who have become disabled has given rise to a proliferation of private rehabilitation providers. However, little has been said and less has been done about providing upward mobility opportunities for employees with disabilities.

The time has come for both the rehabilitation profession and the business community to recognize this need. People with disabilities enter the work force with the same desires, ambitions, and expectations as any other new employee.

Business must accept responsibility to provide career advancement for all employees. However, to do so for employees with disabilities often requires providing reasonable accommodation to the limitations caused by each individual's disability. This can be as sophisticated as providing hi-tech computer software with synthetic speech for people who are blind or as simple as placing a desk on blocks so that a wheelchair may roll underneath.

Unfortunately, many managers in business are unfamiliar with the term "reasonable accommodation," let alone what is meant by it. Thus, if employees with disabilities are to advance, the rehabilitation profession must be prepared to lend the technical assistance necessary to assist employers in making reasonable accommodation a reality. The rewards for providing this support are significant. First, and most importantly, the employee has advanced to a more challenging and rewarding position. In addition, rehabilitation has provided a needed support service to the business community and may as a result, be given the opportunity to fill the entry level vacancy left by the employee who advanced.

Special educators who may see their role as preparing students with disabilities for work can also influence the future career mobility of those individuals. This will be accomplished by educating students with disabilities to take charge of their own lives. Too often in the past, children with disabilities were relegated to segregated institutions where they were cared for and never allowed to make decisions for themselves. Subsequently, when these individuals began employment they expected someone in business to continue to care for them. However, in business it doesn't work that way.

Upward mobility occurs most effectively when directed by those seeking advancement. Special educators have the responsibility to prepare young people with disabilities to be their own advocates.

Business is seeking employees who are interested and motivated in moving up and assuming increased responsibility. Employees with disabilities should not be denied these opportunities and must be considered equally with their peers.

Society benefits whenever any of its members experience an improved quality of life.

IMPLICATIONS

The statement by Jay Rochlin is a good "snapshot" of what is going on in the business community and in the country. The business perspective of utilizing people with special needs revolves around enlightened self-interest. Good public relations aside, the vitality inherent in using workers with disabilities as partners to achieve productivity and profit has been recognized in enlightened business settings. Needless to say, this is just a beginning. Developing partnerships takes time. There are apprehensions on the part of both the business community and the rehabilitation/academic communities in approaching each other. But on the basis of what has happened in the last ten years or so, there is good cause for optimism. Here are some concluding thoughts for consideration.

First, although tremendous strides have been made through legislation to help individuals with special needs, it is crucial that the government provide funds and personnel to fully implement the anti-discrimination laws. We have a long way to go to reach some of the less cooperative members of the corporate world who only conform and do not perform.

Second, business executives who have had experience in this area, need to persuade their not-so-enlightened colleagues to utilize this human resource, as well as showing them how to do it. Of particular importance is the market of emerging small and medium-sized business organizations that will become the major employers in this country. Most employment opportunities will arise in small businesses, and yet that segment remains virtually untouched.

Third, although some unions such as United Automobile Workers, AFL-CIO (Human Resources Institute), Amalgamated Clothing and Textile Workers Union, the Aerospace Workers, and so on have made great contributions to accommodate workers with special needs, many local unions across the country are still not part of the rehabilitation movement. Organized labor can make greater contributions by modifying contract provisions to improve the job retention of workers with disabilities. Furthermore, they can be more aggressive in educating union leaders at the local level that some of the these persons are already union members or are potential union members.

Finally, special education students in training must be believers first. Then they can motivate employers in their respective communities to utilize people with disabilities because they make good employees, if properly placed. The education professionals must learn more about businesses. They may consider taking courses in economics, management, labor law, marketing, and so on in order to fully appreciate the needs of employers and local markets. With such a background, they can help individuals with special needs acquire job-related skills. Without such skills, as previously mentioned, it is extremely difficult for them to find useful jobs in a competitive environment. If businesses can find a product they can use, they will use it. It is the responsibility of educators to make continued efforts to create and market the product called "valuable human resources"—sometimes known as "persons with disabilities."

REFERENCES

American Mutual Insurance Alliance. (Undated). *Hiring the Handicapped: Myths and Facts.* P. 3.

Bowe, Frank, and J. Rochlin. (1984). *The Business-Rehabilitation Partnership.* Arkansas Rehabilitation Research Center, University of Arkansas and Arkansas Rehabilitation Service.

Electronic Industries Foundation. For information, write to PWI, 2001 Eye Street, N.W., Washington, D.C. 20006.

Fair Employment Report. (August 1984).

Human Resources Center. (Undated). "Job Analysis Worksheet." *Module 12: Job Analysis.* Albertson, New York, 1077.

Iacocca, L., with W. Novak. (1984). *Iococca: An Autobiography.* New York: Bantam Books.

Jewish Vocational Services. (May 1978). *Program Models for Projects with Industry.* Research Utilization Laboratory.

Jewish Vocational Services. (February 15, 1980–November 14, 1980. *Projects with Industry: Progress Report.* Chicago. Pp. 4–21.

MABRI. (Undated). When good intentions aren't enough. For more information on MABRI-PWIs, write: 1 South Franklin Street, Chicago, IL 60606.

Pati, C. (March 1978). Countdown on hiring the handicapped. *Personnel Journal,* 149–150.

Pati, C. (October-December 1985). Economics of rehabilitation in the workplace. *Journal of Rehabilitation,* 22–30.

Pati, C. (1982). Industry and rehabilitation: A private-public partnership in utilizing the disabled. An ortale Memorial Lecture, Anaheim, NRA Conference. Portions reprinted in *Disabled U.S.A.* (1983) 2, 13–16.

Pati, C., and J.I. Adkins, Jr. (January-February 1980). Hire the handicapped— Compliance is good business. *Harvard Business Review,* 14–22.

Pati, C., and J.I. Adkins, Jr., with G. Morrison. (1981). *Managing and Employing the Handicapped: The Untapped Potential.* Lake Forest, Ill.: Brace-Park Press. Pp. 35–73.

Pati, C., and E.F. Hinton, Jr. (February 1980). A comprehensive model for a handicapped affirmative action program. *Personnel Journal,* 99–105.

State of Kentucky. Department of Education. (Undated). The major factor determining job success is capability *not* disability. Florence, Ky.

U.S. Civil Service Commission. (1977). *Employment of the Handicapped in State and Local Government.* Washington, D.C.: U.S. Government Printing Office. Pp. 13–143.

U.S. Department of Labor. (1972). *Handbook for Analyzing Jobs.* Washington, D.C.: U.S. Government Printing Office.

U.S. Office of Personnel Management. (1980). *Handbook of Reasonable Accommodation.* Washington, D.C.: U.S. Government Printing Office.

Watkins, L.M. (November 6, 1984). Clearinghouse helps firms accommodate special needs of handicapped employees. *Wall Street Journal.*

Zimmer, A.B. (1981). *Employing the Handicapped: A Practical Compliance Manual.* New York: Amacom.

Part IV Type of Disability and Vocational Education

Although the vocational special education field is largely a generic one, there is a need to address matters dealing with specific disabilities. Hasazi and Cobb describe the major kinds of secondary and postsecondary training and employment programs for students with mild handicaps. Their emphasis on strong interagency collaboration and a planned transition from the secondary to postsecondary years should be noted.

Unfortunately, the vocational potential of persons with severe handicaps has only recently been realized. Previously, it was felt that these individuals were incapable of work, or could accomplish work activity only in a sheltered setting. The current supported employment movement has changed these expectations, as persons with severe handicaps have become employed in regular work settings. Pumpian, West, and Shepard present an ideologically driven chapter that lays out a functional curriculum approach to longitudinal employment training. The basing of their transition and postsecondary programs in the community college is particularly appealing.

Preparing persons with physical disabilities for employment is a challenging endeavor. Because of motor limitations, an individual may not perform fast enough at the job site. Transportation to and from work may also present difficulties. Sowers, Jenkins, and Powers describe a vocational education model that begins in the primary grades and continues on through the transition to adulthood. Their descriptions of vocational adaptations should inspire practitioners in the field.

Persons with sensory impairments also offer unique challenges to vocational training and employment efforts, especially since sight or hearing may be required for particular jobs. The need for innovative job accommodations for persons with sensory limitation is obvious. Sacks and Bullis describe the developments in vocational education programs for hearing-impaired and visually-impaired persons. It is nice to read that a job find program like Job Club has been adapted for hearing-impaired youth. It is also encouraging to read of the manner in which social skill training is being used with visually-impaired children. As vocational education for students with sensory impairments gradually moves from a center and institution base to a community base, there should be a more effective transition to successful employment.

The vocational special education field, and the special education field in general, has recently emphasized generic programs. That is, the vocational processes of assessment, training, and placement, for example, are focused upon as universal matters. Simultaneously, there has been a decreasing emphasis on knowledge of specific disabilities. While this movement toward generic services is sound, there still is a need to present specific, disability-related information. Thus, the four chapters in this section attempt to deal with particular topics like instructional support, accommodations, and mainstreaming, which pertain to specific disabilities. We feel that it is through the combination of generic and specific disability information that the field will progress most successfully.

12 Vocational Education of Persons with Mild Handicaps

Susan Brody Hasazi and R. Brian Cobb
University of Vermont

The purpose of this chapter is to describe current models and practices related to preparing individuals with special needs for employment. This preparation can be categorized as either education or training. Education generally refers to those activities that occur in vocational education classrooms, and whose purpose is to teach generalized work skills. Training generally refers to those activities that occur largely on job sites, and focus on the direct training of job skills. The difference between the two is reflected in the degree of specificity. Ideally, secondary and postsecondary vocational preparation programs for individuals with special needs should contain elements of both education and training since employment preparation requires students to acquire a variety of skills that range a great deal in their complexity. Further, previous research with handicapped individuals (Evans, et. al, 1980) suggests that the complexity of skills to be acquired influences the selection of teaching environments.

Specifically, this chapter defines the characteristics of mildly handicapped and disadvantaged individuals who are commonly considered under the rubric of "individuals with special needs." The chapter then describes typical secondary and postsecondary service delivery systems, including vocational education, vocational training, or some combination of both, that are most appropriately utilized by individuals with special needs. Next comes discussion of those program

331

elements that range across all systems and that exemplify best practices for individuals with special needs. Finally, three case studies are presented that describe how differing systems can cooperatively plan and deliver vocational education and training to best serve handicapped and disadvantaged adolescents and young adults.

DEFINITIONS OF INDIVIDUALS WITH SPECIAL NEEDS

Phelps has defined a special needs learner as an:

> individual who encounters or is likely to encounter difficulty in educational and employment settings because of a disability, economic or academic disadvantage, who has different linguistic or cultural background, or outdated job skills, and who requires individually prescribed and unique teaching strategies; supportive services that vary in type and extent depending on individual need; and additional resources from society for his or her acceptance. (1985, p. 24)

This definition provides a functional orientation to identifying those individuals who are labeled as having special needs. It encompasses individuals generally referred to as mildly handicapped and disadvantaged and who require specialized physical, instructional, or programmatic adaptations to succeed in vocational education and training. As this definition implies, these individuals must meet two criteria in order to receive specialized services. First they must meet the eligibility criteria specified in special education, vocational education, or vocational training legislation for identification as handicapped or disadvantaged. And second, their handicap or disadvantage must interfere with successful acquisition of vocational skills or employment, requiring specialized assistance of some kind.

According to section 602(a)(1) of P.L. 94-142, handicapped students are defined as those children and youth between the ages of 3 and 21 who are eligible for special services under one of the nine categories of handicapping conditions, including mentally retarded, specific learning disability, seriously emotionally disturbed, hard of hearing, deaf, speech- or language-impaired, visually handicapped, orthopedically impaired, and other health impaired. Mildly handicapped students are those individuals traditionally labeled as learning disabled or mildly retarded; behaviorally handicapped students are those individuals traditionally labeled as learning disabled, mildly mentally retarded, or behaviorally disordered.

Disadvantaged individuals who are not handicapped but who require compensatory assistance to succeed in vocational education can be identified to receive services under several eligibility criteria. These individuals qualify for assistance under such criteria as limited English proficiency, membership in economically disadvantaged families, dropouts or potential dropouts, migrant students, and academically disadvantaged. The final regulations of the Carl Perkins Vocational Education Act, P.L. 98-525 (U.S. Department of Education, 1985) provide more detailed criteria for eligibility under these categories.

CURRENT SERVICE DELIVERY SYSTEMS

There are a variety of generic and specialized agencies that have the potential to provide vocational education and training to persons with special needs. These include secondary vocational education, secondary special education, employment and training, apprenticeship programs, vocational rehabilitation, and postsecondary vocational education, A description of each of these systems and the services they offer is given in the following sections.

Secondary Vocational Education

Vocational education at the secondary level is guided by five broad goals:

1. Acquisition of personal skills and attitudes
2. Communication and computational skills and technological literacy
3. Employability skills
4. Broad and specific occupational skills and knowledge
5. Foundations for career planning and lifelong learning (National Commission on Secondary Vocational Education, 1984)

In order to achieve these goals, vocational education is organized around three major components: in-school vocational skills instruction, out-of-school work experience, and vocational student organizations.

In-school skills instruction is delivered in seven program areas, including agriculture education, business and office education, home economics education, industrial arts and technology education, marketing and distributive education, health occupations education, and trade and industrial education. Nationwide, these seven program areas are further classified into more than 400 specific occupational training categories (Malitz, 1981).

Handicapped and disadvantaged individuals have historically had difficulties gaining access to regular vocational education programs. Recognizing this inequity, Congress included initiatives in the Vocational Education Act of 1963 to encourage districts to make their regular vocational education programs more accessible. Successive amendments to this Act, which were passed in 1968, 1976, and 1984, have strengthened these initiatives along both fiscal and programmatic lines. Important gains have been made as a result of these initiatives (Phelps, 1982); however, occupationally specific programs, cooperative education programs, and apprenticeship programs remain significantly underenrolled by both disadvantaged and handicapped youth. In response to these underenrollments, Congress in P.L. 98-524, emphasized these program areas for increased access.

In-school vocational instruction is generally provided for half the day during the junior and senior years of high school. School-based instruction is delivered in laboratories that are designed to simulate the actual work environment for each of the program areas.

Out-of-school work experiences programs are designed to complement classroom learning in actual work environments. These experiences typically occur at the end of a student's program of study, and are generally paid at minimum wage or better. These experiences are often referred to as cooperative vocational education and are supervised by specialized vocational education personnel.

Each vocational program area has associated with it one or more vocational student organizations. P.L. 98-524 defines them as:

> Those organizations for individuals enrolled in vocational education programs which engage in activities as an integral part of the instructional program. These organizations may have state and national units which aggregate the work and purposes of instruction in vocational education at the local level. (Title V, Part B).

These organizations meet after school on a regular basis to prepare projects for state and national competition, engage in community service projects, and provide opportunities for students to learn cooperation and leadership skills. Handicapped and disadvantaged students would apparently benefit greatly from participation in vocational student organizations. However, Birchenall and Wanat (1981) have suggested a number of barriers that serve to exclude students with special needs from these organizations. These include attempts to create separate student organizations for special needs students, lack of support services to accommodate the needs of handicapped and disadvantaged students in student organizations, and the negative attitudes of administrators and supervisors concerning the integration and preparation of special needs students into vocational student organizations.

Vocational education at the secondary level can be delivered in four different settings (American Vocational Association, 1983). The first option is the comprehensive high school. About 90 percent of all vocational education programs nationwide are offered in such schools (National Center for Education Statistics, 1980). Comprehensive high schools offer at least five vocational educational areas, and provide these program areas in the same building that other general and college preparatory curricula are taught.

The second option, area vocational centers, offer only vocational education programs and are typically housed in regional centers serving adjacent school districts. Their programs are usually designed for eleventh and twelfth grade students, who are transported for half the day for their vocational education, receiving the remainder of their education in their home high school during the rest of the day.

Vocational high schools, the third setting, are similar to area vocational centers in that they are housed in separate facilities and serve local school districts on a regional basis. However, their programs are for ninth through twelfth grade students who are interested primarily in a vocational curriculum, and for whom all Carnegie Unit graduation requirements can be provided through vocationally related academic coursework.

The fourth option is the general high school, which offers a minimal array of vocational education or industrial arts programs. It is distinguished from comprehensive high schools in that it provides fewer than five different vocational program options.

A variety of strengths and weaknesses are associated with each of these four settings that have implications for both individuals who require special services and those who do not. For example, students enrolling in vocational education in comprehensive high schools have a greater opportunity to interact with a more diverse group of peers, and become involved in a greater variety of extracurricular activities than students attending area vocational centers and vocational high schools. Conversely, vocational program breadth and depth is typically greater in vocational high schools and area centers, thus allowing the student to learn more technically advanced vocational skills (Benson, 1982; Evans, 1982). Finally, cooperative vocational education programs, which place students during their final year of school in jobs related to their vocational education, are generally more available in separate vocational facilities than in comprehensive high schools (Evans and Herr, 1978).

Under P.L. 98-524 students with special needs who receive secondary vocational education in any of the environments described are entitled to a variety of specialized services. Section 204(b) of the Act mandates that local education agencies receiving federal dollars for vocational education must inform all handicapped and disadvantaged students and their parents of the vocational education programs available, and the accompanying entry requirements, prior to the beginning of the ninth grade. This requirement will increase the information base upon which parents and students with special needs may make informed choices about secondary curriculum options. It will also provide initial program-planning information to vocational and special educators about the potential need for supportive services for prospective classes of students.

Secondary Special Vocational Education

Special vocational education services for handicapped and disadvantaged youth may be provided in any of the setting described. These services are typically delivered in one of two forms. First, specially trained resource teachers assist regular vocational instructors in adapting instruction, curriculum, facilities, or equipment to respond to individual student needs in regular vocational programs. Procedures such as individualized contracts, peer tutoring, and cooperative learning may be introduced into the vocational curriculum, often through team teaching with the regular vocational instructor. In addition, vocational resource teachers may provide individualized instruction around reading, vocabulary, mathematics, and safety concepts specifically related to the vocational curriculum. It is essential that these vocational resource teachers have the skills and knowledge to adapt curriculum and learning environments, and design individualized and group instructional strategies to accommodate student needs. Clearly, it is helpful as well if they are familiar with the different vocational curriculum options, and have an overall understanding of the philosophy and operation of the vocational education system.

Second, special vocational education may be provided in separate classrooms for either handicapped or disadvantaged learners. These classrooms may provide prevocational and vocational curricula designed to replicate regular curricula at a less intensive pace. This model has been used frequently to serve handicapped and disadvantaged learners in many states and has increased the degree of segregation experienced by these students and their teachers (David, 1981; Nacson, 1982). In response to this practice, P.L. 98-524 included financial disincentives and programmatic requirements designed to foster integration of special needs students into regular vocational education programs.

The curriculum expectations of special vocational education differ from those of vocational programs in that the focus is on the acquisition of generic work skills rather than occupationally specific skills. This approach is based on the notion that certain work-related skills have generalized value across a variety of environments and that these skills must be mastered prior to receiving occupationally specific training. Although the notion may have utility for the general student population in vocational education, recent literature and practices have raised questions about this approach for students with special needs (Horner, McDonnell, and Bellamy, 1986). In particular, this readiness approach may inhibit the opportunities for many students with handicaps to participate in occupationally specific training programs, both school- and community-based.

Programs of this nature generally assume that additional vocational training—occupationally specific training—will be provided following graduation or exit from high school. However, recent follow-up studies of former special education students (Hasazi, et al, 1985; Wehman, Kregel, and Seyfarth, 1985) indicate that the majority of handicapped students placed in these specialized programs, in fact, do not receive additional occupationally specific training following high school.

The personnel responsible for providing instruction usually have a background in special education and limited training experience in the content of vocational curricula. These teachers often have little opportunity to interact with their colleagues in regular vocational programs, and the students likewise have minimal contact with their peers in regular vocational programs.

Employment and Training Agencies

Employment and training agencies provide vocational training and placement to youth and adults who are in need of specialized services to overcome serious barriers to employment. These agencies receive their primary funding from the Job Training Partnership Act (JTPA) of 1983 (P.L. 97-300). In order to utilize JTPA funds, each state's governor appoints a State Job Training Coordinating Council (SJTCC), which designates service delivery areas (SDAs). Service delivery areas are local governments with a population of 200,000 or more, or any consortium of contiguous units of local government with a combined population of 200,000 or more. Each SDA in turn appoints a Private Industry Council (PIC) to develop a job-training plan for utilizing the JTPA dollars. Following approval of the plan submitted by the each PIC, the governor distributes JTPA funds for program implementation. Since the focus of this act is on training for employment in the private sector, 70 percent of the funds allocated to each PIC must be used for training individuals for jobs in private business or industry.

All JTPA funds must be utilized for persons who are economically disadvantaged. For those families who have a handicapped family member between the ages of 16- and 21, and who do not meet the income eligibility criterion, the governor of each state may designate that handicapped individual as a "family of one" to allow for participation in JTPA programs. By September, 1985, forty-five of the fifty-seven states and territories had adopted the "family of one" provision in their eligibility criteria (Tindall, 1985). Given that the majority of handicapped young adults will meet the economic criterion at age 22, this "family of one" provision for 16- to 21-year-olds allows for five years of vocational training regardless of the family's income level. The opportunity to receive this vocational training should better prepare handicapped individuals for employment following exit from school programs.

The major source of JTPA funds for use with handicapped and disadvantaged youth are included in the Title IIA, Title IIB, and Title IVB provisions. Twenty-two percent of each state's Title IIA JTPA funds are distributed directly by the governor's SJTCC, and the remaining 78 percent is passed on to the state's PICs. Of this 78 percent distributed to the PICs, 40 percent must be utilized for programs for youth between the ages of 16 to 21. Of the 60 percent remaining for adults, 10 percent may be used for handicapped or hard-to-serve populations. In addition, through Title IIB, the PICs may distribute funds for summer youth employment programs.

Title IVB monies support Job Corps programs, which are administered directly by the U.S. Department of Labor. These programs offer intensive residential and day employment training programs for the most economically disadvantaged youth ages 14 to 22. Participants may receive training for as long as two years.

Both handicapped and disadvantaged youth can benefit from vocational training supported under Titles IIA and IIB. For example, services that can be funded under Title IIA may include: job search assistance, on-the-job training, vocational occupational skill training, job development, literacy and bilingual training, attainment of high school equivalency certificate, follow-up services of participants placed in unsubsidized jobs, and education to work transition activities (Tindall, 1985).

Title IIB summer youth employment programs include some of the same training components as the Title IIA programs. In addition, these funds may support any other employment or job-training activity designed to give employment to eligible individuals or prepare them for and place them in employment, such as tryout employment, vocational exploration, or exemplary youth programs.

Each of these programs must demonstrate adherence to standard performance measures in order to document program effectiveness. In the development of the performance measures for programs designed to serve youth, the U.S. Department of Labor specified in the JTPA regulations that alternative standards may be applied for handicapped and disadvantaged individuals, given the difficulty these youth experience in achieving the general placement standards. These alternative performance measures include attainment of skills within three general competency clusters: basic educational skills, job-specific skills, and preemployment and work maturity skills, including those skills needed to look for, obtain, and retain a job. In order for these standards to be implemented in a given service delivery area, the PIC must first adopt them.

Apprenticeship Programs

Apprenticeships are one of the oldest formal training systems; in these programs both the trainer and trainee have a vested interest in the training process. Apprenticeship programs were established through the National Apprenticeship Act of 1937, commonly referred to as the Fitzgerald Act. This Act remains the statute governing the administration of state apprenticeship programs. Funds to support such programs are administered through the U.S. Department of Labor, Bureau of Apprenticeship Training; programs include occupational areas "that customarily are learned in practical ways through one or more years of experience and training of the job, supplemented by related technical instruction" (U.S. Department of Labor, 1974, p. 3).

Apprenticeship programs offer training to an individual in the form of an agreement between the individual (apprentice) and an employer. Most apprenticeship enrollments are restricted primarily to the construction trades (about 67 percent of all apprentices), some metalworking occupations, and the graphic communications industry (Evans and Her, 1978). Labor unions have been able to maintain almost complete control over most apprenticeship programs, primarily because they occur in trades where there is a powerful union influence.

In order for employers to participate in this wage subsidy and training program, they must agree to provide: equal opportunity; no discrimination in any phase of selection, employment, or training; progressively increased schedule of wages; periodic progress evaluations; organized related instruction; a training plan describing the work processes by which the apprentice will receive training; and experience on the job. In addition, employers may not enroll apprentices who are under the age of 16.

Although guarantees for equal access and opportunity are required of each participating employer, inclusion of individuals with handicaps has been virtually nonexistent. A 1979 Office of Civil Rights (1980) survey of over 10,500 school districts nationwide indicated that only 0.4 percent of school-aged apprentices were handicapped.

Apprenticeship programs hold great potential for handicapped and disadvantaged youth because of their emphasis on on-the-job training, and the commitment by an employer to invest training time and resources with their apprentices through the development of a structured long-range plan. Because of its promise, this service delivery system needs to be explored fully to increase its utilization by special needs individuals.

Vocational Rehabilitation

Vocational rehabilitation is designed to develop and implement through research, training, services, and the guarantee of equal opportunity, comprehensive and coordinated programs of vocational rehabilitation and independent living (Subcommittee on the Handicapped, 1985, p. 45). The major federal statute supporting vocational rehabilitation programs is the Rehabilitation Act of 1973, as amended by P.L. 98–221 in 1984. Vocational rehabilitation is concerned with providing primarily employment-related services to disabled individuals. In order to receive vocational rehabilitation services, an individual must have a physical or a mental impairment that substantially limits one or more major life activities, have a record of such an impairment, or be regarded as having such an impairment. In addition, in order to be determined eligible for services, an individual must reasonably be expected to benefit in terms of employability from vocational rehabilitation services.

Examples of services provided by vocational rehabilitation include, but are not limited to:

1. Evaluation and diagnosis, including psychiatric and psychological examinations

2. Counseling, guidance, referral, placement, and postemployment services, and assistance in securing services from other agencies

3. Vocational training, including personal and vocational adjustment, training materials and services to families

4. Physical and mental restoration services, including corrective surgery or therapeutic treatment, hospitalization, prosthetic and orthotic devices, eyeglasses and visual services, dialysis, artificial kidneys, and diagnoses and treatment for mental and emotional disorders

5. Maintenance

6. Interpreter and reader services

7. Recruitment and training for new employment opportunities

8. Rehabilitation teaching, orientation, and mobility services for the blind

9. Occupational licenses, tools, equipment, and initial stocks and supplies

10. Transportation

11. Telecommunications aids

In addition to providing direct rehabilitation services, P.L. 98–221 contains an important section called the Client Assistance Program. This program is designed to provide information to clients regarding available benefits under the Act and to assist clients in moving through the process of receiving rehabilitation services. In addition, the program helps clients in pursuing legal, administrative, and other appropriate remedies to protect their rights under this Act.

Two other important elements of the Act include the Projects with Industry program and the Centers for Independent Living program. The Projects with Industry program is intended to facilitate a partnership between employers and rehabilitation professionals to increase the employment opportunities for disabled persons. The Centers for Independent Living program provides handicapped individuals with services for independent living, including community group living arrangements, peer counseling, referral and counseling concerning attendant care, attendant care and training or personnel to provide such care, and health maintenance programs.

For the most part, vocational rehabilitation has had limited interaction with secondary school programs although recent initiatives at the federal level have been directed toward increasing the level of collaboration between education and rehabilitation agencies (Albright, et al., 1981). This collaboration should result in identification of needed vocational services for handicapped youth prior to their exit from school, and should facilitate the transfer of service responsibilities from the school to appropriate adult service agencies. States including New York, Massachusetts, and Wisconsin have passed legislation designed to facilitate such collaborative efforts.

Postsecondary Vocational Education

Postsecondary vocational education has been identified as an important option for handicapped and disadvantaged individuals who are not in need of intensive short-term vocational training such as that provided by vocational rehabilitation or employment and training agencies (Will, 1984; Brown, 1985). Historically, individuals with special needs have had difficulty in enrolling and staying in postsecondary vocational education programs. For example, Owens, Arnold, and Costen (1985) indicate that the overall handicapped enrollment in junior and community colleges is 1.1 percent of the general population. Handicapped enrollments in postsecondary vocational education programs are slightly higher, at 2.2 percent. In addition, Brown and Kayser (1985) reported that drop-out rates for handicapped students in postsecondary vocational education programs were disproportionately high because these students were often unaware of the availability of personnel to deliver appropriate special services. No comparable data are generally available for academically or economically disadvantaged individuals.

Postsecondary vocational education programs include those noncollegiate programs provided in community colleges, junior colleges, and vocational and technical schools. Postsecondary vocational education programs are generally two years in duration and result in associate degrees in technical areas. Combinations of laboratory, classroom, and work experience instruction are delivered in a manner similar to that which occurs in secondary vocational schools. In recent years, many postsecondary programs have developed supportive services similar to those found at the secondary level to accommodate handicapped and disadvantaged learners, as well as those with limited English proficiency. These developments have occurred since the late 1970s concurrently with increased access to secondary vocational programs.

BEST PRACTICES IN TRAINING AND EMPLOYMENT

A number of elements characterize programs that result in the greatest likelihood of handicapped and disadvantaged students gaining access to vocational education, training, and employment. These include individualized student planning, interaction with economically and academically diverse peers, vocational training at employment sites, interagency collaboration, parent and consumer participation, job search education, and follow-up of program graduates. Each of these components is essential to ensure a comprehensive service delivery system whose goal is employment.

Cooperative
Individualized
Student
Planning

Most of the service delivery systems described in preceding sections use an individualized student planning process to identify student needs, specify anticipated outcomes, and identify required resources. Individualized student planning at the secondary school level is a practice that has evolved for planning and specifying specialized services primarily for handicapped individuals. Components of this planning process are mandated by law for handicapped students; however, this is not the case for students who are academically or economically disadvantaged.

For students with handicaps at the secondary level, individualized planning is accomplished through the IEP process, as specified in P.L. 94–142. Because the entitlement to educational services ends in most states at age 22, and adult services are not mandatory for all individuals who require such services, it is essential that the IEP include components that focus on vocational and community living concerns. To facilitate this planning process, adult service agencies should be involved. The individualized plans used by these agencies, such as vocational rehabilitation (Individualized Written Rehabilitation Plan) and employment and training (Employability Development Plan), can be developed concurrently with the IEP process.

The goal of this cooperative individualized planning process is to ensure that the secondary school–aged student is placed in one or more of the following options: transitional or competitive employment, vocational training, or postsecondary vocational education. Transitional employment is a paid employment experience that includes short-term, job-specific training and may also include a partially subsidized wage. This option may be provided through employment and training, or vocational rehabilitation agencies. Vocational training is focused primarily on job site training, and may be provided through apprenticeship, employment and training, or vocational rehabilitation agencies. It is distinguished from transitional employment in that it may not involve payment for training time, and may combine classroom and on-site instruction. Postsecondary vocational education is focused primarily on an organized sequence of vocational classes, and may culminate with a paid work experience. It differs from vocational training in that the emphasis is on classroom-related instruction, it usually leads to a degree, and it requires a longer period of instructional time.

At least eighteen months prior to graduation from high school, a transition plan should be included as a component of the IEP. The transition plan should be developed collaboratively by school personnel, parents, the student, and the adult services agencies that can provide the needed services, depending on which of the three above options are selected. In addition, the transition component should consider issues related to residential placement options, recreation and leisure, transportation, medical needs, and income and insurance needs.

Integration

Over the past decade much has been written by professionals and disabled citizens about the importance of living and learning in environments that maximize the interactions between disabled and non-disabled individuals (Blatt, 1981; Bruininks and Lakin, 1985; Wolfensberger, 1977). Situations such as these are particularly important in regard to vocational education and training since the final goal for both is usually employment in integrated work sites. In secondary and postsecondary vocational education, instruction should be delivered in regular vocational classrooms with support services provided to the vocational instructor. These services should be provided in a manner that is unobtrusive and that maximizes the amount of time spent in the regular vocational classroom rather than in a resource room.

In addition to integration in the regular vocational classroom, handicapped students should have opportunities to participate in integrated community-based training programs. For example, the practice of integration is an important within apprenticeship or cooperative vocational education programs as it is with classroom-based instruction. These experiences are important not only for the handicapped student, but also for the nondisabled individuals who have the opportunity to work or learn with a competent disabled person.

Vocational Training at Employment Sites

In order to ensure employment as an outcome of vocational educational and training experiences, community-based instruction should be provided. The range of potential difficulties that may occur at a worksite cannot be anticipated and accommodated in a classroom-based training environment, but can best be addressed at the actual work site. Specific vocational skills are more effectively taught in the environments in which these behaviors are naturally prompted and reinforced (Wehman, 1981).

Vocational training at employment sites can include a variety of support services. For example, an individual might require intensive training by a job coach for a short period of time that would include a planned process for fading the training support. Another individual might require only intermittent follow-along support to monitor potential changes by the employer in the work routine and provide retraining if necessary. A third individual might require no direct training or monitoring but instead need support in relationships with coworkers or supervisors.

Professionals who assist in vocational training at employment sites must have skills that are somewhat different from their colleagues who work in classroom environments. Examples of such skills include job development, job analysis, community resource assessment, individual assessment, job match, and job site training and advocacy (Pitonyak, et al., 1986).

Interagency Collaboration

A secondary or postsecondary level program with employment or further training as one of its primary goals requires the use of resources from both generic and specialized service agencies. An excellent mechanism for identifying human or financial resources is through the development of local interagency agreements between vocational education, special education, vocational rehabilitation, developmental disabilities, and employment and training agencies. Such agreements should specify the services provided by each agency; the conditions under which referrals can be made; provisions for development and delivery of jointly sponsored in-service training for professionals across agencies; and procedures for monitoring, evaluating, and revising the local agreement. In formulating the local agreement, particular attention should be directed toward including generic agencies or programs such as community colleges, evening programs offered at technical schools, adult education programs, and state employment and training services.

A recent follow-up study of handicapped youth in Vermont who left or graduated from high school between 1979 and 1983 indicated that 35 percent of handicapped youth utilized generic employment services agencies, probably because they were familiar with them through family members and friends (Hasazi, Gordon, and Roe, 1985). However, these youth often reported that they were not able to secure jobs or training through these agencies. This suggests that local agreements might consider a provision for placing specialized personnel such as vocational rehabilitation counselors in local employment and training offices to help evaluate client needs and identify appropriate services.

Recent research conducted by Cuenin (1985) into the impact of local interagency agreements on the provision of coordinated vocational services to handicapped individuals suggests that a key element to successful implementation is in-service training given prior to and throughout the process. Specifically, training should focus on the goals and objectives of the interagency agreement and should specify the roles and responsibilities of the various personnel who will be responsible for implementing it.

A process that might be utilized to develop a local interagency includes the following steps:

1. A time commitment from an administrative representative from each agency involved in the development of the agreement; these individuals must have the authority to make decisions regarding resource allocation and modifications to local policies and practices

2. Consensus on a common goal of integrated transitional or competitive employment, or postsecondary vocational training for all handicapped youth

3. An identification of the extent and range of needs at the local level

4. An articulation of the discrepancy between individual needs and services currently available at the local level

5. A definition of the policies, procedures, and practices that serve as barriers to the elimination of discrepancies between services and needs

6. Articulation of policies, procedures, and practices that support the placement of handicapped youth in appropriate vocational and employment programs

7. An evaluation plan to assess the effectiveness of these policies, procedures, and practices (Hull, et al., 1986).

Parent and Consumer Participation

Parent and consumer involvement in the planning and delivery of vocational and employment services should occur at two levels. First, parents and disabled individuals represent the best source of information for developing the individualized service plan. They must be involved in specifying their aspirations and service needs, and in developing goals and objectives designed to meet those needs. Consumers and parents can often provide information about skills and interests not readily observable by professionals through interactions in school and work environments.

Second, the resources needed to ensure long-range employment and community living goals may not be immediately available. Because of limited resources and competing demands for those resources, professionals are not always able to advocate for new or expanded services within their organizations. Because they are outside the system, parents and consumers have open to them other avenues through which to advocate for the services they need to achieve their goals and aspirations.

At least three advocacy processes are available to disabled individuals and their parents. These include legislative advocacy, systems change advocacy, and community organization advocacy (Addison, Haggerty, and Moore, 1976). Legislative advocacy involves using the legislative process to mandate change in order to secure the rights of persons with disabilities. For example, local and state advocacy groups can work with legislators in developing new or revised statutes that support transitional employment services.

Systems change advocacy can be used by consumers and parents to influence policies, practices, and procedures within organizations. An example of this advocacy approach would be the inclusion of parents and consumers on committees designed to develop an interagency agreement, or to review and revise a state-level funding formula to distribute state education dollars.

Community organization advocacy is designed to assist in disseminating information regarding the positive contributions disabled individuals may bring to a community. This can be achieved through interactions of a sustained or short-term nature in generic community service organizations such as church groups, League of Women Voters, the Chamber of Commerce, hospital or school boards, or community-sponsored recreation activities (Addison, Haggerty, and Moore, 1976).

Job Search Education

Over the past few years there has been an increased recognition by secondary level special and vocational educators and by vocational rehabilitation professionals of the need to provide program options characterized by goals and activities closely related to the skills needed in locating and securing work. In their follow-up research, Hasazi et al. (1985) reported that 85 percent of former special education students who were employed found their jobs through the self-family-friend network. This result is similar to the findings of Azrin and Phillip (1979) concerning adult disadvantaged populations.

The job search education approach differs from many job development efforts designed for handicapped and disadvantaged individuals in that the students are taught to utilize job-seeking strategies themselves rather than having a professional work experience coordinator or job counselor find the jobs for them. This approach holds promise for individuals with mild handicaps in that it is a more efficient and self-reliant process.

A number of curricula have been designed primarily for adult job seekers who are both handicapped and disadvantaged. Azrin and Besalel (1980) developed a systematic and structured curriculum to teach job search skills; the curriculum included such elements as identifying and contacting potential employers, resume preparation, and a format where pairs of job-seekers work together on specified activities. The unique aspect of this approach is the intensive skills acquisition focus presented in a supportive partnership learning experience. This approach has been adapted for use by handicapped youth with severe deficits in both reading and written expression (Crane, et al., 1983; Mathews, Whang, and Fawcett, 1984).

Follow-up of Program Graduates

There is a critical need to acquire information on the employment status and use of generic and specialized services by handicapped youth and adults following completion of vocational education, training, and employment services (Bellamy, 1985). Information that should be solicited in follow-up efforts includes current job classification, wages, number of hours worked per week, benefits, satisfaction with employment conditions, duration between jobs, and retraining and social services needs.

Follow-up of individuals in secondary and postsecondary education and training programs should be conducted by the agency delivering these services two to three months after the program is completed and then again one year later. This follow-up activity fulfills two purposes. First, employment data can provide information regarding which elements of an agency's service system appear to be the most effective and which need to be modified. Second, follow-up efforts can identify individuals who are in need of additional services such as retraining or referrals to other agencies.

CASE STUDIES

The remainder of this chapter will present three case studies of individuals who were enrolled in a variety of secondary and postsecondary vocational education and training experiences. These case studies illustrate options available to individuals who are labeled mildly handicapped or disadvantaged.

CASE STUDY: Sara

Description of Student

Sara is a young woman who was labeled learning disabled in elementary school and had a variety of special education services before entering high school. At the time she entered high school she was reading at a fourth grade level and had difficulties comprehending written material. Her computational mathematics skills, however, were equal to those of her peers, and she was involved and accepted in numerous school social activities.

Upon entering high school, Sara was placed in regular ninth grade English and mathematics courses and received special education services through a resource teacher to support those placements. In addition, she attended a regular industrial arts class that included four curriculum modules in drafting, woodworking, electricity/electronics, and small engines. Her industrial arts teachers indicated that she did not need specialized services in those programs.

Description of Vocational Programs and Services

Based on her experience in her industrial arts class, Sara and her parents decided she might want to enroll in a vocational education program at a regional vocational center during her junior and senior years. To assist her in making a final program decision, Sara decided to attend a career exploration class offered to all second semester ninth graders in the high schools that sent their vocational students to that regional center. This program was offered during the summer following the end of the ninth grade, and was delivered for five mornings per week for three weeks. The course was taught by regular vocational educators. Students were allowed to select three one-week experiences from approximately twelve program categories reflecting the range of vocational offerings at the regional center. Each one-week experience included an overview of careers associated with the program; a description of the safety, mathematics, and reading requirements of the program; and a hands-on project to be completed by each student.

Sara selected printing, retailing, and automotive programs for her three one-week experiences. Upon completion of this summer program, Sara decided that she wanted to enroll in a printing program during her junior and senior years. To better prepare her for that program, she enrolled in a graphic arts course during her sophomore year that was taught through the industrial arts program at her home school. The special educator and her graphic arts teacher worked together on an individualized program to minimize the effect of her reading deficits in this course. The program included a weekly review of the vocabulary terms, and training in study skills specifically related to using the graphic arts textbook.

When Sara enrolled in the printing program at the regional center, a meeting was scheduled between her home high school special education teacher, the vocational resource teacher, and the printing teacher at the regional vocational center. It was determined that Sara would require special education services at the center in order to ensure her success in this program. The same strategies that were used to support Sara in her graphic arts class were used in her printing program. In addition, the vocational resource teacher helped the printing teacher develop individualized written materials to be used in her printing classroom.

Transition to Employment

At her IEP meeting during her junior year, Sara and her parents decided that a career in printing was an appropriate goal. A transition plan was developed as a component of her IEP that included a cooperative education work experience at a local publisher during her senior year. To ensure that the necessary resources were available to achieve the work experience and finally employment following graduation, the cooperative education teacher and a job placement specialist from the state employment service were invited to participate in the IEP meeting.

To prepare Sara for her work experience, the cooperative education teacher conducted an analysis of the work requirements at the job site and communicated these to the printing teacher and the vocational resource teacher. These included finishing and binding processes, using screen printing equipment, and operating offset presses. The cooperation education and vocational resource teacher then helped the vocational instructor individualize Sara's projects to focus her work on using processes and equipment that were most similar to those at the job site.

In her senior year, Sara took an advanced printing course during the fall semester and began her work placement during the spring semester. Her cooperative education teacher accompanied her to the work site and facilitated her integration into the work routine. This support included discussions with her supervisor regarding the skills she had acquired in her printing program as well as potential problems she might encounter with reading elements within her work routine. The cooperative education teacher remained with Sara for one day to ensure that she could accomplish her work with a minimum amount of supervision. The cooperative education teacher monitored Sara's work every day for the first week and gradually faded monitoring visits to once weekly. If training problems occurred, the cooperative education teacher was contacted and arranged to send the vocational resource teacher or aide to provide the needed short-term training.

In addition to her work experience during the spring semester, Sara's program included establishing and maintaining regular contact with the job placement specialist, who was searching for a similar printing job in the local community for Sara following graduation. Sara and her parents decided that she would live at home until such time that her job provided her with the resources to live independently in an apartment. Agreements were also made between Sara, her parents, and school personnel that the vocational resource teacher would contact Sara at six- and eighteen-month intervals after graduation to determine her employment status and coordinate appropriate referrals as necessary.

CASE STUDY: Robert

Description of the Student

Robert is a young man labeled mildly mentally retarded. Like Sara, Robert enrolled in regular industrial arts classes in woodworking and small engines during his freshman and sophomore years of high school. During this time he spent the remainder of his school day in regular classrooms and in a resource room. He and his parents refused placement in a regional special class program for mentally retarded youth. Although his reading and math skills were at approximately the fourth-grade level he had good oral comprehension skills and learned well through demonstration and practice.

Description of Programs and Services

During the IEP meeting in his sophomore year, Robert and his parents, together with the home-school special education teacher, the vocational resource teacher, and a representative from the local vocational rehabilitation agency, decided that Robert should be placed in a building trades program during his last two years of high school. This decision followed a two-week shadowing experience in a building trades program at a regional vocational center. This shadowing experience involved pairing Robert with a student he knew while the student was attending vocational class at an actual building site. It was also decided at the IEP meeting that Robert would participate in a summer work program offered through the Job Training Partnership Act following both his sophomore and junior years. In addition, it was decided at his IEP meeting that during the middle of his senior year a vocational rehabilitation counselor would work with Robert and school personnel to determine his need for employment and training services following graduation.

Robert's building trades program at the regional vocational center was an adapted curriculum that included only those competencies associated with building a foundation, rough framing, and roofing. Special education services were provided by the vocational resource teacher and included training on measurement skills, vocabulary, and blueprint reading. The building trades teacher provided modeling and demonstration to small groups of students, some of whom served as peer instructors to Robert when he needed additional assistance.

Robert's summer youth employment programs included training sites in foundation work and roofing. A job coach employed through JTPA funds provided on-site instruction and support to facilitate successful experiences at these training sites.

Transition to Employment

During Robert's senior year a vocational rehabilitation counselor located a full-time job as a roofer and helped Robert through the application and interview processes. The counselor also assigned a job coach to work with Robert and his employer during the first few weeks of employment. At the work site the job coach assessed the skills that Robert would need to learn in order to accomplish the work requirements. Based on this assessment, the job coach provided intensive training until Robert was able to perform these tasks independently. After the job coach faded her presence from the work site, the vocational rehabilitaton counselor contacted Robert and the employer every week to determine if additional resources or training were needed. This follow-up process lasted for three months, at which time the employer indicated that no additional regularly scheduled visits would be required of the vocational rehabilitation counselor. He also reported that Robert would be receiving a wage increase within the next two months.

CASE STUDY: Ann

Description of Student

Ann is a young woman identified as economically disadvantaged and enrolled in a health occupations program at a regional vocational center.

Description of Programs and Services

Because the center she attended was located in an area where 75 percent of the enrolled student population was economically disadvantaged, the school was able to purchase modern technological equipment through a provision in the Carl Perkins Vocational Education Act [Section 201(d) (2)] to prepare her and other students as laboratory technicians.

Prior to graduation Ann indicated an interest in obtaining summer work and receiving additional vocational education in radiation therapy. To help her locate summer work before her postsecondary program, the vocational guidance counselor at the center organized a job search program for a group of ten students including Ann. The guidance counselor also facilitated her placement in a nearby community college and helped her acquire student financial assistance through a federal student loan program.

Transition to Employment

During her second and final year at the community college, Ann participated in a cooperative education program where her wages were subsidized by a Job Training Partnership Program for two months, at which time she demonstrated the skills and knowledge required of a radiation therapist. Prior to this placement, the employer had agreed to employ Ann full time when she had reached this entry level of competence.

SUMMARY

As this chapter has illustrated, there are a variety of programs and services that provide vocational education and training, and employment services at both the secondary and postsecondary levels for mildly handicapped and disadvantaged individuals. Most of these programs and services are available in school districts and local communities.

However, access to many of these programs has been limited by a fragmented approach to referral and service delivery, the lack of a shared philosophy, and minimal incentives for cooperative planning and services delivery. Through collaborative planning and an acceptance of the best practices outlined in this chapter, many more resources will become available to handicapped and disadvantaged individuals. Ultimately, these opportunities should enable handicapped and disadvantaged individuals to become more fully integrated into employment and community life.

REFERENCES

Addison, M.R., D.E. Haggerty, and M.L. Moore. (1976). Advocates on advocacy: Defining three approaches. *Amicus 1*, 9–16.

Albright, L., S.B. Hasazi, L.A. Phelps, and M. Hull. (1981). Interagency collaboration in providing vocational education for handicapped individuals. *Exceptional Children 47*(8), 584–589.

American Vocational Association. (1983). *Fact Sheet*. Arlington, Va.: Author, Publications and Communications Department.

Azrin, N.H., and V.A. Besalel. (1980). *Job Club Counselor's Manual: A Behavioral Approach to Vocational Counseling*. Baltimore: University Park Press.

Azrin, N.H., and R.A. Phillip. (1979). The job club method for job handicapped: A comparative outcome study. *Rehabilitation Counseling Bulletin 47*(2), 144–155.

Bellamy, G.T. (1985). Transition progress: Comments on Hasazi, Gordon, and Roe. *Exceptional Children 51*(6), 474–477.

Benson, C.A. (1982). The question of quality. *VocEd 57*(6), 27–29.

Birchenall, J., and J. Wanat. (1981). Serving the handicapped in vocational student organizations. *VocEd 56*(3), 51–54.

Blatt, B. (1981). *In and Out of Mental Retardation: Essays on Educability, Disability, and Human Policy*. Baltimore: University Park Press.

Brown, J. (September 1985). Issues impacting the education of mildly handicapped learners in postsecondary vocational education programs. Paper presented before the School to Work Transition for Handicapped Youth Forum, University of Illinois, Urbana.

Brown, J.M., and T.F. Kayser. (1985). A proposed model for reducing dropout rates among students in postsecondary vocational education programs. *Journal of Industrial Teacher Education 22*(4), 38–45.

Crane, N., R. Foley, T. Hart, J. Maynard, S. Robinson, and M. Collins. (1983). The job club: Adaptation of a job-seeking skills curriculum for secondary school students. Unpublished manuscript. University of Vermont, Department of Special Education, Social Work, and Social Services.

Cuenin, L. (1985). The impact of cooperative agreements on the coordination of vocational education services for the handicapped. Unpublished doctoral dissertation. University of Maryland, Department of Special Education.

David, H. (September 1981). *The Vocational Education Study: The Final Report.* Vocational Education Study, Publication No. 8. Washington, D.C.: National Institute of Education.

Evans, R.N. (1982). Why vocational education belongs in a comprehensive high school. *VocEd 57*(6), 24–26.

Evans, R.N., and E.L. Herr. (1978).*Foundations of Vocational Eduction* 2d. ed. Columbus, Ohio: Charles E. Merrill.

Evans, R.N. A. Hunter, A. Holter, and J. Miller. (June 1980). *Identification and Validation of Criteria Used for Determining the Best Training Setting for Persons with Handicaps.* Champaign-Urbana: University of Illinois, Bureau of Educational Research.

Hasazi, S.B., L.R. Gordon, and C.A. Roe. (1985). Factors associated with the employment status of handicapped youth exiting high school from 1979 to 1983. *Exceptional Children 51*(6), 455–469.

Hasazi, S.B., L.R. Gordon, C.A. Roe, M. Hull, K. Finck, and G. Salembier. (1985). A statewide follow-up on post high school employment and residential status of students labeled "mentally retarded." *Education and Training of the Mentally Retarded 20*(6), 222–234.

Horner, R.H., J.J. McDonnell, and G.T. Bellamy. (1986). Teaching general skills: General case instruction in simulation and community settings. In R. Horner, L. Meyer, and H. Fredericks (eds.), *Education of Learners with Severe Handicaps: Exemplary Service Strategies.* Baltimore: Paul H. Brookes.

Hull, M., S.B. Hasazi, R.B. Cobb, and M. Collins. (1986). A statewide model for cooperative planning and developing transitional services. Unpublished manuscript. Vermont State Department of Education, Special Education Unit, Montpelier.

Lakin, K.C., and R.H. Bruininks. (eds.). (1985). *Strategies for Achieving Community Integration of Developmentally Disabled Citizens.* Baltimore: Paul H. Brookes.

Malitz, G.S. (1981). *A Classification of Instructional Programs.* Washington, D.C.: National Center for Education Statistics.

Mathews, R.M. P.L. Whang, and S.B. Fawcett. (1984). *Learning Job-finding Skills.* Lawrence: University of Kansas, Research and Training Center on Independent Living.

Nacson, J. (1982, May 5). Prepared statement at the Hearings on the Reauthorization of the Vocational Education Act of 1963 before the House Joint Hearing of the Subcommittee on Elementary, Secondary, and Vocational Education and the Subcommittee on Select Education of the Committee on Education and Labor. Washington, D.C.: U.S. Government Printing Office.

National Center for Education Statistics. (1980). *The Condition of Vocational Education: Review Edition.* Washington, D.C.: U.S. Department of Education.

National Commission on Secondary Vocational Education. (1984). *The Unfinished Agenda: The Role of Vocational Education in the High School.* Columbus: Ohio State University, National Center for Research in Vocational Education.

Office of Civil Rights. (1980, August 27). *Fall 1979 Vocational Education Survey.* (Preliminary unedited data). Washington, D.C.: U.S. Department of Education.

Owens, D., K. Arnold, and J. Costen. (1985). Issues related to administrative planning. *Journal for Vocational Special Needs Education 7*(2), 25–27.

Phelps, L.A. (1982, May 5). Prepared statement at the Hearings on the Reauthorization of the Vocational Education Act of 1963 before the House Joint Hearing of the Subcommittee on Elementary, Secondary, and Vocational Education and the Subcommittee on Select Education of the Committee on Education and Labor. Washington, D.C.: Government Printing Office.

Phelps, L.A. (1985). Special needs students: Redefining the challenge. *VocEd 60*(3), 24–26.

Pitonyak, D., S.B. Hasazi, G. Salembier, R.B. Cobb, and M. Collins. (1986). Competencies for employment training specialists. Unpublished manuscript. University of Vermont, Department of Special Education, Social Work, and Social Services.

Subcommittee on the Handicapped. (March 1985). *A Compilation of Federal Laws for Disabled Children, Youth, and Adults.* Washington, D.C.: U.S. Government Printing Office.

Tindall, L. (September 1985). Utilizing Job Training Partnership Act programs for handicapped individuals. Paper presented before the School to Work Transition for Handicapped Youth Forum, University of Illinois, Urbana.

U.S. Department of Education. (1985, August 16). Final rules and regulations. *Federal Register 50*(159), 33226–33306.

U.S. Department of Labor. (1974). *Comprehensive Employment and Training Act of 1973: Apprenticeship and CETA.* Washington, D.C.: Author, Bureau of Apprenticeship Training.

Wehman, P. (1981). *Competitive Employment: New Horizons for Severely Disabled Individuals.* Baltimore: Paul H. Brookes.

Wehman, P., J. Kregel, and J. Seyfarth. (1985). Transition from school to work for individuals with severe handicaps: A follow-up study. *JASH 10*(3), 132–139.

Will, M. (March–April 1984). *Bridges from School to Work: Programs for the Handicapped.* Washington, D.C.: Clearinghouse on the Handicapped.

Wolfensburger, W. (1977). The principle of normalization. In B. Blatt, D. Biklen, and R. Bogdan (eds.), *An Alternative Textbook in Special Education: People, Schools and Other Institutions.* Denver, Col.: Love Publishing.

13 Vocational Education of Persons with Severe Handicaps*

Ian Pumpian, Elizabeth West,
and Holly Shepard
San Diego State University

OVERVIEW: SERVICES THAT ENHANCE COMPETENCE, PARTICIPATION, ACCEPTANCE, AND RESPECT

Given that all things were equal, *including the availability of resources and the cost of the services,* how would you answer the following questions?

- Should available resources and service delivery models be organized and used to segregate people *or* should they be organized and used to integrate them?

- If people need help, should they be helped to perform useful and valued activities typical of what others in their age group do *or* should they be helped to perform activities typical of those performed by preschoolers, regardless of their age?

- Should persons with severe handicaps be supported to function as productively as possible as workers in the mainstream of our nation's industries *or* should they be massed together and supported to function in "factories and playhouses for the handicapped"? Where would you rather spend your working hours?

*This paper was supported in part by Grant Number G008301455, Number G008430099, and Number G008435102 to the San Diego State University from the U.S. Department of Education, Office of Special Education.

- Should a program not serve an individual capable of performing meaningful work *if* he or she will negatively affect the average earnings reported by the program as a whole?

- Should professionals continue to pay for and use instruments and assessment techniques that would systematically exclude large numbers of people from work environments and jobs in which they now work?

- Should programs and services be evaluated based on improvements in test scores *or* on changes they have made in a person's lifestyle and quality of life?

- Do people with severe handicaps have a right to live, work, and play as equal members of our community even though some people (due to lack of familiarity and experience) feel uncomfortable and awkward in their presence *or* should people with severe handicaps be made second-class citizens?

- Would you find it easier to relate to a group (a crew, an enclave) of say eight or nine people with severe handicaps *or* would you rather get to know people as individuals?

- If it costs more not to provide supported work and living services than to provide them, *then* should we legally mandate the provision of such services?

Consistent answers to these value-laden questions provide the basis for developing and evaluating services for persons with severe handicaps. Such answers are fundamental to understanding the current evolution, direction, and debate concerning training and employment. This chapter is written from the perspective that people with severe handicaps can, and have the right, to live, work, and play as participating, productive, and integrated members of their community. Such a position is essential if one values and respects principles of normalization.

Services should be provided in such a way as to allow people to function as active community members. The major responsibility of the schools should be to prepare people for this participation. The major responsibility of adult agencies is to support this participation. Stated another way, schools teach and, as a function of instruction, provide and identify support needs and systems. Adult services should provide support services and, as a function of providing support, may assume some instructional roles. In the past these distinctions were more difficult to make since both the school and adult system provided services based on the notion of developmental readiness—that is, train then place. Contemporary school and adult services are increasingly being based on the notion of functional training and functional support in valued environments and activities—that is, place then train. As you visit programs and talk to providers, can you determine which basis they use?

Do they use phrases like "he is not ready yet" or "he is too handicapped to be integrated," or do you see sophisticated adaptations and support systems being used to integrate and employ productively people who face severe challenges. Keep in mind that the typical program may be fifteen to twenty years behind the "best existing technology."

SEVERELY DISABLED VS. SEVERE HANDICAPS: CONFUSING TERMINOLOGY

Any attempt to define and describe a group of individuals is dangerous. Such attempts, no matter how well intended, typically are full of overgeneralizations. When such attempts are made to describe a group of persons with disabilities, these overgeneralizations often focus on limitations, or at the other extreme, they become so nebulous that anyone could fall under the definition. The former problem results in reinforcing stereotypes, robbing people of their individuality, and increasing counterproductive self-fulfilling prophecies. The latter problem tends to increase the likelihood that services may not be extended to target populations or that the exchange of program results may be misleading. Both problems arise in trying to define, and provide services to, persons with severe handicaps.

Although often used interchangeably, the phrases *severely disabled* and *severely handicapped* are often distinguished in practice. The phrase *severely disabled* is a categorical reference, typically used by rehabilitation agencies and cited in the Rehabilitation Act of 1973. It is used to refer to a reasonably large and extremely diverse group of individuals with many discernible disabilities and with many discernible categorical and diagnostic labels.

The phrase *severely handicapped* refers to a small subset of the severely disabled population. It is a phrase more common to educators than to rehabilitation specialists. It is typically used to refer to those individuals who tend to manifest the most severe, and often multiple, disabilities in that the disability has a major impact in most areas of functioning. A person whose primary disability is cortical blindness could likely meet the rehabilitation definition of severely disabled but would not likely be considered appropriate for educational services designed for students with severe handicaps.

Although persons with severe handicaps represent a population that is much smaller in numbers, that population still represents a diverse heterogeneous group and therefore is difficult to define. One of the most common characteristics of this group is severe intellectual impairment (that is, mental retardation). In addition, this group has a proportionately larger percentage of individuals with multiple disabilities.

Based on normal distribution curves it is estimated that 1 to 2 percent of the general population could be considered severely handicapped. Severe handicaps are typically observable throughout the life span of an individual (Van Etten, Arkel, and Van Etten, 1980). Severe handicaps are measurable in terms of cognitive, behavioral, and/or physical disabilities; however, many researchers emphasize that such disabilities can be magnified or minimized by the services afforded these individuals and the attitudes others hold toward them (Gold, 1980).

Individuals with severe handicaps represent a very small population, but their service needs in all aspects of functional living (work, play, and family life) and the cost of those services are extensive (Van Etten, Arkel, and Van Etten, 1980). Achieved levels of functioning for individuals with severe handicaps must be evaluated on an individual, rather than categorical, basis. Further, such an evaluation only provides a review of what an individual is currently able to do, not what his or her potential may be. Some persons with severe handicaps have learned to perform many tasks adaptively in integrated community settings, such as crossing a street, and using a city bus or a restaurant (Wilcox and Bellamy, 1982). A small percentage of severely handicapped persons has multiple sensorial deficits; little, if any, volitional movement; and is extremely sedated with chemicals. For individuals who are on life support, or in such states of biological distress, attempts to maintain life should be supplemented by opportunities to participate in normal environments and activities whenever possible. Snell (1982) estimated that only about 7 percent of individuals characterized as profoundly handicapped (that is, 7 percent of 1 percent of the population) fit the description by Landesman-Dwyer and Sachett as being

> (1) incapable of moving through space, even with prosthetic devices and physical assistance; (2) totally lacking all adaptive behaviors as measured by instruments such as the AAMD Adaptive Behavior scale; and, (3) being extremely small for their chronological age (i.e., below the third percentile for height, weight and head circumference. (1978, p.56)

Pumpian, Shepard, and West attempted to demonstrate one way of communicating the diversity of this population when negotiating job-training situations with employers in the following sample dialogue:

> Our program serves individuals labelled severely handicapped who are enrolled in the San Diego Unified School District. The school district provides educational programming for well over 500 individuals identified as severely handicapped. Our responsibility is to provide quality educational experiences to each of these individuals. The group is quite diverse in terms of their age, their individual strengths and interests as well as limitations and challenges they need to overcome. A majority of students could be

characterized as having significant mental retardation. There are some students in the program who walk and others use wheelchairs or other forms of mobility assistance. Some students have very good verbal skills while others may point to a picture book to communicate. Some of our students are requiring extensive assistance to develop control over their behavior while other students act exemplary. Some of our students do not have good oral muscular control and therefore drool, others have good self care skills. Some of our students can eat independently, others need help. It really is a diverse group! However, each is entitled to an appropriate education and it is our responsibility to make sure that each of these individuals has a program designed to prepare them to be active members in their communities. (1986, p. 25).

In sum, people with severe handicaps, as the phrase is used here, do represent the lowest intellectually functioning people in our society. Even so, the range of diversity in interest, ability, family background, and unique challenges is tremendous. Each individual does have extensive service needs that, when unmet, further affect the severity of the disability. However, unless the individual is in such biological distress that acute medical care is required, the adult should be provided integrated, work-oriented support services. Any adult who is included in a day program can be included in one that has this kind of orientation.

INTEGRATED EMPLOYMENT OPTIONS

Supported employment has been discussed and defined throughout this book. The concept of supported employment developed as a result of critical analyses that pointed up the shortcomings of existing adult services afforded to persons with severe disabilities. No doubt, there is interest, determination, and movement for extending supported employment services to persons with other types of disabilities. However, even with the current emphasis and origin of supported employment practices within the severely disabled population, optimism and demonstrations of supported employment services being extended to the most severely disabled adults (those referred to here as severely handicapped) has been extremely limited. This has been exacerbated by definitions of supported employment that focus on hours worked per week and income earned versus changes in overall lifestyle. Consequently, programs are either excluding persons with the most severely disabling conditions or selecting pseudointegration models. These are models that often fail to actually develop and facilitate interactions with nondisabled workers. This has been the case with some enclave and work crew programs. Other programs are choosing to call their attempts to meaningfully employ people in integrated work environments something other than supported employment if all the typical criteria, (e.g,, twenty hours of work per week) are not met. This chapter attempts to delineate philosophies, strategies, and programs that should illustrate the integrated employment options for this entire population.

Numerous measures have already been used to evaluate programs and services. One of the truly unique features associated with the supported employment movement is the focus on outcome as the most important measure of program and service effectiveness. Evaluation criteria include:

1. Is the worker performing meaningful work in an integrated work environment?

2. Is the worker being paid?

3. Is the worker working a minimum twenty hours per week?

4. Is support being provided, and is the support necessary to place, train, and maintain that worker in that job?

These criteria, for the most part, provide an excellent foundation for developing program goals and plans and evaluating program effectiveness. In fact, we applaud attention to outcome measures as a way of analyzing a program's strengths and needs. Furthermore, we could support the strict adherence to these criteria that many vehemently argue for *if* these same advocates did not exclude potential consumers from their programs. Unfortunately, however, they do. These advocates insist on paid employment, but then may exclude persons whom they cannot place in wage-earning jobs. These advocates insist upon at least twenty hours per week of work but then may exclude persons who may not have the stamina or current skills to work that long. We believe strict adherence to supported employment criteria should be used only by programs that have zero exclusion policies. In the interim, and in order to ensure that services are designed to meet an individual's need, we prefer to expand the criteria of supported employment as described below. To reduce confusion and limit semantic debates, we need to note that these criteria cover a range of integrated work options that is broader and more inclusive than that which falls under the rubric "supported employment."

The criteria that should be considered when developing and evaluating adult services for persons with severe handicaps, include:

1. *Is the worker in an integrated vocational environment?* This means integration beyond physical placement in an environment that employs nondisabled workers. Employing eight or fewer disabled workers also appears now to be, at best, a gross indicator of an integrated placement. Specifically, placement in an integrated environment does not in and of itself guarantee that a worker will realize the benefits of that placement. Increased attention must be placed on enhancing the types,

length, and consistency of interactions that occur between the disabled worker and nondisabled coworkers. Attention must be directed toward interactions beyond physical integration in order to critically evaluate the effectiveness of various enclave and work crew models. Many of these models have resulted in supporting no interactions, enhancing no relationships, and developing no natural supervision possibilities. As a result, the social opportunities available in workshops and activity centers have not been replaced by new social opportunities in the integrated workplace. Consequently, work can become an isolating experience. Support services must be designed and provided in a way that encourages, and not limits, social bonding among coworkers.

2. *Is the worker performing meaningful work?* Does the worker have a job description that delineates job skills that the business needs to have performed? Adults should not spend time engaging in makeshift work, pretend work, or prework. Dignity, respect, and value will develop only if the worker performs a needed function and actually makes a contribution to a business. In order to include a significantly larger percentage of adults with severe handicaps in integrated employment situations, attention will have to expand beyond placement in traditional job and job descriptions. Placement of a worker may involve making major modifications in job descriptions and developing new job descriptions and new creative job-sharing plans. In some cases, these situations may limit the number of hours of available work. That is, the individual job description may provide only three hours of employment per day. A fifteen-hour placement may not meet some people's definition of supported work. However, such an individual placement is, at least, more desirable than a segregated program or staying home.

3. *Does the worker receive adequate and fair compensation for his or her work?* There has been much debate and controversy over this criterion. Proponents of supported employment typically require pay— that is, wages—as an absolute necessary component. Others question whether wages are the only and most important form of compensation for all workers in all cases. For example, many citizens volunteer in organizations and agencies throughout the country. They find that volunteer work provides them with other forms and types of compensation, with job experience, and with an opportunity to interact with others and contribute to their community while using and developing job skills and interests. Many of these people do not necessarily depend on wages in order to guarantee comfortable standards of living and quality of life. Is it not possible that a worker with a severe disability: (1) may already have economic security; and (2) may find reward and compensations from exercising his or her right to function as a volunteer? Under these circumstances, and especially when paid compensation is not immediately available, would not volunteer

placement be a reasonable alternative to segregated work and nonwork programs or to remaining at home on a waiting list?

Furthermore, many adults after leaving high school choose and/or find it necessary to develop additional job skills and gain additional job experience. Many valued citizens choose real-life nonpaid internships in order to develop job skills and gain access into the working world. Might not an adult with a severe disability benefit from a nonpaid job-training experience as a way of developing job skills and gaining access into the working world? Is it not reasonable for a program to support an individual in a volunteer or integrated training experience when that individual, because of the severity of the disability, is or would be denied access into other programs that provide only work services in paid employment?

There are certainly more questions here than answers. Rigid adherence to the pay criterion would appear to limit the legal opportunities for training or volunteer placement afforded all other citizens. We do believe in a place-then-train vs. a train-then-place model to the extent that no adults should be placed in a segregated facility or classroom in order to be "prepared" to function in an integrated work environment. Further, in no way, would we ever advocate using nonpaid training or volunteer placements in lieu of integrated paid options, especially for individuals whose wage earning would increase their purchasing power, standard of living, and tax contribution, or who would prefer paid work. In such cases a volunteer placement or a legal nonpaid training experience might be viewed as a successive approximation toward a paid employment goal. There are data that suggest that more individuals will move from an integrated nonpaid situation into an integrated paid situation than will move from a segregated paid situation into an integrated paid situation. Stated another way, if integrated paid employment is a program goal, then segregated paid employment appears to provide a more dead-ended outcome than an integrated nonpaid situation.

In order to truly evaluate whether reasonable compensation is being provided perhaps the following questions should be addressed:

- What type and forms of compensation do nondisabled persons get for the type and amount of work being produced?
- Are any of the conditions of the Fair Labor Standards Act being violated by the circumstances of this placement?
- How does this work situation impact this individual's overall quality of life and lifestyle?

Brown, et al. (1986) and Bellamy, et al., (1986) each have designed instruments that attempt to measure various aspects of a person's lifestyle and overall quality of life. These focus on: where an individual goes and the extent of his or her integration; what an individual does and the overall social, cultural, and age appropriateness of those activities; with whom the individual interacts and the quality of his or her encounters, relationships, and friendships; and, finally, the choices an individual is able to make and how those reflect individual preferences, interests, and abilities. In order to truly measure the appropriateness of the compensation and benefits provided to an individual as a function of his or her work placement, we would suggest that these instruments be used to evaluate the total twenty-four hour lifespace of an individual. If the type of compensation the individual receives for work is not enhancing his or her lifestyle, integration into the community, and relationships with others, then work placement that provides for more and/or additional types of compensation and benefits should be sought. Support services must be organized to review compensation and benefits provided and make sure they meet the worker's needs and interests.

Finally, the question of "who can work?" must be addressed. We have already taken the position that all individuals with severe handicaps, except those in such biological distress that life support is necessary, can and should be provided services that enhance productive participation in integrated work environments. This statement is made despite the fact that many respected researchers and providers have often stated that: "Supported work is not for everybody"; "we include a severely handicapped person to keep our program honest"; "providers must tease out such clients if your program is going to be successful"; "employers are not ready for such individuals"; and "such individuals can only work in segregated environments."

Certainly, school systems are just beginning to evolve to the point where students with severe handicaps can be adequately trained and prepared to work in integrated settings. In order to realize zero exclusion practices, improvements in skill development and technological applications, and changes in policy and attitude must continue. The following section will review some of the major school trends and initiatives that have been a part of this evolution, and then the trends and initiatives in adult services will be described.

VOCATIONAL TRAINING

School Trends   The field of training and employing persons with severe handicaps is relatively new. In the not so distant past only a small portion of these individuals received educational services and an even smaller portion worked. Those that did work were restricted to segregated facilities for "the handicapped." In the late 1950s the notion of educability and instructional technology for these people began to receive more careful attention. This attention led to a series of initiatives that will be reviewed in this section.

Provision of educational services for individuals with severe handicaps is a very young and evolving field. Various trends and initiatives have built upon each other in such a way as to create a more and more sophisticated and effective service system. This section reviews some of these milestones and describes how they led to what is now considered the best existing technology, the so-called state of the art. Each initiative has been the foundation of the next. In addition, none of these initiatives is any less important now than when it was introduced. Rather, we have improved our sophistication and our understanding and delivery of services relative to each. Eventually these initiatives have led to our current attention to: (1) adult functioning; (2) scrutinization of the adult continuum of services that has developed; and (3) attention to supported integrated employment options as an alternative to this continuum. This last will be reviewed in the section after this.

How to Teach. In the late 1950s federal support began to prepare teachers to work with persons who were mentally retarded; this support, which was finally legislated in 1965 (P.L. 89-10), represented a substantial step forward. Personnel preparation has continued to be important ever since. During those early years, teacher preparation focused on instructional technology—that is, how to teach. The phrase *"applied behavioral analysis"* became and continues to be the foundation of this technology (Bellamy, Horner, and Inman, 1979). Basically, applied behavioral analysis provides a foundation for delineating: (1) objectives for behavior change and skill acquisition, and (2) teaching strategies in measurable and observable ways. Data-based instruction (Gaylord-Ross and Holvoet, 1985), prescriptive teaching (Bradfield, 1970), utilization of cues and correction procedures (Falvey et al., 1980), nonpunitive management techniques (LaVigna and Donnellan, 1986), and strategies to teach skill generalization (Horner, Sprague, and Wilcox, 1982) all represent refinements and outgrowths of this movement. During this time the principles of applied behavioral analysis were used to demonstrate that persons with severe handicaps could learn to perform a skill that was previously not in his or her repertoire; the principles also allowed for the planning and documenting of techniques that were associated with that skill acquisition.

What to Teach. As this initiative took hold, and "how to teach" began to be understood, attention turned to a new concern, namely, "what to teach." What curricular content was most important in a program for persons with severe handicaps? Almost by definition, an individual was identified as severely handicapped by comparing him or her to nondisabled age peers. Significant discrepancies could be identified in at least one and usually many developmental areas (e.g., cognitive skills, basic academic skills, self-help skills). Consequently, it seemed clear that the development of such skills needed to be a primary concern for educators.

This led to the next initiative, which was the use of *developmental curriculum*. Educators used and developed sophisticated instruments that delineated the typical development of skills and skill milestones in each of the aforementioned areas. Then the individual skill repertoire was assessed by using this norm-referenced instrument, and a developmental age assigned in each of these skill areas as well as across them. For example, despite the fact that Terri is 18 year old, she may be assessed as having the motor development age of a 2-year-old, the cognitive development of a 20-month-old, and an overall developmental age of a child one year and six months old. After assessment, curriculum would be provided appropriate to her developmental age level. The assumption here was that the prerequisite skills for more sophisticated performance in each of these areas could be taught and that each would build upon the others. In this way, a student could catch up to his or her chronological (that is, real) age peers.

This initiative led to students demonstrating skills gains in many areas and also led to increased participation of professionals from various disciplines. However, although students demonstrated skill gains, these gains failed to make a substantial impact on the quality of their lives and lifestyle. This shortcoming became more and more obvious as the lifespace of adolescents and adults was evaluated (Brown et al., 1979). *Thus, although an educational focus on developing skills remains as a significant attribute of this initiative, the use of a developmental curriculum to organize, identify, and assess skill priorities can no longer be considered appropriate.* A developmental curriculum works on readiness skills and prerequisite skills. Users assume that students will catch up and eventually be ready to learn useful, valued, and age-appropriate skills. Unfortunately, such students typically don't get ready, don't catch up, and consequently, when using such an approach, don't ever engage in useful, valued, and age-appropriate skills. Adults with severe handicaps can no longer be treated as if they were nondisabled preschoolers. These realizations created the momentum for the new initiatives that currently are impacting educational services.

Strategies that generate useful, *functional* curricula content appropriate for a person's *chronological age* are now being used and improved (Brown et al., 1979). This curriculum initiative has led to the consideration and development of individualized adaptations and alternative performance strategies to compensate for major skill deficits. Students with significant disabilities should, at least, participate in age-appropriate activities. This is true even when students cannot demonstrate the prerequisite skills traditionally associated with such activities, and even though others would ascribe them a developmental age of less than 5 years.

Throughout the country students with severe handicaps are now benefiting from school programs that use more functional and age-appropriate curriculum development strategies. In particular, in order for these strategies to focus on preparing these students as integral members of their communities, an initiative to develop *a new curriculum domain strategy* (Brown et al., 1979) has evolved. Basically, rather than using traditional skill areas as curricula domains (e.g., fine motor, gross motor, self-care, communication, functional academics), the lifespace domains of vocational, domestic, recreational/leisure, and general community functioning are used. With this approach, curricular considerations can be comprehensive, and skills can be developed and, when necessary, adapted (Baumgart et al., 1982) to meet the functioning needs and requirements associated with these lifespace areas. These initiatives also led to an expanded need to secure the active involvement of parents and others in selecting and evaluating educational objectives (Brown et al., 1979).

Where to Teach. The utilization of functional and age-appropriate curriculum strategies and the curriculum domain strategy has led educators and consumers to reevaluate current instructional location strategies. Specifically, the question now being asked is: Where should instruction occur? (Falvey, 1986). There is a growing consensus that there are two answers to this question, each associated with a different major initiative. First, in order for students with severe handicaps and their nondisabled age peers to learn to tolerate, accept, and interact with each other, instruction should be given on public school campuses throughout the country. *School integration*, the movement of students from isolated, segregated schools, wings, and trailers onto campuses where their nondisabled age peers learn, represents a major and substantial best practice (Certo, Haring, and York, 1984). The importance of using school campuses to teach interaction skills so that both groups will be prepared to live in the same neighborhoods, eat in the same restaurants, and work in the same businesses, cannot be underscored. Although this issue continues to be controversial, each year more students with severe handicaps are given the opportunity to attend schools with their nondisabled peers. School segregation must end (Association for Persons with Severe Handicaps, 1979).

Second, there is a growing consensus that, in addition to instruction occurring on integrated school campuses, direct and systematic instruction should also be provided in the normalized environments in which students will live, work, and play after school hours, on weekends, and as adults. This has been referred to as *community-based instruction*, community-referenced instruction, or, more recently, *community-intensive instruction* (Falvey, 1986; Sailor et al., 1986).

A wide variety of community environments is now being considered viable extensions of the classroom. The idea of community environments as classrooms goes well beyond the simple notion of a field trip. Rather, when a community environment is selected for instructional use, it is important that individualized objectives, teaching procedures, and measurement strategies be specified and used as fundamental program components (Pumpian, Shepard, and West, 1986). Each selected community environment should be used in a systematic, ongoing manner in order to:

1. Identify critical activities and skills required to function there effectively

2. Design individualized instructional programs to teach students to meaningfully engage in those activities.

This initiative has had a direct impact of vocational training. A growing number of consumers, service providers, advocates, and employers are convinced that most individuals with severe handicaps are capable of performing meaningful work in nonsheltered vocational environments (Brown et al., 1983). Increasing numbers of agencies are providing supported employment services to adults with severe handicaps (Rusch, 1986. At the same time, school agencies are now charged with the responsibility of preparing students to work in the community and benefit from supported work services. The better prepared an individual is during school years, the more likely it is that:

1. She or he will transition from school into a community work placement.

2. Supported work services will be implemented efficiently and effectively. (Wehman, JASH, 1985)

Thus, community-intensive instruction is now regularly occurring within the vocational curriculum domain. Educators are now using actual businesses as extensions of their classrooms. The term *job-training stations* is used here to refer to a business environment that is used as an extension of the classroom. The teacher actually takes part of his or her class to the business and uses it on a regular basis for instruction.

Many school programs have developed a wide variety of job-training stations within their community. These stations are used to provide individualized job and job-related skill instruction to a student throughout his or her years in public instruction. For example:

- A student may be placed in one job station at age 12 for one hour per day and one day per week.

- Each year that student might be placed at a different station. Each year the number of hours per day and days per week would increase.

- When the student has four years left in school, specific transition planning occurs. Transition objectives would utilize data accumulated from all the training experiences in order to plan and actually place the graduating student into an integrated work environment.

The job-training station experiences provide concerned persons with the opportunity to:

1. Develop and assess vocational skills and interests in various types of jobs and job environments.

2. Identify areas of instructional needs.

3. Utilize and assess the efficacy of various training and supervising techniques.

4. Identify and teach the use of viable alternative performance strategies (Wilcox and Bellamy, 1982) and individualized adaptations (Baumgart et al., 1982).

5. Identify the kinds of support that would be necessary to maintain an individual in a particular job environment.

Data related to each of these items are critical for the development of individualized transition plans that will result in the actual movement of individuals from work training to work placement. The use of job-training stations in the community has not only been useful in teaching students valuable job and job-related skills but also in gaining the involvement of significant others who will be instrumental in planning, fostering, and otherwise making adult job placements a reality. Specifically, Pumpian, Shepard, and West (1986) identified the impact school community-based vocational instruction can have on:

1. Employers and employees

2. Parents, family, and other care providers

3. Other school and adult service providers

4. Funding agencies

5. The community at large

Promising Practices in Vocational Training

A Demonstration Transition Class. As previously emphasized, schools have the major responsibility for providing vocational training that will lead students from school into work environments and increase the likelihood that adult programs will be able to support that transition and placement. In 1984, the San Diego Unified School District in cooperation with San Diego State University applied for funding from the Office of Special Education and Rehabilitation Services (OSERS) in order to demonstrate promising instructional and transitional services. One of the outcomes of this effort was the establishment of a secondary age transition class operated by the school district and located on the campus of a continuing education community college. The class was designed to coordinate at least five major promising practices, including:

1. The heterogeneous grouping of students
2. The desegregation of students
3. The provision of functional and age-appropriate curriculum in natural environments
4. The transition of students into adult environments
5. The active involvement of parents and families

First, the class was designed to include students with a variety of severely handicapping conditions. The class consisted of students who were and were not verbal, were and were not ambulatory, were and were not self-feeding, were and were not toilet trained, and so on. Attempts were made to balance the class composition such that the teacher had students in the class who required various types of intervention. Some students required physical prompting to increase their level of participation; some students required systematic behavior management programs infused into their instructional programming in order to reduce and/or monitor aggressive/abusive/fleeting behaviors; and some students who had functional academic needs could learn from modeling and had instructional objectives that focused on independence more than partial participation. Currently, the age range of the twelve students in the program is 17 to 22 years. All twelve students can be classified as mentally retarded, six have moderate to severe levels of retardation, and six are in the severe to profound range of mental retardation. One of the students is also deaf, and three of the students also have severe degrees of cerebral palsy. A teacher and two instructional aides are assigned to the class. This staff allocation is based on the same formula used when grouping students homogeneously—which has resulted in a better staff-to-student ration for students who would be considered higher functioning and a worse staff-to-student ratio for students with more significant challenges.

The second main focus of the demonstration class is related to the district's overall commitment to the desegregation of classes from isolated sites and the movement of students to age-appropriate campuses. Since this class consists of students who are mostly 18 to 22, it is located on a continuing education campus. As a part of each student's educational program, instructional strategies have been designed to increase appropriate interactions between students and their nondisabled peers.

These interactions primarily take place in the hallways, library, cafeteria, grounds, and office rather than in mainstreamed academic classes. In addition, interactions are facilitated between the students in this class and adults enrolled in the occupational skills training program, which also uses this campus. The close proximity of these two programs facilitates transition planning efforts.

Third, the class has been used by the district to help develop and demonstrate functional curricula. Each student has objectives in domestic, vocational, community, and recreation/leisure curriculum areas. Each student has a balanced mix of both school and community-based instruction. Each of the student's weekly schedules includes time spent in a vocational environment. One of the students has a paid job. Seven are registered as volunteers and four are in nonpaid training situations. Seeking paid positions for each student is a part of each student's transition plan. In addition, students receive instruction in a variety of other natural environments. The classroom provides the opportunity to simulate and to provide additional practice and other skill instruction that supplements, but does not replace, instruction in the natural environment.

Fourth, the district has used this class to help develop and demonstrate transition planning and programming. Since the ages of the students vary from 17 to 22, only a few students leave the class each year. As students get closer to this last year of school, efforts intensify to develop a work placement that could continue after leaving school. This effort is based on previously demonstrated interests and abilities of each student and on his or her success with various adaptation strategies, on the aspirations and concerns expressed by family members, and on the communication of this information to adult service providers willing to support the transition and job placement process. Already we have seen a direct correlation between students successfully supported in the adult program (which will be described in the next section) and those who have left the school program with some sort of a job placement intact. In fact, this has been a significant variable in the individual's "level of functioning."

Fifth, and finally, this class has supported the involvement of a parent facilitator in order for the district to develop and demonstrate improved coordination between families and schools, and the development of functional and transitional programming. This parent facilitator: (1) has become more knowledgeable in curriculum development, vocational training, and transitional issues; (2) has catalogued aspirations and concerns that have been voiced by other parents and families; and (3) has assisted in identifying and providing training and family support needs and services.

Examples of Vocational Training Provided Through the Transition Class Although the disabled students in the transition class receive instruction in a wide variety of natural community environments and activities, the primary emphases, due to their age, are on vocational training and the transition of students into a job situation and on the identification of an adult program that will provide necessary support to those students after they leave school. Currently, six vocational job sites are being used by the students. Since the students are enrolled in school, objectives are written to increase the likelihood that their participation at those sites will lead to a successful job situation in the future. Some of the students have now demonstrated their ability to function independently of instructors and under the supervision provided by employers and coworkers on the job. Other students require more direct hands-on instruction by the teacher, and in some cases total hands-on instruction. The six current job sites include the following. Three students are placed at the Pacific movie theater in preemployment training, and one of these has become an employee of the theater. Three students are receiving training at a public library, one at a Travelodge Hotel, one at a preschool, three students at the Department of Motor Vehicles, and one student at the community college. Sites are selected on the basis of geographic location, local job market trends, and in order to expose students to a variety of situations.

CASE STUDY: Pacific Center Three Cinema

Pacific Center Three Cinema is one of the work sites used. This site has been used for the last two years for both nonpaid training as well as competitive job placement. Although their shifts differ, three school-age students and one student from an adult program are involved at the site. Each student has individualized goals for the work, and two students, Robert and Max, now function more independently of their school supervisors. Robert and Max are both employed. Under a traditional classification system, they would be considered trainably mentally retarded. They have now learned to take a city bus from school to work and from work to home. Their job includes stocking the snack bar, getting ice and condiments, taking tickets at the door, and helping work behind the snack bar counter. Their goals are to increase the amount of time they spend at work, unsupported by school staff; to tell time related to beginning and ending their shift; and to increase their interaction with coworkers and their functioning through the supervision of theater staff.

David is another student at the theater; he is involved in a nonpaid training situation. He is nonverbal, has no academic skills, and has learned to use a picture communication system to communicate and follow a sequence of skill responsibilities. Although he still has a teacher on-site, he no longer requires constant supervision. He is learning to get on and off the city bus without physical prompting and to follow a picture sequence card to complete his job skills, which include getting ice, sweeping, cleaning seat backs, and help take tickets at the door. In addition, his communication book is being organized in order to increase interaction with coworkers. Jamie is the fourth student and a trainee at the theater. She will be described in more detail below.

Each of the four students works three days a week. Max and Robert each work a four-hour shift, and David and Jamie receive training under the supervision of their teachers for two hours. The situation provides the opportunity for staff, while working with the trainees, to identify and provide additional support as necessary to the two independent workers. This process has facilitated coordination of supervision between school staff and the theater manager.

Jamie is a student trainee at the theater along with David. The schedules of these two trainees overlap with those of Robert, the other student in the class, who is employed, and Max, who is enrolled in the adult program. The more independent performance of Max and Robert and the now semi independ-ability of David allows more individualized attention to be directed toward Jamie. Jamie currently requires hands-on instruction to complete her job tasks. Although she is ambulatory, she has a very unsteady gait and poor balance due to cerebral palsy and she is nonverbal. Jamie has been ascribed a level of profound mental retardation with an unmeasurable I.Q. Her developmental age has been estimated to be between three and seven months. Her records show a long list of aberrant behavior, including pinching, grabbing everything, mouthing and eating objects, and making inappropriate noises. Her records, prior to entering the community college class last year, indicate little if any instructional progress; in fact, a great deal of her time has apparently been spent in a beanbag chair, mouthing plastic, nonbreakable plates. This has been accepted due to her almost complete noncompliant behavior, and to reduce the likelihood that she would chew and/or swallow more dangerous objects. As a function of her environment at the theater job-training position, she takes a city bus to and from the site and is learning to clean video games, bathroom counters, and theater seat backs. For the first time, Jamie is being required and prompted to use a picture communication card to begin to give her a way of communicating with others in a more appropriate way. At the beginning of the year she required total physical guidance "motoring" through each of these activities. Although she still requires close staff monitoring, she has begun to carry her cleaning supplies without physical prompts at each job area and to clean the seat backs with only partial physical prompting. That is, Jamie has demonstrated progress. There are ways to meaningfully involve Jamie in the theater, and her involvement there necessitates a staff member's presence. In turn, this staff member is able to provide more constant support to each of the other, more independent students and workers. Jamie no longer sits in a beanbag chair chewing on plastic plates. Over the next three years Jamie will receive more training in other work environments. Her transition plan will incorporate information on her skill gains and support needs such that she will continue to function and be supported in an integrated work environment. Examples of promising new practices in adult services, which Jamie will hopefully benefit from in the future, are reviewed in the next section.

ADULT SERVICES

The Continuum of Adult Services

The whole premise of adult day services originated on, and is still intended to focus on, moving people into competitive employment. Over the past several decades different service options and funding agencies have evolved and been used in an attempt to move people into competitive employment. Over time, these service options and funding agencies have been put together in such a way that a continuum of services has been proposed. This current continuum of adult services represents a major attempt to meet the employment needs of adults with disabilities. However, as will be described here, this attempt has many identifiable shortcomings.

Competitive Employment For adults who appear, or have been assessed, to be most ready and most capable of working independently in the community, services are provided by the Department of Vocational Rehabilitation in the form of competitive employment programs and services. These competitive employment services have been designed to be time-limited. That is, after job placement is made, services soon end. The vocational rehabilitation counselor writes an individualized written rehabilitation plan (an IWRP), which delineates the services that need to be provided in order to employ the individual. The Department of Rehabilitation services were originally designed to assess, train, and place a person in a working situation and then, with minimal follow-up, end the services. It was anticipated and expected that, at that point, the individual would be independently, competitively employed. While this has proved successful for many adults with disabilities, those with more substantial disabilities typically have not been able to maintain their employment. Those with the most substantial disabilities were never considered eligible for such competitive employment services. This consideration was reasonable since most adults with substantial disabilities, by definition, require some level of ongoing support. The rehabilitation system was not designed to provide long-term support. As a result, adults with severe handicaps have traditionally not been served in programs receiving federal dollars from the Department of Rehabilitation.

Sheltered Workshops: The Beginning of the Readiness Continuum In the early part of the twentieth century, Samuel Howe established the first sheltered workshop in the United States. Howe, who was interested in persons with visual impairment, conceptualized the sheltered workshop as a place to take persons who were not "job ready" and there provide, in the sheltered setting, the type of training and experience needed to get them job ready. In fact, many vocational rehabilitation counselors, via the IWRP, have purchased the services of workshops to develop job readiness skills in their clients. Although some of these clients, typically those who were not developmentally disabled, demonstrated movement into competitive employment settings within a reasonably short period of time, many with more substantial disabilities did not. Since rehabilitation services were intended to be limited in duration, most states have had to look to additional funding sources for clients who have become extended employees of the workshops. One of the typical funding sources is a state agency that coordinates various federal and state funds. For example, in the state of California, the Department of Habilitation's major mission, up until very recently, was the funding and monitoring of sheltered workshop services.

In summary, sheltered workshops are a major component of the adult service continuum. Workshops have been able to provide services to individuals who require long-term support with better staff-to-client ratios than those available in competitive employment programs sponsored by rehabilitation monies. Nonetheless, workshops are segregated, "for-the-handicapped," environments. Numerous studies have shown that skills are often not learned, substantial wages are often not earned, and normalization principles fail to be realized in segregated environments (Bellamy et al., 1982; Brown et al., 1983). Resources have not resulted in their intended outcomes. The purpose of the sheltered workshop to prepare people to go into competitive employment has been grossly inefficient. Those who continue to believe that workshops represent an appropriate placement have a value system that supports the notion of readiness. Those who continue to believe that workshops represent an appropriate placement have a value system that supports the notion that if you are not "job ready," in a traditional sense, you should be segregated from the rest of the work force. As will be discussed later, supported employment is intended to serve as an alternative to "segregated readiness" services.

The Continuum Grows: Activity Centers Over the past twenty years the adult continuum has grown in many places in the country. California, for example, recognized the fact that many adults with real substantial disabilities were not even being accepted into sheltered workshop programs. After they completed school, they stayed home, were institutionalized, sat on waiting lists, put considerable pressure on their families, and represented a tremendous waste of financial and human resources. Many states still do nothing for those adults; that is, they remain at home, they go to institutions, they represent a waste of twenty-one years of public school programming. The state of California, many years ago, passed legislation titled the Lanterman Act. Basically, the

Lanterman Act states that every adult with developmental disabilities has a right to adult services. Massachusetts has passed transition legislation. More states are going to have to pass similar laws mandating supported services for adults in order to prevent the waste of human lives and public dollars.

In states that offer or mandate adult services, sheltered workshop and work activity programs have grown. However, these programs continue to set entrance criteria such that adults with more extensive severe disabilities are not enrolled. That is, sheltered workshops are for clients who are not ready for competitive employment. Clients who are not ready for sheltered workshops are placed in a variety of "recreational," "behavior," and "skill-building" programs designed to get clients ready to move into the workshop, in order to get clients ready to move into competitive employment! In California, we call these places day treatment activity centers (D.T.A.C.).

Thus, the continuum of adult services has grown on the concept of readiness. If an individual is not ready for competitive employment, he or she is placed in a sheltered workshop. If the individual is not ready for sheltered workshops, he or she placed in an activity center. Funding for activity centers is typically coordinated by another state agency—for example, in the state of California, the State Department of Developmental Services. Activity centers usually have better staff-to-client ratio than workshops. Further, funding for clients is not time-limited. Unfortunately, however, activity centers have been no more successful in moving people upward through the continuum than workshops, and as a result they have provided long-term segregated nonwork experiences for thousands of adults across the country.

The Continuum Keeps Growing As long as our system of adult services is based on readiness, we will continue to find people who are not ready for a service. Thus, not only are workshop clients not ready for competitive employment, and activity center clients not ready from sheltered employment but there is another group of people who are not ready for activity center employment. As a result, we have needed to add to the adult service continuum. We have added on various programs called various things in various states. In California, they are called adult developmental centers (A.D.C). These A.D.C.'s are supposed to prepare people for activity centers so they can get ready to go to the workshop so then can get ready to go out into the real world. Unfortunately, most people do not move out of this A.D.C system either. Many have lost sight of the original purpose of this continuum of services. Now we question whether, in fact, it is a continuum. It does not move people back into community businesses. On that basis, it does not work. Some people would argue it does work because these people just could not be in more normalized settings. But there is another explanation: that is, you cannot segregate to integrate. You cannot experience nonwork in order to learn work; you cannot continue to group people homogeneously and expect to have the resources to meet needs. Adult developmental centers do provide resources for an extensive, long-term service delivery system. However, people have remained segregated, and they have not learned to engage in activities either appropriate to their age or in environments in which their peers function.

It does not matter whether such a continuum has four service options or eight (e.g., a sheltered workshop program, and advanced developmental center program, work activity program, and so on). The continuum is based on work readiness—but the system has failed to make people more job ready; thus, the system has failed to integrate adults with significant disabilities. The system does recognize that people with significant disabilities often require access to services that are extensive, intensive, and/or longitudinal. However, until recently, the system did not recognize that such services should be or could be offered within the context of meaningful activities in integrated environments.

Promising Practices in in Adult Services

Refocusing of Resources: Alternatives to Readiness Many years ago, the continuum of segregated day environments was the best answer for how to meet the needs of an ever-increasing number of adults with disabilities. More adults were living longer, leaving integrated school programs, residing in community residences, and were proportionally represented in the "baby boom." Many of these programs met some very necessary immediate needs. A system was built based on helping people get ready to be integrated. In 1950, there were a handful of workshop and activity center programs. Now over 5,000 exist in the country. A huge financial investment has been incurred. However, the system has proved to be ineffective in major ways, and programs goals have not been realized. Thus, the 1980s has become a time to grow, to change, to analyze the system's shortcomings, and to look at different ways of utilizing resources in order to realize our goals.

Supported employment, as a concept, is an alternative to this segregated readiness continuum. The concept challenges providers to take the resources that have been used to segregate people and use them instead to integrate them. Through this concept, all the ways an individual is not "job ready" are identified, and then existing resources are channeled to provide "support" so as to compensate for those deficits. However, the support must be in an integrated work environment, must promote integration in that environment, must involve performing real work, and must be associated with a fair compensation system (Rusch, 1986).

There are many models for: developing new supported work service vendors; converting existing activity centers and workshops into supported work service providers; and utilizing and coordinating resources from several funding sources. Some supported programs report tremendous cost savings compared to service in the old system. Some report the need for increases during startup, with cost savings realized over time; and some programs report taking the *same* resources and using them to integrate rather than segregate. New models, ideas, and demonstrations are evolving daily.

What is clear is that there are still people who are not "job ready" but who are, nevertheless, working and integrated and, in many cases, at less cost to the taxpayer. It is also clear that demonstrations of integrated employment have included persons with severe and profound multiple handicaps. Such employment options appear to depend *more* on the way client caseloads are grouped; the quality of the trainers; the creativity and commitment of the program and of past educational efforts; and *less* on the biological limitations of an adult. It is clear that there are people functioning productively in integrated work environments who have "developmental twins" restricted to segregated adult development centers. It is clear that quality service programs have generated a level of interest, commitment, and enthusiasm among families, employers, and employees that has made real work, in real-work environments, a more accepted and expected outcome of educational, transitional, and adult programs. And it is clear that when an adult with severe disabilities does receive adequate support in a real-work environment, he or she is in the best place to learn how to interact, produce, and be accepted as an important and valued member of our society.

Employment support services are provided by various agencies and supported by various funding agencies, usually on an individual client basis, called a fee-for-service. For example, an agency such as the Association for Retarded Citizens: (1) can be reimbursed by the Department of Rehabilitation for placing a client in competitive employment; (2) can operate a sheltered workshop utilizing monies from another state agency via a vendorized fee-for-service agreement; and (3) can operate an activity center or an adult development center by establishing a vendorized agreement with a different state agency. Agencies that have traditionally been reimbursed for services and/or entered vendorized agreement with state agencies are now attempting to use these same resources to provide integrated employment options. In addition, new profit and nonprofit agencies, as well as generic agencies that have in the past not provided work services, are also entering into fee-for-service and other vendorized agreements with various state agencies.

One of the most exciting and promising practices is a program's use of resources from more than one agency in order to provide vocational and/or community-integrated support service. For example, one agency may use the resources of the Department of Rehabilitation to fund the actual placement of an individual and then use the resources of another agency, say, the Department of Developmental Services, to provide the long-term support the individual needs in that job placement. In addition, the utilization of resources from various funding sources has allowed some agencies to develop caseloads representing a heterogeneous group of individuals, some of whom in the past would have been placed in developmental centers, others in activity centers, others in workshops, and others even in competitive employment programs. An example of one of these programs, including case histories is provided in a later section.

Employment Services Provided by an Adult Service Vendor One example of a new initiative in adult service for persons with severe handicaps is the Occupational Skills Training program in San Diego, California. Occupational Skills Training (OST) is a collaborative effort between the San Diego Community College District Foundation, Inc., and the San Diego Community College District. The program combines and utilizes resources and funds from a variety of sources in a unique and flexible way. The San Diego Community College District Foundation, Inc., has entered a vendorized agreement with the San Diego Regional Center and with the State Department of Developmental Services. The San Diego Community College District provides resources via adult education classes. Although the purpose, policies, and practices of the foundation and the community college differ, the intention is that they overlap through OST and that they combine resources in order to design and implement individual service plans that meet each individual client's total lifespace needs. The collaborative effort between these agencies is an attempt to meet four major goals:

1. To offer functional age-appropriate services to adults with severe handicaps in a nonexclusionary manner—that is, there are no entrance criteria based on an individual's skill ability

2. To focus those functional and age-appropriate services on supporting persons in individually determined work placements and settings

3. To support each individual's integration into the community at large

4. To meet other independent living needs to be determined on an individual basis

OST provides individuals the opportunity for a six-hour program day. Three of the six hours, or an average of fifteen hours per week, are funded by vendorization or funding by the Department of Developmental Services utilizing monies in an amount similar to that which would be provided to support a traditional day treatment activity center. This vendorization is administered by the San Diego Regional Center through the San Diego Community College District Foundation, Inc., which is a nonprofit organization. The major focus of the vendorization portion of the program is on the development of skills, and provision of support, necessary to allow and enhance each client to function productively in an integrated work environment. A component of this focus is the development of related skills that are necessary and required to allow and enhance community integration in general.

The remaining three program hours, or fifteen hours per week, are provided by a second funding source—the San Diego Community College District—in the form of continuing education classes. Classes generate revenue based on average daily attendance, just as do other classes offered to adults with and without disabilities throughout the community college system. Each individual is enrolled in continuing education classes until full-time employment is available. The major focus of the community college classes is on independent living skills that supplement the client's work placement. One major component of this focus is the development of related skills in domestic, community, and recreation/leisure areas.

In their joint concern with enhancing community integration, the foundation and district program focus overlap. One of the problems traditionally associated with sheltered workshops has been the competition between meeting vocational and other independent living needs. The advantage of this model is that vendorization is allowed to focus on vocational needs while a separate funding source focuses on other independent living needs. In this way neither agency bears a larger service cost, yet the recourses to each individual have nearly doubled.

Individuals are referred to the Occupational Skills Training program by regional center case managers. This process has been facilitated by school transition teams who look to OST as a viable adult service provider. Individuals are referred to the program who in the past would have been referred to the full continuum of adult service options. That is, some of the clients would have been referred to sheltered workshop programs, others to work activity programs, others to day treatment activity centers, and still others to adult developmental centers. The logic behind utilizing a heterogeneous grouping is similar to that which was described for the school program: (1) It provides better staff-to-client ratios for those who would be considered higher functioning, and at the same time, (2) allows for inclusion of students with the most significant challenges—those who in the past would have been excluded from programs that focus on integration and meaningful vocational participation. Other than ensuring that the makeup of any caseload reflects this heterogeneity, the only other priorities for acceptance into the program are:

1. Individuals must have been involved in community-based training in school.

2. The family/guardian must have a commitment to services delivered in the community and integrated vocational environments.

3. The individual's residence must be in close proximity to the program.

4. There must be no history of excessive unexplained absences from past programs.

Given this heterogeneous grouping and funding support from multiple agencies, the program is able to provide a much richer staff-to-client ratio than most traditional work programs, and do so without additional costs to specialized service departments. Specifically, the combined resources of the two programs provide for an average staff-to-client ratio of approximately 1 to 4 including two full-time professional staff positions. Unlike traditional programs, there is no facility to support program activities. However, since the program is associated with the Community College District, space in various college campuses and industrial sites can serve as central meetingplaces. In this way, as the program grows, a large number of individuals will not have to be congregated in one particular environment. Currently, nineteen individuals receive services from OST. They represent a wide range of disabling conditions from moderate to profound as well as a variety of socioeconomic and cultural backgrounds and living arrangements. None of the individuals were involved in nonsheltered employment prior to their enrollment. Eleven were in workshop programs and/or work crews, three were in activity centers, and five were in no programs. The program officially began in March 1986, and at the present time, in addition to their continuing education classes, fourteen of the nineteen individuals are receiving support in integrated vocational environments, five of these receiving minimum wage or better. Given the length of time the program has been in operation, and the fact that many individuals were enrolled with no previous training and/or vocational experience, particular emphasis is now being placed on ensuring that all clients are placed in integrated vocational environments and become employees of those businesses.

Also, given the diversity of individuals, a number of support options are being provided. These are:

1. Continuous on-site support. This is support that requires a program staff member to be on-site the entire time the client is there. In these situations, it is assumed that other individuals may be working in other areas of the business who require one of the forms of other support listed here.

2. Intermittent daily support. This is support provided to individuals who are now capable of working without the direct

supervision of OST staff for short periods of time. The staff contact may occur anywhere from one to five times a day depending on individual need. This daily contact allows staff to provide support at targeted times, spot-check work rate and quality, and coordinate planning with employers and other coworkers.

3. Intermittent weekly support. This level of support is provided to individuals who can work without direct supervision of OST staff for one to five days but still require some level of weekly contact.

4. Intermittent monthly, or as needed, support. Although no clients in OST are now at this level of independence, it is anticipated that as the natural supervision available at a work site is fostered and relationships between other coworkers are enhanced, some clients will be able to significantly reduce the support provided by OST staff.

In all cases, support needs in the community at large and the work environment in particular are individually determined. In no case will a level of support be time determined, nor will individuals who continue to require continuous support be faded or removed from the program. In this way, and unlike other supported employment programs, OST has been designed to not necessarily result in a cost savings (although it is expected that it will), but is designed to take the same resources that would have been used to segregate people and instead integrate them without additional up-front costs.

An additional resource that may be considered in order to provide the program different funding is a state of California habilitation vendorization. The purpose of this vendorization is to provide the program flexibility when particular workers begin to require supervision that could be billed on an hourly rather than daily basis. Furthermore, given the comprehensive set of services afforded to individuals by the program (that is, job placement, training, support, and other lifespace needs), it may be possible to convince individual Department of Rehabilitation counselors that traditionally excluded individuals can now be considered feasible for employment. The advantage of this would be the additional resources that could be provided by the rehabilitation counselors in the program to assist in initial job placement and training. After the initial period of support, depending on the extra service needs and type of job placement, long-term support would be continued via the activity center or habilitation vendorization. Using such combined resources from multiple agencies allows a wide range of individuals to be included, regardless of the number of hours they work, the intensity of their service needs, or the nature of their job placement.

CASE STUDY: Michael

Michael, a 22-year-old individual with autistic-like tendencies, represents an adult worker who requires continuous on-site supervision. He has been ascribed an I.Q. score of 24. Due to his extensive hearing loss and lack of verbal skills, Michael requires the use of a picture communication system. Despite his history of aggressive and self-abusive behaviors, Michael participates in a job-share work program with two other coworkers at a Travelodge Hotel for two hours a day, five days a week. His job sequence includes walking to work, locating the cart and rooms to be cleaned, making the bed(s), cleaning the sink, and vacuuming. Michael's work goals are walking to work with his coworkers without running away, utilizing a picture sequence card independently to complete his job routine, using a vending machine for break skills, and increasing his proximity from the direct supervision of training staff. While his training objectives are being worked on, OST staff continue to seek a paid position for him.

CASE STUDY: Andy

Andy, a 24-year-old who has Down's syndrome, previously required the continual support of staff at his job site. He has been ascribed an I.Q. score of 32. Andy began his work training at Courthouse Racquetball Club as a paid employee at minimum wage. Andy works ten hours a week. During the initial stages of his work training, Andy required the continual support of a staff member for mobility training from his residence to work in the morning and for job activity and sequence instruction. An augmented communication system has been designed to back up his unintelligible speech and to help him remember key sequences of his job routine. He is responsible for mopping ten racquetball courts and doing a variety of other janitorial-type jobs. At the completion of his work, Andy is free to use all the equipment within the facility that is not being used by the customers. Due to an expressed interest in learning how to use the nautilus equipment at work, a coworker has volunteered her work break to show Andy how to use the weights.

Andy now functions more effectively under supervision provided by his employer such that daily support from OST has been faded from continuous to intermittent. This not only allows for support staff to monitor Andy's work behavior at targeted times, while checking production rate and quality of work, but also allows for a more normal employer–employee relationship to develop. There is an ongoing effort to implement strategies that will further reduce the direct supervision provided to Andy such that he may, in the future, require only intermittent weekly or monthly support.

After Andy completes his daily job routine and use of equipment, he takes the bus he has learned to ride to an adult continuing education campus. There he continues to learn additional independent living and community integration skills to meet his individualized needs and expectations. This allows him to increase his social interactions and total lifespace opportunities.

Due to Andy's increased independence at his job site and his acceptance by his employer and coworkers, it is assumed that OST staff will, as noted, be able to further fade themselves to an intermittent weekly contact support system. At this point, habilitation services will be considered as an alternate funding source. This will allow OST support service to be billed on an hourly rather than daily basis.

SUMMARY

The intent of this chapter has been to emphasize that people with severe handicaps have the same needs as less disabled and nondisabled persons. We all have a need to live, work, and play as active members of our communities. But, although the needs are the same, the time, intensity, and duration of training and support service required by people with severe handicaps can differ significantly.

A major function of school training is to prepare students to function as active members of their community. As reviewed in this chapter, contemporary curriculum development strategies focus on vocational, recreational, domestic, and general community functioning. Actual community environments are being used for school instruction and, as a result, functional skills can be taught and the effectiveness of various adaptations, supervision, and support strategies can be evaluated. In the area of vocational training, the utilization of real businesses as classrooms has been highlighted as an exemplary practice. Through this program, preparation takes place in real environments and students learn functional skills while engaging in meaningful job and job-related activities.

As noted, a major role of school agencies is to prepare students for integrated adult life. In turn, the role of adult agencies is to provide services that support an individual's ability to live, work, and play as an active community member. A continuum of adult services has developed over the last few decades. This continuum represents an attempt to place people into segregated environments in order to make them "ready" to move into integrated adult environments. It is now being realized that, unfortunately, there are major flaws in this continuum approach. The programs and services described in this chapter are alternatives to services based on the notion of "readiness." They fall under the heading of "support services." When service delivery models are based on the notion of support, first people are placed in real work and community settings. Then agencies provide the support necessary to enhance an individual's meaningful involvement and interactions in those environments. Examples of programs that provide vocational support to adults with severe handicaps were given. Funding agencies, service providers, consumers, and the community at large are now interacting in new ways that are providing the flexibility necessary to creatively meet the many challenges involved in employing these citizens.

Persons with severe handicaps need some level of support in many aspects of their lives. We must now determine whether the services we provide will help individuals participate in meaningful and valued activities or whether we will perpetuate society's notion of the "eternal child." We must also determine whether we will use our resources to integrate individuals or whether we will use our resources to segregate and systematically exclude them from community environments. What is clear is that people with severe handicaps are citizens first and can benefit from involvement in, and contribute to the integrity of, our communities.

REFERENCES

Association for Persons with Severe Handicaps. (1979). Resolution on deinstitutionalization. Passed by Executive Board, Chicago, Illinois.

Baumgart, D., L. Brown, I. Pumpian, J. Nisbet, A. Ford, M. Sweet, R. Messina, and J. Schroeder. (1982). Principle of partial participation and individualized adaptations. *Journal of the Association for Persons with Severe Handicaps* 7(2), 17–22.

Bellamy, G.T., R.H. Horner, and D.P. Inman. (1979). *Vocational Habilitation of Severely Retarded Adults.* Baltimore: University Park Press.

Bellamy, G.T., J.S. Newton, N.M. LeBaron, and R.H. Horner. (1986). Toward lifestyle accountability in residential service for persons with mental retardation. Unpublished manuscript. University of Oregon, Specialized Training Programs, Eugene.

Bellamy, G.T., L.E. Rhodes, P.E. Bourbeau, and D.M. Mank. (1982). *Mental Retardation Services in Sheltered Workshops and Day Activity Programs: Consumer Outcomes and Policy Alternatives.* Eugene, Ore.: Center on Human Development.

Bellamy, G.T., L.E. Rhodes, B. Wilcox, J. Albin, R.H. Horner, J. Collins, and J. Turner. (1984). Quality and equality in employment for adults with severe disabilities. *Journal of the Association for Persons with Severe Handicaps 9,* 270–278.

Bradfield, R.H. (1970). Precision teaching—a useful technology for special education teachers. *Educational Technology 10*(8), 22–26.

Brown, L., K.V. Albright, A.U. Solner, B. Shiraga, P. Rogan, J. York, and P. Van Deventer. (1986). The Madison strategy for evaluating the vocational milieu of a worker with severe intellectual disabilities. Unpublished manuscript. University of Wisconsin and Madison Metropolitan School District, Madison.

Brown, L., M. Falvey, L. Vincent, N. Kaye, F. Johnson, P. Ferrara-Parrish, and L. Gruenewald. (1979). Strategies for generating longitudinal and age appropriate individual education plans. In L. Brown, M. Falvey, D. Baumgard, I. Pumpian, J. Schroeder, and L. Gruenewald (eds.), *Strategies for Teaching Chronological Age Appropriate and Functional Skills to Adolescent and Young Adult Severely Handicapped Students.* Vol. IX, Pt. 1, 30–60. Madison: Wis.: Madison Metropolitan School District.

Brown, L., B. Shiraga, A. Ford, S. Nisbet, P. Van Deventer, M. Sweet, J. York, and R. Loomis. (1983). Teaching severely handicapped students to perform meaningful work in nonsheltered vocational environments. In L. Brown, A. Ford, J. Nisbet, M. Sweet, B. Shiraga, J. York, R. Loomis, P. Van Deventer (eds.). *Educational Programs for Severely Handicapped Students.* Madison: University of Wisconsin and Madison Metropolitan School District. Pp. 1–100.

Certo, N., N. Haring, and R. York. (eds.). (1984). *Public School Integration of Severely Handicapped Students: Rational Issues and Progressive Alternatives.* Baltimore: Paul H. Brookes.

Falvey, M.A. (1986). *Community-Based Curriculum: Instructional Strategies for Students with Severe Handicaps.* Baltimore: Paul H. Brookes.

Falvey, M., L. Brown, S. Lyons, D. Baumgart, and J. Schroeder. (1980). Strategies for using cues and correction procedures. In W. Sailor, B. Wilcox, and L. Brown (eds.), *Methods of Instruction for Severely Handicapped Students.* Baltimore: Paul H. Brookes. Pp. 109–135.

Gaylord-Ross, R.J. and J.F. Holvoet. (1985). *Strategies for Educating Students with Severe Handicaps.* Boston: Little, Brown and Company. Pp. 125–145.

Gold, M.W. (1980). An alternative definition of mental retardation. In M.W. Gold, *Did I Say That?* Champaign, Ill.: Research Press Company. Pp. 145–150.

Horner, R.H., J. Sprague, and B. Wilcox. (1982). General case programming for community activities. In B. Wilcox and G.T. Bellamy (eds.). *Design of High School Programs for Severely Handicapped Students.* Baltimore: Paul H,. Brookes. Pp. 61–98.

Landesman-Dwyer, S., and G.P. Sackett. (1978). Behavioral changes in nonambulatory profoundly mental retarded individuals. In C.E. Meyers (eds.), *Quality of Life in Severely and Profoundly Mentally Retarded People: Research Foundations for Improvement.* Washington, D.C.: American Association on Mental Deficiency.

LaVigna, G.W., and A.M. Donnellan. (1986). *Alternatives to Punishment: Solving Behavior Problems with Non Adversive Strategies.* New York: Irvington Publishers.

Pumpian, I., H. Shepard, and E. West. (1986). Negotiating job training stations with employers. Manuscript submitted for publication.

Rehabilitation Act of 1973, P.L. 93–112, September 12, 1973. U.S. Code 29, amended 1978.

Rusch, F.R. (1986). *Competitive Employment Issues and Strategies.* Baltimore: Paul H. Brookes.

Sailor, W., A. Halvorson, J. Anderson, L. Goetz, K. Gee, K. Doering, and P. Hunt. (1986). Community intensive instruction. In N.R. Horner, L. Meyer, and H. Fredericks (eds.)., *Education of Learners with Severe Handicaps: Exemplary Service Strategies.* Baltimore: Paul H. Brookes.

Snell, M. (1982). Characteristics, education and habilitation of the profoundly mentally retarded. In P.T. Cegelka and H.J. Prehm (eds.), *Mental Retardation: From Categories to People.* Columbus, Ohio: Charles E. Merrill. Pp. 291–342.

Title 1, Elementary and Secondary Education Act of 1965, Public Law 89–10.

Van Etten, G.V., C. Arkel, and C. Van Etten. (1980). *The Severely and Profoundly Handicapped.* St. Louis: C.V. Mosby.

Wehman, P., and J. Kregel. (1985). A supported work approach to competitive employment of individuals with moderate and severe handicaps. *Journal of the Association for Persons with Severe Handicaps 10,* 311.

Wilcox, B., and G.T. Bellamy. (1982). *Design of High school Programs for Severely Handicapped Students.* Baltimore: Paul H. Brookes.

14 Vocational Education of Persons with Physical Handicaps

Jo-Ann Sowers, Chris Jenkins,
and Laurie Powers
Oregon Research Institute

The term *physical disability* covers an extremely wide and diverse range of disabilities, including cerebral palsy, spina bifida, spinal cord injuries, amputation, muscular dystrophy, arthritis, multiple sclerosis, and polio. Persons who experience any of these disabilities have one important thing in common—their ability to interact with or operate on the environment motorically is to some extent impaired. However, there are many critical differences among and between persons who experience these various disabilities that have important implications for the nature and type of vocational preparation and placement strategies that should be utilized. These differences include the usual onset of the disability, the extent to which the disability is progressive, and the type of other disabilities (e.g., visual, auditory, cognitive) that may accompany the physical disability. This chapter will not address the myriad of issues and strategies pertinent to the broad range of persons

*The authors wish to give credit to Dr. Dean Inman, who influenced much of our thinking with regard to the training of persons with neuromuscular disorders. We also want to thank Phil Bourbeau for his editing expertise and Karen Blais for her assistance in the preparation of this manuscript.

Preparation of this chapter was supported by Grant No. G008430016, awarded to Oregon Research Institute from the Office of Special Education and Rehabilitative Services, U.S. Department of Education. The opinions expressed herein do not necessarily reflect the position of policy of the U.S. Department of Education, and no official endorsement should be inferred.

who may be described as physically disabled. The purpose of this chapter is to discuss the critical issues unique to, and describe a set of strategies for the vocational preparation of, individuals who experience the disability called cerebral palsy. The reason for this focus is that this text is aimed at students who are training to be educators, and some educators may have an opportunity to work with individuals with a variety of physical disabilities (such as a spinal cord injury, arthritis). However, the most common physical disability experienced by students eligible for special education services is cerebral palsy.

PERSONS WHO EXPERIENCE CEREBRAL PALSY: A DESCRIPTION

Like all labels, the designation of "cerebral palsy" carries with it the false implication that a group of individuals is identical or at least highly similar in their abilities and deficits. In fact, this label, like all others, is intended to be only generally descriptive. The one common characteristic shared by persons who are labeled as having cerebral palsy is that they experience some degree of weakness, paralysis, or a decreased ability to execute or control motor movements as a result of damage to one or more part(s) of the brain before, during, or shortly after birth. Beyond this generic etiology, there is a tremendous amount of variation among individuals labeled as cerebral palsy in both the degree and type of motor movement limitation.

Three major classification systems are used to assist in describing these variations (Lindemann, 1981). The first identifies six different types on the basis of what form the motor movements take:

1. Spasticity—Muscles of the affected limbs are tight and held in a "fixed" position; there is usually a paucity of movement, and movements that can be made are frequently jerky due to muscle spasms.

2. Athetosis—Movements of the limbs are slow and twisting in nature, and there is a lack of postural stability.

3. Ataxia—Fine voluntary movements and gait lack coordination in spite of good sensory function and a lack of paralysis; ataxia usually appears in combination with spasticity, athetosis, or atonia.

4. Tremor—Hands, trunk, and head have slight to moderate shake, which is accentuated during movement.

5. Rigidity—Resembles severe spasticity, it is referred to as a "lead pipe phenomenon" due to the tightness of muscles and the difficulty in bending the limbs.

6. Atonia—Extreme flaccidity of muscles; the limbs are limp and the person may not be able to move them at all.

7. Mixed—Any combination of the movement disorders just described.

A second descriptive classification emphasizes the location and number of limbs involved. *Hemiplegia* connotes that one arm and one leg on one side of the body are involved. When all four limbs are involved (although the legs usually more so), the person is classified as *diplegic*. *Quadriplegic* describes a person who has all four limbs involved to a fairly equivalent degree. *Paraplegic* labels the person with leg involvement only. Although such descriptors as "John experiences severe spastic quadriplegic cerebral palsy" may be useful in giving a very general idea of what the person is like physically, the labels provide no useful information about the actual degree of motor control, the functional skills that the individual has mastered, or the person's general level of competence.

In addition to movement difficulties, persons with cerebral palsy frequently experience concomitant disabilities, including mental retardation, vision and hearing loss, epilepsy, and/or speech disorders. These individuals also often have difficulty eating and drinking, as well as controlling drooling. Again, as with motor impairments, the extent to which a particular individual experiences any of these related problems and the degree of each problem varies greatly. The following are descriptions of five individuals who illustrate the extensive variability of persons who experience cerebral palsy. Jane experiences severe quadriplegic athetosis. She has no cognitive disabilities and is mainstreamed into regular classes. Her means of mobility is an electric wheelchair, which she drives using a joystick mounted at her chin. She has no functional use of her hands, a small amount of intelligible speech, but no vision or hearing loss. Steve experiences spastic hemiplegia, in addition to mild mental retardation. He is able to walk short distances but uses a three-wheeled scooter device for longer distances. He has good use of one hand, but is unable to utilize the other. Although he cannot speak, he has no vision or hearing problems. However, he has difficulty eating, drinking, and controlling his drooling. Sara experiences spastic quadriplegic cerebral palsy and has a moderate to severe degree of cognitive disability. She is able to ambulate with a walker and has some functional use of both hands. She has no vision loss. She can speak, although it is difficult to understand her. She also has some difficulty controlling her drooling. Mack is a 14-year-old student with severe spastic quadriplegia. In addition to his physical disability, Mack has a severe visual handicap that limits his ability to read. He operates an electric wheelchair with a joystick mounted at his right hand. Mack's speech is intelligible although somewhat slow. He experiences no cognitive disability. Jim experiences a mixed form of cerebral palsy that combines spastic diplegia with tremor. He, too, is able to operate an electric wheelchair by using a joystick mounted by his right hand. Jim experiences visual problems caused by tremor to the muscles surrounding his eyes. In addition to his visual and motoric disabilities, Jim experiences moderate mental retardation.

HISTORICAL PERSPECTIVE

Over the past two decades, much attention has been focused on the development of vocational training strategies and employment service models for persons with severe disabilities. A vocational training technology has emerged that has proven effective in training critical work and work-related skills. The power of this technology was first illustrated in sheltered work environments (Gold, 1973; Crosson, 1969; Martin and Pallotta, 1978; Bellamy, Horner, and Inman, 1979). More recently, the applicability of this technology has been successfully demonstrated in achieving what was once thought impossible—persons with severe disabilities working successfully and productively in competitive employment (Connis, Sowers, and Thompson, 1979; Rusch and Mithaug, 1980; Wehman, 1981). Motivated by these exciting illustrations of competence, vocational training technology has continued to evolve and expand to include techniques for increasing the degree of generalization (that is, carrying over skills learned in a training setting to the permanent employment setting), procedures to help ensure maintenance of skills when the disabled employee is no longer supervised by a special training staff person, strategies for analyzing complex jobs typical of competitive employment settings, and methods for approaching employers and convincing them to provide job opportunities for severely disabled persons. Finally, there has been the growing realization of the necessity for a spectrum of vocational options for persons with severe disabilities. As a result, program models such as work crews and enclaves have been successfully developed for use with this population (Bourbeau, 1985; Rhodes and Valenta, 1985).

After looking over the large body of literature describing both the vocational training technology and demonstrations of the vocational competence of severely disabled persons, it becomes readily apparent that individuals with physical disabilities such as cerebral palsy have, for the most part, not been represented. Rather, the focus of the effort up to this time has been directed almost exclusively at individuals whose disabilities are cognitive (that is, at persons labeled as experiencing mental retardation). There are a number of explanations as to why persons with physical disabilities have received so little attention with regard to vocational preparation and placement. First, there is a much smaller incidence of cerebral palsy than mental retardation in the population. It is estimated that there are 750,000 individuals in the United States with cerebral palsy compared to 6 million who experience mental retardation (Goldenson, 1978). Second, persons with cerebral palsy have typically had extremely high rates of institutionalization and have been among the last to be deinstitutionalized. Keiter (1979), in a survey of adults with cerebral palsy in Oregon, found that 60 percent were living in institutions. Third, those individuals who have not been institutionalized have had less access to community programs than persons with cognitive disabilities. A survey conducted by the State of Oregon Program for Developmental Disabilities Office (1983) found that 61 percent of individuals with cerebral palsy who were 17 years of age and older were receiving no educational or vocational services compared to 31 percent of persons with mental retardation. Fourth, those educational and vocational services that have been available for persons with cerebral palsy have typically been separate from those provided to the mainstream of developmentally disabled persons. Until recently, many children with cerebral palsy were educated at Easter Seals Society programs. Even today, the programs of United Cerebral Palsy provide sheltered work for a large majority of adults with cerebral palsy. This separation of services is also reflected in personnel preparation programs. Physical and occupational therapists are trained to work with physically disabled individuals while few special education teacher preparation courses provide any significant attention to methods of working with this disability group. In a very informal survey of the teachers in classrooms for students with severe disabilities in Eugene, Oregon, the majority indicated that they felt ill-prepared to work with students who had a significant physical disability.

THE NEED FOR INNOVATIVE PROGRAMS

The vast majority of persons with cerebral palsy have extremely limited vocational options after graduation from school. Few are given access to any vocational programs other than a sheltered workshop or work activity center, where the available work is not challenging, the pay is dismal, the opportunity for interaction with nondisabled persons limited, and the chance for movement out of the sheltered program and into a community-based job is highly unlikely.

It is clear that there is a need for research and program development efforts focused on the unique needs of persons with cerebral palsy that will lead to the development of strategies for preparing these persons for employment in nonsheltered environments. In fact, Virginia

Commonwealth University has begun this important work. The Vocations in Technology Project (Pietruski, et al., 1985) developed and implemented a program to train and place persons with cerebral palsy and mild mental retardation into clerical occupations. In addition, Sowers, Powers, and Jenkins (1986a) are currently conducting a project called the Oregon Transition to Employment Project, which is focused on similar goals.

The Oregon Transition to Employment Project

The purpose of the Oregon Transition to Employment Project (Sowers, Powers, and Jenkins, 1986a), a federally funded grant project, is to develop and implement a set of procedures that schools can use to better prepare those students with severe physical disabilities, such as cerebral palsy, to transition from school to community-based employment settings. The philosophy on which OTEP is founded is that all students, including those with severe physical disabilities, can work productively in nonsheltered community work settings if given proper preparation, opportunity, and the necessary supports. The OTEP model is currently being implemented in two school districts with a total of eighteen middle school and high school students who experience cerebral palsy. These students represent a broad range of intellectual functioning, including students with severe cognitive disabilities and those with normal intelligence. The project has identified four elements that are critical to the vocational preparation of students with severe physical disabilities. These elements, which define the OTEP model, are the following:

1. The work skills trained should be based on the types of jobs available in the local community that students with cerebral palsy can access if given preparation and support

2. Preparation must begin early and continue throughout the students' school careers

3. Only systematic, direct, and behaviorally based vocational instruction will ensure that the students learn to perform to their maximum potential

4. When necessary, adaptations are designed and utilized to assist a student in performing a task

The remainder of this chapter will be devoted to describing each of these program components

IDENTIFYING WORK SKILLS TO TRAIN

One of the most critical steps in developing a vocational preparation and placement program, whether for school-aged or adult severely disabled persons, is to identify those jobs in which there is a high likelihood of employment. Once this is accomplished, the program can focus its training efforts on the specific skills required by the jobs. This "criterion referencing" approach to curriculum or program development has proven effective in preparing many severely disabled persons for a spectrum of community-based situations, including work—especially when compared to traditional approaches that taught generic work-related skills that frequently had little similarity to the skills required in a student's local job market (Brown et al., 1979).

Two criteria should be used when selecting the jobs that students with physical disabilities will be trained in. First, there must be evidence that there will be a fair number of these jobs available when the student graduates. This, of course, will vary from community to community. For example, in Portland, Oregon, there is a large amount of manufacturing work available. However, in Eugene, Oregon, a medium-sized city, very little manufacturing is present. Thus, the wisdom of focusing a training program on the manufacturing-related skills varies greatly between the two locations. Sometimes this variation occurs within a single community over time. Areas of business strength often fluctuate. This has been illustrated by the dramatic decline in the timber industry and the jobs available in that industry in the Northwest during the last five years. So, in addition to looking at current areas of high employment, it is important to obtain employment forecast data. Most city and county employment offices routinely compile current and future forecast data related to employment trends.

The second criterion to be applied when selecting job areas in which to train students is the extent to which the person with a physical disability such as cerebral palsy will be able to adequately perform the required tasks. In many communities, opportunities in service-related occupations such as dishwashers and motel maids are abundant. In fact, the vast majority of the jobs trained and obtained for persons with intellectual disabilities have been in these types of occupations. It is clear, however, that few persons with cerebral palsy would be able to perform such jobs. Generally, jobs with low physical demand requirements would be best suited for these individuals. However, those persons who experience both a substantial degree of motor control problems and some cognitive disabilities are particularly challenging with respect to job identification because physically demanding jobs are not appropriate due to the motor difficulties, while most sedentary jobs usually require more sophisticated cognitive and academic skills than these individuals possess. Possible exceptions are assembly line tasks.

In attempting to identify jobs to target for training for the students in OTEP, project staff first gathered employment forecast data and learned that there were two job areas in the Eugene/Springfield, Oregon, area with high long-term forecasts: service and clerical. The service area was eliminated because of the physically demanding nature of these jobs.

Next, the staff spent several weeks visiting a large number and variety of businesses with clerical positions. Of course, almost every business has at least a small number of clerical staff. Banks, motels, department stores, hospitals, and insurance offices were among the variety of businesses visited. During these visits, employers were questioned about the specific tasks that were performed by the clerical staff, the number of staff hours devoted to them, and the actual physical and cognitive requirements of each task. Employers were also asked to indicate the extent to which they would be open to hiring a person with a severe physical disability to perform various clerical tasks in the company. Many visits also included direct observations of staff performing their work. Based on these visits, the OTEP staff identified five tasks for training:

1. Computer data entry
2. Photocopying
3. Mailing/packaging
4. Phone answering
5. Filing

EARLY AND ONGOING WORK PREPARATION

After the tasks and the specific requirements of each are identified, a school program will have the necessary foundation for preparing students to move successfully from school to a job in the community. It is important to remember that although an attempt has been made to target those jobs that students with cerebral palsy will have some chance of obtaining, there will still be significant barriers presented both by these students' disabilities and society's attitudes. Consequently, work training that will give these students a "head start" cannot begin too soon, and must continue throughout their school careers.

Elementary School

Elementary school teachers can contribute to the future vocational success of a physically disabled person in many ways. Probably the most important of these is instilling in the student the expectation that he or she will work as an adult and a belief in the importance of that work. Here are a few suggestions for accomplishing this.

Identify and create a number of "jobs," which will be assigned to each of the students in the class on a rotating basis These jobs should be short in duration, and (as much as possible) require the student to leave the classroom and interact with nondisabled students and staff. A number of these jobs should be selected so that a child with a severe physical disability will be able to perform them as independently as possible. Children take a great deal of pride in doing things by themselves. This desire to be independent too often is not nurtured in children with disabilities. These "jobs" should also be selected so as to be highly reinforcing so that the students will view work in a positive light. A few examples of the type of clerically related jobs that can be assigned to an elementary-aged student with a physical disability are: (1) taking messages from the teacher to the office or from the office to a number of different teachers, (2) picking up and/or delivering photocopy orders, (3) actually using the photocopy machine to make copies for the teachers, and (4) placing announcements in teachers' mailboxes. In many elementary schools, the older students are permitted to spend a period of the day assisting in the office, library, or school store. Teachers should advocate strongly in order to gain opportunities for their students with severe physical disabilities. Either the teacher, an aide, or a peer tutor can assist the student in the assigned duties.

Make the subject of work an ongoing topic of discussion. Discuss each child's job assignment in front of the class, describe what the child is doing, and how well she or he is performing. In other words, attempt to create a clear sense of how much you feel work is a valued activity.

Discuss with the class what they would like to be when they grow up. Some of these dreams may be unrealistic, as they often are for nondisabled young children (e.g., "I want to be a cowboy"). Although these dreams should not be discouraged in any way, an attempt should be made to help them understand that all types of work are valuable and worthwhile. In other words, even working in a mailroom or delivering messages is important. On the other hand, teachers should expend a great deal of effort to convince students of their competence and of their capacity to aspire to and achieve career goals. Inviting persons (who are vocationally successful in spite of their disabilities) to speak about their work and occupational development may provide students with important role models.

Ask the parents to reinforce the importance of work at home. Parents of students with physical developmental disabilities frequently continue to to view their child as "sick" and treat him or her accordingly. This ongoing high level of overprotectiveness does little to encourage the child's independence and sense of self-worth. Teachers must, to the greatest extent possible, convey to parents the critical importance of breaking this chain of dependence early. Parents should be encouraged to provide at least one or two "chores" at home for which their child is responsible.

Students should be introduced to and trained to use computers as early as possible . In the future computers will be used more and more in all aspects of our daily lives. A large proportion of jobs will include the use of computers to some degree. It has been estimated that by 1990, 75 percent of all jobs will involve computers (Cain, 1983). Consequently, students with physical disabilities should be provided maximum exposure to computers.

**Middle/Junior
High School**

When a student with a physical disability, such as cerebral palsy, enters the middle school years, systematic vocational instruction should begin on the specific tasks identified through the local business survey. Many individuals may feel that the middle school level is too early for such a high degree of focus on vocational preparation. However, by beginning training in the middle schools, the student will have sufficient time to acquire and master the skills, both motor and cognitive, required by vocational tasks. Too often, if a person with a disability does not show significant gains in learning a new skill within a few weeks or months, it is assumed that the person will not be able to learn the skill. Experiences with the students in the OTEP project, however, have shown that students often can learn if the training takes place over long periods of time.

During the middle school years. student should be provided with the opportunity to try many of the different jobs identified by the local business survey. This will permit an assessment of which job(s) the student may best be suited for in terms of both performance and preference. One of the advantages of the clerical work is that most of these jobs are actually performed in school settings. The teacher should attempt to enlist the cooperation of the school staff in providing access to these jobs by the students with physical disabilities. However, if a certain job is not available in the school, or the teacher cannot access it, it might still be taught in a simulated fashion in the classroom. In fact, some jobs, such as computer data entry and telephone answering, may best be taught in a simulated and controlled setting before a student performs it in the "real" work setting. For example, the goal for Mack was that he would answer the phones in his middle school's main office one hour per day. Since Mack had no experience answering the phone and because a number of adaptations would need to be devised and tried out to enable him to accomplish this task, training began in the classroom. A phone headset with a microphone was purchased; this permitted him to speak to a caller without holding the receiver. In addition, an electronic device was made that, with a hit of a switch by Mack, lifted the receiver arm on the telephone, again allowing Mack to answer the phone without picking up the receiver. Training was provided in the classroom in a role-play type format on the appropriate responses he was to make for each of the different types of phone calls that were received in the main office. After Mack demonstrated that he could, with the adaptive devices, appropriately handle phone answering, he took over this job in the office.

High School

The high school years should be the time for increased emphasis on vocational preparation. The amount of time allocated to vocational training activities will vary among students. A student who may have the potential for going on to college will want to continue to take college preparatory courses. For other students, courses such as science and history may need to be sacrificed. In addition, an assessment should be made to determine if a student can be expected to continue making significant gains in reading and math. If the answer is yes, then instruction should continue because of the vocational importance of these skills for a student with a physical disability. However, if no large gains are projected, then the student's time may be more fruitfully devoted to specific vocational training activities. Even in those cases where college preparatory or academic skill training is continued, time should be allocated in the student's schedule for vocational training.

During the first year or two of high school, students may continue to receive vocational training in the school, as they did during the middle school years. However, as soon as possible, students should be given the opportunity to receive training at business sites in the community. Although school-based jobs provide excellent initial training opportunities, the importance of experience in environments in which the student will eventually be placed cannot be overemphasized.

One of the major difficulties that school districts face in providing community-based vocational training to students with severe disabilities is staffing. Students with milder disabilities are frequently placed in work experience sites, where the employer is expected to provide the bulk of the training, and the school staff simply checks on the student once or twice a week. In most cases, this approach will not be adequate for students with severe physical disabilities. A trainer will need to provide intensive and ongoing instruction in order for the student to profit from the experience. Schools obviously do not have the personpower to provide a trainer for every high school student who may need this level of instruction. In response to this problem, OTEP has created what is called a "central training site." One large business was identified that had at least one of each of the jobs targeted for instruction. The employer agreed to permit several students with physical disabilities to receive vocational training at the business. Currently, a total of nine students is receiving vocational training several hours each day given by two part-time vocational trainers. So that a trainer is required to supervise only two students at any one time, the hours when students arrive and leave work are staggered. This arrangement ensures that students receive a high degree of quality instruction that is, at the same time, cost-efficient for the district.

Training in an actual community business provides students the chance to experience the stresses and demands in these settings, to observe mature and appropriate work-related behaviors, and to realize that they can perform competently in and be a part of such a setting. Each of the students who work at the OTEP central training site is assigned to at least two different tasks in the business. For example, one hour each day Jane enters the business's accounts payable (which is a computer data-entry task) and does filing for another hour each day. Sara fills and delivers supply orders to each of the departments in the business and does photocopying. In addition to the task assignments, students also receive systematic instruction and feedback on such work-related behaviors as appropriate dress, time management, and social interactions. Each student also is given time in his or her schedule to take a short break, which provides them with the opportunity to interact socially with the nondisabled employees. As part of their vocational training, most of the students in OTEP have been taught to use the public transportation system to get from school to work and back.

CLOSING THE PERFORMANCE GAP

Figure 14-1 provides a general conceptual framework of vocational preparation for persons with significant physical disabilities. Before work preparation occurs, a performance gap exists between the job requirements and the student's skills. The goal of all preparation efforts is to close this gap. The performance gap can be closed by increasing the student's ability to perform the task and by decreasing the difficulty of the task. Thus, there are two major strategies for closing the performance gap: (1) training and (2) adaptations.

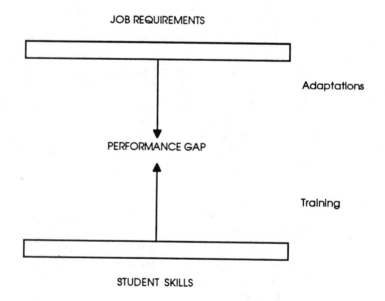

Figure 14.1 Vocational preparation conceptual overview

Systematic Training

As stated at the beginning of this chapter, a powerful technology of vocational training exists for persons with cognitive disabilities. This vocational training technology can be characterized as behavior analytic (Rusch and Mithaug, 1980). The behavior analytic approach is based on the belief that a person's behavior and the skills a person has mastered are determined as much, if not more, by the experiences that she or he has had than by innate and inborn traits or characteristics. Before the behavioral approach was adopted, it was commonly believed that persons with mental retardation were born with a limited and set ability to acquire new skills; thus, there was little motivation to try to teach these people. Today, through the use of systematic and careful instructional technologies, even persons who experience severe cognitive disabilities can learn sophisticated skills.

Although this behavior analytic approach toward the habilitation of persons with cognitive disabilities has become widely accepted, such is not the case with persons who have physical disabilities such as cerebral palsy. Instead, for persons with cerebral palsy, there is a continuation of the traditional philosophy that they cannot learn new motor responses through direct intervention. Because cerebral palsy is caused by defects to the central nervous system, it is generally believed that the only way to improve the motor control of these persons is to actually impact the central nervous system. This view is reflected in the widespread use of neuromotor and sensorimotor therapies. The goal of these therapies with children who have cerebral palsy is to "normalize" the central nervous system. These approaches are typically utilized until the person reaches the early teens, when it is felt that the central nervous system can no longer be modified. At this time the focus of therapy becomes stretches, exercises, and braces or splints, the purpose of which is to maintain the movements that the person does have.

Recently, interest has developed in the possibility that motor control for persons with cerebral palsy could be modified through direct behavioral interventions. This interest was generated by experiments using what is commonly called biofeedback. Biofeedback (in this application) refers to a strategy of providing explicit feedback to the person regarding the level of tension (tone) in the muscles of his or her body. The technique used to provide this feedback is called electromyography (EMG). Information about the tone in a muscle can be measured via electrodes placed on the muscle that are attached to the EMG equipment. The EMG equipment can then be used to operate a device (e.g., radio, light) that provides feedback to the person. The threshold level of tension required to activate the radio or light can be adjusted (raised or lowered), thereby requiring increased or decreased levels of tension in the muscles. Biofeedback has been demonstrated experimentally in persons with cerebral palsy to increase muscle control (Bird, Cataldo, and Cunningham, 1978; Gallenstein, Osternig, and

Skrotzky, 1978; McCaughey and Nielson, 1982; Inman, 1979). However, even with these demonstrations, there is a surprising dearth of studies that have attempted to use direct behavioral techniques to train functional motor responses (that is, independent living or vocational skills) in persons with motor movement difficulties (Denney, McDonald, and Rice, 1968; Iwata, Poynter, and Thompson, 1979; Horner, 1971).

Based on experiences in the OTEP project, two things appear clear regarding the use of behavioral training strategies to teach students with cerebral palsy to perform vocational tasks: (1) the technology developed for persons with mental retardation is highly transferable (and there is a great need to demonstrate this), but (2) there are some important differences between persons who experience mental retardation and those with cerebral palsy, and these differences require modifications and variations in the training technology.

In the remainder of this section, we attempt to elucidate the extent to which the major vocational training strategies are applicable to persons with cerebral palsy, and, based on our experiences in the OTEP project, to suggest critical variations that trainers should implement when working with these individuals.

General Overview of Training When teaching a new skill to any individual, there are two major goals to be achieved. For illustration purposes, we use the skill of bussing tables (that is removing dishes from customers' tables) as an example. First, the person must learn *how* to perform the skill. In the table bussing example, the person will have to be taught to pick up dishes and put them in a tub or tray, and to use a rag to wipe the tables. In addition to learning *how* to bus tables, the individual must also learn *when* to bus tables. It is not appropriate to bus tables when customers are still eating or when a customer has left the table for a few minutes to use the restroom or the phone. The person must learn to bus tables only when the customer has completed a meal. In most cases, the first goal is not very difficult to achieve when training individuals who experience only mental retardation. Most persons, even those with a severe cognitive disability, can rapidly learn to pick up dishes, put them in a bin, and wipe tables. The challenge in training these individuals is to achieve the second goal: to teach them to discriminate *when* it is appropriate to respond. The situation is just the opposite for a person who experiences only a physical disability. This individual will find it easy to determine when to respond (e.g., to bus tables). However, it may be extremely difficult to learn to pick up a dish or to wipe a table because of the motor movement difficulties. Of course, many persons with cerebral palsy experience both cognitive and physical disabilities, and the extent of the challenge that these individuals face in learning new skills and the challenge for those who take on their training is extremely high.

Task Analysis When training a worker in a new skill, the first thing a trainer must do is to perform a task analysis. Task analysis is the process by which a skill or task is broken down into its component parts. The trainer uses the task analysis to ensure that the person receives instruction on each component of the skill. In addition, the task analysis serves as a basis for assessing which skills the student acquires as training proceeds, and on which she needs further training. The importance of task analysis to the vocational training of persons with mental retardation has been widely demonstrated (Gold, 1972; Gold & Pomerantz, 1978). Figure 14-2 illustrates a typical task analysis that would be constructed to teach a person with a cognitive disability to perform a very simple computer data-entry task. Task analysis is equally important in teaching persons with cerebral palsy. However, the trainer must be prepared to break a task into much smaller steps. These steps will define each of the individual motor responses required to execute a behavior. Figure 14-3 presents an example of a step analysis (in this case, step 1 of the computer data-entry task shown in Figure 14-2) designed for a person with a physical disability. For a student with cerebral palsy, each of these minute movements may be a step that must be individually learned.

STEPS

1.	Put start-up disk in drive 1
2.	Put data disk in drive 2
3.	Turn computer on
4.	Put program disk in drive 1
5.	Type in customer's name
6.	Type in date
7.	Type in account number
8.	Press Open-Apple-S to save
9.	Remove disks/place in sleeves
10.	Turn computer off

Figure 14.2 General task analysis of a basic computer data-entry task

STEPS

1.	Put disk on table with top toward table edge
2.	Place edge of left hand on bottom of paper sleeve
3.	Place finger of right hand on top of disk
4.	Pull disk away from sleeve toward table edge
5.	Grasp edge of disk between thumb and forefinger
6.	Position disk into drive opening
7.	Push disk gently into drive
8.	Release disk
9.	Using thumb, push drive down to close

Figure 14.3   Detailed task analysis of putting a start-up disk into a drive.

Student: __Sara__   Trainer: __Rich__

Date: __1/10/86__   Task: __Photocopying__

STEP		D	M	D	M
1.	Obtain original from request basket on worktable	+	+	+	+
2.	Remove paper clip	+	−	+	−
3.	Carry original to machine	+	−	+	−
4.	Turn quantity knob to number of copies requested	+	+	+	+
5.	Open copier door	+	+	+	+
6.	Place original on window	+	+	+	+
7.	Align paper	+	−	+	−
8.	Close door	+	+	+	+
9.	Push start button	+	+	+	+
10.	Open copier door	+	+	+	+
11.	Remove original	+	+	+	+
12.	Repeat steps 5–11 until all pages are copies				
13.	Remove copies	+	+	+	+
14.	Take copies back to worktable	+	−	+	−
15.	Even copy/original stacks	+	−	+	−
16.	Place clip on each copy/original	+	−	+	−

Figure 14.4   OTEP data collection form

Data Collection   The goals of vocational training are (1) to teach the disabled person new skills; (2) to perform these skills as closely as possible to community standards; (3) to maintain these skills over time; and (4) to generalize these skills from training to performance settings. In order to determine the extent to which these goals are being achieved, information about the student must be systematically and consistently obtained. Figure 14-4 is the data collection form used in the OTEP project. This form is very similar to that typically used in vocational programs for persons with mental retardation, with one exception. On traditional data collection forms, the trainer simply indicates if a step is performed correctly or incorrectly. On the OTEP form, the trainer indicates two things for each step. First, did the student discriminate (D) which step he or she was supposed to perform, and second, was the student able to motorically (M) perform the step. For example, the data in Figure 14-4 show that Sara "knows" what she is supposed to do. She always attempted to initiate the correct step. However, she had difficulty completing several steps correctly because of motor problems. In step 2, she had difficulty removing paper clips because of the necessity to grasp, pull, and hold the paper in place, all simultaneously. In steps 3 and 14— when she carried papers from the table to the machine and back—she would crumble the paper. Sara was only able to grasp the papers with one hand while walking, and this hand had a fairly high degree of tension spasticity in it. In step 7, she couldn't get the paper aligned and then remove her hand without pushing or knocking it out of alignment. In step 15, she would drop papers when she tried to even the papers in a copy or original group. In step 16, she could not get the clip around the pages. Thus, the trainer recorded a (+) under the D and a (-) under the M for each of these steps. These data tell the trainer that Sara "knows" or "understands" what she was supposed to do, but she could not execute the steps motorically. This type of information is extremely important when training persons with physical disabilities, since different training techniques may be required, depending on whether a person cannot perform a step because of a discrimination or motor difficulty.

Prompting Prompts can be thought of as instructions in *how* to perform a task or step in a task. There are four major methods of prompting or providing a person with task completion instructions:

1. Verbal—Tell the person what to do (e.g., "put the disk in drive 1").

2. Gesture—Indicate to the worker what to do by pointing to some important aspect of the task (e.g., point to the disk to prompt the worker to pick it up.

3. Model—Demonstrate for the worker how to perform the task (e.g., have the worker watch as the trainer puts the disk into the drive).

4. Physical assistance—Physically guide the person through the step (e.g., the trainer helps hold the worker's hand steady while pushing the disk into the drive).

The first two types of prompts are most appropriately used when a person is having a discrimination problem; the other two prompt types are best used to help a person to learn how to perform a specific motor response. In fact, when training persons with cognitive disabilities, physical prompts are usually the least frequently used. However, persons with severe physical disabilities require a large amount of physical guidance to learn to perform the basic motor movements required by the task. Consequently, trainers should have a high degree of facility in using physical guidance.

Modifying Materials   In the next section of this chapter, we will discuss the issues surrounding adaptations that can be utilized to make a job more "do-able." We will discuss modifications to equipment, persons, or environments that are intended to be permanent. There are also other modifications that help an individual in learning a task, and then are faded out and removed so that the person eventually performs the task as anyone else would. Bellamy, Horner, and Inman (1979) describe the use of this strategy for teaching subtle discriminations required by a step in a vocational task. For example, if a worker is required to discriminate which side of a nut is flat and which side is raised slightly, the worker could be assisted in learning this discrimination by painting the raised side. Then, as the paint is slowly faded, the worker should begin to attend to the raised feature of the nut.

Modifications can also be used to help a person learning to perform a difficult motor manipulation and then be faded out. For example, to assist Sara in aligning the paper on the photocopy machine, a strip of rubber was affixed to the glass surface to form a guide for the paper. As she became more proficient at placing the paper on the machine, the rubber strip was gradually reduced in size until it was completely removed.

Consequences   The events that follow a person's response determine, to a great extent, whether or not the person will continue to perform that response in the future. There are, of course, many different types of consequences, including social (e.g., praise, smiles, reprimands), money, breaks, privileges (e.g., extra time off), and the like. One of the most important functions of consequences in vocational training is feedback—that is, ensuring that the person understands when the response was performed correctly or incorrectly. Feedback is particularly important when working with persons with physical disabilities, who are attempting to learn new and difficult motor behaviors.

The consequence used most frequently when teaching persons with disabilities is praise. A good trainer is one who gives immediate and enthusiastic praise for a new step correctly performed—"Good job!" However, anyone who has worked with a person with cerebral palsy can attest to the mixed effects that may result from such feedback. Here is an example. Sara had just aligned paper on the copier when the trainer said,

"All right." This praise unfortunately caused her to lose motor control, and she pushed the paper off the machine. The motor system of persons with cerebral palsy (with the exception of those who are of the flaccid nature) is extremely sensitive to external stimuli, especially those that occur suddenly or are potentially excitatory. Trainers should be aware of this and should strive to deliver praise in a careful, low-key fashion *after* a worker's hands have been removed from task-related objects.

Alternative Motor Movements   When provided with the opportunity to perform a simple task that requires basic motor movement, most people will use the same or very similar movements. For example, if 100 nondisabled individuals were asked to turn on a computer (e.g., activate the ON switch), probably all 100 would use their index finger to push the switch. When working with individuals with cognitive disabilities, an effort is usually made to train these individuals to perform tasks using motor movements that are typical or "normal," since these are usually the most efficient movements. However, nearly all tasks or steps can be accomplished using any number of different movements, one of which may be preferable for training a person with cerebral palsy. For example, if a student does not have enough control or cannot apply enough pressure with the finger to activate the switch, an alternative movement probably could be devised—such as using the thumb, the heel of the hand, or even the elbow—to accomplish the objective. In many cases, individuals with motor difficulties are very proficient in figuring out how to accomplish a step using a different motor movement. In addition, trainers need to be prepared (when the student is having difficulty performing a movement as instructed) to think of and try out some other possible movements that result in the same end product but are easier for the worker to perform.

Adaptations

In the previous section, we discussed training methods that can be used to close the gap between the requirements of a job or task and the student's present performance level. In this section, we describe another strategy for closing the gap—adaptations.

Recent technological developments have already begun to have an impressive impact on the lives of persons with physical disabilities. Even more exciting is the fact that these developments are only embryonic; new and important refinements and discoveries are occurring literally every day. In this section, we describe critical issues related to the selection and design of adaptations to assist in closing the gap between a worker's skills and the requirements of a task.

Identifying and Selecting Adaptations   There are a large number of commercially available adaptations that can assist disabled persons in a wide variety of ways, including vocationally. However, commercial products represent only a very small sample of the adaptations possible.

In fact, the number and type of adaptations that can be used to decrease the performance gap between job requirements and worker skills is limited only by one's creativity and resources. For any given problem, there may be a number of different adaptations that could help the disabled worker perform the job more easily. The trainer's task is to determine, given a variety of factors, which one is the most appropriate. We have identified a process that will help a trainer systematically select the adaptation that is most appropriate for a particular worker who wishes to perform a specific task or job.

1. Identify what aspects of the task may need adaptation.
2. Identify as many adaptive options as possible.
3. Choose the "best" adaptation among these options.

Identify what aspects of the task the worker may need adapted. In order to select an "appropriate work-related adaptation," a trainer must first identify exactly what it is about a task that may cause a given worker difficulty due to the physical disability experienced. To do this, the trainer first observes the task being done by a nondisabled worker. If possible, the trainer herself or himself also performs the task several times. While observing and performing the task, the trainer always keeps the worker in mind, imagining for each step of the task what difficulty the worker may encounter. If the situation permits, the trainer should allow the worker the opportunity to perform the task. Observing him or her perform the task will provide even better information regarding the specific nature of any difficulties. During these observations, the trainer should construct a task modification analysis (TMA), like that shown in Figure 14-5. This TMA was conducted to determine the type of adaptations that Sara might require to perform photocopying. The TMA includes a task analysis of photocopying as it is currently done by nondisabled persons. Next, each step in the task analysis that may prove difficult for the student is identified and a brief description of what specifically makes that step difficult is given. When completing the TMA, the trainer should consider such variables as the weight of materials that must be lifted or transported, pressure that must be exerted to move or activate something, the height of an object or piece of equipment that must be accessed, and the fine motor dexterity that is required to manipulate something.

Identify possible adaptations for each problem. After the specific problem(s) that a worker may encounter are pinpointed, the next step is to attempt to identify several adaptation options that may help the worker perform the task more easily. There are two major types of adaptations. First are those adaptations that assist the individual in performing the task as it is currently designed. These are *assistive devices* adaptations. An example of an assistive device is a mouthstick or headstick that a worker who has limited hand control but good head control can use to strike the keys on typewriter or computer. Another example of an assistive device is a splint that is devised for a worker's hand to make it easier for the worker to grasp objects such as papers. Still another example of an assistive device is a "reacher," a mechanical device that permits an individual to obtain objects while remaining in a stationary position. A reacher is often used by individuals who are in wheelchairs who find it difficult to stand or reach out or up for objects.

OTEP Task Modification Analysis

Student: _Sara_   Task: _Photocopying_

STEP	DIFFICULT STEPS	DESCRIBE DIFFICULTY
1. Obtain original from request basket on worktable		
2. Remove paper clip	√	Requires two hands; one to hold paper, one to remove clip; she difficulty grasping and pulling clip simultaneously; clip won't come off because she is grasping it too hard
3. Carry original to machine	√	Squeezes paper while she walks
4. Turn quantity knob to number of copies requested		
5. Open copier door		
6. Place original on window		
7. Align paper	√	With her degree of spasticity, very difficult to precisely align paper on the "slippery" glass
8. Close door		
9. Push start button		
10. Open copier door		
11. Remove original		
12. Repeat steps 5–11 until all pages are copied		
13. Remove copies		
14. Take copies back to worktable	√	Same as for step 3
15. Even copy/original stacks	√	Drops papers when she picks up to knock on table surface to even; needs a strategy that does not require two hands
16. Place clip on each copy/original	√	Similar to step 2. Needs two hands to hold paper and put clip on. She squeezes clip so tightly it won't slip onto the papers.

Figure 14.5 Example of OTEP Task Modification Analysis for Sara's Photocopy Task

The second major type of adaptations is those used to change the work environment by modifying equipment used as part of the task, or by actually modifying the manner in which the task is done. These adaptations are referred to as *environmental modifications.* Examples of environmental modifications include raising a table to permit a person in a wheelchair to fit under it, or lowering a shelf to permit a worker to retrieve papers from it.

As stated earlier, the number and type of adaptations is limited only by one's creativity and resources. In fact, the greatest limitation may be simply the trainer's lack of knowledge of what is available commercially and what noncommercial devices and modifications are possible. There are a variety of resources from which a trainer can gain help in thinking of adaptation options. If the individual being trained is still in school, one of the best sources for adaptation suggestions is the physical or occupational therapist assigned to the school. Although these individuals may have little or no experience in vocational settings, therapists usually have a wealth of experience with adaptations. In addition, therapists will also be able to show the trainer catalogues from major companies that produce and sell adaptations for persons with physical disabilities. For adult clients, the local vocational rehabilitation agency may have a rehabilitation engineer with experience in designing work modifications. Rehabilitation engineers are professionals whose specialty is the design and production of adaptations for persons with disabilities. Still another resource, and probably one of the very best sources of help, is a craftsperson in the community who is interested in volunteering his or her expertise. These individuals can be located in many ways: through service agencies, by putting a notice up at a retirement center, asking parents of the disabled persons, and enlisting the help of your own friends and relatives.

OTEP has compiled a catalogue of commercial and noncommercial assistive devices and environmental modifications specifically related to clerical tasks (Sowers, Powers, and Jenkins, 1986b). Figure 14-6 shows an example of the format that is used in the OTEP Vocational Adaptation Catalogue. First, specific functional problem that an individual might encounter in performing a certain clerical task is noted. The assistive device or modification is then described, along with where it might be purchased or the materials to build it found, the cost, how to install it, how the worker uses it, and, finally, any other important characteristics of the adaptation.

Select adaptations. After a number of adaptations have been identified, the trainer must select the one that will be purchased, built, or implemented. A number of factors must be taken into consideration when making this decision, including:

1. The relative effectiveness of each with regard to decreasing the performance gap
2. Cost
3. Availability of someone to construct it if this is necessary
4. Its acceptability to the employer.

In the best of circumstances, the first factor should be the only one considered. However, this is often not possible. Many commercial products are extremely expensive, and the cost of labor and materials to build a device or to make a modification may also be costly. If the person is a client of a vocational rehabilitation agency, the cost of the adaptation may be covered if it can be clearly determined that the device will help the person obtain a competitive employment position. Financial assistance may also be obtained through foundations or community organizations. To help build a device or modification, the trainer can try the same sources suggested earlier for helping to generate adaptation ideas. Finally, before designing or purchasing an adaptation, the trainer must find out if it will be acceptable to an employer. In most cases, assistive devices are more acceptable to employers than environmental modifications. Assistive devices require no changes in the equipment or in how the work is currently done in the company, while environmental modifications do. Most employers will have little objection to minor modifications such as moving a table or lowering a shelf, but the more the changes impact other workers or accepted work routines, the more

Curriculum Area:	Phone Use
Functional Problem:	Student is unable to old telephone handset
Adaptation Strategy	
Device:	Telephone headset with attached microphone
Where Available:	Radio Shack
Cost:	$55
How Installed/Applied:	Conventional phone headset jack is disconnected and jack from RS headset plugged in its place; headset placed on student's head with earpiece and microphone properly positioned.
Student Use:	Student speaks into microphone as with conventional handset
Important Characteristics	

— "Transparent Modification": is temporary and requires no modifications to phone system
— Size: lightweight, easily stored
— Cost/Benefit: inexpensive, flexible, and temporary modification

Figure 14.6 Example of the format used in the OTEP Vocational Adaptation Catalogue.

employers will resist. The perfect adaptation is the one that is extremely effective for the worker, costs little money, is very easy to make, and requires few or no changes in the work environment. It is surprising how often an adaptation can be found that meets all these specifications.

CASE STUDY: Sara
Decreasing the Performance Gap

From Figure 14–5, it is clear that the gap between Sara's motor ability to perform photocopying and the requirements of the job was quite large. To close the performance gap, both training and adaptations were implemented. To assist her in removing paper clips, she was provided with a paperweight, which eliminated the necessity for her to hold the paper while she removed the clip. In addition, she was taught an alternative method for removing the clip to that normally used (which is to grasp and pull it off). She was trained to simply push the clip off with her thumb, which was fairly simple with the paperweight holding the papers in place.

With regard to her difficulty in carrying paper to and from the worktable and photocopier without wrinkling the pages, the trainer had to make a decision between trying to teach her to do this, or using an adaptation. The adaptations considered were: moving the worktable closer to the machine or giving Sara a box for carrying papers. Due to her young age, the trainer opted for training. Training consisted of providing her with repeated opportunities to carry papers to locations that at first, were only a short distance apart and then, as she began to master this skill, were increasingly further apart. The trainer watched her hand carefully as she walked and gave her feedback on when she was not crumbling the paper: "Good, your hand is relaxed"; "Good, good, keep it going." After several months of training, her ability to carry papers had improved dramatically.

Earlier, the strategy that was used to help Sara learn to align papers on the photocopier was described. Briefly, a piece of rubber was affixed to the surface that acted as a guide. As she gained more motor skill in performing this step, the piece of rubber was slowly decreased in size until it was gone altogether.

Sara also found it difficult to straighten or even out the pages of a copy or original before clipping them. Most persons would pick up the papers together and knock them on a table surface. Since Sara had use of only one hand, however, this method was not possible. After considering and trying a number of alternative motor methods, the trainer opted for an adaptation—a cardboard box. Sara was trained to place the pages into the box, pick up the box and shake it until the pages fell together.

Putting paper clips on a group of pages was also particularly difficult for Sara. (To experience her problem, try to put on a paper clip using only one hand.) Even given two hands—one to hold the paper and one to put on the clip—the operation still requires a tremendous amount of finger dexterity and strength to position the clip around the papers, pull the clip apart, and push it on—all simultaneously. To solve this problem, the trainer first had Sara use the heavy paperweight to hold the papers in place during the clipping operation. Then he gave Sara repeated daily practice putting clips on. The trainer started with a large clip, which he opened up for her slightly. As she became more proficient, the clips were no longer opened and the size of the clip was reduced. At the present time, Sara, after many months of training and the implementation of these adaptations, is able to photocopy with a high degree of independence.

Closing the Performance Gap: A Summary

We have described two major strategies for closing the gap between a job's requirements and a worker's ability to perform a job: (1) training and (2) adaptations. Two important issues must be addressed with regard to these strategies. First, should a worker be trained for new motor skills, and when should an adaptation be used? This, of course, is a complex question. One rule of thumb is that the younger the student, the more motor skill training should be considered. Successful acquisition of a motor skill will make it easier for the person to obtain a job in the future, since the need for potentially expensive or difficult to construct adaptations will be eliminated or at least decreased. However, if an individual is nearing graduation or is out of school, the choice begins to shift much more toward adaptations that will permit the individual to access and perform the job as quickly as possible.

Second, even when adaptations are selected, the worker must still receive training. Despite an adaptation, a worker must still perform certain motor behaviors. In many cases, the first attempt at an adaptation may demonstrate that the worker cannot use it at all or that it must be modified to some extent. Adaptation design and implementation is a trial and error process. Using the three-step process described earlier, an adaptation is designed and implemented, the worker is trained, a determination of its effectiveness is made, and the adaptation is modified. This cycle of assessment, design, training, assessment, and modification is repeated until the worker is able to perform the task to the standards established by the employer.

ADULT SERVICE PROGRAMS

The most important measure of the effectiveness of a vocational preparation program is the extent to which the students who participate in it gain meaningful employment (that is, community-based, integrated, well-paid employment) after graduation from the program. However, as *necessary* as good preparation is to achieving this outcome, it is not *sufficient* with regard to persons with severe disabilities. Madeline Will of the Office of Special Education and Rehabilitation Services (OSERS) stated:

> The transition from school to work and adult life requires sound preparation in the secondary school, adequate support at the point of school living, and secure opportunities and service, if needed, in adult situations. (1984, pp. 6–7)

Most persons with severe developmental disabilities, including cerebral palsy, need to have support and assistance not only at the point of transition, but long-term. This is the reason the recent OSERS-supported work initiative was founded (U.S. Department of Education, 1985). This initiative reflects the realization that a need exists for the development and widespread implementation of vocational program options that provide alternatives to those currently available. In most communities, only two options are typically available today for persons with disabilities. First, a person can be competitively employed and expected to function at regular business standards without any special assistance or support. For many persons with severe disabilities, this option is not viable. The second option is sheltered employment. This is the option to which persons with severe disabilities have most frequently been assigned. Unfortunately, sheltered employment does not provide community-based, integrated, or well-paid work. In many communities, persons with severe disabilities do not even have access to a sheltered workshop or work activity center.

As noted earlier, some progress has been made with regard to the development of vocational program options for persons whose primary disability is cognitive. In particular, three models have appeared to be particularly promising: (1) work crews, (2) enclaves, and (3) individual, supported employment. Crew programs [see Bourbeau, (1985) for a detailed description of crew programs] operate in a similar way to regular, commercial janitorial or groundskeeping services. In the crew, a small group (typically four to six) of workers with disabilities perform cleaning and yard maintenance work at a number of different locations, including private businesses, homes, and public facilities. A program staff person provides the necessary training and supervision for each job, in addition to transporting the workers from job to job.

The enclave [see Rhodes and Valenta (1985) for a detailed description of enclaves] differs from the crew in that the program operates in one business. Like the crew, a small number of workers with disabilities are trained and supervised by a program staff person. Enclaves have typically been established in electronic or manufacturing companies. In most cases, disabled workers have worked together in one location in the company. A preferred option would be for the disabled workers to be dispersed throughout the company in order to increase the extent of integration.

The third work option is the individual, supported employment model [see Connis, Sowers, and Thompson (1979); Mithaug and Rusch (1980); and Wehman (1981) for a detailed description of the individual, supported employment model]. In this type of program, persons with disabilities are placed into individual businesses throughout a community. The vast majority of the positions in which persons have been placed are janitorial and food service. Initial training and long-term follow-up is provided by program staff. However, the amount of ongoing program support and assistance in this option is usually significantly less than that typically provided by either the crew or enclave programs. In fact, to this time, the expectation is that persons in this type of program will require only minimal amounts of support after the first six to nine months of placement.

Applicability of Models to Persons with Physical Disabilities

The extent to which the program models just described are appropriate for persons with physical disabilities must be examined and evaluated. "Special" programs that serve only persons with physical disabilities are probably not the best approach. Rather, these individuals should have access to programs that are available to other individuals with similar employment assistance and support needs. The question then is which of these existing vocational models may be appropriate for persons with significant physical disabilities.

At first glance, the crew program appears to be the least appropriate model for persons with physical disabilities, give the mobile nature of the crew and the physical type of work usually done. However, the extent to which the crew moves from business to business is really not a factor, except for persons who are in wheelchairs and require special transport vehicles. In addition, given that most crews assign only a small part of each job to individual workers and that a staff person is available for assistance and support, the nature of the work usually done by crews should not serve as a barrier to the person with physical disability might be assigned the job of bringing needed supplies to other crew members who are cleaning throughout a building. The same worker may also serve in a quality control role, checking each room after other workers have finished cleaning it.

The enclave model is also appropriate for persons with physical disabilities, especially those who may be confined to a wheelchair, since the enclave does not require the worker to move from business to business. In addition to eliminating the logistical difficulties inherent in moving around, the enclave provides workers with a sense of working for and belonging in a company, which the crew model does not. This stability in many cases also increases the likelihood that the employer will be willing to make environmental modifications. The enclave approach is particularly applicable for a group of workers trained in clerical skills, since large corporations frequently have numerous tasks that must be done on a daily basis.

For many persons with cerebral palsy, individual, supported employment is the best option. This work model provides the most normalized working situation of the three, and for that reason should be selected if an individual can function with a relatively small degree of support and assistance. However, for a large number of persons, much higher levels of support will be required. For these individuals, a model variation that may still allow them to work in an individual work placement would be to maintain a higher level of follow-up than is currently provided. This degree of follow-up could be achieved by assigning three or four workers to one trainer/supervisor, whose job would be to spend an hour or two each day with each worker. The major drawback of this model option is, of course, money. Current levels of program funding will, in most cases, not permit such a model to be employed.

CONCLUDING REMARKS

This chapter has attempted to provide some insight into the unique vocational preparation and employment needs of persons who experience severe physical disabilities, such as cerebral palsy. Until recently, this group of persons has received little attention with respect to being provided with appropriate preparation or employment services. It is our hope that the professional efforts made on behalf of persons with severe cognitive disabilities will begin to also be made on behalf of individuals with severe physical disabilities. Many of the behavior analytic training strategies and work models developed primarily with cognitively disabled persons in mind have a great deal of applicability to persons with significant physical disabilities. However, some modifications and variations of these techniques and work models will need to be made in order to accommodate the unique needs of these persons with motor performance difficulties.

REFERENCES

Bellamy, G.T., R.H. Horner, and D.P. Inman. (1979). *Vocational Habilitation of Severely Retarded Adults.* Baltimore: University Park Press.

Bourbeau, P.E. (1985). Mobile work crews: An approach to achieve long-term supported employment. In P. McCarthy, J. Everson, S. Moon, and M. Brius (eds.), *School-to-Work Transition for Youth with Severe Disabilities.* Richmond, Va.: Virginia Commonwealth University, Rehabilitation and Training Center.

Brown, L., M. Branston-McClean, D. Baumgart, L. Vincent, M. Falvey, and J. Schoeder. (1979). Using the characteristics of current and subsequent least restrictive environments in the development of content for severely handicapped students. *AAESPH Review 4*, 407–424.

Cain, E.J. (March, 1983). Expanding horizons-current and future potentials of microcomputer technology for all handicapped. Paper presented at the National Conference on the Use of Microcomputers in Special Education, Hartford, Conn.

Cataldo, M., B. Bird, and C. Cunningham. (1978). Experimental analysis of EMG feedback in treating cerebral palsy. *Journal of Behavioral Medicine 1*, 311–322.

Crosson, J.E. (1969). A technique for programming sheltered workshop environments for training severely retarded workers. *American Journal of Mental Deficiency 73*, 814–818.

Gold, M. (1972). Stimulus factors in skill training of the retarded on a complex assembly task: Acquisition, transfer and retention. *American Journal of Mental Deficiency 76*, 517–526.

Gold, M.W. (1973). Research in the vocational habilitation of the retarded: The present, the future. In N. Ellis (ed.), *International Review of Research in Mental Retardation*. Vol. 6. New York: Academic Press. (Pp. 97–148).

Gold, M., and D. Pomerantz. (1978). Issues in prevocational training. In M. Snell (ed.), *Systematic Instruction of the Moderately and Severely Handicapped*. Columbus, Ohio: Charles E. Merrill.

Goldenson, R. (1978). Cerebral palsy. In R. Goldenson, J. Dunham, and C. Dunham (eds।)., *Disability and Rehabilitation Handbook*. New York: McGraw-Hill.

Horner, R. (1971). Establishing use of crutches by a mentally retarded spina bifida child. *Journal of Applied Behavior Analysis 4*, 183–189.

Inman, D.P. (1979). Gaining control over tension in spastic muscles. In G. Hammerlynch (ed.), *Behavioral Systems for the Developmentally Disabled: II. Institutional, Clinic and Community Environments*. New York: Brunner-Mazel.

Keiter, J. (1979). Characteristics of the AADD population. Presented at the annual meeting of the American Academy on Mental Retardation.

Lindemann, J.E. (1981). *Psychological and Behavioral Aspects of Physical Disability: A Manual for Health Practitioners*. New York: Plenum Press.

Martin, G., and A. Pallotta. (1978). Behavior modification in sheltered workshops and community homes for the retarded: Current status and future considerations. In G. Hammerlynch (ed.), *Applied Behavior Analysis Techniques for the Developmentally Disabled*. New York: Brunner-Mazel.

Nielson, P., and J. McCaughey. (1982). Self-regulation of spasm and spasticity in cerebral palsy. *Journal of Neurology, Neurosurgery and Psychiatry 45*.

Pietruski, J. Everson, R. Goodwyn, and P. Wehman. (1985). Vocational training and curriculum for multihandicapped youth with cerebral palsy. *Vocations in Technology*. Richmond, Va,.: Virginia Commonwealth University, School of Education.

Rhodes, L., and L. Valenta. (1985). Industry-based supported employment: An enclave approach. *Journal of the Association for Persons with Severe Handicaps 10*, 12–20.

Rice, H., B. McDonald, and S. Denney. (1968). Operant conditioning techniques for use in the physical rehabilitation of the multiply handicapped retarded patient. *Physical Therapy 48*, 342–346.

Rusch, F.R., and D.E. Mithaug. (1980). *Vocational Training for Mentally Retarded Adults*. Champaign, Ill.: Research Press.

Skrotzky, K., J. Gallenstein, and L. Osternig. (1978). Effects of electromyographic feedback training on motor control in spastic cerebral palsy. *Physical Therapy* 50, 547–551.

Sowers, J., L. Powers, and C. Jenkins. (1986). *The Oregon Transition to Employment Project*. Eugene, Ore.: Oregon Research Institute, Special Education Group.

Sowers, J., L. Powers, and C. Jenkins. (1986). *The OTEP Transition to Employment Project*. Eugene, Ore.: Oregon Research Institute, Special Education Group.

Sowers, J., L. Thompson, and R. Connis. (1979). The food service vocational training program. In G.T. Bellamy, G.O. O'Connor, and O.C. Karan (eds.), *Vocational Rehabilitation of Severely Handicapped Persons: Contemporary Service Strategies*. Baltimore: University Press.

State of Oregon Program for Developmental Disabilities Office. (1983). Survey report: Services to persons with cerebral palsy. Salem: State of Oregon Program for Developmental Disabilities Office, Mental Health Division, Department of Human Resources.

Thompson, G., B. Iwata, and H. Poynter. (1979). Operant control of pathological tongue thrust in spastic cerebral palsy. *Journal of Applied Behavior Analysis* 12, 325–333.

U.S. Department of Education. (1985). *Cooperative Programs for Transition from School to Work*. Washington, D.C.: U.S. Department of Education, Office of Special Education and Rehabilitative Services, National Institute of Handicapped Research.

Wehman, P. (1981). *Competitive Employment: New Horizons for Severely Disabled Persons*. Baltimore: Paul H. Brookes.

15 Vocational Education of Persons with Sensory Handicaps

Sharon Zell Sacks
San Francisco State University

Michael Bullis
Oregon State System of Higher Education

INTRODUCTION

The impact of a sensory impairment (hearing loss, deafness, visual impairment, or blindness) places certain limitations on one's ability to develop and maintain a set of requisite behaviors or experiences that allow an individual to prepare for the world of work. Such limitations are contingent upon the degree or severity of the impairment, the individual's ability to effectively master the environment with some degree of independence, the availability of adaptive devices, and the perceptions of significant others within the disabled person's social environment. Graves (1983) asserts that such limitations are influenced by *intrinsic and extrinsic factors*. These elements may control the direction one encounters in the development of career experiences or job training outcomes. Other career development theorists (Bailey and Stadt, 1973; Healy, 1982) allude to the importance of a positive self-concept, a realistic view of one's disability, motivation, an awareness of social nuances, and an ability to make choices and take responsibility. These theorists contend, however, that such factors are not always controlled by the individual, but are influenced by social barriers, economic constraints, and labor market availability. Despite the vocational education advances that have been made for special needs populations, programs that directly affect persons with sensory deficits are in a formative stage of development. It is only within recent years that educators, parents, and other professionals have come to recognize that these individuals require more than an academically based educational program, and that the integration of a functionally based curriculum is equally important.

The purpose of this chapter is twofold. The first is to explain and examine the unique vocational needs of students with sensory handicaps. The second is to present exemplary vocational education programs in order to illustrate how such strategies can be implemented with youngsters who exhibit auditory and visual impairments. Each disability area will be treated separately, but the format will be similar. Each section will include a needs statement, population characteristics, brief historical overview, program descriptions, and a case study. Additionally, program descriptions will distinguish between elementary, secondary, and adult programs within residential, public school, and community-based sites for normally functioning as well as multihandicapped students.

TRAINING AND EMPLOYMENT OF PERSONS WITH HEARING IMPAIRMENTS

This section addresses the training and employment of persons with hearing impairments. In order to provide a comprehensive overview of this area, three major topics are discussed. First, a brief description of the characteristics of this population is given. Second, a review of habilitation/rehabilitation services and issues for this population is given. Finally, a case study is presented depicting the employment-related experiences of a young man with deafness.

Characteristics The population of persons with hearing impairments is extremely diverse. In order to provide a common frame of reference, three topics are reviewed: the classification of hearing impairments, communication modes and philosophies, and pertinent demographic information. The reader is encouraged to consult other references for a more complete treatment of these subjects (Babbidge, 1965; Bolton, 1976; Davis and Silverman, 1970; Mindel and Vernon, 1971; Moorse, 1978; Schein and Delk, 1974; Schlesinger and Meadow, 1972).

Classification *Hearing impaired* is a general term that can be used to describe the entire population of individuals who have hearing limitations. Within this group, however, persons may possess a hearing loss that ranges from complete to minimal. Two primary divisions of the population can be made: deaf and hard of hearing. Deafness refers to inability to hear and understand speech (Schein and Delk, 1974), and hard of hearing refers to deviations from the norm in hearing abilities.

This broad demarcation can be further specified according to the degree of hearing loss, the type of auditory dysfunction, and the age at which the loss is incurred.

Thorough auditory testing the hearing threshold level [that is, the faintest sound in decibels (db) at a given frequency of sound or hertz (Hz) that a person can hear in 50 percent of the hearing test trials] is specified for both of a client's ears. The degree of impairment is based on the amount of hearing loss in the *best* ear. It is established by averaging the subject's db thresholds at 250, 500, and 1,000 Hz. The levels of hearing loss are termed normal (0–25 db loss), slight (25–40 db loss), mild (40–55 db loss), marked (55–70 db loss), severe (70–90 db loss), and profound (+ 90 db loss). Further, these levels of hearing disability can be established through two transmission modes: air conduction (sound transmitted through the auditory canal), or bone conduction (sound transmitted through the skull to the auditory nerves).

The age at which the individual experiences the hearing loss will dramatically affect his or her communication development. The earlier that the loss occurs, the more likely it is that the client's communication and language abilities will be impeded. Thus, the earlier in life (e.g., before 3 years of age) that the loss of hearing occurs, the more likely it is that the individual will fail to develop language. If the loss occurs after the person has developed language, though, that ability may remain with that person and be utilized to communicate—at least to some degree. In recognition of this fact, students with deafness are classified commonly as having prelingual deafness (onset prior to 3 years of age) or prevocational deafness (onset prior to 19 years of age) (Schein and Delk, 1974). The other major factor that determines the communication mode that is used by the individual relates to the educational philosophy and training orientation to which he or she is exposed.

Communication: Philosophy There is controversy over the correct way to train communication skills in persons with auditory handicaps. Three distinct camps exist: oral/aural, manual, and total communication.

The oral/aural philosophy embraces the notion that children with hearing impairments should be taught language (that is, the spoken word), should be taught to read lips (speech-read), and should be trained to speak. Ideally, this treatment orientation would enable students to engage successfully in the hearing world. Unfortunately, many persons with hearing difficulties lack the fundamental capacities to acquire such skills.

The manual orientation strives to teach children to communicate through hand or finger representation of letters, words, or concepts. This mode of communication is termed broadly "sign language." There are several different types of sign language; the type that is used most widely for the population of persons who are considered to be deaf is

American Sign Language (ASL). ASL is a true language in that it possesses its own form and structure, and it appears to be a suitable communication avenue for most persons with deafness. ASL in particular, and the manual communication mode in general, have been criticized for being unrelated to English. It is argued that reliance on manual communication may isolate individuals from the hearing society.

Total communication is a blend of the oral/aural and manual philosophies (Gerretson, 1976). It is an approach that is designed to build on the strengths of the individual and accommodate his or her auditory and communication limitations. For example, by integrating training in speechreading and training in manual signs it may be possible for a person with profound deafness to interact with an individual who speaks and signs minimally, as well as with another person with profound deafness who only signs. This philosophy appears the most comprehensive and, logically, the most powerful. Further, several studies exist to support this approach (Delaney, Stuckless, and Walter, 1984).

Demographics   The last complete census of persons with hearing impairments in this country was conducted in 1974 by Schein and Delk. Recent statistics have been compiled on the present population of adolescents who are considered to be deaf (Karchmer, 1984). These documents are too voluminous to summarize here; thus, only data related to prevalence, demographics of the present adolescent group, and unemployment/underemployment rates are reported.

In the last census (Schein and Delk, 1974) it was estimated that approximately 13.4 million persons possessed some type of hearing impairment. The prevalence rate at that time was calculated to be approximately 203 per 100,000. Of the total population persons with hearing impairments, it was found that 1.8 million could be considered as deaf. Obviously, due to an increase in the general population these totals will have grown since the time of that investigation.

The survey conducted by Gallaudet College's Center for Assessment and Demographic Studies (Karchmer, 1984) on the current population of adolescents with hearing impairments may shed greatest light on the group most relevant to the thrust of this discussion. Drawing from the child count supplied to the U.S. Department of Education by the states under the requirements of P.L. 94-142 and P.L. 89-313, it was estimated that 75,000 students between the ages of 3 and 21 were categorized as hard of hearing or deaf in school year 1982–1983. Karchmer (1984) suggests that this figure may be conservative, with the actual number of students receiving special services because of their hearing loss being around 90,000. Some 55,000 of these students were included in Gallaudet's survey. A few of the more salient results of this study follow: 54 percent of the sample was male; 48 percent of the total population received some instruction in a mainstreamed educational setting with hearing students;

28 percent attended residential schools; 66 percent received training in sign language; and over 94 percent were reported to have lost their hearing prior to age 3 and have minimal English and language skills.

Finally, based on the 1974 census it can be stated that unemployment rates among persons with hearing impairments were, *at that time*, roughly equivalent to national norms. Specifically, males with deafness experienced an unemployment rate of 3 percent, while the unemployment rate of all males in the general population was 4.9 percent. It can be speculated that the economic downturn that has occurred since that investigation has had a negative impact on these persons and has increased unemployment among this group (Passmore, 1983). What must be kept in mind, though, is the extreme variance of these people and that no one unemployment index fully describes the entire population. What is glaringly apparent from the last census and from recent writings (Passmore, 1983), is that persons in this population tend to be woefully underemployed. Indeed, persons who are auditorially impaired are virtually unrepresented in administrative and management positions, and are employed primarily in skilled, semiskilled, and unskilled positions. Further, many persons with deafness tend to be employed only part-time. As pointed out by Passmore (1983), this state of affairs is regrettable in that it alienates these persons from the rest of society, lowers their self-esteem, and limits their economic options.

Habilitation/ Rehabilitation
This section introduces exemplary training programs and crucial issues related to the career/employment preparation of persons with hearing impairments. A brief review of the history of the career education movement for this population is presented first. Then three exemplary training and service models are summarized, and several crucial issues related to the career preparation and employment of persons with hearing impairments are described.

History The progression of the career preparation movement for persons with deafness has roughly paralleled that for persons with other types of handicaps (Dwyer, 1985). The National Research Conference of Behavioral Aspects of Deafness was the seminal meeting on career education in this field. In the keynote address to this conference, Gellman (1965) discussed three factors that affect the work orientation and capacity of persons with deafness: perceptual differences, restricted lifespace, and sociocultural immobility or self-segregation. He suggested that these problems could be remediated through a comprehensive work preparation program that was based in the school setting. In a major initial study, Lerman and Guilfoyle (1970) examined the career development and employment patterns of 340 students who had resided and been educated in residential schools. It was found that language and communication deficits in this population played a major role in vocational success. Echoing Gellman's earlier views (1965), Lerman and Guilfoyle concluded that much more emphasis on career preparation in the school setting was necessary in order to prepare students to meet the demands of society.

As a consequence of the clear need for students with hearing impairments to receive effective and viable vocational programming, conferences and projects related to this need were initiated. Some of the efforts (Egelston-Dodd, 1980; Gallaudet College, 1982; Galloway, 1979) related to defining the concept and philosophy of career education. Other projects focused on direct service delivery concerns. One such project began in 1975 at Gallaudet College and was manifested in the Model Secondary School for the Deaf (MSSD). The goals of this project were to develop a comprehensive program of career education for students with hearing impairments, staff development programming, and a career planning system. The particulars of this effort are described in detail in other references (Cobb and Egbert, 1981; Fitch, 1975; Galloway, 1979; Johnson and Newman, 1978; Steffan, 1975).

The second endeavor was larger in design. The National Project on Career Education (NPCE) began in 1979 as a joint effort coordinated and funded by the MSSD and the National Technical Institute for the Deaf (NTID). The focus of this project was to train educators throughout the country to develop and deliver career education programming. Sixty schools from different parts of the United States participated in eight training workshops, and follow-up services were afforded these participants. Several products from this program have been published that delineate content and process issues in the career education of students with deafness (Cobb and Egbert, 1981; Egelston-Dodd, 1980; Egelston-Dodd et al., 1985; Updegraff and Egelston-Dodd, 1982).

Finally, a recent survey (Ouellette and Dwyer, 1985) documents the growth and integration of career education philosophy in programs serving adolescents and young adults with hearing impairments. This investigation included 345 secondary and postsecondary institutions, and indicates that career/vocational preparation has become anchored in the philosophical framework of the educational community. This concept is broad and encompasses self-development, career awareness, career exploration, specific vocational preparation, and job placement. By and large, it was found that most career education classes and efforts begin during the secondary years. It is interesting to note that semiskilled and skilled trades in industry were listed by the majority of the respondents as the most likely fields that the students would enter, and the areas in which more training would be necessary.

Model Programs Three exemplary training and service programs that service persons who could be considered severely involved, postschool job-seekers, and community college/university students are described here.

The programs reviewed here serve an older clientele, but the respective procedures and components of these programs have applicability to other settings and other age groups.

Southwest Center for the Hearing Impaired—The Southwest Center for the Hearing Impaired is located in San Antonio, Texas, and serves clients who are deaf and who possess secondary or multiple handicapping conditions (Torretti, 1983). It is a comprehensive residential facility that provides training in independent living skills and competitive employment. Services include vocational evaluation, work adjustment classes, independent living classes, job placement, and follow-up.

The vocational evaluation component (Cheung, 1983) is comprehensive and uses both informal (e.g., observation) and formal (e.g., vocational evaluation system) assessment procedures. It is designed to gather indices of the client's communication level in various work and living situations, as well as indices of physical abilities, academic skills learning style (that is, the medium through which the subject learns best), work habits, independent living skills, and vocational skills. The assessments provide a clear blueprint of the individual's abilities and deficits, and serve as a baseline from which to plan training interventions and document progress.

Classes and individualized training are offered to clients in self-care and independent living skills. Training in the domain of personal and social adjustment is given through both individual and group counseling procedures. This aspect of training is particularly important in that the bulk of employment problems for this population seems to stem from impairment in social functioning (DiFrancesca, 1980; DiFrancesca and Hurwitz, 1969). Under the general umbrella of vocational training, classes are offered in vocational exploration, rudimentary work skills, and job-seeking skills. When judged ready for competitive placement students are moved into the job placement component of the Center.

The job placement component consists of the Job Club and follow-along services. The Job Club is based on a small-group training model described by Azrin and Besalel (1980). Essentially, the Job Club is an intensive training program designed to teach clients how to locate and secure their own jobs through a group (usually eight to twelve) instruction format. It provides a training and support millieu that both educates and motivates the clients to find his or her own employment. Although the basic structure of the Job Club has been followed at the Southwest Center, some adaptations have been made to address the communication issues and problems faced by this particular group of clients (e.g., using interpreters, filling out job applications). Once the client secures competitive employment, follow-along services are provided to the worker and the employer to ensure that the placement is successful.

Data on the effectiveness of the program has been positive (Torretti, 1983). In 1981–1982, seventy-three clients were placed in competitive jobs in the community. The bulk of these placements were in service (43.8 %, N=32) or processing (16.4 %, N =12) trades. Only 20% of the clients were terminated from their jobs. Overall, this comprehensive training and placement approach appears to be a viable system for facilitating the employment and community integration of persons with deafness and other handicapping conditions.

Tulsa Speech and Hearing Association/Projects with Industry—In 1983 the Tulsa Speech and Hearing Association received a grant from the Rehabilitation Services Administration to establish a Projects with Industry (PWI) service program. The objectives of this effort are:

I.   To provide hearing-impaired clients with the social and personal adjustment skills necessary to secure and maintain employment.

II. To provide job ready clients with the skills necessary to conduct a self-directed job search.

III. To develop employment opportunities among Tulsa area industries targeted for above average growth during the next decade.

IV. To ensure success after placement by providing follow-up services to employees/employers as needed for up to one year.

V.   To provide specialized training and placement activities for special populations of hearing-impaired clients.

VI. To coordinate activities with all community resources/agencies which provide direct services, or information and referral for hearing-impaired clients. (Long, in press, pp. 4–5)

In conjunction with these goals the PWI has strong ties with the department of vocational rehabilitation job placement services, and an industry/employer advisory council, and maintains an active community-based advisory board.

Demographic data indicate that the "average" person involved in this project is a young adult male who has been unemployed for at least a year, who has little successful employment experience, and who has no secondary disability or a minimally restrictive secondary condition. In general, the trainees have profound or severe deafness and communicate through sign language. Clients are brought into the program approximately every four to five weeks in groups of ten to twelve. The trainees are screened prior to entry to ensure that they are emotionally stable and have rudimentary work skills.

Training consists of classes, offered four days a week, in both social skills and job-seeking skills. Social skills training is provided two mornings a week and includes training focused on communication, job retention, and personal concerns (e.g., banking, budgeting). The afternoons of these two days are reserved for tours of work places, interviews, and structured teaching (e.g., interviewing). Two mornings a week are devoted to learning independent job-seeking skills through a modified Job Club approach (Azrin and Besalel, 1980), developed specifically for persons who are deaf (Justi, McMahon, and Lewis, 1983). The afternoons of these days are reserved to allow subjects to practice job-seeking skills and engage in job search endeavors.

Staff support is offered the trainees in the form of individual counseling, development of jobs in the community, and the identification of job leads. Perhaps most importantly, once a trainee secures employment, agency staff provide ongoing, intensive follow-up to both the trainee and the employer to ensure a successful placement.

To date, eighty-one trainees have been referred to the PWI and forty-five have been placed in competitive jobs (Davis, 1986). This outcome is excellent given the unemployment histories of the bulk of the clients.

National Technical Institute for the Deaf—The National Technical Institute for the Deaf (NTID) is located on the campus of the Rochester Institute of Technology (RIT) in Rochester, New York. It was established in 1965 and receives federal funds to provide technical and professional training to persons with hearing impairments. NTID is one of nine colleges within RIT. As a separate entity, NTID trains students in four career areas: business, applied science/allied health, engineering technology, and visual communications. Students with hearing impairments may take coursework under the umbrella of NTID, or in programs at RIT. A comprehensive support system for the students is maintained by NTID that includes tutoring, notetaking, counseling, and interpreting. Moreover, exemplary student outreach and recruitment programs (Egelston-Dodd and DeCaro, 1986), career preparation and guidance services (DeCaro and Areson, 1983), job placement (Martin, 1983), and institutional research components are maintained. In fact, the close empirical scrutiny that permeates the institution and its services may account, in large part, for its fine program.

Approximately 1,000 persons are enrolled as students at NTID. Individuals are recruited nationally to attend. In order to be admitted students must be U. S. citizens; have a 70-db hearing loss in the better ear without a hearing aid; have "good" high school grades and references; and possess an eighth grade achievement level in reading, language, and math (Egelston-Dodd and DeCaro, 1986). Review of past records indicate that most NTID students tend to earn either certificates of training (one year of training to become employable), diplomas (two years of training designed for job preparation), or associate degrees (specific level of achievement in a technical area). Roughly 18 percent of the students go on to receive bachelor's or master's degrees under the aegis of RIT.

A summary of follow-up data of 1,831 NTID graduates (Martin, 1983) indicates that 94 percent are working and the majority (around 80 percent) are employed in white collar jobs. Salary analyses of these graduates show that the mean earnings growth in 1979–1980 exceeded the Consumer Price Index for those years. As of 1980 the mean income figure for NTID/RIT graduates was $14,072, with a range of $4,108–$36,400. Comparisons of graduates versus dropouts of NTID demonstrates the consistent superiority of the former group in employment rate, salaries, and involvement in high-level positions (that is, white versus blue collar placements).

Issues and Directions   The career preparation of persons with hearing impairments is a young field. Excellent instructional programs do exist, but they are not widely discussed or examined empirically in the professional literature. Other areas for improvement in this field also deserve mention.

First, it appears that there are few, if any, career/vocational assessment tools that are valid for use with this population. In a comprehensive review Sligar (1983) demonstrates that most of the commercially available work evaluation inventories were not developed for, nor standardized on, persons with hearing impairments. Further, some research indicates that the utility of these tools is minimal for persons who are deaf (Bullis and Marut, in press). In addition, commercially available instruments designed to assess career knowledge and maturity in the general population apparently have little validity for individuals who are hearing impaired (White and Slusher, 1978). In sum, there is a considerable need to direct efforts to construct career/vocational assessment tools for use with this population.

Second, there is a dearth of published studies directed at what vocational training methods are effective with these people. It has been suggested (Bullis, 1985b; Bullis and Anderson, in press) that this fact may be due to an overreliance on traditional group research methods. A single-case experimental method is advocated as a strategy for investigating career/vocational training with this population.

Third, virtually no studies document empirically whether career/vocational preparation programs are effective—that is, what the long-range impact of these programs is on the community adjustment of these persons. Such scrutiny is long overdue and should be encouraged.

In conclusion, the career/vocational preparation of persons with hearing impairments is a field that has developed rapidly, but possesses numerous gaps. Fortunately, there is a growing interest in developing and investigating methods to foster the community integration of adolescents and adults with hearing impairments. It will only be through such efforts that the all-too-pervasive problems of unemployment and under-employment that plague this population will be addressed and remediated.

CASE STUDY: Lee*

Lee is a 20-year-old male who has been profoundly deaf from birth and possesses no other disabilities. The cause of his auditory impairment is not known. He wears hearing aids, but because of the degree of his hearing loss they are only minimally effective and allow him to comprehend only isolated words and pieces of conversations. His parents and brother all hear, and it has only been in the past few years that his mother has learned to communicate with him in sign language. His father and brother both use gestures or pantomime to transfer information and directives.

Lee completed the elementary grades in a school for nonhandicapped students. His parents had been told that it would be best if he could learn to lipread and to speak. In school, he seldom understood the teacher and rarely received special attention. The other children could not communicate with him and did not include him in their play. Prior to beginning the eighth grade Lee's parents decided that he was not receiving appropriate training and elected to send him to the state residential school for the deaf. The school was over 100 miles from their home and it was necessary for him to live at the institution. Upon entry to the school Lee found that he could not communicate with most of the children, who were fluent in sign language. He began to learn American Sign Language in a special class, and in a short time was able to converse with the other students. His academic training included basic academic skills with some emphasis on career and vocational preparation. For instance, during his junior year he was involved in a job exploration class that included many field trips to see where other persons with deafness worked. During his senior year Lee was placed in a part-time job in the cafeteria at the school, and later in the year he was placed as a janitor in an office building.

After graduation Lee returned home. He helped his father and mother out around the house but soon grew bored, missing his friends and other persons with whom he could communicate. His parents contacted the state department of vocational rehabilitation to see if they could help Lee find a job. The counselor at the agency was able to communicate with Lee via sign language. After several counseling sessions the counselor suggested that Lee attend a one-year program at a local community college that was designed to teach persons with handicaps to find employment.

Lee entered the program the following fall after waiting at home for almost seven months. He was somewhat surprised that not all the students were deaf; instead, many were physically impaired, and others seemed to have difficulty reading and learning. Aides who were fluent signers helped him and the other students with deafness to understand what the teachers were saying. Classes were offered for a half-day and were structured to teach basic academic skills, but in a much different way than Lee had been accustomed to. In his math class, paychecks and checking accounts were used to teach adding and subtracting; in the reading class, the students were required to read and understand job listings; and in this writing class, the students were asked to fill out job forms and write notes to hypothetical job

---

*Lee is a fictitious character. His experiences, however, are representative of many persons who are auditorily impaired.

supervisors to express needs. The other part of the day was devoted to working in various departments asround the school (e.g., food service, janitorial, grounds crew).

About halfway through the year a meeting was held by the rehabilitation counselor with Lee and his parents and teachers to focus the remainder of the training. Lee told the group that he liked working around cars and wanted to work in a garage. Consequently, he began to receive training at the college in rudimentary mechanic skills and body work. He clearly had a knack for the work, but often did not understand what the instructor or the other students wanted. Luckily, his aide was able to help in many instances, and by the end of the year he was able, with gestures and notes, to communicate with most of the people in the class.

At the end of the school year the rehabilitation counselor found Lee a part-time job in an auto garage that paid just above minimum wage. Lee began the job and encountered many problems. Although he tried to do his work well, he did not understand directions and could not communicate his requests except through notes. This isolation made Lee extremely unhappy and several times at work he reacted in an extremely violent manner (e.g., throwing tools) for no apparent reason. The rehabilitation counselor contacted Lee and the employer each week, and tried to help work through these problems by assisting in the development of a dual communication avenue that consisted of pantomime, fundamental signs, and notes. After several months Lee had caught on to the job and was relatively happy with his work and the paycheck that he received. Moreover, as time went on it became very apparent that his skills in bodywork were excellent.

Unfortunately, despite Lee's obvious competence it was virtually impossible for the employer to train him in more advanced and better paying jobs. He just did not have the time or the expertise to give to Lee. The employer did talk to the rehabilitation counselor about further training for Lee, but it was found that such programs would conflict with his work hours and it was doubtful if public support could be secured to pay for the additional classes. Consequently, Lee's future probably looks much like the present. It is likely that he will continue to work at this job, or at this level of employment, for some time.

THE TRAINING AND EMPLOYMENT OF PERSONS WITH VISUAL IMPAIRMENTS

Over the past twenty years, visually handicapped children and youth have had greater opportunities to participate more fully within the sighted environment. Special educators and other professional who understand the unique needs of this population have come to realize that skills such as orientation and mobility, personal hygiene, home management, problem solving, self-advocacy, and social competence are essential elements for independent living and future planning (Morrison, 1974; Best, 1977; Gardner, 1977). Many attempts have been made to incorporate such subject matter into the educational structure for visually impaired youngsters in residential and integrated sites (Yeadon, 1974; Hanson, 1979; Naughton and Sacks, 1977). A number of programs have been relatively successful, but they have been limited in their longevity and in their ability to provide a continuum of functional learning experiences. Service providers have also recognized the importance of implementation programs that emphasize career education and vocational readiness as a bridge toward independent functioning (Ethridge, 1978; Graves, 1983a; Wolfe, 1973; Wurster, 1983; Uxer, 1973). However, these programs have undergone fluctuations in funding and support (Spungin, 1983), and are weak in their methodological approach (Bagley, 1984). In addition, the paucity of research that exists in this area makes it difficult to substantiate the effectiveness of such programming. Before one can examine the vocational educational models that have been developed for visually handicapped children and adolescents, it is important to have some knowledge about this diverse group.

Visually Handicapped Persons

The heterogeneity that exists among visually impaired persons makes it difficult to develop programs and to implement curricular strategies that can be useful with a wide variety of students. Traditionally, distinctions were made between those students who were "legally blind" and those who were "partially sighted." Such classifications created discrepancies in placement and in instructional implementation. As a result, many children were misplaced and taught in a mode that was inconsistent with their appropriate learning style. For example, many children were taught braille even though they demonstrated high levels of visual ability. However, many programs for the visually handicapped have adopted a more functional definition of visual disability that integrates the medical-rehabilitative definition along with a more functionally based approach. Such a perspective may encourage the use of residual vision for independent living tasks, but recognize the importance of using auditory and tactile skills for academic endeavors. It should be noted, however, that the definition of "legal blindness" still establishes criteria for service provision and funding, especially for the adult visually handicapped population.

It is also important to consider the differences between those individuals who have *congenital* visual impairments (a vision loss that is present at birth or manifests itself in early childhood) and those who have an *adventitious* visual loss (a loss that usually occurs later in life—during adolescence or adulthood). Most visually impaired children and youth have congenital losses, or lost their vision at an early age. The simple presence of some vision, or having a sense of visual imagery, makes a difference in conceptual development, negotiation of the environment, and understanding of abstract ideas such as personal space or appropriate physical appearance. Additionally, the nature of the visual disability affects functioning. For example, individuals who have retrolental fibroplasia (RLF) (retinal damage as a result of premature birth and excessive amounts of oxygen administered shortly after birth) often exhibit an inability to understand abstract concepts. In addition, these students need to have ideas presented to them in a concrete fashion; they also seem to exhibit fine and gross motor deficits. However, the degree of dysfunction seems to depend on the amount of residual vision.

Multihandicapped visually impaired persons are another group that requires some discussion. Perhaps, of all the students who are served, we understand this group the least. It is the most diverse, and probably has the widest variety of unique needs. There are a growing number of such students with visual disabilities and other anomalies; however, the loss of visual function compounds an individual's inability to learn tasks. Alternate approaches must be initiated, but a clear decision needs to be made as to whether visual disability is the primary source of concern. Again, the degree and nature of the multiple impairments must be taken into consideration. Educators with expertise in visual disability need to work alongside specialists who have extensive training in behavior management, functional skills, positioning, and environmental adaptations.

Program Models

While educators of visually handicapped students have been instrumental in pioneering mainstreaming efforts, less emphasis has been given to the implementation of programs that encourage career development or vocational readiness in traditional educational settings. As illustrated earlier, such gaps in providing these services may be the direct result of the diversity of the population as well as the low incidence nature of this group. It is estimated that nearly 35,000 youngsters across the nation are legally blind (American Printing House for the Blind, 1983), and that 1 out of every 1,000 school-age children has a severe visual impairment requiring special support. The development of educational programs for visually handicapped students, however, has paralleled a shift in philosophy from a more academic orientation to one that incorporates the elements of a critical skills model. In the following sections are detailed descriptions of program models that have helped to mold the career development needs of visually handicapped youth.

Residential School Programs Vocational education programs that were initially developed in residential schools focused attention on the secondary level student. The implementation of such programming took the form of specific courses that emphasized work skill development, specific work training, interviewing techniques, personal management skills, and some off-campus work experience. Tremble and Campbell (1973) developed a federally funded project that provided students with some community-based instruction. However, the program continued to emphasize academic skills along with specific job training on the school site. Once the students gained the requisite skills to perform the job within the community, they were placed in part-time employment. Tremble and Campbell suggest that as a result of the project, *some* of the students obtained full-time employment. Carroll and La Barre (1974) initiated a similar program, but their model included speakers, field experiences, and job shadowing (observing an individual perform a specific job task) to help students gain greater exposure to the world of work.

Huber (1973) coordinated a work experience program between the Western Pennsylvania School for Blind Children and the Pittsburgh Association for the Blind. Each student received a six-week paid position. After the initial work period, the students were evaluated on production rate, work behavior and motivation, and appropriateness of placement. The program was originally designed to improve community attitudes toward the blind and visually impaired. However, the program was limited in its ability to justify its original intent because the students received their work experience only within a sheltered work-shop setting.

Coker (1974) describes a vocational education model that permeated all aspects of the education framework at the Tennessee School for the Blind. Coker designed his program to meet the individual needs of the students at all grade levels. In his description, Coker discussed the importance of a functionally based program that includes career awareness and career development strategies for younger children. Such programs stress personal and social development, the acquisition of basic academic skills to promote a sense of pride and responsibility in one's accomplishments, and exposure to the world of work through simulation of specific job tasks as well as actual exposure to real jobs in the community. Coker encouraged varied work experiences for students during the secondary years, along with specific training in the use of leisure time and independent living. Coker also stressed the importance of traditional educational programs allowing for flexibility in scheduling and giving students a wide range of vocational experience throughout their high school years. Finally, Coker encouraged the need for close cooperation between the school and the employer to ensure job success for the student once gainfully employed. Such an approach involved ongoing follow-up.

Clayton (1973) stressed similar components as factors in achieving job success for the students at the Maryland School for the Blind. In a survey distributed to employers in the Baltimore area and to former students at the Maryland School, the following suggestions for program development were made:

1. that the student be exposed to the world of work earlier through off-campus and on-campus work experience,

2. that greater emphasis be placed on social development through activities with other, sighted children,

3. that students be provided greater opportunities in making decisions regarding their conduct and future,

4. that greater involvement of parents regarding the students' future be developed, and

5. that students be provided more information about available job opportunities.

From the information provided in the initial survey, Clayton developed a comprehensive vocational education program that focused attention on social skills related to job acquisition and retention, community-based work experience, and a prevocational program that allowed students to explore a variety of occupations while developing generic work skills (punctuality, following directions, taking breaks) (Clayton, 1977, 1979, 1983).

More recently, residential school programs have shifted from an on-campus emphasis to training students within the community. Such transition programs are the direct result of recognizing that independent living skills and crucial work behaviors cannot easily be acquired in an artificial setting (classroom), but rather must occur in the "real" environment for generalization to take place. The Perkins School for the Blind, for example, has initiated an apartment living program within the community for its older students. Similarly, vocational experiences occur in real work sites. An exemplary vocational educational program for deaf-blind and multihandicapped students will be described in a later section.

The California School for the Blind has redesigned its curriculum to emphasize skills of daily living, career and vocational education, and use of leisure time. These goals have become the primary curricular strategy throughout the school. The implementation of a "life skills team" has allowed specialists in the areas of daily living skills, social skills, vocational education, and orientation and mobility to work together to provide an individualized functional learning experience for students. The vocational education program provides a continuum of programs for all levels. Younger students (elementary aged) are given chores, such as making their beds or taking out the trash. In return, the students receive an allowance, just as normally sighted children do. Older students participate in a "job shop" program on campus, where they learn generic work skills. Once students master skills in the job shop (xeroxing, collating, simple assembly), they receive real work experience on campus (janitorial, dishwashing) and participate in ROP (Regional Occupational Programs) off-campus in the community. These experiences include janitorial and landscaping. A number of more severely impaired students participate in workshop programs in the immediate area. When students prepare for off-campus experiences, the life skills team works together to ensure appropriate and positive social behavior, functional mobility skills, and appropriate personal management acquisition.

Public School Programs Few reports are available that describe vocational education programs for the visually handicapped in the public schools, but in the early 1970s, a task force of experts in special education, career education, vocational education, and vocational rehabilitation joined forces to develop career education programs suitable for the visually impaired. These programs took the elements of existing career education strategies utilized at the elementary and secondary levels, and adapted them to meet the needs of the visually impaired. One such program that gained wide acceptance was the CI-TAB curriculum (Career Information and Training Activities for the Blind) (Abrams, 1974). This program emphasized job search skills, job behavior, hygiene and grooming, purchasing habits, budgeting, banking, home management, and health care. It also outlined a continuum of teaching strategies for career development that paralleled grade equivalent activities. For example, students in kindergarten through sixth grade developed skills in career awareness (understanding the world of work and work-related values). Such programs were infused into the regular academic curriculum.

Although the CI-TAB program began to identify some of the more critical skills necessary to enhance career awareness, its basic structure relied heavily on academic achievement as a requisite for passing through each phase of the curriculum. Additionally, there were no research data available to substantiate the effectiveness of such a program over time. More recently, Kirkman (1983) developed a career education curriculum specifically for blind and visually impaired children. Like the CI-TAB program, this curriculum is infused into academic subject matter such as language arts, reading, and mathematics. The program has been field-tested with several visually impaired children in public school and residential sites throughout the nation. Again, no preliminary data are available as to its effectiveness.

Ethridge (1978) implemented an innovative career education program at the elementary level that incorporated career exploration activities, introduction of job responsibilities, experimentation with job tasks, use of tools, and use of leisure time. In addition, students gained experience keeping track of hours worked, learning money management skills, and developing an ability to make realistic decisions about career choices.

Woal (1974) provided career education experiences for blind and visually impaired children through a series of career awareness and self-exploration books and activities. Eighteen different job clusters were introduced to visually impaired and sighted children in a classroom setting. The children discussed their strengths and limitations with reference to their unique needs. Additionally, the program gave the students the opportunity to meet and to learn more about visually impaired adults who were employed. The thrust of the program was to help students develop a sense of identity and to instill greater understanding about their visual impairments.

Storey, Sacks, and Olmstead (1985) introduced a visually impaired high school student to a series of operator call tasks at a local AT&T office by initiating a community-classroom approach (Gaylord-Ross, Forte, and Gaylord-Ross, 1986). The student received vocational instruction in the natural work setting rather than at the school site. Using a multiple-probe research design, the student learned, maintained, and generalized ten different telephone calls at high rates of performance. In addition, the student acquired a number of generic work behaviors and was given critical feedback regarding his social competence on the job. As a result of this experience, the student's educational program has undergone significant changes. His school day now focuses on acquiring basic occupational skills, including functional math and reading skills, continued acquisition of operator call tasks through AT&T training, as well as introduction to other job experiences within the community.

Vocational Programs for the Multihandicapped/Visually Impaired
Traditionally, lower functioning visually impaired individuals have participated in workshop programs or work activities centers. These facilities provided a structured environment for many individuals whose social and mental abilities prohibited them from functioning in a regular work setting. However, numerous studies with severely handicapped adults have demonstrated positive effects when an individual is allowed to participate in work activities alongside nonhandicapped peers (Brown, et al., 1984; Wehman, 1981). This shift has met with resistance from proponents of the workshop structure. In a position paper prepared by the National Industries for the Blind regarding the multihandicapped visually impaired, it was stated that

> if full or partial economic self-sufficiency is to be attained at all by blind persons with serious vocational limitations, it is most likely that this will occur primarily under the conditions of the special workshop for the blind. (Compare Winkley, 1985, p. 7.)

However, other individuals realize the need to provide options for severely handicapped, visually impaired individuals. Winkley (1984), over a five-year period, has transformed his workshop at the El Paso Lighthouse for the Blind into an enclave in industry. Visually impaired workers perform similar tasks in the "real-work" environment within an industrial complex (Converters). They are given extensive support by trained staff from the Lighthouse so that effective social integration and work production can occur between the disabled and the nondisabled.

Long-term effects of the program (five years) have been excellent. Indeed, the program has been so successful that the Lighthouse has returned its workshop funds to the National Industries for the Blind. Additionally, the Lighthouse has moved its work activities center to the industrial site, allowing for greater exposure to the "real world." Other work activities programs (e.g., Pittsburgh Association for the Blind) have effectively utilized "general case" strategies (instruction of a set of tasks that can be transferred to a similar set of tasks in varied environments, or with slightly different materials) with severely handicapped visually impaired adults to teach a set of sorting tasks (Lengel and Woolcock, 1984). Such techniques can certainly be initiated in other environments with the visually handicapped. Lengel and Woolcock report that such training has been used on a limited basis at community work sites (convalescent hospitals) with severely handicapped/visually handicapped clients.

Thus far, the programs illustrated have focused on the adult multihandicapped/visually impaired population. The Perkins School for the Blind, however, has created an in-depth community-based vocational education program for its deaf-blind multihandicapped students. Project ADVANCE (Action for the Development of Vocational Alternatives and New Concepts in Education) provided community-based job training for twenty-seven multihandicapped students ages 16 to 22, with fourteen private sector employers and in three sheltered workshops within the metropolitan Boston area. Job sites varied, and over two-thirds of the students experienced more than one job placement. The students were exposed to a variety of entry-level jobs that included baker's helper, food service personnel, dishwashers, housekeeping staff, laundry workers, coin tellers, file clerks, greenhouse worker, and maintenance worker. The students were supported by three full-time plus one half-time vocational instructors. The teachers provided intense on-the-job training for at least a three-month period. Then they faded and transferred responsibility to the employer personnel. A large component of the program also included training in work-related behaviors. During the three-year lifetime of the project, 40 percent of the participants received minimum wage, 40 percent received subminimum wage, and 20 percent were paid at piecerate. All participants were paid by the employer. As of 1983, two participants have graduated from Perkins, and both have been hired by their employer for full-time, permanent employment.

The Impact of Social Skills Training on Vocational Readiness

As trends in education of the visually handicapped have shifted from a developmentally based model to a more functionally based curriculum, vocational education programs have initiated curricula that encourage the acquisition of appropriate social behavior, independent living skills, and activities to enhance independent thinking and problem-solving ability. Laurence (1973), Rossi and Marotta (1974), Dickson (1979), and

Lombana (1980) all designed programs that encouraged clients to improve job-seeking skills. Laurence (1973) initiated the Self-Reliance Institute, where high school–aged, visually impaired students participated in a summer career development seminar. The primary goal of the program was to develop skills that enhanced independence and a positive self-identity. The students were given work experiences in the community and lived in apartments while participating in the program. Marotta and Rossi (1974) and Dickson (1979) worked with adult visually impaired clients to develop a set of job-seeking skills. Inclusive in these models were job search skills, interviewing techniques, appearance and grooming skills, and skills to enhance assertive behavior in the job search phase and on the job.

Wolf (1984) has created the Job Readiness Clinic at the University of Texas, Austin. While recognizing the importance of job search skills, Wolf strongly believes that visually impaired adolescents and adults are not ready to tackle such sophisticated skills. Rather, the focus of her program emphasizes the acquisition of appropriate social behavior and the development of a positive self-image. Over a four-week period, the students progress through a series of life exploration activities. The program encourages the client to take responsibility for his own actions and to begin making choices regarding life pursuits. Through self-exploration, group feedback and individual counseling, the client will hopefully gain a sense of control over his own destiny. In a recent presentation at the Association for Education and Rehabilitation for the Blind and Visually Impaired (AER) Southwestern Regional Conference in San Diego, Wolf indicated that a similar model was used with school-aged youth. The results, however, were less successful. She attributed the weakness of the program to a lack of training carryover from school to home for the students. Although the initial training was successful, there was inconsistent support from families and educators.

Further recognition of social skill deficits within the visually impaired population was identified by Hoben and Lindstrom (1979) and by Van Hasselt, et al., (1983). The latter program initiated an assessment procedure to determine specific skill deficits and to implement a training procedure that would enhance social skill acquisition among visually impaired adolescents in a residential school setting. Such services were extended to public school students during a five-week Community Adjustment Program (Stewart, et al., 1984). This program emphasized training in orientation and mobility, daily living skills, recreation and leisure skills, and a social skills training program. Students were given an extended apartment living experience that fostered independence and self-advocacy.

Finally, programs that encourage the inclusion of adult visually impaired role models seem particularly effective. For example, gifted students from the Austin, Texas, area participated in a mentorship program at the Texas School for the Blind. Visually handicapped adolescents were paired with adult role models who had similar vocational and personal interests. Not only were students given opportunities to observe the lifestyle of the visually impaired mentor, but some longlasting friendships resulted. A similar program, Adventures in the Future (Bonner, 1985), employed visually handicapped adults to facilitate open discussions among visually impaired adolescents and their parents during a series of weekend transition workshops in the greater Long Island area. Both the parents and the students valued the information provided by the visually impaired adults. It gave them a more realistic perspective regarding the skills and behaviors needed to succeed in competitive employment as a visually impaired individual. Further, such experiences helped the adolescents identify with individuals who have similar disabilities, yet who have strived for, and gained, independence, employment, and a positive sense of self.

SUMMARY

The impact of vocational education programs for visually handicapped children and youth has been somewhat inconsistent over time. Although many innovative and exciting programs have been implemented, high rates of unemployment and underemployment continue to plague this group. The initiation of educational programs that provide students with a continuum of life experiences and ongoing exposure to the world of work in the adolescent years can facilitate vocational success as adults. With greater commitment among educators of visually handicapped students to incorporate alternative educational strategies, these youngsters will have greater opportunities to achieve a level of independence equal to their sighted peers.

CASE STUDY: John

John, age 17, has been visually handicapped since birth. Congenital cataracts, which were removed at age 2, left him with light perception in his left eye and usable residual vision in the right eye. John is able to read standard print with a hand-held magnifier or specially prescribed lenses, but his reading rate is slow and extremely labored. John has received the services of a teacher of visually handicapped students throughout his school years, first in an elementary resource room and later from itinerant teachers. John has been mainstreamed into regular education classes since the third grade even though his skill levels range from fourth grade in math comprehension to eighth grade in spelling. His reading comprehension, organization, and note-taking skills are particularly weak and require constant support, yet his educational program has continued to emphasize academic pursuits.

Although John attends his neighborhood high school, he has few friends. He spends much of his leisure time alone, and finds interaction with peers difficult and sometimes rather awkward. Encouraged by his VH teacher, John has begun to participate in the drama club. He is quite verbal and enjoys acting a variety of roles; however, he is easily intimidated when questioned about his visual impairment or difficulty with reading. At home, John is responsible for his personal needs, but does not consistently perform other job tasks around the house. He has repeatedly volunteered to help mow the lawn or prepare meals, but his parents are hesitant to allow him to perform such jobs because of his limited vision. Although John's parents recognize the importance of allowing him to become more independent, they are fearful of his safety and have not allowed him to travel by himself throughout the community or spend his own money as readily as his siblings or same-aged peers.

At a recent IEP meeting, John's VH teacher, along with other team members (orientation & mobility specialist, vocational coordinator, vocational rehabilitation counselor, school psychologist, John, and his parents) discussed future educational and vocational goals for him. As they spoke, it was apparent that John's parents perceived his academic performance much differently from other team members. His parents believed that John was functioning at or above grade level on most academic tasks and felt that he would be able to attend college. Conversely, team members did not recognize John's desire to develop more independent living and travel skills, as well as wanting to secure a job for himself. When questioned about job preference, John seemed interested in working at a radio station or developing his acting skills. At the suggestion of the vocational coordinator, John was asked to participate in a series of community vocational experiences, where he would be able to explore and to learn about a variety of jobs through hands-on experience. Reluctantly, John's parents allowed him to do so.

Instead of full participation in a regular education setting, John now spent half of his school day in a community classroom at a real job site. Assisted by a vocational special education teacher, and his VH teacher, John gained exposure to landscape gardening, sorting and packaging, and basic office skills. Each experience lasted approximately three months. In addition, he developed a set of generic work behaviors and social skills (basic greetings and conversational skills, appropriate eye contact and body posture, interpretation of nonverbal behavior and cues by others, and enhanced assertion skills through role plays and modeling) that transferred to other settings. In the community classroom environment, time was also spent developing functional math and reading skills that included money management, time management, and completion of job applications. John was expected to travel to work independently in the morning, and back to his local high school in the afternoon. As a result of this initial vocational experience, John's educational program has shifted from a purely academic focus to one that is more functionally based. He will continue to participate in the community classroom program during his final year of high school, while working with his special education teachers and vocational counselor to secure employment after high school.

REFERENCES

Abrams, K. (1974). CI-TAB: VIEW for the blind. *Education of the Visually Handicapped* 2(1), 23–27.

American Printing House for the Blind. (1983). *Report on National Quota of Blind and Visually Impaired Children in the United States.* Louisville, Ky.

Azrin, N., and V. Besalel. (1980). *Job Club Counselor's Manual.* Baltimore: University Park Press.

Babbidge, H.D. (1965). *Education of the Deaf.* Washington, D.C.: Department of Health, Education, & Welfare.

Bagley, M. (1984). The career development needs of blind and visually impaired students and rehabilitation clients and the resources available to meet those needs. Mississippi State University, Rehabilitation Research and Training Center on Blindness and Low Vision. To be submitted to the American Foundation for the Blind for publication.

Bailey, L.J., and R. Stadt. (1973). *Career Education: New Approaches to Human Development.* Bloomington, Il.: McKnight Publishing.

Best, J. (1977). The relevance of normalcy. *Education of the Visually Handicapped* 8(4), 115–119.

Bolton, B. (1973). *Introduction to Rehabilitation of Deaf Clients.* Hot Springs, Ark.: Research and Training Center.

Bolton, B. (Eds.). (1976). *Psychology of Deafness for Rehabilitation Counselors.* Baltimore: University Park Press.

Bonner, M.A. (1985). Adventures in the future: State of New York. *Journal of Visual Impairment and Blindness 79,* 460–470.

Brown, L., B. Shiraga, J. York, K. Kessler, B. Strohm, P. Ragan, M. Sweet, K. Zanella, P. Van Deveuter, and R. Loomis. (1984). Integrated work opportunities for adults with severe handicaps: The extended training option. *Journal of the Association for Persons with Severe Handicaps 9,* 262–269.

Bullis, M. (1985a). Decision-making: A theoretical frame of reference in the career education of students with deafness. In G. Anderson & D. Satson (eds.), *The Habilitation and Rehabilitation of Deaf Adolescents* Washington, D.C.: The National Academy of Gallaudet College. Pp. 304–316.

Bullis, M. (1985b). Where do we go from here? In M. Bullis & D. Watson (eds.), *Career Education for Hearing Impaired Students: A Review.* Little Rock, Ark.: Research and Training Center on Deafness and Hearing Impairment. Pp. 97–112.

Bullis, M. and G. Anderson. (In press). Single subject research methodology: An under utilized tool. *American Annals of the Deaf.*

Bullis, M., and P. Marut. (In press). Evaluation recommendations and rehabilitation outcomes. In L. Stewart (ed.), *Clinical Rehabilitation and Hearing Impairment: A Guide to Quality Assurance.* Washington, D.C.: National Association of the Deaf.

Carroll, L.R., and A. La Barre. (1974). A cooperative vocational guidance course for visually impaired students-clients. *The New Outlook for the Blind 68,* 163–169.

Cheung, F.M. (1983). Vocational evaluation of severely disabled hearing-impaired rehabilitation clients. In D. Watson, G. Anderson, P. Marut, S. Ouellette, and N. Ford (eds.). *Vocational Evaluation of Hearing-impaired Persons: Research and Practice.* Little Rock, Ark.: Research and Training Center on Deafness and Hearing Impairment. Pp. 57–68.

Clayton, I.P. (1973). Career opportunities for visually impaired persons in Maryland. *The New Outlook for the Blind 67,* 210–215.

Clayton, I.P. (1983). Career preparation and the visually handicapped student. *Education of the Visually Handicapped 14*(4), 121–125.

Clayton, I.P. (1977). The work experience program at the Maryland School for the Blind. *Education of the Visually Handicapped 9*(3), 91–94.

Clayton, I.P. (1979). An expanded program in prevocational education at the Maryland School for the Blind. *Education of the Visually Handicapped 3*(3), 80–81.

Cobb, S.R. and A.M. Egbert. (1981). *A Career Education Bibliography: Annotation of Studies and Programs for Handicapped Americans.* Washington, D.C.: Gallaudet College.

Coker, D.G. (1974). The development of a vocational program in a residential school for the visually handicapped. *The New Outlook for the Blind 68,* 25–28.

Corn, A.L. (1983). Visual function: A theoretical model for individuals with low vision. *Journal of Visual Impairment and Blindness 77,* 375–377.

Corn, A.L., and V. Bishop. (1984). Acquisition of practical knowledge by blind and visually impaired students in grades 8–12. *Journal of Visual Impairment and Blindness 78,* 353–356.

Davis, G. (1986). *Year End Report: Projects with Industry.* Tulsa, Okla.: Tulsa Speech and Hearing Association.

Davis, H. and S.R. Silverman. (eds.). (1970). *Hearing and Deafness.* New York: Holt, Rinehart and Winston.

DeCaro, J., and A. Areson. (1983). Career assessment and advisement of the technical college student. In D. Watson, G. Anderson, P. Marut, S. Ouellette, and N. Ford (eds.), *Vocational Evaluation of Hearing-impaired Persons: Research and Practice.* Little Rock, Ark.: Research and Training on Deafness and Hearing Impairment. Pp. 77–92.

Delaney, M., E. Stuckless, and G. Walter. (1984). Total communication effects—a longitudinal study of a school for the deaf in transition. *American Annals of the Deaf 129,* 481–486.

Dickson, M. (1979). Job seeking skills program for the blind. *Journal of Visual Impairment and Blindness 73,* 20–24.

DiFrancesca, S. (1980). Developing thinking skills in career education. *Volta Review 80,* 351–354.

DiFrancesca, S., and S. Hurwitz. (1969). Rehabilitation of hard core deaf: Identification of an affective style. *Journal of Rehabilitation of the Deaf 3,* 34–41.

Dwyer, C. (1985). Career education: A literature review. In M. Bullis and D. Watson (eds.), *Career Education for Hearing Impaired Students: A Review.* Little Rock, Ark.: Research and Training Center on Deafness and Hearing Impairment. Pp. 3–25.

Egelston-Dodd, J. (ed.). (1980). *Trainers' Manual on Career Education/Planning Skills.* Rochester, N.Y.: National Technical Institute for the Deaf.

Egelston-Dodd, J., and J. DeCaro. (1986). The role of special education Institutions: NTID as a special program model. Unpublished manuscript. Rochester, N.Y.: National Technical Institute for the Deaf.

Egelston-Dodd, J., M. Young, D. Lichty, J. Lutz, and S. Cobb. (1985). *Evaluation of an Inservice Program: Final Project Report.* Rochester, N.Y.: National Technical Institute for the Deaf.

Ethridge, E.B. (1978). An approach to career development for visually impaired students on the elementary level. *Education of the Visually Handicapped* 10(3), 87–91.

Fitch, B. (1975). What is career education? In R.R. Davila and D.R. Tweedie (eds.), *Report of the Proceedings of the Forty-seventh Meeting of the Convention of American Instructors of the Deaf.* Washington, D.C.: U.S. Government Printing Office. Pp. 219–222.

Gallaudet College (1982). *Career Education Matrix: Arizona Department of Education.* Washington, D.C.: Gallaudet College, Department of Counseling.

Galloway, V. (1979). *Overview of a Career Development Model: N.P.C.E. Pre Workshop Proceedings.* Washington, D.C.: Gallaudet College.

Gannon, J., and L. Gilbert. (1976). What's happening in career development? *Gallaudet Today: Career Development* 6(4), 8–11.

Gardner, R. (1977). Quality of life education program. *Journal of Visual Impairment and Blindness* 71, 435–437.

Gaylord-Ross, C., J. Forte, and R. Gaylord-Ross. (1986). The community classroom: Technological vocational training for students with serious handicaps. *Career Development for Exceptional Individuals* 9, 24–33.

Gellman, W. (1965). Vocational adjustment and guidance of deaf people. In R.E. Stuckless (ed.), *Research on Behavioral Aspects of Deafness.* Washington, D.C.: Department of Health, Education, & Welfare. Pp. 1–21.

Gerretson, M.D. (1976). Total communication. *Volta Review 78,* 88–95.

Graves, W.H. (1983a). Career development theory applied to the delivery of services to blind and visually impaired persons. In *Yearbook of the Association for Education and Rehabilitation of the Blind and Visually Impaired,* American Foundation for the Blind, 2–17.

Graves, W.H. (1983b). Rehabilitation research and educational services for blind and visually impaired individuals. *Education of the Visually Handicapped* 14(4), 126–132.

Graves, W.H. (1983c). Rehabilitation research and training center in blindness and low vision: A progress review for 1982-1983. In *Yearbook of the Association for Education and Rehabilitation of the Blind and Visually Impaired.* American Foundation for the Blind, 70–76.

Hanson, T. (1979). The acquisition of prevocational independent living skills by blind adolescents during their attendance in a residential school for the blind and visually impaired. Doctoral dissertation. *Case Western Reserve University Dissertation Abstracts International* 40(5), 2592A.

Healy C.C. (1982). *Career Development Counseling through the Life Stages.* Boston: Allyn and Bacon.

Hoben, M. and V. Lindstrom. (1979). Evidence of isolation in the mainstream. *Journal of Visual Impairment and Blindness* 74, 239–296.

Hoyt, K.B. (1980). Career education for exceptional individuals: Challenge for the future. Remarks prepared for a presentation at the CEC National Conference on Career Education for Exceptional Individuals, American Foundation for the Blind.

Hoyt, K.B. (1980). Career education for persons with visual handicaps. Paper presented at the Helen Keller Centennial Conference, Boston, Massachusetts. American Foundation for the Blind.

Huber, D. (1973). Learn to earn: A school work-experience program. *The New Outlook for the Blind 67*, 219–220.

Johnson, J. and D. Newman. (eds.). (1978). *Resource Guide for Career Education.* Columbus, Ohio: National Center for Research on Vocational Education, Ohio State University.

Justi, J., B. McMahon, and F. Lewis. (1983). *Curriculum for Employability Skill Training of Deaf/Hearing Impaired Persons.* Tallahassee, Fla.: Department of Health and Rehabilitative Services.

Karchmer, M. (1984). Demographics and deaf adolescence. In G. Anderson and D. Watson (eds.), *The Habilitation and Rehabilitation of Deaf Adolescents.* Washington, D.C.: National Academy of Gallaudet College. Pp. 28–46.

Kirkman, R.E. (1983). Career awareness and the visually impaired student. *Education of the Visually Handicapped 14*(4), 105–114.

Laurence, M. (1973). The self-reliance institute: Filling the gap in work experience. *The New Outlook for the Blind 67*, 221–225.

Lengel, M., and W. Woolcock. (1984). A general case simulation of national zip code sorting by first and second digits: Acquisition, maintenance, and extension. Research proposal, University of Pittsburgh, Department of Special Education.

Lerman, A.M., and G.R. Guilfoyle. (1970). *The Development of Prevocational Behavior in Deaf Adolescents.* New York: Teachers College Press.

Lombana, J.H. (1980). Career planning with visually handicapped students. *The Vocational Guidance Quarterly 28*, 219–244.

Long, N. (In press). Self directed job seeking skills training: Utilization in a project with industry program for deaf persons. In G. Anderson and D. Watson, *Proceedings of the 1986 Conference of the American Deafness and Rehabilitation Association.* Little Rock, Ark.: Research and Training Center on Deafness and Hearing Impairment.

Martin, K. (1983). Innovations in the placement of hearing-impaired technical college graduates. In D. Watson, G. Anderson, N. Ford, P. Marut, and S. Ouellette (eds.), *Job Placement of Hearing Impaired Persons: Research and Practice.* Little Rock, Ark.: Research and Training Center on Deafness and Hearing Impairment. Pp. 41–56.

Mindel, E.D. and M. Vernon. (1971). *They Grow in Silence: The Deaf Child and His Family.* Silver Springs, Md.: National Association of the Deaf.

Moorse, D. (1978). *Education of th Deaf: Psychology, Principles, and Implications.* Boston: Houghton-Mifflin.

Morrison, M. (1974). The other 128 hours a week: Teaching personal management to blind young adults. *The New Outlook for the Blind 68*(10), 454–459, 460.

Naughton, F. and S. Sacks. (1977). Hey! What's cooking? A kitchen curriculum for parents of visually impaired children. Unpublished paper. South Metropolitan Association for Low Incidence Handicapped Children.

Ouellette, S. and C. Dwyer. (1985). A current profile of career education programs. In M. Bullis & D. Watson (eds.), *Career Education for Hearing Impaired Students: A Review.* Little Rock, Ark.: Research and Training Center on Deafness and Hearing Impairment. Pp. 27–54.

Passmore, D. (1983). Employment of deaf people. In D. Watson, G. Anderson, N. Ford, P. Marut, and S. Ouellette (eds.), *Job Placement of Hearing Impaired Persons: Research and Practice.* Little Rock, Ark.: Research and Training Center on Deafness and Hearing Impairment. Pp. 5–15.

Perkins School for the Blind. (1983). Advancements: An implementation guide to a community-based vocational training program for deaf-blind youth. Edited by D.L. Gross and M. Kowalski-Glickman. Watertown, Mass.

Rossi, P. and M. Marotta. (1974). Breaking blind stereotypes through vocational placements. *The New Outlook for the Blind 68,* 29–32.

Schein, J., and M.T. Delk. (1974). *The Deaf Population of the United States.* Silver Springs, Md.: National Association of the Deaf.

Schlesinger, H., and K. Meadow. (1972). *Sound and Sign: Childhood Deafness and Mental Health.* Berkeley, Ca.: University of California Press.

Scott, R.A. (1969). *The Making of Blind Men.* New York: The Russel Sage Foundation.

Sligar, S. (1983). Commercial vocational evaluation systems and deaf persons. In D. Watson, G. Anderson, P. Marut, S. Ouellette, and N. Ford (eds.), *Vocational Evaluation of Haring-impaired Persons: Research and Practice.* Little Rock, Ark.: Research and Training Center on Deafness and Hearing Impairment. Pp. 35–55.

Spungin, S.J. (1983). Career development: The educational context. In *Yearbook of the Association for Education and Rehabilitation of the Blind and Visually Impaired.* New York: American Foundation for the Blind. Pp. 18–29.

Steffan, R. (1975). Implementation of career education at MSSD. In R.E. Davila and D.R. Tweedie (eds.), *Report of the Proceedings of the Forty-seventh Meeting of the Convention of the American Instructors of the Deaf.* Washington, D.C.: U.S. Government Printing Office. Pp. 228–321.

Stewart, I., V.B. Van Hasselt, J. Simon, and W. Thompson. (1984). The community adjustment program (CAP) for visually handicapped adolescents. *Journal of Visual Impairment and Blindness 79,* 49–54.

Storey, K., S.Z. Sacks, and J. Olmstead. (1985). Community-referenced instruction in a technological work setting: A vocational education option for visually handicapped students. *Journal of Visual Impairment and Blindness 79,* 481–486.

Torretti, W. (1983). The placement process with severely disabled deaf people. In D. Watson, G. Anderson, N. Ford, P. Marut, and S. Ouellette (eds.), *Job Placement of Hearing-impaired Persons: Research and Practice.* Little Rock, Ark.: Research and Training Center on Deafness and Hearing Impairment.

Tremble, J.T., and L.F. Campbell. (1973). A diversified work experience programs for blind and multi-handicapped blind students. *The New Outlook for the Blind 67,* 216–219.

Twyman, L., and S. Ouellette. (1978). Career development programs in residential schools for the deaf: A survey. *American Annals of the Deaf 12,* 10–12.

Updegraff, D.R., and J. Egelston-Dodd. (1982). The national project on career education: Past, present, and future. *Directions 2*(4), 15–23.

Uxer, J.R. (1973). Career education and visually handicapped persons: Some issues surrounding the state of the art. *The New Outlook for the Blind 67,* 200–206.

Van Hasselt, V.B., M. Hersen, and A.E. Kazdin. (1985). Assessment of social skills in visually handicapped adolescents. *Behavior Research and Therapy 23,* 53–63.

Van Hasselt, V.B., M. Hersen, A.E. Kazdin, J.A. Simon, and A.K. Mastanuono. (1983). Social skills training for blind adolescents. *Journal of Visual Impairment and Blindness 77,* 99–103.

Wehman, P. (1981). *Competitive Employment New Horizons for Severely Disabled Individuals.* Baltimore: Paul H,. Brookes.

Wehman, P., and J. Kregel. (1983). A supported work approach to competitive employment of individuals with moderate and severe handicaps. Unpublished paper.

White, K., and N. Slusher. (1978). *Measuring Career Development among Post Secondary Deaf Students.* Research manuscript #25. Rochester, N.Y.: National Technical Institute for the Deaf.

Winkley, W. (1985). Worlds without workshops. *Journal of Visual Impairment and Blindness 79.*

Woal, S.T. (1974). A career education program for visually handicapped students. *Vocational Guidance Quarterly 73*(2), 172–173.

Wolf, K. (1984). Major issues in counseling visually handicapped youth and adults toward independent living. Austin: University of Texas, Department of Special Education, Job Readiness Clinic.

Wolfe, H. (1973). Career education: A new dimension in education for living. *The New Outlook for the Blind 67,* 193–199.

Wurster, M.V. (1983). Career education for visually impaired students: Where we've been and where we are. *Education of the Visually Handicapped 14*(4), 99–104.

Yeadon, A. (1974). *Toward Independence: The Use of Instructional Objectives in Teaching Daily Living Skills to the Blind.* New York: American Foundation for the Blind.

Index

Accommodations, in placement, 298-
300, 317-318
Activity centers for severely handicapped, 374-375
Adaptations for training the disabled,
396, 405-411
resources for, 408–409
Administrative support for secondary
training, 193
Adult development centers (A.D.C.),
375-376
Adult employment programs, 205-233
Adult services:
continuum of, 373-376
for physically handicapped, 411-414
promising practices in, 376
for severely handicapped, 375-383
Adult Skills Development Programs
(ASDP), 103
ADVANCE (Action for the
Development of Vocational
Alternatives and New Concepts
in Education), 435
Adventures for the Future, 437
Advocacy processes, 346
Advocacy strategies, knowledge of, 77
Age appropriateness for vocational
education, 73
American Sign Language (ASL), 420
Application component in vocational
assessment, 118-120, 121-123
Apprenticeship programs, 339
Architectural Barriers Act (1968), 9
Area Redevelopment Act (1961), 9

Arizona State University, 25-26
Ashton, Paul, 296n, 304-309
Assessment component in vocational
assessment, 117-118, 120-121
Assessment variables:
in physical ecology, 238-240
in production skills, 240-241,
243-244, 250-251
in social skills, 241-242, 245-248,
250-251
See also Vocational education
Assistance:
amount of, 156-157
fading, 159-161
method of, 156
purpose of, 155-156
Assistive device adaptations,
406-407
Association for Educational Rehabilitation of the Blind and
Visually Impaired (AER), 436
Ataxia, 388
Athetosis, 388
Atonia, 389

Bank of Indiana, 296n, 309
Barrier-free environment, 16
Behavior analysis, 143-148
case study, 144-145
Behavior analytic aproach, 399
Behavioral strategies for voca-
tional training, 400
Bellevue, WA, 288
Benchwork model, 289-291

Bend, OR, 290
Benefits, social, 211, 262-263
Berkeley, CA, 259
Berkeley Planning Associates
    (BPA), 275
Bilingual training, 12
Biller, Ernest, 30-63
Biofeedback, for motor control, 399
Blind, programs for, 16
Blindness:
  legal, 429
  See also Visual impairment
Brolin, Donn, 174
Bullis, Michael, 417-444
Bureau of Education for the Handi-
    capped, 22
Burien, WA, 290
Business, benefits from disabled
    employment, 211
Business perspective on disabled
    employment, 296-328
Business sites, vocational training
    at, 297

California, adult services, 374-375
California Automobile Associa-
    tion, 197
California Institute on Human
    Services, 24
California School for the Blind, 432
Career assessment:
  approaches to, 48-55
  nontraditional techniques, 51-55
Career counseling, 184-185
Career development, 41-45
  career education and, 39-41
  defined, 40-41
Career education, 30-63
  career development in, 39-41
  case study, 57-59
  concept of, 32-35
  of hearing impaired, 421-428
  implementation of, 45
  life-centered model, 45-46
  mainstream, 57
  plan case example, 56-59
  rationale for, 35-39
  secondary school, 184-187
  separate programming vs. infusion,
    55-56

sequence for, 182-183
Career Education Incentive Act
    (1977), 32
Career Information and Training
    Activities for the Blind
    (CI-TAB), 433
Career mobility for the disabled,
    325-326
Career options, limitation, 44
Career preparation, placement and, 45
Career readiness, 44-45
  See also Readiness
Career stages, development tasks
    and, 42
Carl D. Perkins Vocational Education
    Act (1984). *See* Perkins Act
Center for Career Education, 32
Center for Independent Living
    (Berkeley), 264
Centers for Independent Living
    Programs (of P.L. 98-221), 340-341
Central training sites, 397
Cerebral palsy:
  description, 388-390
  terminology, 388-389
  vocational training strategies
    for, 400-414
CETA. *See* Comprehensive Employment
    and Training Act
Chadsey-Rusch, Janis, 234-256
Clark, Gary, 174
Client Assistance Program (of P.L.
    98-221), 340
Close, Daniel W., 87-108
Cobb, R. Brian, 331-354
Cognitive disabilities, training
    technology for, 390, 399
Colorado, 208
Commission on National Aid to Voca-
    tional Education, 7
Communication:
  ability for, 77
  for hearing impaired, 419-420
Community:
  living and work in, 87-108
  vocational education and, 67-69
Community and Family Living
    Amendments, 100
Community-based instruction,
    366-367

Community-based organization (CBO), 273
Community integration, 219-220
Community-intensive instruction, 367
Community linkage, 319-326
Community living, 87-108
    empirical basis, 92-93
    research findings, 91-97
Community resources, 182
Compensation for work, 361-362
Competencies, core, 270-271
Competitive employment, 216-218
    for severely handicapped, 373
    supported, 220-224
Comprehensive Employment and Training Act (CETA), 11, 16, 271-272
Computers, 401-402
    for physically handicapped, 395-396
Conceptual model of vocational assessment, 116-118
Consequences, in training, 404
Consumer economics, 182
Consumer participation in employment and training, 345-346
Contingencies:
    managing, 147-148
    in vocational instruction, 157-158
Cooperative agreements, 21-23
Cooperative individualized student planning, 342-347
Correction, 156-157
Costs:
    disability related, 279-283
    to society, 211, 262-263
    of supported employment, 288-290
Council on Exceptional Children (CEC), 71, 135
Coworkers, ability to work with, 76
Craft, Richard, 185
Crews. See Mobile work crews
Curricula/Curriculum:
    age-appropriate, 365-366
    for severely disabled, 364-366
    vocational education, 66-67
Curriculum-based assessment, 115-116, 133-134
Curriculum-based model, 115-116
Curriculum domains, 366

Curriculum model for the mildly handicapped, 181-182

Data collection for training, 402-403
Day treatment activity centers (D.T.A.C.), 375
DCD. See Division on Career Development
Deaf, program for, 16
Deafness:
    definition, 418-419
    See also Hearing impairment
Deficit Reduction Act (1984), 276
Developmental curriculum for the severely handicapped, 365
Developmental programs for the adult handicapped, 212-213
Dignity, 210
Diplegic, 389
Disability/Disabilities:
    severe, 222
    statistics on, 258-259
    types and vocational education, 329-444
Disability Rights Education and Defense Fund, 259
Disabled employment:
    advantages to business, 300-309
    business perspective on, 296-328
    economic issues, 257-295
    rationale, 206-207
Disadvantaged, 332-333
    case study, 351
Discrimination, 308-309
    in private employment, 274-275
Discriminative stimulus (SD), 146, 150
Disincentives, 267
Division on Career Development (DCD), 112-114, 135

Earning power, 211
Easter Seals Society, 391
ECLS. See Exploration career life stage curriculum
Ecological approaches to vocational assessment, 67-68
Ecology:
    defined, 236-237

organizational, 250-253
perspective, 235-236
physical, 237-243
social, 243-249
Economic Development Act (1964), 10
Economic issues:
in disabled employment, 257-295
problems in studying, 259-262
Economic Opportunity Act, 10, 11
Economic Recovery Tax Act (1981)
(ERTA), 18, 275
Education, Department of, 39
Education, job search, 346-347
See also Vocational education
Education, Office of, 12, 22, 39
Education Amendments of 1975, 32
Education Amendments of 1976, 12,
13, 32
Education for All Handicapped
Children Act (1975), 12, 14-18,
66, 79, 87, 100, 175-177, 179, 180,
258, 332
Education of the Handicapped Act,
175, 259
Education for the Handicapped Act
Amendments (1983), 20, 27
Education for the Handicapped
Amendments (1983), 18
Educators, training, 69-72
Electromyography (EMG), 399
Electronic Industries Foundation
(EIF), 323
Elementary school:
physically disabled in, 394-395
work preparation in, 394-495
El Paso Lighthouse for the Blind,
434-435
Employers, ability to work with, 76
Employment:
benefits to society, 211, 262-263
best practices in, 342-347
competitive. *See* Competitive
employment
in disabled lifestyle, 206-207
discrimination in, 274-275
options for integrated, 359-363
supported, 219-231, 285-291,
376-377, 412-414
transition to, 392-403, 407-409
Employment programs, adult disabled,
203-328, *especially* 205-233

Employment and training agencies, 337
Employment and Training Programs, 11
Employment Development Plan, 342
Employment Opportunities for
Disabled Americans Act
(proposed), 266
Employment sites, vocational training
at, 343
Enclaves, 412
for blind work, 434
model, 288
outcomes from, 227-228
for physically disabled work, 413
for supported work, 226-227
Environmental modifications, 408
Epilepsy, 389
Eugene, OR, 289-290
Eugene Precision Manufacturing
Service, 289-290
Evaluation of severely handicapped,
198-199
Evaluation procedures in vocational
assessment, 74
Exploration career life stage curriculum
(ECLS), 46-47

Fair Labor Standards Act, 214
Families:
of the disabled, 210
role in community living, 100-101,
102-103
Family education in community
living, 103
Family-of-one rule, 18
Family support:
in community living, 97-105
rationale for, 98-100
Federal Unemployment Tax Act
(FUTA), 275
Feedback in training, 404
Fitzgerald Act, apprenticeship
programs, 339
Follow-up:
after placement, 318-319
after training and employment, 347
Frasier, James R., 1, 3-29

Gallaudet College, 420, 422
Gaylord-Ross, Robert, 109, 174-202
Generic services, 330, 347
George-Barden Acts (1946, 1956, 1959), 6

George-Deen Act (1936), 6
Gilbreth, Frank, 238
Gilbreth, Lillian, 238
Government and law, skill, 182

Habilitation. *See* Rehabilitation
Halpern model, 88-89
Handicapped:
  definitions and categories, 332
  occupational characteristics, 39
Hard of hearing, definition,
  418-419
Hasazi, Susan Brody, 331-354
Headstick, 406
Health, 182
Health Act, amendments (1956), 6
Hearing impaired:
  case study of, 427-428
  rationale for career education
    of, 37-38
  training and employment of, 418-428
Hearing impairment:
  characteristics of, 418-428
  classifications of, 418-419
  degree of, 419
  demographics of, 420-421
  issues and directions concerning,
    426-428
  model programs for, 422-426
  statistics, 420
Hearing loss, in cerebral palsy, 389
Hemiplegia, 389
High school, work preparation in,
  396-397
Historical perspective, 5-12
Honer, Robert H., 109, 142-173
Hoyt, Kenneth, 174
Human resource management model,
  310-311

IEP. *See* Individualized educational
  programs
Illinois, University of, 24
Implementation, in secondary vocational training, 196-197
Incentives, transfer payments and,
  263-267
Independent living for hearing
  impaired, 423
Individualization of vocational
  education, 73-74

Individualized educational programs
  (IEP), 11, 14, 19, 22, 51, 179-180,
  342, 343
  in secondary vocational training, 194
Individualized written rehabilitation
  program (IWRP), 14, 22, 342,
  373, 374
Industry:
  benefits from disabled employment,
    211
  projects with, 319-322, 340-341,
    424-425
Infusion, in career education, 55-56
Innovations for the physically
  handicapped, 391-392
Institute for the Crippled and Disabled
  (ICD), 50
Instruction:
  in secondary vocational training, 197
  strategies, 162-164
Instructional options in vocational
  assessment, 123-125
Instructional programming in vocational education, 142-143
Insurance in vocational training, 193
Integration:
  of employment, 359-363
  school, 366
  in training and employment, 343
  in vocational environment, 360-361
Interagency agreements, 81-83
  case study, 83
Interagency collaboration, 78-83
  in training and employment, 344-345
Interagency resources for the severely
  handicapped, 377-380
Intervention methodology in vocational education, 74-75
Intervention strategies:
  in production skills, 240-244, 251-253
  in social skills, 242-243, 248-249,
    251-253
Irvin, Larry K., 109, 111-141
IWRP. *See* Individualized written
  rehabilitation program

JAN. *See* Job Accommodation
  Network
Jenkins, Chris, 387-416
JEWEL program, 248-285

Jewish Vocational Services (JVS), 319, 320, 322-329
Job(s):
  at central training sites, 397-398
  in elementary school, 394-395
  in middle school, 396
Job Accommodation Network (JAN), 298-300
Job analysis, 148-152
  in physical ecology, 238-240
  sample, 151-152, 153
  in selective placement, 309-310, 315-316
  summary, 153
  worksheet, 154
Job coach for mentally retarded, 228-231
Job Corps, 10, 11, 23, 263
  program, 16
  training programs, 338
Job creation, training and wage subsidies vs., 271-284
Job Entry Work Experience Laboratory (JEWEL), 284-285
Job Readiness Clinic, 436
Job search education, 346-347
Job sharing, 262-263
Job Training Partnership Act (JTPA), 16-18, 23, 25, 263, 272-273, 336-338
  support services, 17
Job-training stations, 367-368
Joysticks, 389
JTPA. See Job Training Partnership Act
Junior high school, 396

Keating, Thomas J., 2, 87-108
Kregel, John, 205-233

Labor queue theory, 270, 276
Lanterman Act, 374-375
Laws, 5-27, 175-181
LCCE. See Life-centered career education
LEA. See Local education agency
Leadership Development Program, 24
Learning, work as context for, 284-285
Learning-disabled persons, rationale for career education, 38-39

Least restrictive environment (LRE), 14, 19-20, 178-179
Liability, in vocational training, 193
Life-centered career education (LCCE), 45-46
Life skills, 182
Lindsay, Dolores, 284-285
Lip reading, 419-420
Local education agency (LEA), in vocational assessment, 118, 121-122
LRE. See Least restrictive environment

Maintenance programs, 273
Maintenance-promoting strategies, 165-169
Mank, David M., 109, 142-173
Mann, Horace, 5
Manpower Development and Training Act (MDTA) (1962), 9, 10, 11
Manual communication, 419-420
Marland, Sidney P., Jr., 31
Maryland School for the Blind, 431
MDTA. See Manpower Development and Training Act
Medical examinations in selective placement, 316-317
Mental retardation, 357, 389
  in historical perspective, 390-391
  training technology for, 399
Mentally retarded, rationale for career education of, 36
Middle school:
  for the mildly handicapped, 183-184
  work preparation in, 396
Midwest Association of Business, Rehabilitation, and Industry (MABRI), 323
Mildly handicapped:
  career readiness of, 44-45
  case studies, 347-351
  secondary vocational training for, 181-188
  vocational education of, 331-354
Mobile work crews, 224-226, 288-289, 412-413
  outcomes, 227-228
  for physically disabled, 413
Model Secondary School for the Deaf (MSDD), 422

Modifying materials, 404
Moe, Gary, 185
Morrill Act (1856), 5
Motor disabilities, vocational training for, 400-411
Motor impairments, 389
Motor limitations, 329
Motor movements, alternative, 405
Mouthstick, 406
Multihandicapped, vocational programs for, 434-435

National Advisory Council on Career Education, 32
National Apprenticeship Act (1937), 339
National Association for Retarded Citizens, 264
National Association of Secondary School Principals, 31
National Commission on Architectural Barriers, 9
National Council on the Handicapped, 16, 267
National Education Act (1958), 7
National Industries for the Blind, 434-435
National Institute of Education (NIE), 13
National Institute for Handicapped Research, 16
National Project on Career Education (NPCE), 422
National Research Conference of Behavioral Aspects of Deafness, 421-422
National Technical Institute for the Deaf (NTID), 422, 425-426
National Vocational Guidance Association (NVGA), 42
Native Americans
  programs for, 16
  vocational education, 12
Natural proportion, vocational education and, 73
Neighborhood Youth Corps, 10
New Jobs Credit, 18
Newark, CA, 284
Nisbet, Jan, 1, 2, 65-86

North Dakota, cooperative activities, 23
Nystrom, D.C., 7

O'Brien, Justin, 257-295
Occupational knowledge, 182
Occupational Skills Training (OST), 378-381
Occupational training, secondary, 185
Office of Career Education, 32
Office of Education, 12, 22, 39
Office of Special Education and Rehabilitative Services (OSERS), 22-25, 87, 102, 259, 266, 273, 286, 287, 369, 411, 412
Olympus Electronics, 290
Omnibus Reconciliation Act (1981), 32
On-the-job training, 269-271
On-the-job tryouts, 51
Operant chains in behavior, 144-147
Oral/aural communication, 419-420
Oregon, University of, 91-93, 102-103, 287
Oregon Transition to Employment Project (OTEP), 392-403, 407-409
Organizational ecology, 250-253
OSERS. See Office of Special Education and Rehabilitative Services
Outcomes, as criteria of vocational education, 360
Outreach in selective placement, 312-315

Pacing in training, 159
Paraplegic, 389
Paraprofessionals in secondary vocational training, 193
Parent(s):
  in community living, 102-103
  in work preparation, 395
Parent facilitator, 370
Parent participation in training and employment, 345-346
Parents Graduation Alliance (PGA), 103-105
Park, Hyun Sook, 174-202
Parsons, Frank, 41
Partnership programs, 273
Pay criterion, 361-362

Performance gap:
  closing, 398-411
  closing case study, 410-411
  summary of closing strategies, 411
Performance-promoting strategies,
  161-164
Perkins Act (P.L. 98-524), 12-14, 19,
  26-27, 175-179, 258, 333-336
  sequence chart, 178
Perkins School for the Blind, 432, 435
Phelps, L. Allen, 1, 3-29
Physical disabilities, 329
  historical perspective, 390-391
Physical ecology, 237-243
Physically disabled, innovative program needs, 391-392
Physically handicapped, vocational
  education of, 387-416
Physio-Controls, Inc., 288
PIC. See Private industry councils
Pittsburgh Association for the Blind,
  431, 435
P.L. numbers. See Public Law numbers
Placement:
  career preparation and, 45
  in competitive employment, 216-218
  credibility in, 307
  external and internal sources, 313-315
  for the hearing impaired, 423-424
  selective, 309-319
  techniques, knowledge of, 75-76
Pleasant Valley, OR, 56-59
Policy aspects of vocational educa-
  tion, 3-29
Policy issues, 262
Political involvement in community
  living, 104
Positive values, development of,
  72-74
Postemployment services, 218
Postsecondary vocational education,
  341-342
Powers, Laurie, 387-416
Praise in training, 404-405
Prejudice against the handicapped, 258
Preplacement services, 217-218
President's Commission on Employ-
  ment of the Handicapped, 15,
  67, 78, 259
Private industry councils (PIC), 17-18,
  25, 272-273, 337

Private sector employment, factors
  associated with, 274-275
Production skills, 238
  intervention strategies, 240-241,
  243-244, 251-253
  in organizational ecology, 250-253
  in physical ecology, 238-241
  in social ecology, 243-244
Professional development, recent and
  future, 23-24
Professionals:
  in community living, 102-103
  in vocational education, 65-86
Program implementation, 180-181
Program improvement, 104
Project INTERFACE, 25-26
Project Transition into Employment
  (TIE), 26
Project Work-ability, 25
Projects with industry, 319-322, 340-341
  for hearing impaired, 424-425
Prompting in training, 403-404
Psychological tests in career
  assessment, 49
Public Law numbers. Refer to titles
  listed below:
  P.L. 88-210. See Vocational Educa-
    tion Act
  P.L. 91-230. See Education of the
    Handicapped Act
  P.L. 93-112. See Rehabilitation
    Act (1973)
  P.L. 93-380. See Education Amend-
    ments of 1975
  P.L. 93-516. See Rehabilitation Act
    Amendments (1974)
  P.L. 94-142. See Education for All
    Handicapped Children
    Act (1975)
  P.L. 94-482. See Education Amend-
    ments of 1976
  P.L. 95-207. See Career Education
    Incentive Act
  P.L. 95-602. See Rehabilitation,
    Comprehensive Services, and
    Developmental Disabilities
    Amendments (1978)
  P.L. 98-199. See Education for the
    Handicapped Amendments
    (1983)
  P.L. 98-221. See Rehabilitation Acts
    (1973) Amendments (1974)

P.L. 98-524. *See* Perkins Act
Public school programs for the visually impaired, 433-434
Public sector employment, 271-272
Pumpian, Ian, 355-386
PWI. *See* Projects with industry

Quadriplegic, 389

Reacher, 407
Readiness, 44-45, 357, 374-375, 383
alternatives to, 376-378
social skills and, 435-438
Readiness component in vocational assessment, 117, 118-120
Reading disability, case study, 53-55
Recruitment in selective placement, 312-315
Rehabilitation:
business and, 319-326
of hearing impaired, 421-428
industry connection, 306-307
See also Vocational rehabilitation
Rehabilitation, Comprehensive Services, and Developmental Disabilities Amendments (1978), 16
Rehabilitation Acts, 6, 8, 12, 14, 134, 147, 257, 259, 266, 308, 340, 357
Amendments (1984), 16, 340-341
services in, 15-16, 79-80
Rehabilitation programs, vocational assessment in, 111-141
Rehabilitation Services Administration, 22, 266, 424
Reinforcement, promoting, 157-158
Residential school program, for visually impaired, 430-433
Resources for vocational education, 74
Response analysis, 144
Retrolental fibroplasia (REP), 430
Revenue Act (1978), 18
Richmond, CA, 185
Rigidity, 388
Rochester Institute of Technology (RIT), 425-426
Rochlin, Jay, 296n, 325-326
Rusch, Frank R., 234-256

Sacks, Sharon Zell, 417-444
Salitore, Robert, 296n, 309

San Diego Community College District, 378-380
San Diego Unified School District, 358-359, 368-369
San Francisco, CA, 187
Scheduling in secondary vocational training, 196-197
Scher, Paul, 296n, 303-304
School-based career education model, 47
School programs, vocational assessment in, 111-141
School trends in vocational training, 363-368
SD. *See* Discriminative stimulus
SDA. *See* Service delivery areas
Sears, Roebuck & Co., 302-304
Secondary and Transition Services Program, 23, 27
Secondary vocational education, 333-336
Secondary vocational training, case study, 188-191
Segregation, 258
Self-management, 156-169
Semi-independent living programs (SILP), 91-93, 100
Sensory handicaps, vocational education for, 417-444
Sensory impairments, 329-330
Separate programming, in career education, 55-56
Service delivery areas (SDA), 17, 337
Severe handicaps, 329
Severely disabled:
case studies, 222-231
rationale for career eduction of, 36-37
severely handicapped vs., 357-359
supported employment for, 220
Severely handicapped:
case study, 198-199
rights of, 356
secondary vocational training for, 191-199
services for, 335-357
severely disabled vs., 357-359
sheltered workshops for, 373-374
support service case studies, 382-383
supported work transition model for, 47-48
vocational education of, 355-386

vocational training for, 363-372
Sheltered workshops, 208-210,
    212-216
  future of, 216
  operational problems, 215-216
  for severely handicapped adults,
      373-374
Shepard, Holly, 355-386
Siegel, Shepherd, 109, 174-202
Sign language, 419-420
SILP. See Semi-independent living
      programs
Site procurement for secondary
      vocational training, 195
Site selection for secondary vocational
      training, 196
Situational assessment, 50-51
Skill demands in vocational assess-
      ment, 124-125
Skill gains of severely handi-
      capped, 365
Smith-Hughes Act (1917), 6
Smith-Sears Act (1918), 6
Social Darwinists, 257
Social ecology, 243-249
  summary on, 249
Social Security Act Amend-
      ments, 258
Social Security Disability Amend-
      ments (P.L. 96-265), 258,
      266-267
Social skills:
  intervention strategies, 242-243,
      248-249, 251-253
  in organizational ecology, 250-253
  in physical ecology, 241-243
  in social ecology, 244-248
  vocational readiness and, 435-438
Society, benefits from disabled
      employment, 211, 262-263
Sonoma (CA) State University, 24
Southwest Center for the Hearing
      Impaired, 423-424
Sowers, Jo-Ann, 387-416
Spasticity, 388
Special education:
  "aging out" of, 286
  contemporary legislation, 18-20
  employment outlook after, 296-298
  historical perspective, 11-12
  outlook after, 327
  secondary, 336-337

vocational, 336-337
  in vocational education, 79
Special needs:
  defined, 332
  individuals with, 331-333
Special projects, 24-25
Specialized Training Program (STP),
      287, 289, 290
Specific services, 330, 347
Speech disorders, in cerebral
      palsy, 389
Speech reading, 419-420
Splint, assistive, 407
SSI. See Supplemental Security
      Income
Staffing:
  for severe disabilities, 397
  for supported employment, 222-223
State Job Training Coordinating
      Council (SJTCC), 337-338
Stern, David, 257-295
Stigmatization, 257
STP. See Specialized Training Program
Student characteristics in vocational
      assessment, 123
Substantial gainful activity
      (SGA), 264
Supplemental Security Income (SSI),
      65-66, 264-266
Support, ongoing, 220
Support services, degrees of, 380-381
Support systems, 88-81, 383-384
Supported employment, 219-220,
      285-291
  in adult services for severely
      handicapped, 376-377
  case studies, 228-231
  individual, 412, 413-414
  model, 220-224
  need for services, 221-222
  settings for, 223-224
  for severely disabled, 220
  staffing for, 222-223
Supported jobs model, 287
Supported living, 89-96
  case studies, 94-97
Supported work, 363
  transition model (SWTM), 47-48
System change, 77

Targeted Jobs Tax Credits (TJTC), 258,
      263, 275-284

Targeted programs, 273
Task analysis, 149-151
  for cognitive disability, 401
  for physically handicapped,
    401-402
Task design, 149
Task modification analysis (TMA),
    405-406
Tax Equity and Fiscal Responsibility
    Act (TEFRA) (1982), 18, 275-276
Tax Reduction and Simplification Act
    (1977), 18
Tax Reform Act (1985), 277
Taylor, Frederick W., 238
Teaching of severely disabled, 364-368
Tennessee School for the Blind, 431
Tennessee Valley Authority (TVA),
    314-315
Tests, 49, 129-133
Texas, University of (Austin), 436
Texas School for the Blind, 437
Texas School for the Deaf, 37
TJTC. See Targeted Jobs Tax Credits
Trainers, need for, 397
Training:
  best practices in, 342-347
  general, 268-271
  job creation and wage subsidies vs.,
    271-284
  specific, 268-271
  for vocational instruction, 152-161
  See also Vocational training
Transfer payments, incentives and,
    268-267
Transition, in secondary
    training, 187
Transition-focused programs, 25-26
Transition to employment, 392-403,
    407-409
  case study, 371-372
  demonstration class for, 368-372
Tremor, 388
Tulsa Speech and Hearing Associa-
    tion/Projects with industry,
    424-425

Unemployment, 207-210
  costs of, 210-212
  of hearing impaired, 421
  rates of, 259
Unemployment tax, 275

Unions, in rehabilitation move-
    ment, 327
United Cerebral Palsy, 391
U.S.D.E. See Education, Department of
U.S. Employment Service Act (1933), 9
USSR, influence of, 7

VCU. See Virginia Commonwealth
    University
Vendors, in adult servics for the
    severely handicapped, 376-383
Vermont, 234
Virginia, 208, 221, 224
Virginia Commonwealth University,
    26, 391-392
Visual impairment:
  in cerebral palsy, 389
  program models for, 430-435
  variety and degree of, 429-430
Visually impaired:
  case study of, 437-439
  multihandicapped, 434-435
  program models for, 430-435
  training and employment of, 428-435
Vocational alternatives, for the
    disabled, 212-218
Vocational assessment:
  approaches to, 67-68
  case study, 132-133
  comprehensive model of, 116
  curriculum based, 115-116, 133-134
  definition, 111
  guiding principles, 111-112
  implementing, 125
  in instruction/training, 158-159
  instrumentation, 129-131
  personnel in, 135
  procedures, 74
  process of, 123-129
  program related, 126
  in rehabilitation programs, 111-141
  school-based models of, 114-123
  in school programs, 111-141,
    especially 114-123
  tests, 129-133
  vocational rehabilitation in, 136-140
Vocational assessment and preparation,
    109-202
Vocational education:
  contemporary legislation and policy
    framework, 12-14
  disability types and, 329-344

future directions in, 126-127
historical perspective, 6-8
instructional programming in,
    142-173
interagency collaboration in, 78-83
legislative and policy framework,
    12-21
of the mildly handicapped,
    331-354
objective, 142-143
postsecondary, 341-342
professionals in, 69-72, 72-77
recent and future developments,
    21-27
secondary, 333-336
secondary special, 336-337
settings, 334-335
Vocational Education Act (1963) 7, 78,
    175, 177
    Amendments, 79
Vocational Education Resources System
    (VERS), 24
Vocational Evaluation Center
    Model, 115
Vocational Evaluation Final
    Report, 50
Vocational evaluation for the hearing
    impaired, 423
Vocational instruction:
    case study in, 160-161
    technology of, 143-148
    training procedures for, 152-161
Vocational rehabilitation, 79-81,
    339-341
    case recording in, 136-138
    historical perspective, 8-9
    program-related assessment in,
        138-140
    vocational assessment in, 136-140
    See also Rehabilitation
Vocational Rehabilitation Acts, 6, 8,
    12, 14-16, 79-80, 134, 257, 259,
    266, 308, 340, 357
Vocational special education:
    defined, 45
    legislative and policy aspects, 3-29
    recent and future directions, 21-27
Vocational training:
    bilingual, 12
    business sites, 397

demonstration transition class,
    368-370, 371-372
employment sites, 343-344
historical perspective, 390-391
implementing, 125-129
promising practices in, 368-370
secondary, 174-202
of the severely handicapped,
    363-372
systematic, 399-405
technology development, 390
See also Training

Wages:
    for disabled, 211
    pay criterion, 361-362
    in secondary vocational training, 194
    subminimum, 214-215
    subsidies, training and job creation
        vs., 271-284
    supported employment, 219
Washington Day Service Agency, 289
Wehman, Paul, 205-233
West, Elizabeth, 355-386
Western Pennsylvania School for
    Blind Children, 431
Westside Center for Independent
    Living, 264
White, Warren J., 30-63
White House Conference on Handi-
    capped Individuals, 264
Will model, 87-89
Wilson, William, 174-202
Wilson Woodrow, 6
Wisconsin, University of
    (Madison), 272
Woodward, Calvin, 5
Work, meaningful, 73, 361
Work crews. See Mobile work crews
Work environment, 238, 240
Work experiences, in secondary
    training, 186-187
Work preparation for physically
    disabled, 394-398
Work sample evaluation, in career
    assessment, 49-50
Work skills:
    identifying, 392-394
    specific vs. general, 267-271

Workplace ecology, 234-256
  case study, 252-253

Young Adult Conservation Corps, 11
Youth Community Conservation and
  Improvement Projects, 11

Youth Employment and Demonstration
  Projects Acts (1977), 11
Youth Incentive Entitlement
  Projects, 11

Zittel, Gail, 186